GUIDE TO
REFERENCE
IN MEDICINE
AND HEALTH

GUIDE TO REFERENCE IN MEDICINE AND HEALTH

CHRISTA MODSCHIEDLER and
DENISE BEAUBIEN BENNETT, Editors

AN IMPRINT OF THE
AMERICAN LIBRARY ASSOCIATION
CHICAGO • 2014

© 2014 by the American Library Association

Printed in the United States of America

18 17 16 15 14   5 4 3 2 1

Extensive effort has gone into ensuring the reliability of the information in this book; however, the publisher makes no warranty, express or implied, with respect to the material contained herein.

ISBNs: 978-0-8389-1221-8 (paper); 978-0-8389-1982-8 (PDF); 978-0-8389-1983-5 (ePub); 978-0-8389-1984-2 (Kindle). For more information on digital formats, visit the ALA Store at alastore.ala.org and select eEditions.

Library of Congress Cataloging in Publication Control Number: 014005002.

Cover design by Alejandra Diaz. Image ©jongjet303 / Shutterstock, Inc.

Text design in the Berkeley and Helvetica typefaces. Composition by Scribe, Inc.

♾ This paper meets the requirements of ANSI/NISO Z39.48-1992 (Permanence of Paper).

CONTENTS

FOREWORD

The American Library Association has long been a source for authoritative bibliographies of the reference literature for practicing librarians, library educators, and reference service trainers. ALA's *Guide to Reference Books* was printed in eleven editions over nearly a century, and was succeeded in 2009 by the online *Guide to Reference* (www.guidetoreference.org). The *Guide to Reference* segments, drawn from the online *Guide*, continue that tradition with expertly compiled, discipline-specific, annotated bibliographies of reference works and serve as snapshots of the evolving content of the *Guide*.

Although intended for use largely in North American libraries serving institutions of higher education, the segments will also be valuable to public and school librarians, independent researchers, publishers and book dealers, as well as librarians outside North America, for tasks such as identifying sources that will answer questions, directing researchers, creating local instructional materials, educating and training LIS students and reference staff, and inventorying and developing reference collections. These guides provide a usably comprehensive, rather than exhaustive, repertory of sources as the foundation for reference and information services in today's higher education settings. They include works that can most usefully satisfy the vast majority of demands made on a reference service, while not altogether excluding "exotic" or little-known works that will meet only the unusual need.

In addition to providing classified annotated bibliographies, topical sections include editors' guides that orient readers to each discipline, its scope and concerns, and the types of sources commonly consulted. The editors' guides will be useful to the generalist librarian and to the LIS student as background to the bibliographies or as intellectual frameworks for addressing reference questions.

The reader will find entries for works that are, for the most part, broadly focused; works on individual persons or with a narrow geographical or chronological focus are generally not included. Selection criteria favored titles published in the last twenty years; the reader may consult earlier printed bibliographies and indexes, such as the numerous print editions of the *Guide to Reference Books*, for many earlier and still important works. As libraries shift their print reference works to the general stacks or to remote locations, the online *Guide* and its older print editions may help to identify reference works that are no longer close at hand.

Sources in the *Guide* include websites, search engines, and full-text databases as well as the traditional array of encyclopedic, bibliographic, and compendious works. Online sources have replaced their printed versions for most librarians under most circumstances. A source only appears in one format; its annotation will identify the format options and describe the relationships between online and print versions. New reference works or editions are not automatically included in the *Guide*. Selection criteria favor sources that have stood some test of time and utility, as well as sources that are free but authoritative or sources that require purchase or licensing but are held at enough libraries to be reasonably available to readers of the *Guide*. The topical sections do not include universal sources that are covered in the General Reference Works division such as *Wikipedia* or *Ulrich's Periodicals Directory*; please consult the *Essential General Reference* volume or the online *Guide* for general sources that are common to all disciplines.

The reader is encouraged to peruse the annotations of entries in the same subcategory as known items. An annotation may contain extensive cross references to related sources that are not described separately as well as comparisons to related sources, indications of appropriate audiences for the source, and other details that provide significant added value. In an attempt to balance inclusion and exhaustion, a source may be included in several but not necessarily all relevant subcategories.

This segment on Medicine and Health includes sources for each patron in every type of library. The subsection on Consumer Health is rapidly growing and provides guidance to authoritative sources, which may be the aspect for which most patrons request assistance. The Division Editor's choice for most entertaining subsection is "Medical illustration and images" in the Medicine category, where records lead to atlases, photos, drawings, videos, reusable images and more, potentially matching every level of patron need from consumer to student to researcher.

We on the *Guide to Reference* team hope you find the segments helpful, and we welcome your comments at *guidetoreference@ala.org*. To get the full benefit of the comprehensive compilation in a wide range of subject areas as well as updates to each segment, we also encourage you to subscribe to the online *Guide*, where you have access to updated entries, annotations, user comments, and special features such as personal notes and lists. We regularly seek new editors, especially those who believe they can improve existing sections or develop new ones. Please check the website at *www.guidetoreference.org* for details on subscribing or volunteering to participate in the continuing development of the *Guide to Reference*.

Denise Beaubien Bennett
General Editor, *Guide to Reference*
Division Editor for Science, Technology, and Medicine

CONTRIBUTORS

Christa Modschiedler, retired Biomedical Librarian from the University of Chicago, has served as the Contributing Editor for the Medical and Health Sciences section of the Guide to Reference since the 11th print edition (1996). **Denise Beaubien Bennett**, Engineering Librarian at the University of Florida, is the Division Editor for the Science, Technology, and Medicine sections since 2005 and also has served as the General Editor of the Guide to Reference since 2009.

EDITOR'S GUIDE

The Medicine and Health category provides an annotated list of print and electronic biomedical and health-related reference sources, including Internet resources and digital image collections. The original purpose of the Guide to Reference remains (i.e., to provide a wide selection of bibliographic and information resources relevant to the provision of reference services in a biomedical library). It is intended to help users find relevant research, clinical, and consumer health information resources. As with previous editions of the Guide, the current edition cannot claim to be exhaustive in coverage; coverage in the medical section/subsections remains rather selective. Following previous editions of the Guide, some of the resources in this section are not strictly reference materials in the traditional sense. Emphasis is on U.S. resources, with a few representative examples from other countries. With few exceptions, materials in the medicine section would generally be found in the Library of Congress classification R. The intended audience is biomedical researchers, clinicians, and allied health professionals, as well as health consumers and the general public.

Consumer Health is the fastest-growing section within the medicine and health category, and it offers a wide range of options for public and academic librarians to assist patrons with varying levels of health care literacy skills.

The majority of reference resources included in this edition have been published between 1995 and 2013. Some of the classic selections were retained from the previous edition of the Guide, regardless of publication date; others are updated to the most recent editions. For older editions that have not been updated, an attempt was made to locate and substitute web-based resources with similar content. Print indexing and abstracting services have largely been replaced with online services, and Guide entries for bibliographic databases and digital database resources reflect this trend. Highly specialized databases have been kept to a minimum. Information on several high-profile print indexes is still included, but in summary format rather than with the full description found in the 11th edition of the Guide.

As a result of the rapid growth of the Internet, increased focus is on electronic resources, with inclusion of many relevant web-based electronic-only resources. The large number of biomedical websites dictates selective coverage. As a leading provider of information and information resources, the National Library of Medicine (NLM), the National Center for Biotechnology Information (NCBI), and the Centers for Disease Control and Prevention (CDC) have set the tone with the provision of a large number of highly useful web-based resources. Other U.S. government agencies, the World Health Organization (WHO), the Pan American Health Organization (PAHO), and professional and other noncommercial medical organizations also provide many relevant web-based reference sources.

Though it appears that Internet access is the preferred way for users to access biomedical reference materials, print reference collections continue to play a role at this time. In many cases, reference sources are published both in print and as an e-book. Electronic-only resources appear in steadily rising numbers. Though online reference is the desired future, much of the information that is needed today is still located in "trusted" print reference resources. The trend, however, is toward online reference resources.

— Christa Modschiedler
Contributing Editor for Medical and Health Sciences

1 Medicine

1 Encyclopedia of immunology. 2nd ed.
Peter J. Delves, Ivan M. Roitt. San Diego,
Calif.: Academic Press, 1998. 4 v., ill.
(some color). ISBN 0122267656
616.07903   QR180.4.E53

First ed., 1992. While due for an update, the 2nd
ed. of the encyclopedia expanded from three to four
volumes. Provides comprehensive coverage of the
field of immunology with significant additions to the
1st ed., including sections of color photographs and
more figures and illustrations. Each volume includes
a glossary from Roitt's 1997 text *Essential immunology*. Available as an e-book. Appropriate for research
libraries.

2 Health on the Net Foundation (HON).
http://www.hon.ch/. Health on the Net
Foundation. Geneva, Switzerland: Health
on the Net Foundation (HON). 1995–
                         R859.7.E43

Health On the Net Foundation (HON) is a nonprofit, nongovernmental organization known for
its HONcode, which defines rules and ethical standards for website developers on how information is
provided in terms of the source and data provided.
The HONcode is not considered an award or quality rating system for websites.

Provides a "portal to medical information on the
Internet" (*Website*). Searchable website provides
access to resources for individuals/patients and medical professionals. Includes HON's history and current

contact information, access to listservs, newsgroups,
and FAQs. For medical and health queries, HON's
Search HON (http://www.hon.ch/HONHunt/Adv
HONHunt.html) and HONselect© (http://www.hon
.ch/HONselect/) help locate quality websites and
support groups, medical terminology, journal articles,
and healthcare news. HONmedia (http://www.hon
.ch/HONmedia/) is a growing and searchable repository of medical images and videos (currently contains
6,800 medical images and videos, pertaining to 1,700
topics and themes).

**3 National Center for Biotechnology
Information**. http://www.ncbi.nlm.nih
.gov. National Center for Biotechnology
Information (U. S.), National Library of
Medicine, National Institutes of Health.
Rockville, Md.: National Center for
Biotechnology Information. 1995(?)–
660.6; 574.873282   TP248.2

Covers the National Center for Biotechnology Information (NCBI), an organization that advances science and health by providing access to biomedical
and genomic information. Its mission is to develop
"new information technologies to aid in the understanding of fundamental molecular and genetic
processes that control health and disease" (http://
www.ncbi.nlm.nih.gov/About/glance/ourmission
.html). Provides links to NCBI's literature databases, molecular databases, genomic resources, and
tools for data mining as well as information about

the work of the NCBI. Includes lists and links to NCBI resources in various helpful groupings, e.g., a complete list of all NCBI resources; a listing of databases, tools ("analyze data using NCBI software"), downloads ("get NCBI data or software"), how-to's ("learn how to accomplish specific tasks at NCBI"), and submissions ("submit data to Genbank or other NCBI databases"), in the following subcategories: chemicals & bioessays; data & software; DNA & RNA; domains & structures; genes & expression; genetics & medicine; genomes & maps; homology; literature; proteins; sequence analysis; taxonomy; training & tutorials; variation. The most popular database is PubMed. NCBI site search is at http://www.ncbi.nlm.nih.gov/ ncbisearch/; "GQuery" (http://www.ncbi.nlm.nih .gov/gquery/) allows a "global cross-database" search of NCBI databases. Other helpful links include an overview of NCBI resources ftp://ftp.ncbi.nih.gov/ pub/factsheets/Factsheet_NCBI_Overview.pdf, an annual update of NCBI databases, services, and tools in the special database issue of *Nucleic acids research* http://www.ncbi.nlm.nih.gov/pmc/articles/ PMC3531099/, selected databases, tools, help documents and educational materials http://www .ncbi.nlm.nih.gov/. "NCBI news link" (http://www .ncbi.nlm.nih.gov/news/) provides the latest information about NCBI services and activities, with "follow us" links to the "NCBI insights" blog and NCBI's social media outlets on Twitter, Facebook, and YouTube.

Guides

4   Alternative medicine. Christine A. Larson. Westport, Conn.: Greenwood Press, 2007. xv, 215 p. ISBN 0313337187
610   R733.L37
Contents: "The origins of alternative medicine"; "The theories underlying alternative medicine"; "The business of alternative medicine"; "Why consumers seek alternative treatments"; "Do alternative therapies work?"; "Should alternative medicine be regulated by the government?"; "Should managed care provide coverage for alternative therapies?"; "Pharmaceuticals versus alternative therapies"; "Culture and health: Who bears responsibility for health and healthcare?"; "The future of health and healthcare."

Guide to alternative medicine, covering practical

and also controversial issues, with recommendations on using safe alternative medicine practices together with Western medicine. Annotated primary source documents, alternative medicine timeline, and glossary. Includes bibliographical references (p. [201]–208) and index. For researchers, clinicians, consumers, and academic and medical libraries. Also available as an e-book.

The Medical Library Association guide to finding out about complementary and alternative medicine by Crawford provides an overview of resources, with emphasis on consumer health resources.

5   Alternative medicine resource guide. Francine Feuerman, Marsha J. Handel. Lanham, Md.: Medical Library Association, 1997. 335 p.
ISBN 0810832844
615.5   R733.F48
Provides information on alternative systems of medicine—Ayurvedic, Chinese, and herbal medicine, homeopathy, naturopathy—and various manipulative (e.g., chiropractic and osteopathy) and other therapies, such as biofeedback and sensory therapies. Organized into two main sections: pt. I, a resource guide with reference information on specific services and products, organizations, and companies; pt. II, a selective, evaluative, annotated bibliography of books, journals, and newsletters, limited to English-language print sources published in the U.S. since 1988. Appendix lists book publishers. Index.

A more recent resource, *The Medical Library Association guide to finding out about complementary and alternative medicine* provides an overview of resources, with emphasis on consumer health resources. Includes books, periodicals, and websites.

6   Current practice in health sciences librarianship. Alison Bunting, Medical Library Association. Chicago; New York: Medical Library Association; Forbes Custom Publishing, 1994–2001. 8 v., ill.
First ed. (1943)–4th ed. (1982–1988) had title *Handbook of medical library practice*, 3 v.
Rev. ed. in 8 v.
Contents: v. 1 (1994), *Reference and information services in health sciences libraries*, ed. M. Sandra Wood; v. 2 (1995), *Educational services in health sciences libraries*, ed. F. Allegri; v. 3 (1996), *Information access and delivery in health sciences*

libraries, ed. Carolyn E. Lipscomb; v. 4 (1997), *Collection development and assessment in health sciences libraries*, ed. Daniel T. Richards and Dottie Eakin; v. 5 (1996), *Acquisitions in health sciences libraries*, ed. David H. Morse; v. 6 (2001), *Bibliographic management of information resources in health sciences libraries*, ed. Laurie L. Thomson; v. 7 (1999), *Health sciences environment and librarianship in health sciences libraries*, ed. Lucretia W. McClure; v. 8 (2001), *Administration and management in health sciences libraries*, ed. Rick B. Forsman.

A guide to library standards, practices, policies, and institutional issues in biomedical libraries, written by library specialists.

More recently published titles in this subject area include, for example, *Introduction to health sciences librarianship* (325) by Wood and *The Medical Library Association guide to managing health care libraries* (329).

7 Doody's review service. http://www
.doody.com/drs/. Doody Enterprises, Inc.
Chicago: Doody Enterprises, Inc. 2006–
Comprehensive database of expert reviews of books and software in the health sciences (basic science, clinical medicine, nursing, allied health, and other health-related disciplines), with bibliographic information and links to suppliers of digital versions of titles, a weekly literature update with timely reviews by professionals from major North American academic institutions, and ratings (Doody's Star Rating®) of newly published titles. Integrates the annually updated list of "Doody's Core Titles in the Health Sciences (DCT)" which "distills the perspectives of academic healthcare professionals and health sciences librarians into a core list" (*Publ. website*). DCT (http://www.doody.com/dct), first issued in 2004 and published each May, is a collection development and management tool created as a replacement for the discontinued "Brandon/Hill Selected Lists" (1965–2004).

**8 Introduction to reference sources in
the health sciences. 5th ed.** Jeffrey
T. Huber, Jo Anne Boorkman, Jean C.
Blackwell. New York: Neal-Schuman,
2008. 386 p. ISBN 9781555706364
016.61072   Z6658.I54; R118.6
First ed., 1980; 4th ed., 2004.

Contents: pt. 1, "The reference collection" (ch. 1); pt. 2, "Bibliographic sources" (ch. 2–6); pt. 3, "Information sources" (ch. 7–14).

Discusses various types of bibliographic and information sources, both print and electronic, and their use in reference work. Written for library-school students, practicing librarians, and health science library users. Each of the chapters covers specialized topics such as building, organizing, and managing a reference collection; bibliographic sources for monographs and periodicals; indexing, abstracting, and digital databases; terminology; medical and health statistics; history sources; and additional relevant areas. Contains figures and tables. Includes bibliographical references and index.

**9 The Medical Library Association
encyclopedic guide to searching and
finding health information on the
Web.** P. F. Anderson, Nancy J. Allee. New
York: Neal-Schuman Publ., 2004. 3 v.
ISBN 1555704948
025.06/61   R859.7.I58M436
Contents: v. 1, Search strategies/quick reference guide; v. 2, Diseases and disorders/mental health and mental disorders; v. 3, Health and wellness/life stages and reproduction, and cumulative index. A comprehensive guide written by experienced health sciences librarians. Recommends search terms, search strategies, and search engines for checking the Internet for answers to health-related questions. Useful for both health care consumers and librarians involved in teaching health information literacy. Companion website at http://www
-personal.umich.edu/~pfa/mlaguide/indextest
.html. Also available on CD-ROM, with search capability and links to over 11,000 web sites.

**10 The Medical Library Association's
master guide to authoritative
information resources in the health
sciences.** Laurie L. Thompson, Mori Lou
Higa, Esther Carrigan, Rajia Tobia, Medical
Library Association. New York: Neal-
Schuman Publishers, 2011. xv, 659 p.
ISBN 9781555707194
610.711   R118.2.M38
Contents: 1. Allied health; 2. Biomedical engineering; 3. Chiropractic; 4. Dentistry; 5. Environmental health; 6. Health services administration; 7. Hospital

administration; 8. Medical illustration; 9. Medicine; 10. Medical specialties; 11. Surgical specialties; 12. Nursing; 13. Nursing specialties; 14. Nutritional sciences; 15. Optometry; 16. Orthoptics; 17. Pharmacology; 18. Pharmacy; 19. Podiatry; 20. Medical psychology; 21. Medical sociology; 22. Pharmaceutical technology; 23. Veterinary medicine; 24. Anatomy; 25. Biochemistry; 26. Biology; 27. Genetics; 28. Biotechnology; 29. Physiology; 30. Analytical, diagnostic, and therapeutic techniques; 31. Ethics; 32. History of the health sciences; 33. Health education; 34. General reference.

This bibliography "is intended to offer an updated option to the iconic publication, 'Brandon/Hill selected list of print books and journals for the small medical library'" http://library.mssm.edu/brandon -hill/history.shtml (*Pref.*) which ceased publication in 2003. It expands the original list by also including works in the basic sciences, as well as digital and online publications. Covers both monographic and journal literature, also online formats, online databases, and other electronic resources. Entries indicate whether the work is appropriate for a particular collection or collections (e.g., hospital, academic, specialized collections, and/or consumer health collection). Describes 2,011 selected titles in the health sciences literature, including the clinical specialties, basic sciences, and emerging subject areas. Arranged by the "health occupations" (G02) and "biological sciences" tree schedules (G01) of NLM's MeSH: Medical subject headings (858). A companion online version will be regularly updated with new edition information (cf. *Pref.*). Index of monographs; Index of journals; Index of databases and electronic resources. Useful for academic and public libraries.

11   Medical reference works, 1679-1966: A selected bibliography. Supplement.
Mary Virginia Clark, Joy S. Martyniuk, John Ballard Blake, Medical Library Association. Chicago: Medical Library Association, 1970–. v.
016.61   Z6658.B63 Suppl.; R129
(Medical Library Association publication no. 3). Suppl., 1 comp. by Mary Virgina Clark; suppl. 2–3, comp. by Joy S. Richmond.

The 1st suppl. follows the pattern of the main work (Medical reference works, 1679–1966: A selected bibliography) but excludes references on the history of medicine "since material of this sort is listed in the annual *Bibliography of the history of medicine*" (*Pref.*, 16). Includes more than 300 references with the emphasis on works published 1967–68. The 2nd and 3rd suppl. are computer-produced from the National Library of Medicine's *Current catalog;* therefore, these citations are arranged by author and subject. "General historical works, pharmacopoeias, reviews, and popular works have been excluded" (*Pref.*), suppl. 2. A total of about 750 citations are added for the periods 1969–72 and 1973–74. Most references of the suppl. are annotated.

12   National Library of Medicine guide to finding health information. http:// www.nlm.nih.gov/services/guide.html. National Library of Medicine. Bethesda, Md.: National Institutes of Health. 2001–
Contents: How can the National Library of Medicine help me with my research?; Why should I go to a public library, and what can I find there?; What other resources can I find at a medical library, and how do I find one that is open to me?; How can I get information from other government or health-related organizations?; How do I search for other medical information on the Web?; How do I evaluate the information I find?

Overview and starting points for researchers concerning services provided by the National Library of Medicine, other government agencies, and health-related organizations. Provides links to consumer health information resources and professional health literature resources.

13   The new Walford guide to reference resources: Volume 1: Science, technology, and medicine. 9th ed.
Ray Lester. London: Facet, 2005–. xix, 827 p., ill. ISBN 1856044955
011.02   Z1035.1
"This book is the first volume of a series that succeeds *Walford's guide to reference material*, published.1959 and 2000 by Library Association Publishing (271)." The scope and format of this guide is much different from the "old Walford," and thus it would behoove librarians to keep both eds. on the shelf. This version concentrates on websites and on general interest resources, including many that aren't specific to science and technology. Includes

current awareness sources and many monographs that aren't traditional reference sources, but rather are popular introductions to topics.

Volume 2: The social sciences was published January 2008; and *Volume 3: Arts, humanities, and general reference* is expected in 2009. For more information, see publisher's page at http://www .facetpublishing.co.uk/search.php?search_keyword =walford.

14   Science.gov. http://www.science.gov/. U.S. Department of Energy, Office of Scientific and Technical Information. Oak Ridge, Tenn.: U.S. Dept. of Energy, Office of Scientific and Technical Information. 2002–

"Science.gov is a gateway to over 50 million pages of authoritative selected science information provided by U.S. government agencies, including research and development results."—*website*. Provides a single interface for searching major government-sponsored indexes; for example, NTIS, AGRICOLA, PubMed, STINET (http://stinet.dtic.mil/), and United States Patents. Also searches science-related websites of federal agencies. One can browse by major discplines and subjects or search one or all areas of Science.gov. A very good portal to government information.

Bibliography

15   ARBA in-depth: Health and medicine. Martin Dillon, Shannon Graff Hysell. Westport, Conn.: Libraries Unlimited, 2004. xiii, 252 p.
         016.61   Z6658.A648;R129
(ARBA in-depth series)

Contains 473 signed reviews for health-related and medical reference titles, taken from the last six editions of *American reference books annual* (*ARBA*). Includes reviews of print and Internet sites. Detailed table of contents, author/title, and subject indexes. Also available online. Intended for "reference librarians, collection development specialists, scholar, researcher, and patron."—*Cover*. Online version available via ARBAonline (http:// www.arbaonline.com/).

16   Bibliography of the history of medicine. National Library of Medicine

(U.S.), United States; Public Health Service. Bethesda, Md.; Washington: U.S. Dept. of Health and Human Services, Public Health Service, National Institutes of Health, National Library of Medicine; For sale by the Supt. of Docs., U.S. G.P.O, 1966–[1994]. 28 v.
    016.61/09 0067-7280   Z6660.B582

Produced by National Library of Medicine (NLM). Annual, each 5th issue being a quinquennial cumulation. Cumulations: 1964/69 (publ. 1972. 1475 p.); 1970/74 (1976. 1069 p.); 1975/79 (1980. 924 p.); 1980/84 (1985. 1300 p.); 1985/89 (1990. 1454 p.). Supt. of Docs classification: HE 20.3615. Consists of citations drawn from NLM's now discontinued HISTLINE database (cf. "FAQ Retired Databases" http://www.nlm.nih.gov/services/past databases.html) monographs, analytic entries for symposia, congresses, etc., and chapters in general monographs. Works on the general history and philosophy of science are largely excluded. Attempts to avoid extensive duplication of topics regularly covered in "Critical bibliographies" section of *Isis* (now merged into *History of Science, Technology and Medicine Database* (402), but there is considerable duplication with *Current work in the history of medicine* (later called *Wellcome bibliography for the history of medicine*.) Subject and author listings. Remains useful for pre-1993 material. NLM's History of Medicine Historical Collection webpages, "Rare Books and Journals" (http:// www.nlm.nih.gov/hmd/collections/books/index. html) and "Printed Catalogs and Guides" (http:// www.nlm.nih.gov/hmd/help/printed/index.html) provide further help in searching the literature in the history of medicine.

17   CAM resources project. http:// camresources.pbworks.com/. CAM Special Interest Group, Medical Library Association. Chicago: Medical Library Association. 2008-

Complementary and Alternative Medicine (CAM) Special Interest Group (SIG), Medical Library Association (MLA)

"The goal of the project is to have members.contribute to a bibliography of authoritative and informative books, databases, and websites that libraries can use to build their collections and to recommend to their users."—*Home page*. Arranged by subject categories (e.g., acupuncture, Ayurveda, energy medicine, herbal medicine, homeopathy, naturopathic medicine, osteopathic medicine, etc.). Presented in wiki format which allow participants to contribute directly. Website contains criteria for inclusion and instructions on how to contribute to the wiki. Includes both professional and consumer health titles.

18   A catalogue of seventeenth century printed books in the National Library of Medicine. Peter Krivatsy, National library of Medicine (U.S.). Bethesda, Md.: U.S. Dept. of Health and Human Services, Public Health Service, National Institutes of Health, National Library of Medicine, 1989. xiv, 1315 p.
016.61/09/032   Z6659.N38; R128.7
Shipping list no.: 89-261-P. Item 508-F.

For some 13,300 books printed 1601–1700, "monographs, dissertations and corresponding program disputations, broadsides, pamphlets and serials" (*Introd.*), provides title page transcription, physical description, and reference to standard bibliographies. Entries are alphabetical by author, editor, compiler, occasionally by corporate body, and in a few instances by title. Most authors' names are in vernacular form with cross-references to latinized or other names. There is no index, but the National Library of Medicine's History of Medicine Division maintains indexes of printers, publishers, and vernacular imprints.

Complements earlier catalogs of pre–19th-century holdings of NLM: *A catalogue of incunabula and manuscripts in the Army Medical Library,* by Dorothy M. Schullian and Francis E. Sommer, ([1948?]); *A catalogue of sixteenth century printed books in the National Library of Medicine,* comp. by Richard J. Durling (1967); *A catalogue of incunabula and sixteenth century books in the National Library of Medicine: first supplement,* comp. by Peter Krivatsy (1971); and *A short title catalogue of eighteenth century printed books in the National Library of Medicine,* comp. by John Ballard Blake (1979, 11).

19   The development of medical bibliography. Estelle Brodman. [Washington]: Medical Library Association, 1954. ix, 226 p., ports., diagrs.
016.61   Z6658.B7

(Publication [Medical Library Association]; no. 1)

Comprehensive survey of medical bibliography since 1500, covering printed medical bibliographies in Western languages that pertain to medicine in general rather than to its subdivisions or specialties. Personal bibliographies and bibliographies that do not make up the main portion of a work have been excluded, as have catalogs (with the exception of the *Index-catalogue of the Library of the Surgeon General's Office*). No distinction made between indexes and abstracts as bibliographies.

"For each bibliography discussed there is a biographical sketch of the compiler, a description of the work emphasizing advances in technique, and a discussion of the importance of the work in the history of medical bibliography."—*Introd.* Appendix 1 lists references; appendix 2 lists medical bibliographies since 1500 which were not discussed in the body of the text, arranged by century. General and author indexes. A digitized version of this book is available at http://www.nlm.nih.gov/hmd/collections/digital/brodman/brodman.html as part of the National Library of Medicine's History of Medicine digital collections. Like this work, *The great medical bibliographers: A study in humanism,* by John F. Fulton, identifies important medical bibliographies and bio-bibliographies.

20   Disease and destiny: A bibliography of medical references to the famous. Judson Bennett Gilbert. London: Dawsons of Pall Mall, 1962. 535 p.
016.92   Z6664.A1G5
Drawn largely from *Index-catalogue of the library of the Surgeon General's office* (IndexCat), *Index medicus,* and *Quarterly cumulative index medicus* (81).

A bibliography of writings that treat the medical history of famous people in history, the humanities, and the arts and sciences in all countries from ancient to modern times. Personalities are listed alphabetically and identified by dates of birth and death and a brief descriptive phrase. Books and papers about them are listed in chronological order. Introduction contains a bibliography of monographic literature of medicobiographical writing.

21   Doody's review service. http://www .doody.com/drs/. Doody Enterprises, Inc. Chicago: Doody Enterprises, Inc. 2006–

Comprehensive database of expert reviews of books and software in the health sciences (basic science, clinical medicine, nursing, allied health, and other health-related disciplines), with bibliographic information and links to suppliers of digital versions of titles, a weekly literature update with timely reviews by professionals from major North American academic institutions, and ratings (Doody's Star Rating®) of newly published titles. Integrates the annually updated list of "Doody's Core Titles in the Health Sciences (DCT)" which "distills the perspectives of academic healthcare professionals and health sciences librarians into a core list" (*Publ. website*). DCT (http://www.doody .com/dct), first issued in 2004 and published each May, is a collection development and management tool created as a replacement for the discontinued "Brandon/Hill Selected Lists" (1965–2004).

22 Grey literature report. http://www .greylit.org/. New York Academy of Medicine Library. New York: New York Academy of Medicine. [1999]– 362.1
1931-7050

A publication of the New York Academy of Medicine Library http://www.nyam.org/library/

Grey literature is defined as "that which is produced on all levels of government, academics, business and industry in print and electronic formats, but which is not controlled by commercial publishers" (Cf. *Website*, New York Academy of Medicine "What is Grey Literature?" http://www.greylit.org/about. Considered an alerting service to new grey literature in health services research and various public health topics, assisting researchers and librarians with the identification of this literature for both reference and collection development purposes. The Academy's entire Grey Literature Collection can be searched by keyword(s), with further refinements being offered. Also included on the website is an A–Z list of grey literature producing publishers (http://www.greylit.org/publishers/list), the New York Academy of Medicine Library's collection policy for grey literature (http://www.greylit.org/about/collection-development-policy), and other relevant links. The publications are cataloged in the New York Academy of Medicine Library online catalog.

23 History and bibliography of artistic anatomy: Didactics for depicting the human figure. Boris Röhrl. Hildesheim, Germany: Olms, 2000. xx, 493 p., ill. ISBN 3487110741
743.4/9   NC760.R65

Contents: pt. 1, History: ch.1, Introd., ch. 2, Anatomy in the art of the Ancient World and the Middle Ages; ch. 3, From the 13th to the 15th cent.; ch. 4, 16th cent.; ch. 5, 17th cent.; ch. 6, 18th cent.; ch. 7, 19th cent.; ch. 8, 20th cent.; ch. 9, definition of genres; pt. 2, Bibliography: (1) Bibliography and description of books A–Z; (2) Appendices: Selected list of secondary literature; Index of ill.; Index of persons; Index of places and schools of art.

Considered a reference book which contains the didactical structure and content of specific teaching manuals. Presents the different subgroups of medically oriented teaching and how anatomy was taught in schools. Includes, for example, Leonardo da Vinci's anatomical sketchbooks. The bibliography in pt. 2 contains "books on osteology, myology, morphology, and locomotion for artists. Treatises accompanying écorchés and theoretical essays. Manuals on proportions, expression and portrait drawing" (*t.p.*).

24 Institute of Medicine (IOM). http://www.iom.edu/. Institute of Medicine. Washington: National Academy of Sciences. 1998–

The Institute of Medicine (IOM), one of the U.S. National Academies, has the mission to "serve as adviser to the nation to improve health" and "provides independent, objective, evidence-based advice to policymakers, health professionals, the private sector, and the public"—*main page*. Offers a list of all publications by the IOM since 1970 (http://www .iom.edu/Reports.aspx), which cover a broad range of topics, including aging, child health, a variety of diseases, global health, health care quality, minority health, nutrition, public health, public policy, preventive medicine, women's health, and many other areas. The National Academies Press (http://www .nap.edu, 31) provides online access to the publications of the four National Academies, i.e., National Academy of Sciences (456), National Academy of Engineering, IOM, and National Research Council.

25 Medical and health care books and serials in print. R. R. Bowker Co. New York: Bowker, 1985–
016.61 0000085X   Z6658.B65R129

Medical and Health Care Books and Serials in Print. Title varies: 1972–77, *Bowker's medical books in print;* 1978–84, *Medical books and serials in print: An index to literature in the health sciences.* Derived from *Books in print, Ulrich's periodicals directory,* and related Bowker databases.

Description based on 2013 ed. (2 v.)

Contents: Vol. 1, Books—subject index; Books—title index A-M; v. 2, Books—title index N-Z; Books—author index; Publisher name index; Wholesaler and distributor index; Serials—subject index; Serials—title index.

A comprehensive and authoritative source for information on books published and distributed in the United States. Subjects include medicine, dentistry, nursing, nutrition, veterinary medicine, psychology, behavioral health, and other subject areas. Also included are U.S. and foreign serials, with full ordering and publishing information and also selected international series publications.

26   Medical heritage library. http://www
.medicalheritage.org/. Internet Archive
(Firm). San Francisco: Internet Archive.
2000–

Continually updated resource.

Digital collection of materials compiled collaboratively by many of the world's leading medical libraries (e.g., National Library of Medicine, Francis A. Countway Library of Medicine, Cushing/Whitney Medical Library, New York Public Library, and others) with historical resources in medicine. A growing and freely accessible collection of digitized medical rare books, pamphlets, journals, and films, with works from the past six centuries. Searchable and browsable.

See further details and list of contributors on the "About" page at http://www.medicalheritage .org/about/.

27   Medical humanities dissertations.
http://www.hsls.pitt.edu/histmed/
dissertations/. Jonathon Erlen, University
of Pittsburgh Health Sciences Library
System. Pittsburgh: Health Sciences
Library, University of Pittsburgh Medical
Center. 2001–

Provides a monthly current awareness service for selected recent medical dissertations and theses. Arranged by topics, currently covers the following areas: AIDS (social and historical contexts); alternative medicine (social and historical contexts); art and medicine; biomedical ethics; history of medicine prior to 1800; history of medicine and health care; history of science and technology; literature/theater and medicine; nursing history; pharmacy/pharmacology and history; philosophy and medicine; psychiatry/ psychology and history; public health/international health; religion and medicine; women's health and history. To view complete citations, abstracts, and full-text of dissertations requires a subscription to Proquest dissertations and theses (PQDT).

**28   The Medical Library Association's
master guide to authoritative
information resources in the health
sciences.** Laurie L. Thompson, Mori
Lou Higa, Esther Carrigan, Rajia Tobia,
Medical Library Association. New York:
Neal-Schuman Publishers, 2011. xv, 659
p. ISBN 9781555707194

610.711   R118.2.M38

Contents: 1. Allied health; 2. Biomedical engineering; 3. Chiropractic; 4. Dentistry; 5. Environmental health; 6. Health services administration; 7. Hospital administration; 8. Medical illustration; 9. Medicine; 10. Medical specialties; 11. Surgical specialties; 12. Nursing; 13. Nursing specialties; 14. Nutritional sciences; 15. Optometry; 16. Orthoptics; 17. Pharmacology; 18. Pharmacy; 19. Podiatry; 20. Medical psychology; 21. Medical sociology; 22. Pharmaceutical technology; 23. Veterinary medicine; 24. Anatomy; 25. Biochemistry; 26. Biology; 27. Genetics; 28. Biotechnology; 29. Physiology; 30. Analytical, diagnostic, and therapeutic techniques; 31. Ethics; 32. History of the health sciences; 33. Health education; 34. General reference.

This bibliography "is intended to offer an updated option to the iconic publication, 'Brandon/Hill selected list of print books and journals for the small medical library'" http://library.mssm.edu/ brandon-hill/history.shtml (*Pref.*) which ceased publication in 2003. It expands the original list by also including works in the basic sciences, as well as digital and online publications. Covers both monographic and journal literature, also online formats, online databases, and other electronic resources. Entries indicate whether the work is appropriate for a particular collection or collections (e.g., hospital, academic, specialized collections, and/or consumer health collection). Describes 2,011 selected titles in the health sciences literature, including the clinical specialties, basic sciences, and emerging subject areas. Arranged by the "health occupations" (G02) and "biological sciences" tree schedules (G01) of NLM's MeSH: Medical subject headings (858). A companion online version will be regularly updated with new edition information (cf. *Pref.*). Index of monographs; Index of journals; Index of databases and electronic resources. Useful for academic and public libraries.

29   Medicine, health, and bioethics: Essential primary sources. K. Lee Lerner, Brenda Wilmoth Lerner. Detroit: Thomson/Gale, 2006. lvii, 513 p., ill. ISBN 1414406231
174.2   R724.M313
(Series: Social issues primary sources collection)

Contains complete primary sources or excerpts of documents and publications published 1823–2006, illustrating major biomedical issues. Each entry includes the complete text or an excerpt with complete original citation, subject area, historical context, significance. For students, health professionals, and also general readers. Available online via Gale virtual reference library.

30   Medicine: A bibliography of bibliographies. Theodore Besterman. Totowa, N.J.: Rowman and Littlefield, 1971. 409 p. ISBN 0874710502
016.01661   Z6658.A1B4
Rather than listing citations alphabetically as they were in the parent publication, this source lists them topically as follows: medicine, anatomy, hygiene, pharmacology, pharmaceutics, psychiatry, and special subjects such as adrenal glands, balneology, and yaws. "Useful to those who seek primary signposts to information in varied fields of inquiry" (*Pref.*). Wide subject and language coverage.

31   National academies press. www.nap .edu/. National Academies Press (U.S.), National Academies (U.S.), National Academy of Sciences (U.S.). Washington: National Academies Press. 1999–
Z1217.N37
Contains free online access to over 3,700 monographs, mainly reports of the academy on issues of importance to the science community and society—for example, future trends in employment opportunities in different fields, analyses of discrepancies in gender/racial makeup of scientists in discplines, as well as the prospects of scientific projects or programs. Overall, it provides a wealth of information on the state of science. The National Academies are made up of the National Academy of Sciences (456), National Academy of Engineering, the Institute of Medicine (24), and the National Research Council.

32   Repertorium commentationum a societatibus litterariis editarum. Jeremias David Reuss. New York: B. Franklin, 1961. 16 v.
Z5051.R44
Originally publ. 1801–21; repr., 1961. Contents: (1) Historia naturalis, generalis et zoologia; (2) Botanica et mineralogia; (3) Chemia et res metallica; (4) Physica; (5) Astronomia; (6) Oeconomia; (7) Mathesis, mechanica, hydrostatica, hydraulica, hydrotechnia, aerostatica, pnevmatica, technologia, architectura civilis, scientia navalis, scientia militaris; (8) Historia; (9) Philologia, linguae, scriptures graeci, scriptores latini, litterae elegaritiores, poesis, rhetorica, ars antiqua, pictura, musica; (10-16) Scientia et ars medica et chirurgica.

A very valuable index to the publ. of the learned societies of various countries from the time of the founding of each society to 1800, thus preceding the Royal Society of London's Catalogue of scientific papers. Sections are arranged topically and include an author index. Freely available online at http://www-gdz.sub.uni-goettingen.de/cgi-bin/digbib.cgi?PPN366452967.

33   Thornton's medical books, libraries, and collectors: A study of bibliography and the book trade in relation to the medical sciences. 3rd rev. ed. John Leonard Thornton, Alain Besson, John Leonard Thornton. Aldershot, Hants, U.K.; Brookfield, Vt.: Gower, 1990. xxi, 417 p., ill. ISBN 0566054817
381.45002   Z286.M4T47
First ed., 1949, and 2nd ed., 1966, had title: *Medical books, libraries and collectors: A study of bibliography and the book trade in relation to the medical sciences.*

An introductory history of the literature of medicine from the earliest times through the 19th century. A separate chapter treats medical writings before the invention of printing. Medical literature of the 20th century is included in chapters on growth of the medical periodical literature and medical libraries of today. Intends "to record the chief writings of every prominent author and to chart the growth and development of ancillary subjects such as periodicals, bibliographies and libraries"—*Introd.*

Includes a bibliography and indexes of personal and institutional names, journal titles, and subjects.

34   Women in medicine: A bibliography of the literature on women physicians.
Sandra L. Chaff. Metuchen, N.J.: Scarecrow Press, 1977. v. ISBN 0810810565
016.61069/52   Z7963.M43W65; R692
"Comprehensive coverage of the literature about women physicians in all parts of the world" (*Introd.*). Includes 4,000 citations (books, medical and non-medical journal articles, alumnae and alumni magazine articles, doctoral dissertations), representing the literature from 1750 through 1975. Entry provides bibliographical information and annotation. Author, subject, and personal name indexes; appendixes of directories and special library collections.

Audiovisual materials

35   Fact sheet, access to audiovisual materials. http://www.nlm.nih.gov/pubs/factsheets/lrc.html. National Library of Medicine (U.S.). Bethesda, Md.: National Library of Medicine. 2001–
Provides a description of NLM's audiovisual collection covering biomedical subjects: "60,000 audiovisual programs in almost 40 formats . . . over 3,500 . . . of historical interest"—*main page*. Includes instructions for on-site access, copyright restrictions for audiovisual materials, and other information. Online catalog access to identify audiovisual materials via Locator-Plus (52).

36   Guide to mental health motion pictures. http://www.nlm.nih.gov/hmd/collections/films/mentalhealthguide/index.html. National Library of Medicine (U.S). Bethesda, Md.: National Library

of Medicine U.S. Dept. of Health, Education, and Welfare, National Institutes of Health. 2012
Administered by the National Library of Medicine's Historical Audiovisuals Collection (HAV). Compiled and Edited by: Sarah Eilers; Technical Assistance: Nancy Dosch, Anatoliy Milikhiker, Anthony Vu.

This online guide contains references to approximately 200 films and videorecordings produced from the 1930s to 1970 dealing "with mental or psychiatric disorders as defined or recognized at the time the films were produced, as well as their corresponding causes and treatments. . . . The mental disorders found in these productions include anxiety, depression, psychosis, schizophrenia, substance abuse, and bipolar, dissociative, and personality disorders. Some films also consider as mental disorders topics that are not so classified today, such as alcoholism, homosexuality, and marital or maternal dissatisfaction. Therapies and treatments include psychiatric interviews, counseling and talk therapy, electro-convulsive therapy, frontal lobe surgery (lobotomy), pharmaceuticals, art therapy, residential treatment programs, and community-based treatment programs."—*Introd. and Scope*. Includes title, date of publication, running time, conditions/therapies, names, abstract, and link to the full catalog record in LocatorPlus (52) for each item. Subject index.

Further information on additional content and a selected list of notable titles can be found at http://www.nlm.nih.gov/hmd/collections/films/mentalhealthguide/scope.h tml. It is part of the NLM films and video collections http://www.nlm.nih.gov/hmd/collections/films/index.html#A0 which includes more than 5,300 films and video recordings from 1900 to the present.

Other online guides to NLM's historical audiovisual collections include, for example, *Guide to tropical disease motion pictures and audiovisuals* http://www.nlm.nih.gov/hmd/collections/films/tropicalguide/index.html and *National Library of Medicine's Motion pictures and videocassettes about the Public Health Service and its agencies* http://www.nlm.nih.gov/hmd/pdf/motionpicture.pdf. A print title is *Mental health motion pictures*.

37   Videos of surgical procedures (MedlinePlus). http://www.nlm.nih.gov/medlineplus/surgeryvideos.html.

National Library of Medicine (U.S.). Bethesda, Md: National Library of Medicine, National Institutes of Health, U.S. Dept. of Health and Human Services. 2004?–

Pt. of MedlinePlus®. Provides links to prerecorded webcasts of surgical procedures, that is, actual operations performed at medical centers in the U.S. since Jan. 2004. Intended for educational purposes.

Government publications

38 Current bibliographies in medicine. http://www.nlm.nih.gov/ archive/20120907/pubs/resources.html. National Library of Medicine (U.S.); Reference Section. Bethesda, Md.: U.S. Dept. of Health & Human Services, National Institutes of Health, National Library of Medicine, Reference Section. 1996–2007

Publ. in print format between 1988–97, continuing in part *Literature search* of the National Library of Medicine (NLM) which ceased in 1988. In 1989, absorbed NLM's "Specialized bibliography series." Selected bibliographies also published in online format under title *NLM resource lists and bibliographies: current bibliographies in medicine* 1992–2007.

Bibliographies prepared in support of National Institutes of Health Consensus Development Conferences (cf. website). Each bibliography covers a subject area of biomedicine of current popular interest. 2000–2007 offered in both HTM and PDF formats. Also referred to as CBM.

39 National Library of Medicine publications catalog. http://www.nlm .nih.gov/pubs/pubcat.html. National Library of Medicine (U.S.). Bethesda, Md.: U.S. National Library of Medicine, National Institutes of Health, Dept. of Health & Human Services. 2000–

A–Z listing of publications in a variety of formats, publ. by and available from the National Library of Medicine (NLM). Includes, for example, all NLM fact sheets, audiovisuals, bibliographies, books, booklets, brochures, catalogs, monographs, online

resources, pamphlets, reports, etc. Provides bibliographic, ordering, pricing, and related information.

Previously publ. in print format. Title varies: 1981–90, *Publications/National Library of Medicine (U.S.)*; 1991–?, *Catalog of publications, audiovisuals, & software.*

Incunabula

40 Incunabula scientifica et medica: Short title list. Arnold C. Klebs. Bruges, Belgium: Saint Catherine Press, 1938 [i.e., 1937]. 359 p.

Z240.K62

Repr. from *Osiris*, v. 4 (1938): [1]–359.

"Intended . . . to offer . . . a survey in the briefest possible terms" (*Introd.*). Arranged alphabetically by the names of authors (approx. 650 names) or by keyword in the case of anonymous works. The vernacular form of personal name is used whenever possible, otherwise the latinized name. Editions are arranged in ascending chronological order. There are approx. 3,000 editions, with dubious editions excluded. Cross-references at the end.

Periodicals

41 Chemical Abstracts Service source index. American Chemical Society. [Columbus, Ohio]: Chemical Abstracts Service

016.5405 0001-0634   Z5523.A52QD1

Now freely available online at http://cassi.cas.org/ search.jsp.

Also cited as *CAS source index* and *CASSI.*

CASSI provides complete bibliographical details for any publication cited in *Chemical Abstracts* or the CAS databases. This cumulation contains information concerning more than 80,000 scientific and technical serial and nonserial source publications, proceedings of nonrecurring meetings, and other compilations of articles; including cross-references, there are over 175,000 entries.

Invaluable for determining full titles from abbreviations and variant names; for publication history, including discontinuations, name changes, and title twigging. Until 1998, CASSI listed library holding information, making it valuable to locate obscure publications. Although this is no longer done, CASSI has preserved the pre-1998 holdings information.

Coverage is defined broadly because *Chemical Abstracts* covers not only the chemical sciences but also related biological, engineering, and physical sciences. Moreover, CASSI has added source material cited in *Beilstein handbook of organic chemistry* prior to 1907 and *Chemisches Zentralblatt* from 1830 to 1969.

Each entry includes the full title with its abbreviated portions printed in boldface; entries are alphabetized letter-by-letter according to this abbreviated title. All titles are printed in the roman alphabet; for titles not in Western European languages, a translation is included. Entries also include CODEN; ISSN; ISBN; previous and succeeding titles; original language(s) of publication, summaries, and table of contents; history and frequency of publication; current volume/year correlation; address of publisher or source (or abbreviation if a standard source); AACR2 standard entry; date and place of meeting information for nonserial titles; cross-references, including references to title-to-title translations journals if extant; pre-1998 library holdings information; and CAS Document Delivery Service availability.

CASSI updates are available as quarterly supplements for a period of 5 years between cumulations. Electronic versions: available as a CD-ROM and online database. These versions are searchable by title, abbreviated title, keyword in title, CODEN, ISSN, ISBN, meeting data, source information, holdings information, and publication details.

42   Directory of open access journals.
http://www.doaj.org. Lund University Libraries. Lund, Sweden: Lund University Libraries. 2003– 011.34

Directory of free, full-text, scholarly journals spanning most disciplines. Journals are international and multilingual in scope and must be peer reviewed or have an editorial review board. The database includes more than 10,000 journals, the majority of which are searchable at the article level. Browsable by title and subject tree. Entries link out to full-text content at the journal's homepage; records include title, subject, ISSN, publisher, language, related keywords, and year of first online issue available.

43   EMBASE list of journals indexed.
Excerpta Medica. Amsterdam,

Netherlands: Elsevier Science, 1979–2006 0929-3302

Previous title, 1979–82: *Excerpta medica: List of journals abstracted*; 1983–92: *List of journals abstracted.*

Description based on 2006 ed. A later print version is no longer available.

Complete list of journals (more than 5,000) indexed in EMBASE and its print equivalent, *Excerpta medica.* Provides information on new, changed, and discontinued titles. Arranged in alphabetical order by full journal title, with ISSN, CODEN, the abbreviated journal title, and an indication if the journal is indexed cover-to-cover or selectively and if it is a "priority journal" (currently 1,835 titles are considered the most important in biomedicine by the publisher). Also provides several other listings: number of journals per classification; list of journals per subject classification; number of journals per country of publication; list of journals per country of publication.

Information about the number of journals indexed in EMBASE and related information at http://www.embase.com/info/helpfiles/search-forms/journals. "Browse journals" to view an alphabetic list and browse through individual volumes, issues, and table of content. However, journals that are unique to MEDLINE do not appear in this listing.

44   Encyclopedia of global health. Yawei Zhang. Los Angeles: Sage, 2008. 4 v. (xli, 1938, 1-64 p.), ill. ISBN 9781412941
362.103   RA441.E53

Major headings listed in "Reader's guide": children's health; countries: Africa, Americas, Asia, Europe, Pacific; diseases, cancers; diseases, localized; diseases, systemic; drugs and drug companies; health sciences; men's health; mental health; organizations and associations; procedures and therapies; research; society and health; women's health.

Interdisciplinary reference to physical and mental health topics and current health status for countries worldwide. A–Z arrangement. Includes entries on national health policies, biographies of physicians, researchers, medical institutes and other organizations, drugs, surgical operations, etc. Chronology of major medical advances (8000 BCE–2007 CE), a glossary of health-related definitions, cross-references, and bibliographic citations.

For both health professionals and general readers. Available online via Sage eReference.

45   Encyclopedia of health care management. Michael J. Stahl. Thousand Oaks, Calif.: Sage, 2004. xxxvii, 621 p., ill. ISBN 0761926747
362.1068   RA971.E52

Alphabetical list of entries at the beginning of the book provides an overview of the terminology and variety of subject areas covered in this resource including business and economics, statistics, law, clinical research, informatics, and others. A reader's guide with the following major headings is provided: Accounting and activity-based costing, Economics, Finance, Health policy, Human resources, Information technology, Institutions and organizations, International health care issues, Legal and regulatory issues, Managed care, Marketing and customer value, Operations and decision making, Pharmaceuticals and clinical trials, Quality, Statistics and data mining, and Strategy. The main section, consisting of approximately 650 entries, is alphabetically arranged. Each entry contains the term's definition, background, and other relevant information. Includes tables on health care acronyms, medical degrees, medical legislation, and others. Cross-references, list of further readings, and websites. Index. Also available as an e-book.

46   Encyclopedia of pestilence, pandemics, and plagues. Joseph Patrick Byrne, Anthony S. Fauci. Westport, Conn.: Greenwood Press, 2008. 2 v. (xxv, 872 p.), ill., maps. ISBN 9780313341014
614.4003   RA652.E535
Contents: v. 1. A-M — v. 2. N-Z.

Covers both historical and modern infectious diseases (e.g., HIV/AIDS; SARS; influenza epidemics, etc.) and historical epidemics (e.g., black death; bubonic plague; great plague of London; public health in the Islamic world 1000-1600; syphilis during the 16th century, etc.), including social, economic, and political factors. Sidebars within entries contain information from primary sources. Also includes entries on persons considered important in historical epidemiology. List of all entries and a guide to related topics in front of v. 1. Glossary, bibliography of both print and electronic resources, and index in v. 2. For

students, health professionals, and also general readers. Also available as an e-book.

By the same author, *Encyclopedia of black death*, is "a collection of 300 interdisciplinary entries covering plague and its effects on Western society across four centuries" (*Introd.*), with main focus on the second plague pandemic for the years 1340-1840. However, also includes some pre-1340s and post-1840s subjects, a timeline of events, glossary, cross-references, and a bibliography. Considered a useful resource for undergraduates and above and also for general readers. *Encyclopedia of plague and pestilence: From ancient times to the present* (374) is another resource in this area.

The following two Internet resources provide details on the influenza epidemic of 1918-1919: *The Great pandemic: The United States in 1918-1919* http://www.flu.gov/pandemic/history/1918, with historical details (and also a link to current information http://www.flu.gov/index.html) and *Influenza encyclopedia* (University of Michigan Center for the History of Medicine) http://www.influenzaarchive.org/, an excellent, comprehensive searchable collection of primary source documents, images, timelines, reference lists, etc. which provides details of the impact of the epidemic on 50 U.S. cities.

The Centers for Disease Control and Prevention (CDC) provides maps and statistics of cases of human plague in the U.S. and worldwide at http://www.cdc.gov/plague/maps/.

47   List of serials indexed for online users. http://www.nlm.nih.gov/tsd/serials/lsiou.html. National Library of Medicine (U.S.). Bethesda, Md.: National Library of Medicine. [2000]–
016.6105 1555-2403   Z6660.L56
1983–2005 print ed. (2002–2012 publ. by Bernan, Lanham, Md.). Continues: *List of serials and monographs indexed for online users* (publ. 1980–2). Also called LSIOU. Updated annually. Description based on the 2013 ed.

Arranged alphabetically by abbreviated title followed by full title, with bibliographic information for serials which are indexed with MeSH® (858) terms and cited in MEDLINE®/PubMed®. The 2013 list contains 14,555 serial titles, including 5,648 titles currently indexed for MEDLINE. Indicates titles which are selectively indexed (symbol used: "s") and "core clinical journals" subset limit (symbol used: "*"). Further bibliographic information can be found via LocatorPlus® (52).

A separate list previously available for the titles indexed for MEDLINE, entitled *List of journals indexed for MEDLINE*, ceased with the 2008 edition.

48 **PMC (PubMed Central)**. http://www.pubmedcentral.nih.gov. National Library of Medicine, National Center for Biotechnology Information (U.S.), National Institutes of Health (U.S.). Bethesda, Md.: National Center for Biotechnology Information. 2000–
025174570610.7   R11

Produced by National Library of Medicine (NLM) and National Institutes of Health (NIH); developed and managed by NIH's National Center for Biotechnology Information (NCBI). Previously called PubMed central: An archive of life science journals.

NLM's free and open-access online digital archive of peer-reviewed full-text research papers in the medical and life sciences. The continuously growing PMC journals list (http://www.ncbi.nlm.nih.gov/pmc/journals/) includes, for example, titles from the Public Library of Science (PLoS, 49) and BioMed central (BMC, 100)(http://www.biomedcentral.com/), publishers of many open-access journals. Also includes the complete back files of many important medical journals that NLM has digitized in collaboration with the Wellcome Trust and the Joint Informations Systems Committee (JISC). The list is alphabetically arranged and available as a full or tabbed list, used to find journals added to PMC in the last 60 days. Other helpful links are provided, e.g., NIH public access (http://publicaccess.nih.gov/) and NIH manuscript submission system (http://www.nihms.nih.gov/). Further information at PMC Frequently asked questions (http://www.pubmedcentral.nih.gov/about/faq.html). The NLM fact sheet (http://www.nlm.nih.gov/pubs/factsheets/dif_med_pub.html) explains the differences between MEDLINE, PubMed, and PubMed central. Help with the "PMCID-PMID-Manuscript ID-DOI converter" tool at http://www.ncbi.nlm.nih.gov/pmc/pmctopmid/.

49 **Public library of science (PLoS)**. http://www.plos.org/. Public Library of Science. [San Francisco]: Public Library of Science. 2000–

PLoS is a non-profit organization of scientists and physicians who are committed to promote free and timely online access to the international scientific and medical literature. Since 2003 a nonprofit scientific and medical publishing venture. Publishes high-profile open-access journals (e.g., *PLoS biology*, *PLoS medicine*, *PLoS ONE*, and several others), funded by authors and participating institutions. The full content of every PLoS issue is placed into PubMed central (PMC, 48). PLoS titles can also be accessed via Directory of open access journals: DoAJ (42).

Library catalogs

50 **The Cole Library of early medicine and zoology: Catalogue of books and pamphlets.** Nellie B. Eales. Oxford, U.K.: Alden P. [for] the University of Reading Library, 1969–1975. v, plate, facsim.
016.59   Z6676.R35

Contents: v. 1, 1472–1800; v. 2, 1800 to present day and supplement to v. 1.

A descriptive catalog of a distinguished collection. Chronological arrangement, with subject and author indexes.

51 **IndexCat**. http://www.nlm.nih.gov/hmd/indexcat/ichome.html. U.S. National Library of Medicine, Library of the Surgeon-General's Office, Army Medical Library, Armed Forces Medical Library, National Library of Medicine. Bethesda, Md.: U.S. National Library of Medicine, National Institutes of Health, Health and Human Services. 2004-

Z6676

IndexCat™ is the digitized version of the *Index-catalogue of the library of the Surgeon General's office* (Army Medical Library), ser. 1–5, 61 v. Washington: U.S. Govt. Printing Office (16), 1880–1961. Ser. 1, A–Z (1880–95); ser. 2, A–Z (1896–1916); ser. 3, A–Z (1918–32); ser. 4. v. 1–11, A–Mn (1936–55); ser. 4 is incomplete, last half was never published; 5th series (1959–61).

"A collaborative project initiated by the American Association for the History of Medicine with support from the Wellcome Trust, the Burroughs Wellcome Fund, and the U.S. National Library of Medicine."—*Website*

Content and coverage is the same as the printed catalog, e.g., from early times through 1950 imprints, including books, journal articles, dissertations, pamphlets, reports, newspaper clippings, case studies, obituary notices, letters, and portraits, as well as rare books and manuscripts. Recently, two new collections, involving medieval scientific English and Latin texts, were made available through IndexCat. Further detailed information about content and coverage of *IndexCat* is at http://www.nlm.nih.gov/hmd/indexcat/aboutic .html and http://www.nlm.nih.gov/services/faqic .html.

Subject headings in IndexCat do not conform to the Medical subject headings (MeSH®, 858). Searchable by keywords (subject, author, title, journal title, note content, and by year of publication).

IndexCat and LocatorPlus™ (52), NLM's online public catalog, may be searched at the same time. LocatorPlus contains NLM holdings and current information for books, pamphlets, dissertations, and journal titles.

52 LocatorPlus. http://purl.access.gpo .gov/GPO/LPS4582. National Library of Medicine (U.S.). Bethesda, Md.: National Library of Medicine. 1998–

LocatorPlus is the National Library of Medicine (NLM) continuously updated online public catalog. Includes catalog records for books, journals, audiovisuals, and other materials in NLM's collections. Provides holdings information for journals and other materials; links from catalog records to Internet resources, including online journals; and access to other NLM resources. Can be searched by keyword, author, title, journal title, MeSH (858), call number, etc. See LocatorPlus fact sheet at http:// www.nlm.nih.gov/pubs/factsheets/locatorplus.html for additional information. The NLM catalog provides another search interface to NLM bibliographic records for journals, books, audiovisuals, electronic resources, etc.

53 Medical heritage library. http://www .medicalheritage.org/. Internet Archive (Firm). San Francisco: Internet Archive. 2000–

Continually updated resource.

Digital collection of materials compiled collaboratively by many of the world's leading medical libraries (e.g., National Library of Medicine, Francis A. Countway Library of Medicine, Cushing/Whitney Medical Library, New York Public Library, and others) with historical resources in medicine. A growing and freely accessible collection of digitized medical rare books, pamphlets, journals, and films, with works from the past six centuries. Searchable and browsable.

See further details and list of contributors on the "About" page at http://www.medicalheritage .org/about/.

54 New York Academy of Medicine Library online catalog. http://www .nyam.org/library/search-collections/. New York Academy of Medicine, New York Academy of Medicine Library. New York: New York Academy of Medicine

Z680.3

Contains the library's complete journal collection, and portions of rare books, manuscript collections, and government documents. "Records for some, but not all, of the archival and manuscript collections in the New York Academy of Medicine Library can be found in the Library's online catalog, although many of the small manuscript holdings can only be found at the present time by consulting the printed catalog"—Website. For materials not found in the online catalog, the New York Academy of Medicine's card catalog or printed catalogs (images of all cards filed in the card catalog through approximately 1970) still need to be consulted. They include *Subject catalog of the library* (1969; 34 v. and 4-v. supplement), *Author catalog of the library* (1969; 43 v. and 5-v. supplement), *Illustration catalog* (1976), and *Portrait catalog* (5 v., 1960).

A prominent title published by the New York Academy of Medicine is *Grey literature report* (22). "Resource guide for disaster medicine and public health" (http://disasterlit.nlm.nih.gov/, 1443), developed in collaboration with the National Library of Medicine, is described "gateway to freely available online resources related to disaster medicine and public health . . . resources include expert guidelines, factsheets, websites, research reports, articles, and other tools aimed at the public health community."—Website.

55 **NLM catalog**. http://www.ncbi.nlm
.nih.gov/nlmcatalog. National Library
of Medicine (U.S.), National Center
for Biotechnology Information (U.S.).
Bethesda, Md.: National Library of
Medicine. 2004–

"The NLM Catalog provides access to NLM bibliographic data for journals, books, audiovisuals, computer software, electronic resources and other materials. Links to the library's holdings in LocatorPlus (52), NLM's online public access catalog, are also provided"—*main page*.

56 **The Wellcome library: The library at
Wellcome collection**. http://library
.wellcome.ac.uk/. Wellcome Library.
London: Wellcome Library

The Wellcome Library website provides several links to its holdings. The online library catalog contains records for all Wellcome Library collections in all formats, covering both the history of medicine and current biomedical topics. It also provides access to the growing Wellcome images, with more than 160,000 images; Moving image and sound Collections, Iconographic collections (more than 100,000 prints, drawings, paintings, photographs, and other media); and Archives and manuscripts of persons and organizations in medical science and health care. Links to MetaFind, which allows cross-searching of various catalogs and databases, and MedHist.

57 **WHOLIS**. http://www.who.int/
library/databases/en/. World Health
Organization. Geneva, Switzerland:
World Health Organization

Title varies: WHOLIS; WHOLIS Webcat. Formerly known as World Health Organization library catalogue; WHO library catalogue; World Health Organization library catalog; WHO library catalog;

WHO library & information networks for knowledge (LNK)

The WHO LNK (http://www.who.int/library/en/) offers worldwide online access to WHOLIS, WHO's online catalog. "WHOLIS indexes all WHO publications from 1948 onwards and articles from WHO-produced journals and technical documents from 1985 to the present. An on-site card catalogue provides access to the pre-1986 technical documents. It contains bibliographic information with subject headings and, for some records, abstracts. For some records, full text links are available. An online tutorial for guidance in using WHOLIS is available"—*main page*.

Classification

58 **AJCC cancer staging manual.
7th ed.** Stephen B. Edge, American
Joint Committee on Cancer. New York:
Springer, 2010. xiv, 648 p., ill., port.
ISBN 9780387884400
616.9940012   RC258.A333

First ed.–4th ed. (1977–92) had title: *Manual for staging of cancer*; 5th ed., 1997; 6th ed., 2002. Prepared by the American Joint Committee on Cancer (AJCC), first organized in 1959 as the American Joint Committee for Cancer Staging and End-Results Reporting (AJC), in cooperation with the UICC (Union internationale contre le cancer = International Union against Cancer, 220). "Since the 1980s, the work of the UICC and AJCC has been coordinated, resulting in the simultaneous publication of TNM classification of malignant tumors by the UICC and the AJCC Cancer staging manual."—*Pref*. Also available as a handbook: *AJCC cancer staging handbook: From the AJCC cancer staging manual*.

Designed to facilitate uniform classification and description of cancer and information on staging cancer at various anatomic sites. Some non-anatomic factors (e.g., relevant important markers which may be required to make treatment decisions) have also been added to the classification. A historical overview, with information on the founding organizations, is provided in the introduction. UICC TNM history can be found at http://www.uicc.org/aboutuicc. Organized into 13 parts (e.g., head and neck, musculoskeletal sites, central nervous system, ophthalmic sites, etc.) and 57 chapters, with changes since the previous edition summarized at the beginning of each chapter. Black-and-white illustrations and line drawings which ".depict the anatomic extent of disease for tumor (T), regional lymph node (N), and distinct metastasis (M) for multiple sites.and allow the reader to. visualize the progressive extent of malignant disease".—*Publ. note*. Includes new or revised classifications for tumor staging for melanoma and breast, bone, kidney, prostate, and thyroid cancer.

Related classifications and publications include the *World Health Organization classification of tumours series*, publ. by IARC since 2000, which is a continuation of the *International histological classification of tumours series*, publ. between 1967–99 (commonly referred to as "Blue Books"), with definitions, descriptions, and illustrations of tumor types and proposed nomenclature; WHO's *International classification of diseases for oncology: ICD-O* (62), a numerical coding system for neoplasms; SNOMED; *TNM classification of malignant tumours; TNM atlas: Illustrated guide to the TNM classification of malignant tumours; UICC manual of clinical oncology*, and others. Also available as an e-book.

AJCC cancer staging atlas: A companion to the seventh editions of the AJCC cancer staging manual and handbook and *Cancer grading manual* by Damjanov et al., a "quick reference for surgical pathologists and trainees" (*Preface*) with microscopic grading of tumors, are designed for consultation rather than for systematic reading.

59 Application of the international classification of diseases to neurology: ICD-NA. 2nd ed.
World Health Organization. Geneva, Switzerland: World Health Organization, 1997. xi, 574 p., ill. ISBN 924154502X
616.8001/2   RC346.A66
First ed., 1987 (developed in 1984–85) related to the International Classification of Diseases (ICD)-9. One of the adaptations of the Tenth Revision of the International Statistical Classification of Diseases and Related Health Problems (ICD-10), developed "to respond to the needs of specialist disciplines such as neurology" (*Pref.*). Contains outline of the history and structure of the ICD and ICD-NA, and the "ICD Family of Classifications." Other specialty-based adaptations of the ICD include oncology (*International classification of diseases for oncology: ICD-O*, dentistry (*Application of the international classification of diseases to dentistry and stomatology: ICD-DA*), dermatology, psychiatry (*The ICD-10 classification of mental and behavioural disorders: clinical descriptions and diagnostic guidelines*), and others.

60 Guides to the evaluation of permanent impairment. 6th ed.
Robert D. Rondinelli, Elizabeth

Genovese, Christopher R. Brigham, American Medical Association. Chicago: American Medical Association, 2008. xxiv, 634 p., ill. ISBN 9781579478889
614.1   RA1055.5.G85
First ed., 1965 (repr. *Journal of the American Medical Assoc.*, Feb. 15, 1958, special ed.); 5th ed., 2001.

Contents: ch. 1, "Conceptual foundations and philosophy"; ch. 2, "Practical application of the guides"; ch. 3, "Pain-related impairment"; ch. 4, "The cardiovascular system"; ch. 5, "The pulmonary system"; ch. 6, "The digestive system"; ch. 7, "The urinary and reproductive systems"; ch. 8, "The skin"; ch. 9, "The hematopoietic system"; ch. 10, "The endocrine system"; ch. 11, "Ear, nose, throat, and related structures"; ch. 12, "The visual system"; ch. 13, "The central and peripheral nervous system"; ch. 14, "Mental and behavioral disorders"; ch. 15, "The upper extremities"; ch. 16, "The lower extremities"; ch. 17, "The spine and pelvis"; appendix; glossary; index.

"Defines an innovative new international standard for impairment assessment . . . The goal is to provide an impairment rating guide that is authoritative, fair, and equitable to all parties . . ." (*Pref.*), applying terminology and a framework based on the World Health Organization's International Classification of Functioning, Disability, and Health (ICF). Five impairment classes allow patient rating from no impairment to impairment considered most severe. Also includes diagnosis-based grids for each organ system. Employs a peer-review process, with guidance from an editorial panel and input from state medical associations and national medical specialty societies.

Intended as a tool to understand the changes between the 5th and 6th ed. of this resource, *Transition to the AMA guides sixth: Guides to the evaluation of permanent impairment, sixth edition* by Rondinelli et al. ". . . introduces the new and experienced *Guides* user to the fundamentals and the changes for impairment ratings . . ."—*Pref.* Provides, for example, comparisons of changes between the 5th and 6th edition tables, a summary of key points in each chapter, analysis of rating procedures, and other helpful information.

Related titles are *AMA guides to the evaluation of ophthalmic impairment and disability*, *AMA guides to the evaluation of work ability and return to work, Guide to the evaluation of functional ability,* and *Guides to the evaluation of disease and injury causation.*

61 **The ICD-10 classification of mental and behavioural disorders: Clinical descriptions and diagnostic guidelines.** World Health Organization. Geneva, [Switzerland]: World Health Organization, 1992. xii, 362 p.
ISBN 9241544228
616.890012   RC455.2.C4I34

Adopted by the World Health Organization, Jan. 1993. A related title is *The ICD-10 classification of mental and behavioural disorders: Diagnostic criteria for research*, published by WHO in 2003.

Developed from ch. 5 of the *International statistical classification of diseases and related health problems.* An internationally agreed-upon psychiatric classification system, with descriptions of clinical features for each disorder, diagnostic guidelines, and codes for mental and behavioral disorders.Includes index. Full text available online at http://www.who.int/classifications/icd/en/bluebook.pdf. A companion volume is *Lexicon of psychiatric and mental terms.*

Another major title in the area of classification of mental disorders is *{record}Diagnostic and statistical manual of mental disorders.*

Development of ICD-11 is underway with expected completion in 2015. See details at http://www.who.int/classifications/icd/en/.

62 **International classification of diseases for oncology: ICD-O. 3rd ed.** April G. Fritz. Geneva, Switzerland: World Health Organization, 2000. vii, 240 p. ISBN 9241545348
616.9920012   RC258.I44

First ed., 1976; 2nd ed., 1990. Also referrred to as ICD-O-3. Based to a large extend on WHO's International Histological Classification of Tumours.

Used for coding the site (topography) and the histology (morphology) of neoplasms, usually obtained from a pathology report. Combined alphabetical index for topography and morphology. Detailed information about the classification, structure, and relationship to other classifications (e.g., correspondence tables are available between ICD-O revisions, and between ICD-9 and ICD-10) and

terminologies (e.g, SNOMED) can be found at http://www.who.int/classifications/icd/adaptations/oncology/en/print.html.

In five main sections: (1) general instructions and rules for using the coding systems and gives rules for their implementation in tumour registries and pathology laboratories; (2) numerical list of topography codes; (3) numerical list of morphology codes; (4) alphabetical index gives codes for both topography and morphology and includes selected tumour-like lesions and conditions; (5) a guide to differences in morphology codes between the second and third editions, lists of all new code numbers, new terms, and synonyms added to existing code definitions, and changed terms.

A related title is the *AJCC cancer staging manual*, prepared by the American Joint Committee on Cancer (AJCC, 58).

The National Cancer Institute SEER (Surveillance Epidemiology and End Results) provides ICD-O-3 coding (e.g., http://seer.cancer.gov/icd-o-3/) and related web-based training materials.

63 **International classification of diseases, ninth revision, clinical modification**. http://www.cdc.gov/nchs/icd/icd9cm.htm. National Center for Health Statistics (U.S.). Hyattsville, Md.: U.S. Dept. of Health and Human Services, Centers for Disease Control and Prevention, National Center for Health Statistics. 199?–

Contents: v. 1, Tabular list of diseases and external injuries; v. 2, Alphabetical index to diseases; v. 3, Tabular list of procedures.

ICD-9-CM is based on the World Health Organization's (WHO) *International classification of diseases, ninth revision (ICD-9),* "designed to promote international comparability in the collection, processing, classification, and presentation of mortality statistics" (*Website*). In addition it also provides morbidity detail for indexing of medical records and health statistics and for assigning codes to diagnoses associated with inpatient, outpatient, and physician utilization in the U.S. ICD-9-CM is considered the official system for assigning codes to diagnoses and procedures associated with hospital (inpatient and outpatient) and physician office utilization in the U. S. The National Center for Health Statistics (NCHS) and the Centers for Medicare and Medicaid Services are responsible for all changes to the ICD-9-CM.

ICD-10-CM is due in October 2014; details at http://cdc.gov/nchs/icd/icd10cm.htm.

Previously available in various print and CD-ROM editions.

64 International classification of functioning, disability and health (ICF). http://www.who.int/classifications/icf/en/index.html. World Health Organizations. Geneva, Switzerland: World Health Organization (WHO). 2001–

World Health Organization (WHO); International Classification of Functioning, Disability and Health (ICF).

"Describes how people live with their health condition. ICF is a classification of health and health related domains that describe body functions and structures, activities and participation. The domains are classified from body, individual and societal perspectives. Since an individual's functioning and disability occurs in a context, ICF also includes a list of environmental factors. ICF is useful to understand and measure health outcomes. It can be used in clinical settings, health services or surveys at the individual or population level" (*Website*). ICF complements the *International statistical classification of diseases and related health problems* (ICD-10, 59) and is part of the WHO Family of International Classifications: WHO-FIC website which provides access to WHO's reference and other classifications.

65 International statistical classification of diseases and related health problems. http://www.who.int/classifications/apps/icd/icd10online/. World Health Organization. Geneva, Switzerland: World Health Organization. 1994–2007

Title varies: International classification of diseases; ICD-10. The original three-volume print version, publ. 1992–94, has title *International statistical classification of diseases and related health problems* (v. 1, *Tabular list*; v. 2, *Instruction manual*; v. 3, *Alphabetical index*).

Contents: ch. 1, "Certain infectious and parasitic diseases"; ch. 2, "Neoplasms"; ch. 3, "Diseases of the blood and blood-forming organs and certain disorders involving the immune mechanism"; ch. 4, "Endocrine, nutritional and metabolic diseases"; ch. 5, "Mental and behavioural disorders"; ch. 6, "Diseases of the nervous system"; ch. 7, "Diseases of the eye and adnexa"; ch. 8, "Diseases of the ear and mastoid process"; ch. 9, "Diseases of the circulatory system"; ch. 10, "Diseases of the respiratory system"; ch. 11, "Diseases of the digestive system"; ch. 12, "Diseases of the skin and subcutaneous tissue"; ch. 13, "Diseases of the musculoskeletal system and connective tissue"; ch. 14, "Diseases of the genitourinary system"; ch. 15, "Pregnancy, childbirth and the puerperium"; ch. 16, "Certain conditions originating in the perinatal period"; ch. 17, C"ongenital malformations, deformations and chromosomal abnormalities"; ch. 18. "Symptoms, signs and abnormal clinical and laboratory findings, not elsewhere classified"; ch. 19, "Injury, poisoning and certain other consequences of external causes"; ch. 20, "External causes of morbidity and mortality"; ch. 21, "Factors influencing health status and contact with health services"; ch. 22, "Codes for special purposes."

"Standard diagnostic classification for all general epidemiological and many health management purposes . . . used to classify diseases and other health problems recorded on many types of health and vital records including death certificates and hospital records . . . [and] provide the basis for the compilation of national mortality and morbidity statistics by WHO member states"—*WHO summary* (http://www.who.int/classifications/icd/en/). Additional information and links to several full-text ICD publications, updates, and ICD adaptations can be found, e.g., *Application of the international classification of diseases to dentistry and stomatology*, *International classification of functioning, disability and health*, International classification of diseases for oncology, *International classification of external causes of injury*, *International classification of health interventions* (currently under development), *International classification of primary care*. Additional related information can be found on the WHO family of international classifications website. Its purpose is to promote the appropriate selection of classifications in various health care settings around the world.

History of the statistical classification of diseases and causes of death by Moriyama et al. describes the historic development of the disease nomenclatures that resulted WHO's international classification of diseases. It is accessible at (http://www.cdc.gov/nchs/data/misc/classification_diseases2011.pdf.

66   National Library of Medicine Training Center. http://nnlm.gov/ntc/. National Library of Medicine (U.S.). Bethesda, Md.: National Library of Medicine. 2003–

Produced by National Library of Medicine (NLM).

Provides access to online training materials used in conjunction with classes and courses offered by the National Training Center and Clearinghouse (NTCC), e.g., for PubMed{/record and {record} TOXNET.

67   NLM classification. http://wwwcf. nlm.nih.gov/class. National Library of Medicine (U.S.). Bethesda, Md.: National Library of Medicine. 2002–

HE20.3602

"A product of the National Library of Medicine for the arrangement of library materials in the field of medicine and related sciences used internationally" (main page), with hyperlinks between class numbers in the index and the schedules. The 2013 edition includes, for example, all recent new additions and changes to the schedules and to the MeSH (858) concepts in the index. About the NLM classification (http://www.nlm.nih.gov/class/nlmclassintro.html) provides further information on the structure of the NLM classification, its relationship to MeSH, and its index, as well as on the history of the development of the classification. Fact sheet: NLM classification (http://www.nlm.nih.gov/pubs/factsheets/nlmclassif.html) gives further details, such as a summary outline for the "preclinical sciences" and "medicine and related subjects." The home page provides links to related NLM resources, e.g., the NLM cataloging section homepage, LocatorPlus (52), and MeSH.

68   Nursing interventions classification (NIC). 6th ed. Gloria M. Bulechek. St. Louis: Elsevier/Mosby, 2013. xxviii, 608 p. ISBN 9780323100113

610.7301/2   RT42

First edition, 1992; 5th ed., 2008.

Contents: pt. 1, Overview and use of the classification; pt. 2, Taxonomy of nursing interventions; pt.3, The classification; pt. 4, Core interventions for nursing specialties areas; pt. 5, Estimated time and education level necessary to perform NIC intervention; pt. 6, NIC interventions linked to NANDA-I diagnosis; pt. 7, Appendixes: (A) Interventions: New revised and retired since the fifth edition; (B) Guidelines for submission of a new and revised intervention; (C) Timeline and highlights for NIC; (D) Abbreviations; (E) Previous editions and translations.

Provides an overview of the interventions performed by all nurses and of the NIC taxonomy, with different groupings representing the areas of nursing practice and coding guidelines. Includes 554 interventions. Interventions can be used with diagnostic classifications, e.g., NANDA (North American Nursing Diagnosis Association), ICD (International Classification of Diseases), DSM (*Diagnostic and statistical manual*), and those included in clinical information systems (e.g., SNOMED International, 69). Interventions are listed alphabetically, and each intervention has been assigned a unique number. Appendixes include new, revised, and retired interventions since the last edition, selected publications, abbreviations, and several other resources. Has associated website and companion book, *NANDA, NOC, and NIC linkages: Nursing diagnoses, outcomes, and interventions* by Johnson.

69   SNOMED CT. http://www.snomed.org/. College of American Pathologists International Division, International Health Terminology Standards Development Organisation. Copenhagen, Denmark: International Health Terminology Standards Development Organisation. 2002–

Published in several print editions 1993–2001, with title *SNOMED International: The systematized nomenclature of human and veterinary medicine*.

SNOMED CT is a clinical reference terminology. It can be described as a global, comprehensive, and precise clinical terminology, sharing health data across clinical specialties, which can be adapted for national purposes. Compatible with key health care standards (e.g., HL7, DICOM, ANSI, and ISO).

SNOMED CT was transferred from College of American Pathologists (CAP) to IHTSDO (International Health Terminology Standards Development Organisation) in April 2007 and remains under development. Representatives from nine nations are working with CAP and its SNOMED international division and offer services and products for the adoption and use of SNOMED CT. Detailed information about SNOMED CT is provided at the IHTSDO website(http://www.ihtsdo.org/about -ihtsdo/faq/).

The National Library of Medicine (NLM) is the U.S. member of IHTSDO. NLM's Unified Medical Language System (UMLS, 70), a metathesaurus containing biomedical concepts and terms from many controlled vocabularies and classifications, includes SNOMED CT FAQs at http://www.nlm .nih.gov/research/umls/Snomed/snomed_faq.html.

70   Unified medical language system (UMLS). http://purl.access.gpo.gov/ GPO/LPS2400. National Library of Medicine (U.S.). Bethesda, Md.: National Library of Medicine. 1999–

The purpose of the UMLS is to facilitate the development of computer systems concerned with the use of the biomedical and health-related language. NLM produces and distributes the UMLS knowledge sources (Metathesaurus [http://www .nlm.nih.gov/pubs/factsheets/umlsmeta.html], the Semantic network [http://www.nlm.nih.gov/ pubs/factsheets/umlssemn.html], and the SPECIALIST lexicon [http://www.nlm.nih.gov/pubs/ factsheets/umlslex.html]) and associated software tools and programs for the use of various systems developers in building or enhancing electronic information systems (e.g., electronic patient record, public health data, scientific literature, etc.) and informatics research. The lexical tools work in combination with the UMLS knowledge sources but can also be used independently. The UMLS Fact Sheet (http://www .nlm.nih.gov/pubs/factsheets/umls.html) provides further detailed information and explanation. Questions concerning the inclusion of SNOMED CT: Systematized nomenclature of medicine— clinical terms in UMLS are answered in FAQs: SNOMED CT in the UMLS (http://www.nlm.nih .gov/research/umls/Snomed/snomed_faq.html).

71   WHO family of international classifications. http://www.who.int/ classifications/en/. World Health Organization. Geneva: World Health Organization. 2007

Provides information and explanation on various internationally recognized and endorsed reference classifications and links to their full text: International statistical classification of diseases and related health problems (ICD), International classification of functioning, disability and health (ICF), and International classification of health interventions (ICHI) (http://www.who.int/classifications/ ichi/en/index.html), currently under development. Also provides information about or links to full-text and updates for WHO's derived and related classifications and terminologies.

Derived classifications include International classification of diseases for oncology (ICD-O-3); ICD-10 classification of mental and behavioural disorders: Clinical descriptions and diagnostic guidelines; Application of the international classification of diseases to dentistry and stomatology (ICD-DA); Application of the international classification of diseases to neurology (ICD-10-NA).

Related classifications include: International classification of primary care (ICPC); International classification of external causes of injury (ICECI); Anatomical, therapeutic, chemical (ATC) classification system with Defined Daily Doses (DDDs); ISO 9999 Technical aids for persons with disabilities— classification and terminology.

Volumes tracing the history of disease classification 1903–38 are available at http://www.who .int/library/collections/historical/en/index1.html as part of the WHO Library Historical Collection.

The North American Collaborating Center (NACC), part of the National Center for Health Statistics (63), serves as WHO's Collaborating Center for the Family of International Classifications for North America (http://www.cdc.gov/nchs/icd.htm).

Indexes; Abstract journals; Databases

72   BIOSIS previews. http://www.thomson reuters.com/biosis-previews. Thomson

Reuters, Biological Abstracts, inc. Philadelphia: Thomson Reuters

QH301

Online edition of *Biological abstracts*, BIOSIS Previews includes *Biological abstracts/RRM*, which stands for reports, reviews, and meetings. Long regarded as the most thorough source for indexing in all areas of biology and biomedicine, BIOSIS Previews covers research reports in journals and other publications, reviews, books, and conference papers. Over the years, coverage has expanded to include interdisciplinary fields of biochemistry, biotechnology, genetics, and molecular biology. Nearly 6,000 journals and 1,500 international meetings are indexed. Online subscriptions are available from various providers; most content is updated weekly, and backfiles are available from 1926 to the present. Database available through several vendors.

73   CAM on PubMed. http://nccam.nih.gov/ research/camonpubmed/. Alternative Medicine, National Library of Medicine. Bethesda, Md.: National Center for Complementary and Alternative Medicine; National Library of Medicine

CAM (Complementary and Alternative Medicine) is jointly developed by the National Library of Medicine (NLM) and the National Center for Complementary and Alternative Medicine (NCCAM). "NCCAM defines complementary and alternative medicine (CAM) as those health care practices not currently considered an integral part of conventional medicine. It covers a broad range of healing therapies, approaches, and systems. Some examples of CAM include acupuncture, herbs, homeopathy, chiropractic, hypnosis, and traditional Oriental medicine"—*NCCAM website*. CAM can be searched either as a subset of PubMed, which provides citations to the journal literature of complementary and alternative medicine, or from the NCCAM website (http://nccam.nih.gov/), with citations back to 1966, including different CAM therapies and therapeutic systems.

74   The Cochrane Library. http://www .thecochranelibrary.com/. Cochrane Collaboration. Hoboken, N.J.: Wiley Interscience. 1996– 1465-1858   R723.7

Acronyms: Evidence-based   medicine   (EBM); Evidence-based health care (EBHC).

Imprint varies: 1996–2003, Update Software Ltd., Oxford, U.K.; publ. by Wiley Interscience 2004–. Produced by contributors to the Cochrane Collaboration (founded in 1993 and named after the British epidemiologist, Archie Cochrane) and consists of a group of experts in the various clinical specialties who apply EBM criteria to the review and selection of studies, perform meta-analyses, and then write detailed topical reviews.

The Cochrane Library consists of several online databases that provide systematic reviews, meta-analyses of the literature, and randomized clinical trials: Cochrane database of systematic reviews (CDSR)—Cochrane reviews and protocols; Database of abstracts of reviews of effectiveness (DARE)—Other Reviews; Cochrane central register of controlled trials (CENTRAL)—Clinical trials; Cochrane methodology register (CMR)—Methods studies; Health technology assessment database (HT)—Health technology; and NHS economic evaluation database (NHSEED).

The major product of the Cochrane Collaboration is the *Cochrane database of systematic reviews*, prepared mostly by healthcare professionals who work as volunteers in one of the many Cochrane Review Groups. Editorial teams oversee the preparation and updating of the reviews and applying quality standards. Provides access to full-text articles that review the effects of health care.

Other examples of EBM and EBHC resources include ACP journal club and ACP PIER (American College of Physicians), Clinical evidence (BMJ), DynaMed (EBSCO), Evidence matters, PubMed/ PubMed clinical queries (systematic reviews and meta-analyses) (http://www.ncbi.nlm.nih.gov/pub med/clinical), Turning research into practice (TRIP) database, Health services technology assessment text (HSTAT), NLM gateway, National guideline clearinghouse (335), and others.

Many websites from various organizations and universities provide EBM and EBHC-related subject guides, e.g., EBM Resource Center, New York Academy of Medicine (http://www.ebmny.org/), "Evidence-based practice" subject guide (Hardin Library for the Health Sciences, The University of Iowa, http://guides.lib.uiowa.edu/ebp), "Evidence based medicine," Johns Hopkins University (http://www.hopkinsmedicine.org/gim/research/method/ebm.html), and many others.

Print EBM/EBHC resources are, for example, *Evidence-based medicine: How to practice and teach EBM* and *Clinical epidemiology: How to do clinical practice research.*

75 Computer medical databases: The first six decades (1950-2010). Morris F. Collen. New York: Springer, 2011. xix, 288 p. ISBN 9780857299611
610.28/5   R859.7.D36

Contents: ch. 1, "Prologue: The evolution of computer databases"; ch. 2, "The development of medical databases"; ch. 3, "Processing text in medical databases"; ch. 4, "Primary medical record databases"; ch. 5, "Specialized medical databases"; ch. 6, "Secondary medical research databases"; ch. 7, "Biosurveillance and claims databases"; ch. 8, "Medical knowledge databases"; ch. 9, "Medical bibliographic databases: Knowledge discovery/data mining"; ch. 10, "Epilogue."

Describes the development of medical digital databases. Each chapter has examples of early databases, a summary and commentary, and a comprehensive list of references. Describes the gradual changes of the traditional medical library into a virtual library, with credit being given to the National Library of Medicine {http://www.nlm.nih.gov/} for providing a leading role. Also mentions the influence of Canada, Europe, and Japan on the computer databases developments in the United States. Includes extensive information on specialized medical registries and diseases databases and addresses the emergence of bioinformatics as a new field in health informatics to support developments in molecular biology. Not included are computer processing of digital images (radiographs), of photographs (dermatology), and of analog signals (electrocardiograms).—Cf. *Pref.* Projections for the next decade include the development of "larger computer database-management systems . . . to support clinical decisions with evidence-based practice guidelines readily accessible from bibliographic and knowledge databases . . ."—*Epilogue.* Also mentioned are wireless communications of physicians and patients, benefits of using telemedicine technology, Internet and World Wide Web to facilitate broadband communications, common shared EMR when receiving care in different

medical centers, and handheld portable devices with increased wirelss capacity. Subject index; author index. Also available as an e-book.

76 EMBASE. http://www.embase.com/. Elsevier Science. Amsterdam, Netherlands: Elsevier Science. 1974–

EMBASE.com (originally launched in 1999, now release 6.0) is a biomedical and pharmaceutical database containing bibliographic records with abstracts from EMBASE (1974–present) and MEDLINE (1966–present, deduplicated and searchable with EMTREE [857]). Indexes 7,000 journals. About half of records have full-text links.

EMBASE is the online version of *Excerpta Medica: The international medical abstracting service*, an abstracting journal with approximately 52 subsections (44 currently in use), providing author and subject access to the biomedical literature and published since 1947, searchable in EMBASE since 1974. With few exceptions, EMBASE section headings correspond to the titles of the *Excerpta Medica* abstract journals. "EMBASE Classic" refers to the EMBASE backfile (1947-73), with citations from more than 3,000 international titles. User support is provided by Elsevier regional offices (http://www.elsevier.com/online-tools/embase/training-and-support#our-offices).

Bibliographic database for the biomedical literature, with extensive coverage of pharmacology, drug research, and toxicology; also covers veterinary medicine, dentistry, and nursing. Also covers conference abstrats. Indexes 7,600 journals. Titles indexed are listed in the *EMBASE list of journals indexed.* International in scope, with coverage of 2,000 titles not indexed in MEDLINE. *EMTREE thesaurus* provides a controlled vocabulary for EMBASE, with all MeSH (858) terms having been converted to EMTREE index terms. Records contain bibliographic information, controlled terms (EMTREE medical and drug descriptors, EMTREE codes), drug trade names and manufacturers, and medical device trade names and manufacturers. Most records include abstracts, and many include a CAS registry number. Also available from several commercial vendors.

77 GenBank. http://www.ncbi.nlm.nih.gov/Genbank/. National Center for Biotechnology Information (U.S.).

Bethesda, Md.: National Center for Biotechnology Information, National Library of Medicine, National Institutes of Health, U.S. Dept. of Health and Human Services. 1990s–

Genetic sequence database, an annotated collection of all publicly available nucleotide (DNA and RNA) sequences and their protein translations. Laboratories around the world contribute sequence data to GenBank, and more than 100,000 organisms are represented. The overview gives current status of number of records and nucleic acid bases in the database and also instructions for submitting, revising, or updating sequence data. Maintained by NCBI, Gen-Bank joins the DNA Databank of Japan (DDBJ) and the European Molecular Biology Laboratory (EMBL) in forming the International Nucleotide Sequence Database Collaboration (INSCD, http://www.insdc.org/), based on continual exchange of data among these organizations. For libraries supporting genetics and molecular biology teaching and research.

78   GeneTests. http://www.genetests.org/. Children's Hospital and Medical Center (Seattle, Wash.), Univ. of Wash., School of Medicine; National Library of Medicine (U.S.). Seattle, Wash.: Univ. of Washington. 1993–

Contents: Home page; Disorders; GeneReviews; Panel Directory; Laboratory directory; Clinic directory.

Provides authoritative information on genetic testing and its use in diagnosis, disease management, and genetic counseling. Promotes use of genetic services in patient care and decision making by individuals. GeneReviews and Laboratory directory can be searched by disease, gene symbol, protein name, etc. Contains context-sensitive illustrated glossary, teaching tools, and other resources.

79   Genetic testing registry (GTR). http://www.ncbi.nlm.nih.gov/gtr/. National Center for Biotechnology Information (U.S.). Bethesda, Md.: National Center for Biotechnology Information, National Library of Medicine (U.S.). 2012-

RB155.6

Operated by NLM's National Center for Biotechnology Information (NCBI).

"Provides a central location for voluntary submission of genetic test information by provider. The scope includes the test's purpose, methodology, validity, evidence of the test's usefulness, and laboratory contacts and credentials. The overarching goal of the GTR is to advance the public health and research into the genetic basis of health and disease."—*Home page, About*.

Contains AMA's CPT (Current procedural terminology codes, 856) for molecular pathology, genetic tests, and molecular diagnostic services; incorporates SNOMED CT (Systematized Nomenclature of Medicine—Clinical Terms, 69), and clinical terminology produced by the International Health Terminology Standards Development Organisation (IHTSDO, 69) and LOINC® (Logical Observation Identifiers Names and Codes), produced by the Regenstriet Institute, which provides standardized terms and codes for identifying laboratory and clinical observations. NLM is the U.S. member of the IHTSDO and provides support for the development and free US-wide use of both SNOMED CT and LOINC.

CPT, SNOMED CT, and LOINC are required standards in the certification criteria for electronic health record products issued by the Office of the National Coordinator for Health Information Technology (ONC), Dept. of Health and Human Services at http://www.healthit.gov/. GTR tutorials can be found at http://www.youtube.com/playlist?list=PL1C4A2AFF811F6F0B

80   Health services technology assessment texts (HSTAT). http://hstat.nlm.nih.gov. National Library of Medicine (U.S.). Bethesda, Md.: National Library of Medicine (U.S.), National Institutes of Health, Dept. of Health and Human Services. 1994?–

Coordinated by the National Library of Medicine's National Information Center on Health Services Research and Health Care Technology (NICHSR). Part of the "NCBI Bookshelf" (http://www.ncbi.nlm.nih.gov/books).

Searchable collection of full-text documents containing results of health services research, evidence reports and technology assessments, consensus conference reports, clinical practice guidelines (e.g., HIV/AIDS approved guidelines and information), reports of the Surgeon General, and other health information in support of health care decision making. Intended for health care providers, health service researchers, policymakers, payers, consumers, and information professionals. Further details in the *HSTAT fact sheet* (http://www .nlm.nih.gov/pubs/factsheets/hstat.html).

81 Index medicus. U.S. Dept. of Health, Education and Welfare, Public Health Service, National Institutes of Health, National Library of Medicine. Bethesda, Md.: U.S. Dept. of Health, Education and Welfare; Public Health Service; National Institutes of Health; National Library of Medicine, 1960–2004

016.61 0019-3879   Z6660.I42

Title varies; imprint varies. *Index medicus*: series I,1879–99; series II, 1903–20; series III, 1921–27; 1916–26, *Quarterly cumulative index to current medical literature*, publ. by the American Medical Association (AMA, 60); 1927–56, *Quarterly cumulative index medicus* (AMA) and *Cumulated index medicus* (AMA); 1941–59, *Current list of medical literature* (Army Medical Library, now National Library of Medicine [NLM]); 1960–2004 again called *Index medicus* (n.s., cumulated annually as *Cumulated index medicus* until 2000), available online as PubMed®/MEDLINE® and currently used exclusively in its online version. For a review of the scope of coverage for *Index medicus*–related titles see *Introduction to reference sources in the health sciences* (8).

Provides subject and author access. Remains useful for researching the biomedical, healthcare, and related literature from other disciplines for which online access is not yet available in PubMed/MEDLINE.

Related titles: *Bibliographia medica (Index Medicus): Receuil mensuel* (Institut de Bibliographie, Paris), by Marcel Baudouin, publ. 1900–02 while publication of *Index medicus* was temporarily suspended; IndexCat, the online version of *Index catalogue of the Library of the Surgeon-General's Office*: 1st series, 1880–95; 2nd series, 1896–1916; 3rd series, 1918–32; 4th series A–Mez, 1936–48; 4th series Mh–MN, 1955; 5th series, 1959–61; *Bibliography of medical reviews* (separate publication, 1955–67; 1968–77 publ. separately and also as pt. of *Index medicus*; 1978– publ. only as pt. of *Index medicus*); 1970–97, *Abridged index*

medicus (NLM), intended for individual physicians and small libraries. "Index Medicus Chronology" (http://www.nlm.nih.gov/services/indexmedicus .html) provides further details.

82 International clinical trials registry platform search portal (ICTRP). http://www.who.int/trialsearch/. World Health Organization. Geneva, Switzerland: World Health Organization. 200?–

Produced by World Health Organization (WHO).

Database to locate information about clinical trials. Described by Tim Evans (WHO) as a "collaborative international initiative led by WHO that facilitates the identification of all clinical trials, regardless of whether or not they have been published." For health care researchers.

83 Literature, arts, and medicine database. http://litmed.med.nyu.edu/ Main?action=new. New York University School of Medicine. New York: New York University School of Medicine. 1993–

Part of Medical Humanities, New York University (NYU) School of Medicine (http://medhum.med .nyu.edu), Division of Educational Informatics (DEI). Previously part of the Hippocrates Project (NYU School of Medicine), a media laboratory that applies information technology to medical education. Established 1993 in Gopher; Web-based since 1994.

Contains selected annotations for works of literature, art, and performing arts pertaining to the illness experience, medical education, and medical practice, i.e., their placement in a medical context. Each annotation provides a summary, including a description for works of art, critical commentary, publishing information, and relevant keywords. Provides a "viewing room" (for digital resources), a "listening room" (for literary texts), and a "screening room" (excerpts of videos or theater productions). Annotations are searchable by words or phrases, title, work category (art, film, literature, theater), art form, genre, or medium; also provides search capability for people, keyword, annotator, and free text. Intended for an academic audience. This website also provides links to syllabi in medical humanities from other institutions as well as a directory (organized by country, state, and institution) of individuals engaged in various aspects of medical humanities work.

84 LiverTox. http://www.livertox.nih.gov/. National Institute of Diabetes and Digestive and Kidney Diseases.; Liver Disease Research Branch., National Institutes of Health (U.S.), National Library of Medicine (U.S.). Specialized Information Services Division. Bethesda, Md.: National Institutes of Health. 2012-

Joint project of the Liver Disease Research Branch of the National Institute of Diabetes and Digestive and Kidney Diseases (NIDDK) and the Division of Specialized Information Services of the National Library of Medicine (NLM), National Institutes of Health.

Provides freely accessible up-to-date information on the diagnosis and management of liver injury which may be caused by prescription & nonprescription medications, dietary supplements, and herbal remedies. Derived from the scientific literature and public databases, the content of this database reflects the professional expertise of the authors. Also includes a case registry which allows scientific and clinical analysis of liver injury. Can be searched for a specific medication, herbal, or supplement and also allows browsing by first letter of medication, herbal, or supplement. Further information about the major components of this database, drug record format, status of the development, etc., can be found at http://www.livertox.nih.gov/aboutus.html. Resource for physicians, medical specialists, researchers, and patients.

85 MEDLINE. http://purl.access.gpo.gov/GPO/LPS4708. National Library of Medicine (U.S.). Bethesda, Md.: National Library of Medicine (U.S.). 1900s-

MEDLINE®—Medical literature analysis and retrieval system online (National Library of Medicine®—NLM), primary subset of PubMed® and part of the databases provided by the National Center for Biotechnology Information (NCBI, 3). Coverage extends back to 1946, with some older material.

Bibliographic database, providing comprehensive access to the international biomedical literature from the fields of medicine, nursing, dentistry, veterinary medicine, allied health, and the preclinical sciences. It is also a primary source of information from the international literature on biomedicine, including the following topics as they relate to biomedicine and health care: Biology, environmental science, marine biology, plant and animal science, biophysics, and chemistry. For indexing articles, NLM uses MeSH: Medical subject headings® (858), a controlled vocabulary of biomedical terms. An increasing number of MEDLINE citations contain a link to the free full-text articles.

The MEDLINE database is the electronic counterpart of *Index medicus®* (81), *Index to dental literature* (780), and the *International nursing index* (782). The databases is offered at no additional cost on a variety of indexing platforms.

For detailed information, see the MEDLINE fact sheet at http://www.nlm.nih.gov/pubs/factsheets/medline.html, which also includes a list of related fact sheets (e.g., "MEDLINE, PubMed, and PMC (PubMed Centeral): How are they different?").

86 National Center for Biotechnology Information. http://www.ncbi.nlm.nih.gov. National Center for Biotechnology Information (U. S.), National Library of Medicine, National Institutes of Health. Rockville, Md.: National Center for Biotechnology Information. 1995(?)–
660.6; 574.873282 TP248.2

Covers the National Center for Biotechnology Information (NCBI), an organization that advances science and health by providing access to biomedical and genomic information. Its mission is to develop "new information technologies to aid in the understanding of fundamental molecular and genetic processes that control health and disease" (http://www.ncbi.nlm.nih.gov/About/glance/ourmission.html). Provides links to NCBI's literature databases, molecular databases, genomic resources, and tools for data mining as well as information about the work of the NCBI. Includes lists and links to NCBI resources in various helpful groupings, e.g., a complete list of all NCBI resources; a listing of databases, tools ("analyze data using NCBI software"), downloads ("get NCBI data or software"), how-to's ("learn how to accomplish specific tasks at NCBI"), and submissions ("submit data to Genbank or other NCBI databases"), in the following subcategories: chemicals & bioessays; data & software; DNA & RNA; domains &

structures; genes & expression; genetics & medicine; genomes & maps; homology; literature; proteins; sequence analysis; taxonomy; training & tutorials; variation. The most popular database is PubMed. NCBI site search is at http://www.ncbi.nlm.nih.gov/ ncbisearch/; "GQuery" (http://www.ncbi.nlm.nih .gov/gquery/) allows a "global cross-database" search of NCBI databases. Other helpful links include an overview of NCBI resources ftp://ftp.ncbi.nih. gov/pub/factsheets/Factsheet_NCBI_Overview. pdf, an annual update of NCBI databases, services, and tools in the special database issue of *Nucleic acids research* http://www.ncbi.nlm.nih.gov/pmc/ articles/PMC3531099/, selected databases, tools, help documents and educational materials http://www .ncbi.nlm.nih.gov/. "NCBI news link" (http://www .ncbi.nlm.nih.gov/news/) provides the latest information about NCBI services and activities, with "follow us" links to the "NCBI insights" blog and NCBI's social media outlets on Twitter, Facebook, and YouTube.

87 **National Library of Medicine**. http:// www.nlm.nih.gov/. National Library of Medicine (U.S.), National Institutes of Health. Bethesda, Md.: National Library of Medicine. 1993–

Homepage of the U.S. National Library of Medicine (NLM). Contains information about NLM's databases and other electronic resources, e.g., Pub Med/MEDLINE, ClinicalTrials.gov (276), LocatorPlus (52), MedlinePlus, MeSH (858), NLM Catalog (55), NLM classification (67), NLM gateway, TOXNET, Unified medical language system (UMLS, 70), and the Visible human project (539), to name a few of NLM's important resources. An annotated list of NLM databases and electronic resources (http://www.nlm.nih .gov/databases/) provides access to additional resources. Also includes a link to NLM's numerous "retired databases" (http://www.nlm.nih.gov/services/past databases.html). Health information and NLM's products and services are presented for several different user groups: the public, health care professionals, researchers, librarians, and publishers. A listing and link to NIH clinical alerts, which are "provided to expedite the release of findings from the NIH-funded clinical trials where such release could significantly affect morbidity and mortality" (*Clinical Alerts and Advisories page*) are available at http://www.nlm.nih.gov/databases/alerts/ clinical_alerts.html. Milestones in NLM history

(http://apps.nlm.nih.gov/175/milestones.cfm) and the NLM fact sheets (http://www.nlm.nih.gov/pubs/ factsheets/nlm.html) provide further information.

88 **National Organization for Rare Disorders, Inc.** http://www.rarediseases. org/. National Organization for Rare Disorders. Danbury, Conn.: National Organization for Rare Disorders. 1999–

RC48

The National Organization for Rare Disorders (NORD) provides alphabetical Index of rare diseases and several searchable databases—namely, Rare disease database, Index of organizations (list of organizations), and Organizational database (patient organizations)—as well as advice on how to interpret search results. Other resources in this area can be located via *NORD guide to rare disorders* (338) and NIH's Office of Rare Diseases (338).

89 **NLM gateway**. http://gateway.nlm. nih.gov/. National Library of Medicine (U.S.). Bethesda, Md.: National Library of Medicine. 2000–

RA11

As announced in 2011, "the NLM® gateway has transitioned to a new pilot project from the Lister Hill National Center for Biomedical Communications (LHNCBC, 392)."—*Website* The new site focuses now on two databases: Meeting abstracts and Health services research projects. All of the other resources previously accessed through the NLM gateway are available through their individual sites. For a list of these databases previously available via the NLM gateway see http://gateway. nlm.nih.gov/about.jsp.

The NLM gateway previously allowed simultaneous searching of information resources at the National Library of Medicine (NLM)/National Center for Biotechnology Information (NCBI, 3) with an overview of the search results presented in several categories (bibliographic resources, consumer health resources, and other information), with a listing of the individual databases and the number of results within these categories. Previously included were, for example, MEDLINE/PubMed and the NLM Catalog as well as other resources, including information on current clinical trials and consumer health information (MedlinePlus) and many others.

90   **OLDMEDLINE data**. http://www.nlm
.nih.gov/databases/databases_oldmedline
.html. National Library of Medicine
(U.S.). Bethesda, Md.: National Library of
Medicine. 2003–

Journal article citations from *Cumulated index
medicus* and the *Current list of medical literature*
(see *Index medicus*), covering medicine, preclinical sciences, and allied health sciences from 1946
through 1965. Most of these OLDMEDLINE
records are included in the MEDLINE database and
can be searched via PubMed.

A chart is provided for the OLDMEDLINE
data. It contains information on date added, citations added, and the title and year of the printed index. Website also provides a brief history
of NLM's use of MEDLARS (Medical Literature
Analysis and Retrieval System) and introduction
of Medline.

91   **PMC (PubMed Central)**. http://
www.pubmedcentral.nih.gov. National
Library of Medicine, National Center
for Biotechnology Information (U.S.),
National Institutes of Health (U.S.).
Bethesda, Md.: National Center for
Biotechnology Information. 2000–
025174570610.7   R11

Produced by National Library of Medicine (NLM)
and National Institutes of Health (NIH); developed
and managed by NIH's National Center for Biotechnology Information (NCBI). Previously called
PubMed central: An archive of life science journals.

NLM's free and open-access online digital
archive of peer-reviewed full-text research papers
in the medical and life sciences. The continuously
growing PMC journals list (http://www.ncbi.nlm
.nih.gov/pmc/journals/) includes, for example, titles
from the Public Library of Science (PLoS, 49) and
BioMed central (BMC, 100)(http://www.biomed-
central.com/), publishers of many open-access journals. Also includes the complete back files of many
important medical journals that NLM has digitized
in collaboration with the Wellcome Trust and the
Joint Informations Systems Committee (JISC). The
list is alphabetically arranged and available as a full
or tabbed list, used to find journals added to PMC
in the last 60 days. Other helpful links are provided, e.g., NIH public access (http://publicaccess
.nih.gov/) and NIH manuscript submission system

(http://www.nihms.nih.gov/). Further information
at PMC Frequently asked questions (http://www
.pubmedcentral.nih.gov/about/faq.html). The NLM
fact sheet (http://www.nlm.nih.gov/pubs/factsheets/
dif_med_pub.html) explains the differences between MEDLINE, PubMed, and PubMed central.
Help with the "PMCID-PMID-Manuscript ID-DOI
converter" tool at http://www.ncbi.nlm.nih.gov/
pmc/pmctopmid/.

92   **Public library of science (PLoS)**.
http://www.plos.org/. Public Library of
Science. [San Francisco]: Public Library
of Science. 2000–

PLoS is a non-profit organization of scientists and
physicians who are committed to promote free and
timely online access to the international scientific
and medical literature. Since 2003 a nonprofit scientific and medical publishing venture. Publishes
high-profile open-access journals (e.g., *PLoS biology*, *PLoS medicine*, *PLoS ONE*, and several others),
funded by authors and participating institutions.
The full content of every PLoS issue is placed into
PubMed central (PMC, 48). PLoS titles can also
be accessed via Directory of open access journals:
DoAJ (42).

93   **PubMed**. http://www.ncbi.nlm.nih.gov/
pubmed. U.S. National Center for
Biotechnology Information, National
Library of Medicine, National Institutes
of Health. Bethesda, Md.: U.S. National
Center for Biotechnology Information.
1996–

PubMed®, developed and maintained by the
National Center for Biotechnology Information
(NCBI, 3) at the National Library of Medicine®
(NLM). Provides a search interface for more than
20 million bibliographic citations and abstracts in
the fields of medicine, nursing, dentistry, veterinary medicine, health care systems, and preclinical
sciences. It provides access to articles indexed for
MEDLINE® and for selected life sciences journals.
PubMed subsets found under the "Limits" tab are:
MEDLINE and PubMed central®, several journal
groups (i.e., core clinical journals, dental journals,
and nursing journals), and topical subsets (AIDS,
bioethics, cancer, complementary medicine,
dietary supplements, history of medicine, space
life sciences, systematic reviews, toxicology, and

veterinary science). "Linkout" provides access to full-text articles.

For detailed information see the PubMed fact sheet at http://www.nlm.nih.gov/pubs/factsheets/pubmed.html and also MEDLINE®/PubMed® resources guide (http://www.nlm.nih.gov/bsd/pmresources.html) which provides detailed information about MEDLINE data and searching PubMed.

Information regarding the mobile version of this resource is part of NLM's Gallery of mobile apps and sites.

94 PubMed health. http://www.ncbi.nlm .nih.gov/pubmedhealth/. National Center for Biotechnology Information (U.S.); National Library of Meidcine (U.S.). Bethesda, Md.: National Center for Biotechnology Information U.S.); National Library of Medicine (U.S.). 2011-

Based on systematic reviews of clinical trials which help to determine which treatments and preventive measures work. Searchable database which allows access to clinical effectiveness research and reviews (CER). Easy-to-read summaries as well as full-text reviews & reports can help consumers and clinicians understand and use clinical research results. Information is drawn, for example, from NCBI bookshelf (http://www.ncbi.nlm.nih.gov/sites/entrez?db=books), PubMed, and published systematic reviews from the Agency for Health Care Research and Quality (335), National Cancer Institute (99), The Cochrane Collaboration (see related entry Cochrane Library, and many others. A comprehensive listing of collaborators and other information about this resource at http://www.ncbi.nlm.nih .gov/pubmedhealth/about/.

95 SciFinder. http://www.cas.org/products/scifinder. Chemical Abstracts Service. Columbus, Ohio: Chemical Abstracts Service. 1998?–
QD9

SciFinder and its academic version SciFinder Scholar have become the primary searching interfaces for the Chemical Abstracts Service (CAS) databases: Chemical Abstracts; the CAS Registry file of over 33 million substances, many with structural and property information; CASREACT, a file of over 14 million single and multistep reaction sequences; CHEMLIST, about

250,000 regulated chemicals; CHEMCATS, sources of over 17 million commercially available chemicals; MARPAT, a patent file of over 750,000 searchable Markush structures. In addition to the CAS databases, SciFinder also provides access to MEDLINE. The client software was replaced by SciFinder Web in 2011, then changed name to SciFinder.

The SciFinder searching interface allows exploring by natural language query, author or organizational name, chemical structure/substructure, or molecular formula. Specific literature queries can be done using bibliographic details, patent number, or CA abstract number. Specific substances can be located using the CAS Registry number. Text search results can be further analyzed, refined, or categorized by a variety of criteria. Structure searches are carried out graphically, and the results can also be refined in a variety of ways. The interface requires individual logon for all searching as well as for access to personalized features.

96 Scopus. http://www.scopus.com/. Elsevier Science Publishers. [s.l.]: Elsevier B. V.

Scopus provides powerful, user-friendly searching of the STM journal literature (21,000 titles), as well as websites, patents (25 million), conference proceedings, and book series. Includes tools to analyze, visualize, and compare research productivity based on publication output, such as *Citation Overview/Tracker*, *Author Identifier*, *Author Evaluator*, and *Journal Analyzer*. Scopus exceeds the Web of Science (97) in its breadth of coverage of the current journal literature but has inconsistent citation searching before 1996. See more details at http://www.elsevier.com/online-tools/scopus.

97 Web of science. http://wokinfo.com/products_tools/multidisciplinary/webofscience/. Thomson Reuters. Philadelphia: Thomson Reuters. 2001-
Z7401

The Web of Science (WoS) database is the platform for Thomson Reuter's suite of databases. The *Web of Science Core Collection Citation Indexes* include the Science Citation Index, the Social Sciences Citation Index, the Arts and Humanities Citation Index and Book Citation Index, which are available separately. Other databases are available on the platform, such as chemical indexes, Journal Citation Reports, Essential Science Indicators, and nonproprietary databases such as Medline and CAB Abstracts. In addition to standard indexing, "Cited Reference Search" discovers all the articles in the database that have cited a particular article. "Related Records" retrieves records that have cited a source common to the chosen record. The "Author Search" function is a work in progress, attempting to cluster results to provide author name disambiguation. Offers strong analytical tools to assess a results set: "Analyze Results" to rank records by selected fields, and the "Create Citation Report" function includes a calculation of the h-index impact measurement of records in the set. Includes access to EndNote Basic bibliographic management software and to ResearcherID to manage author name disambiguation. Permits cross searching of all subscribed databases. One of the greatest strengths and weaknesses of the WoS is that coverage is largely restricted to core and high-impact journals. Coverage years vary by database. The Web of Science supercedes the Web of Knowledge platform name in January 2014.

Specialized indexes

98   Aerospace medicine and biology.
http://purl.access.gpo.gov/GPO/
LPS1988. United States National
Aeronautics and Space Administration,
Scientific and Technical Information
Branch. Washington: Scientific and
Technical Information Branch, National
Aeronautics and Space Administration.
1964–2000?

Supersedes an earlier publication of the same title, issued 1952–63 (1952–53 called *Aviation medicine*). Supt. of Docs. classification: NAS 1.21:7011 (NASA-SP-7011). 1964-2000 distr. to depository libraries in microfiche. Sep. 1995–July 12, 1999 accessible via the Internet. Current research in this subject area (i.e., biological and physiological effects of atmospheric and space flight on humans) can be located via the NASA technical reports server.

A selection of annotated references to unclassified reports and journal articles that were introduced into the NASA Scientific and Technical Information System and announced in *Scientific and technical aerospace reports (STAR)* and *International aerospace abstracts (IAA)*. Although emphasis is placed on applied research, references to fundamental studies are also included. International coverage; signed annotations in English.

99   Cancer.gov. http://www.cancer.gov/.
National Cancer Institute. Bethesda, Md.:
National Cancer Institute. 1990s–

A metasite for cancer information for health care professionals as well as patients. Provides extensive information on all aspects of cancer as a disease and current cancer treatment, including, for example, complementary and alternative medicine, screening, prevention, and genetics. Links for searching the PubMed cancer literature subset and PDQ Query at http://www.cancer.gov/cancertopics/pdq/cancerdatabase.

100   CasesDatabase. http://www.casesdata
base.com/. BioMed Central Ltd. London:
BioMed Central. 2012–
RC66
CasesDatabase; Cases database

Continuously updated database, developed by BioMed Central (BMC) (http://www.biomed-central.com/), a well-known publisher of open-access biomedical journals, to identify medical case reports in support of clinical practice and research. "Cases Database is not a journal and does not directly publish case reports . . . [it] uses text mining technology to make published case reports more discoverable and valuable."—*About/FAQ page*. Provides basic & advanced search and limits/filtering capabilities (e.g., by condition, symptom, medication, etc.), allowing for fast identification of relevant case reports. To make the database more comprehensive, BMC is working with other publishers (e.g., Springer [58], BMJ Group, and others) to include case reports, both open access and non-open access (a search can be limited by "open access" and "non-open access" content), from a large number of journals from multiple publishers. Supports registration to receive alerts and to save cases. For clinicians, researchers, students, educators, and patients.

101   CINAHL. http://www.ebscohost.com/
cinahl/. Cinahl Information Systems,
EBSCO. Ipswich, Mass.: EBSCO. 1982–
CINAHL® [database]. Title varies. Online version: 1984–1992 (with coverage 1982–), publ. by

Cinahl Information Systems; 1993– , publ. jointly by EBSCO and Cinahl Information Systems. Also available in different enhanced versions: CINAHL® with Full Text, CINAHL® Plus™, and CINAHL® Plus with Full Text. Comparisons of the different versions at http://www.ebscohost.com/uploads/thisTopic-dbTopic-592.pdf.

Print version: 1956–76 entitled: *Cumulative index to nursing and allied health literature*; 1977– *Cumulative index to nursing and allied health literature®* (continues to be published in print).

Authoritative database for the professional literature of nursing and allied health. Provides references to journal articles, books, book chapters, pamphlets, audiovisual materials, dissertations, educational software, selected conference proceedings, standards of professional practice, and more. Some full-text material is included. Currently indexes a large number of journals, as well as publications from the American Nurses' Association and the National League for Nursing (837). Allows for application of specific interest category filter, e.g., evidence-based practice, informatics, patient safety, public health, women's health, and others. Subject access is provided by *CINAHL . . . subject heading list: Alphabetic list, tree structures, permuted list*. Complements *International nursing index* (782), publ. 1966–2000.

102 Computer medical databases: The first six decades (1950-2010). Morris F. Collen. New York: Springer, 2011. xix, 288 p. ISBN 9780857299611
610.28/5   R859.7.D36
Contents: ch. 1, "Prologue: The evolution of computer databases"; ch. 2, "The development of medical databases"; ch. 3, "Processing text in medical databases"; ch. 4, "Primary medical record databases"; ch. 5, "Specialized medical databases"; ch. 6, "Secondary medical research databases"; ch. 7, "Bio-surveillance and claims databases"; ch. 8, "Medical knowledge databases"; ch. 9, "Medical bibliographic databases: Knowledge discovery/data mining"; ch. 10, "Epilogue."

Describes the development of medical digital databases. Each chapter has examples of early databases, a summary and commentary, and a comprehensive list of references. Describes the gradual changes of the traditional medical library into a virtual library, with credit being given to the National Library of Medicine

{http://www.nlm.nih.gov/} for providing a leading role. Also mentions the influence of Canada, Europe, and Japan on the computer databases developments in the United States. Includes extensive information on specialized medical registries and diseases databases and addresses the emergence of bioinformatics as a new field in health informatics to support developments in molecular biology. Not included are computer processing of digital images (radiographs), of photographs (dermatology), and of analog signals (electrocardiograms).—Cf. *Pref*. Projections for the next decade include the development of "larger computer database-management systems . . . to support clinical decisions with evidence-based practice guidelines readily accessible from bibliographic and knowledge databases . . ."—*Epilogue*. Also mentioned are wireless communications of physicians and patients, benefits of using telemedicine technology, Internet and World Wide Web to facilitate broadband communications, common shared EMR when receiving care in different medical centers, and handheld portable devices with increased wirelss capacity. Subject index; author index. Also available as an e-book.

103 HealthSTAR (Ovid). http://www.ovid .com/site/products/ovidguide/hstrdb. htm. National Library of Medicine (U.S.). Sandy, Utah: Ovid Technologies. 2000–
Ovid HealthSTAR (HSTR); HealthSTAR (Health Services Technology, Administration, and Research).

"Comprised of data from the National Library of Medicine's (NLM) MEDLINE and former HealthSTAR databases . . . contains citations to the published literature on health services, technology, administration, and research. It focuses on both the clinical and non-clinical aspects of health care delivery. . . . Offered by Ovid as a continuation of NLM's now-defunct HealthSTAR database. Retains all existing backfile citations and is updated with new journal citations culled from MEDLINE. Contains citations and abstracts (when available) to journal articles, monographs, technical reports, meeting abstracts and papers, book chapters, government documents, and newspaper articles from 1975 to the present." —*Publ. notes*. A list of NLM's retired databases, including the original HealthSTAR database, can be found at http://www.nlm .nih.gov/services/pastdatabases.html.

Relevant content on health services research, health technology, health administration, health policy, health economics, etc., can also be found in MEDLINE®/PubMed®, NLM® Gateway, and also CINAHL® (101).

104   Hospital and health administration index. American Hospital Association., American Hospital Association.; Resource Center., National Library of Medicine (U.S.). Chicago: American Hospital Association, 1995–1999
016.36211 1077-1719   Z6675.H75H67; RA963

1945–54, *Index of current hospital literature;* 1955–57, *Hospital periodical literature index;* 1957–94, *Hospital literature index,* cumulated at five-year intervals for the 1945–77 volumes as *Cumulative index of hospital literature.* Discontinued; last published in 1999. Described as a "primary guide to literature on hospital and other health care facility administration, including multi-institutional systems, health policy and planning, and the administrative aspects of health care delivery . . . Special emphasis is given to the theory of health care systems in general; health care in industrialized countries, primarily in the United States; and provision of health care both inside and outside of health care facilities" (*Introd.*). A separate online database, HealthSTAR (Health Services Technology, Administration, and Research) for this literature, previously maintained by NLM, is no longer available (cf. list of NLM's retired databases at http://www.nlm.nih.gov/services/pastdatabases.html). Relevant content is available via MEDLINE/PubMed or HealthSTAR (Ovid, 103), and also CINAHL (101).

105   Nutrition abstracts and reviews series A. http://www.cabi.org/publishing-products/online-information-resources/nutrition-abstracts-and-reviews-series-ahuman-and-experimental/. CAB International. Wallingford, U.K: CAB International. 1990–

Vol. 1 (Oct. 1931) through v. 46 (1976), *Nutrition abstracts and reviews* (NARA), Commonwealth Agricultural Bureau (CAB) International (CABI). Split into ser. A (Human and experimental) and ser. B (Livestock feeds and feeding). Since 1977, available in print. A searchable online back file,

derived from *CAB abstracts*, is available going back to 1990; also included in the full CAB abstracts database, available though multiple vendors.

A searchable international abstract database that includes a variety of biomedical and agricultural subject areas, with papers relevant to all aspects of human nutrition selected from approximately 1,000 journals, books, reports, and conferences. Covers techniques (analytical methodologies for carbohydrates, fiber, lipids, proteins, etc.); foods (functional foods, food additives, supplements; beverages, food processing, food contamination, etc.); physiological and biochemical aspects (endocrinology and nutritional immunology, fasting, vitamins, phytochemicals, minerals, etc.); nutrition and health (diet studies, infant feeding, sports nutrition, nutritional status, etc.); clinical nutrition (e.g., malnutrition, obesity, food allergies, cancer, etc.); and many other subjects.

106   POPLINE. http://www.popline.org/. Johns Hopkins University Bloomberg School of Public Health, Information and Knowledge for Optimal Health Project. Baltimore: Johns Hopkins University Bloomberg School of Public Health
HQ766

A free resource, maintained by the Knowledge for Health Project http://www.k4health.org/ at the Johns Hopkins Bloomberg School of Public Health/Center for Communication Programs and funded by the United States Agency for International Development (USAID) http://www.usaid.gov/.

Database on reproductive health with international coverage. Provides bibliographic citations with abstracts to English-language published and unpublished biomedical and social science literature, with links to full-text documents, RSS feeds for topical searches, and other special features. POPLINE subjects (http://www.popline.org/poplinesubjects) in 12 main categories: Adolescent reproductive health; family planning methods; family planning programs; gender; health communication; HIV/AIDS; maternal and child health; population dynamics; population law and policy; population, health, and environment; reproductive health; sexually transmitted infections.

107   PubChem. http://purl.access.gpo.gov/GPO/LPS61236. National Center for

Biotechnology Information, National Library of Medicine (U.S.). Bethesda, Md.: National Center for Biotechnology Information; National Library of Medicine

Three databases, integrated with the NCBI databases, provide information on the biological activities of small molecules: bioactivity data (PubChem BioAssay); compound structures (PubChem Compound); and substance information (PubChem Substance). PubChem Compound and PubChem Substance databases, where possible, provide links to bioassay description, literature, references, and assay data points. The PubChem BioAssay database also includes links back to the substance and compound databases. Also provides compound neighboring, substructure, superstructure, similarity structure, bioactivity data, and other search features. Provides announcements and updates through social media tools such as Twitter, Facebook, a blog, and more, as well as RSS, an Announcements page, and "share" fucntions. Further detailed information is found at http://pubchem.ncbi.nlm.nih.gov/help.html.

108 **SPORTDiscus**. http://www.ebscohost. com/academic/sportdiscus. Sport Information Resource Centre, Coaching Association of Canada. Ipswich, Mass.: EBSCO

Produced by Sport Information Resource Centre, Ottawa (SIRC); and SPORTDiscus via EBSCOhost platform.

Multidisciplinary full-text database, with comprehensive bibliographic coverage of sports, fitness, and related disciplines. Includes monographic literature dating back to 1949, journal coverage back to 1975. References from journal and magazine articles, books, book chapters, conference proceedings, dissertations, theses, and websites. Useful research tool for health professionals researching the sports medicine literature. Training documentation and help guides available.

Encyclopedias

109 **Current medical diagnosis and treatment.** Marcus A. Krupp, Milton J. Chatton, Lawrence M. Tierney, Stephen J.

McPhee, Maxine A. Papadakis. New York: McGraw-Hill, 1974–. ill.
  616.07505 0092-8682   RC71.A14
Imprint varies: 1962–86 publ. by Lange Medical Publ.; 1987–2003, Appleton and Lange. Supersedes: *Current diagnosis and treatment* (1962–73). Also known as *CMDT*.

Description based on 51st ed., 2012, edited by Stephen J. McPhee, Maxine A. Papadakis, and Michael W. Rabow. Also available online through multiple services. 52nd ed., 2013 is available.

Provides concise and up-to-date information on diseases and disorders and widely accepted methods currently available for diagnosis and treatment. Covers internal medicine, gynecology/obstetrics, dermatology, ophthalmology, otolaryngology, psychiatry, neurology, and imaging procedures. Includes information on nutrition, medical genetics, and an annual update on HIV infection and AIDS. Several chapters are available only online: "Anti-infective chemotherapeutic & antibiotic agents"; "Basic genetics"; "Complementary & alternative medicine"; "Information technology in patient care"; and "Women's health issues." An appendix provides therapeutic drug monitoring and laboratory reference ranges. Index. For health professionals and also general readers seeking information on specific diseases and their diagnosis and treatment.

110 **Encyclopaedic companion to medical statistics. 2nd ed.** Brian Everitt, Christopher Ralph Palmer. Chichester, West Sussex, U.K.: Wiley, 2011. xxii, 491 p., ill. ISBN 9780470684191
  610.7203   RA409.E527
First ed., 2005.

"The aim of this new edition remains . . . to aid communication between medical researchers and statisticians."—*Pref*. Contains approximately 400 statistical topics and cross-referenced articles, considered important and accessible to medical researchers and not necessarily requiring a technical background. Includes useful examples from the biomedical literature. Also available as an e-book.

111 **Encyclopedia of AIDS: A social, political, cultural, and scientific record of the HIV epidemic.** Raymond A. Smith. Chicago: Fitzroy Dearborn,

1998. xli, 601 p., ill., ports.
ISBN 1579580076
362.1969792003   RA644.A25E5276
Covers the time period 1981–96 of the AIDS epidemic, with particular focus on 1991–96. Information is presented in eight major areas: basic science and epidemiology; transmission and prevention; pathology and treatment; impacted populations; policy and law; politics and activism; culture and society; and the global epidemic. Contains 250 entries listed in alphabetical order, with keywords helpful in searching the literature, and references for further reading, and also a resource guide pointing to a variety of additional resources. For undergraduate and graduate students, health professionals, and general readers. Also available as an e-book.

Another resource in this subject area for general readers is *The encyclopedia of HIV and AIDS* (137) by Watstein et al.

Current HIV/AIDS literature citations can be accessed via MEDLINE®/PubMed® (AIDS subset).

112   Encyclopedia of aging. David J. Ekerdt. New York: Macmillan Reference USA, 2002. 4 v., ill. ISBN 0028654722
305.2603   HQ1061.E534
A basic, interdisciplinary gerontology encyclopedia for general readers. Entries cover a broad range of sociological, psychological, legal, economic, medical, biological, and public policy subjects. Includes source documents, cross-references, bibliographies at the end of each article, and a list of articles grouped by topical areas. Not so comprehensive as to be overwhelming, this is a basic resource which can serve as a good starting point for some researchers, even for middle and high school students, as well as for older levels. Available as an e-book.

113   Encyclopedia of aging. 4th ed. Richard Schulz. New York: Springer, 2006. 2 v., 720 p. ISBN 0826148433
305.2603   HQ1061.E53
From the 1st ed. in 1987, this encyclopedia has provided a thorough presentation of a wide range of items, issues, and facts dealing with aging. Now in its 4th ed., it documents in thoughtful essays many aspects of the lives of older persons, as well as issues and services for the elderly. Made up of some 600 essays, including 200 that are entirely new, with others significantly updated. Multidisciplinary, covering relevant materials from biology, physiology, genetics, medicine, psychology, nursing, social services, sociology, economics, technology, and political science. Extensive listing of further resources, cross-references, and thorough index. Definitive work on gerontology and geriatrics. A must-have reference title for general and research collections. Available as an e-book.

114   Encyclopedia of aging and public health. Sana Loue, Martha Sajatovic. New York: Springer, 2007. 843 p.
0387337539
Interdisciplinary resource for professionals in the fields of public health and geriatrics. Contains entries on health and diseases of adults as they age, and quality and accessibility of care for an aging population. Includes biological, psychosocial, historical, ethical, and legal aspects. Entries include references and resource lists. Also available as an e-book.

115   The encyclopedia of Alzheimer's disease. 2nd ed. Carol Turkington, Deborah R. Mitchell, James E. Galvin. New York: Facts On File, 2010. xvi, 302 p. ISBN 9780816077663
616.831003   RC523
Part of Facts on File library of health and living series (137); also available online via Health Reference Center (Facts on File, Inc., 712) and others. Alphabetically-arranged entries discuss Alzheimer's disease, its causes, symptoms, treatments, related conditions, both physical and emotional, sufferers, and more. Several appendixes list resources, international associations and agencies, legal and financial issues, clinical trials, etc. Includes cross-references, glossary, bibliography, and index. For general readers, but also useful for health professionals. Another encyclopedia on Alzheimer's disease is Elaine A. Moore's *Encyclopedia of Alzheimer's disease: With directories of research, treatment, and care facilities* (116).

116   Encyclopedia of Alzheimer's disease: with directories of research, treatment and care facilities. 2nd ed.

Elaine A. Moore, Lisa Moore. Jefferson, N.C.: McFarland, 2012. viii, 447 p, ill. ISBN 9780786464586

616.8/31003   RC523.M665

"Comprehensive reference work intended for anyone involved in the care, treatment, and day-to-day concerns of patients with Alzheimer's disease and related disorders . . . for anyone who is interested in learning more about the genetic and environmental factors that contribute to both early onset and late onset Alzheimer's disease" (*Pref.*). Entries on the different basic science and medical aspects of this disease, research and treatment, caregiving, and many other topics. Contains sections on long-term and day-care treatment centers, arranged by state and city, research facilities by state, listing of resources (books, booklets, pamphlets, caregiver resources, legal assistance, Internet support groups, etc.). This updated edition includes more nursing home facilities, also more information regarding prevention, alternative & novel therapies, environmental triggers, and clinical drugs & vaccines trials. Also available as an e-book. For public, academic, and medical libraries. Another encyclopedia on Alzheimer's disease is Carol Turkington's *The encyclopedia of Alzheimer's disease* (115).

117 Encyclopedia of behavioral medicine.
Marc D. Gellman, J. Rick Turner. New York: Springer, 2013. Four vols., ill. (some color)

616.89003   R726.5.E495

The interdisciplinary field of behavioral medicine is based on the understanding of relationships among behavior, psychosocial processes, and sociocultural contexts. Includes 1,200 entries on behavioral medicine concepts and topics, behavioral (e.g., lifestyle: diet, physical activity, smoking; medication adherence), psychosocial (e.g., temperament and personality, marital and work stressors, social support), and sociocultural variables as potential risk factors for chronic diseases. Includes, for example, articles on alcohol consumption, psychosocial treatment of cancer, gene-environment interaction, history of behavioral medicine, evidence-based behavioral medicine (EBBM) and practice, lipid abnormalities, translational behavioral medicine, etc. Entries include definition, synonym(s), cross-references, references, and citations for further reading. Available as an e-book.

118 Encyclopedia of biomaterials and biomedical engineering. 2nd ed.
Gary E. Wnek, Gary L. Bowlin. New York: Informa Healthcare USA, 2008. 4 v. (various pagings), ill. ISBN 9781420078022

610.28403   R857.M3E53

Provides an "important and continual resource for the many individuals whose work touches, and is touched by, biomaterials and biomedical engineering in order to further stimulate, create, and deliver improvements in quality of life" (*Pref.* Topics include facets of biosensors, implants, orthopedic devices, and tissue engineering. Intended to be multidisciplinary and comprehensive. Second edition has doubled in size and contains nearly 300 articles averaging about ten pages in length. Articles are signed. Contributors (more than 500, largely from the U.S.) are predominantly from academia, but some are from industry. Arranged alphabetically. Includes brief contents (inside front cover), table of contents, cross-references, article references, and index. Published in print and online formats.

119 The encyclopedia of blindness and vision impairment. 2nd ed.
Jill Sardegna. New York: Facts on File, 2002. xiii, 333 p., ill. ISBN 0816042802

362.4/1/03   RE91.S27

First ed., 1991.

Treats all aspects of blindness, including health issues, education, legal questions and organizations. This updated ed. contains over 500 entries, with more than 100 updated entries and revised appendixes that reflect new developments and information (cf. *Pref.* to the 2nd ed.). Includes both brief definitions and main articles (1–2 pages in length), some of which include a short list of references. Twelve appendixes list updated information, including websites for relevant companies, organizations, schools, federal agencies, publications, and services related to blindness and vision impairment. Bibliography and index. Also available as an e-book.

120 Encyclopedia of cancer. 2nd ed.
Joseph R. Bertino. San Diego, Calif.: Academic Press, 2002. 4 v., ill. (some col.) ISBN 0122275551

616.99/4/003   RC262.E558

First ed., 1996.
Vol. 1, A–Cm; v. 2, Co–K; v. 3, L–Q; v. 4, R–Z, Index.

This enl. ed. covers a broad range of cancer-related topics from both basic science and clinical science. Includes recent advances in the etiology, prevention, and the various imaging modalities and treatments currently available. Extensive cross-referencing.

An online version of the Encyclopedia of Cancer is available via Elsevier ScienceDirect at

http://www.sciencedirect.com/science/referenceworks/9780122275555

121 Encyclopedia of cancer. 3rd ed.
M. Schwab. Heidelberg, Germany; New York: Springer, 2011. 7 v. (lxxxvi, 3984 p.), ill. (some col.) ISBN 9783642164828
616.99/4003   RC254.5.E475
First ed., 2001 had title: *Encyclopedic reference of cancer*; 2nd ed., 2008.

This revised and expanded edition provides comprehensive information in the fast developing field of basic and translational cancer research, molecular medicine, and personalized medicine, with information on the major cancers (e.g., breast, colorectal, prostate, ovarian, renal, lung, and hematological malignancies, such as leukemia and lymphoma). For each of these cancers, includes topics describing the pathology, clinical oncology, and targeted therapies. In addition to detailed essays, also provides brief explanations of commonly used acronyms and terms. Alphabetical arrangement, with approximately 7,000 entries (keywords and detailed entries) and cross-references. For clinical and basic science research scientists, clinicians, advanced students, and also general readers. Also available as an e-book.

122 Encyclopedia of cancer and society.
Graham A. Colditz. Thousand Oaks, Calif.: Sage, 2007. 3 v., ill. (some col.) ISBN 9781412949
616.994003   RC254.5.E48

Addresses the issues surrounding cancer and its effects on society. Describes the different types of cancer; possible causes; suspected carcinogens; cancer treatments, including alternative treatments and diets; and controversies in treatment and research. Contains information on the relationship between race and ethnicity and cancer risk, socioeconomic

factors, cancer researchers, cancer associations, hospitals and treatment centers, health and medical policy issues, cancer incidence rates for other countries, and many other related topics. Includes a chronology of cancer from 3000 BCE to the present as well as an "Atlas of cancer" (p. A1–A16). Intended for students, practitioners, and researchers. Also available as an e-book and via Credo reference.

123 The encyclopedia of complementary and alternative medicine. Tova Navarra, Adam Perlman. New York: Facts On File, 2004. xxiii, 276 p., ill. ISBN 0816049971
615.503   R733.N38

Provides information concerning medicines and treatments that may supplement Western medical practices. Approx. 400 entries and appendixes, with lists of organizations, herbs, and a historic time line of complementary and alternative therapies. Glossary, bibliography, and index.

Pt. of Facts on file library of health and living series (137); also available online via Health reference center (Facts on File, Inc.) and netLibrary.

124 Encyclopedia of complementary health practice. Carolyn Chambers Clark, Rena J. Gordon, Barbara Harris, Carl O. Helvie. New York: Springer, 1999. xxi, 638 p., ill. ISBN 0826112390
615.503   R733.E525

"Comprehensive, authoritative, and concise information in the application of complementary health practices that supplement traditional medical procedure . . . as a vehicle for communication across traditional and complementary disciplines . . ."— *Pref.* Divided into four parts: pt. I, Contemporary issues in complementary health practices; pt. II, Conditions; pt. III, Influential substances; pt. IV, Practices and treatments. Cross-references, contributor directory, resource directory, and extensive references. Subject index and contributor index.

125 Encyclopedia of disability. Gary L. Albrecht. Thousand Oaks, Calif.: Sage Publications, 2006. 5 v., ill. ISBN 0761925651
362.403   HV1568.E528

"Conceived as an effort to bring current knowledge of and experience with disability across a wide variety of places, conditions, and cultures to both the general reader and the specialist."—*Introd.* In the first four volumes of this landmark new reference work, more than 500 scholars have contributed some 1,000 entries, which span history far back into antiquity up to the present time, cover cultures and peoples from all over the world, and delve into topics both expected and unexpected, with clarity, insight, and extensive documentation. Entries range from one paragraph to ten pages, and conclude with a bibliography of both print and electronic resources. The fifth and final volume includes a wealth of primary documents drawn from religious texts, including the Bible, literature and poetry, medicine, diaries, and legislation, all divided into three time periods: the ancient world; historical time from 1500 to 1800; and the modern era from 1945 to the present. Documents are annotated and lavishly illustrated. A superb resource at both basic and advanced levels. Available as an e-book.

126 Encyclopedia of drugs, alcohol and addictive behavior. http://www.gale.cengage.com/. Pamela Korsmeyer, Henry R. Kranzler. Detroit: Macmillan Reference USA. 2009 ISBN 9780028660646
362.2903   HV5804

Third ed. with 133 new articles and extensive revision of more than 200 others. New coverage of the Internet as a factor in addictions; drugs and alcohol in the media and in sports and fashion industries; and connections between terrorist groups and the drug trade. Wider regional and international coverage, and updated content on medical, chemical and physiological aspects of addiction. Includes addictive behaviors such as eating disorders and compulsive gambling. Over 500 signed entries, with bibliographies. Multidisciplinary perspective includes legal, behavioral and pharmacological aspects; extensive listings of organizations that deal with various aspects of alcoholism, drug abuse, and addictive behaviors. The sweeping coverage and certain authority of the 1st ed. has been preserved and enhanced. Also available in print format.

127 Encyclopedia of endocrine diseases. Luciano Martini. Amsterdam, Netherlands; Boston: Elsevier Academic Press, 2004. 4 v. (xxxiv, 2400 p.), ill. ISBN 0124755704
616.4003   RC649.E476

Contents: v. 1. A–D; v. 2. E–Im; v. 3. In–Pl; v. 4. Po–Z, Index.
"Intended to provide a comprehensive reference work on the extensive spectrum of diseases and disorders that can occur within the endocrine system . . ."—*Pref.* Approx. 500 topics. Each entry begins with a defining paragraph and has cross-references listed at the end of each article. Further readings and subject index. Written to be accessible to both the health professional and general reader.

Also available online via Elsevier Science Direct http://www.sciencedirect.com/science/referenceworks/9780124755703.

128 Encyclopedia of family health. Martha Craft-Rosenberg, Shelley-Rae Pehler. Thousand Oaks, Calif.: Sage, 2011. 2 v. (xxxvi, 1083 p.)
610 9781412969185   RA418.5.F3E45
Vol. 1: A–G; v. 2: H–Z

Provides brief articles on various health, psychosocial, and societal issues affecting families, with definitions and descriptions on a wide range of topics, with length of the description and depth of coverage varying by topic. Alphabetical list of entries at the front of each volume, each covering the entire set and a "Readers guide" in the first volume, with articles organized under 11 topics (e.g., "at-risk conditions and at-risk situations," "factors influencing family health," "families and the health care system," "family interventions," "genetics and families," and others). Index at the end of v. 2. Written for health care providers, researchers, educators, and students in a variety of health sciences and social sciences disciplines, including medicine, nursing, allied health, social & behavioral sciences, and policy, assisting with assessment and treatment of diseases and conditions utilizing a family-centered approach. Also available as an e-book.

129 Encyclopedia of folk medicine: Old world and new world traditions. Gabrielle Hatfield. Santa Barbara, Calif.: ABC-CLIO, 2004. xx, 392 p, ill. ISBN 1576078744
615.8803   R733.H376

Collection of folk medicine and remedies derived from animals, plants, and minerals; themes and contributions from many cultures and disciplines with examples from Britain, Ireland, and North America.

Each entry includes a bibliography of selected books and journal articles. Cross-references to related subjects. Index. Also available as an e-book.

130 **Encyclopedia of gastroenterology.**
Leonard R. Johnson. Amsterdam,
Netherlands; Boston: Academic Press,
2004. 3 v., ill. (some col.)
ISBN 9780123868602
616.33003   RC802.E513
Contents: v.1, A–E; v.2, F–N; v.3, O–Z.

Articles covering various aspects of gastroenterology and hepatology in both the basic sciences and the clinical areas. Articles have been classified into 25 different subject areas. Entries on specific diseases and their treatment, including nutritional aspects and specific anatomical sites (e.g., esophagus, stomach, and liver). 477 entries. Each entry begins with a glossary of cross-referenced terms and an abstract and has a list of references for further reading. Subject index. Clinical and academic audiences. Available online from publisher at http://www.sciencedirect .com/science/referenceworks/9780123868602.

131 **Encyclopedia of genetics.** Sydney
Brenner, Jeffrey H. Miller, William
Broughton. San Diego, Calif.: Academic
Press, 2002. 4 v. (lxx, 2257 p.), ill.
ISBN 0122270800
576.503   QH427.E532

More than 700 expert authors contributed articles (arranged alphabetically) that range from glossary items, definitions, and short articles to full articles of five pages or longer (many with further reading lists). Many entries are accessible to nonspecialists, while others are written for expert researchers. Cross-references and liberal inclusion of figures and tables enhance the text. A thorough table of contents provides an overview of the set's coverage, while a more detailed index is also available. Appropriate for academic and large public libraries, this title has an online edition available for an added fee.

132 **Encyclopedia of genetics, genomics,
proteomics, and bioinformatics.** Lynn
B. Jorde. Hoboken, N.J.: John Wiley and
Sons, 2005. 8 v. ISBN 9780470849743
599.935   QH431.E62

Each of the four two-volume pairs of this work is devoted to one of the main topics in the title; the review articles are categorized as introductory, specialist, or basic techniques and approaches. A sampling of the many broad topics includes gene mapping, complex traits and diseases, genetic medicine and clinical genetics, structuring and integrating data, and modern programming paradigms in biology. Studies in human and mouse genomes predominate, although other model eukaryotes and some pathogenic bacteria are also presented throughly. An online edition is available from the publisher for an additional fee.

133 **The encyclopedia of genetic disorders
and birth defects. 3rd ed.** James
Wynbrandt, Mark D. Ludman. New York:
Facts On File, 2008. xix, 682 p.
ISBN 9780816063963
616.04203   RB155.5.W96
First ed., 1991; 2nd ed., 2000.

With many entries revised or updated in this edition, presents some 1,000 articles written for both health care professionals and general readers. Entries for disorders, selected on the basis of incidence and historical and clinical importance, discuss prognosis, prevalence, mode of inheritance, and the availability of both carrier screening and prenatal diagnosis; many include addresses of private organizations that can provide further information. Also included are brief discussions of subjects and terminology related to genetic disorders and congenital anomalies. If known, the biochemical and molecular basis of a disease is given. The introduction provides a brief history of human genetics. Numerous cross-references. Appendixes provide statistics and tables on congenital malformations and infant mortality, directory information for private and state, regional, and federal government organizations, and selected Web resources. Bibliography; subject and name index.

Part of Facts on File library of health and living series (137). Also available online via Health Reference Center (Facts on File, Inc., 712).

134 **Encyclopedia of gerontology. 2nd ed.**
James E. Birren. Oxford, U.K.; San Diego,
Calif: Academic Press/Elsevier, 2007. 2 v.
ISBN 0123705304
                              RC952.5.E58
First ed., 1996.

Alphabetical arrangement of 181 articles on all

aspects of aging, the aged, old age, with topics such as theories of aging, biological, behavioral, social, and environmental influences on aging, etc. Written in a standard format, each chapter includes a brief table of contents, a glossary of words with definitions as used in the chapter, and brief bibliography. Cross-references; subject index. Intended for students and professionals.

Other well-regarded, but less recent or comprehensive gerontology encyclopedias are Ekhardt's *Encyclopedia of aging* (112), or Schulz' *Encyclopedia of aging*.

135   Encyclopedia of health and aging.
Kyriakos S. Markides. Thousand Oaks, Calif.: Sage Publications, 2007. 650 p.
ISBN 9781412909495
613.043803   RA777.6.E534
Resource on health and aging in the United States and abroad. "Reader's Guide" lists entries by key themes and topics, with entries contributed from different disciplines (e.g., biology, epidemiology, health psychology, public policy, sociology, and others) related to health and aging: aging and the brain; diseases and medical conditions; drug-related issues; function and syndromes; mental health and psychology; nutritional issues; physical status; prevention and health behaviors; sociodemographic and cultural issues; studies of aging and systems of care. Also addresses economic issues and provides recent research results and facts on health and aging. Includes further readings, bibliographical references, a list of online resources, and index. Appropriate for academic, various types of health sciences libraries, and public libraries. Also available as an e-book.

136   Encyclopedia of health and behavior.
Norman B. Anderson. Thousand Oaks, Calif.: Sage, 2004. 2 v. ISBN 0761923608
610.3   R726.5.E53
Contents: v.1, A–G; v.2, H–W.
Health and behavior as an area of study can be defined as an interdisciplinary field of health science, health care, and public health that focuses on the interaction of behavioral, psychological, emotional, social, cultural, and biological factors with physical health outcomes. Approximately 200 entries such as stress and health, pain management, social support, health, smoking, health promotion and disease prevention, and HIV/AIDS. Includes

policy and organizational issues, including health care costs. Cross-references. Appendix with online resources and an annotated listing of organizations. Author and subject indexes. For scholars, health professionals, and also general readers. Also available as an e-book.

137   The encyclopedia of HIV and AIDS.
3rd ed. Stephen E. Stratton, Evelyn J. Fisher, Sarah Watstein. New York: Facts On File, 2012. xiii, 414 p.
ISBN 9780816077236
362.196/9792003   RC606.6.W385
First ed. (1998) had title: *The AIDS dictionary*.; 2nd ed., 2003.
While the previous edition also included general medical terminology not specifically related to HIV and AIDS, the focus in this edition is on HIV and AIDS, with many new and revised entries from the previous edition, covering the medical conditions and drugs associated with HIV/AIDS, its science aspects, and vaccine development in greater depth. Also includes cultural and social sciences topics. Revised appendixes with frequently used abbreviations, HIV/AIDS statistics in the U.S. (recent data from the Centers for Disease Control and Prevention's 2007 *HIV/AIDS surveillance report* http://www.cdc.gov/hiv/topics/surveillance/resources/reports/2007report/pdf/2007surveillancereport.pdf) and worldwide by country (2010 United Nations *UNAIDS Report on the global AIDS epidemic* http://www.unaids.org/globalreport/), and other selected resources. Includes bibliography and index. For students and general readers.

Part of the Facts on File library of health and living series. Available online via Health reference center (Facts on File, Inc., 172) and also as an e-book.

Another resource in this subject area for general readers is *Encyclopedia of AIDS: a social, political, cultural, and scientific record of the HIV epidemic* (111).

138   Encyclopedia of hormones. Helen L. Henry, Anthony W. Norman. Amsterdam, Netherlands; Boston: Academic Press, 2003. 3 v., ill. ISBN 0123411033
571.7403   QP571.E52
This set presents 300 articles, six to eight pages long, that cover topics in plant and animal (vertebrate and invertebrate) hormones, growth factors,

interleukins, and hormone receptors and action mechanisms. Aspects of hormones presented include chemical structure and biological synthesis; major physiological systems in which they operate; cellular and subcellular sites of their action; nature of signal transduction mechanisms in hormone action; and biological consequences of an excess or deficiency of specific hormones. Articles begin with a topical outline, abstract, and glossary of key terms. They provide cross-references and list of suggested readings.

Each volume contains the table of contents, foreword, preface, and guide to using the entire set as well as the individual volume's contents. Vol. 3 provides a glossary containing nearly all terms defined in individual articles and an alphabetical index of broad subjects and more specific keywords. Appropriate for academic and research libraries.

Also available online from publisher for an additional fee.

139 Encyclopedia of infectious diseases: Modern methodologies. Michel Tibayrenc. Hoboken, N.J.: Wiley-Liss, 2007. 747 p., [24] p. of plates: ill. (some color), maps (some color).
ISBN 0471657328
362.1969003   RA643.E53

Provides coverage of modern multidisciplinary approaches and applications of newly developed technologies to the study of infectious diseases and their surveillance and control. Emphasis is on medical applications. Articles on AIDS, malaria, SARS and influenza, evolution of pathogens and the relationship between human genetic diversity and the spread of infectious diseases, uses of various technologies, and various specialized topics (e.g., bioterrorism, antibiotics, using a geographic information system to spatially investigate infectious disease, representation of infectious diseases in art, and others). Includes list of web resources. For an academic audience. Also available as an e-book.

Encyclopedia of infectious diseases, by Turkington et al. (part of the Facts on File library of health and living series, 115), is also a useful resource, intended for health professionals, general readers, and public libraries.

140 Encyclopedia of life sciences. Nature Publishing Group. London; New York: Nature Publishing Group, 2002. 20 v., ill.

(some color), maps, color plates.
ISBN 1561592749
       QH302.5.E525

Aimed at academic libraries, this comprehensive encyclopedia has 20 volumes, including an index volume. Topic areas with thorough coverage include molecular biology, physiology, evolution, and ecology; however, treatment of descriptive biology on animals and plants is minimal. Several articles address medical subjects but agriculture and biotechnology are excluded. The 3,300 articles are categorized by the specificity of material presented; designations are elementary, secondary (more specialized), and supplementary, which cover special topics. Detailed index volume includes a list of articles in alphabetical order and classified by topic. Each article begins with a short definition. Cross-references appear at the paragraph level, and each article includes further reading recommendations and bibliographies of material current as of 2002. Most articles have illustrations, though color images are limited to a section of plates in each volume. The online edition is not regularly updated, but the graphics and navigation enhance the content. Six additional volumes published by Wiley (110) in 2007 (v. 21–26), with index in v. 26 to the new material. The publisher will integrate this title with *Encyclopedia of the human genome.*

141 Encyclopedia of life sciences. 2nd ed. Anne O'Daly. Tarrytown, N.Y.: Marshall Cavendish, 2004. 13 v. (1872 p.), ill. (some color), color maps.
ISBN 0761474420
570.3   QH302.5.E53

Written to appeal to those lacking strong scientific backgrounds, this revised 2nd ed. is accessible to middle school readers and above. The 13-volume set is rich with illustrations, color photographs and diagrams, and color-coded sidebars. The sidebars expand on content of the articles featuring facts to add depth to some topics, biographical highlights about scientists, tidbits from evolutionary history, alerts to risks arising from pollution, threats to species, and explanations of how topics in life science relate to industry, medicine, and human activity. Many topics that surface frequently in introductory high school and college biology classes receive thorough treatment (e.g., abortion, animal experimentation, and recycling). An index appears in each volume. Vol. 13 has a comprehensive index, indexes by broad subtopics such as botany and medicine, a bibliography, and glossary. Articles provide recommendations for further reading, cross-references among keywords and topics, and explicit connections to interdisciplinary concepts. Valuable for high school, public, and undergraduate library collections.

142 Encyclopedia of medical anthropology: Health and illness in the world's cultures. Carol R. Ember, Melvin Ember. New York: Kluwer Academic/Plenum, 2004. 2 v. (xliv, 1071 p.), ill. ISBN 0306477548

362.103   RA418.E354

Medical anthropology as part of cultural anthropology is concerned with the application of anthropological and social science theories and methods to questions about health, illness, and healing. Vol. 1, "Health and illness in the world's cultures," contains essays grouped into five sections: general concepts and perspectives; medical systems; political, economic, and social issues; sexuality, reproduction, and the life cycle; and health conditions and diseases. Vol. 2, "Cultures," describes the state of health and illness around the world. Subject index. Also available as an e-book and via Credo reference.

143 Encyclopedia of medical decision making. Michael W. Kattan, Mark E. Cowen. Thousand Oaks, Calif.: SAGE Publications, 2009. 2 v. (xxxvi, 1229 p.), ill. ISBN 9781412953726

610.3   R723.5.E53

Approx. 300 signed essays on concepts and methods in the patient-care decision-making process. Entries cover topics such as mathematical and statistical aspects of decision-making, biostatistics, clinical decision-making and analysis, clinical epidemiology, and outcome measures. Also includes essays on process and technology in medical decision-making. Contains a reader's guide, bibliographical references, "see also" references, tables, charts, and further readings. Index. Useful for graduate students, physicians, and other health professionals. Also available as an e-book.

144 Encyclopedia of medical devices and instrumentation. 2nd ed. John G. Webster. Hoboken, N.J.: Wiley, 2006. ISBN 0471263583

610.2803   R856.A3E53

First ed., 1988, 4 v.

Contents: v. 1, Alloys, shape memory—Brachytherapy, Intravascular; v. 2, Capacitive microsensors for biomedical applications–Drug infusion systems; v.3, Echocardiography and Doppler echocardiography–Human spine, biomechanics of; v.4, Hydrocephalus, tools for diagnosis and treatment of–Monoclonal antibodies; v. 5, Nanoparticles–Radiotherapy accessories; v.6, Radiotherapy, heavy ion–X-rays, production of.

An alphabetically arranged collection of approximately 300 articles by experts, providing a comprehensive treatment of the contributions of engineering, physics, and computer science to the various areas of medicine. Discusses function and use of diagnostic and therapeutic devices. Articles include many illustrations and substantial bibliographies of the primary literature. Cross-references; index. Also available as an e-book.

145 Encyclopedia of medical genomics and proteomics. Jürgen Fuchs, Maurizio Podda. New York: Dekker, 2005. 2 v. (xxviii, 1359 p., xxix), ill. ISBN 0824755022

616.04203   RB155.E54

Presents an overview of medical applications of current nucleic acid and protein technology for diagnosis, treatment, and management of human diseases, including infections, neoplastic, and genetic diseases. Contains 400 entries, with figures and tables. Topics include, among others, diagnostic microbiology, genetic testing, genomic and proteomic medicine, pharmacogenetics, and tissue and cell typing. Bibliographic references, including website references, and index. For researchers, clinicians, science and medical students, and general readers. Also available in a continually updated online edition.

146 Encyclopedia of medical physics. Slavik Tabakov. Boca Raton, Fla.: CRC Press, 2013. 2 v. (xiv, 822, 17 p.), ill. (some col.) ISBN 9781466555501

616.07/54803   R895.A3 E53

Co-published by the European Medical Imaging Technology EMITEL e-encyclopedia for lifelong learning (EMITEL) consortium, with support from the International Organization for Medical Physics.

Includes approx. 2,800 entries, with topics in the following categories: "General terms; "diagnostic radiology; "nuclear medicine"; "radiotherapy"; 'magnetic resonance imaging"; "ultrasound imaging"; "radiation protection." Contains articles with black-and white images, graphs, and diagrams, also a few color plates. Useful for medical physicists at all levels and related professions. Also available as an e-book.

All content of this encyclopedia is also made available as a searchable database (title: *EMITEL e-encyclopedia for lifelong learning*), additionally also a digital multilingual translation dictionary (approx. 3,200 terms in 25 languages; cross-translation to/from any two languages from its database; hyperlinked to an appropriate article) with explanatory articles for each term. These two online resources can be searched either separately or combined. Content of both resources is freely accessible at http://www.emitel2.eu/.

147 Encyclopedia of molecular cell biology and molecular medicine.
2nd ed. Robert A. Meyers. Weinheim, Germany: Wiley-VCH Verlag, 2004–2005. 16 v., ill. (some col.)
ISBN 3527305432
572.803   QH506.E534
First ed., 1996–97 (6 v.).

Contents: Vol. 1, adipocytes to biological regulation by protein phosphorylation; v. 2, bioorganic chemistry to chamydomonas; v. 3, chromosome organization within the nucleus to e-cell: computer simulation of the cell; v. 4, electric and magnetic field reception to FTIR of biomolecules; v. 5, fungal biotechnology to growth factors; v. 6, growth factors and oncogenes in gastrointestinal cancers to informatics (computational biology); v. 7, innate immunity to mass spectrometry, high speed DNA fragment sizing; v. 8, mass spectrometry-based methods of proteome analysis to mucoviscidosis (cystic fibrosis), molecular cell biology of; v. 9, mutagenesis, malignancy, and genome instability to organic cofactors as coenzymes; v. 10, origins of life, molecular basis of to programmed cell death; v. 11, proteasomes to receptor, transporter, and ion channel diseases; v. 12, recombination and genome rearrangements to serial analysis of gene expression; v. 13, sex hormones (male): analogs and antagonists to synchrotron infrared microspectroscopy; v. 14, syngamy and cell cycle control to triacylglyerol storage and mobilization, regulation

of; v. 15, triplet repeat diseases to zebrafish (Danio rerio) genome and genetics; v. 16, index (including acronyms, cross-references, organizations, and some species names), cumulative table of contents, and list of authors.

Considered an interdisciplinary authoritative, peer-reviewed encyclopedic reference work with comprehensive treatment of molecular biology, cell biology, molecular genetics, and molecular medicine topics, with focus on molecular medicine. This edition has 150 new articles and 250 from the first edition. Each article begins with a keyword section, including definitions, and references to the primary and secondary literature. Articles are organized by the following broad, primary topical categories: nucleic acids; structure determination technologies for biomolecules; biochemistry; proteins, peptides, and amino acids; biomolecular interactions; cell biology; molecular cell biology of specific organisms, organs, or systems, and diseases; pharmacology; and biotechnology. Articles vary in length, typically ten to forty pages, most with an extensive list of references. Cross-references help the reader to find relevant entries. Each volume has a section of color plates, a glossary, figures depicting DNA base pairing, and tables listing the amino acids with their chemical structures, abbreviated names, and RNA codes, and the same glossary that appears in all volumes. Aimed at specialists and investigators in other disciplines who are interested in this field, the work is edited by fifteen international experts, including ten Nobel Prize (447) winners.

Appropriate for academic and other research library collections. Also available online.

148 Encyclopedia of neuroscience.
3rd ed., rev. and enl. ed. George Adelman, Barry H. Smith. Amsterdam, Netherlands: Elsevier BV, 2004. 1 CD-ROM. ISBN 0444514325
612.803   RC334.E53
Print editions: 1st ed., 1987, supplemented by *Neuroscience year: Supplement . . . to the Encyclopedia of neuroscience*, v. 1–3, 1989–93; 2nd rev. and enl. ed., 2 v., 1999; 3rd ed., 2004, not issued in print, only CD-ROM. CD-ROM editions: 2nd rev. and enl. ed. (e.g., [1st] CD-ROM ed., 1997); 3rd rev. and enl. ed. (e.g., [2nd] CD-ROM ed.), 2004.

Description based on the 2nd rev. and enl. CD-ROM ed. (1997) and 2nd rev. print ed. (1999).

Contains alphabetically arranged articles covering clinical and basic aspects of neuroscience, its many subfields, new research findings, and many recently developed tools and techniques such as neuroimaging and functional imaging. Both volumes begin with a list of all entries and end with a subject index. Vol. 2 contains two appendixes: I. "Concise biographies of contributors to neuroscience, 300 B.C. to 1960 A.D.," and II. "Society for neuroscience policies on the use of animals and human subjects in neuroscience." The 2nd ed. was originally published in CD-ROM format, with 800 contributions, over 14,000 EMBASE abstracts, and direct access to relevant websites, illustrations, animations, and videos. Readers are encouraged to use the CD-ROM edition with its additional capabilities. It is viewed by the publisher "as the foundation of a revisable and updatable neuroscience database."—*Pref.*

More recently published encyclopedias in this area, available in both print as well as e-books, include *Encyclopedia of neuroscience* by Binder et al. (Springer) and *Encyclopedia of neuroscience* by Squire (Elsevier).

149 Encyclopedia of obesity. Kathleen Keller. Los Angeles: Sage, 2008. 2 v., ill., port. ISBN 9781412952385
362.196398003   RC628.E53

"Reader's guide" topics: biological or genetic contributions to obesity; children and obesity; dietary interventions to treat obesity; disordered eating and obesity; environmental contributions to obesity; health implications of obesity; medical treatments for obesity; new research frontiers on obesity; obesity and ethnicity/race; obesity and the brain or obesity and behavior; obesity as a public health crisis; psychological influences and outcomes of obesity; societal influences and outcomes of obesity; women and obesity; worldwide prevalence of obesity.

This interdisciplinary resource explores a variety of topics on obesity, health conditions, and issues related to obesity. Written in nontechnical language and intended as a starting point for different audiences, from scholars to the general public. References at the end of each entry. Glossary and index in both volumes. Available online via Sage eReference.

150 Encyclopedia of obesity and eating disorders. 3rd ed. Dana K. Cassell, David H. Gleaves. New York: Facts on File, 2006. 362 p. ISBN 0816061971
616.8526003   RC552.E18.C37

First edition, 1994; 2nd ed., 2000.

Provides concise entries on the causes, symptoms, and treatments, including pharmacotherapy, of obesity and the various eating disorders (e.g., anorexia nervosa, bulimia, etc.). Lists sources of information, websites, audiovisuals, and other resources. Bibliography and index. For general readers and health professionals.

Part of *Facts on File library of health and living* series. Available online via Health Reference Center (712).

151 Encyclopedia of pain. Robert F. Schmidt, William D. Willis. Berlin; New York: Springer, 2007. 3 v., ill. (some col.) ISBN 9783540439578
616/.047203   RB127.E523

Contents: v. 1, A–G; v. 2, H–O; v. 3, P–Z.

Approx. 3,000 alphabetically arranged entries, with color images and figures as appropriate, on all aspects of pain and pain management. Includes bibliographic references and A–Z listing of entries at the end of each volume. No index. Online ed. (http://www.springer.com) provides keyword searching. For academic health sciences libraries.

152 Encyclopedia of respiratory medicine. 1st ed. Geoffrey Laurent, Steven Shapiro. Amsterdam, Netherlands; Boston: Academic Press, 2006. 4 v. ISBN 0124383602
                              RC732

In 4 v. Covers various aspects of respiratory medicine, including basic science and clinical aspects, and treatment of diseases that affect the respiratory system. Uniform layout of entries. Written for students, researchers, and health professionals. Diagrams and illustrations. Subject index. Also available as an e-book.

153 Encyclopedia of sports medicine. Lyle J. Micheli. Thousand Oaks, Calif.: SAGE Publications, 2011. 4 v. (xliii, 1758 p.), ill. ISBN 9781412961158
617.1/02703   RC1206.E53

Authoritative entries of varying length and depth on the diagnosis and treatment of various health conditions related to sports medicine, including the psychological needs of the injured athlete. Alphabetic list of entries and a reader's guide, illustrations, see-also references, further readings, glossary, and index. Also includes an annotated list of sports medicine organizations and step-by-step instructions and images for various taping and bracing techniques. Written for medical students and various health professionals & practitioners. Also considered useful to health consumers. Also available as an e-book.

Two other encyclopedias, *Encyclopedia of exercise, sport and health* by Brukner et al. and *Encyclopedia of sports medicine* by Oakes et al., are both written for general readers.

154   Encyclopedia of stress. 2nd ed.
George Fink. Boston: Elsevier, 2007.
p. cm 0120885034
First ed., 2000.

"Comprehensive reference source on stressors, the biological mechanisms involved in the stress response, the effects of activating the stress response mechanisms, and the disorders that may arise as a consequence of acute or chronic stress . . . includes a wide range of related topics such as neuroimmune interactions, cytokines, enzymatic disorders, effects on the cardiovascular system, immunity and inflammation, and physical illnesses. It also goes beyond the biological aspects of stress to cover topics such as stress and behavior, psychiatric and psychosomatic disorders, workplace stress, post-traumatic stress, stress-reduction techniques, and current therapies" (*Publ. notes*). For researchers, clinicians, professionals, and students. Available online via Elsevier ScienceDirect.

The encyclopedia of stress and stress-related diseases by Kahn et al., part of the Facts on File Library of health and living series and available online via Health reference center (Facts on File, Inc., 712), provides accessible content on stress and stress-related diseases for all types of readers and libraries.

155   Encyclopedia of substance abuse prevention, treatment, & recovery. Gary L. Fisher, Nancy A. Roget. Los Angeles: SAGE, 2009. 2 v. (xxxiii, 1092 p.), ill. ISBN 9781412950848
362.2903   RC563.4

350 signed entries in alphabetical order deal with the classification of drugs, diagnosis, treatment and prevention, the criminal justice system, impacts

on families and communities, special populations, and substance abuse on the job and in school. Suggestions for further reading. Includes behavioral addictions and alcohol. Theoretical, sociological, medical, historical, neurobiological and public policy aspects. Identifies substances, organizations, and methods. Aimed at professionals in social work, the criminal justice system, medicine, and education. Bibliography. Index. Available as an e-book.

156   The encyclopedia of the brain and brain disorders. 3rd ed. Carol Turkington, Joseph R. Harris. New York: Facts On File, 2009. xi, 434 p. ISBN 9780816063956
612.8203   QP376.T87

First ed., 2006, has title: *The brain encyclopedia*; 2nd ed., 2002.

Accessible reference about the brain and brain disorders for general readers. Clear and concise entries on elements and functions of the brain and its various disorders and diseases. Increased amount of material on memory in this edition. Also includes three directories (of self-help, professional, and governmental organizations), helpful websites, a glossary, an extensive list of references, and an index to a wide range of terms.

Part of the *Facts on File library of health and living series.* Available online via Health Reference Center (712) and other providers.

157   Encyclopedia of the human brain.
V. S. Ramachandran. San Diego, Calif.: Academic Press, 2002. 4 v., xxxv, 903 p., ill. ISBN 0122272102
612.8303   QP376.E586

More than 220 signed entries authored by leaders in neuroscience and psychology cover topics ranging from anatomy, physiology, neuropsychology, and clinical neurology to neuropharmacology, evolutionary biology, genetics, and behavioral science. Each entry consists of an outline and definition paragraph, glossary, cross-references, and a list of suggested readings. Detailed subject index is the main point of access. Valuable for life sciences collections and academic libraries. Available as an online database.

158   Encyclopedia of the neurological sciences. 1st ed. Michael J. Aminoff,

Robert B. Daroff. Amsterdam; Boston: Academic Press, 2003. 4 v., ill. (some col.) ISBN 0122268709

612.8/03   RC334.E535

v. 1, A–De; v. 2, Di–L; v. 3, M–Ph; v. 4, Pi–Z, index.

Approx. 1,000 concise entries in 32 subject areas deal with basic science aspects and clinical issues of the neurological sciences, including neurology, neuroanatomy, neurobiology, neurosurgery, psychiatry, and other related areas. Alphabetical sequence by title, with groupings according to specific discipline. Suggestions for further reading at the end of each entry. Includes biographies of famous neuroscientists. Some graphics. Outline of contents in v. 4. Extensive cross-references. Subject index. Written for readers from other disciplines, not necessarily for the specialist. Also available online via ScienceDirect.

A second edition is planned to be published in 2014.

159   Encyclopedia of women's health.
Sana Loue, Martha Sajatovic, Keith B. Armitage. New York: Kluwer Academic/ Plenum, 2004. vii, 710 p. ISBN 0306480735

613.04244   RA778.E5825

Covers the history of women's health as well as current topics and issues. Interdisciplinary resource, including topics from medicine, psychology, law, and other areas and perspectives. Also includes alternative and complementary health topics. Suggested readings. Written for both general readers and health professionals. Also available as an e-book and via Credo reference.

160   The encyclopedia of women's health. 6th ed. Christine Ammer. New York: Facts On File, 2009. xiii, 480 p., ill. ISBN 9780816074075

613/.0424403   RA778.A494

First ed. (1983) has title *A to Z of women's health*; [2nd] ed. (1989) through 4th ed. (2000) have title *The new A to Z of women's health*. Title for 5th ed. varies; issued both as *The new A to Z of women's health: A concise encyclopedia* and *The encyclopedia of women's health*. Pt. of *Facts on file library of health and living series* (137).

Some revised and a few new entries in this edition. Entries cover a broad range of women's health issues and changing health needs during the different stages of their lives. Also gives attention to social and emotional issues. Appendix, topically arranged, provides contact information for associations and organizations. Alphabetical arrangement, cross-references, and index. Also available as an e-book.

161   Encyclopedia of women's health issues. Kathlyn Gay. Westport, Conn.: Oryx Press, 2002. xvii, 300 p., ill. ISBN 157356303X

613.0424403   RA778.G39

Goes beyond the description of the various health problems and diseases that women experience and also includes social, political, legal, economic, and ethical aspects of women's health. Treats contemporary issues and also provides a historical perspective when appropriate. Can serve as a starting point for research on gender issues in health care policy and politics. Alphabetical arrangement, bibliography, and a selection of websites. Index. For an academic audience and also general readers.

162   Encyclopedic reference of immunotoxicology. Hans-Werner Vohr. Berlin; New York: Springer, c2005. xxi, 730 p., ill. (some col.) ISBN 3540441727

616.07/903   QR180.4.E55

"Immunotoxicology . . . focuses on the undesirable effects of chemicals on the immune system. The exposure of humans . . . to such agents may be intentional (drugs) or unintentional (environment) . . . The side effects may lead to over-activation of the immune system, or equally to immunosuppression. The end points of dysregulation are therefore also varies: allergies, cancer, autoimmunity, poor resistance to infection." (*Pref.*). Intended for scientists and advanced students. Also available as an e-book.

163   French's index of differential diagnosis: An A-Z. 15th ed. Mark Kinirons, Harold Ellis, Herbert French. London: Hodder Arnold, 2011. x, 786 p., ill. (some col.) ISBN 9780340990711

616.07503   RC71.5

First ed., 1912: *An index of differential diagnosis of main symptoms;* 14th ed., 2005.

Also called *Index of differential diagnosis*.

Based on symptoms patients might present to their physicians, offers a description of the different diagnoses, supported in many cases by illustrations, lists, and tables. Diagnoses are described in order of importance, with emphasis on the more common diagnoses. Intended to provide decision support for clinicians. Also available as an e-book.

164 The Gale encyclopedia of alternative medicine. 3rd ed. Laurie J. Fundukian. Detroit: Gale, Cengage Learning, 2009. 4 v. (xxii, 2688 p.), ill. (some col.)
ISBN 9781414448725
615.503   R733.G34
First ed., 2001; 2nd ed., 2005.
Contents: v. 1, A–C; v. 2, D–K; v. 3, L–R; v. 4, S–Z.

This expanded edition presents information and covers all aspects of alternative and complementary practices, therapies, and remedies, and their effect on various diseases and disorders. Entries also include conventional treatments.

Alphabetically arranged entries, sidebar glossary of key terms, websites, suggestions for further readings, list of selected organizations, etc. Each volume contains a list of all entries in the set. Color illustrations and photographs. Bibliography. General index. Available online in the Gale Virtual Reference Library. Intended for general readers and nonspecialist professionals.

165 The Gale encyclopedia of cancer: A guide to cancer and its treatments. 3rd ed. Jacqueline L. Longe. Detroit: Gale, Cengage Learning, 2010. 2 v. (xxxvii, xxxvii, 1724 p.), color ill.
ISBN 9781414475981
616.994003   RC254.5.G353
First ed., 2002; 2nd ed., 2005.
Contents: v. 1, A–K; v. 2, L–Z.

This updated ed. provides a detailed guide to cancer topics and issues. Following a standardized format, entries on a variety of cancers, treatments, diagnostic procedures, cancer drugs and their side effects, also on cancer biology, carcinogenesis, and cancer genetics. Entries for cancer types include definition, description, demographics, causes and symptoms, diagnosis, clinical staging, treatments and treatment team, prognosis, coping with cancer treatment, clinical trials, prevention, special concerns, and resources. For cancer drugs: definition, purpose, description, recommended dosage, precautions, side effects, and drug interactions are

included, also traditional and alternative treatments and information on clinical trials. A resources section provides additional information. Contact information for organizations, support groups, government agencies, and research groups in an appendix at the back of v. 2. Alphabetical arrangement, cross-references, color images for many malignancies, and anatomical illustrations of the major body systems affected by cancers. List of contents; general index.

Also available as an e-book as part of Gale Virtual Reference Library. Intended for general readers and nonspecialist professionals.

166 Gale encyclopedia of children's health: Infancy through adolescence. 2nd ed. Jacqueline L. Longe. Detroit: Gale, 2011. 4 v., col. ill. ISBN 9781414486413
618.920003   RJ26.G35
V. 1, A–C; v.2, D–K; v.3, L–R; v.4, S–Z.

Includes approximately 600 articles, presented in a standardized format. Covers common medical conditions and also rare diseases, developmental issues, immunizations, drugs, and various procedures. Each entry provides definition and description of various diseases, disorders and other problems, their causes, symptoms, diagnosis, treatment, prognosis, etc. Glossary, color photos, illustrations, charts (growth charts), tables, childhood medications, and resources for further reading and study. General index. For use by general readers and health professionals. Also available as an e-book.

167 The Gale encyclopedia of genetic disorders. 3rd ed. Laurie J. Fundukian. Farmington Hills, Mich.: Gale, 2010. 2 v., ill. (chiefly color)
ISBN 9781414476025
616.04203   RB155.5.G35
First ed., 2002; 2nd ed., 2005.
Contents: v. 1, A–L; v. 2, M–Z.

Signed entries with detailed information for genetic or congenital diseases, disorders, and conditions. A standardized format provides for each entry as appropriate: Definitions, description, genetic profile, demographics, signs and symptoms, tests, diagnosis, treatment and management, prognosis, resources, and key terms. Written for the non-specialist. Available as an e-book as part of the Gale virtual reference library.

168 The Gale encyclopedia of medicine.
4th ed. Laurie J. Fundukian, Gale
Group. Detroit: Gale, 2011. 6 v., col. ill.
ISBN 9781414486468
616.003   RC41.G35
First ed., 1999; 2nd ed., 2002; 3rd ed., 2006.
Revised edition, with comprehensive coverage of
basic medical information, with articles on diseases, common conditions and disorders, various
treatments, including alternative treatments, and
tests. Diets and preventive measures are also covered. Includes sidebars with biographical information of prominent individuals in medicine. Articles
are written in a standardized format, in alphabetical
arrangement, with definitions of key terms, contact
information for organizations and support groups,
resources section for additional information, full-color
illustrations, photographs, and tables. General index.

Encyclopedias in other medical subjects published by Gale also following this type of arrangement and a standardized format include *The Gale
encyclopedia of alternative medicine* (164), *The Gale
encyclopedia of cancer: A guide to cancer and its treatments* (165), *The Gale encyclopedia of genetic disorders* (639), *The Gale encyclopedia of mental health*
(708), and *The Gale encyclopedia of nursing and
allied health* by Longe. Also available as an e-book.

169 The Gale encyclopedia of
neurological disorders. 2nd ed.
Brigham Narins. Detroit: Gale Cengage
Learning, 2012. 2 v. (xxii, 1330 p.), ill.
(some col.) ISBN 9781414490083
616.8003   RC334.G34
First ed., 2005.
Contents: v. 1, A–L; v. 2, M–Z, glossary, index.

Includes 400 alphabetically arranged entries on
disorders of the nervous system, with articles on
neurological diseases, disorders and syndromes,
tests, treatments, diagnostic equipment, and medications. Also includes articles on the brain and nervous system anatomy. A typical entry for a disease
includes, e.g., definition, description, demographics, causes and symptoms, diagnosis, treatment
team, treatment, recovery and rehabilitation, clinical trials, prognosis, special concerns, resources,
and key terms. Also included are resource lists
of books, periodical articles, organizations, and
websites. Both volumes include a complete list
of entries. Intended for patients, their families,

allied health students, and general readers. Drug
and treatment data also provide structured entries,
with definition, purpose, description, recommended dosage, precautions, side effects, interactions,
resources, and key terms. Available online in the
Gale Virtual Reference Library.

170 The Gale encyclopedia of senior
health: A guide for seniors and their
caregivers. Jacqueline L. Longe. Detroit:
Gale, c2009. 5 v. (2120 p.), ill. (chiefly
col.) ISBN 9781414403830
618.97003 22   RC952.5.G3485
2009
Comprehensive encyclopedia, alphabetically organized, with approx. 600 illustrated entries and
arranged in five categories: diseases and conditions;
treatment, rehabilitation, recovery; aging, general
health, death and dying; healthy living: nutrition,
exercise, prevention; and community care giving. A
typical entry provides definition, description, causes
and symptoms, diagnosis, treatment, various resources, etc. Glossary of key terms, appendix listing organizations, and general index. Intended as a resource
for senior patients/health consumers to educate
themselves about their condition. It is not intended
to replace a doctor's visit. It is also considered a useful
reference source for librarians. Also available online
through Gale virtual reference library.

Some overlap of content with other Gale encyclopedias, e.g., *Gale encyclopedia of medicine* and
Gale encyclopedia of nursing, can be expected.

Encyclopedia of aging (112) and *Encyclopedia
of health and aging* (135) address the biological,
psychological, social, and economic aspects of
health and aging and are intended for health care
professionals who work with an aging population.

171 Macmillan encyclopedia of death and
dying. Robert Kastenbaum. New York:
Macmillan Reference USA, 2003. 2 v.
(xxi, 1017 p.) ISBN 002865689X
306.9   HQ1073.M33
Scholarly multidisciplinary resource on all aspects
of death and dying and also related contemporary
psychosocial issues, such as bereavement, grief
and mourning across cultures, etc. Alphabetically arranged signed entries. Useful resource for
health professionals and also for general readers.
Suitable for academic library collections and large

public libraries. An appendix provides information on organizations. Illustrations, bibliographies and index. Also available as an e-book through Gale Virtual Reference Library and more.

Similar recent titles include *Encyclopedia of death and dying* by Howarth et al. and *Handbook of death and dying* by Bryant.

172 Medical encyclopedia (MedlinePlus).
http://www.nlm.nih.gov/medlineplus/encyclopedia.html. National Library of Medicine (U.S.). Atlanta; Bethesda, Md.: A.D.A.M.; National Library of Medicine. 1999–

RC81.A2

Title varies: A.D.A.M. Medical Encyclopedia; MedlinePlus, Medical Encyclopedia.

Articles about diseases and conditions, injuries, nutrition, poisons, surgeries, symptoms, tests, and other special topics. Contains medical illustrations and images. Editorial processes and policy at http://www.adam.com/editorialGuidelines.aspx.

173 Medicine, literature and eponyms: An encyclopedia of medical eponyms derived from literary characters. Alvin E. Rodin, Jack D. Key. Malabar, Fla.: R.E. Krieger, 1989. xxii, 345 p., ill.
ISBN 0894642774
610.321   R121.R62

Defines more than 350 medical eponyms derived from literary characters; among the sources are mythology, fables, and cartoons. Each entry includes a synopsis of the medical condition, a description of the associated literary character and of how specific characteristics correspond to symptoms of the condition, further literary references to the medical state, and other related material. A list of references to both the literary character and the medical condition appear with each entry. Subject index.

174 The MIT encyclopedia of communication disorders. Raymond D. Kent, Massachusetts Institute of Technology. Cambridge, Mass: MIT Press, 2004. vii, 618 p., ill. ISBN 0262112787
616.85/5/003   RC423.M56

Areas covered include audiology, speech-language pathology, communication sciences and various disorders (such as hearing, language, speech), and voice abnormalities. With basic science entries (normal anatomy and physiology, physics, psychology, psychophysics, linguistics), disorders entries (specific disorders, methods for the identification and assessment of disorders), and clinical management entries (behavioral, pharmacological, surgical, prosthetic) (Cf. *Introd.*). Separate chapters for adults and children for many topics. References, further reading, and bibliographies. For health professionals, researchers, students, and educated laypersons. Also available as an e-book and via MIT CogNet.

175 Nature encyclopedia of the human genome. David N. Cooper, Nature Publishing Group. London; New York: Nature Publishing Group, 2003. 5 v., ill. (some color). ISBN 0333803868
611.0181603   QH447.N38

Designed not only for researchers but also for teachers and students, this broad-ranging treatment provides an important overview of a field that is highly technical and subject to rapid change. A topical outline of all the peer-reviewed articles in the five volumes serves as a beefed-up table of contents. Some of the areas covered include structural and functional genomics; proteomics; bioinformatics; ethical, legal, and social issues; mathematical and population genetics; and history. Articles are labeled as introductory, intermediate, and advanced; each begins with a box showing article contents. All provide references, most have cross-references, and some offer suggested further reading and links to websites. Blind entries help the reader find articles (e.g., chimpanzee nucleotide diversity redirects to human and chimpanzee nucleotide diversity). The table of contents and indexing are thorough; the glossary in the final volume is useful. Excellent illustrations and sections of color plates enhance the text. Soon to be integrated with *Encyclopedia of life sciences* (140). Important for academic and medical library collections.

176 The Oxford illustrated companion to medicine. 3rd ed. Stephen Lock, John M. Last, George Dunea. Oxford; New York: Oxford University Press, 2001. xiv, 889 p., ill. ISBN 0192629506
610/.3   R121.O884

Title varies. 1st ed., 1986 had title: *The Oxford companion to medicine*; 2nd ed., 1994 had title: *The Oxford medical companion*.

Restructures, updates, and revises information originally published in the *Oxford medical companion*.

Not entirely alphabetic arrangement. Entries cover both historical and contemporary topics in the medical, nursing, and allied health sciences. Four indexes: Topics, grouped under major headings (p. 879–81); alphabetic "List of Individual Conditions and Diseases" (p. 883–4); "People Index"—inclusion in this list of deceased persons implies a separate biography (page no. in bold face) or a substantial mention in the text. Includes bibliographical references. Large number of illustrations and color plates. General index of alphabetically arr. broader topics. For general readers and professionals. Also available aas an e-book. Electronic version via Oxford reference online has title: *The Oxford companion to medicine*.

177   Wiley encyclopedia of biomedical engineering. Metin Akay. Hoboken, N.J.: Wiley, 2006. ISBN 047124967X
610/.2803   R856.A3.W55

Approx. 350 alphabetically arranged signed articles in 6 v., with tables, figures, and illustrations. Covers areas such as biochemical engineering, biomedical devices and instrumentation, rehabilitation and orthopedic engineering, and biomedical education (including Internet learning and distance education). Also available in electronic format, with some of the color graphics only available in the online ed. A similar title is *Encyclopedia of biomaterials and biomedical engineering* (118).

178   Wiley encyclopedia of molecular medicine. Haig H. Kazazian, John Wiley & Sons. New York: John Wiley & Sons, 2002. 5 v. (xxix, 3699 p.), ill. ISBN 0471374946
572.8/03   QH506.W535

Comprehensive resource in molecular medicine, with coverage "ranging from the organ to the cell to the molecular." (*Publ. notes*). Considered an essential resource for geneticists, biochemists, molecular biologists, medical researchers, and clinicians. Available as an e-book.

Dictionaries

179   The American Heritage medical dictionary. Boston: Houghton Mifflin, 2007. xxxii, 909 p., ill. ISBN 0618824359
610.3   R121.A4446

First ed., 1995, to 2nd ed., 2004, had title *The American Heritage Stedman's medical dictionary*; 2007 ed. is rev. ed. of the 2nd ed. Provides clear definitions for approx. 45,000 medical words and phrases, including tests, diseases, treatments, technology, and prescription and nonprescription drugs. Also includes health policy terms. Intended for health care consumers, students, and health professionals. Also available online via Credo reference (http://corp.credoreference.com/).

180   Black's medical dictionary. 42nd ed. Harvey Marcovitch. London: A. & C. Black, 2010. viii, 764 p., 16 p. of plates, ill. ISBN 9780713689020
610.3   R121

First ed., 1906. 40th ed., 2002; 41st ed., 2005. A standard dictionary of British terminology, with clear explanation of medical terms. This revised edition contains approximately 5,000 medical terms, including new terms and concepts (e.g., new diagnostic imaging techniques, minimally invasive surgery, gene therapy) and revisions. Many cross-references. Several appendixes provide information on subjects such as basic first aid, travel and health, measurements in medicine, health policy organizations, and others. Intended for nurses, healthcare professionals, students, and consumers. Available online via Credo reference.

181   The Cambridge historical dictionary of disease. Kenneth F. Kiple. Cambridge, U.K.; New York: Cambridge University Press, 2003. xiii, 412 p.; 25 cm. ISBN 9780521808347
616/.009   RC41.C365

International and interdisciplinary resource for medical history of human disease, originally published as pt. VIII of the Cambridge world history of human disease, rewrites and edits essays into shorter and up-to-date entries and also takes information from other parts of the original publication.

Available online to subscribers via Gale virtual reference library.

182 Concise dictionary of modern medicine. Joseph C. Segen. New York: McGraw-Hill, 2006. xix, 765 p. ISBN 0838515355

R121.S42

A revision of *Current med talk: A dictionary of medical terms, slang, and jargon*.

Illustrated dictionary, with 20,000 current medical terms, covering clinical and basic science aspects, also jargon and casual speech not necessarily found in other reference sources. Intended to supplement standard medical dictionaries. Also available in a 2002 ed. with the same title and as *Dictionary of modern medicine* which contains 40,000 entries.

183 Dictionary of biomedical sciences. Peter J. Gosling. London; New York: Taylor & Francis, 2002. 444 p. ISBN 0415241383

610/.3   R121.G623

Concise guide to a wide range of technical terms, abbreviations, and acronyms in the biomedical sciences and related disciplines. Not intended to be a dictionary of medical laboratory scientific techniques (cf. *Pref.*). American spelling where it differs from current use in the U.K. Cross-references. Several appendixes, covering reference ranges of blood and urinary constituents, metric conversions, biomedical science organizations, a select bibliography and further reading. Entries in alphabetical order, with no inverted headings. Also available as an e-book.

184 A dictionary of biomedicine. J. M. Lackie. Oxford: Oxford University Press, 2010. 608 p. ISBN 9780199549351

610.28   R856.A3L335

(Oxford paperback reference series)

In the interdisciplinary field of biomedicine where "vocabularies of clinicians and molecular bioscientists do not necessarily overlap" (*Pref.*), this dictionary provides concise definitions and explanation of biomedical terms, and diseases and disorders that are helpful to both basic scientists and clinicians. Contains 9,600 entries and cross-references. Web links for entries are available on a companion website. Appendixes contain prefixes for SI (International System) units, the Greek alphabet, and

single-letter and three-letter codes for amino acids. Intended for biomedical scientists, clinicians, and medical students. Also available as an e-book.

185 A dictionary of the history of medicine. Anton Sebastian. New York: Parthenon Publ. Group, 1999. vi, 781 p., ill. ISBN 1850700214

610.9   R121.S398

This illustrated medical history dictionary, a scholarly work, includes terms, with Latin and Greek origins of terms, brief biographies of notable people in medicine, eponymic information, important events, conditions, procedures, and other historical information for a broad range of subjects. Includes anecdotes and background material on both well- and little-known facts of medical history. Drawings and photographs of antique medical instruments and rare medical conditions. A negative review (*Journal of the history of medicine and allied sciences* 56, no. 2 [2001]: 182–83) cites factual errors, omissions, and "overly broad coverage." Users are cautioned to double check facts in other sources.

By the same author, *Dates in medicine: A chronological record of medical progress over three millennia* provides important milestones in the development of medicine. It is part of the Landmarks in Medicine series (publ. 2000–2002 by Parthenon), which also includes several other titles, including *Dates in ophthalmology: A chronological record of progress in ophthalmology over the last millennium,* by Daniel Albert, and several other titles by Helen S. J. Lee: *Dates in cardiology, Dates in gastroenterology, Dates in infectious disease, Dates in obstetrics and gynecology, Dates in neurology, Dates in oncology,* and *Dates in urology,* all with the subtitle *A chronological record of progress . . . over the last millennium.*

186 Dorland's illustrated medical dictionary. 32nd ed. W. A. Newman Dorland. Philadelphia: Saunders/Elsevier, 2012. xxvii, 2147 p., ill. (chiefly color). ISBN 9781416062578

R121.D73

First–22nd ed., 1900–51 had title: *The American illustrated medical dictionary*; 31st ed., c2007.

Designed to satisfy the conventional use of a dictionary; that is, to discover spelling, meaning, and derivation of specific terms and to assist in the creation of words by defining prefixes, suffixes, and stems.

Includes a section on "Fundamentals of medical etymology." Reflects standard and current terminology, with official nomenclatures from various fields, e.g., for anatomy, *Terminologia Anatomica* (Federative International Committee on Anatomical Terminology), for enzymology (Nomenclature Committee of the International Union of Biochemistry and Molecular Biology on the Nomenclature and Classification of Enzymes), and several others as listed in the preface. Also includes eponyms, acronyms, abbreviations, pronunciation, cross-references, etc. 1,525 illustrations in this edition. Eight appendixes include, for example, selected abbreviations used in medicine, symbols, phobias, table of elements, units of measurements, and others. Accompanying CD-ROM contains supplementary appendixes, e.g., selected terms in anatomy, a listing of surgical equipment not covered in the main section (A-Z) of the dictionary, also audio phonetics for over 35,000 terms. Internet access to this dictionary is available for subscribers at http://www.dorlands.com. For health professionals and students in medicine, nursing, and allied health. Index to tables; Index to plates; Index to appendixes; extensive "notes on the use of this dictionary" in the beginning pages of the dictionary.

187 Encyclopedia and dictionary of medicine, nursing, and allied health. 7th ed. Benjamin Frank Miller. Philadelphia: Saunders, 2003. xxxi, 2262 p., [40] p. of plates, ill. (chiefly col.) ISBN 0721697917

610.3   R121.M65

First ed. (1972) had title *Encyclopedia and dictionary of medicine and nursing*; 6th ed. (1997) had title *Miller-Keane encyclopedia and dictionary of medicine, nursing, and allied health*.

A concise work intended for students and workers in the nursing and allied health fields. Clear definitions and explanations of the current multidisciplinary terminology. This edition has 3,900 new terms, including the "latest changes for diagnosis-related groups, nursing diagnoses, and key nursing taxonomies."—*Foreword*; for example, definitions are provided for the complete vocabulary of the Unified Nursing Language System. Pronunciation guides; a list of stems, prefixes, and suffixes; and a 32-page color atlas of human anatomy.

The print resource is supplemented by a CD-ROM that contains spellchecker software, derived from *Dorland's medical speller*.

188 Encyclopedic reference of genomics and proteomics in molecular medicine. Detlev Ganten, Klaus Ruckpaul. New York: Springer, 2005. ISBN 3540442448

An effective blend of dictionary and encyclopedia formats, this two-volume set covers the proliferating terminology in the fields of genomics and proteomics, elucidating how these fields relate to molecular medicine. Some entries explain familiar terms in this context (e.g., addiction, gene, informed consent). Definition entries are short, provide thorough explanations, and list cross-references to related entries or, in the case of acronyms, to the full term or phrase. This title is also available online.

Article-length encyclopedic entries are signed and provide author affiliation and contact information. All articles include synonyms and definition sections followed by material appropriate to the topic, such as characteristics, description, clinical applications, clinical relevance, molecular interactions, regulatory mechanisms, therapeutic consequences, and more specific subheadings as appropriate. Cross-references enhance articles' interrelationships. Articles are beautifully illustrated with figures, tables, and photographs, many in color. All articles list references and many include Internet resources. Also available as an e-book.

Most appropriate for academic libraries, especially those supporting molecular biology and medical research. Public libraries might find the Encyclopedic dictionary of genetics, genomics, and proteomics a sufficient alternative.

189 Medical dictionary (MedlinePlus). http://www.nlm.nih.gov/medlineplus/ mplusdictionary.html. National Library of Medicine (U.S.). Bethesda, Md.: National Library of Medicine. 2002–

R121

Part of MedlinePlus. This online dictionary, based on *Merriam-Webster's medical dictionary* (192), can be searched from the MedlinePlus home page (via "Dictionary" tab). Contains definitions for words and phrases used by health care professionals, a pronunciation guide, and brief biographies of individuals (after whom particular diseases are named). Most MedlinePlus

Health Topics pages contain a link or links to additional online dictionaries and/or glossaries from various sources.

Numerous online medical dictionaries and glossaries are also available from many other sources. They include titles made available from various government agencies, organizations, and commercial publishers. Some examples include online medical dictionaries accessible via Credo reference (currently 24 titles), Deciphering medspeak (http://www.mlanet.org/resources/medspeak/; MLANET), Diabetes dictionary (http://diabetes.niddk.nih.gov/dm/pubs/dictionary/index.htm; National Institute of Diabetes and Digestive and Kidney Diseases), Dictionary of cancer terms (National Cancer Institute), mediLexicon tools (http://www.medilexicon.com/), Talking glossary of genetics terms (http://www.nhgri.nih.gov/glossary.cfm; National Human Genome Research Institute), and many others.

190 Medical phrase index: A comprehensive reference to the terminology of medicine. 5th ed. Jean A. Lorenzini, Laura Lorenzini Ley. Los Angeles, Calif.: Practice Management Information Corp. (PMIC), 2006
First ed., 1978; 4th ed., 2001.

"For medical transcribers, medical records librarians, medical assistants, legal secretaries, insurance claims examiners—for anyone who must capture medical terminology accurately and quickly" (*Publ. notes*). Includes both formal and informal phrases which are cross-indexed for each major word. Entries are arranged alphabetically. For words with more than one spelling, gives directions to common usage; sound-alikes are indicated.

191 Melloni's illustrated medical dictionary. 4th ed. Ida Dox, Biagio John Melloni. New York: Parthenon, 2002.
xiii, 764 p., ill. (some color).
ISBN 185070094X
610.3   R121.D76
First ed., 1979; rev. ed. of: *Melloni's illustrated medical dictionary,* Ida G. Dox, B. John Melloni, Gilbert M. Eisner. 3rd ed., 1993.

Includes 30,000 terms, with 4,000 new terms in this rev. ed. More than 3,000 color ill. are keyed to terms, with color coordination between the illustration and the specific term. Phonetic pronunciations

are included in a separate list at the front of the book, also a list of abbreviations, prefixes, suffixes, and combining form. Fewer entries but more ill. than Dorland's illustrated medical dictionary. For students in the health sciences. Also available as an e-book and in a "pocket" version entitled *Melloni's pocket medical dictionary: Illustrated* (Parthenon, 2004).

192 Merriam-Webster's medical dictionary. Enl. print ed. Merriam-Webster. Springfield, Mass.: Merriam-Webster, 2007. ISBN 9780877796
610.3   R121.M565
Abridged version of *Merriam-Webster's medical desk dictionary.*

Brief definitions for medical and scientific terms, including definitions of diseases, medical tests, and popular medical terms. Also includes eponyms and short biographies of famous doctors. No illustrations. Available online via Medical dictionary (MedlinePlus) and Credo reference. A related title is *Webster's new world medical dictionary.*

193 Mosby's dictionary of medicine, nursing & health professions. 9th ed. Mosby, Inc. St. Louis: Elsevier/Mosby, 2013. xiv, A-43, 1989 p., ill. (chiefly col.) ISBN 9780323074032
610.3   R121
First ed., 1982 and 2nd ed., 1986, had title: *Mosby's medical and nursing dictionary*; 3rd ed., 1990 and 4th ed., 2002, had title: *Mosby's medical, nursing, and allied health dictionary*; 5th ed., 1998 and 6th ed., 2001, had title: *Mosby's medical, nursing, and allied health dictionary*; 7th ed., 2006; 8th ed., 2009.

Reflects recent developments in medical and healthcare terminology. Encyclopedic-style definitions and approx. 2,450 color illustrations, photographs, and a "color atlas of human anatomy," organized by organ system. Numerous appendixes include, for example, reference information such as normal laboratory values for children and adults, units of measurement, dietary guide and U.S. dietary reference intakes, complementary and alternative medicine, herbs and natural supplements, American sign language guidelines, major nursing classifications, online resources, etc. Available online via Credo reference.

194 Mosby's medical dictionary. 9th ed. Marie T. O'Toole. St. Louis: Elsevier/

Mosby, 2013. xiv, A1-A43, 1921 p., col. ill. ISBN 9780323085410

610.3   R121

First ed., 1982; 8th ed., 2009.

Contains over 56,000 terms and over 2,450 color illustrations. Includes a color atlas of human anatomy and other ready-reference information, such as "American sign language and manual communication;" "Common abbreviations used in writing prescriptions;" "Spanish-French-English equivalents of commonly used medical terms and phrases;" "Commonly used abbreviations;" "Joint Commission do not use list." For physicians, nurses, and allied health professionals. Also useful for health consumers.

195   PDR medical dictionary. Medical Economics Company. Montvale, N.J.: Medical Economics, 1995–. v., ill.

616 1094-4176   R121.P275

Description based on 3rd ed., 2006. Contains terms and definitions for the medical and health science specialties, images and illustrations, and color anatomical plates with Latin and English anatomical terms for gross anatomy and neuroanatomy. Also contains a cross-reference table of generic drugs and brand-name drugs, and other reference charts (e.g., metric and SI units, temperature equivalents, and weights and measures).

196   Sloane's medical word book: a spelling and vocabulary guide to medical transcription. 5th ed. Ellen Drake, Sheila B. Sloane. St. Louis: Elsevier/Saunders, 2012. xiii, 1191 p., col. ill. ISBN 9781416048794

610.1/4   R123

First ed., 1973; 3rd ed., 1991, had title: *Medical word book: A spelling and vocabulary guide to medical transcription*; 4th ed., 2002

Outdated material has been updated or replaced in this edition. Designed for purposes of medical transcription, providing lists of terms without definitions. In three major parts: Pt. 1, a list of general medical terms, general surgical terms, and laboratory, pathology, and chemistry terminology; pt. 2, terms associated with 17 specialties; pt. 3, abbreviations and symbols, a list combining forms, and rules for forming plurals in medical terminology. Appendix contains anatomy plates of the human body, table of elements, and table of weights and measures. Useful for medical transcription.

197   Stedman's medical dictionary. 28th ed. Thomas Lathrop Stedman. Baltimore: Lippincott, Williams & Wilkins, 2006. 1 v. (various pagings); 1 CD-ROM, ill. (chiefly color). ISBN 0781733901

610.3   R121.S8

1st ed., 1911, titled *A practical medical dictionary;* title of later editions varies slightly. 27th ed., 2000.

A standard work, frequently revised. Offers approx. 107,000 terms and definitions (5,000 terms new in this edition) and 1,500 images. Many color illustrations, including a 40-page anatomy atlas. Contains "extensive system of usage notes . . . alerting users to common errors of sense, spelling, and pronunciation, including confusion between words of similar form or meaning."—*Pref.* Appendixes include cancer classification systems, body mass and body surface calculations, abbreviations to use in medication orders, and others. This ed. includes CD-ROM, including the "Stedman's plus spellchecker 2006" and 300 LifeArt® medical clipart four-color images. Also available online via Credo Reference. The 29th ed. is due to be published in 2013.

Recent editions of other Stedman's dictionaries include *Stedman's medical dictionary for the health professions and nursing* (6th ed., 2008); *The American Heritage medical dictionary* (2007 ed., 179), formerly titled *The American Heritage Stedman's medical dictionary;* and *Stedman's medical abbreviations, acronyms and symbols* (4th ed., 2008).

198   Stedman's medical dictionary for the health professions and nursing. Illustrated 7th ed. Thomas L. Stedman. Philadelphia: Wolters Kluwer Health/ Lippincott Williams & Wilkins, 2012. xxxix, 512 p., 59 p. of plates, ill. (chiefly col.) ISBN 9781608316922

610.3   R121.S8

Title varies. 1st ed., 1986, had title *Stedman's pocket medical dictionary;* 2nd ed., 1994, *Stedman's concise medical dictionary;* 3rd ed., 1997, *Stedman's concise medical dictionary: Illustrated;* 4th ed., 2001, *Stedman's concise medical dictionary for the health professions;* 5th ed., 2005, *Stedman's medical dictionary for the health professions and nursing;* 6th ed., 2008.

Provides concise definitions with pronunciation keys. Contains 56,000 entries, 68 appendixes with extensive information (e.g., nursing classifications), and many color and black-and-white illustrations. CD-ROM contains the full text of the print edition, with audio-pronunciation, anatomy animations, various images, and medical/pharmaceutical spellchecker. Also available as an online edition: Stedman's Online: Stedman's medical dictionary for the health professions and nursing includes all the content from the print dictionary, audio pronunciations, and 48 videos; along with a free version of Stedman's Plus Medical/Pharmaceutical Spellchecker.—Cf. *publ. description*.

Recent editions of other Stedman's dictionaries include, for example, *Stedman's medical dictionary* (28th ed., 2006); *The American Heritage medical dictionary* (2007 ed.), formerly titled *The American Heritage Stedman's medical dictionary*; and *Stedman's medical abbreviations, acronyms and symbols* (4th ed., 2008). Also available via Credo reference.

199 Stedman's medical eponyms.
2nd ed. Susan L. Bartolucci, Thomas Lathrop Stedman, Pat Forbis. Baltimore: Lippincott, Williams & Wilkins, 2005.
xix, 899 p. ISBN 0781754437
610/.1/48   R121.F67
1st ed., 1998.

Developed from entries found in Stedman's medical dictionary and supplemented with terminology found in the current medical literature. Provides concise definitions of approx. 18,000 terms "to both frequently encountered and hard-to-find eponyms" (**Publ. notes**). Entries include biographical information (e.g., nationality, specialty, and birth/death dates) in most cases. Included are equipment names, diagnostic and therapeutic procedures, operations, techniques and maneuvers, incisions, methods and approaches, syndromes and diseases, anatomic terms, and more. Intended for health care professionals, students, transcriptionists, and medical editors. Organized alphabetically; cross-references; keyword index. Provides variant spellings and phrasings.

200 Taber's cyclopedic medical dictionary.
Clarence Wilbur Taber, Clayton L. Thomas. Philadelphia: F.A. Davis Co., 1940–. ill.
610 1065-1357   R121.T18

Nineteenth ed., 2001; 21st ed., 2009. Description based on 22nd ed., 2013.

An updated edition of this standard work, giving definitions of medical terms and words. Pronunciation for all but very common terms and the etymology of most words is included. Appendixes include such information as emergency treatment, dietetic charts, Latin and Greek nomenclature, and normal reference laboratory values. Taber's online, available by subscription, provides full-text searching and hyperlinks to cross-references, ill., tables, "interactive nutritional value of foods" application, etc. Detailed product information at http://www.tabers.com/tabersonline/ub.

201 Webster's new world medical dictionary. 3rd ed. William C. Shiel, Melissa Conrad Stöppler. Hoboken, N.J.: Wiley, 2008. 470 p. ISBN 9780470189283
610.3   R121
First ed., 2000; 2nd ed., 2003.

"From the doctors and experts at WebMD."

This new "fully revised, updated" edition provides definitions of 8,500 medical terms, including diseases, treatments, scientific terms, abbreviations and acronyms, pharmaceuticals, herbal supplements, etc. Intended to support clear communication of health consumers with their physicians. Online access via Credo reference, MedicineNet.com's MedTerms dictionary (http://www.medterms.com/), and also available as an e-book.

Abbreviations

202 Elsevier's dictionary of abbreviations, acronyms, synonyms, and symbols used in medicine. 2nd, enl. ed.
Samuel A. Tsur. Amsterdam, Netherlands; San Diego, Calif: Elsevier, 2004. 843 p.; 25 cm. ISBN 0444512659
610/.1/48   R121.T787
First ed., 1999.

This enlarged edition contains more than 30,000 entries, gathered from medical articles, books, and encyclopedias. Includes all abbreviations, synonyms, and symbols from the first edition. Explains briefly what a term stands for, but gives no definitions. Includes cross-references. No index.

203 Jablonski's dictionary of medical acronyms and abbreviations. 6th ed. Stanley Jablonski. Philadelphia, Pa.: Saunders/Elsevier, 2009. xviii, 525 p. ISBN 9781416058991
610.14   R123.J24
First ed., 1987; 4th ed., 2001; 5th ed., 2004 has title: *Dictionary of medical acronyms and abbreviations*.

A pocket-size dictionary of commonly-used acronyms and abbreviations from all medical specialties, alphabetically arranged. Each entry is followed by a phrase for the abbreviation or acronym. Includes many recent additions from the fields of medical informatics, computer technology, molecular biology, virus nomenclature, and others. Comparable titles are *Melloni's illustrated dictionary of medical abbreviations* and Sloane's *Medical abbreviations and eponyms* (204). An expanded list of symbols and their meaning in this edition can be found in front. Identifies abbreviations which appear on the Joint Commission's (JCAHO) "Do not use" list. JCAHO's list was compiled with patient safety in mind to minimize ambiguities when interpreting acronyms and abbreviations. Includes searchable CD-ROM. Recommended for health professionals, medical students, and also general readers. Also available as an e-book.

204 Medical abbreviations and eponyms. 2nd ed. Sheila B. Sloane. Philadelphia, Pa.: Saunders, 1997. x, 905 p. ISBN 0721670881
610/.148   R123.S569
First ed., 1985.

Rev. ed., with approx. 10,000 new abbreviations and 1,000 new eponyms. In two main sections: alphabetical listings of medical abbreviations; and spellings and definitions of medical eponyms. Appendixes include anticancer drug combinations; table of elements; symbols; position of the fetus; and the Greek alphabet. Intended to answer the needs of transcriptionists and healthcare personnel.

205 Melloni's illustrated dictionary of medical abbreviations. Biagio John Melloni, June L. Melloni. New York: Parthenon Publ. Group, 1998. 485 p., ill. ISBN 1850707081
610/.1/48   R121.M539

Abbreviations compiled from recent medical texts and journals. Approx. 15,000 entries and 150 ill. A–Z arrangement.

206 Stedman's medical abbreviations, acronyms & symbols. 5th ed. Thomas Lathrop Stedman. Philadelphia: Wolters Kluwer Health/Lippincott Williams & Wilkins, 2013. 1 v. (various pagings). ISBN 9781608316991
610.1/48   R123.S69
Title varies: First ed., 1992, had title *Stedman's abbrev.: Abbreviations, acronyms and symbols*; 2nd ed., 1999, *Stedman's abbreviations, acronyms, and symbols*; 3rd ed., 2003, *Stedman's abbrev.: Abbreviations, acronyms and symbols*.

Contains abbreviations, acronyms, and symbols for medical, health, and nursing professionals; and medical transcriptionists, medical editors, and copy editors; and others. Includes professional titles and degrees, hospital abbreviations, abbreviations for specialties, and professional organizations & associations. Also includes abbreviations for viruses, medical informatics, molecular biology, and other subject areas. Abbreviations in boldface; multiple meanings listed alphabetically, with explanatory material in parentheses. Includes "do not use" abbreviations and slang terms. Nine appendixes. Also comes with three months of free access to *Stedman's online*.

Recent editions of other Stedman's dictionaries include *Stedman's medical dictionary* (28th ed., 2006), *Stedman's medical dictionary for the health professions and nursing* (7th ed., 2012), and *The American heritage medical dictionary* (2007 ed.), formerly titled *The American heritage Stedman's medical dictionary*.

Multilingual

207 Elsevier's dictionary of medicine and biology: In English, Greek, German, Italian, and Latin. Giannis Konstantinidis, Stavroula Tsiantoula. Amsterdam [The Netherlands]; Boston: Elsevier, 2005. ISBN 0444514406
610.3   R121.E47
In 2 v. Contents: pt. 1, basic table: English and Latin; pt. 2, indexes: Greek, Italian, and German.

Covers the life sciences, with emphasis on "cell biology, biochemistry, molecular biology, immunology, developmental biology, microbiology, genetics, and also the fields of human anatomy, histology, pathology, physiology, zoology, and botany" (*Pref.*) and other fields. The basic table is "an active English to target languages dictionary" (*Note to the reader*) and also includes Latin terms; pt. 2 contains Greek, Italian, and German indexes with reference numbers to the English terms contained in pt. 1. Contains approximately 27,500 main English entries and more than 130,000 translations. All main entries are followed by grammatical information. For scientists, teachers, and students. Pt. 1 is available online via netLibrary.

208   Medical dictionary in six languages.
Bert Spilker. New York: Raven Press, 1995. xx, 665 p. ISBN 0781701821
610/.3   R121.S685

A dictionary for medical professionals to be able to translate terms that are difficult to find in a dictionary. Includes translations for words, terms, and common phrases. Entries are listed in alphabetical order in English and each has been assigned an entry number. Five indexes (i.e., French, Italian, Spanish, German, and Japanese) with reference to the main listing by entry number.

209   Multilingual glossary of technical and popular medical terms in nine European languages. http://users .ugent.be/~rvdstich/eugloss/welcome .html. European Commission, Heymans Institute of Pharmacology, Mercator School. Gent, Belgium: Heymans Institute of Pharmacology. 2000
610.3   R121

Currently contains eight glossaries, with 1,830 scientific, technical, and popular medical terms in eight of the nine official European languages: English, Dutch, French, German, Italian, Spanish, Portuguese, and Danish. One list for each language, containing an index of all the medical terms, with cross-references between technical and popular terms. The "multilingual lemma collection" provides translations of the term in the seven other languages. Also contains an dictionary with the English definition of all terms. Glossaries contain notes and comments from translators and users. Makes

available a "guide for first time users" (http://users .ugent.be/~rvdstich/eugloss/firsttime.html). A revision is planned, starting September 2007.

210   A practical dictionary of Chinese medicine. 1st ed. Nigel Wiseman, Ye Feng. Brookline, Mass.: Paradigm Publications, 1998. xxiv, 945 p. ISBN 0912111542
610.951   R601.W57

Language: English; text in English and Chinese, with pinyin. Definitions for words and concepts used in Chinese medicine. Includes synonyms and cross-references to other entries. Alphabetical arrangement. A more recent dictionary by Nigel Wiseman is *Dictionary of Chinese medicine: English-Chinese, Chinese English*. Other publications by the same author include *Chinese medical characters*, *Chinese medical Chinese*, and *Introduction to English terminology on Chinese medicine*.

211   Say it in Spanish: A guide for health care professionals. 3rd ed. Esperanza Villanueva Joyce, Maria Elena Villanueva. St. Louis: Saunders, 2004. xiii, 440 p., ill. ISBN 0721604242
468.2/421/02461   R121.J69
First ed., 1996; [2nd ed.], 1999.

Contains commonly used English words and phrases in healthcare settings, with their Spanish translation and pronunciation. Includes information on Hispanic culture and popular health beliefs. For health-care workers who communicate with Spanish-speaking patients. Alphabetical word index; phrase and sentence index. Includes audio CD.

212   Southwestern medical dictionary: Spanish-English, English-Spanish. 2nd ed. Margarita Artschwager Kay. Tucson, Ariz.: University of Arizona Press, 2001. xxi, 308 p., ill. ISBN 0816521557
610/.3   R121.K238
First ed., 1977.

Contents: pt. I, Spanish to English; pt. II, English to Spanish. Appendix (A) Food items; (B) Kinship terms; (C) Plants reported to the Arizona Poison and Drug Information Center; (D) Anatomical illustrations with bilingual labels.

Brief definitions for standard Spanish terminology and for words relating to medicine and current health-related problems, with examples on how a word is used in a sentence, with translation.

213   Standard acupuncture nomenclature. http://whqlibdoc.who.int/wpro/-1993/ 9290611057.pdf. World Health Organization. Manila, Philippines: World Health Organization, Regional Office for the Western Pacific. 1993

First print edition, 1984. Description based on the web PDF edition.

"Efforts to develop a uniform nomenclature have been going on for some time . . . with a view to achieving global agreement on a standard acupuncture nomenclature"—*Introd*. Entry for each of the classical acupuncture points has three parts: (1) the standardized name of the classical point, (2) a brief explanation of the name of the point, and (3) a multilingual comparative list of the names of the point.

Specialized and specialist dictionaries

214   Atlas of anatomy: Latin nomenclature. Anne M. Gilroy, Brian R. MacPherson, Lawrence M. Ross, Michael Schünke, Erik Schulte, Udo Schumacher. New York: Thieme Medical, 2009. xv, 656 p., col. ill. ISBN 9781604060997

QM25.A79

Provides labeled anatomical color illustrations of the regional anatomy of the body: back, thorax, abdomen and pelvis, upper and lower extremities, head and neck, and neuroanatomy. Valuable for medical students and health professionals who wish to review the key anatomical relationships. Regional anatomy and dissection approaches are discussed throughout the book, in different chapters. Includes tables and schematic diagrams.

Other recently published atlases include, for example, *Atlas of human anatomy* by Netter, *Thieme atlas of anatomy* by Schünke et al., and *Grant's atlas of anatomy*, to name a few.

215   The cancer dictionary. 3rd ed. Michael J. Sarg, Ann D. Gross, Roberta Altman. New York: Facts On File, 2007. xv, 416 p., ill. ISBN 0816064113

616.994003   RC262

First ed., 1992; [2nd] rev. ed., 2000. Designed for general readers, attempts to provide definitions for every term connected with cancer, with many new terms, drugs, and treatments since the previous edition. Includes many cross-references, and capitalized terms within a definition have their own entry. Appendixes include websites of national cancer and AIDS organizations, and listings of both comprehensive and clinical cancer centers by state. Includes bibliographic references and index. Also available as an e-book.

216   Churchill Livingstone's international dictionary of homeopathy. Jeremy Swayne, Faculty of Homoeopathy (London); Homoepathic Trust, Homoeopathic Trust (London). Edinburgh, Scotland, U.K.; New York: Churchill Livingstone, 2000. xix, 251 p., ill. ISBN 0443060096

615.53203   RX41.C48

Provides definitions and explanations of terms and concepts related to the principles and practice of homeopathy. Includes bibliographic references (p. [232]–233) and index. Available online via Credo Reference as *International dictionary of homeopathy*.

217   A clinician's dictionary of pathogenic microorganisms. James H. Jorgensen, Michael A. Pfaller. Washington: ASM Press, 2004. viii, 273 p. ISBN 1555812805

616.904103   QR81.J67

"This booklet catalogues the current state of microbial taxonomy as of mid-2003."—*Pref*. Concise reference for pathogenic microorganisms (bacteria, fungi, parasites, and viruses) that affect humans. Entries include common and also less frequent pathogens. Reflects current microbial taxonomy and covers recent changes in terminology. Old and obsolete species names are included, with cross-references to older terms. Also available in PDA format and as e-book from publisher at http://www.asmscience.org/.

218   Companion to clinical neurology. 3rd ed. William Pryse-Phillips. Oxford; New York: Oxford University Press, 2009. xvi, 1214 p., ill. ISBN 9780195367720

616.8003   RC334.P79

1st ed., 1995; 2nd ed., 2003.

Alphabetically arranged terms and definitions used in neurology. Includes accepted diagnostic criteria, assessment tools, descriptions, eponymic disorders, Internet sites, etc. Also contains brief biographies and portraits of well-known neurologists. Contains extensive list of bibliographical references. Also available as an e-book.

219   Comprehensive dictionary of audiology, illustrated. 2nd ed.
Brad A. Stach. Clifton Park, N.Y.: Thomson/Delmar Learning, 2003. xvi, 363 p., ill. ISBN 1401848265
617.8003   RF291.S73
First ed., 1997.

Described as a source of terminology for the profession, practice, and science of audiology. This expanded ed. contains 7,000 terms, abbreviations, acronyms, and cross-references, including many older terms ("if they are generic enough to stand the test of time"—*Pref.*), but emphasizing modern terminology concerning hearing disorders and diseases or disorders affecting the auditory system and speech. Cross-references, tables, and illustrations. Several appendixes include, for example, audiometric symbols, list of toxins which can affect hearing, a glossary with codes for report writing, and associations and other organizations.

220   Comprehensive tumour terminology handbook. Phillip H. McKee, C. J. M. de Wolf, International Union against Cancer. New York: Wiley, 2001. xx, 362 p. ISBN 0471184853
616.99/2/0014   RC254.6.C66

Includes synonyms, eponyms, and pathologic descriptions to classify tumors. Organized in 44 sections; each section provides the tumor terminology related to one organ or organ system of the human body. Follows a consistent tabular format in all sections. Tumor terminology is presented in three columns: preferred and recommended terms (shown in bold), synonyms, and comments. Useful as a reference for researchers, health professionals, and patients.

221   Concise dictionary of biomedicine and molecular biology. 2nd ed.
Pei-Show Juo. Boca Raton, Fla.: CRC Press, 2002. 1154 p., ill. ISBN 0849309409

610.3   R121.J86
First ed., 1996.

Includes terminology commonly used in biomedicine, biotechnology, biochemistry, molecular biology, and related fields. 30,000 entries in this edition. Includes definitions, chemical structures, abbreviations, equations of enzymatic reactions and restriction endonucleases, and integrates "terminology and abbreviations from a variety of disciplines . . . and fill the need for a handy reference volume."—*Pref.* Useful for students and professionals in the allied health fields. Also available as an e-book.

222   Dermatology lexicon project. http://people.rit.edu/grhfad/DLP2/aboutDLP/abtFAQS.htm. Art Papier, Lowell Goldsmith, University of Rochester, Dept. of Dermatology. Rochester, N.Y.: University of Rochester. 2005–

International online open-source project with the goal of creating a standardized and reliable dermatology vocabulary. Provides diagnostic concepts, definitions, morphologic terminology, with illustrations and interactive animations. Includes dermatologic diagnoses and their synonyms, therapies, procedures, lab tests, etc. Also provides links to lexical/medical informatics resources, dermatology research, and organizations as well as patient information.

223   Dictionary for clinical trials. 2nd ed.
Simon Day. Chichester, U.K.; Hoboken, N.J.: John Wiley & Sons, 2007. xii, 249 p., ill. ISBN 0470058161
610.72/4   R853.C55D39
First ed., 1999.

This rev. and expanded ed. includes definitions for terms and short phrases from a variety of fields (e.g., medicine, statistics, epidemiology, ethics, and others) and from publications related to clinical trials, such as trial protocols, regulatory guidelines, reports, etc. Cross-references, line figures, and graphs. Also available as an e-book.

A more recently published dictionary, available both in print and as an e-book, *Clinical trials dictionary: Terminology and usage recommendations* by Meinert, provides precise terms and clear definitions for the large vocabulary needed to describe the methods and results of clinical trials.

224 Dictionary of alternative medicine.
J. C. Segen. Stamford, Conn.: Appleton & Lange, 1998. vi, 407 p., ill. ISBN 0838516203
615.5/03 R733.S44

Derived, in part from *Dictionary of modern medicine,* publ. 1992, and *Current MedTalk,* publ. 1995.

Defines and describes the alternative and complementary medicine terminology, including slang, acronyms, synonyms, and cross-references. Bibliographical references (p. 406–407).

Other recent titles in this subject area include *Mosby's dictionary of complementary and alternative medicine* which covers the terminology of alternative healthcare systems, mind-body interventions, biologically based therapies, manipulative and body-based health methods, and energy therapies, with 24 appendixes (Acupuncture–Yoga) and bibliography (available in print and online via Credo), and *Stedman's alternative & complementary medicine words*, an A–Z list of 53,000 words intended for medical transcriptionists, medical editors, and others.

225 Dictionary of cancer terms. http://www.cancer.gov/dictionary/. National Cancer Institute, National Institutes of Health. Bethesda, Md.: National Cancer Institute

Contains more than 4,000 terms related to cancer and medicine. Available in both English and Spanish. Detailed instructions on how to search this dictionary are available on the website. Other cancer vocabulary resources include the NCI Thesaurus, NCI Metathesaurus, and NCI Terminology Browser, made available via NCI Enterprise Vocabulary Services (EVS) at http://evs.nci.nih.gov.

226 Dictionary of developmental disabilities terminology. 3rd ed.
Pasquale J. Accardo, Barbara Y. Whitman, Jennifer A Accardo. Baltimore: Paul H. Brookes Pub, 2011. xx, 512 p., ill. ISBN 9781598570700
618.92/85889003 RJ135.A26
First ed., 1996; 2nd ed., 2002.

Interdisciplinary resource with terminology from medicine, genetics, mental retardation, pediatrics, psychology, social work, physical therapy, and others. This revised edition defines more than 4,000 terms. Provides concise definitions for neurodevelopmental disorders and developmental disabilities, with brief descriptions of medical syndromes. Includes tests and published instruments, key legislation, associations and organizations, and public laws relating to disabilities. Synonyms and acronyms, with cross-references to full name of acronyms. Includes bibliographical references.

227 Dictionary of environmental health.
David Worthington. New York: Spon Press, 2002. ISBN 0415267242
616.9803 RA566.W68
(Clay's library of health and the environment)

"Provides a one-stop reference to over 3,000 common and not so common terms, concepts, abbreviations, acronyms, and a wealth of supporting data . . . suitable for . . . environmental and public health practitioners and students . . ."—*Publ. description.* Appendix I: Units and measurements; Appendix II: Abbreviations and acronyms. Cross-references, bibliographical references, and index. Available as an e-book.

228 Dictionary of eye terminology. 6th ed.
Barbara Cassin, Melvin L. Rubin. Gainesville, Fla.: Triad Publ., 2012. 302 p., ill. ISBN 9780937404737
617.7003 RE21.C37

First ed., 1984; 4th ed., 2001; 5th ed., 2006. Provides brief definitions, with pronunciation guides only for difficult words. Each term is also assigned a general category—e.g., pathologic condition, optical device, or surgical procedure—which provides a context for each definition. Includes surgical techniques, laser technology, drugs, and systemic diseases with ocular manifestations. Includes approx. 5,000 terms and 1,000 abbreviations. Intended to make ophthalmic terminology understandable to those not familiar with the field. For students and health professionals.

A digital version, *Eye terms: The dictionary of eye terminology*, is available as a mobile app.

229 A dictionary of genetics. 7th ed.
Robert C. King, William D. Stansfield, Pamela Khipple Mulligan. New York: Oxford University Press, 2006. ISBN 9780195307627
576.503 QH427.K55

This edition of a respected dictionary presents expanded information in the rapidly changing field of genetics and includes valuable supplementary material. Entries include acronyms and common words adopted by geneticists; entries for organisms include scientific and common names and explain their economic importance or advantageous use for elucidating genetic phenomena. Appendixes add value to the dictionary by providing a list of the scientific names of 240 domesticated species grouped by common name; a table showing genome size and gene numbers of organisms and organelles included in the dictionary; recommended Internet sites; 512 periodicals relevant to genetics; a bibliography of 140 books; a chronology of genetics from 1590 to 2001; and a list of Nobel Prize (447) winners in the field with references to their key publications. Available as an e-book.

230　The dictionary of health economics.
2nd ed. A. J. Culyer. Chelthenham, U.K.; Northampton, Mass.: Edward Elgar, 2010. xix, 694 p., ill.
ISBN 9781849800419
362.103　　　　　　　　　RA410.A3C85
Concise definitions of terms, concepts, and methods from the field of health economics and related fields, such as epidemiology, pharmacoeconomics, medical sociology, medical statistics, and others. Expanded number of words and phrases relating to health economics of poor and middle-income countries (cf. *Pref.*). Increased number of entries in this edition (from 1,586 in the previous edition to 2,130). Many cross-references. An appendix contains "100 economic studies of health interventions." For health services researchers and professionals. Also available as an e-book. A similar title is *Dictionary of health economics and finance.*

231　Dictionary of health economics and finance. David E. Marcinko, Hope R. Hetico. New York: Springer Publ., 2006. 436 p. ISBN 0826102549
338.47362103　　　　　　RA410.A3D53
Definitions, abbreviations and acronyms, and eponyms of medical economics and health care sector terminology. Bibliography. A similar title is *The dictionary of health economics* (230).

232　The dictionary of health education.
David A. Bedworth, Albert E. Bedworth. Oxford; New York: Oxford University

Press, 2010. xi, 539 p.
ISBN 9780195342598
613.03　　　　　　　　　　RA440.D53
Defines and illustrates the language of the health education field and its subspecialties. Includes a brief symbols and abbreviation section (p. IX). A bibliography at the end of the volume lists those sources which have used the terms and expressions included in this dictionary. Also available as an e-book.

233　Dictionary of health insurance and managed care. David Edward Marcinko. New York: Springer Pub. Co., 2006.
ISBN 0826149944
368.382003　　　　　　　　RA413.D53
Health insurance, managed care plans and programs, health care industry terminology and definitions, abbreviatons, and acronyms. Also available as e-book.

234　Dictionary of medical eponyms.
2nd ed. Barry G. Firkin, Judith A. Whitworth. New York: Parthenon Publ. Group, 1995. viii, 443 p., ill., ports.
ISBN 1850704775
610/.3　　　　　　　　　　R121.F535
First ed., 1987.
This corrected edition offers explanations of approx. 2,300 eponyms currently used in internal medicine; in general, eponymous terms from subspecialties have been excluded. Alphabetical arrangement. Each entry includes a brief definition of the term, and provides biographical information about the person from whom the term is derived; some entries include a photograph or a portrait. Although the orientation is Australian, these terms are used in most English-speaking countries. Includes some cross-references, but there is no index. The introduction provides a brief list of reference sources, but individual entries do not provide bibliographic citations. Not as comprehensive but continually updated is an online resource entitled Who Named It? (http://www.whonamedit.com/), a biographical dictionary of medical eponyms.

235　Dictionary of medical sociology. William C. Cockerham, Ferris Joseph Ritchey. Westport, Conn.: Greenwood Press, 1997. xxvi, 169 p. ISBN 0313292698
306.46103　　　　　　　　RA418.C655
Positioned at the intersection of arguably the softest of the soft sciences (sociology) and the hardest

of the hard sciences (medicine), medical sociology has developed at a rapid pace over the last two decades to richly inform both of its parent disciplines. This dictionary from 1997 defines key terms from the newly-emerging field at that time, but also demonstrates how each discipline informs and expands the other. A useful reference tool, and also an informal guide to the newly-created field. Includes bibliographical references and index.

236 Dictionary of medical syndromes.
4th ed. Sergio I. Magalini, Sabina C. Magalini. Philadelphia: Lippincott-Raven, 1997. vii, 960 p. ISBN 0397584180
616/.003   RC69.M33
First ed. 1997; 3rd ed., 1990.

Alphabetical arrangement by name of syndrome, giving for each as appropriate: synonyms, symptoms and signs, etiology, pathology, diagnostic procedures, therapy, prognosis, and bibliography. Index (p. 865–960). Less inclusive, the *Dictionary of syndromes and inherited disorders* by Patricia Gilbert (3rd ed.) is written in nontechnical language.

237 A dictionary of neurological signs.
3rd ed. A. J. Larner. New York: Springer, 2011. xvi, 381 p. ISBN 9781441970947
616.8003   RC348.L37
First ed., 2001; 2nd ed., 2006

Alphabetical listing of neurological signs encountered during history taking and physical examination, from "Abadie's sign" to "zoom effect." Entries provide brief definitions, describe the clinical technique to elicit the particular sign, its treatment, and related information, such as neuroanatomical information when appropriate. Cross-references. Also available as an e-book.

Details of many neurological disorders mentioned only briefly in this dictionary may be found in a companion volume, available both in print and as an e-book, *The A-Z of neurological practice: A guide to clinical neurology* by Larner.

238 Dictionary of ophthalmology. Michel Millodot, Daniel M. Laby. Oxford; Boston: Butterworth-Heinemann, 2002. xx, 313 p., ill. (chiefly col.) 617.7003
0750647973

Alphabetical arrangement of approx. 4,000 key terms and definitions on eye diseases and related ophthalmic vocabulary. Includes synonyms, cross-references, and color illustrations. Another title by the same author is *Dictionary of optometry and visual science* (239).

239 Dictionary of optometry and visual science. 7th ed. Michel Millodot. Edinburgh, Scotland, U.K.; New York: Elsevier/Butterworth-Heinemann, 2009. xxix, 409 p., ill. (some color). ISBN 9780702029585
617.75003   RE939.7.M54
First–4th eds. (1986–97) had title *Dictionary of optometry*; 6th ed., 2004.

This revised and expanded edition contains 5,400 terms, 89 tables, and 241 illustrations. In concise entries, defines terms commonly used in optometry, ocular pathology, ocular pharmacology and therapeutics, and other visual science terminology from the basic sciences, optics, refraction, and other related areas. All definitions from previous editions have been revised and in many cases expanded. Many cross-references. Mostly British spelling. Available online via Credo Reference. Another title by the same author is *Dictionary of ophthalmology* (238).

240 A dictionary of virology. 4th ed. Brian W. J. Mahy. Amsterdam ; Boston: Elsevier/Academic Press, 2009. 510 p., ill. ISBN 9780123737328
579.203   QR358
First ed., 1981; 2nd ed., 1997; 3rd ed., 2001. This updated and rev. ed. includes, for example, terms used in virology; virus names with taxonomic status and, if known, the genus to which the virus belongs; newly discovered viruses; reclassification schemes of viruses; new technologies for virus discovery; commonly used cell lines; and explanations of molecular biology terminology as related to viruses. Includes only viruses affecting vertebrates; viruses that infect only bacteria, fungi, invertebrates, or plants are not in scope for this dictionary. Also contains references to antiviral drugs used clinically and experimentally. Appendix of virus families, reference list, and cross references. For biologists, clinicians, researchers, and veterinary virologists. Also available as an e-book.

241 Dictionary of visual science and related clinical terms. 5th ed.
Henry W. Hofstetter. Boston: Butterworth-Heinemann, 2000. xviii, 630 p., ill. ISBN 0750671319
617.7003   RE21.D42
First ed. (1960) through 4th ed. (1989) had title *Dictionary of visual science*.

A comprehensive dictionary providing succinct definitions for terms in all fields of visual science, including anatomy and physiology of the eye, optics, and ocular pharmacology. Includes entries for syndromes with ocular manifestations. In this edition, expanded coverage of ocular disease and therapeutic pharmacologic agents, and 400 new terms on optics and refractive surgery. Compound and eponymous terms are listed alphabetically under the noun, and pronunciation is given for more difficult terms. An appendix lists terms, symbols, and abbreviations, and there are reference tables related to visual science. Includes CD-ROM.

242 Encyclopaedic companion to medical statistics. 2nd ed. Brian Everitt, Christopher Ralph Palmer. Chichester, West Sussex, U.K.: Wiley, 2011. xxii, 491 p., ill. ISBN 9780470684191
610.7203   RA409.E527
First ed., 2005.
"The aim of this new edition remains . . . to aid communication between medical researchers and statisticians."—*Pref.* Contains approximately 400 statistical topics and cross-referenced articles, considered important and accessible to medical researchers and not necessarily requiring a technical background. Includes useful examples from the biomedical literature. Also available as an e-book.

243 Encyclopedic dictionary of AIDS-related terminology. Jeffrey T. Huber, Mary L. Gillaspy. New York: Haworth Information Press, 2000. 246 p. ISBN 9780789012074
616.97/92   RC607.A26 H8955
Defines words, phrases, and medical terms associated with HIV and AIDS, including related legal, social, psychological, and religious terminology. Also available as an e-book. Another resource is the online

"AIDSinfo (648) glossary" (http://www.aidsinfo .nih.gov/education-materials/glossary), a dictionary of HIV/AIDS-related terms, provided as part of AIDSinfo (648).

244 Illustrated dictionary of immunology. 3rd ed. Julius M. Cruse, R. E. Lewis. Boca Raton, Fla.: CRC Press, 2009. 801 p., ill. ISBN 9780849379871
616.07903   QR180.4C78
First ed., 1995; 2nd ed., 2003.
Updated ed., with many new entries from the contemporary literature of immunology and its subspecialties (for example, autoimmunity, immunopathology, transplantation). Concise definitions of current terms and illustrations of various kinds provide an understanding of the current specialized immunologic vocabulary and concepts. Includes photographs of historical figures. Alphabetical arrangement. No cross-references within entries. Intended for both immunologists and non-immunologists. Also available as an e-book.

245 Jablonski's dictionary of syndromes and eponymic diseases. 2nd ed.
Stanley Jablonski. Malabar, Fla.: Krieger, 1991. ix, 665 p., ill. ISBN 0894642243
616.003   R121.J24
Rev. ed. of *Illustrated dictionary of eponymic syndromes and diseases and their synonyms*, 1969.

Entries under personal names may provide brief biographical information. Many cross-references, and some entries include references.

246 Lewis' dictionary of occupational and environmental safety and health.
Jeffrey W. Vincoli. Boca Raton, Fla.: Lewis, 2000. 1093 p., ill. ISBN 1566703999
363.1103   T55.L468
Comprehensive resource for the terminology of the interdisciplinary area of industrial safety and environmental health. Includes approximately 25,000 definitions.
Available online via CRCnetBASE.

247 The managed health care dictionary. 2nd ed. Richard Rognehaugh. Gaithersburg, Md.: Aspen Publ., 1998. xii, 261 p. ISBN 0834211440

362.1/04258/03 RA413.R58
Forst ed., 1996.

Includes over 1,000 terms with definitions, including slang, acronyms, etc., many with cross-references. Does not include medical specialties and health professions. Intended for health professionals, patients, and others. Another more recent title is Dictionary of health insurance and managed care.

248 A manual of orthopaedic terminology. 7th ed. Fred R. T. Nelson, Carolyn Taliaferro Blauvelt. Philadelphia: Mosby/ Elsevier, 2007. 496 p.
616.7001/4 RD723.B53
First ed., 1977; 6th ed., 1998.

Contents: (1) Classifications of fractures, dislocations, and sports-related injuries; (2) Musculoskeletal diseases and related terms; (3) Imaging techniques; (4) Orthopaedic tests, signs, and maneuvers; (5) Laboratory evaluations; (6) Casts, splints, dressings, and traction; (7) Prosthetics and orthotics; (8) Anatomy and orthopaedic surgery; (9) The spine; (10) The hand and wrist; (11) The foot and ankle; (12) Physical medicine and rehabilitation: physical therapy and occupational therapy; (13) Musculoskeletal research. Appendixes: (A) Orthopaedic abbreviations and acronyms; (B) Anatomic positions and directions; (C) Etymology of orthopaedics; (D) ICD codes for eponymic musculoskeletal disease terms.

Vocabulary of orthopedics, with brief definitions. Arranged in 13 topical chapters and various appendixes. Bibliographic references and index. Also available from publisher in a searchable web version.

249 Medical meanings: A glossary of word origins. 2nd ed. William S. Haubrich. Philadelphia: American College of Physicians, 2003. p. ISBN 1930513496
610/.14 R123.H29

First ed., 1984; rev. & expanded ed., 1997.

An etymological dictionary of medical terms, relating word origins to their current meaning. Cross-reference index.

250 Melloni's illustrated dictionary of the musculoskeletal system. Biagio John Melloni. New York: Parthenon

Publ. Group, 1998. 308 p., ill. ISBN 1850706670
611/.7/03 QM100.M44

Dictionary with 4,600 terms and definitions, with color illustrations, covering the musculoskeletal system. Contains tables of the muscles and bones of the human body, with description of each bone and insertion and action of each muscle. For physical therapy and occupational therapy students.

251 Melloni's illustrated dictionary of obstetrics and gynecology. June L. Melloni, Ida Dox, Harrison H. Sheld. New York: Parthenon Publ. Group, 2000. 401 p., ill. (some col.) ISBN 1850707103
618/.03 RG45.M45

Contains over 15,000 concise definitions, including terms from other disciplines that are related to female health. Includes 280 ill., with color correlation of a defined term and its illustration. Cross-references, pronunciation guide, and relevant abbreviations. For health professionals and students.

252 National Cancer Institute. http://www .cancer.gov/. National Cancer Institute, U.S. National Institutes of Health. Bethesda, Md.: National Cancer Institute

Website created by the National Cancer Institute (NCI), a division of the National Institutes of Health (NIH).

Contents: NCI home, Cancer topics, Clinical trials, Cancer statistics, Research and funding, News, About NCI.

Links to cancer-related information for health professionals, medical students, and patients. Provides guidance to searching the cancer literature in PubMed by searching the "cancer subset" and access to already prepared searches on more than 100 different topics. Non-PubMed citations previously found in CANCERLIT, a database no longer being maintained, consist primarily of meeting abstracts from the annual meetings of the American Society of Clinical Oncology (ASCO) and the American Association for Cancer Research (AACR). ASCO abstracts for recent years are available via http://www.asco.org, AACR abstracts at http:// aacrmeetingabstracts.org/. Also provides access to PDQ: Physician data query (http://www.cancer .gov/cancertopics/pdq), a database with the latest information about cancer treatment, screening, prevention, genetics, etc.

The NCI website includes descriptions of various types of cancer (A–Z list of cancers: http://www.cancer.gov/cancertopics/alphalist/) and related topics, with links to diagnosis and treatment information and supportive care, information on clinical trials, cancer prevention, cancer statistics (e.g., SEER cancer statistics review), cancer statistics tools, cancer mortality maps and graphs, and related NCI websites. Links to the Dictionary of cancer terms and various cancer vocabulary resources (e.g., NCI thesaurus, NCI metathesaurus, and NCI terminology browser), NCI drug dictionary, NCI publications, etc. Available both in English and Spanish.

253 Neurological eponyms. Peter J. Koehler, G. W. Bruyn, John Pearce. Oxford; New York: Oxford University Press, 2000. xiv, 386 p., ill. ISBN 0195133668
616.8/01/4   RC343.N434

Collection of short essays that describe the derivations of many common neurological eponyms, derived from *Eponyms in neurological examination* (Netherlands Society of Neurology, 1995), but revised and expanded (*Pref.*).

Contents: Pt. I, Structures and processes (ch. 1–10); pt. II, Symptoms and signs (ch. 11–17); pt. III, Reflexes and other tests (ch. 18–27); pt. IV, Syndromes (ch. 28–39); pt. V, Diseases and defects (ch. 40–55). Each chapter deals with one or two people's association with the eponym, with brief biography and reference to the publication important for the naming of a particular syndrome. For medical professionals and others with an interest in medical history. Includes bibliographical references and index. Also avaialble as an e-book.

254 Ophthalmic eponyms: An encyclopedia of named signs, syndromes, and diseases in ophthalmology. Spencer P. Thornton. Birmingham, Ala.: Aesculapius, [1967]. ix, 324 p.
617.7003   RE21.T54

In two sections: (1) "Signs, syndromes, and diseases in medical, pediatric, and neuro-ophthalmology"; and (2) "Eponyms in ophthalmic surgery." Arrangement is alphabetical within each section.

Bibliographic references are included with most entries.

255 Oxford dictionary of medical quotations. Peter McDonald. Oxford; New York: Oxford University Press, 2004. 212 p. ISBN 0192630474
610   R705.S565

Source of quotations (mostly from the English-speaking countries: Great Britain, Ireland, and North America, with just a few from other countries) from books, plays, poems, ballads, etc., covering a variety of topics related to medicine, "selected on the basis of their usefulness to modern medical authors, journalists, politicians, nurses, physios, lecturers, and even health managers . . . something for everyone within these pages" (*Pref.*). Quotations are listed under author (with biographical information in many cases) in alphabetical order, reference to the source when possible, and an index of keywords. "How to use the dictionary" provides further helpful information. Also available as an e-book. Another resource is *Oxford dictionary of scientific quotations* by Bynum et al.

256 The Oxford dictionary of sports science and medicine. 3rd ed. Michael Kent. Oxford; New York: Oxford University Press, 2006. vii, 612 p., ill. ISBN 9780198568506
617.102703   RC1206.O94

Includes clearly written, scientific definitions of nearly 8,000 terms related to sports medicine and sports science. Offers updated entries of terms covering sports nutrition, drug and doping regulations, and gene technology. Illustrated with drawings and photographs. Electronic version via Oxford reference online.

257 The progressive era's health reform movement: A historical dictionary. Ruth C. Engs. Westport, Conn.: Praeger, 2003. xxii, 419 p. ISBN 0275979326
362.1/0973/03   RA395.A3E547

Covers 1880–1925, the time period labeled the Progressive era of the United States. Entries cover individuals (biographical information/assessment of historical importance), events, crusades (e.g., exercise, vegetarian diets, alternative health care), legislation, publications, and terms. Includes entries on the health reform movement and campaigns against alcohol, tobacco, drugs, and sexuality. For scholars, students, and general readers. "Selected chronology" (p. [371]–407), bibliographical references, and index. Also available as an e-book.

258   Slee's health care terms. 5th ed.
Debora A. Slee, Vergil N. Slee, H. Joachim Schmidt. Sudbury, Mass.: Jones and Bartlett Publ., 2007. 700 p.
ISBN 9780763746155
362.103   RA423.S55
First ed., 1986; 4th ed., 2001. Also called *Health care terms.*

Provides concise definitions for terms from a wide range of disciplines in the healthcare field, including administration, organization, finance, statistics, law, and governmental regulation. Many cross-references. Pays particular attention to acronyms. Terms used in definitions are italicized to indicate the term is defined elsewhere in the dictionary; related terms may be grouped together under one term, such as the many entries under the term "hospital." Intended for all types of healthcare consumers.

259   Standard acupuncture nomenclature.
http://whqlibdoc.who.int/wpro/-1993/9290611057.pdf. World Health Organization. Manila, Philippines: World Health Organization, Regional Office for the Western Pacific. 1993
First print edition, 1984. Description based on the web PDF edition.

"Efforts to develop a uniform nomenclature have been going on for some time . . . with a view to achieving global agreement on a standard acupuncture nomenclature"—*Introd.* Entry for each of the classical acupuncture points has three parts: (1) the standardized name of the classical point, (2) a brief explanation of the name of the point, and (3) a multilingual comparative list of the names of the point.

260   Terminology of communication disorders: Speech-language-hearing. 5th ed. Lucille Nicolosi, Elizabeth Harryman, Janet Kresheck. Baltimore: Lippincott, Williams & Wilkins, 2004. p.
ISBN 0781741963

616.85/5/003   RC423.N52
First ed., 1978; 4th ed., 1996.
Updated edition, intended as a comprehensive dictionary and sourcebook for the terminology of speech, language, and hearing disorders. Alphabetical arrangement, brief definitions, illustrations, many cross-references for synonyms and related terms. Includes charts, lists, tables, and several appendixes.

261   The words of medicine: Sources, meanings, and delights. Robert Fortuine. Springfield, Ill.: Charles C. Thomas, 2001. xvi, 434 p.
610/.1/4 0398071322   R123.F64
Provides a brief history of the English medical vocabulary from its Indo-European roots to the modern era. Addresses medical word formation from Greek and Latin roots, prefixes, suffixes, Latin and Greek verbs and adjectives, spelling, euphemisms, etc. Contains several chapters on "word-imagery" (*Introd.*), including obsolete words still encountered in literary works and historical documents, "loan words" borrowed from other languages, and historical and modern terms (for example, drug names, managed care, and medical genetics). Also contains chapters on eponyms, folk etymology, and acronyms. "Not considered a handbook for learning terminology, nor a word list, nor a dictionary." Although the book is not in dictionary format, it provides succinct, accurate definitions for many of the words discussed. Intended for physicians and other health professionals who are already familiar with most of the terms discussed. Also available as an e-book.

Directories

262   The directory of complementary and alternative medicine. Hugh P. Greeley, Anne M. Banas. Marblehead, Mass.: Opus Communications, 2000. xxi, 530 p.
ISBN 1578390656
615.5   R733.D563
Contents: (1) Mind-body medicine (Mind-body methods, Religious healing and spirituality, Social and contextual areas); (2) Alternative medical systems (Oriental medicine and acupuncture, Traditional indigenous systems/folk medicine, Unconventional western systems, Naturopathic

medicine/naturopathy); (3) Lifestyle and disease prevention therapies (Clinical preventive practices, Lifestyle therapies); (4) Biologically based therapies (Herbal medicine and phytotherapy, Special diet therapies, Orthomolecular medicine, Pharmacological, biological, and instrumental interventions); (5) Manipulation and body-based systems (Chiropractic medicine, Massage and bodywork, Naprapathy, Osteopathic medicine, Unconventional physical therapies); (6) Biofield therapeutics/vibrational medicine; (7) Therapies for specific health conditions. Appendix: International CAM organization. Index.

Organization of this directory is based on the classification scheme of the National Institutes of Health's (NIH) Center for Complementary and Alternative Medicine (NCCAM), which groups CAM practices into seven major categories. Entries include description, title, education and training requirements, licensing, certification, professional associations, and practice sites.

Canada

263   AAMC curriculum inventory and reports. https://www.aamc.org/initiatives/cir/. Association of American Medical Colleges. Washington: Association of American Medical Colleges. 2002–

Describes medical student education programs and institutional characteristics at 125 medical schools in the United States and 17 schools in Canada. Presents comparable data about required courses, U.S. Medical Licensing Exams, clerkships, electives, and combined degree programs, and reports on curriculum design and policies (https://www.aamc.org/initiatives/cir/curriculumdesignandpolicies/). Also provides a graphic representation of each medical school program. Related titles, also published by the AAMC, are *Directory of American medical education* (266) and *Medical school admission requirements, U.S.A. and Canada* (268).

Print version ceased with 2000 ed. Title varied: also called *Curriculum directory*.

264   Best . . . medical schools. Princeton Review (Firm). New York: Random House, 2004–
610.13 1553-8761   R745.C875

Title varies. 1997–1999: *The best medical schools*; 2000–Title varies. 1997–1999: *The best medical schools*; 2000–2003: *Complete book of medical schools*.

Description based on 2012 ed., published in 2011.

Subtitle: *The best 168 medical schools*.

Based on student input regarding the curriculum, teaching, and student life, rates accredited medical and osteopathic schools. Includes profiles of 133 accredited allopathic schools in the United States, including Puerto Rico, 17 allopathic schools in Canada, and 26 osteopathic schools. Six accredited naturopathic schools in the U.S. and Canada are also profiled. Presents profiles and statistical data (student body, faculty, admission requirements, application costs, and financial aid) for the different schools. Alphabetical index, index by location, and index by cost.

265   Canadian medical directory. Don Mills, Ont., [Canada]: Seccombe House, 1955–
610.695202571   R713.01.C3
0068-9203

Imprint varies. Published annually. Description based on 57th ed., 2011; 58th ed., 2012 available.

Section (1) Physicians in Canada; (2) General practitioners and certificants of the College of Family Physicians of Canada; (3) Certified specialists listed geographically according to specialty; (4) Hospitals in Canada; Index of hospitals; (5) Resource section; (6) Canadian health care associations; (7) 2010 year in review; Canadian medical hall of fame.

Brief biographical information for Canadian physicians; alphabetical arrangement, with address, telephone number, medical school and year of degree, professional memberships, position, and hospital affiliation. A "resource section" contains related miscellaneous information, such as listings of worker's compensation boards, departments of health and health units, cancer centers and clinics, medical associations, university faculties of medicine, 2010 graduates, etc. Also includes a section "Year in Review" with a summary of major medical news from the Canadian Medical Association Journal.

More detailed information on hospitals, long-term care facilities, medical clinics, and laboratories can be found in its annual companion volume, *Guide to Canadian health care facilities: Guide des établissements de santé du Canada.* Information regarding administrative and medical personnel, bed size, annual budgets, etc., can be found in the annual companion volume, *Directory of Canadian healthcare personnel*, 2008-, previously called *Canadian health facilities directory*.

266 Directory of American medical education. Association of American Medical Colleges. Washington: Association of American Medical Colleges, 1995–
610.71173   R712.A1A8
DAME

Title varies: 1951/52–1966/67, *Association of American Medical Colleges. Directory*; 1968–1995, *AAMC directory of American medical education*. Description based on 2012 ed. 2013 ed. available.

Provides alphabetical and geographical listings of U.S. medical schools and Canadian affiliate institutional members, and information on AAMC's organizational structure, activities, and its various member organizations. Related titles, also published by the AAMC, are *AAMC curriculum inventory and reports* (263) and *Medical school admission requirements, U.S.A. and Canada* (268).

267 Find a library (MedlinePlus). http://www.nlm.nih.gov/medlineplus/libraries.html. National Library of Medicine (U.S.). Bethesda, Md.: National Library of Medicine. 200?–
Part of Directories (MedlinePlus).

Clickable map of the United States and Canada for locating health sciences/medical libraries. Medical/Health Sciences Libraries on the Web provides further information for finding medical libraries internationally.

268 Medical school admission requirements, U.S.A. and Canada. Association of American Medical Colleges. Evanston, Ill.: Association of American Medical Colleges, 1964–
371.215 0738-6060   R745.A8

First–14th ed., 1947–63: *Admission requirements of American medical colleges*. Title varies.

2012–13 ed. has title: Medical school admission requirements (MSAR®). Subtitle: The most authoritative guide to U.S. and Canadian medical schools.

Description based on the 2012-13 ed.; 2013-14 ed. available.

Contents: Ch. 1, So . . . You want to be a doctor; ch. 2, Building a strong foundation: Your undergraduate years; ch. 3, From here to there: The medical education process; ch. 4, All about the MCAT® exam; ch. 5, Choosing the school that's right for you; ch. 6, Applying to medical school; ch. 7, The admissions decision; ch. 8, Building toward greater diversity; ch. 9, Be in the know: AAMC; ch. 10, Applicant and acceptee data; ch. 11, Financing your medical education; ch. 12, Information on combined undergraduate/M.D. programs; ch. 13, M.D.-Ph.D. dual degree programs; ch. 14, Information about U.S. medical schools accredited by the LCME; ch. 15, Information about Canadian medical schools accredited by the LCME and by the CACMS.

Provides information about 134 accredited U.S. and 17 accredited Canadian medical schools and details about each school's curriculum, its entrance requirements, selection factors, and other relevant information. A website, maintained by the AAMC (http://www.aamc.org/students/start.htm), provides various resources and related information for medical students, residents, and others interested in a medical career. The current print version comes with a subscription to an online version, MSAR® Online, which offers access to more comprehensive information and data. Web-only access is also available to individuals via a subscription. Further MSAR information is provided at https://www.aamc.org/students/applying/requirements/msar/.

The annual *Directory of American medical education* (title varies) lists member institutions, with information on their facilities and administration.

The Official guide to the MCAT® exam (Association of American Medical Colleges) is a valuable resource for medical students. This edition has been updated to reflect recent changes re MCAT exam. Offers insight, tips, and guidance to help students prepare for the exam. Provides current data on MCAT scores and GPAs, and score changes on retake exams.

269 Peterson's graduate programs in business, education, health, information studies, law and social work. Peterson's (Firm). Princeton, N.J.: Peterson's, 1997–. ill.
378.15530257 1088-9442   L901.P459

The standard guide to graduate schools, with information on programs offered; degree requirements; number and gender of faculty; number, gender, and ethnicity of students; average student age; percentage of students accepted; entrance requirements; application deadlines; application fee; costs; and financial aid. Also available online.

270 Research centers directory. Gale Research Co., Gale Research Inc., Gale Group. Detroit: Gale Research, 1965–
001 0080-1518   AS25.D5
(Based on 34th ed.) This annual publ. contains listings of more than 14,300 North American laboratories, including full contact information, e-mail, and URLs, when available. Listings also include short descriptive statements about the laboratories. Divided by subject category, the first part contains the descriptive listings, while the second part consists of subject, geographic, personal name, and master indexes. Available as an e-book.

Great Britain

271 Directory of health library and information services in the United Kingdom and the Republic of Ireland. 11th ed. Library Association. London: Library Association, 2002–
Z675.M4
First ed. (1957) through 4th ed. (1976) had title *Directory of medical libraries in the British Isles*; 5th ed. (1982) through 10th ed. (1997–98) *Directory of medical and health care libraries in the United Kingdon and Republic of Ireland*.

"Compiled for the Health Libraries Group of the Library Association."

Alphabetical arrangement by name of library and various other information services (e.g., NHS Direct Online). For each library or other service listed gives, as appropriate, location, stack policy, hours, holdings, classifications, computer facilities and availability, and user accessibility. Three indexes: index by towns, index of personal names, and a general index. Glossary of acronyms and abbreviations.

Superseded by the web-based, searchable *Health library information services directory* (HSLISD) at http://www.hlisd.org with more than 850 entries.

272 Guide to libraries and information sources in medicine and health care. 3rd ed. Peter Dale. London: British Library, Science Reference & Information Service, 2000. 209 p. 026.610941 0712308563
First ed., 1995; 2nd ed., 1997; 3rd paperback ed., 2002.

"Aims to provide useful and informative coverage of leading sources of information in order to facilitate the work of librarians, information workers, and researchers . . . [and] covers those libraries and information services which are prepared to accept serious enquiries from outside" (*Pref.*). The various organizations are listed alphabetically. Entries provide detailed contact information, summary of the purpose of the organization, subject coverage, and services. Appendix provides medical Internet resources. Organisation acronym index; organisation index; subject index.

273 List of registered medical practitioners. http://www.gmc-uk.org/register/search/index.asp. General Medical Council. London: General Medical Council. 2005–
General Medical Council (Great Britain). Pub. in print format as *Medical register*, 1859–2004; 2005– also available on CD-ROM.

Provides access to a list of registered medical practitioners, a listing of all doctors who are registered to practice in the United Kingdom, with the doctor's reference number, name, any former name, gender, year and place of primary medical degree, registration status, date of registration, entry in GP/Specialist Register, and any publicly available fitness-to-practice history since October 20, 2005.

274 The Medical directory: London, provinces, Wales, Scotland, Ireland, abroad, Navy, Army & Air Force . . . London: J. & A. Churchill Ltd., 1845–. v.
0305-3342   R713.29.M4
Publ. varies. Publ. in association with the Royal Society of Medicine (RSM). Description based on ed. 167th ed., 2013.

Contains a listing of registered medical practitioners in the U.K., giving brief biographical information. Also provides information on U.K. healthcare organizations, including an alphabetical listing of all NHS trusts and hospitals, educational institutions, medical associations, and medical societies.

International

275 Avicenna directory for medicine. http://avicenna.ku.dk/database/medicine. Københavns Universitet., World Federation for Medical Education, World Health Organization. Copenhagen, Denmark: University of Copenhagen. 1953–

"The Avicenna Directory for medicine includes the latest information from the new survey in progress of all the world's medical schools, as well as information from the 7th edition (2000) of the WHO *World Directory of Medical Schools*, with updates submitted to the WHO Directory between 2000 and 2007. Each entry is marked to show if the information is new, or is from before 2007."—*Avicenna page*.

Print editions published by World Health Organization: 1st ed., 1953; 7th ed., 2000, with title *World directory of medical schools*.

Print edition arranged by country, lists institutions of basic medical education in 157 countries and also provides information on obtaining a license to practice medicine in 14 countries that do not have medical schools. Provides name and address, year instruction started, language used in teaching, and duration of medical education to obtain a degree, including practical training.

276 ClinicalTrials.gov. http://clinicaltrials .gov. National Institutes of Health, National Library of Medicine (U.S.), United States. Bethesda, Md.: National Institutes of Health. 2000–
   R853.C55

Provides information about federally and privately funded research in human volunteers for patients, their families and other consumers, and health care professionals. Contents include clinical trials, experimental treatments, experimental and new diagnostic procedures, patient enrollment

and recruitment, and all study phases. Explains who may participate, location (U.S. and other countries), and contact information. Searchable by key terms, disease, location, treatment, age group, study phase, etc. Trial listings by condition, sponsor, and status. For additional information and various links to related websites, consult the NLM fact sheet on ClinicalTrials.gov at http://www.nlm .nih.gov/pubs/factsheets/clintrial.html.

As of 2012, new homepage and graphic design, with core functions of the site remaining unchanged. Recent enhancement introduced and described in detail in "New style and new content for ClinicalTrials.gov" http://www.nlm.nih.gov/ pubs/techbull/ja12/ja12_clinicaltrials.html.

277 Directory of the Medical Library Association. Medical Library Association. Hampden, Conn.: Shoe String Press, 1959–
   026 0543-2774   WMLCL833577

Publ. in print 1959–2001; title and imprint vary. From 2002-2006, only available online in PDF format and users were able to sign up for updates. This is no longer the case. Directory information is currently only available via MLA's member center (https://service.mlanet.org/mlassa/censsacustlkup .query_page) to MLA members.

Detailed information about MLANet/MLA is available at MLANET: The Medical Library Association's Network of Health Information Professionals.

278 GeneTests. http://www.genetests. org/. Children's Hospital and Medical Center (Seattle, Wash.), Univ. of Wash., School of Medicine; National Library of Medicine (U.S.). Seattle, Wash.: Univ. of Washington. 1993–

Contents: Home page; Disorders; GeneReviews; Panel Directory; Laboratory directory; Clinic directory.

Provides authoritative information on genetic testing and its use in diagnosis, disease management, and genetic counseling. Promotes use of genetic services in patient care and decision making by individuals. GeneReviews and Laboratory directory can be searched by disease, gene symbol, protein name, etc. Contains context-sensitive illustrated glossary, teaching tools, and other resources.

279   International research centers directory. Detroit: Gale Research, 1981–
001.4025 0278-2731   Q179.98.I58

"*International Research Centers Directory* provides unparalleled access to government, university, independent, nonprofit, and commercial research and development activities in countries worldwide. Entries include English and foreign name of center, full mail and electronic address, personal contact, organizational affiliates, staff, description of research program, publications, services, and more. Master, subject, personal name, and country indexes are provided." —*Publisher website.*

280   Medical/health sciences libraries on the Web. http://www.lib.uiowa.edu/hardin/hslibs/. Eric Rumsey, Hardin Library of the Health Sciences, University of Iowa. Iowa City, Iowa: Hardin Library of the Health Sciences, University of Iowa. 1997– 026.61
Part of Hardin MD.

Geographical arrangement. Provides links to the websites of individual libraries in the United States, Canada, Australia, Germany, the United Kingdom, and others. List does not claim to be complete and allows for individual libraries not currently on the list to be added. *Directory of health library and information services in the United Kingdom and the Republic of Ireland* is another resource in this area.

United States

281   AAMC curriculum inventory and reports. https://www.aamc.org/initiatives/cir/. Association of American Medical Colleges. Washington: Association of American Medical Colleges. 2002–

Describes medical student education programs and institutional characteristics at 125 medical schools in the United States and 17 schools in Canada. Presents comparable data about required courses, U.S. Medical Licensing Exams, clerkships, electives, and combined degree programs, and reports on curriculum design and policies (https://www.aamc.org/initiatives/cir/curriculumdesignandpolicies/). Also provides a graphic representation of each medical school program. Related titles, also

published by the AAMC, are *Directory of American medical education* (266) and *Medical school admission requirements, U.S.A. and Canada* (268).

Print version ceased with 2000 ed. Title varied: also called *Curriculum directory*.

282   AHA guide to the health care field. American Hospital Association. Chicago: Healthcare Infosource, Inc., 1997-98 –
RA977.A1

Title varies: 1949–71, pt. 2 of Aug. issue (called "Guide issue," 1956–70) of *Hospitals*, which superseded *American hospital directory* (1945–48); 1972–73, *The AHA guide to the health care field*; 1974–96, *American Hospital Association guide to the health care field*.

Description based on 2011-2012 ed.; 2014 ed. available.

"Provides basic data reflecting the delivery of health care in the United States and associated areas, and is not to serve as an official and all-inclusive list of services offered by individual hospitals."—*Acknowledgements and Advisements*. Four major sections, each with table of contents and explanatory information: (A) Hospitals, institutional, and associate members; (B) networks, health care systems, and alliances; (C) lists of health organizations, agencies, and providers; and (D) indexes. Also available in CD-ROM format. Additional information about this resource is available at http://www.AHAdata.com. Statistical information concerning hospitals is published in AHA hospital statistics.

A web-based resource, American hospital directory® (AHD®) http://www.ahd.com/ (by a Kentucky Company) provides data for over 6,000 hospitals, with data derived from Medicare claims, hospital cost reports, Centers for Medicare and Medicaid Services, and other sources (further details at http://www.ahd.com/data_sources.html). While most features of this website are only available to subscribers, free access is provided to "hospital profiles."

283   Barron's guide to medical and dental schools. Barron's Educational Series, Inc. Woodbury, N.Y.: Barron's Educational Series, Inc., 1982–
610 1935-7559   R735.A4B37

Based on *Barron's guide to medical, dental, and allied health science careers* [1974], and its updated versions, published in 1975 and 1977. 13th ed., 2012. Description based on 12th ed., 2009.

Contents: pt. 1. Medicine; pt. 2. Dentistry; Appendixes A-K.

Intended as a guidance manual for pre-professional students. Presents basic data and detailed information for accredited medical, dental, and osteopathic schools in the U.S. and Canada, such as admissions requirements, curriculum, grading and promotion policies, facilities, and special features of an institution, etc. Includes a full-length model Medical College Admission Test (MCAT) with answers, and selected questions from recent Dental College Admission Tests (DAT), sample essays for medical student applications, and other advice for students considering a medical or dental career. Includes a chapter on "physicians and medicine in the twenty-first century," addressing many issues facing physicians today, including cybermedicine and medical informatics. Bibliography and indexes (index of medical school profiles; subject index).

284   Best . . . medical schools. Princeton Review (Firm). New York: Random House, 2004–

610.13 1553-8761   R745.C875

Title varies. 1997–1999: *The best medical schools*; 2000–Title varies. 1997–1999: *The best medical schools*; 2000–2003: *Complete book of medical schools*.

Description based on 2012 ed., published in 2011.

Subtitle: *The best 168 medical schools*.

Based on student input regarding the curriculum, teaching, and student life, rates accredited medical and osteopathic schools. Includes profiles of 133 accredited allopathic schools in the United States, including Puerto Rico, 17 allopathic schools in Canada, and 26 osteopathic schools. Six accredited naturopathic schools in the U.S. and Canada are also profiled. Presents profiles and statistical data (student body, faculty, admission requirements, application costs, and financial aid) for the different schools. Alphabetical index, index by location, and index by cost.

285   Directories (MedlinePlus). http://www .nlm.nih.gov/medlineplus/directories .html. National Library of Medicine

(U.S.), National Institutes of Health (U.S.). Bethesda, Md.: U.S. National Library of Medicine, National Institutes of Health, Dept. of Health and Human Services. 200?–

RC48

Pt. of MedlinePlus.

Contents: Doctors and dentists—general; Hospital and clinics—general; Doctors and dentists—specialists; Other healthcare providers; Hospitals and clinics—specialized; Other healthcare facilities and services; Libraries.

Links to directories to help find health professionals, services, and facilities. Includes, for example, access to the American Medical Association's DoctorFinder, how to find a dentist, a Medicare participants physicians directory, and many others.

286   Directory of American medical education. Association of American Medical Colleges. Washington: Association of American Medical Colleges, 1995–

610.71173   R712.A1A8

DAME

Title varies: 1951/52–1966/67, *Association of American Medical Colleges. Directory*; 1968–1995, *AAMC directory of American medical education*. Description based on 2012 ed. 2013 ed. available.

Provides alphabetical and geographical listings of U.S. medical schools and Canadian affiliate institutional members, and information on AAMC's organizational structure, activities, and its various member organizations. Related titles, also published by the AAMC, are *AAMC curriculum inventory and reports* (263) and *Medical school admission requirements, U.S.A. and Canada* (268).

287   Directory of physicians in the United States. American Medical Association; Survey & Data Resources, American Medical Association.; Division of Data Base Products and Licensing. Chicago: American Medical Association, Div. of Survey and Data Resources, 1992–2011. ISBN 10963588

610.257   R712.A1A6

Continues: *American medical directory,* 1st ed. (1906)–32nd ed. (1990). 33rd ed.– issued in four vols.: v. 1, Alphabetical index of physicians; v. 1. Alphabetical index of physicians — v. 2. Geographical register of physicians: Alabama through Indiana — v. 3. Geographical register of physicians: Iowa through New York — v. 4. Geographical register of physicians: North Carolina through US Military Postal Service.

Description based on 42nd ed., 2011. Last print ed.; publisher recommends DoctorFinder online.

For more than 900,000 physicians located in the United States, Puerto Rico, Virgin Islands, and certain Pacific Islands, gives school and year of graduation, practice specialties, type of practice, and licensing and American Board of Specialties (ABMS) certification information. Includes Doctors of Osteopathy, and both members and non-members of the American Medical Association (AMA), as well as administrators, teachers, residents, researchers, and retired physicians. Each entry contains codes, e.g., U.S. medical school and foreign medical school codes, codes for type of practice and certification. "A guide to codes" appears in each part of the directory.

This edition is also issued in a CD-ROM edition which provides additional functionality and search capabilities.

288 DoctorFinder. https://extapps.ama-assn. org/doctorfinder/home.jsp. American Medical Association. Chicago: American Medical Association. 1997–

R712.A1

Also called AMA Doctor Finder; earlier title was AMA Physician Select: On-Line Doctor Finder.

Tool for locating licensed physicians (doctors of medicine [M.D.] and doctors of osteopathy [D.O.]) in the United States and information about them. Can be searched by physician name or medical specialty. Listings include address, medical school and year of graduation, residency training, primary practice, specialty, and indication of AMA membership. AMA member listings generally include more information.

Other sites to find doctors include, for example, a search engine created by the Administrators In Medicine (AIM) National Organization for State Medical and Osteopathic Board Executive Directors, entitled Docfinder Searches (http://www.docboard. org/) and links identified through Healthfinder.gov.

289 Encyclopedia of medical organizations and agencies: A subject guide to organizations, foundations, federal and state government agencies, research centers, and medical and allied health schools.
Donna Batten. Detroit: Gale Research Co., 1983–. v.

362.1/025/73 0743-4510   R712.A1E53
First ed., 1983; 15th ed., 2005. Subtitle varies. Description based on 24th ed., 2012.

Arranged by medical subjects, in 69 chapters. Major divisions include national and international associations, state and federal agencies, research centers, and computer-based information and database services. Entries provide contact and descriptive information, such as the organization's name, address, website, telephone number, key officials, founding year, number of members, number of employees, and publications. Includes websites and email addresses. Name, keyword, and subject indexes. Derived from *Encyclopedia of associations* and available online in aggregated sources in the Gale Virtual Reference Library.

290 Find a library (MedlinePlus). http:// www.nlm.nih.gov/medlineplus/libraries .html. National Library of Medicine (U.S.). Bethesda, Md.: National Library of Medicine. 200?–
Part of Directories (MedlinePlus).

Clickable map of the United States and Canada for locating health sciences/medical libraries. Medical/Health Sciences Libraries on the Web provides further information for finding medical libraries internationally.

291 FREIDA online. http://www.ama-assn .org/ama/pub/education-careers/graduate -medical-education/freida-online.page?. American Medical Association American Medical Association, Accreditation Council for Graduate Medical Educati Accreditation Council for Graduate Medical Educati, American Medical Association, Accreditation Council for Graduate Medical Education (U.S.). Chicago: American Medical Association. 1997–
FREIDA Online®: Fellowship and Residency

Electronic Interactive Database. Online version of the *Graduate medical education directory* (292).

Online database containing graduate medical education programs accredited by the Accreditation Council for Graduate Medical Education, as well as combined specialty programs. Allows a search of programs and a comparison of programs regarding length of training, program size, number of faculty, etc. Provides graduates' career plan statistics and links to related resources.

292 Graduate medical education directory. American Medical Association. Accreditation Council for Graduate Medical Education (U.S.). Chicago: American Medical Association, 1993– 610 1079-0519   R840.D56

Title varies: 1948–51, *Approved internships and residencies in the United States*; 1952–73/74, *Directory of approved internships and residencies*; 1974–75, *Directory of approved residencies*; 1975/76–77/78, *Directory of accredited residencies*; 1978/79–86/87, *Directory of residency programs accredited by the Liaison Committee on Graduate Medical Education*; 1987/88–92/93, *Directory of graduate medical education programs*. Also known as "The green book," available both in print and as an e-book.

Description based on 2012–13 edition.

"Including programs accredited by the Accreditation Council for Graduate Medical Education"— *Cover*. This revised and updated edition contains information on 9,000 programs accredited by the Accreditation Council for Graduate Medical Education (GME) in the U.S., including residency, fellowship, and combined programs, 215 new programs and 3,000 teaching institutions. The Web-based version has title: FREIDA Online (Fellowship and Residency Electronic Interactive Database Access [291]), made available by the American Medical Association. Provides essential information on residency programs. Contains information on the Electronic Residency Application Service (ERAS provided by the AAMC: American Association of Medical Colleges), National Resident Matching Program (http://www.nrmp.org/), and the Educational Commission for Foreign Medical Graduates (http://www.ecfmg.org/). Has sections for: (I) Graduate medical education information; (II) Specialty/subspecialty information and programs; (III) New and withdrawn

programs; (IV) Graduate medical education teaching institution. Appendixes: A, Combined specialty programs; B, Medical Specialty Board certification requirements; C, Medical schools in the United States; D, Graduate medical education glossary; E, Listings of subspecialty and fellowship programs; F, Medical licensure information. A companion publication, *GMED companion: An insider's guide on selecting a residency program,* also published by the American Medical Association, contains supplemental data on specialty and subspecialty programs and several appendixes listing medical specialty websites, core competencies in genetics, medical licensure information, and a glossary.

293 Health care careers directory. American Medical Association. Chicago: American Medical Association, 2008– 610.73 2157-3743   R847.D57

Title varies: *Directory of accredited allied medical education programs,* 1969/70; *Directory of approved allied medical education programs,* 1971; *Allied medical education directory, 1972–76*; 7th ed. (1978)– 23rd ed., 1996 *Allied health education directory*; 24th ed. (1996–97) *Allied health and rehabilitation professions*; 25th–27th ed., 1997/98–1999/2000 *Health professions education directory*; 2000-2008 *Health professions career and education directory*.

Updated annually.

Description based on 39th ed. (2011-12) "8,400 programs, 2,600 sponsoring institutions, 82 health care careers."—*Pref.* 2012-2013 is available.

Contains information on educational programs in health care occupations, and data from accrediting agencies, including licensure, certification, and registration for practicing in a particular profession. Educational programs are listed alphabetically by state and by city, with contact information, annual class capacity, program length, tuition cost, etc. Provides details on the history and development of the various health professions.

Similar data available online at http://www.ama-assn.org/ama/pub/education-careers.page.

294 Health.gov. http://www.health.gov/. Office of Disease Prevention and Health Promotion. Washington: U.S. Department of Health and Human Services

Coordinated by the Office of Disease Prevention and Health Promotion, Office of Public Health Service, U.S. Dept. of Health and Human Services (HHS).

"Portal to the Web sites of a number of multi-agency health initiatives and activities of the U.S. Department of Health and Human Services (HHS) and other Federal departments and agencies."—*Main page* Provides links to general health information (e.g., Healthfinder, National Health Information Center [http://www.health.gov/nhic/], MedlinePlus, and others), special initiatives (e.g., Healthy People, Dietary guidelines for Americans 2010, and others), health news, the major federal agencies (U.S. Dept. of Health and Human Services and its agencies, Office of Disease Prevention and Health Promotion [http://odphp.osophs.dhhs.gov/], Office of the Surgeon General [http://www.surgeongeneral.gov/]), and other key government agencies with "direct health responsibilities" (e.g., Dept. of Defense [DoD], Environmental Protection Agency [EPA], Dept. of Veterans Affairs [VA], Occupational Safety and Health Administration [OSHA], and others).

295 Health professions education standards. American Medical Association. Chicago: American Medical Association, 1999. v. 0899709885

Provides details for educational standards and guidelines for accredited programs of the professions listed in the companion Health professions career and education directory. Includes mission statements, policies, professional ethics and responsibilities, etc. (cf. *Publ. notes*).

Another American Medical Association publication, *Health professions library: Educational programs, standards, and careers,* provides similar and additional information on 6,100 programs in 52 health professions professions.

296 Medical and health information directory. Anthony Thomas Kruzas. Detroit: Gale Research Co., 1977–
610.72073 0749-9973   R118.4.U6M43
Editor varies. Description based on 25th ed., 2011. Edited by Donna Batten (project editor). 27th ed., 2012 is available.

Subtitle: A guide to organizations, agencies, institutions, programs, publications, services, and other resources concerned with clinical medicine,

basic biomedical sciences and the technological and socioeconomic aspects of health care.

Contents: v. 1, National and international organizations; v. 2, State and regional organizations; v. 3, Foundations and other funding organizations; v. 4, Consultants and consulting organizations. Alphabetical name and keyword index.

Entries include name, address, including e-mail and website information if available, membership, the year when a particular organization was founded, purpose, meeting, and publications.

297 Medical school admission requirements, U.S.A. and Canada. Association of American Medical Colleges. Evanston, Ill.: Association of American Medical Colleges, 1964–
371.215 0738-6060   R745.A8
First–14th ed., 1947–63: *Admission requirements of American medical colleges.* Title varies.

2012–13 ed. has title: Medical school admission requirements (MSAR®). Subtitle: The most authoritative guide to U.S. and Canadian medical schools.

Description based on the 2012-13 ed.; 2013-14 ed. available.

Contents: Ch. 1, So . . . You want to be a doctor; ch. 2, Building a strong foundation: Your undergraduate years; ch. 3, From here to there: The medical education process; ch. 4, All about the MCAT® exam; ch. 5, Choosing the school that's right for you; ch. 6, Applying to medical school; ch. 7, The admissions decision; ch. 8, Building toward greater diversity; ch. 9, Be in the know: AAMC; ch. 10, Applicant and acceptee data; ch. 11, Financing your medical education; ch. 12, Information on combined undergraduate/M.D. programs; ch. 13, M.D.-Ph.D. dual degree programs; ch. 14, Information about U.S. medical schools accredited by the LCME; ch. 15, Information about Canadian medical schools accredited by the LCME and by the CACMS.

Provides information about 134 accredited U.S. and 17 accredited Canadian medical schools and details about each school's curriculum, its entrance requirements, selection factors, and other relevant information. A website, maintained by the AAMC (http://www.aamc.org/students/start.htm), provides various resources and related information for medical students, residents, and others interested in a medical career. The current print version comes with a subscription to an online version, MSAR® Online, which offers access to more comprehensive information and data. Web-only access is also available to individuals via a subscription. Further MSAR information is provided at https://www.aamc.org/students/applying/requirements/msar/.

The annual *Directory of American medical education* (title varies, 266) lists member institutions, with information on their facilities and administration.

The Official guide to the MCAT® exam (Association of American Medical Colleges) is a valuable resource for medical students. This edition has been updated to reflect recent changes re MCAT exam. Offers insight, tips, and guidance to help students prepare for the exam. Provides current data on MCAT scores and GPAs, and score changes on retake exams.

298 **The official ABMS directory of board certified medical specialists**. http://www.abmsdirectory.com/abms/static/home.htm. American Board of Medical Specialties. Amsterdam, Netherlands; Chicago: Elsevier; American Board of Medical Specialties. 2013

R729.5.S6

American Board of Medical Specialties (ABMS)

An electronic directory, rather than a companion website to the print directory which ceased publication in 2012. Updated quarterly with data from the ABMS, as well as other updates received from physicians. New physicians and new certifications will be displayed with each update.

Provides access to "professional information about more than 800,000 board certified physicians in 50+ specialties and 100+ subspecialties from the 24 member boards of the ABMS, with their contact information."—*Publ. description*. Searchable by physician's name, by board certified specialty, by location, etc. Answers questions whether or not a physician is board certified, where to find a specialist within a geographic location, information about physicians' education and training, their various hospital and academic appointments, contact information, etc. A brief overview and guided tour of this reference tool is provided at http://www.abmsdirectory.com/html/abms-demo.html.

Additional supplementary resources (e.g., "Information about ABMS," "Approved specialty boards," "Codes and abbreviations," "Guide to medical specialties, "Directory of U.S, and Canadian medical schools," etc.) can be located under the "Resources" tab.

Further information about the American Board of Specialties is at http://www.abms.org. FAQs provide further details.

299 **Peterson's graduate programs in business, education, health, information studies, law and social work.** Peterson's (Firm). Princeton, N.J.: Peterson's, 1997–. ill.

378.15530257 1088-9442   L901.P459

The standard guide to graduate schools, with information on programs offered; degree requirements; number and gender of faculty; number, gender, and ethnicity of students; average student age; percentage of students accepted; entrance requirements; application deadlines; application fee; costs; and financial aid. Also available online.

300 **Research centers directory.** Gale Research Co., Gale Research Inc., Gale Group. Detroit: Gale Research, 1965–

001 0080-1518   AS25.D5

(Based on 34th ed.) This annual publ. contains listings of more than 14,300 North American laboratories, including full contact information, e-mail, and URLs, when available. Listings also include short descriptive statements about the laboratories. Divided by subject category, the first part contains the descriptive listings, while the second part consists of subject, geographic, personal name, and master indexes. Available as an e-book.

301 **Who's who in medicine and healthcare.** New Providence, N.J.: Marquis Who's Who, 1996–

0000-1708   R153.W43

Description based on 2011–12 edition. Compilation of biographical information on medical professionals, including administrators, educators, researchers, clinicians, and other medical and healthcare personnel. This edition contains 27,150 biographical profiles. Listings include full name, occupation, date/place of birth, family background, education summary, writings, and association memberships and awards.

The biographical profiles included in this

resource are also available online as part of Marquis biographies online through a subscription.

Handbooks

302 Atlas of cancer. 2nd ed. Maurie Markman. Philadelphia: Current Medicine LLC, 2008. x, 662 p., color ill. ISBN 9781573402897

616.99400223   RC262.A846

Contents: (I) Head and neck; (II) Gynecologic cancer; (III) Lung cancer; (IV) Upper gastrointestinal cancers; (V) Lower gastrointestinal cancers; (VI) Leukemia; (VII) Lymphoma; (VIII) Sarcoma; (IX) Breast cancer; (X) Genitourinary cancers; (XI) Skin cancer; (XII) Neuro-oncology.

"The intent.is to present information in a highly visual format, both to showcase the dynamic nature of the topics and to ensure that important messages are conveyed."—*Pref.* Each section provides a summary introduction to a particular cancer, with U.S. statistics, epidemiology and etiology, histology, genetics, staging, major risk factors, imaging, surgical management, treatment modalities, prevention, and other information as appropriate to the specific cancer. Each chapter includes a list of references. Index.

303 Bates' guide to physical examination and history-taking. 11th ed. Lynn S. Bickley, Peter G. Szilagyi, Barbara Bates. Philadelphia: Wolters Kluwer Health/ Lippincott Williams & Wilkins, 2013. xxv, 994 p., ill. (chiefly col.) ISBN 9781609137625

616.07/54   RC76.B38

Covers the essential process of obtaining a patient history and performing a comprehensive physical examination, with the goal of providing the best care for patients. Imparts basic knowledge of human anatomy and physiology. Includes case studies, examples of evidence-based practice, with step-by-step techniques. Intended for medical and advanced nursing students. Also a useful resource for health professionals. *Bates' nursing guide to physical examination and history taking* by Hogan-Quigley et al. is intended for beginning nursing students.

Also available as a set of DVDs or in a streaming video version: *Bates' visual guide to physical examination* (4th ed., 2005) is currently the only edition which includes the complete set of videos. A new edition/online product is under development: *Bates' visual guide to physical examination* or *Bates' visual guide* for short, with new video content will be available and include the following modules: Approach to the patient; Head to toe assessment (adult); Pediatric head-to-toe assessment (infant); Pediatric head-to-toe assessment (child); Head-to-toe assessment (Older adult); General survey and vital signs; Examination of the skin; Head, eyes, and ears; Nose, mouth , and neck; Thorax and lungs; Cardiovascular system; Peripheral vascular system; Breasts and axillae; Abdomen; Male genitalia, hernias, rectum, and prostate; Female genitalia, anus, and rectum; Musculoskeletal system; Nervous system: cranial nerves and motor system; Nervous system: sensory system and reflexes. Further information at http://www.batesvisualguide.com/.

304 Bergey's manual of systematic bacteriology. 2nd ed. David R. Boone, Richard W. Castenholz, George M. Garrity. New York: Springer, 2001–. v. 1-2, 4-5; in 7, ill. ISBN 9780387987712

579.3012   QR81.B46

The most comprehensive work in the field of bacterial taxonomy, this extensive revision of this authoritative manual is ongoing. The Bergey's Manual Trust is working with more than 150 international authorities to expand and update content. This new edition will reflect growth in the field; more than 2,200 new species and 390 new genera have been described since the first edition was published in 1984. Advances in molecular sequencing techniques have generated this new information, and elucidation of genes in highly conserved regions of the prokaryotic genome lead to a natural classification reflective of the evolutionary history of bacteria and archaea. The second edition presents bacterial taxonomy following a phylogenetic organizational scheme. Volumes of the second edition will be available individually and, eventually, as a complete set. Available as e-books.

305 The biomedical engineering handbook. 3rd ed. Joseph D. Bronzino. Boca Raton, Fla.: CRC/Taylor and Francis, 2006. 3 v., ill. ISBN 0849321247

610.28   R856.B513

First ed., 1995; 2nd ed., 2000.

Contents: v. 1, Biomedical engineering fundamentals; v. 2, Medical devices and systems; v. 3, Tissue engineering and artificial organs.

Provides a comprehensive overview of the field of biomedical engineering, with many revisions from the previous edition, reflecting technological changes in recent years. Includes new sections, for example, on biomimetics (defined as the imitation of biological processes), ethical issues associated with medical technology, and a new chapter on virtual instrumentation. Includes bibliographical references and index.

Also available as an e-book.

306 Biomedical informatics: Computer applications in health care and biomedicine. 3rd ed. Edward Hance Shortliffe, James J. Cimino. New York: Springer, 2006. xxvi, 1037 p., ill.
ISBN 9780387289861
610.28   R858.M397

First ed., 1990 (Reading, Mass.: Addison-Wesley) had title *Medical informatics: Computer applications in health care*; 2nd ed., 2001, *Medical informatics: Computer applications in health care and biomedicine*.

(Health informatics series)

"The field of biomedical informatics sits at the crossroads of computer science, decision science, cognitive science, and biomedicine . . . [and this book] provides the conceptual framework and practical know-how to navigate this integral discipline."—*Cover*

Provides an overview of concepts in biomedical informatics and biomedical information management. Bibliography, glossary, name index, and subject index. Also available as an e-book.

307 The bioterrorism sourcebook. Michael R. Grey, Kenneth R. Spaeth. New York: McGraw-Hill Medical Publ. Div., 2006. xxxiii, 549 p., ill. ISBN 0071440860
303.625   RC88.9.T47; G746

Contents: section I, Clinical principles and practices (ch. 1–9); section II, Infectious agents (ch. 10–16); section III, Biotoxins and category B and C agents (ch. 17–20); section IV, Chemical weapons (ch. 21–26); section V, Nuclear and radiation syndromes (ch. 27–30).

Clinical and public health guidance preparing for and responding to immediate and long-term bioterrorism-related conditions. Provides concise and essential information on the various aspects and agents of a bioterrorist attack and the expected consequences, with synopses, illustrations, tables, charts, and practical tips. Selected bibliography; index. Also available as an e-book.

The CDC's "Emergency Preparedness and Response" site, "intended to increase the nation's ability to prepare for and respond to public health emergencies" (http://www.bt.cdc.gov/) provides extensive information resources for bioterrorism, chemical, and radiation emergencies, natural disasters, and other threats.

Additional resources in this area include, for example, *Bioterrorism and public health* (2002, 1432), *Bioterrorism preparedness* (2006), also available in print and online, and others.

308 Catalog of human cancer genes: McKusick's Mendelian inheritance in man for clinical and research oncologists (onco-MIM). John J. Mulvihill. Baltimore: Johns Hopkins University Press, 1999. xxv, 646 p.
ISBN 0801847990
616.99/4042   RC268.42.M84

Provides a subset of cancer-related (or "neoplasia" in Mendelian inheritance in man [MIM] nomenclature) citations selected from McKusick's *Mendelian inheritance in man: Catalog of autosomal dominant, autosomal recessive, and x-linked phenotypes*. Includes entries on phenotypes, disorders & conditions, discussion of genes and proteins, etc. Entries grouped by organ system. Considered a valuable starting point in research, but needs to be supplemented with more recent citations from *OMIM: Online Mendelian inheritance in man* (339) and PubMed. Of interest to health professionals.

309 The cancer handbook. 2nd ed. Malcolm Alison. Chichester, U.K.; Hoboken, N.J.: John Wiley & Sons, 2007. 2 v. ISBN 9780470018521
616.99/4   RC263.C29168

First ed., 2002.

Contents: pt. I, The molecular and cellular basis of cancer; pt. II, The causation and prevention of cancer; pt. III, Systematic oncology; pt. IV, Pre-clinical models for human cancer; pt. V, The treatment of cancer.

Overview of scientific and clinical information of all the major areas in cancer research and oncology. Glossary of terms, extensive cross-referencing, references, further readings, black and white illustrations and color plates, tables, and figures. Resource for medical and life sciences students, researchers, clinicians, and scientists. Online access via Wiley Online Library (http://onlinelibrary.wiley.com/) is restricted to subscribers.

310   Clinical research manual: Practical tools and templates for managing clinical research. R. Jennifer Cavalieri, Mark E. Rupp, Sigma Theta Tau International. Indianapolis, Ind.: Sigma Theta Tau International, 2013.
ISBN 9781937554637
610.72/4   R853.C55
Contents: ch. 1, Introduction to clinical research operations; ch. 2, Site administration; ch. 3, Managing financial processes; ch. 4, Managing regulating activities and documents; ch. 5, Working with institutional review boards (ethics committees); ch. 6, Managing clinical trial activities and processes; ch. 7, Managing data and research records; ch. 8, Professional development; Appx. A, Your go-to regulatory reference tool; Appx. B, Keeping track of things; Index.

Explains the research process, answers questions about the details of conducting clinical research/clinical trial research, and offers practical advice on how to carry out study activities effectively and efficiently. Covers all important aspects and provides a comprehensive description of all steps, various forms, and tips. Useful for a wide variety of professionals involved in clinical research. Also available as an e-book.

311   The complete writing guide to NIH behavioral science grants. Lawrence M. Scheier, William L. Dewey. New York: Oxford University Press, 2007. 506 p.
ISBN 9780195320275
362.1079   RA11.D6C65
Contents: ch. 1, Peer review at the National Institutes of Health; ch. 2, Drug abuse research collaboration in the 21st century; ch. 3, A brief guide to the essentials of grant writing; ch. 4, Sample size, detectable difference, and power; ch. 5, Exploratory/developmental and small grant award mechanisms; ch. 6, Funding your future: what you need to know to develop a pre- or postdoctoral; training application; ch. 7, Unique funding opportunities for underrepresented minorities and international researchers; ch. 8, R01 grants: the investigator-initiated cornerstone of biomedical research; ch. 9, P50 research center grants; ch. 10, P20 and P30 center grants: developmental mechanisms; ch. 11, The K award: an important part of the NIH funding alphabet soup; ch. 12, T32 grants at the NIH: tips for success; ch. 13, SBIR funding: a unique opportunity for the entrepreneurial researchers; ch. 14, Federal grants and contracts outside of NIH; ch. 15, The financing and cost accounting of science: budgets and budget administration; ch. 16, Documenting human subjects protections and procedures; ch. 17, Navigating the maze: electronic submission; ch. 18, Revisions and resubmissions; ch. 19, Concluding remarks: the bottom line. Appendix 1: The NIH Web sites; Appendix 2: NIH institutes, centers, and their websites.

Presents important considerations in developing research proposals and funding mechanisms for both junior and established researchers. Provides practical information on how to construct and write successful grants, electronic grant submission, revising research proposals, etc. Useful to researchers, clinicians, and educators in a wide variety of subject areas who are interested in submitting grants to the NIH.

312   Conn's current therapy. Howard F. Conn, Robert E. Rakel. Philadelphia: W. B. Saunders, 1984–. ill.
615.505 8755-8823   RM101.C87
Title varies: 1949–1983, *Current therapy*. 1949–1983 ed. Howard F. Conn; 1984– ed. Robert E. Rakel.

Revised annually. Description based on 2013 ed., by Edward T. Bope and Rick D. Kellerman.

Presents authoritative current advances and methods of therapeutics and diagnostics. Arranged in 23 chapters, offering broad coverage of diseases (e.g., infectious diseases, diseases of allergy, etc.) and disorders of the various organ systems (e.g., respiratory system, cardiovascular system, etc.). Each section contains articles by specialists on more specific topics. Evidence is included where it exists.—*Pref.* List of approx. ten references for each chapter. Contains tables and boxes of information, graphs, figures, several appendixes and index. Also available as an e-book. Online access to previous editions is also available, with keyword searchability (cf. *Pref.*).

313 **The enzyme reference: A comprehensive guidebook to enzyme nomenclature, reactions, and methods.** Daniel L. Purich, R. Donald Allison. San Diego, Calif.: Academic Press, 2002. ix, 929 p., ill. ISBN 0125680414
572.7   QP601.P87

"The aim of this work is to provide a fuller spectrum of information in a single source on enzyme-catalyzed reactions than is currently available in any published reference work or as part of any Internet database."—*Publ. notes*

Enzymes chosen for inclusion are those classified by the Enzyme Commission and others for which the chemical reaction is known. Includes 6,000 enzyme reactions (with Enzyme Commission numbers, alternative names, substrates, products, alternative substrates, and properties) and chemical structures of key metabolites and cofactors. Describes catalyzed reactions, reaction stoichiometry, and cofactors. Provides extensive references to literature and the most comprehensive index available to *Methods in enzymology*. The index lists enzyme names. Appropriate for academic, medical, and other special libraries. Also available as an e-book.

314 **The family practice desk reference. 4th ed.** Charles E. Driscoll, Edward T. Bope. Chicago: AMA Press, 2003. xi, 1035 p., ill. ISBN 1579471900
610   RC55.F22

First ed., 1986 had title: *Handbook of family practice;* 3rd ed., 1996.

Includes aspects of health and illness management for common conditions and diseases encountered by family physicians. Organized by "life-cycle approach" (*Pref.*), e.g., care of children, maternity care, women's health, men's health, and by body system (e.g., cardiovascular, respiratory, gastrointestinal, etc.). Entries in standardized format, each with a table of contents and list of references, and organized by conditions. Each chapter

presents symptoms using differential diagnosis tables, laboratory values, and diagnostics.

315 **First aid manual. 4th ed.** Gina M. Piazza, American College of Emergency Physicians. London; New York: DK Pub, 2011. 288 p., col. ill. ISBN 9780756672355
616.0252   RC86.8.F565

Published by American College of Emergency Physicians® (ACEP)

Contents: (1) Becoming a first aider; (2) Managing an incident; (3) Assessing a victim; (4) The unconscious victim; (5) Respiratory problems; (6) Wounds and circulation; (7) Bone, joint, and muscle injuries; (8) Nervous system problems; (9) Effects of heat and cold; (10) Foreign objects, poisoning, bites, & stings; (11) Medical problems; (12) Techniques and equipment; (13) Emergency first aid; First aid regulations; Index.

"A comprehensive guide to treating emergency victims of all ages in any situation" (*Cover*). Step-by-step explanation and color photographs of life-saving procedures (e.g., cardiopulmonary resuscitation, treatment of blocked airway, etc.), treatments and techniques, following current first-aid guidelines. Section for the most critical emergencies at the end of the book.

316 **GeneTests**. http://www.genetests. org/. Children's Hospital and Medical Center (Seattle, Wash.), Univ. of Wash., School of Medicine; National Library of Medicine (U.S.). Seattle, Wash.: Univ. of Washington. 1993–

Contents: Home page; Disorders; GeneReviews; Panel Directory; Laboratory directory; Clinic directory.

Provides authoritative information on genetic testing and its use in diagnosis, disease management, and genetic counseling. Promotes use of genetic services in patient care and decision making by individuals. GeneReviews and Laboratory directory can be searched by disease, gene symbol, protein name, etc. Contains context-sensitive illustrated glossary, teaching tools, and other resources.

317 **Guides to the evaluation of permanent impairment. 6th ed.** Robert D. Rondinelli, Elizabeth

Genovese, Christopher R. Brigham, American Medical Association. Chicago: American Medical Association, 2008. xxiv, 634 p., ill. ISBN 9781579478889

614.1   RA1055.5.G85

First ed., 1965 (repr. *Journal of the American Medical Assoc.*, Feb. 15, 1958, special ed.); 5th ed., 2001.

Contents: ch. 1, "Conceptual foundations and philosophy"; ch. 2, "Practical application of the guides"; ch. 3, "Pain-related impairment"; ch. 4, "The cardiovascular system"; ch. 5, "The pulmonary system"; ch. 6, "The digestive system"; ch. 7, "The urinary and reproductive systems"; ch. 8, "The skin"; ch. 9, "The hematopoietic system"; ch. 10, "The endocrine system"; ch. 11, "Ear, nose, throat, and related structures"; ch. 12, "The visual system"; ch. 13, "The central and peripheral nervous system"; ch. 14, "Mental and behavioral disorders"; ch. 15, "The upper extremities"; ch. 16, "The lower extremities"; ch. 17, "The spine and pelvis"; appendix; glossary; index.

"Defines an innovative new international standard for impairment assessment . . . The goal is to provide an impairment rating guide that is authoritative, fair, and equitable to all parties . . ." (*Pref.*), applying terminology and a framework based on the World Health Organization's International Classification of Functioning, Disability, and Health (ICF). Five impairment classes allow patient rating from no impairment to impairment considered most severe. Also includes diagnosis-based grids for each organ system. Employs a peer-review process, with guidance from an editorial panel and input from state medical associations and national medical specialty societies.

Intended as a tool to understand the changes between the 5th and 6th ed. of this resource, *Transition to the AMA guides sixth: Guides to the evaluation of permanent impairment, sixth edition* by Rondinelli et al. ". . . introduces the new and experienced *Guides* user to the fundamentals and the changes for impairment ratings . . ."—*Pref.* Provides, for example, comparisons of changes between the 5th and 6th edition tables, a summary of key points in each chapter, analysis of rating procedures, and other helpful information.

Related titles are *AMA guides to the evaluation of ophthalmic impairment and disability, AMA guides to the evaluation of work ability and return to work, Guide to the evaluation of functional ability,* and *Guides to the evaluation of disease and injury causation.*

318   Handbook of environmental health. 4th ed. Herman Koren, Michael S. Bisesi. Boca Raton, Fla.: Lewis Publ., 2003. 2 v., ill. ISBN 1566705363

363.7   RA565.K67

First ed., 1980; 3rd ed., 1996.

Contents: v. 1, Biological, chemical, and physical agents of environmental related disease; v. 2, Pollutant interactions in air, water, and soil.

Includes various environmental health topics, issues, and hazards such as emerging infectious diseases and microorganisms, air quality and its effect on ecosystems, toxicology, and effects of the environment on humans. Describes interactions between humans and the environment and how they affect health and welfare of individuals of individuals. Comprehensive bibliography (v. 1, p. 647–702) and indexes. Also available as an e-book.

319   The handbook of health behavior change. 3rd ed. Sally A. Shumaker, Judith K. Ockene, Kristin A. Riekert. New York: Springer Pub. Co, 2009. xxxi, 827 p., ill. ISBN 9780826115454

613   RA776.9.H36

First ed., 1988; 2nd ed., 1998.

Contents: Sect. I, Health behavior change and maintenance: theory and techniques; sect. II, Interventions for lifestyle change; sect. III, Measurement; sect. IV, Obstacles and predictors of lifestyle change and adherence; section V, Lifestyle change and adherence issues within specific populations; Sect. VI, Lifestyle change and adherence issues among patients with chronic diseases; Sect. VII, Lifestyle change and adherence : the broader context.

It is recognized that many acute and chronic diseases can be prevented or lessened by increased attention to adopting and maintaining healthy behaviors. Health behavior change is considered the key to preventable diseases. This excellent handbook addresses health behavior change both in theory and practice, with current studies, interventions, and strategies, e.g., alteration of lifestyle, such as no longer smoking, changing eating habits, increasing physical activity, adherence to a medication regimen, practicing safe sex, etc. A valuable resource for both graduate and undergraduate students and health professionals. Includes tables and figures. Index. Also available as an e-book. A new edition is expected to be published in 2014.

320 Handbook of health behavior research. David S. Gochman. New York: Plenum Press, 1997. 4 v., ill.
ISBN 0306454432
613   RA776.9.H363
Contents: (I) Personal and social determinants; (II) Provider determinants; (III) Demography, development, and diversity; (IV) Relevance for professionals and issues for the future.

Interdisciplinary resource, presenting and explaining health behavior concepts and research findings. Includes a glossary, bibliographical references, and index. For an academic audience.

321 Handbook of neurologic rating scales. 2nd ed. Robert M. Herndon. New York: Demos Medical Publ., 2006. xiv, 441 p.
ISBN 1888799927
616.8/0475   RC348.H296
First ed., 1997.
Contents: ch. 1, Introduction to clinical neurologic scales (Robert M. Herndon and Gary Cutter); ch. 2, Generic and general use scales (Robert M. Herndon); ch. 3, Pediatric developmental scales (Roger A. Brumback); ch. 4, Pediatric neurologic and rehabilitation rating scales (Raphael Corcoran Sneed, Edward L. Manning, and Cathy F. Hansen); ch. 5, Amyotrophic lateral sclerosis clinimetric scales: Guidelines for administration and scoring (Benjamin Rix Brooks); ch. 6, Scales for the assessment of movement disorders (Stephen T. Gancher); ch. 7, Multiple sclerosis and demyelinating diseases (Robert M. Herndon and Jeffrey I. Greenstein); ch. 8, Assessment of the elderly with dementia (Richard Camicioli and Katherine Wild); ch. 9, Clinical stroke scales (Wayne M. Clark and J. Maurice Hourihane); ch. 10, Peripheral neuropathy and pain scales (Robert M. Herndon); ch. 11, Diagnostic headache criteria and instruments (Elcio J. Piovesan and Stephen D. Silberstein); ch. 12, Scales for assessment of ataxia (Robert M. Herndon); ch. 13, Assessment of traumatic brain injury (Risa Nakase-Richardson, Frances Spinosa,

Charles F. Swearingen, and Domenic Esposito); ch. 14, Health-related quality-of-life scales for epilepsy (James J. Cereghino); ch. 15, Rehabilitation outcome measures (Samuel T. Gontkovsky and Risa Nakase-Richardson); ch. 16, Human immunodeficiency virus–associated cognitive impairment (Giovanni Schifitto and Michelle D. Gaugh); ch. 17, Summary and conclusions (Robert M. Herndon).

Reference source on methods of measurement and rating scales used in neurology to assess neurologic disease. Useful in the design of clinical trials and for interpreting the literature of clinical trials in neurology.

322 Handbook of physical measurements. 2nd ed ed. Judith G. Hall. Oxford; New York: Oxford University Press, 2007. xii, 507 p., ill. ISBN 9780195301496
573.6   QM28.H23
First ed., 1989 had title: *Handbook of normal physical measurements*.

Contents: 1. Introduction; 2. Measurement; 3. Proportional growth and normal variants; 4. Height and length; 5. Weight; 6. Head circumference (occipitofrontal circumference, OCF); 7. Craniofacies; 8. Limbs; 9. Chest and trunk; 10. Genitalia; 11. Skin and hair; 12. Dermatoglyphics and trychoglyphics; 13. Use of radiography for measurement; 14. Developmental data; 15. Prenatal ultrasound measurements; 16. Postmortem organ weights; 17. Measurements for specific syndromes; 18. An approach to the child with dysmorphic features; Glossary; Index.

Provides a collection of reference data (e.g., normal growth curves; graphs or tables of standard growth parameters; standards for body structures) and also practical methods for use in the evaluation of children and adults with "dysmorphic features and/or structural anomalies."— *Introd.* Each chapter includes an introduction with the embryology of the particular area of the body, the sources from which the measurements are taken, and the necessary instruments and instructions to obtain the appropriate measurements, growth charts, and references which are useful in better understanding of statistics, methodology, and anthropometrics in patient care. Considered an important resource for a variety of health professionals. Also available as an e-book.

323 HIV InSite knowledge base. http:// hivinsite.ucsf.edu/InSite.jsp?page=KB. Laurence Peiperl, Paul Volberding, P. T. Cohen, Merle A. Sande, University of California, San Francisco, San Francisco General Hospital (Calif.). San Francisco: University of California. 1996(?)– 025.174; 616.9792; 362.1969792; 616.979201

Online adaptation of *The AIDS Knowledge Base* (AKB), which appeared in several print editions (1st ed., 1990; 2nd ed., 1994; 3rd ed., 1999).

Contents: Epidemiology of HIV; Natural Science of HIV; Diagnosis and Clinical Management of HIV; Clinical Manifestations of HIV; Infections Associated with HIV; Malignancies Associated with HIV; Transmission and Prevention of HIV; HIV Policy.

Continually updated online resource covering HIV/AIDS clinical topics and also access to selected related materials (e.g., guidelines, fact sheets, journal articles, etc.), including both links within the HIV InSite and outside resources. For academic libraries.

324 Interpreting the medical literature. 5th ed. Stephen H. Gehlbach. New York: McGraw-Hill, 2006. x, 293 p., ill. ISBN 0071437894
610.7222   R118.6.G43
First edition, 1982; 4th ed., 2002.

Contents: ch. 1, "Tasting an article"; ch. 2, "Study design: General considerations"; ch. 3, "Study design: The case-control approach"; ch. 4, "Study design: The cross-sectional and follow-up approaches"; ch. 5, "Study design: The experimental approach"; ch. 6, "Study design: Variations"; ch. 7, "Making measurements"; ch. 8, "Analysis: Statistical significance"; ch. 9, "Analysis: Some statistical tests"; ch. 10, "Interpretation: Sensitivity, specificity, and predictive value"; ch. 11, "Interpretation: Risk"; ch. 12, "Interpretation: Causes"; ch. 13, "Cases series, editorials, and reviews"; ch. 14, "A final word"; Index.

Assists with understanding and utilizing the information presented in medical studies and reports and also with the critical reading and interpretation of conflicting studies. Provides clinical examples from the published medical and public health literature. Also available as an e-book.—CM

325 Introduction to health sciences librarianship. M. Sandra Wood. Binghamton, N.Y.: Haworth Information Press, 2008. xvii, 494 p., ill. (some col.) ISBN 9780789035
026.61   Z675.M4.I58

Contents: sec. 1, "Introduction/overview"; sec. 2, "Technical services"; sec. 3, "Public services"; sec. 4, "Administration"; sec. 5, "Special topics."

Overview of health sciences librarianship and the different types of health sciences libraries, reflecting current trends in the health care field; the important influence of many organizations, particularly the Medical Library Association (MLA, 6), the Association of Academic Health Sciences Libraries (AAHSL), and the National Library of Medicine (NLM); and the pervasive role of advances in information technology. Addresses concepts such as information literacy, evidence-based librarianship, and health informatics. Glossary; index. Also available as an e-book.

326 Laboratory tests and diagnostic procedures. 6th ed. Cynthia C. Chernecky, Barbara J. Berger. St. Louis: Elsevier, c2013. x, 1222 p. ISBN 9781455706945
616.07/5   RB38.2.L33
First ed., 1993; 5th ed., 2008.

Updated edition. Pt. 1, "Diseases, conditions, and symptoms," contains an alphabetical list of diseases and conditions, with mention of the appropriate test and/or procedure for each disease. Pt. 2 lists laboratory and diagnostic procedures in alphabetical order, norms for different age groups and all known national and international units, usage of a particular test for a specific condition, causes of abnormal laboratory test results, and a description of the test or procedure with an interpretation of test results and post-procedure care. Alphabetically organized, with thumb tabs, with cross-references for alternative test names and acronyms. Includes information on herbal supplements which might affect test results. Appendixes list "reportable diseases" and "informed consent for genetic testing." Written as a guide for healthcare professionals and students caring for patients. Bibliography and index.

Similar print titles include *Interpretation of diagnostic tests* by Wallach, *Manual of laboratory and diagnostic tests* by Fischbach et al., *Mosby's manual of diagnostic and laboratory tests* (344), and *Tietz clinical guide to laboratory tests* (344) by Wu; a web-based resource is *Lab tests online: A public resource on clinical lab testing from the laboratory professionals who do the testing* (327).

327 Lab tests online. http://www.labtests online.org. American Association for Clinical Chemistry. Washington: American Association for Clinical Chemistry. 2001–

Produced and maintained by the American Association for Clinical Chemistry, in collaboration with several other professional societies.

Provides patients and other health consumers with reliable information on clinical laboratory tests that are commonly used to diagnose various diseases and conditions and their interpretation. Also provides links to additional resources and websites.

Print titles containing information about lab tests include *Interpretation of diagnostic tests* by Wallach, *Laboratory tests and diagnostic procedures* (327) by Chernecky et al., *Manual of laboratory and diagnostic tests* by Fischbach et al., *Mosby's manual of diagnostic and laboratory tests* (344) by Pagana et al., and *Tietz clinical guide to laboratory tests* (344).

328 The Medical Library Association guide to health literacy. Marge Kars, Lynda M. Baker, Feleta L. Wilson. New York: Neal-Schuman Publ., 2008. xiv, 314 p., ill. ISBN 9781555706258
026/.610973   Z675.M4; M497

Overviews issues related to health literacy and approaches to effective health communication. A practical guide, including best practices for librarians working in hospital and consumer health settings and providing health/patient education and appropriate services for persons with low literacy or illiterate persons. Intends to empower patients to understand their health care information. Explains different types of health literacy. Includes reference interview techniques, collaboration between libraries, exploration of the role of the librarian in promoting health literacy, etc. Addresses the special needs of senior citizens and adolescents.

Each chapter has a thorough list of current references. Resources for health professionals; upper-level and graduate-level health care students.

Useful for librarians working in hospital and consumer health settings.

329 The Medical Library Association guide to managing health care libraries. 2nd ed. Margaret Bandy, Rosalind F. Dudden, Medical Library Association. New York: Neal-Schuman Publishers, 2011. xxiii, 424 p., ill. ISBN 9781555707347
026.61   Z675.M4M5

Based on *Hospital library management,* 1983.

Contents: Ch. 1, Introduction: Libraries in health care settings (Margaret Moylan Bandy, Rosalind Farnam Dudden); ch. 2, The health care environment (Margaret Moylan Bandy, Barbara Jahn); ch. 3, Topics in management (Jacqueline Donaldson Doyle, Kay E. Wellek); ch. 4, Financial management (Mary Fran Prottsman); ch. 5, Human resources management (Dixie A. Jones); ch. 6, Evaluation and improvement management (Rosalind Farnam Dudden); ch. 7, Collection planning management (Craig C. Haynes); ch. 8, Collection technical management (Gretchen Hallerberg, Michelle Kraft, Marlene Englander, Marian Simonson); ch. 9, Library space management (Elizabeth Connor); ch. 10, On-site and web-based information services (Susan Lessick); ch. 11, Educational services (Lisa K. Traditi); ch. 12, Information practice (Michele Klein-Fedyshin); ch. 13, Knowledge services (Lorri Zipperer); ch. 14, Health information for patients and consumers (Michele Spatz); ch. 15, Associated services (Hope Leman, Donna Beales, Daniel Sokolow, Alison Aldrich, Marlene Englander); ch. 16, Solo librarian (Jerry Carlson).

This revised edition presents an overview of current trends in health sciences libraries and highly relevant topics in health sciences librarianship. Accompanying CD-ROM with MLA policy statements, policy and procedure templates, bibliographies, and various other resources. Intended as a resource and practical guide for librarians in different types of healthcare libraries and for library & information sciences students.

330 MEDLINE: A guide to effective searching in PubMed and other interfaces. 2nd ed. Brian S. Katcher. San Francisco: Ashbury Press, 2006. xi, 136 p., ill. ISBN 0967344514

025.0661 Z699.5.M39K373
First ed., 1999.
Contents: ch. 1, Origins of MEDLINE and why it works the way it does; ch. 2, Working in MED-LINE; ch. 3, Medical subject headings (MeSH, 858); ch. 4, Publication types and other limiting strategies; ch. 5, Framing questions and other practical tips; Appendix A: MEDLINE interfaces and related resources on the World Wide Web; Appendix B: Journals in the Abridged Index Medicus (AIM); Index.

A medical informatics resource for librarians, students, and others to become more informed about MEDLINE® searching via PubMed® and additional interfaces (e.g., Ovid, Medscape, Infotrieve, Paperchase, and others). Includes step-by-step examples for effective searching. *The Medical Library Association essential guide to becoming an expert searcher* by Jankowski is another helpful resource.

331 **The Merck manuals**. http://www.merck manuals.com//. Merck and Co.
Whitehouse Station, N.J.: Merck and Co. 1995–
"A trusted source for medical information . . . ."
—*Website*
Overview of the various titles and editions of the Merck manuals, organized in categories by user group, with information about online availability, online in other languages, as printed book or PDA download, and appropriate links. Under "patients and caregivers" lists the *Merck manual of medical information—home edition* (available online, online in other languages, and also as printed book) and the *Merck manual of health and aging* (available online and as printed book). Under "healthcare professionals" lists the *Merck manual of diagnosis and therapy* (available online, online in other languages, as PDA download, and as printed book); *Merck manual of geriatrics* (available online, online in other languages, and as printed book. The listing also includes under "chemists" the *Merck index* (available online and as printed book) and the *Merck veterinary manual* (available online, as PDA download, and as printed book).

MerckEngage® http://www.merckengage.com/, (formerly Mercksource), is a related website intended for healthcare consumers as a good starting point, together with MedlinePlus. It provides information concerning medical conditions, health news, searches topics in Spanish. Its "resource library" and "health tool" tabs provide additional useful information.

332 **The Merck manual of diagnosis and therapy.** Merck & Co., Merck Sharp & Dohme., Merck Research Laboratories. Rahway, N.J.: Merck, 1950–
615.5805 0076-6526 RC55.M4
Title varies: *Merck's manual of the materia medica* (varies slightly), 1899–1940. 18th ed., 2006; 19th ed., 2011.

Also issued 1987– as two soft cover volumes: *Merck manual of diagnosis and therapy*. Vol. I, General medicine; and: *Merck manual of diagnosis and therapy*. Vol. II, Gynecology, obstetrics, pediatrics, genetics.

Periodically revised to provide up-to-date medical information that will facilitate accurate diagnosis and promote effective treatment. Most entries include a definition or description, etiology, symptoms and signs, diagnosis, prognosis, and treatment. Surgical procedures are rarely described. Includes tables and ill. Indexed. The current edition is also available online (http://www.merck manuals.com).

The Merck Manuals page provides further information about this and several other Merck publications.

333 **Money for graduate students in the health sciences.** Reference Service Press. El Dorado Hills, Calif.: Reference Service Press, 2007–
LB2337.2M653;
1547-822X LB2337.2.M6532
Provides unique information for graduate students in health related fields seeking funding for graduate study, training, research, and creative activities. Includes more than 900 fellowships, grants, and awards; only scholarships and grants that require no repayment or interest; travel projects; and competitions, prizes, and honoraria. Excludes study or research outside the United States and very restrictive programs (specific geographic area or limited applicant eligibility, e.g., children of union members).

For funding in other subject areas, see also *Money for graduate students in the arts and humanities*; *Money for graduate students in the social &*

behavioral sciences; *Money for graduate students in the biological sciences*; and *Money for graduate students in the physical and earth sciences*. Available as an e-book.

334 Mosby's manual of diagnostic and laboratory tests. 4th ed. Kathleen Deska Pagana, Timothy James Pagana. St. Louis: Mosby/Elsevier, 2010. xi, 1245 p., col. ill.
9780323057479   RB38.2.P34
First edition, 1998; 3rd ed., 2006.

Contents: "Guidelines for proper test preparation and performance"; "Blood studies"; "Electrodiagnostic tests"; "Endoscopic studies"; "Fluid analysis studies"; "Manometric studies"; "Microscopic studies"; "Nuclear scanning"; "Stool tests"; "Ultrasound studies"; "Urine studies"; "X-ray studies"; "Miscellaneous studies"; bibliography; appendixes: (A) "Alphabetical list of tests"; (B) "List of tests by body systems"; (C) "Disease and organ panels"; (D) "Abbreviations for diagnostic and laboratory tests." Index, with names of all tests and their synonyms and other terms within tests.

Provides information and explanation on clinically relevant laboratory and diagnostic tests, including procedures and patient care before, during, and after a particular test, contraindications, and potential complications. Includes bibliographical references (p. 1215-17) and index. Another publication by the same author, is *Mosby's diagnostic and laboratory test reference* (11th ed., 2012).

Similar print titles include *Interpretation of diagnostic tests* by Wallach, *Laboratory tests and diagnostic procedures* (326) by Chernecky et al., *Tietz clinical guide to laboratory tests* (344); a Web-based resource is *Lab tests online: A public resource on clinical lab testing from the laboratory professionals who do the testing* (327).

335 National guideline clearinghouse. http://www.guideline.gov/. Agency for Healthcare Research and Quality, American Medical Association, American Association of Health Plans. Rockville, Md.: Agency for Healthcare Research and Quality. 1998–
R723.7
Originally created by Agency for Healthcare Research and Quality (AHQR), American Medical Association (AMA), and American Association of Health Plans (now America's Health Insurance Plans [AHIP], http://www.ahip.org/).

Contains evidence-based clinical practice guidelines, protocols, and related documents, with searching and browsing options. Searchable by keyword, disease/condition, treatment/intervention, guideline category, organization and organization type, intended user, clinical specialty, methods to assess and analyze evidence, etc. Related resources (http://www.guideline.gov/resources/index.aspx) include annotated bibliographies, bioterrorism resources, a glossary, guideline archive (lists withdrawn or superseded guidelines), guideline index (complete listing of the guideline summaries available on the website), National Library of Medicine (NLM) and National Center for Biotechnology Information (NCBI) links (PubMed, Health services technology assessment texts (HSTAT, 80), part of the NCBI bookshelf http://www.ncbi.nlm.nih.gov/books?itool=toolbar), patient resources links, and others.

A related site is National Quality Measures Clearinghouse (NQMC).

336 National Library of Medicine Training Center. http://nnlm.gov/ntc/. National Library of Medicine (U.S.). Bethesda, Md.: National Library of Medicine. 2003–
Produced by National Library of Medicine (NLM).

Provides access to online training materials used in conjunction with classes and courses offered by the National Training Center and Clearinghouse (NTCC), e.g., for PubMed{/record and {record} TOXNET.

337 The NCBI handbook. http://www.ncbi.nlm.nih.gov/books/NBK143764/. National Center for Biotechnology Information. Bethesda, Md.: National Center for Biotechnology Information. 2013-
Produced by National Center for Biotechnology Information (NCBI).

Contents: Literture; Genomes; Variation; Health; Genes and Gene Expression; Nucleotide; Tools; and Metadata.

In-depth guide to NCBI bioinformatics resources, including a variety of databases and search engines. Describes both well-known (e.g., GenBank, PubMed,

OMIM, and others) and also less well-known NCBI databases (e.g., the macromolecular structure databases, GEO, and many others) and gives details on how they work. Intended for biomedical researchers, health professionals, and students.

338   NORD guide to rare disorders.
National Organization for Rare Disorders. Philadelphia: Lippincott, Williams & Wilkins, 2003. lxiv, 895 p., [16] p. of plates, ill. (some col.) ISBN 0781730635
616   RC48.8.N385
NORD (National Organization for Rare Disorders) is "a non-profit voluntary health agency dedicated to the identification, treatment, and cure of all orphan diseases" (*Pref.*).

Contents: ch. 1, Autoimmune & connective tissue disorders; ch. 2, Cardiovascular disorders; ch. 3, Chromosomal disorders; ch. 4, Dermatologic disorders; ch. 5, Dysmorphic disorders; ch. 6, Emerging/infectious diseases; ch. 7, Endocrine disorders; ch. 8, Gastroenterologic disorders; ch. 9, Hematologic/oncologic disorders; ch. 10, Inborn errors of metabolism; ch. 11, Neurologic disorders; ch. 12, Neuromuscular disorders; ch. 13, Ophthalmologic disorders; ch. 14, Pulmonary disorders; ch. 15, Renal disorders; ch. 16, Skeletal disorders.

At what point a disease is considered rare differs among countries. In the U.S., a disease is considered a rare or an "orphan" disease if it is a low-incidence disease that affects fewer than 200,000 people. This resource "covers about 800 of the estimated 6,000 rare diseases . . . [and] presents many of the sign and symptoms that can be an aid in the diagnosis and differentiation of rare diseases in addition to possible treatment" (*Foreword*). Lists resources which provide help to patients and families affected by a rare disorder. Includes a "List of orphan products approved for marketing." Index. For physicians and other health professionals, patients, and students. Other resources in this area can be located via National Organization for Rare Disorders, Inc. and NIH's Office of Rare Diseases.

NORD compendium of rare diseases and disorders provides updated quick-reference information and data.

339   OMIM. http://www.ncbi.nlm.nih.gov/omim/. Victor A. McKusick, National Center for Biotechnology Information.

Bethesda, Md.: National Center for Biotechnology Information. 2000–
                           QH442.4
OMIM and Online Mendelian inheritance in man are trademarks of the Johns Hopkins University (JHU, 339); OMIM is a continuously updated catalog of human genes and genetic disorders compiled by Dr. Victor A. McKusick and colleagues at JHU and developed for the Web by the National Center for Biotechnology Information (NCBI). OMIM has its origins in the print *Mendelian inheritance in man: Catalogs of autosomal dominant, autosomal recessive, and X-linked phenotypes*. A related title is John J. Mulvihill's *Catalog of human cancer genes: McKusick's Mendelian inheritance in man for clinical and research oncologists* (308).

The OMIM help pages (http://omim.org/help) provide guidance for basic and advanced searches. FAQs help to explain the OMIM numbering system, symbols, the OMIM gene map and morbid map, as well as provide answers to a variety of additional specific questions.

Records provide descriptions of genetic traits, references to the literature, and extensive links to MEDLINE, protein, and DNA sequence records in NCBI's system and from other data repositories.

"OMIM is intended for use primarily by physicians and other professionals concerned with genetic disorders, by genetics researchers, and by advanced students in science and medicine. While the OMIM database is open to the public, users seeking information about a personal medical or genetic condition are urged to consult with a qualified physician for diagnosis and for answers to personal questions."—*FAQ - Note at bottom*

340   Professional guide to signs & symptoms. 6th ed. Lippincott Williams & Wilkins. Philadelphia: Wolters Kluwer/ Lippincott Williams & Wilkins, 2011. ix, 801 p., color ill.
ISBN 9781608310982
616.047   RC69.P77
First ed., 1993; 5th ed., 2007.
Alphabetically-organized reference tool helpful for identification and interpretation of selected signs and symptoms of various diseases, agents of bioterrorism, signs and symptoms associated with herbs, and laboratory test results. Includes a table of English-Spanish translations (on inside front and

back cover). Selected references and index. Also available as an e-book. A related title, *Professional guide to diseases*, has been regularly updated since 1981. Also available as an e-book.

341   The Sage handbook of health psychology. Stephen Sutton, Andrew Baum, Marie Johnston. Thousand Oaks, Calif: SAGE Publ., 2004. xiii, 432 p., ill. ISBN 0761968490

616.0019   R726.7.S24

Contents: ch. 1, Context and perspectives in health psychology; ch. 2, Epidemiology of health and illness: a socio-psycho-physiological perspective; ch. 3, Biological mechanisms of health and disease; ch. 4, Determinants of health-related behaviours: theoretical and methodological issues; ch. 5, Health-related cognitions; ch. 6, Individual differences, health and illness: the role of emotional traits and generalized expectancies; ch. 7, Stress, health and illness; ch. 8, Living with chronic illness: a contextualized, self-regulation approach; ch. 9, Lifespan, gender and cross-cultural perspectives in health psychology; ch. 10, Communicating about health threats and treatments; ch. 11, Applications in health psychology: how effective are interventions?; ch. 12, Research methods in health psychology; ch. 13, Assessment and measurement in health psychology; ch. 14, Professional issues in health psychology.

Comprehensive interdisciplinary handbook reflecting international health psychology research and issues. For advanced students, researchers, and practitioners. Includes bibliographical references and index. Also available as an e-book.

342   The SAGE handbook of mental health and illness. David Pilgrim, Bernice A. Pescosolido, Anne Rogers. Los Angeles: SAGE, 2011. xviii, 547 p., ill. ISBN 9781847873828

362.196/89   RA790.5.S24

Contents: sect. 1, Mental health and mental disorders in social context (ch. 1-14); sect. 2, Clinical and policy topics (ch. 15-25).

Scholarly essays on a wide range of mental health topics and issues, research findings, and practice. Looks at mental health from both biological and social points of view. Index. Important resource for scholars, advanced students, researchers, practitioners. Also available as an e-book and via Credo reference.

343   Studying a study & testing a test. 6th ed. Richard K. Riegelman. Philadelphia: Wolters Kluwer/Lippincott Williams & Wilkins Heath, 2013. xii, 338 p., ill. ISBN 9780781774260

610/.72   R118.6.R54

First ed., 1981; 5th ed., 2005. Subtitle varies: Earlier editions "How to read the medical literature"; this 6th ed., "Reading evidence-based health research."

Provides decision support and step-by-step help for health sciences students and health professionals to critically assess and interpret the primary research literature and to translate evidence into clinical practice. Based on the M.A.A.R.I.E. (method, assignment, assessment, results, interpretation, extrapolation) framework. Includes bibliographical references and index.

344   Tietz clinical guide to laboratory tests. 4th ed. Alan H. B. Wu. St. Louis: Saunders/Elsevier, 2006. li, 1798 p. ISBN 0721679757

616.07/5   RB38.2.C55

First ed., 1983–3rd ed., 1995 had title: *Clinical guide to laboratory tests.*

Contents: section 1, Preanalytical aspects; section 2, General clinical tests; section 3, Molecular diagnostics; section 4, Therapeutic drugs and drugs of abuse; section 5, Clinical microbiology; section 6, Immunophenotyping markers; section 7, Pharmacogenomics; section 8, Allergy testing; Test index; Disease index.

Presents diagnostic information on commonly used tests as well as specialized tests and procedures, with discussion of biological variables and drug interferences that may affect test results. Provides reference ranges for most laboratory tests and clinical interpretation of laboratory data. For health professionals. Similar print titles include *Interpretation of diagnostic tests* (by Wallach), *Laboratory tests and diagnostic procedures* (by Chernecky, et al, 326), *Mosby's manual of diagnostic and laboratory tests;* a web-based resource is *Lab tests online: A public resource on clinical lab testing from the laboratory professionals who do the testing* (327).

345   Wallach's interpretation of diagnostic tests. 9th ed. Mary A. Williamson, L. Michael. Snyder, Jacques B. Wallach. Philadelphia: Wolters Kluwer/Lippincott

Williams & Wilkins Health, 2011. xvi, 1143 p, ill. ISBN 9781605476674

616.07/56   RB38.2.W35

First ed., 1970; 8th ed., 2007. Previous editions had title: *Interpretation of diagnostic tests*.

Provides information about tests and diseases, also new technologies and techniques used in testing. Includes sections on normal values, specific laboratory examinations, diseases of organ systems, and drugs and laboratory test values. This revised edition has been reorganized into two sections: (1) Listing of laboratory tests in alphabetical order, with indication of their sensitivity, specificity, and positive and negative probabilities (cf. *Pref.*). Separate listing for microbiology tests. (2) Disease states (infectious diseases; cardiovascular disorders; central nervous system disorders; digestive diseases; endocrine diseases; renal and urinary tract diseases). Appendixes include a list of abbreviations and acronyms and a glossary. Subject index. Designed for clinicians, but also useful for health consumers. Also available as an e-book.

Similar print titles include *Laboratory tests and diagnostic procedures* (327), *Manual of laboratory and diagnostic tests* (by Fischbach, et al.), *Mosby's manual of diagnostic and laboratory tests* (344), and *Tietz clinical guide to laboratory tests* (344); a web-based resource is *Lab tests online: A public resource on clinical lab testing from the laboratory professionals who do the testing* (327).

Style manuals

346 AMA manual of style: A guide for authors and editors. 10th ed.
Cheryl Iverson, American Medical Association. New York: Oxford University Press, 2007.
ISBN 9780195176339

808.06661   R119.A533

Title varies: 1st ed., 1962, called *AMA stylebook*; 6th ed., 1976, called *Stylebook: Editorial manual*; 7th ed., 1981, called *Manual for authors and editors*; 8th ed., 1989, called *American Medical Association manual of style*; 9th ed., 1998, called *American Medical Association manual of style: A guide for authors and editors*. Comp. varies.

Contents: Section 1, Preparing an article for publication; Section 2, Style; Section 3, Terminology; Section 4, Measurements and quantitation; Section 5, Technical information. Index.

Presents guidelines for medical authors and editors in writing and preparing manuscripts for publication. Offers advice on style, usage, nomenclature, statistics, and mathematical composition; also considers types of articles, fraud and plagiarism, inclusive language, grammar, and the publishing process, with information on electronic publishing, style recommendations for electronic references, and copyright issues. Ch. 24 is a "Glossary of Publishing Terms."

Also available as an e-book, *AMA manual of style online: A guide for authors and editors* (http://www.amamanualofstyle.com). The online edition includes the most recent version of the entire print 10th ed., with search functionality, browse options, web-only material, and other supplementary features.

347 Citing medicine. http://www.nlm.nih.gov/citingmedicine. Karen Patrias, Dan Wendling, National Library of Medicine (U.S.), National Center for Biotechnology Information. Bethesda, Md.: National Library of Medicine. 2007

R119

Updates and supersedes *National Library of Medicine recommended format for bibliographic citation*, publ. 1991; National Library of Medicine recommended formats for bibliographic citation: Internet supplement, publ. 2001.

Contents: Citing published print documents; Citing unpublished material; Citing audio and visual media (audio cassettes, video cassettes, slides, photographs, etc.); Citing material on CD-ROM, DVD, or disk; Citing material on the Internet. Appendixes: (A) Abbreviations for commonly used English words in journal titles; (B) Additional sources for journal title abbreviations; (C) Abbreviations for commonly used English words in bibliographic description; (D) ISO country codes for selected countries; (E) Two-letter abbreviations for Canadian Provinces and U.S. States and Territories; (F) Notes for citing MEDLINE/PubMed.

Provides information on how to construct and format citations. Describes rules and exceptions for specific citations, as well as recent rule changes. Includes examples. Additions and changes to this edition at http://list.nih.gov/archives/citingmed.html.

Part of the NCBI Bookshelf (http://www.ncbi
.nlm.nih.gov/books), a searchable, growing collection of online books.

**348 The complete guide to medical
writing.** Mark Stuart. London; Chicago:
Pharmaceutical Press, 2007. 491 p.
ISBN 0853696675
808.06661   R119

Contents: sec. 1, "Medical writing essentials"; sec.
2, "Reviews and reports"; sec. 3, "Medical journalism and mass media"; sec. 4, "Medical writing
in education"; sec. 5, "Medical writing for medical professionals"; sec. 6, "Medical publishing";
appendixes: (1) "Common medical abbreviations";
(2) "Measurements"; (3) "Normal values for common laboratory tests"; (4) "Proof correction marks";
(5) "A to Z of medical terms in plain English."

Covers aspects of scientific and medical writing, medical journalism, and medical publishing.
Resource for medical professionals and students
to provide help with writing, communicating,
and presenting scientific and medical information
clearly and accurately, with examples from the
pharmaceutical sciences. Covers copyright and
patient confidentiality. For authors and editors.
Also available as an e-book.

**349 The complete writing guide to NIH
behavioral science grants.** Lawrence
M. Scheier, William L. Dewey. New York:
Oxford University Press, 2007. 506 p.
ISBN 9780195320275
362.1079   RA11.D6C65

Contents: ch. 1, Peer review at the National Institutes
of Health; ch. 2, Drug abuse research collaboration in
the 21st century; ch. 3, A brief guide to the essentials
of grant writing; ch. 4, Sample size, detectable difference, and power; ch. 5, Exploratory/developmental
and small grant award mechanisms; ch. 6, Funding your future: what you need to know to develop
a pre- or postdoctoral; training application; ch. 7,
Unique funding opportunities for underrepresented
minorities and international researchers; ch. 8, R01
grants: the investigator-initiated cornerstone of biomedical research; ch. 9, P50 research center grants;
ch. 10, P20 and P30 center grants: developmental
mechanisms; ch. 11, The K award: an important part
of the NIH funding alphabet soup; ch. 12, T32 grants
at the NIH: tips for success; ch. 13, SBIR funding: a

unique opportunity for the entrepreneurial researchers; ch. 14, Federal grants and contracts outside of
NIH; ch. 15, The financing and cost accounting of
science: budgets and budget administration; ch. 16,
Documenting human subjects protections and procedures; ch. 17, Navigating the maze: electronic submission; ch. 18, Revisions and resubmissions; ch. 19,
Concluding remarks: the bottom line. Appendix 1:
The NIH Web sites; Appendix 2: NIH institutes, centers, and their websites.

Presents important considerations in developing research proposals and funding mechanisms
for both junior and established researchers. Provides practical information on how to construct
and write successful grants, electronic grant submission, revising research proposals, etc. Useful
to researchers, clinicians, and educators in a wide
variety of subject areas who are interested in submitting grants to the NIH.

350 Health professionals style manual.
Shirley H. Fondiller, Barbara J. Nerone.
New York: Springer, 2006.
ISBN 0826102077
808.06661   R119.F66

Rev. ed. of *Health professionals stylebook*, 1993.

Contents: ch. 1, "Style and substance: The dynamic duo"; ch. 2, "From principles to practice: The art
of effective writing"; ch. 3, "Understanding usage: An
alphabetical guide to specific writing tips and pitfalls";
ch. 4, "Be clear and direct: How to avoid redundancies, euphemisms, and cliches"; ch. 5, "Harness the
potential of computers and the Internet." Appendixes:
A, "Common abbreviations and acronyms in health
care"; B, "Commonly misspelled words"; C, "Using
prefixes and suffixes"; D, "Common proofreader's
marks"; E, "Electronic resources"; F, "Referencing."
Includes references for further reading and index.

Provides guidelines about writing clearly and
effectively, covering American usage only. Addresses style, style errors, English grammar, composition techniques, and other areas of technical
writing. Can be used as a supplement to other style
manuals. For researchers and students in the various health professions. Also available as an e-book.

**351 How to report statistics in medicine:
Annotated guidelines for authors,
editors, and reviewers. 2nd ed.**
Thomas A. Lang, Michelle Secic. New

York: American College of Physicians, 2006. p. cm. ISBN 1930513690

610.72   RA409.L357

First ed., 1997.

Rev. ed., with new and updated content. Considered a standard guide to interpreting and reporting statistics in scientific and medical writing. Provides guidelines for reporting statistical analyses, research, and trial design used in biological sciences and medical research, how to display data, and explanation of statistical terms and tests. Also available as an e-book.

352   How to write and publish a scientific paper. 7th ed. Robert A. Day, Barbara Gastel. Santa Barbara, Calif.: Greenwood Press, 2011. xxi, 300 p., ill. ISBN 9780313391958

808.0665   T11

Contents: What is scientific writing? — Historical perspectives — Approaching a writing project — What is a scientific paper? — Ethics in scientific publishing — Where to submit your manuscript — How to prepare the title — How to list the authors and addresses — How to prepare the abstract — How to write the introduction — How to write the materials and methods section — How to write the results — How to write the discussion — How to state the acknowledgments — How to cite the references — How to design effective tables — How to prepare effective graphs — How to prepare effective photographs — Rights and permissions — How to submit the manuscript — The review process (how to deal with editors) — The publishing process (how to deal with proofs) — How to write a review paper — How to write opinion (book reviews, editorials, and letters to the editor) — How to write a book chapter or a book — How to write for the public — How to present a paper orally — How to prepare a poster — How to write a conference report — Use and misuse of English — Avoiding jargon — How and when to use abbreviations — Writing clearly across cultures and media — How to write science in English as a foreign language — How to write a thesis — How to prepare a curriculum vitae — How to prepare grant proposals and progress reports — How to write a recommendation letter- and how to ask for one — How to work with the media — How to provide peer review — How to seek a scientific-communication career. Appendixes (1) Selected journal title word abbreviations, (2) Words and expressions to avoid, (3) Prefixes and abbreviations for SI (Système International), (4) Some helpful websites; Includes cartoons; glossary; references; index.

This updated ed. emphasizes the communication of science beyond writing skills. For beginning students, nonnative English speakers, and researchers.

353   How to write, publish, & present in the health sciences: A guide for clinicians & laboratory researchers. Thomas A. Lang. Philadelphia: American College of Physicians, 2009. xx, 389 p., ill. (some color). ISBN 9781934465141

808.06661   R119.L365

Guide to practical information, tips, and techniques, with detailed examples on how to communicate effectively. Provides guidelines for writing and submitting scientific articles, preparing and documenting drawings, photographs, laboratory images, etc. Also addresses grant writing and ethical issues in research and publishing. Also available as an e-book.

354   ICMJE recommendations for the conduct, reporting, editing, and publication of scholarly work in medical journals. http://www.icmje.org/urm_main.html. International Committee of Medical Journal Editors. Philadelphia: International Committee of Medical Journal Editors

Also called "ICMJE recommendations."

The International Committee of Medical Journal Editors (ICMJE) (http://www.icmje.org/index.html), established in 1978, originally known as the Vancouver Group. Further details at http://www.icmje.org/about_c.html

Formerly called: "Uniform requirements for manuscripts submitted to biomedical journals: Writing and editing for biomedical publication," first published in 1979, with multiple updated versions since then published in *Annals of internal medicine*.

I. About the recommendations; II. Roles and responsibilities of authors, contributors, reviewers, editors, publishers, and owners; III. Publishing and editorial issues related to publication in medical journals; IV. Manuscript preparation and submission.

Provides guidelines and recommendations for the format of manuscripts submitted to journals that agree to use the ICMJE style. Answers to frequently asked questions are provided at http://www.icmje.org/faq_urm.html. Links to journals following ICMJE recommendations (http://www.icmje.org/journals.html). Further explanation found at http://www.icmje.org/new_recommendations.html.

The *ICMJE recommendations* serve as a model for publishers, editors, and authors in non-medical disciplines as well.

355   A manual for writers of research papers, theses, and dissertations: Chicago style for students and researchers. 7th ed. Kate L. Turabian, Wayne C. Booth, Gregory G. Colomb, Joseph M. Williams. Chicago: University of Chicago Press, 2007. xviii, 466 p., ill. ISBN 9780226823362
808.02   LB2369.T8

Presents the "Chicago style" for formal papers; a significant revision of previous editions. In three parts: pt. I, adapted from *The craft of research* (2003), provides practical advice on the research and writing process; pt. II covers citation forms (including those for electronic materials); and pt. III covers writing mechanics (punctuation, capitalization, quotations, etc.). Appendix gives general guidelines for formatting and submitting dissertations. Bibliography lists sources on finding and presenting information.

Revised to be in conformity with the 15th ed. of *The Chicago manual of style*. Standard source to consult before using the *Manual*.

356   Medical writing: A guide for clinicians, educators, and researchers. 2nd ed. Robert B. Taylor. New York: Springer, 2011. xiv, 372 p., ill. ISBN 9781441982339
808.06661   R119.T395

First ed., 2005 had title: *Clinician's guide to medical writing*.

Contents: (1) Getting started in medical writing; (2) Basic writing skills; (3) From page one to the end; (4) Technical issues in medical writing; (5) What's special about medical writing?; (6) How to write a review article; (7) Case reports, editorials, letters to the editor, book reviews, and other publication models; (8) Writing book chapters and books; (9) How to write a research protocol; (10) How to write a grant proposal; (11) How to write a report of a clinical study; (12) Getting your writing published; Appendix 1, Glossary of terms used in medical writing, words and phrases; Appendix 2, Proofreader's marks; Appendix 3, Commonly used medical abbreviations; Appendix 4, Laboratory reference values for adults; Appendix 5, Methodological and statistical terms used in research studies. Index.

The author provides a brief introduction, valuable practical advice, and various models and examples for medical writing. Intended to teach clinicians about the basics of medical writing and publishing. Also available as an e-book. Comparable to an older resource, *Why not say it clearly: A guide to scientific writing* by King.

357   Scientific style and format: The CSE manual for authors, editors, and publishers. 7th ed. Council of Science Editors. Reston, Va.: Council of Science Editors; Rockefeller University Press, 2006. xvi, 658 p., ill. ISBN 097796650X
808.066   T11.S386

Desk reference useful to anyone writing, editing, publishing, or peer reviewing scientific in disciplines. Content reflects the interdisciplinary relationships among many scientific fields and discusses print and electronic publishing and basics of copyright. Explains conventions of punctuation, abbreviation, capitalization, symbols, and required format and contents of citations to references. Chapters address electromagnetic spectrum; chemical names, elements, and formulas; drugs, cells, chromosomes, and genes; viruses, bacteria, taxonomy, and nomenclature; the earth; and astronomical objects and time systems. Gives rules for abbreviating journal titles and publisher names, and an annotated bibliography of other style manuals, dictionaries, handbooks, and guides to word usage and prose style. Discusses technical elements of publishing books, journal articles, conference papers and proceedings, technical reports, and other types of monographs in science. Useful to authors, editors, publishers, students, and translators, this title is appropriate for academic libraries.

358 Publishing and presenting clinical research. 3rd ed. Warren S. Browner. Philadelphia: Lippincott Williams & Wilkins, 2012. ix, 214 p., ill. ISBN 9781451115901

808/.06661 R852.B77

First ed., 1999; 2nd ed., 2006.

Contents: 1. Overview; 2. Title and abstract; 3. Introduction; 4. Methods; 5. Results; 6. Tables; 7. Figures; 8. Discussion; 9. References and publishing; 10. Authorship; 11. Posters; 12. Oral presentation; 13. Choosing a journal and responding to reviews; 14. Suggestions for writing well; Appx. A, Uniform requirements for manuscripts submitted to biomedical journals; Appx. B, List of resources; Additional suggestions about style and presentations; Some suggested books about biostatistics; Index.

Provides help with getting work accepted in medical journals and at scientific meetings. Shows investigators how to organize research results and how to prepare a manuscript for publication. Also shows how to produce posters, oral presentations, etc. With this edition, there is access to a companion website with fully searchable text. A companion volume is *Designing clinical research* (by Hulley).

359 Writing a biomedical research paper: A guide to structure and style. Brian Stephen Budgell. Tokyo ; New York: Springer, 2009. vi, 66 p., ill. ISBN 9784431880363

808.06/661 R119.B85

Contents: Ch. 1, "Beginning a manuscript"; ch. 2, "The title: Your last chance to make a first impression"; ch. 3, "Writing an effective introduction"; ch. 4, "Ensuring the flow of discourse: Conjunctions and conjuncts"; ch. 5, "Hedging your bets and minding your modals"; ch. 6, "Writing an effective methods section"; ch. 7, "The passive voice and I"; ch. 8, "Writing an effective results section"; ch. 9, "The special case of case studies"; ch. 10, "Writing an effective discussion"; ch. 11, "Is it a discussion or a systematic review"; ch. 12, "Writing an effective abstract"; ch. 13, "The process of manuscript submission and review"; "Epilogue — Our shared biomedical language"; Index.

"Intended as a practical guide to writing good, publishable biomedical manuscripts."—*Pref*. This concise guide, with short chapters, provides helpful information regarding grammar, structure, and style. It describes the writing patterns and submission of manuscripts of successful authors. Supplementary materials (readings and self-directed learning) accessible at the website of the Centre for Biomedical and Health Linguistics at http://www.bmhlinguistics.org. Also available as an e-book.

360 Writing and publishing in medicine. 3rd ed. Edward J. Huth. Baltimore: Williams & Wilkins, 1999. ix, 348 p. ISBN 0683404474

808/.06661 R119.H87

First ed., 1982 and 2nd ed., 1990 had title: *How to write and publish papers in medicine*.

This rev. and reorganized ed. details the steps in writing and publishing a paper and offers specific suggestions on content likely to be needed in papers reporting several types of research: in clinical trials, observational studies, and reports of laboratory research (cf. *Introd.*). Provides information on punctuation, abbreviation, citation, formats for references, etc. Follows recommendations from an earlier version of the *Uniform requirements for manuscripts submitted to biomedical journals*.

Histories

361 American surgery: An illustrated history. Ira M. Rutkow, Stanley B. Burns. Philadelphia: Lippincott-Raven Publ., 1998. xiv, 638 p., ill. (some col.), col. map. ISBN 0316763527

617/.0973 RD27.3.U6R87

Contents: ch. 1, Native American surgery; ch. 2, Surgical practice in colonial America, 1607–1783; ch. 3, English and French influences, 1784–1845; ch. 4, Surgical anesthesia, 1846–1860; ch. 5, Civil War surgery, 1861–1865; ch. 6, Professionalization and antisepsis, 1866–1889; ch. 7, German authority and scientific advancement, 1890–1916; ch. 8, World War I surgery, 1917–1918; ch. 9, Consolidation and specialization, 1919–1940; ch. 10, World War II surgery, 1941–1945; ch. 11, American surgical supremacy, 1946–1974; ch. 12, Socioeconomic and political transformation, 1975–1997; Surgical specialties and biographies; ch. 13, General surgery; ch. 14, Cardiothoracic surgery; ch. 15, Colorectal surgery; ch. 16, Gynecologic surgery; ch. 17, Neurologic surgery; ch. 18, Ophthalmologic surgery; ch. 19, Orthopedic surgery; ch. 20, Otorhinolaryngologic surgery; ch. 21, Plastic surgery; ch. 22, Urologic surgery; References; Index.

Chronological arrangement, describing the development of American surgery, starting with Native American surgery and a description of practices of the various tribes. Includes biographies of important figures for the different time periods. Describes the development of the surgical subspecialties. Other titles by Ira Rutkow include *History of surgery in the United States* and *Surgery: an illustrated history* (391).

Another recommended title for both general readers and physicians is *History of surgery in the U.S. from pre-Columbian and colonial times to the present* by Schwartz.

362 The Army Medical Department, 1917-1941. Mary C. Gillett. Washington: Center of Military History, United States Army : For sale by the Supt. of Docs., U.S. G.P.O, 2009. xx, 644 p., ill. (some col.), col. maps. ISBN 9780160839702
355.3/45097309041 22   UH223.G544
(Army historical series)

Official military history, with information about the structure and organization of the US Army's medical branch. This volume places particular emphasis on WWI. It includes a discussion of the army's involvement and problems of dealing with the 1918-19 influenza pandemic. Also available online (PDF http://www.history.army.mil/html/books/medical_department_1917-1941/index.html). Other titles in this four-vol. set by the same author are *Army medical department, 1775-1818* (e.g., Revolutionary War—PDF version http://www.history.army.mil/catalog/pubs/30/30-7.html), *Army medical department, 1818-1865* (e.g., Mexican War and Civil War information—PDF version http://www.history.army.mil/catalog/pubs/30/30-8.html) and *Army medical department, 1865-1917*, with army doctors dealing with epidemics of cholera, yellow fever, typhoid, dysentery, and malaria (PDF version http://www.history.army.mil/html/books/030/30-9-1/index.html). Considered important titles for researchers and for all libraries with medical history collections.

363 A biographical encyclopedia of medical travel authors. Edward A. Martin, Peter Froggatt. Lewiston, N.Y.: Edwin Mellen Press, 2010–. v. 1–6. ISBN 9780773436817
610.922   R134.M325
Vol. 1, The Americas and Canada; v. 2, Australia and New Zealand, South Africa, and the Pacific and Antarctica; v. 3, Continental Europe; v. 4, England and Wales; v. 5, Ireland; v. 6, Scotland.

Biographical sketches with often little-known travel descriptions of doctors and other medical professionals, with ".selection targeted on medical travel authors of the Western Hemisphere between the Poles" (*Pref.*), mostly from recent centuries and mostly men. The author's sources include published materials, both in print and on the Web. Also available as an e-book.

364 The Cambridge historical dictionary of disease. Kenneth F. Kiple. Cambridge, U.K.; New York: Cambridge University Press, 2003. xiii, 412 p.; 25 cm. ISBN 9780521808347
616/.009   RC41.C365
International and interdisciplinary resource for medical history of human disease, originally published as pt. VIII of the Cambridge world history of human disease, rewrites and edits essays into shorter and up-to-date entries and also takes information from other parts of the original publication. Available online to subscribers via Gale virtual reference library.

365 The Cambridge world history of human disease. Kenneth F. Kiple, Rachael Rockwell Graham. Cambridge, U.K.; New York: Cambridge University Press, 1993. xxiv, 1176 p., ill. ISBN 0521332869
610/.9   R131.C233
Repr., 2001.

Modeled to a certain extent after *Handbook of geographical and historical pathology* by A. Hirsch (London: New Sydenham Soc., 1883–86), tr. by Charles Creighton from the 2nd German ed. of *Handbuch der historisch-geographischen Pathologie* (2 v., Stuttgart: Enke, 1881–86). A major work, the result of the Cambridge History and Geography of Human Disease project which began in late 1985. Pt. I covers the "major historical roots and branches of medical thought from ancient times to the twentieth century," while pt. II "deals with concepts of disease in the East and West, as well as with concepts of complex physical and mental ailments" (*Introd.*). Other sections treat medical specialties and disease prevention, the measurement of health, the history of human disease in Asia and elsewhere, and the geography of human disease. The final section, pt. VIII (rewritten into shorter and up-to-date entries in Cambridge historical dictionary of disease), covers major human diseases, past and present. A list of tables, figures, and maps is provided, and also a bibliography for each topic covered. Names index includes proper names, dates, and brief biographical sketches of all historical figures in medicine mentioned by more than one author. Also available as an e-book.

366   A century of surgeons and surgery: The American College of Surgeons 1913-2012. David L. Nahrwold, Peter J. Kernahan. Chicago: American College of Surgeons, 2012. iv, 389 p., ill.
9781880696996   RD1

"Documents the changing needs of surgeons, hospitals, and the general public over the 100 years since its founding."—*Introd.* Well-documented history of the American College of Surgery. Intended for surgeons and for readers interested in the history of surgery in North America. Earlier histories of the American College of Surgeons are *Fellowship of surgeons: A history of the American College of Surgeons* by Davis and *Fifty years of surgical progress, 1905-1955* by Davis.

367   Companion encyclopedia of the history of medicine. W. F. Bynum, Roy Porter. London; New York: Routledge, 1993. 2 v., ill. ISBN 0415047714
610/.9   R133.E5
1997, 1993 1st. paperback ed.

Contents: pt. 1, The place of medicine; pt. 2, Body systems; pt. 3, Theories of life, health and disease; pt. 4, Understanding disease; pt. 5, Clinical medicine; pt. 6, Medicine in society; pt. 7, Medicine, ideas, and culture.

Comprehensive survey of all aspects of the history of medicine. Includes 72 essays on the development of medical science, the medical profession and institutions, and medicine's interrelationship with society, culture, religion, etc. Bibliographical notes for each article. Cross-references and index.

368   A dictionary of the history of medicine. Anton Sebastian. New York: Parthenon Publ. Group, 1999. vi, 781 p., ill.
ISBN 1850700214
610.9   R121.S398

This illustrated medical history dictionary, a scholarly work, includes terms, with Latin and Greek origins of terms, brief biographies of notable people in medicine, eponymic information, important events, conditions, procedures, and other historical information for a broad range of subjects. Includes anecdotes and background material on both well- and little-known facts of medical history. Drawings and photographs of antique medical instruments and rare medical conditions. A negative review (*Journal of the history of medicine and allied sciences* 56, no. 2 [2001]: 182–83) cites factual errors, omissions, and "overly broad coverage." Users are cautioned to double check facts in other sources.

By the same author, *Dates in medicine: A chronological record of medical progress over three millennia* provides important milestones in the development of medicine. It is part of the Landmarks in Medicine series (publ. 2000–2002 by Parthenon), which also includes several other titles, including *Dates in ophthalmology: A chronological record of progress in ophthalmology over the last millennium,* by Daniel Albert, and several other titles by Helen S. J. Lee: *Dates in cardiology, Dates in gastroenterology, Dates in infectious disease, Dates in obstetrics and gynecology, Dates in neurology, Dates in oncology,* and *Dates in urology,* all with the subtitle *A chronological record of progress . . . over the last millennium.*

369   Digital collections (NLM). http://collections.nlm.nih.gov/muradora/. National Library of Medicine (U.S.). Bethesda, Md.: U.S. National Library of Medicine, National Institutes of Health, Dept. of Health and Human Resources

Repository for access and preservation of biomedical resources from NLM's collections, including books and films & videos. This continually updated resource contains several collections and "featured items from the collection," e.g., "Cholera online: A modern pandemic in text and images," "Medicine in the Americas," and others. This site can be browsed by collections, titles, subjects, authors, years, and languages. Further information can be found on the NLM Digital Repository Project information page (http://www.nlm.nih.gov/digitalrepository/index .html). It complements PMC (PubMed Central, 48), the digital archive of electronic journal articles.

Related sites are "Digital resources" from NLM's historical collections (http://www.nlm.nih.gov/ hmd/collections/digital/index.html) and its digital manuscripts program (http://www.nlm.nih.gov/ hmd/collections/archives/dmp/index.html).

370 The DOs: Osteopathic medicine in America. 2nd ed. Norman Gevitz. Baltimore: Johns Hopkins University Press, 2004. xiv, 242 p., ill., map. ISBN 0801878330
615.5330973   RZ325.U6G48
First ed., 1982.

A history of osteopathic medicine, from its beginning in the 19th century to the present, detailing its philosophy, practice, and relationship with the medical profession. This revised edition has 11 chapters, with two new chapters on recent developments and growth of the profession. Includes bibliographic notes and index.

371 Encyclopaedia of the history of science, technology, and medicine in non-western cultures. Helaine Selin. Dordrecht, Netherlands; Boston: Kluwer Academic, 1997. xxvii, 1117 p., ill., maps (some color). ISBN 0792340663
509   Q124.8.E53

Contains 600 signed entries with references. Includes major topics (e.g., agriculture, maps, and medicine) in several cultures/geographic areas. Also includes famous scientists. List of entries, index, list of authors.

372 Encyclopedia of medical history. Roderick E. McGrew, Margaret P. McGrew. New York: McGraw-Hill, 1985. xiv, 400 p. ISBN 0070450870
610/.9   R133.M34

Intends "to provide an easily accessible historical treatment of important medical topics" (*Pref.*). Includes 103 essays, each with a bibliography of additional readings. Topical entries are arranged in alphabetical order. No biographical articles, but

individuals' contributions to medical science are discussed in the essays. Index.

373 Encyclopedia of pestilence, pandemics, and plagues. Joseph Patrick Byrne, Anthony S. Fauci. Westport, Conn.: Greenwood Press, 2008. 2 v. (xxv, 872 p.), ill., maps. ISBN 9780313341014
614.4003   RA652.E535
Contents: v. 1. A-M — v. 2. N-Z.

Covers both historical and modern infectious diseases (e.g., HIV/AIDS; SARS; influenza epidemics, etc.) and historical epidemics (e.g., black death; bubonic plague; great plague of London; public health in the Islamic world 1000-1600; syphilis during the 16th century, etc.), including social, economic, and political factors. Sidebars within entries contain information from primary sources. Also includes entries on persons considered important in historical epidemiology. List of all entries and a guide to related topics in front of v. 1. Glossary, bibliography of both print and electronic resources, and index in v. 2. For students, health professionals, and also general readers. Also available as an e-book.

By the same author, *Encyclopedia of black death*, is "a collection of 300 interdisciplinary entries covering plague and its effects on Western society across four centuries" (*Introd.*), with main focus on the second plague pandemic for the years 1340-1840. However, also includes some pre-1340s and post-1840s subjects, a timeline of events, glossary, cross-references, and a bibliography. Considered a useful resource for undergraduates and above and also for general readers. *Encyclopedia of plague and pestilence: From ancient times to the present* (374) is another resource in this area.

The following two Internet resources provide details on the influenza epidemic of 1918-1919: *The Great pandemic: The United States in 1918-1919* http://www.flu.gov/pandemic/history/1918, with historical details (and also a link to current information http://www.flu.gov/index.html) and *Influenza encyclopedia* (University of Michigan Center for the History of Medicine) http://www.influenzaarchive .org/, an excellent, comprehensive searchable collection of primary source documents, images, timelines, reference lists, etc. which provides details of the impact of the epidemic on 50 U.S. cities.

The Centers for Disease Control and Prevention (CDC) provides maps and statistics of cases of human plague in the U.S. and worldwide at http://www.cdc.gov/plague/maps/.

374   Encyclopedia of plague and pestilence: From ancient times to the present. 3rd ed. George C. Kohn. New York: Facts On File, 2007. ISBN 9780816069354; 0816069352
614.403   RA649.E53
First ed., 1995; rev. ed., 2001. Description based on 2001 rev. ed.

Alphabetical listing by geographical location of major epidemic diseases (700 main entries), with the exception for names in common use (e.g., black death, HIV/AIDS epidemic, etc.). Same name but different dates are listed in chronological order. Cross-references. Further reading at the end of entry. Bibliography of selected secondary sources; index. Appendix 1: Entries by disease; Appendix 2: Geographical list of entries; Appendix 3: Timetable of plague and pestilence. Intended for general readers. *The Cambridge world history of human disease* provides further and more scholarly information in this subject area. Also available as an e-book.

Encyclopedia of pestilence, pandemics, and plagues is another resource in this area.

375   The evolution of surgical instruments: An illustrated history from ancient times to the twentieth century. John Kirkup. Novato, Calif.: Historyofscience.com, 2006. xviii, 510 p., [16] p. of plates, ill. (some col.) ISBN 0930405862
617/.9178/09   RD71.K53
Norman surgery series, no. 13; Norman science and technology series, no. 8; Norman science technology series, no. 8.

Contents: (1) Historical introduction; (2) Materials; (3) Structure & form; (4) Applied instrumentation.

General illustrated history of surgical instruments and apparatus. Instruments are grouped by forms and use. Each chapter covers the history of the instrument category up to the present time, identifying the surgeons and technology that made each advance possible. Ill. are mostly black and white; section with color plates. Appendix provides a list of museums worldwide exhibiting

surgical instruments. Bibliographical references (p. 449–465). Index.

Earlier titles on the subject include C. J. S. Thompson's *The history and evolution of surgical instruments,* Elisabeth's Bennion's *Antique medical instruments,* with focus on the aesthetic aspects of medical surgical instruments to 1879, and *American surgical instruments: The history of their manufacture and a directory of instrument makers to 1900 (Publ. notes).* Smith's *reference and illustrated guide to surgical instruments* is the result of a review of manufacturers' catalogs and contains "2,397 competitive pattern instruments with 7,560 variations and 2,210 exclusive pattern instruments . . . and over 140,000 entries of information" (*Pref.*) in use at the time.

376   Fact sheet, access to audiovisual materials. http://www.nlm.nih.gov/pubs/factsheets/lrc.html. National Library of Medicine (U.S.). Bethesda, Md.: National Library of Medicine. 2001–
Provides a description of NLM's audiovisual collection covering biomedical subjects: "60,000 audiovisual programs in almost 40 formats . . . over 3,500 . . . of historical interest"—*main page.* Includes instructions for on-site access, copyright restrictions for audiovisual materials, and other information. Online catalog access to identify audiovisual materials via LocatorPlus (52).

377   History of medicine. http://www.nlm.nih.gov/hmd/index.html. National Library of Medicine (U.S.). Bethesda, Md.: National Library of Medicine
610.02; 610.09   R131
"The NLM's History of Medicine Division collects, preserves, makes available, and interprets for diverse audiences one of the world's richest collections of historical material related to human health and disease.i}About Us page{/i} This website provides access to many full-text digitized books and collections (e.g., "Cholera online: a modern pandemic in texts and images," "FDA notices of judgment collection, 1906-1964," "Medicine in the Americas 1610-1920," and many others), images (Images from the history of medicine), and manuscripts (Digital manuscripts program) from its collections. Also provides quick links to NLM's catalogs (LocatorPlus [52], NLM catalog, IndexCat),

MEDLINE/PubMed, Profiles in science, archives and manuscripts finding aids (http://oculus.nlm.nih.gov/cgi/f/findaid/findaid-idx?c=nlmfindaid;page = simple), manuscripts, a "History of medicine finding aids consortium" (https://www.nlm.nih.gov/hmd/consortium/index.html), online exhibitions, Directory of history of medicine collections, and other resources. *Circulating now* (http://www.nlm.nih.gov/news/circulating_now_blog.html) is NLM's History of Medicine's blog featuring its historical collections. For scholars, researchers, and the general public.

378   History of medicine finding aids consortium. http://www.nlm.nih.gov/hmd/consortium/index.html. National Library of Medicine (U.S.), National Institutes of Health (U.S.). Bethesda, Md.: National Library of Medicine U.S. Dept. of Health, Education, and Welfare, National Institutes of Health. 2010- Continually updated resource.

This history of medicine finding aids consortium pilot project was created by archivists from different U.S. institutions to provide information about the content of their archival collections and also to provide inventories and links to finding aids to assist researchers in locating materials (e.g., historical documents, personal papers, business records, etc.). Currently includes "3,600 finding aids from 35 institutions that collect broadly in the area of the history of medicine and its allied sciences and more general special collections and archives."—*Website*.

379   History of the health sciences World Wide Web links. http://www.mla-hhss.org/histlink.htm. Patricia Gallagher, Stephen Greenberg, Medical Library Association, History of Medicine Section. [Chicago?]: Medical Library Association

Electronic access to the resources listed in ch. 4 ("What a tangled Web: World Wide Web resources in the history of the health sciences") of the print edition of *History of the health sciences*, under the following headings: "Organizations in the history of the health sciences," "History of the health sciences library collections," "History of the health sciences educational programs," "Organizations and museums with history of the health sciences interests," "Important figures in medicine—their lives and works," "Databases," "Link pages," "Oaths, prayers and declarations," "For children," "The history of diseases," "Bibliographies/chronologies/histories," "Listservs and newsgroups," and "Journals."

380   A history of the National Library of Medicine: The nation's treasury of medical knowledge. Wyndham D. Miles, National Library of Medicine (U.S.). Bethesda, Md.; Washington: U.S. Dept. of Health and Human Services, Public Health Service, National Institutes of Health, National Library of Medicine; For sale by the Supt. of Docs., U.S. G.P.O, 1982. viii, 531 p., ill., ports.
026/.61/0975284   Z733.N3M54

Presents a detailed history of the NLM (or its earlier official name, the Library of the Office of the Surgeon General, United States Army) from its beginnings in 1818 to the early 1980s, with chapters, for example, on the development of the Library during the Civil War, biographies of John Shaw Billings and Fielding Garrison, the beginning of indexing, the Index-catalogue and Index Medicus, the Library during WWI and WWII, modernizing the library and its services, and many others. Several appendixes include, for example, members of the Board of Regents, a selected chronology, biographies of staff members, etc. This title is also available online in a pdf edition at http://www.nlm.nih.gov/hmd/manuscripts/miles/miles.html.

A website, "The story of the NLM historical collections" (http://www.nlm.nih.gov/hmd/about/collectionhistory.html), provides related information.

381   The illustrated history of surgery. 2nd rev. and updated ed. Knut Hæger. London; Chicago: Fitzroy Dearborn Publ., 2000. 295 p., ill. (some col.)
ISBN 1579583199
617/.09   RD19.H34

Contents: ch. 1, The beginnings of medicine; ch. 2, The rise of Western surgery; ch. 3, Medieval medicine; ch. 4, Surgery in the Renaissance; ch. 5, Medicine becomes a science; ch. 6, The surgeons of the Enlightenment; v. 7, Surgery in the Age of Revolutions; ch. 8, The human face of surgery; ch. 9, The triumph of complex operations; ch. 10, The world of modern surgery. Detailed contents: http://www.loc.gov/catdir/toc/fy031/2001268056.html.

Survey of the development of surgery and the profession of surgery, from prehistoric to modern times. Includes information on herbal remedies, early anesthetics and procedures related to surgery, and the use of drugs. Includes portraits of famous surgeons. Contains approx. 200 color illustrations. Chronological table; bibliography; illustration sources; index. For specialists and general readers.

382   Images from the history of medicine. http://www.nlm.nih.gov/hmd/ihm/. National Library of Medicine (U.S.). Bethesda, Md.: National Library of Medicine

Images from the History of Medicine (IHM): "Database of over 70,000 images in the National Library of Medicine's (NLM) historical prints and photographs collection. The collection of portraits, photographs, fine prints, caricatures, genre scenes, posters, and other graphic art illustrates the social and historical aspects of medicine from the Middle ages to the present."—*IHM Fact Sheet* (http://www.nlm.nih .gov/pubs/factsheets/ihmfact.html). The IHM database can be searched by keyword or by browsing a list of terms. Further details via the IHM fact sheet.

383   Information sources in the history of science and medicine. Pietro Corsi, Paul Weindling. London; Boston: Butterworth Scientific, 1983. xvi, 531 p., ill.
ISBN 0408107642
509   Q125.I46
Consists of 23 topical chapters (e.g., "The history of technology," "Scientific instruments," "Medicine since 1500") written by authorities. Each chapter includes background and history, a discussion of the literature, and an extensive list of references. Remains the best guide and overview of the field. Indexed.

384   Medical discoveries: Who and when; a dictionary listing thousands of medical and related scientific discoveries in alphabetical order, giving in each case the name of the discoverer, his profession, nationality, and floruit, and the date of the discovery. J. E. Schmidt. Springfield, Ill.: Thomas, [1959]. ix, 555 p.
610.9   R131.S35
Lists biomedical and related scientific discoveries. Each entry contains the elements listed in the

descriptive subtitle. Information found in this resource could possibly be supplemented by *Medical firsts: From Hippocrates to the human genome* and *Medical discoveries: Medical breakthroughs and the people who developed them,* by Travers et al. written in nontechnical language.

385   Medical firsts: From Hippocrates to the human genome. Robert E. Adler. Hoboken, N.J.: John Wiley & Sons, 2004. vii, 232 p., ill. ISBN 0471401757
610/.9   R133.A43
Contents: Hippocrates: A principle and a method; Herophilus and Erasistratus: The light that failed; Marcus Varro: The germ of an idea; Dioscorides: The herb man of Anazarbus; Soranus: The birthing doctor; Galen of Pergamon: Combative genius; The enlightened mind of Abu Bakr al-Razi; Ibn al-Nafis, Galen's nemesis; Fracastoro: The poet of pestilence; Paracelsus, renaissance rebel; Andreas Vesalius, driven to dissection; Johann Weyer, a voice of sanity in an insane world; William Harvey and the movements of the heart; Edward Jenner, a friend of humanity; Such stuff as dreams are made on: The discovery of anesthesia; Antisepsis: Awakening from a nightmare; The quiet Dr. Snow; Pasteur and the germ theory of disease; Out of the corner of his eye: Roentgen discovers x-rays; Sigmund Freud's dynamic unconscious; Beyond bacteria: Ivanovsky's discovery of viruses; The prepared mind of Alexander Fleming; Margaret Sanger and the pill; Organ transplantation, a legacy of life; A baby's cry: The birth of in vitro fertilization; Humanity eradicates a disease—smallpox—for the first time; Cannibals, kuru and mad cows: A new kind of plague; Self, non-self and danger: Deciphering the immune system; Discovery can't wait—cracking the human genome; Into the future.

Presents medical discoveries and the famous and also less well-known individuals associated with these "medical firsts." Organized chronologically. Illustrations; references and further reading; index. Available online via Questia.

386   Medical heritage library. http://www .medicalheritage.org/. Internet Archive (Firm). San Francisco: Internet Archive. 2000–

Continually updated resource.

Digital collection of materials compiled collaboratively by many of the world's leading medical libraries (e.g., National Library of Medicine, Francis A. Countway Library of Medicine, Cushing/Whitney Medical Library, New York Public Library, and others) with historical resources in medicine. A growing and freely accessible collection of digitized medical rare books, pamphlets, journals, and films, with works from the past six centuries. Searchable and browsable.

See further details and list of contributors on the "About" page at http://www.medicalheritage.org/about/.

387   Medicine: An illustrated history.
Albert S. Lyons, R. Joseph Petrucelli. New York: H. N. Abrams, [1978]. 616 p., ill. ISBN 0810910543

610/.9   R131.L95

Reprint, ©1987.

Contents: Early types of medicine; Ancient civilizations; Greece and Rome; Medieval medicine; The fifteenth and sixteenth centuries; The seventeenth century; The eighteenth century; The nineteenth century (The beginnings of modern medicine); The twentieth century. Bibliography, p. 604–607.

Approx. 1,000 photographs from ancient to modern times, with explanatory text. Includes works of art, archaeological discoveries, mummies, portraits of famous physicians and scientists, and 19th and 20th century medical discoveries and developments.

388   Medicine in America: A short history.
James H. Cassedy. Baltimore: Johns Hopkins University Press, 1991. xi, 187 p. ISBN 0801842077

610/.973   R151.C375

Overview of the history of medicine and health care in America (colonial period through the 1980s), with broad coverage and emphasis on social history and medical developments being presented in their social and political context. Chronological arrangement. Bibliographical essay, arranged by subject headings, which includes only monographs. Index. For health professionals and also general readers, and considered a good starting point for students.

389   Medieval science, technology, and medicine: An encyclopedia. Thomas F. Glick, Steven John Livesey, Faith Wallis.

New York: Routledge, 2005. xxv, 598 p., ill. ISBN 0415969301

509.02   Q124.97.M43

Entries range from one to a few pages, focusing on European and Islamic topics. Entries include bibliographies and cross-references. A unique resource for this slice of science and technology development. One section of the *Routledge encyclopedias of the middle ages* series.

390   The progressive era's health reform movement: A historical dictionary.
Ruth C. Engs. Westport, Conn.: Praeger, 2003. xxii, 419 p.

RA395.A3E547 362.1/0973/03

0275979326

Covers 1880–1925, the time period labeled the Progressive era of the United States. Entries cover individuals (biographical information/assessment of historical importance), events, crusades (e.g., exercise, vegetarian diets, alternative health care), legislation, publications, and terms. Includes entries on the health reform movement and campaigns against alcohol, tobacco, drugs, and sexuality. For scholars, students, and general readers. "Selected chronology" (p. [371]–407), bibliographical references, and index. Also available as an e-book.

391   Surgery: An illustrated history. Ira M. Rutkow. St. Louis: Published by Mosby-Year Book Inc. in collaboration with Norman Publ., 1993. xiii, 550 p., ill. (some color), color maps. ISBN 0801660785

617.09   RD19.R88

Pictorial record of the history of surgery. Traces the development of surgery from its primitive beginnings. Includes brief biographies of famous surgeons, charts, and timelines. Other titles by Ira Rutkow include *American surgery: An illustrated history* and *The history of surgery in the United States, 1775–1900*.

Another title, *The Cambridge illustrated history of surgery* (revised edition of *History of surgery*, 2001) by Harold Ellis, written in an entertaining style for general readers and students, provides an introductory history of surgery. Of reference value is the chronological survey of surgical history from prehistoric times to the end of the 20th century. Contains, however, no notes and bibliography.

392 Turning the pages online. http://
archive.nlm.nih.gov/proj/ttp/intro.htm.
Lister Hill National Center for Biomedical
Communications, National Library of
Medicine (U.S.). Bethesda, Md.: National
Library of Medicine. 2003–
Produced by National Library of Medicine (NLM).

Turning the Pages Information System (TTPI),
initially created by the British Library (272). TTP
at NLM is the result of collaboration between the
British Library and NLM, with refinement of the
original technology. Detailed information about
research, design, system development, software,
and content available on website.

Web version provides access to the digitized
images of rare historic books in the biomedical sciences. Includes many important and influential
works in the history of medicine. Provides the ability to browse titles and bibliographic information, to
turn the pages, and to use zoom images. Information
regarding the mobile version of this resource is part
of NLM's Gallery of mobile apps and sites.

Bibliography

**393 Bibliotheca Osleriana a catalogue
of books illustrating the history of
medicine and science.** Sir William Osler,
Osler Library. Montreal: McGill-Queen's
University Press, 1969. xli, 792 p.
ISBN 0773590501
016.61   Z6676.O86
Catalog of the Osler Library. An earlier version
(Oxford: Clarendon Pr., 1929) described the basic
collection and had nearly as many entries as the
1969 ed. Some 8,000 entries in classed arrangement
with index. Particularly valuable for its annotations.

**394 A catalogue of printed books in the
Wellcome Historical Medical Library.**
Wellcome Historical Medical Library.
London: Wellcome Historical Medical
Library, 1962–2007. 5 v.
ISBN 1888262044 (set)
016.61   Z6676.W4
(Publications of the Wellcome Historical Medical
Library. Catalogue series)

Complete in 5 v. Spine title of v. 1–4, *A cata-
logue of printed books in the Wellcome Historical*
Library, v. 5, *A catalogue of printed books in the*
Wellcome Library.

Contents: v. 1, Books printed before 1641
(publ. 1962); v. 2, Books printed from 1641 to
1850 A–E (publ. 1966); v. 3, Books printed from
1641 to 1850 F–L (publ. 1976); v. 4. Books printed
from 1641 to 1850 M–R (publ. 1995); v. 5, Books
printed from 1641 to 1850 S–Z (publ. 2007).

Catalog of early printed books in the Wellcome
library. Reference source for medical historians and
bibliographers.

**395 A catalogue of seventeenth century
printed books in the National Library
of Medicine.** Peter Krivatsy, National
library of Medicine (U.S.). Bethesda,
Md.: U.S. Dept. of Health and Human
Services, Public Health Service, National
Institutes of Health, National Library of
Medicine, 1989. xiv, 1315 p.
016.61/09/032   Z6659.N38; R128.7
Shipping list no.: 89-261-P. Item 508-F.

For some 13,300 books printed 1601–1700,
"monographs, dissertations and corresponding
program disputations, broadsides, pamphlets and
serials" (*Introd.*), provides title page transcription,
physical description, and reference to standard
bibliographies. Entries are alphabetical by author,
editor, compiler, occasionally by corporate body,
and in a few instances by title. Most authors' names
are in vernacular form with cross-references to latinized or other names. There is no index, but the
National Library of Medicine's History of Medicine
Division maintains indexes of printers, publishers,
and vernacular imprints.

Complements earlier catalogs of pre–19th-
century holdings of NLM: *A catalogue of incunabula and manuscripts in the Army Medical Library,*
by Dorothy M. Schullian and Francis E. Sommer,
([1948?]); *A catalogue of sixteenth century printed*
books in the National Library of Medicine, comp. by
Richard J. Durling (1967); *A catalogue of incunabula*
and sixteenth century books in the National Library
of Medicine: first supplement, comp. by Peter Krivatsy (1971); and *A short title catalogue of eighteenth*
century printed books in the National Library of
Medicine, comp. by John Ballard Blake (1979, 11).

**396 Catalogue of Western manuscripts on
medicine and science in the Wellcome**

Historical Medical Library. S. A. J. Moorat, Wellcome Historical Medical Library. London: Wellcome Historical Medical Library, 1962–1973. 2 v. in 3, col. front

016.61 Z6611.M5W44

(Publications of the Wellcome Historical Medical Library; Catalogue series; MS1–MS3).

Contents: v. 1, Mss. written before 1650 A.D.; v. 2, Mss. written after 1650 A.D. (2 v.).

A group of titles not included in *A catalogue of printed books in the Wellcome Historical Medical Library. Catalogue of Western manuscripts in the Wellcome Library for the History and Understanding of Medicine: Western manuscripts 5120–6244*, publ. in 1999 and curated by Richard Palmer, is a continuation of the original two volumes.

397 A chronology of medicine and related sciences. Leslie T. Morton, Robert J. Moore. Aldershot, U.K.; Bookfield, Vt: Scolar Press; Ashgate Publ. Co, 1997. 784 p. ISBN 1859282156

610/.9 R133.M717

"Does not claim to be exhaustive but aims to portray the broad development of a wide field over a long period." (*Introd.*). Each year's entries are divided into three groups: a) Events (e.g., Nobel Prizes, the establishment of institutions, hospitals, etc., significant publications), b) Births: descriptive biographical entries for individuals; c) Deaths: name, year of birth, and subject keywords. Entries in groups a and b include a brief annotation and a bibliographic reference, and when available the citation number of Morton's medical bibliography. Index of personal names (listing of birth entry); subject index (subjects and corporate/institutional names); journal code list.

398 The Cole Library of early medicine and zoology: Catalogue of books and pamphlets. Nellie B. Eales. Oxford, U.K.: Alden P. [for] the University of Reading Library, 1969–1975. v, plate, facsim.

016.59 Z6676.R35

Contents: v. 1, 1472–1800; v. 2, 1800 to present day and supplement to v. 1.

A descriptive catalog of a distinguished collection. Chronological arrangement, with subject and author indexes.

399 Encyclopedia of medical sources. Emerson Crosby Kelly. Baltimore: Williams & Wilkins Co., 1948. v, 476 p.

016.61 Z6658.K4

The author "kept a list of references to medical eponyms and original works . . . A search for the earliest or best article has been conducted and great care has been exercised in copying the correct title with exact reference" (*Pref.*). This bibliography of first-to-publish articles is arranged alphabetically by investigator/author and gives the contribution with its citation in the literature. Includes an index to the specific condition, disease, medication, treatment, test, etc.

400 Health and British magazines in the nineteenth century. E. M. Palmegiano. Lanham, Md.: Scarecrow Press, 1998. ix, 282 p. ISBN 0810834863

016.6 Z6673.P288; RA776.5

Bibliography of 2,604 entries based on headlines and captions in major British Victorian serials (selected mainly from the *Wellesley index to Victorian periodicals 1824–1900*), providing a synopsis of health issues during this period that demonstrates "the evolution of popular thinking about the practice of human health . . . and outlines major concepts and investigates the formation of essential categories still in use, such as ideas of wellness and unwellness, the meaning of care and care-givers, and the productive status of being healthy"—*Publ. notes*. Indexed by author and subject.

401 History and bibliography of artistic anatomy: Didactics for depicting the human figure. Boris Röhrl. Hildesheim, Germany: Olms, 2000. xx, 493 p., ill. ISBN 3487110741

743.4/9 NC760.R65

Contents: pt. 1, History: ch.1, Introd., ch. 2, Anatomy in the art of the Ancient World and the Middle Ages; ch. 3, From the 13th to the 15th cent.; ch. 4, 16th cent.; ch. 5, 17th cent.; ch. 6, 18th cent.; ch. 7, 19th cent.; ch. 8, 20th cent.; ch. 9, definition of genres; pt. 2, Bibliography: (1) Bibliography and description of books A–Z; (2) Appendices: Selected list of secondary literature; Index of ill.; Index of persons; Index of places and schools of art.

Considered a reference book which contains the didactical structure and content of specific teaching manuals. Presents the different subgroups of medically oriented teaching and how anatomy was taught in schools. Includes, for example, Leonardo da Vinci's anatomical sketchbooks. The bibliography in pt. 2 contains "books on osteology, myology, morphology, and locomotion for artists. Treatises accompanying écorchés and theoretical essays. Manuals on proportions, expression and portrait drawing" (*t.p.*).

402   History of science, technology, and medicine database. http://www.hss online.org/teaching/teaching_database .html. History of Science Society, Society for the History of Technology, Istituto e museo di storia della scienza (Italy), Wellcome Library for the History and Understanding of Medicine, Research Libraries Group. Mountain View, Calif.: Research Libraries Group

"*History of Science, Technology, and Medicine* (402) is the definitive international bibliography on the development and influence of science, from prehistory to the present. It integrates four premier tools for historians: *Isis Current Bibliography of the History of Science*, *Current Bibliography in the History of Technology*, *Bibliografia Italiana di Storia della Scienza*, and citations from the Wellcome Library for the History and Understanding of Medicine (incorporating the former Wellcome Bibliography for the History of Medicine)."—*Publisher Website* Contains over 250,000 records, indexing journals since 1975.

403   History of the health sciences. 2nd rev. ed. Stephen J. Greenberg, Patricia E. Gallagher. Chicago: Medical Library Association, 2002. 142 p.

Z6660.8.G74

First ed. (1999) has title: *Bibkit: History of the health sciences.*

(MLA BibKit; no. 5).

Contents: ch. 1, In case of emergency, break glass: ready reference sources in the history of the health sciences; ch. 2, Medicine's greatest hits: primary sources in the history of the health sciences; ch. 3, Knowledge is of two kinds: secondary sources in the history of health sciences; ch. 4, What a tangled web: world wide web resources in the history of the health sciences: section 1, Organizations in the history of the health sciences; section 2, History of the health sciences library collections; section 3, History of the health sciences educational programs; section 4, Organizations and museums with history of the health sciences interests; section 5, Important figures in medicine—their lives and works; section 6, Databases; section 7, Link pages; section 8, Oaths, prayers and declarations; section 9, For children; section 10, The history of diseases; section 11, Bibliographies/chronologies/histories; section 12, Listservs and newsgroups; section 13, Journals.

Collaboration of a librarian and a historian in compiling this resource. Includes resources in medicine, nursing, and the allied sciences. Intended for reference librarians and library users, but not necessarily for history of medicine specialists. Accompanying computer disk provides links to the websites listed in chapter four. *History of the health sciences world wide web links*, a continually updated website, also provides electronic access to the resources listed in chapter 4.

404   Medical humanities dissertations. http://www.hsls.pitt.edu/histmed/ dissertations/. Jonathon Erlen, University of Pittsburgh Health Sciences Library System. Pittsburgh: Health Sciences Library, University of Pittsburgh Medical Center. 2001–

Provides a monthly current awareness service for selected recent medical dissertations and theses. Arranged by topics, currently covers the following areas: AIDS (social and historical contexts); alternative medicine (social and historical contexts); art and medicine; biomedical ethics; history of medicine prior to 1800; history of medicine and health care; history of science and technology; literature/theater and medicine; nursing history; pharmacy/pharmacology and history; philosophy and medicine; psychiatry/psychology and history; public health/international health; religion and medicine; women's health and history. To view complete citations, abstracts, and full-text of dissertations requires a subscription to Proquest dissertations and theses (PQDT).

405   Morton's medical bibliography: An annotated check-list of texts illustrating the history of medicine

(Garrison and Morton). 5th ed.
Leslie T. Morton, Jeremy M. Norman.
Aldershot, Hants, U.K.; Brookfield, Vt.:
Scolar Press; Gower, 1991. xxiv, 1243 p.
ISBN 0859678970
016.61   Z6660.8.M67; R131
First ed., 1943; 4th ed., 1983. Title varies.

A major revision of this classic work. A bibliography of 8,927 books and periodical articles in various languages and periods, early times to the present. Classed arrangement with brief annotations indicating the significance of the work in the history and development of the medical sciences; chronological arrangement within each subject category. Name and subject index.

406 Secondary sources in the history of Canadian medicine: A bibliography.
Charles G. Roland. Waterloo, Ont., [Canada]: Hannah Institute for the History of Medicine, 1984–2000. xxiii, 190 p. ISBN 088920182X
016.610971   Z6661.C3R64; R461
Vol. 2 has special title: *Bibliographie de l'histoire de la médecine*. Publ. varies.

Broad, enumerative retrospective bibliography, categorized by biographical listing, subject entries, and author listing. Contains published sources about events or persons. Entries do not contain annotations or library location(s). Further inclusions, exclusions, and omissions are mentioned in the introduction. Bibliographic references, list of journal abbreviations. Vol. 2 continues and also expands v. 1. It includes 1984–98 publications, and also many pre-1984 publications not included in v. 1. Vol. 2 contains more French-language material and is also available as an e-book.

Continuously maintained data files are available to scholars at McMaster University.

407 Sir William Osler: An annotated bibliography with illustrations.
Richard L. Golden, Charles G. Roland. San Francisco: Norman Publ., 1988. xv, 214 p., ill. ISBN 0930405005
016.61   Z8647.8.S55; R464
(Norman bibliography series; no. 1)
Revised and updated ed. of Maude E. Abbott's *Classified and annotated bibliography of Sir William Osler's publications,* 2nd ed. (Montreal: The Medical Museum, McGill Univ., 1939).

Contains 1,493 citations, some with annotations, arranged chronologically in 11 categories. This ed. includes a checklist of Osler's papers published under his pseudonym (Egerton Yorrick Davis) and a list of editions, printings, and translations of *The principles of medicine.* Supplemented by *Addenda to Sir William Osler: An annotated bibliography with illustrations,* with addenda and its index limited to new and revised entries.

408 Wellcome bibliography for the history of medicine. http://bibpurl.oclc.org/web/24. Wellcome Library for the History and Understanding of Medicine. [London]: Wellcome Library for the History and Understanding of Medicine. 2003–Jun. 2004
Publ. from May 2003 (no issues Jan.–Apr. 2003) until it ceased in Jul. 2004.

Continues: *Current work in the history of medicine,* publ. 1954–99. 1991–99, available both in print and online and continued as online publication with the same title, 2000–Dec. 2002.

Index of articles on the history of medicine, arranged by subject, with international coverage. Wellcome bibliography archive files (May 2000–Jun. 2004) are freely available via the Wellcome Library website, as will the entries created in the Library catalogue (cf. Wellcome website).

Now subsumed into Wellcome Library Catalogue. At http://wellcomelibrary.org/search-the-catalogues/search-by-subject, search for "history of medicine" to retrieve the collection.

409 WHO historical collection. http://www.who.int/library/collections/historical/en/print.html. World Health Organization. Geneva, Switzerland: World Health Organization. 2000s–
Produced by World Health Organization (WHO); part of WHO Library and Information Networks for Knowledge (LNK).

Covers conferences before the founding of the WHO, WHO official records, International Sanitary Conventions (since 1851), and official records, reports, and other published materials from the Office International d'Hygiène Publique (OIHP), the health organization of the League of Nations (UNRRA). Includes materials on plague, cholera, and yellow fever, and also more recent epidemics; international classifications and nomenclatures of diseases; and public health and medicine monographs on public health in different countries and languages. Related links are, for example, WHO-LIS: World Health Organization library database and WHO archives (http://www.who.int/archives/en/index.html). The distinctions between the WHO library, the WHO archives, and WHO records are described at http://www.who.int/archives/fonds_collections/partners/en/index.html.

Directories

410   Directory of history of medicine collections. http://wwwcf.nlm.nih.gov/hmddirectory/index.cfm/. Crystal Smith, National Library of Medicine (U.S.), History of Medicine Division. Bethesda, Md.: U.S. Dept. of Health & Human Services, National Institutes of Health, National Libray of Medicine, History of Medicine Division

Developed by the History of Medicine Division (HMD) of the the National Library of Medicine (NLM).

Contains locations and descriptions of medical history collections in the U.S., Canada, and other parts of the world. Subjects include, for example, dentistry, veterinary medicine, nursing, military medicine, and pharmacy. Collections are arranged alphabetically by U.S. state and city, followed by collections in foreign countries. Records provide the name and type (e.g., libraries, archives, museums) of collection, address, contact information, a detailed description of the collection, holdings, subject strengths, and services provided. Helpful to researchers in identifying medical history collections throughout the world. Participating institutions are able to keep their record up-to-date. New and revised data can be sent directly to the History of Medicine Division via the "Edit Your Collection" link below. A help page can be found at http://www.nlm.nih.gov/hmd/directory/help/advancedsearch.html, FAQs at http://www.nlm.nih.gov/hmd/about/faqs/hmddirectory/advancedsearch.html

Directory of history of medicine collections is also available as a print edition, published biennially since 1990. The 17th print edition was published in 2010.

Historical surveys

411   The Cambridge illustrated history of medicine. Roy Porter. Cambridge, U.K.; New York: Cambridge University Press, 1996. 400 p., ill. (some col.), col. maps. ISBN 0521442117
610/.9   R131.C232

A history of Western medicine from antiquity to the present in ten chapters. Includes a brief reference guide with chronology, major human diseases (in tabular format, listing disease, cause, and means of transmission), notes, further reading, and index of medical personalities. Ill. with prints, paintings, photographs, diagrams, maps, and tables. Written for general readers. *The Cambridge history of medicine* (Cambridge, 2006), also ed. by Roy Porter, contains a ten-page update, with the same text as the 1996 ed. but no ill.

412   Chiropractic: History and evolution of a new profession. Walter I. Wardwell. St. Louis: Mosby-Year Book, 1992. xv, 358 p., ill. ISBN 0801668832
615.5/34/0973   RZ225.U6W37

Includes bibliographical references (p. 289–340) and index.

Scholarly work on the history of chiropractic since its beginning in 1895, with chapters on the early leaders in the field, their schools, the struggle for licensing legislation and resulting medical opposition, and acceptance of chiropractic. Other titles in the history of chiropractic include *Chiropractic in America: the history of a medical alternative by Moore, Chiropractic: an illustrated history by Peterson et al.,* and *A history of chiropractic education in North America: Report to the Council on Chiropractic Education* (417).

413   Fragments of neurological history. John Pearce. London: Imperial College Press, 2003. xvii, 633 p., ill., ports.
616.809   RC338.P436

A collection of articles in the history of neurology and medicine. Includes, for example, biographical reviews (e.g., Galen and Vesalius), chapter entitled "Illness of the famous, and some medical truants," and chapters on anatomical and neurophysiological phenomena, dementias, headaches, cranial nerve and various other neurological disorders, and the origins of insulin and aspirin. For neurologists, neuroscientists, physicians, and general readers. Includes bibliographical references and index. Also available as an e-book.

414   The genesis of neuroscience.
A. Walker, Edward Laws, George Udvarhelyi, American Association of Neurological Surgeons. Park Ridge, Ill.: American Association of Neurological Surgeons, 1998. ISBN 1879284626
616.8009   QP353
Contents: ch. 1, Origins of neuroscience; ch. 2, From Galen through the 18th century: an overview; ch. 3, The evolution of encephalization; ch. 4, The spinal cord; ch. 5, The peripheral nerves; ch. 6, Clinical and pathological examination of patients with neurological disorders; ch. 7, Manifestation of cerebral disorders: headache, epilepsy, sleep disorders, and cerebrovascular disease; ch. 8, Congenital anomalies of the nervous system; ch. 9, Infections and inflammatory involvement of the central nervous system; ch. 10, The evolution of neurosurgery; ch. 11, Neuroscience comes of age. Appendixes (A)The arts in the evolution of neuroscience; (B) Medical fees throughout the ages; (C) Historical glossary of neurological syndromes; (D) Bibliography of writings by A. Earl Walker; Index.

Describes the origins of neurology and neurosurgery from prehistoric times until the 19th century. Includes portraits of many neurologists and neurosurgeons. Other titles in this area include *Fragments of neurological history* (413) and *History of neurology* (421).

415   The greatest benefit to mankind: A medical history of humanity. 1st American ed. Roy Porter. New York: W. W. Norton, 1998. xvi, 831 p., ill. ISBN 0393046346
610/.9   R131.P59
British ed. publ. with subtitle: *A medical history of humanity from antiquity to the present.*

Contents: (I) Introduction; (II) The roots of medicine; (III) Antiquity; (IV) Medicine and faith; (V) The medieval west; (VI) Indian medicine; (VII) Chinese medicine; (VIII) Renaissance; (IX) The new science; (X) Enlightenment; (XI) Scientific medicine in the nineteenth century; (XII) Nineteenth-century medical care; (XIII) Public medicine; (XIV) From Pasteur to penicillin; (XV) Tropical medicine, world diseases; (XVI) Psychiatry; (XVII) Medical research; (XVIII) Clinical science; (XIX) Surgery; (XX) Medicine, state and society; (XXI) Medicine and the people; (XXII) The past, the present and the future.

Explores the evolution of medicine through the ages and the development of medical specialties and medical practice. While viewpoint is global, emphasis is on Western medicine. Chronological table of contents, illustrations, bibliographical references (p. 719–764), and index.

416   Guardians of medical knowledge: The genesis of the Medical Library Association. Jennifer Connor. Chicago; Lanham, Md: Medical Library Association; Scarecrow Press, 2000. xi, 190 p., ill. ISBN 0810834707
026.61/06/073   Z673.M5C66
Medical Library Association (MLA), established in 1898.

Focuses on the early history of MLA and the physicians who founded and led the MLA. "Portrays the genesis of the Medical Library Association (MLA) through analysis of its origins, its dominant medical culture, and its intricate network of physician leaders" (*Author's descr.*). Includes a listing of MLA presidents, 1898–1998, officers of national associations, and other tables. Ill. Includes bibliographical references (p. [153]–180) and index.

417   A history of chiropractic education in North America: Report to the Council on Chiropractic Education. Joseph C. Keating, Alana K. Callender, Carl Service Cleveland, Association for the History of Chiropractic., Council on Chiropractic Education (U.S.). Davenport, Iowa: The Association, 1998. ix, 516 p., ill., ports. ISBN 0965913112
615.5/34/071173   RZ225.U6K425

"The story of the Council on Chiropractic Education (CCE) is an important piece of the saga of chiropractic education" (*Foreword*) and its struggles and successes in the development of the profession, quality education and training of doctors, and standard-setting and recognized accreditation.

Chronology of Events and Activities Related to the Application for Correspondent Status of the Sherman College of Chiropractic: p. 471–472. Includes bibliographical references (p. 473–494) and index.

418 A history of medicine. 2nd ed. Lois N. Magner. Boca Raton, Fla.: Taylor & Francis, 2005. xii, 611 p., ill.
ISBN 0824740742
610/.9   R131.M179
First ed., 1992.

Contents: Paleopathology and paleomedicine; Medicine in ancient civilizations: Mesopotamia and Egypt; The medical traditions of India and China; Greco-Roman medicine; The middle ages; The Renaissance and the scientific revolution; Native civilizations and cultures of the Americas; The Americanization of old world medicine; Clinical and preventive medicine; The medical counterculture: unorthodox and alternative medicine; Women and medicine; The art and science of surgery; Medical microbiology and public health; Diagnostics and therapeutics.

Survey of the major areas, themes, and important events of medicine and its famous men and women. Useful for students and general readers. Also available as an e-book.

Another well-regarded title by the same author is *History of infectious diseases and the microbial world*, available both in print and also as an e-book.

419 A history of medicine. 2d ed., rev. and enl. ed. Arturo Castiglioni, E. B. Krumbhaar. New York: Knopf, 1947. xxx, 1192, lxi p., illus., ports.
610.9   R131.C272

Translation of: *Storia della medicina* (rev. and enl. ed. Milan: A. Mondadori, 1936).

A comprehensive and readable source, especially strong in coverage of Greek and Roman history of medicine. Includes a useful bibliography (p. 1147–1192) arranged by subject. Index of subjects and index of names. Serves to supplement Fielding H. Garrison's Introduction to the history of medicine (421).

420 History of medicine in the United States. Francis R. Packard, Robert P. Parsons. New York: P. B. Hoeber, Inc., 1931 [i.e. 1932]. 2 v, front., ill., plates, ports., facsims.
R151.P12
Repr.: N.Y.: Hafner, 1963.

An enlargement of the author's earlier work (1901). Contains much useful reference material, in both text and ill., on American medical history, biography, and bibliography. Gives a bibliography of pre-Revolutionary medical publications and a general bibliography.

421 History of neurology. Fielding H. Garrison, Lawrence C. McHenry. Springfield, Ill.: Thomas, [1969]. xv, 552 p., ill., facsims., ports.
616.809   RC338.G36

Contents: ch. 1, Ancient origins; ch. 2, The Middle Ages and the Renaissance; ch. 3, The seventeenth century; ch. 4, The eighteenth century; ch. 5, The nineteenth century: Neuroanatomy; ch. 6, The nineteenth century: Neurophysiology; ch. 7, The nineteenth century: Neurochemistry; ch. 8, The nineteenth century: Neuropathology; ch. 9, Clinical neurology; ch. 10, The neurological examination; ch. 11, Neurological diseases.

A re-publication of Garrison's *History of neurology*, previously published in 1925 as a historical chapter in Charles L. Dana's *Textbook of nervous diseases*.

Presents a broad survey of neurology from antiquity to the beginning of the 20th century. Other more recent titles in the history of neurology are, for example, *A short history of neurology: The British contribution*, *The genesis of neuroscience*, *Fragments of neurological history*, and Stanley Finger's *History of neurology*, to name a few.

422 Illustrated history of medicine. Jean-Charles Sournia. London: Harold Starke Publ., 1992. 585 p., ill.
ISBN 1872457053
610.9   R131

Engl. language ed. of *Histoire de la médecine et des médecins* by Jean-Charles Sournia.

Contents: ch. I, The diseases of prehistory; ch. II, The continued existence of ethnomedicine; ch. III, The archaeology of medicine; ch. IV, The Greeks establish our system of medicine; ch. V,

The Middle Ages in the Mediterranean countries; ch. VI, Different types of medicine; ch. VII, Anatomy in the Renaissance; ch. VIII, The seventeenth century and the Age of Reason; ch. IX, Medicine in the Age of the Enlightenment; ch. X, Conversion to clinical medicine; ch. XI, Laboratory medicine; ch. XII, From X-rays to penicillin; ch. XIII, The explosion of knowledge and techniques; Appendices.

Extensive pictorial history of medicine. Includes bibliographical references (p. 562–63) and index.

423 An introduction to the history of medicine: With medical chronology, suggestions for study and bibliographic data. 4th ed., rev. and enl. ed. Fielding H. Garrison. Philadelphia: W.B. Saunders, 1929. 996 p., ill., ports. ISBN 0721640303
R131.G3
Errata slip tipped in after t.p. Repr., 1967. 1st ed., 1913; 3rd ed., 1921.

Valuable reference history, covering the whole history of medicine from the earliest times to the 1920s. Much biography and bibliography are included for every period. Appendixes include: a chronology of medicine and public hygiene; hints on the study of medical history; bibliographic notes for collateral reading including histories of medicine, medical biography, and histories of medical subjects. Index of personal names and index of subjects.

424 Science and technology in medicine: An illustrated account based on ninety-nine landmark publications from five centuries. Andras Gedeon. New York: Springer, 2006. vii, 551 p., ill. (some col.) ISBN 0387278745
610   R131.G43
Each of the 99 essays ("landmark publications") includes a brief biographical sketch, a description of the particular scientific and technological discovery, excerpts, and a summary of the original publication. Explains the significance and gives historical perspective and background for many medical techniques, 1528 to the present. Includes bibliography and timeline. Index of personal names. Also available as an e-book.

425 The Western medical tradition: 1800 to 2000. W. F. Bynum, Anne Hardy, Stephen Jacyna, Christopher Lawrence, E. M. Tansey. New York: Cambridge University Press, 2006. xiii, 614 p., ill. ISBN 0521475244
610   R131.W472
Contents: ch. 1, Medicine in transformation, 1800–49 (Stephen Jacyna); ch. 2, The rise of science in medicine, 1850–1913 (W. F. Bynum); ch. 3, Continuity in crisis: Medicine, 1914–45 (Christopher Lawrence); ch. 4, Medical enterprise and global response, 1945–2000 (Anne Hardy and E. M. Tansey).

"Gives an account of the last two centuries of the development of 'Western' medicine . . . [and a description of] important people, events, and transformations, . . . [and] explanations for why medicine developed as it did. . . . It contains . . . historical summaries of the development of medicine after the Second World War."—*Introd.* Considered a companion vol. to *The Western medical tradition, 800 B.C. to A.D. 1800.*

426 Western medicine: An illustrated history. Irvine Loudon. Oxford; New York: Oxford University Press, 1997. xvi, 347 p., [24] p. of plates, ill. (some color), facsims. (some color), maps, ports. (some color). ISBN 0198205090
610.9   R131.W47
Emphasis on art and visual representation. The Wellcome Iconographic Collections videodisc, containing 56,000 images on the history of medicine was used in designing this resource. Videodisc was made 1990–93 at the Wellcome Institute for the History of Medicine which was dissolved as of Oct. 2000 and is now called The Wellcome library: The library at Wellcome collection. Ranging from "Medicine in the classical world" to "Medicine in the second half of the twentieth century," with coverage of various medical themes related to the social history of medicine, medical education, the medical profession, public health, medical genetics, and molecular medicine. Further reading, chronology, glossary, and list of ill. sources. Index. Also available as an e-book.

427 Women, health, and medicine in America: A historical handbook. Rima D. Apple. New York: Garland Publ., 1990. xxii, 580 p., ill. ISBN 0824084470
610/.82   RA564.85.W664

Includes chapters on a wide variety of subjects, including Childbirth in America, 1650–1990, Historical perspectives on women and mental illness, and Race as a factor in health. Extensive bibliography and index.

Biography

428   African American firsts in science and technology. Raymond B. Webster. Detroit: Gale Group, 1999. xiii, 461 p., ill.
ISBN 0787638765
508.996073   Q141.W43
Chronology of firsts in various fields: Agriculture and Everyday Life, Dentistry and Nursing, Life Science, Math and Engineering, Medicine, Physical Science, and Transportation. Includes bibliography, index by year, occupational index, general index, and citations for first achievents. Over 1200 entries, 100 illustrations.

429   Bailey and Bishop's notable names in medicine and surgery. 4th ed.
Hamilton Bailey, W. J. Bishop, Harold Ellis. London: Lewis, 1983. xv, 272 p., ill. (some col.), ports. ISBN 0718604660
610/.92/2   R134
First ed., 1944–3rd ed., 1959, had title: *Notable names in medicine and surgery.* Includes biographical sketches (with portraits) of persons whose names are associated with particular diseases or medical discoveries, e.g., Potter's disease, Thomas's splint. Includes a list of biographies for additional reading. Indexed.

430   Blacks in science and medicine. Vivian O. Sammons. New York: Hemisphere, 1990. xii, 293 p. ISBN 0891166653
509.22B   Q141.B58
Presents biographical information, based on published sources, for more than 1,500 living and deceased individuals who have contributed to the development of science, medicine, and technology, focusing on contributions by African Americans in the United States. Entries are brief, in who's-who style, but include citations to the source material. Extensive bibliography. A very useful index to biographees is arranged by such categories as occupation, discipline, and

invention and notes "first black" and "first (black or white)" achievements.

431   Doctors and discoveries: Lives that created today's medicine. John Galbraith Simmons. Boston: Houghton Mifflin, 2002. xx, 459 p., ill.
ISBN 0618152768
610.922B   R134.5.S56
Profiles 86 individuals who are considered important and influential to contemporary medicine. In addition to the "figures of constant reference" (pt. III) from the past, also includes contemporary researchers. Source notes, bibliography, and index.

432   Doctors: The biography of medicine. 1st ed. Sherwin B. Nuland. New York: Knopf, 1988. xxi, 519 p., ill.
ISBN 0394551303
610.92/2B   R134.N85
Traces the development of modern medicine through the lives of famous physician-scientists (e.g., Hippocrates, Galen, Andreas Vesalius, Ambroise Paré, William Harvey, Giovanni Morgagni, and others) and discoveries and inventions (e.g., stethoscope, anesthesia, microscope, antiseptic surgery, "blue-baby operation, heart transplantation, and others). Includes "anecdotes and colorful episodes" (*Introd.*). Bibliography; index.

433   Germ theory: Medical pioneers in infectious diseases. Robert P. Gaynes. Washington: ASM Press, 2011. xii, 329 p., ill. ISBN 9781555815295
616.9/0410922   RB153.G39
Contents: Ch. 1, Introduction; ch. 2, Hippocrates, the father of modern medicine; ch. 3, Avicenna, a thousand years ahead of his time; ch. 4, Girolamo Fracastoro and contagion in renaissance medicine; ch. 5, Antony van Leeuwenhoek and the birth of microscopy; ch. 6, The demise of the humoral theory of medicine; ch. 7, Edward Jenner and the discovery of vaccination; ch. 8, Ignaz Semmelweis and the control of puerperal sepsis; ch. 9, Louis Pasteur and the germ theory of disease; ch. 10, Robert Koch and the rise of bacteriology; ch. 11, Joseph Lister, the man who made surgery safe; ch. 12, Paul Ehrlich and the magic bullet; ch. 13, Alexander Fleming and the

discovery of penicillin; ch. 14, Lillian Wald and the foundations of modern public health; ch. 15, Conclusions.

Covers the beginnings of Western medicine in ancient Greece to the discovery of penicillin and the beginnings of modern antimicrobial therapy. Includes well-researched biographies of the medical scientists who changed what is now known as infectious disease medicine and germ theory of disease. "Each of the individuals profiled . . . was responsible . . . for a paradigm shift in medical knowledge."—*Introd.* The concluding chapter provides an overview of current challenges in infectious disease medicine. References at the end of each chapter; index. For physicians, medical students, researchers, and general readers interested in the history of medicine. Also available as an e-book.

Another resource in this area, *Pioneers of bacteriology: Dictionary of the great scientists* by Renaud et al., is considered a quick reference tool to the history of bacteriology, with biographies of both well-known and also lesser-known scientists.

434   Profiles in science. http://www.profiles .nlm.nih.gov. National Library of Medicine (U.S.). Bethesda, Md: U.S. National Library of Medicine. 1998–
509.20904   Q141.P76

Profiles in Science® (National Library of Medicine), a collaboration of NLM's Lister Hill National Center for Biomedical Communications (http://www.lhncbc.nlm.nih.gov/) and NLM's History of Medicine Division.

Includes a growing number of scientists, physicians, and other leaders in biomedical research and health, providing access to the digitized archival collections of the papers, and other published and unpublished materials of the individual scientists. Further information at http://profiles.nlm.nih.gov/Help/About/.

435   Women and medicine. 3rd ed.
Beatrice Levin. Lanham, Md.: Scarecrow Press, 2002. x, 205 p., ill.
ISBN 0810842386
610/.82/0973   R692.L49
First ed., 1980; 2nd ed., 1988.

Contents: The dinosaur is twitching: famous firsts; To be a doctor in America: overcoming obstacles;

Shattering the glass ceiling: surgeons general and presidents' doctors; Historical perspectives: midwives and doctors around the globe; Women on the march: civil war heroines; Pioneers, o pioneers!: then and now; One university's contributions: those remarkable Johns Hopkins women; Oh, brave new world: Nobel Prize winners in medicine; Women's proper place: our biological selves; A peaceful revolution: the fight for birth control; What was the doctor wearing?: from white coats to space suits.

Comprehensive history of women experiencing and overcoming sexism in medical schools and the medical profession. Biographical chapters on many famous women in medicine, for example, on Elizabeth Blackwell, Janet Travell, Mary Putnam Jacobi, Marie Curie, and also other Nobel Prize (447) winners.

Bibliography

436   A bibliography of medical and biomedical biography. 3rd ed.
Leslie T. Morton, Robert J. Moore. Aldershot, England; Burlington, Vt.: Ashgate, 2005. xi, 425 p.
ISBN 0754650693
016.610922   Z6660.5.M67;R134
First ed., 1989; 2nd ed., 1994.

First ed., 1989 (begun as a 3rd ed. of John L. Thornton's *A select bibliography of medical biography*); 2nd ed., 1994.

Includes biographical references to 3,740 individuals in the biomedical sciences as well as in clinical medicine and surgery. Lists only English-language publications and provides references to biographies published in book form, among others to entries in *Dictionary of scientific biography* (449), *Biographical memoirs of fellows of the Royal Society*; *Obituary notices of fellows of the Royal Society*, Biographical memoirs of the National Academy of Sciences (456), and selected periodical references. An initial section of individual biographies is alphabetic by biographee, giving nationality, field, and notable accomplishments; location of archival materials is also indicated. A list of collective biographies follows, usually giving a brief description of the work, while a third section provides a short list of books on the history of medicine and related works, arranged by subject. Indexed by discipline; biographees are listed within each discipline by birth date. This edition also includes the names of individuals listed in Morton and Moore's *Chronology of medicine and related sciences (397)*.

437 The development of medical bibliography. Estelle Brodman. [Washington]: Medical Library Association, 1954. ix, 226 p., ports., diagrs.

016.61   Z6658.B7

(Publication [Medical Library Association]; no. 1)

Comprehensive survey of medical bibliography since 1500, covering printed medical bibliographies in Western languages that pertain to medicine in general rather than to its subdivisions or specialties. Personal bibliographies and bibliographies that do not make up the main portion of a work have been excluded, as have catalogs (with the exception of the *Index-catalogue of the Library of the Surgeon General's Office*). No distinction made between indexes and abstracts as bibliographies.

"For each bibliography discussed there is a biographical sketch of the compiler, a description of the work emphasizing advances in technique, and a discussion of the importance of the work in the history of medical bibliography."—*Introd.* Appendix 1 lists references; appendix 2 lists medical bibliographies since 1500 which were not discussed in the body of the text, arranged by century. General and author indexes. A digitized version of this book is available at http://www.nlm.nih.gov/hmd/collections/digital/brodman/brodman.html as part of the National Library of Medicine's History of Medicine digital collections. Like this work, *The great medical bibliographers: A study in humanism*, by John F. Fulton, identifies important medical bibliographies and bio-bibliographies.

438 Disease and destiny: A bibliography of medical references to the famous. Judson Bennett Gilbert. London: Dawsons of Pall Mall, 1962. 535 p.

016.92   Z6664.A1G5

Drawn largely from *Index-catalogue of the library of the Surgeon General's office* (IndexCat), *Index medicus*, and *Quarterly cumulative index medicus*.

A bibliography of writings that treat the medical history of famous people in history, the humanities, and the arts and sciences in all countries from ancient to modern times. Personalities are listed alphabetically and identified by dates of birth and death and a brief descriptive phrase. Books and papers about them are listed in chronological order. Introduction contains a bibliography of monographic literature of medicobiographical writing.

439 Doctors, nurses, and medical practitioners: A bio-bibliographical sourcebook. Lois N. Magner. Westport, Conn.: Greenwood Press, 1997. xiii, 371 p. ISBN 0313294526

610/.92/2B   R153.D63

Biographical information on 56 "significant but lesser known individuals . . . outside their own country . . . extraordinary . . . yet unsung" (*Introd.*), covering the time period 1710–1924, with essays focusing on the life and career. Bibliographic references include archival materials and works written by and about the particular individual. Appendixes: (A), Listing by occupations and special interests; (B), Listing by date of birth; (C), Listing by place of birth; (D), Listing of women practitioners. Intended for students and scholars.

Great Britain

440 Biographical memoirs of fellows of the royal society. Royal Society (Great Britain). London: Royal Society, 1955–. 49+ vols., ill.

0080-4606   Q41.L8476

Continues *Obituary notices of fellows of the royal society* (1932–54), and previous notices were published in *Proceedings of the royal society*. Vol. 75 (1905) of the *Proceedings* contained obituaries of deceased fellows chiefly for 1898–1904 with a general index to previous notices from 1860–99. Contains long biographical articles with excellent autographed ports. of deceased members of the Royal Society, including foreign members. Usually includes bibliographies, some quite extensive. Also available online through JSTOR.

441 Plarr's lives of the fellows of the Royal college of surgeons of England. Victor Plarr. Bristol; London: Printed and publ. for the Royal College of Surgeons by J. Wright & Sons Ltd.; London, Simpkin, Marshall Ltd., 1930. 2 v.

R489.A1P5

At head of title: *Thelwall Thomas memorial.*

Biographies of fellows from those elected in 1843 (founding date of the fellowship) through those who died before 1930. Much of the information was obtained from obituary notices or from friends and relatives of the fellows. For each fellow, includes references to publications sufficient to indicate the subjects in which each was interested.

Continued by: Sir D'Arcy Power and William Richard Le Fanu, *Lives of the fellows of the Royal College of Surgeons of England, 1930–1951,* publ. 1953 (biographies of fellows who died from 1930 to the end of 1951, including some who died before 1930 but were omitted from Plarr's list; includes lists of publications); R.H.O.B. Robinson and W. R. Le Fanu, *Lives of the fellows of the Royal College of Surgeons of England, 1952–1964,* publ. 1970; James Paterson Ross and W.R. Le Fanu, *Lives of the fellows of the Royal College of Surgeons of England, 1965–1973,* publ. 1981; *Lives of the fellows of the Royal College of Surgeons of England, 1983–1990,* ed. by Ian Lyle and Selwyn Taylor, publ. 1995; John P. Blandy, *Lives of the fellows of the Royal College of Surgeons of England, 1991–1996,* publ. 2000; *Lives of the fellows of the Royal College of Surgeons of England, 1997–2002* (with a cumulated index to the previous volumes).

International

442 Biographical dictionary of medicine.
Jessica Bendiner, Elmer Bendiner. New York: Facts on File, 1990. 284 p.
ISBN 0816018642
610/.92/2B   R134.B455

Subjects are included on the basis of their importance to the history of medicine. Entries vary in length from one paragraph to several pages. Includes a chronology of important events in the history of medicine and a brief bibliography. Separate name and subject indexes.

443 A biographical dictionary of women healers: Midwives, nurses, and physicians. Laurie Scrivener, J. Suzanne Barnes. Westport, Conn.: Oryx Press, 2002. x, 340 p., ports.

ISBN 157356219X
610.820922B21   R692.S38

Alphabetically arranged brief entries include names, dates, education, professional organizations, etc., from Colonial times to the present. Includes 240 American and Canadian women. Appendix 1 is a listing of individuals by occupation (nurses, midwives, physicians); appendix 2 provides a time line of events and the historical context in which women practiced. Provides a starting point for further research. *Dictionary of American nursing biography, Women in medicine: An encyclopedia* (455), and *American midwives: 1860 to the present* provide added information on women in the health professions.

444 A biographical encyclopedia of medical travel authors. Edward A. Martin, Peter Froggatt. Lewiston, N.Y.: Edwin Mellen Press, 2010–. v. 1–6.
ISBN 9780773436817
610.922   R134.M325

Vol. 1, The Americas and Canada; v. 2, Australia and New Zealand, South Africa, and the Pacific and Antarctica; v. 3, Continental Europe; v. 4, England and Wales; v. 5, Ireland; v. 6, Scotland.

Biographical sketches with often little-known travel descriptions of doctors and other medical professionals, with ".selection targeted on medical travel authors of the Western Hemisphere between the Poles" (*Pref.*), mostly from recent centuries and mostly men. The author's sources include published materials, both in print and on the Web. Also available as an e-book.

445 Biography index. http://www.ebscohost.com/academic/biography-index-past-and-present. EBSCO Publishing. Ipswich, Mass.: EBSCO Publishing. 2006

Z5301

Indexes English-language biographical material found in periodicals, individual and collective biographical books, selected *New York Times* obituaries, and other sources. Published until 2011 by the H. W. Wilson Company. Successor to the print format *Biography index* by Joseph publ. quarterly with annual cumulations and index by profession, which has been indexed in Biography and Genealogy Master Index (Gale/Cengage Learning). Earlier content is offered in Biography Index Retrospective: 1905-1982.

446 Catalog of biographies. Boston: G. K. Hall, 1960. 165 p.
016.9261 R134.N4
A photographic reproduction of the New York Academy of Medicine Library's shelflist (54), containing "single biographies of physicians and scientists, with a few autobiographies, family histories, and occasional biographies written by physicians."—*Introd.*
Available online at http://hathitrust.org.

447 A century of Nobel prize recipients: Chemistry, physics, and medicine.
Francis Leroy. New York: Marcel Dekker, 2003. 380 p., ill. (chiefly color), ports. (some color). ISBN 0824708768
509.22B Q141.C252
Provides biographical profiles of Nobel laureates from 1901–2001. Contains many graphics and descriptions of models, making the content available to a nontechnical audience. Each discipline also contains an introd. describing the advances in the field over the past cent., providing context for the award winners. Also available as an e-book.

448 Dictionary of medical biography. W. F. Bynum, Helen Bynum. Westport, Conn.: Greenwood Press, 2006. 5 v. (xl, 1415 p.), ill. ISBN 0313328773
610 R134.D57
Contents: v. 1, A–B; v. 2, C–G; v. 3, H–L; v. 4, M–R; v. 5, S–Z.

Biographies, with mention of relevant scientific and social context, of healers, medical practitioners, and physicians from all cultures from ancient times to the present. Emphasis is on Western medicine, but also includes essays that provide an introduction to Chinese, Islamic, Japanese, South Asian, and Southeast Asian medicine, and entries on traditional and alternative medicine. Each entry includes brief bibliographies of primary and secondary literature references. Illustrations, name, and subject index. Also available as an e-book.

449 Dictionary of scientific biography.
Charles Coulston Gillispie, Frederic Lawrence Holmes, American Council of Learned Societies. New York: Scribner, 1980–1990. 18 v. ISBN 0684169622
509.22B Q141.D5

New ed. publ. in December 2007, available as eight new print vols. Available online in two e-book versions, as the 8-vol *New Dictionary of Scientific Biography* or as the 26-vol. *Complete Dictionary of Scientific Biography* that consists of the 18-vol. original set plus the 8 new vols. See details at http://www.gale.cengage.com/ndsb/about.htm.

Description based on set publ. 1980–90. Work is internat. in coverage, including scientists from all periods of history (excluding living persons), and encompassing the fields of astronomy, biology, chemistry, earth sciences, mathematics, and physics. Technology, medicine, and social sciences are only included as they relate to the above sciences. Focuses on scientists whose work made a difference to the discipline. Signed articles include bibliographies of original and secondary works. In some cases the article is the first or most comprehensive study of a figure's total contribution to science.

Vols. 15–18 are suppl., including more recent scientists or those whose entries were not ready for the main edition of the work, and including supplementary features, such as topical essays on the achievements of ancient civilizations.

New dictionary of scientific biography contains new articles about scientists dying after 1980 and earlier figures omitted from the original Dictionary together with articles updating, but not replacing, entries in the original. Unlike the original, psychology and anthropology are covered, with some sociology and economics.

450 The founders of neurology: One hundred and forty-six biographical sketches by eighty-eight authors.
2nd ed. Webb Haymaker, Francis Schiller. Springfield, Ill.: Thomas, [1970]. xxi, 616 p., ports
616.80922 R134.H29
First ed., 1953 had subtitle: One hundred and thirty-three biographical sketches prepared for the Fourth International Neurological Congress in Paris by eighty-four members, ed. by Webb Haymaker and Karl A. Baer.

Rev. ed. Contents: section I, Neuroanatomists of earlier times (born before 1850); section II, Neuroanatomists in more recent times; section III, Neurophysiologists; section IV, Investigators of neural transmission and neurochemistry; Neuropathologists; section VI, Clinical neurologists; section VII,

Neurosurgeons; section VIII, A neurohistorian; section IX, Other sources for the history of neurology.

Short biographies with brief historical information and portraits. Arrangement is alphabetical within subspecialties. A chapter on "The meaning of some of the academic terms used in the biographies" explains the academic hierarchies in France, Germany, and Great Britain. Name index; subject index.

451 **The global history of paleopathology: Pioneers and prospects.** Jane E. Buikstra, Charlotte A. Roberts. Oxford; New York: Oxford University Press, 2012. xvii, 798 p., ill. ISBN

560.92/2   R134.85.A1G56

Contents: Pt. I, "Biography"; pt. II, "Moments"; pt. III, "Regions"; pt. IV, "Topics"; pt. V, "Organizations, key congresses, and education in paleopathology; pt. VI, "Future developments."

Compendium on the history of paleopathology, defined as the interdisciplinary study that focuses on the study of ancient disease. Regions include Africa, the Americas, and Eurasia. Topics explored are, for example, the first dental pathologists and paleopathologists, and mummies & bog bodies. Also addresses nonhuman paleopathology and recent developments, such as using DNA techniques to study human disease and current and future trends in imaging techniques.

452 **The medical practitioners in medieval England: A biographical register.** C. H. Talbot, Eugene Ashby Hammond. London: Wellcome Historical Medical Library, 1965. x, 503 p.

610.922   R489.A1T3

Inspired by Ernest Wickersheimer's *Dictionnaire biographique des médecins en France au Moyen Age* (Paris: E. Droz, 1936), but entries are generally longer than in that work. The period covered is from Anglo-Saxon times to about 1518, and physicians of England, Scotland, and Wales are included. Bibliographical references follow the articles, and the general index offers geographical and a wide variety of topical subject approaches.

453 **Nobelprize.org**. http://nobelprize.org. Nobelstiftelsen; Nobel Web AB. Stockholm, Sweden: Nobel Foundation

Official website of the Nobel Foundation. Contains comprehensive list of winners since 1901; biographies; history of prizes; award ceremonies; and interesting facts about the laureates.

See also *Nobel Foundation directory*.

Although dated, *Who's who of Nobel Prize winners, 1901–2000* by Sherby et al., is useful for its topical index and cites the nationality, religion, and education of the winners, which is not consistently listed in other sources.

Ig Nobel Prizes, an internationally-acclaimed parody of the venerable Nobel Prize ceremony and awards, is held at Harvard University every October and receives wide press coverage and attention.

454 **A select bibliography of medical biography: With an introductory essay on medical biography. 2nd ed.** John Leonard Thornton. London: Library Assoc., 1970. 170 p., 7 plates, illus., ports. ISBN 0853652422

016.61/0922   Z6660.5.T5

First ed., 1961, by Thornton, A. J. Monk, and E. S. Brooke.

Contains citations to books in English published in the 19th and 20th centuries. Includes more than 400 biographees. Nearly 100 collective biographies are listed in a separate section. Indexed.

455 **Women in medicine: An encyclopedia.** Laura Lynn Windsor. Santa Barbara, Calif.: ABC-CLIO, 2002. xx, 259 p., ports. ISBN 1576073920

610/.82/0922B   R692.W545

Includes biographies of "women who throughout history have made a significant impact on medicine" (*Pref.*). Arranged alphabetically, with cross-references. Each entry concentrates on the woman's accomplishments. Focus on women physicians, nurses, and researchers, but also includes entries on related information such as "institutions, medical terms, and social issues relevant to women in medicine" (*Pref.*). Includes women from outside North America and Western Europe. Ill., bibliography, and index.

Comparable sources are *American nursing: a biographical dictionary* (1119); *Dictionary of American nursing biography*; *American midwives: 1860 to the present*, and (as a good starting point for high school and college students) *Biographical dictionary of women healers: midwives, nurses, and physician* (443).

Kate Campbell Hurd-Mead's *A history of women in medicine from the earliest times to the beginning of the nineteenth century* continues to be a useful resource.

United States

456 Biographical memoirs of the national academy of sciences. http://www.nas online.org/publications/biographical -memoirs. National Academy of Sciences. Washington: National Academy of Sciences
Q141

This website provides free access to all the *Biographical memoirs* of the National Academy of Sciences, since 1995, of deceased members of the academy. The academy is actively digitzing volumes from 1877 to 1995. The print vols. will remain valuable until all are available online. Memoirs can be the most authoritative and detailed account of the lives of selected scientists, and include selective bibliographies of their works.

457 Dictionary of American medical biography. Martin Kaufman, Stuart Galishoff, Todd Lee Savitt. Westport, Conn.: Greenwood Press, 1984. 2 v. (xvi, 1027 p.) ISBN 031321378X
610/.92/2B   R153.D53

Includes over 1,000 persons from the 17th century to those of the 20th century who had died prior to Dec. 31, 1976. "The major contribution of [this] work is the inclusion of biographical sketches representing developments which occurred after the publication of Kelly and Burrage [*Dictionary of American medical biography*. N.Y.: Appleton, 1928]" (*Pref.*). Coverage extends outside the medical mainstream—blacks and women; nonphysicians such as biochemists, medical educators, administrators; and "health faddists, patent medicine manufacturers, unorthodox practitioners, and others whose major role was to provide alternatives to traditional medicine."

A typical entry gives full name, date and place of birth, date and place of death, occupation and area of specialization, parents' names and occupations, marital information, career information, contributions, and a maximum of five citations to important or representative works. The appendix gives a listing by date of birth, place of birth, state where

prominent, occupation and specialty, medical college or graduate level college, and females. Indexed.

A companion work is *Dictionary of American nursing biography*.

458 Dictionary of American medical biography: Lives of eminent physicians of the United States and Canada, from the earliest times. Howard A. Kelly, Walter L. Burrage. New York, London: D. Appleton and Co., 1928. 2 p.l., vii-xxx, 1364 p
R153.K3

Publ. in 1912 under title *A cyclopedia of American medical biography: Comprising the lives of eminent deceased physicians and surgeons from 1610 to 1910*, 2 v., and in 1920 under title *American medical biographies*. Repr.: Boston: Milford House, 1971.

Biographies with bibliographies of 2,049 deceased American and Canadian physicians and surgeons from colonial days to 1927. Supersedes Howard A. Kelly's *Cyclopedia of American medical biography* and *American medical biographies* (1920), although each edition includes new biographical sketches, some material is dropped from each; therefore, the earlier editions may still be useful.

459 Who's who in medicine and healthcare. New Providence, N.J.: Marquis Who's Who, 1996–
0000-1708   R153.W43

Description based on 2011–12 edition. Compilation of biographical information on medical professionals, including administrators, educators, researchers, clinicians, and other medical and healthcare personnel. This edition contains 27,150 biographical profiles. Listings include full name, occupation, date/place of birth, family background, education summary, writings, and association memberships and awards.

The biographical profiles included in this resource are also available online as part of Marquis biographies online through a subscription.

Statistics

460 AAMC data book. Association of American Medical Colleges, Division of Medical School Services and Studies,

AAMC Data Services. Washington: Association of American Medical Colleges, 1990-. v.

610.71 2150-8720   R745

Subtitle varies. Description based on 2013 ed. Subtitle: Medical schools and teaching hospitals by the numbers. Full data tables are available only to AAMC Councils, organizations, group members, and other members of the medical school community and requires to sign in at http://www .aamc.org.

2013 table of contents available at https:// www.aamc.org/download/280206/data/tableof contents.pdf

Covers data and trends on U.S. medical schools and teaching hospitals, provides current and historical statistical data on U.S. medical schools and teaching hospitals, with revisions posted to the Association of American Medical Colleges (AAMC) website. According to the publisher, answers questions concerning accredited medical schools, medical school applicants and students, medical school faculty, medical school revenue, graduate medical education, tuition, financial aid, & student debt. Also provides information on health care financing, research expenditures, physicians, faculty compensation, and general/historical price indexes.

461   AHA hospital statistics. American Hospital Association, Health Forum (Organization). Chicago: Healthcare InfoSource, 2005–

0090-6662   RA981.A2A6234

Title varies: Prior to 1971 issued as part 1 of the annual guide issue of *Hospitals*; 1971–90, *Hospital statistics*; 1991–97, *American Hospital Association hospital statistics*; 1998–2004, *Hospital statistics*. Editions starting in 1998 draw data from the 1996– *AHA annual survey of hospitals*. Statistical complement to the AHA guide to the health care field.

Description based on 2012 ed. Subtitle: *The comprehensive reference source for analysis and comparison of hospital trends*.

Compilation of data on trends, including emerging trends, in the hospital field through 2010. Additions in recent years include community health indicators, utilization, personnel, and finance by all metropolitan statistical areas (MSAs), five-year trend data, breakdowns between inpatient and outpatient care, and facilities and services information.

Includes "Historical trends in utilization, personnel, and finances for selected years from 1946-2010." Includes section on "Statistics for multihospital health care systems and their hospitals." A glossary explains specific terms used in the tables and text of this volume. Hospitals included are not necessarily identical to those included in the *AHA guide to the health care field* (282).

462   American health: Demographics and spending of health care consumers. New Strategist Publications, Inc. Ithaca, N.Y.: New Strategist Publications, 2005–. xvi, 504 p., ill. ISBN 1885070748

614.4273   RA445.A442

Publ. 1998–2000 as *Best of health: demographics of health care consumers*.

(American consumer series)

1st, 2005 ed.; 2nd ed., 2007. Description based on 3rd ed., 2010.

Contents: ch. 1, Addictions; ch. 2, Aging; ch. 3, Alternative medicine; ch. 4, Attitudes towards health care; ch. 5, Births; ch. 6, Coverage and cost; ch. 7, Deaths; ch. 8, Disability; ch. 9, Diseases and conditions; ch. 10, Health care visits; ch. 11, Hospital care; ch. 12, Mental health; ch. 13, Sexual attitudes and behavior; ch. 14, Weight and exercise.

Data on health care consumers from many different sources, including information from the federal government (e.g., National Center for Health Statistics, (63) incl. *Health, United States* (481), Consumer Expenditure Survey (http://www.bls.gov/cex/), MEPS Medical Expenditure Panel Survey (493), to name a few). Contains more than 300 tables, graphs, a glossary, bibliographical references, and index. Also available as an e-book.

463   American hospital association. http://www.aha.org/aha_app/index.jsp. American Hospital Association. Chicago: American Hospital Association

Founded in 1898, the association represents hospitals, health care networks, and their consumers. The website provides "Fast Facts on U.S. Hospitals," reports and studies, trends, testimony, regulations, and a section for members only. Some information is only available for a fee.

464   Atlas of cancer. 2nd ed. Maurie Markman. Philadelphia: Current

Medicine LLC, 2008. x, 662 p., color ill.
ISBN 9781573402897

616.99400223   RC262.A846

Contents: (I) Head and neck; (II) Gynecologic cancer; (III) Lung cancer; (IV) Upper gastrointestinal cancers; (V) Lower gastrointestinal cancers; (VI) Leukemia; (VII) Lymphoma; (VIII) Sarcoma; (IX) Breast cancer; (X) Genitourinary cancers; (XI) Skin cancer; (XII) Neuro-oncology.

"The intent.is to present information in a highly visual format, both to showcase the dynamic nature of the topics and to ensure that important messages are conveyed."—*Pref.* Each section provides a summary introduction to a particular cancer, with U.S. statistics, epidemiology and etiology, histology, genetics, staging, major risk factors, imaging, surgical management, treatment modalities, prevention, and other information as appropriate to the specific cancer. Each chapter includes a list of references. Index.

465 Atlas of health in Europe. 2nd ed.
World Health Organization.; Regional Office for Europe. Copenhagen, Denmark: WHO Regional Office for Europe, 2008. vii, 126 p., col. ill., maps.
ISBN 9789289014106

614.4/24   G1797.21.E55 W5

First ed., 2003.

Contents: 1. Demography; 2. Life and death; 3. Diseases; 4. Lifestyles and environment; 5. Health care.

The WHO Regional Office for Europe consists of 53 member states.

This resource updates the 2003 ed. It pulls together health and disease-related statistics, with "new data on relevant health issues in the WHO European Region . . . to better reflect the new challenges confronting public health. Rich and elaborate data from various sources have been gathered, systematized, grouped and reformatted to help readers to go through them and gain an overall picture of health in the Region, to the extent it can be expressed in figures."—*Foreword.* Data covered are from 1980 at the earliest to 2006 at the latest, depending on the data available in countries. For undergraduates through faculty/researchers, also general readers. A freely available PDF version available at http://www .euro.who.int/__data/assets/pdf_file/0011/97598/ E91713.pdf

466 The Cambridge dictionary of statistics. 4th ed. Brian S. Everitt, Anders Skrondal. Cambridge, U.K.; New York: Cambridge University Press, 2010. ix, 468 p., ill.
ISBN 9780521766999

519.503   QA276.14

Includes nearly 4000 entries. Covers medical, survey, theoretical, and applied statistics, including computational aspects, and standard and specialized statistical software. The 4th ed. expands on Bayesian statistics, causality and machine learning. Also includes brief biographies of more than 100 noteworthy statisticians. Definitions include mathematical detail and graphical material for completeness and clarity. Many definitions include references to other books and articles for further information. Useful for specialist and nonspecialist alike. Also available as an e-book.

467 The Cambridge dictionary of statistics in the medical sciences. Brian Everitt. Cambridge, U.K.; New York: Cambridge University Press, 1995. 274 p., ill.
ISBN 0521473829

610/.21   RA407.E94

Concise definitions and brief explanations of approx. 2,000 statistical terms and concepts used in the biomedical sciences. Also includes relevant mathematical, computing, and genetic terms. Graphical illustrations and numeric examples. *The Cambridge dictionary of statistics* (3rd ed., 2006) by the same author also covers medical statistics.

468 Cancer facts and figures. http://www .cancer.org/Research/CancerFactsFigures/ CancerFactsFigures/index. American Cancer Society. Atlanta: American Cancer Society. 1997–

Part of the services provided by American Cancer Society (ACS), a nationwide, community-based voluntary health organization. Also publ. in print format since 1956.

Description based on the 2013 ed. http:// www.cancer.org/research/cancerfactsfigures/ cancerfactsfigures/c ancer-facts-figures-2013

Contents: Cancer: Basic facts; Selected cancers; Special section: Pancreatic cancer; Cancer disparities; Tobacco use; Nutrition and physical activity; Environmental cancer risks; The global fight against cancer; The American Cancer

Society; Sources of statistics; Screening guidelines for the early detection of cancer in average-risk asymptomatic people

Provides basic facts and data about cancer in general and selected cancers, cancer incidence, risk factors, mortality, and survival. Annual estimates of expected new cases and deaths. Each issue also has a special section that addresses different topics (e.g., 2012, cancers with increasing incidence in the U.S., 1999-2008; 2011, cancer disparities and premature death; 2010, prostate cancer; 2009, multiple primary cancers; 2008, insurance and cost-related barriers to cancer care; 2007, cancer-related pain; 2006, environmental pollutants and cancer; 2005, cancers linked to infectious diseases; 2004, cancer disparities, etc.). Also includes, for example, trends in cigarette smoking, fruit and vegetable consumption, physical inactivity, overweight and obesity, and screening exams. Additional statistics on various topics and estimates of new cases and a glossary of cancer-related terms are provided at http://www.cancer.org/docroot/stt/stt_0.asp.

SEER cancer statistics review and the National Cancer Institute's SEER (Surveillance Epidemiology and End Results) program (http://seer.cancer.gov) are other sources for authoritative information on cancer statistics.

469   County health rankings & roadmaps.
http://www.countyhealthrankings.org/. Robert Wood Johnson Foundation, University of Wisconsin Population Health Institute. Madison, Wisc.: University of Wisconsin Population Health Institute. 2010–

RA407.3

Part of the County Health Rankings & Roadmaps program, a collaboration between the Robert Wood Johnson Foundation and the University of Wisconsin Population Health Institute. Further information at http://www.countyhealthrankings.org/about-project.

A map of the U.S. allows to click on individual states to show county-by-county health data and the rank of the health of "nearly every county in the nation."—*Website*. Provides data of the overall health of each county and helps with understanding the factors that affect health (e.g., income, limited access to health foods, air and water quality, smoking, obesity, etc.) Offers various display options for data. FAQs (http://www.countyhealthrankings

.org/faq-page) answer general and methodology questions. For all audiences.

470   Diversity in the physician workforce.
https://members.aamc.org/eweb/ DynamicPage.aspx?webcode=PubByTitle. Association of American Medical Colleges. Washington: Association of American Medical Colleges. 2006-
331.6 2162-3791   R693
(Facts & figures data series [AAMC])

2006- editions published in this series are accessible from AAMC's "browse by title" publications page https://members.aamc.org/eweb/DynamicPage.aspx?webcode=PubByTitle.

Description based on the 2010 edition.

Contents: I, "Introduction: Diversity, disparities, and data"; II, "Current status of physician graduates from U.S. MD-granting medical schools"; III, "Trends among physician graduates from U.S. MD-granting medical schools and implications for health care"; IV, "Detailed tables"; "Supplemental tables."

"Provides physicians, medical students, faculty, administrators, researchers, and policy makers with a compendium of detailed statistical information on the demographics and practice patterns of the physician workforce that graduated from U.S. MD-granting medical schools between 1978 and 2008."—*Introd.* In addition, selected data are included from the U.S. Census Bureau and statehealthfacts.org(http://www.statehealthfacts.org/).

Another title in AAMC's Facts & figures series providing minorities in medicine statistics is *Diversity in medical education. Minority graduates of U.S. medical schools: Trends, 1950-1998* is a related title.

471   Encyclopaedic companion to medical statistics. 2nd ed. Brian Everitt, Christopher Ralph Palmer. Chichester, West Sussex, U.K.: Wiley, 2011. xxii, 491 p., ill. ISBN 9780470684191
610.7203   RA409.E527
First ed., 2005.

"The aim of this new edition remains . . . to aid communication between medical researchers and statisticians."—*Pref.* Contains approximately 400 statistical topics and cross-referenced articles, considered important and accessible to medical researchers and not necessarily requiring a technical background. Includes useful examples from the biomedical literature. Also available as an e-book.

472 Encyclopedia of statistical sciences.
2nd ed. Samuel Kotz, N. Balakrishnan, Campbell B. Read. Hoboken, N.J.: Wiley-Interscience, 2006. v. 1–14, ill.
ISBN 9780471150442
519.503   QA276.14.E5

The second edition is expanded by about 50 percent over the first and encompasses materials included in supplement and update volumes issued between editions. Entries are signed, most include bibliographies, and most are multipage. Over 600 contributors. Includes some biographical articles. Aim is to provide articles that are accessible to the student and the nonspecialist. Enough depth to impart basic understanding and facilitate rudimentary application of the concepts with references to more detailed readings. Good, broad coverage of the mathematical aspects of statistical theory and the application of statistical methods. Appropriate for collections supporting instruction and research in statistics as well as those supporting users in other disciplines who use statistical methods in their research.

Also available in an online edition through Wiley InterScience.

473 Faststats A to Z. http://www.cdc.gov/nchs/fastats/Default.htm. National Center for Health Statistics (NCHS). Hyattsville, Md: U.S. Dept. of Health and Human Services, Centers for Disease Control and Prevention, National Center for Health Statistics

Provides topic-appropriate public health statistics (e.g., birth data, morbidity and mortality statistics, and health care use) and relevant links to further information and publications. Includes state and territorial data, with clickable map for individual state data. Also includes data derived from the "Behavioral Risk Factor Surveillance System (BRFSS)," which compiles data for 16 negative behaviors.

474 FedStats. http://www.fedstats.gov/. U.S. Federal Interagency Council on Statistical Policy. Washington: Interagency Council on Statistical Policy
HA37.U55

FedStats provides a portal to publicly available statistics produced by more than 100 U.S. government agencies, including agriculture, census, education, health and human services, interior, justice, labor, transportation, and the treasury. It permits several access points to the agency sites, including an A–Z subject index, keyword searching, and federated searching across agency websites. This outstanding resource also provides a link to online versions of frequently requested publications such as the *Statistical abstract of the United States* and the *State and metropolitan area data book*.

475 Finding and using health statistics. http://www.nlm.nih.gov/nichsr/usestats/. National Information Center on Health Services Research and Health Care Technology, National Library of Medicine (U.S.). Bethesda, Md.: National Library of Medicine. 2008–

Contents: "Introduction"; "About health statistics" ("Importance"; "Uses"; "Sources"; "Health statistics enterprise"); "Finding health statistics" ("Challenges"; "Natural structure"; "Strategies"; "Internet strategies"); "Supporting material" (including a glossary, exercises, and examples).

"This course describes the range of available health statistics, identifies their sources and helps you understand how to use information about their structure as you search."—*Main page*

Reviews various approaches to finding health statistics and provides help with developing search strategies. Links to numerous relevant examples of statistical web resources and portals from federal and state governments, universities, and private organizations. Provides a good introduction and overviews for health professionals, students, and reference librarians.

476 The global burden of disease: A comprehensive assessment of mortality and disability from diseases, injuries, and risk factors in 1990 and projected to 2020. Christopher J. L. Murray, Alan D. Lopez, Harvard School of Public Health., World Health Organization., World Bank. Cambridge, Mass.: Publ. by the Harvard School of Public Health on behalf of the World Health Organization and the

World Bank, 1996. xxxii, 990 p.
ISBN 0674354486
614.4/2   RA441.G56

(Global burden of disease and injury series; v. 1) "The Global Burden of Disease Series provides, on a global and regional level, a detailed and internally consistent approach to meeting . . . information needs . . . concerning epidemiological conditions and disease burden" (*Foreword*). GDB is considered to have set new standards for measuring population health. It also attempts to provide a comparative index of the burden of each disease or injury, i.e., the number of disability-adjusted life years lost as a result of either premature death or years lived with disability. The findings attempt to provide a comprehensive assessment of the health of populations. Results are only approximate, with the reliability of data considered poor for some regions of the world; with estimates of causes of death, incidence and prevalence of disease, injury, and disability, measures and projections of disease burden, and measures of risk factors. Other titles in this series include, e.g., Global health statistics: a compendium of incidence, prevalence, and mortality estimates for over 200 conditions, *Health dimensions of sex and reproduction: the global burden of sexually transmitted diseases, HIV, maternal conditions, perinatal disorders, and congenital anomalies,* and *The global epidemiology of infectious diseases*. Another related title is Global burden of disease and risk factors and the World Health Organization's "Global burden of disease estimates" website (http://www.who.int/health info/bodestimates/en/index.html), with recent results and links.

477   Global burden of disease and risk factors. Alan D. Lopez, Disease Control Priorities Project. New York; Washington: Oxford University Press; World Bank, 2006. xxix, 475 p., ill. ISBN 9780821362
362.1   RA441.G5613

Disease Control Priorities Project is a partnership of the Fogarty International Center (U.S. National Institutes of Health), the World Bank, The World Health Organization, and the Population Reference Bureau).

Contents: ch. 1, Measuring the Global Burden of Disease and risk factors, 1990–2001; ch. 2, Demographic and epidemiological characteristics of major regions, 1990–2001; ch. 3, The burden of disease and mortality by condition: data, methods, and results for 2001; ch. 4, Comparative quantification of mortality and burden of disease attributable to selected risk factors; ch. 5, Sensitivity and uncertainty analyses for burden of disease and risk factor estimates; ch. 6, Incorporating deaths near the time of birth into estimates of the Global Burden of Disease.

Presents the results of the "Global Burden of Disease Study" (quantification of the impact of diseases, injuries, and risk factors on population health) and the CEA (Cost-Effectiveness Analysis) Study and a description of the global epidemiology of diseases, injuries, and risk factors. Resource for researchers interested in the development of methods to measure disease burden and in global and regional health policy.

Related titles are, e.g., The global burden of disease: A comprehensive assessment of mortality and disability from diseases, injuries, and risk factors (476), Global health statistics: A compendium of incidence, prevalence, and mortality estimates for over 200 conditions, and the World Health Organization's "Global burden of disease estimates" website(http://www.who.int/healthinfo/bodestimates/en/index .html), with recent results and links.

Available online at http://bibpurl.oclc.org/web/13502.

478   Globalhealth.gov. http://globalhealth. gov/index.html. U.S. Dept. of Health and Human Services. Washington: U.S. Dept. of Health and Human Services. 1990s–

Produced by HHS Office of Global Health Affairs (OGHA). Title varies: Global Health.gov; GlobalHealth.

Provides access to information about major global health topics, such as avian influenza, HIV/AIDS, malaria, etc. and links to partner organizations (e.g., WHO, PAHO, and others) and information on international travel, health regulation, refugee health, and related areas. CDC's Coordinating Office for Global Health (http://www.cdc.gov/cogh/) provides additional information and resources.

479   Global health observatory (GHO). http://www.who.int/gho/en/. World Health Organization. Geneva, Switzerland: World Health Organization
RA427

Pt. of the World Health Organization (WHO).

Provides access to data and analysis for monitoring the global health situation. Serves as a health statistics repository. Includes major statistical reports (e.g. *World health statistics*, *Global health risks*; *Women and health*; *Global burden of disease: 2004 update*) by Mathers et al. and links to other reports on a variety of topics from various WHO programs. Also provides access to "country statistics" with health data and statistics for each country, a "map gallery" with an extensive list of maps on major health topics (e.g., environmental health, global influenza virology surveillance, mortality and global burden of disease, violence against women, and others).

480   Global health statistics: A compendium of incidence, prevalence, and mortality estimates for over 200 conditions. Christopher J. L. Murray, Alan D. Lopez, World Health Organization., World Bank., Harvard School of Public Health. Boston; Cambridge, Mass.: Publ. by The Harvard School of Public Health on behalf of the World Health Organization and the World Bank ; Distributed by Harvard University Press, 1996. vii, 906 p. ISBN 0674354494
614.4/2   RA407.M87
(Global burden of disease and injury series; 2)

Provides information on the underlying epidemiological statistics for over 200 conditions and several chapters with detailed data for each condition.

Part of the Global burden of disease series which "provides, on a global and regional level, a detailed and internally consistent approach to meeting . . . information needs . . . concerning epidemiological conditions and disease burden . . . volumes summarize epidemiological knowledge about all major conditions and most risk factors" (*Foreword*).

Other titles in this series include, for example, The global burden of disease: A comprehensive assessment of mortality and disability from diseases, injuries, and risk factors in 1990 and projected to 2020 (476), *Health dimensions of sex and reproduction: the global burden of sexually transmitted diseases, HIV, maternal conditions, perinatal disorders, and congenital anomalies,* and *The global epidemiology of infectious diseases.* Other related titles

are Global burden of disease and risk factors and the World Health Organization's "Global burden of disease estimates" website (http://www.who.int/healthinfo/global_burden_disease/en/index.html), with recent results and links.

481   Health, United States. http://purl.access.gpo.gov/GPO/LPS2649. National Center for Health Statistics, National Center for Health Services Research. Rockville, Md.: National Center for Health Statistics. 1975–
An annual report on trends in health statistics.

The report consists of several main sections: complete report; "at a glance" table; highlights; a chartbook containing text and figures that illustrate major trends in the health of Americans; and a trend tables section that contains 150 detailed data tables. Includes extensive appendixes and an index. Hyperlinks to tables and graphs, which are available in formats such as Excel, PowerPoint, and PDF.

New for the 2012 edition is a special feature on emergency care.

Easy access to related online resources provided by the National Center for Health Statistics (NCHS).

482   Health and healthcare in the United States: County and metro area data. Richard K. Thomas, NationsHealth Corporation. Lanham, Md.: Bernan Press, c1999–c2001. 2 v., maps
362 1526-1573   RA407.3.H415
First ed., 1999–2nd ed., 2000; 2nd ed. technical consultant, Russell G. Bruce. Compendium of health-related statistics and reference maps for each of the 3,000 counties and the 80 metropolitan areas in the U.S.—demographics, vital statistics, healthcare resources, and Medicare data. Based on information from the National Center for Health Statistics (63) and the U.S. Bureau of the Census. Accompanying CD-ROMs make it possible to manipulate the data. Also available as an e-book.

483   Healthcare cost and utilization project (HCUP). http://www.hcup-us.ahrq.gov/home.jsp. Agency for Healthcare Research and Quality

(AHRQ). Rockville, Md.: Agency for Healthcare Research and Quality, U.S. Dept. of Health and Human Services
"Family of health care databases and related software tools and products . . . made possible by a Federal-State-Industry partnership sponsored by the Agency for Healthcare Research and Quality (AHRQ)" (*Website*).

Website designed to answer HCUP-related questions. Provides information on HCUP databases (e.g., Nationwide Inpatient Sample, State Inpatient Databases, State Ambulatory Surgery Databases, and others), tools and software products (e.g., HCUPnet, an interactive tool for identifying, tracking, analyzing, and comparing statistics on hospital care (e.g.,*HCUP statistical briefs* http://www.hcup -us.ahrq.gov/reports/statbriefs/statbriefs.jsp); Clinical classifications software, and others), and offers technical assistance to HCUP users.

484   Health data tools and statistics from PHPartners. http://phpartners.org/ health_stats.html. Partners in Information Access for the Public Health Workforce, National Library of Medicine (U.S.). Bethesda, Md.: U.S. National Library of Medicine, National Institutes of Health, Dept. of Health and Human Services
Contents: County and local health data; State health data; Individual state data; National health data; Global health data; Statistical reports; Demographic data; Geographic information systems (GIS); Training and education; Health information technology and standards; Tools for data collection and planning.

Provides lists of selected links with brief annotations to assist in locating public health data and statistics. Part of The Partners in Information Access for the Public Health Workforce (PHPartners) website (http://phpartners.org/index.html) which is described as "a collaboration of U.S. government agencies, public health organizations and health sciences libraries, with the mission of helping the public health workforce find and use information effectively to improve and protect the public's health."—*About page.* Its topics pages include, for example, bioterrorism, dental public health, HIV/AIDS, nutrition, obesity, public health genomics, and other relevant information for public health professionals and researchers.

Additional highly useful sites in this area are, for example, Health services research and public health information, HSR information central (492), and National Information Center on Health Services Research and Health Care Technology.

485   Health statistics (MedlinePlus). http://www.nlm.nih.gov/medlineplus/ healthstatistics.html. National Library of Medicine (U.S.). Bethesda, Md.: National Library of Medicine. 2000–
Part of MedlinePlus; National Library of Medicine (NLM).

Contents: Overviews; Latest News; Related Issues; Research; Journal Articles; Directories; Organizations; Newsletters/Print Publications; Law and Policy; Children; Teenagers; Men; Women; Seniors.

Provides helpful links to various types of health and vital statistics for consumers and health professionals. FAQ Statistics (http://www.nlm.nih.gov/ services/statistics.html) is another website made available by NLM that answers questions on how to find statistics for U.S. and global health and medicine topics.

486   Healthy people. http://www.cdc.gov/ nchs/healthy_people.htm. National Center for Health Statistics (NCHS). Hyattsville, Md.: Centers for Disease Control (U.S.), National Center for Health Statistics
RA395.A3
Contents: Healthy people 2000; Healthy People 2010; Healthy People 2020; Progress Reviews; Publications.

"Healthy People provides science-based, national goals and objectives with 10-year targets designed to guide national health promotion and disease prevention efforts to improve the health of all people in the United States." —*Home Page.* Previous reports include *Healthy people 2000* (http:// purl.access.gpo.gov/GPO/LPS3745) and *Healthy people: The Surgeon General's report on health promotion and disease prevention: Background papers: Report to the Surgeon General on health promotion and disease prevention.* "Healthy People DATA 2010," an interactive database system accessible via CDC WONDER provides various reports and data. A search interface providing searches for published literature related to Healthy People 2010 was added to the "special queries" section of PubMed.

Also available in print format: *Tracking healthy people 2010*. Progress Reviews and publications are added to the website regularly.

487 Health statistics: An annotated bibliographic guide to information resources. 2nd ed. Frieda Weise. Lanham, Md.: Medical Library Association and Scarecrow Press, 1997. x, 178 p. ISBN 0810830566
016.3621/0973/021   Z7553.M43W444; RA407.3
First ed., ©1980.

Rev. ed. Contents: Ch. 1, General references; ch. 2, Compilations of health statistics; ch. 3, Vital statistics; ch. 4, Morbidity; ch. 5, Health resources; ch. 6, Health services utilization; ch. 7, Health care costs and expenditures; ch. 8, Population characteristics; Appendixes A–D; Glossary; Index.

Annotated bibliography of basic vital and health statistics. "Health statistics include a wide spectrum of information: vital statistics (birth, death, marriage, and divorce); morbidity and other measures of health status; health care facilities, health personnel and health professions education; use of health care services; and health care costs and expenditures, . . . linked to population and demographic data . . ." (*Pref.*). Contains mostly print, but also electronic resources. Several appendixes include, for example, newsletters and journals, lists of government agencies, and private associations from which information can be obtained.

488 Healthy women. http://www.cdc.gov/ nchs/data/healthywomen/womenschart book_aug2004.pdf. Centers for Disease Control and Prevention (U.S.); National Center for Health Statistics (U.S.). Hyattsville, Md.: National Center for Health Statistics, Centers for Disease Control and Prevention, U.S. Dept. of Health and Human Services. 2004
RA408.W65
Title varies: Suggested title for website: *Healthy women: State trends in health and mortality;* suggested citation for print version, publ. in 2004 as *Women's health and mortality chartbook* by K. M. Brett and Suzanne G. Hayes.

PDF of *Women's Health and Mortality Chartbook,* developed by NCHS with support from the Office on Women's Health. It describes the health of people in each state in the U.S. by sex, race, and age by reporting current data on critical issues of relevance to women.

Other publications in this area include *Women's health data book: A profile of women's health in the United States,* ed. by D. Misra, a collaborative publication by the Jacobs Institute of Women's Health and the Henry J. Kaiser Family Foundation (Kaiser Family Foundation) since 1992, complemented by *State profiles on women's health: Women's health issues,* publ. since 1998.

489 HHS Data Council. http://aspe.hhs.gov/ datacncl/. United States.; Dept. of Health and Human Services.; Data Council. Washington: U.S. Department of Health and Human Services. 200?–
RA407.3
"The HHS Data Council coordinates all health and human services data collection and analysis activities of the Department of Health and Human Services, including an integrated data collection strategy, coordination of health data standards and health and human services and privacy policy activities."—*Website.*

Provides access to key health and human services data and statistics. Covers information sponsored by federal, state, and local governments. Complements other government resources such as USA.gov and FedStats. Links to health and human services surveys and data systems sponsored by federal agencies and leads to websites and other key resources that contain statistics and data. Additionally, HealthData.gov http://www.hhs.gov/ open/datasets/index.html provides access to datasets, various tools, and applications using data about health and healthcare.

490 Historical statistics of the United States. http://hsus.cambridge.org/. Richard Sutch, Susan B. Carter. New York: Cambridge University Press
Standard source for American historical data. No uniform end date for tables, but many end in the late 1990s. Examples of tables include population, work, labor, education, health, and government finance. Tables are easily searched and can be downloaded into Excel or CSV formats. Also in print as a five-vol. set.

491 How to report statistics in medicine: Annotated guidelines for authors, editors, and reviewers. 2nd ed.
Thomas A. Lang, Michelle Secic. New York: American College of Physicians, 2006. p. cm. ISBN 1930513690

610.72   RA409.L357
First ed., 1997.

Rev. ed., with new and updated content. Considered a standard guide to interpreting and reporting statistics in scientific and medical writing. Provides guidelines for reporting statistical analyses, research, and trial design used in biological sciences and medical research, how to display data, and explanation of statistical terms and tests. Also available as an e-book.

492 HSR information central. http://www .nlm.nih.gov/hsrinfo/. Bethesda, Md.: National Library of Medicine (U.S.), National Institutes of Health, Dept. of Health and Human Services. 1993–

HSRIC = Health Services Research Information Central

Contents: HSR general resources: Data, tools, and statistics; HSR social media resources; Education and training; Grants, funding, and fellowships; Guidelines, journals, other publications; Key organizations; Legislation; Meetings and conferences; State resources. HSR topics: Aging Population Issues; Comparative effectiveness research (CER); Child health services research; Evidence-based practice and health; Technology assessment; Health care reform, health economics, and health policy; Health disparities; Health informatics; Public health systems and services research; Quality; Rural health. Alphabetic index (all websites in alphabetic order).

Developed by the National Library of Medicine to serve the information needs of the health services research community, in partnership with other government agencies and institutes (e.g., Agency for Healthcare Research and Quality (AHRQ, 335), National Cancer Institute, the Cecil C. Sheps Center for Health Services Research, and the Health Services Research and Development Service [HSR&D] at the Veterans Administration, and others). Provides selected links which are intended to represent a sample of available information.

493 MEPS Medical Expenditure Panel Survey. http://www.meps.ahrq.gov/meps web/. U.S. Agency for Healthcare Research and Quality. Bethesda, Md.: Agency for Healthcare Research and Quality. 1996–

RA408.5
Produced by Agency for Health Care Research and Quality (AHRQ).

"Set of large-scale surveys of families and individuals, their medical providers (doctors, hospitals, pharmacies, etc.), and employers across the United States. MEPS collects data on the specific health services that Americans use, how frequently they use them, the cost of these services, and how they are paid for, as well as data on the cost, scope, and breadth of health insurance held by and available to U.S. workers" (*Website*). Provides information on health expenditures, utilization of health services, health insurance, and nursing homes, and reimbursement mechanisms. MEPS topics include access to health care, children's health, children's insurance coverage, health care disparities, mental health, minority health, the uninsured, and other topics. Further details concerning the survey background, data overview, and frequently asked questions are provided at the website. Provides full-text access to MEPS publications: highlights, research findings, statistical briefs, etc.

494 Munro's statistical methods for health care research. 6th ed. Stacey Beth Plichta, Elizabeth A. Kelvin, Barbara Hazard Munro. Philadelphia: Wolters Kluwer Health/Lippincott Williams & Wilkins, 2012. vii, 567 p., ill. ISBN 9781451115611

610.72/7   RT81.5.M86
First edition, 1986 to 5th ed. 2005 had title: *Statistical methods for health care research*.

Explains statistical methods and techniques frequently used in the health care literature. Includes charts, graphs, and examples from the literature. Contains, for example, principles underlying statistical inference, material on statistical model building and logistic regression, structural equation modeling, writing and presenting for publication, and other areas. Written for students and teachers.

495 National Cancer Institute. http://www .cancer.gov/. National Cancer Institute,

U.S. National Institutes of Health.

Bethesda, Md.: National Cancer Institute
Website created by the National Cancer Institute (NCI), a division of the National Institutes of Health (NIH).

Contents: NCI home, Cancer topics, Clinical trials, Cancer statistics, Research and funding, News, About NCI.

Links to cancer-related information for health professionals, medical students, and patients. Provides guidance to searching the cancer literature in PubMed by searching the "cancer subset" and access to already prepared searches on more than 100 different topics. Non-PubMed citations previously found in CANCERLIT, a database no longer being maintained, consist primarily of meeting abstracts from the annual meetings of the American Society of Clinical Oncology (ASCO) and the American Association for Cancer Research (AACR). ASCO abstracts for recent years are available via http://www.asco.org, AACR abstracts at http://aacrmeetingabstracts.org/. Also provides access to PDQ: Physician data query (http://www.cancer.gov/cancertopics/pdq), a database with the latest information about cancer treatment, screening, prevention, genetics, etc.

The NCI website includes descriptions of various types of cancer (A–Z list of cancers: http://www.cancer.gov/cancertopics/alphalist/) and related topics, with links to diagnosis and treatment information and supportive care, information on clinical trials, cancer prevention, cancer statistics (e.g., SEER cancer statistics review), cancer statistics tools, cancer mortality maps and graphs, and related NCI websites. Links to the Dictionary of cancer terms and various cancer vocabulary resources (e.g., NCI thesaurus, NCI metathesaurus, and NCI terminology browser), NCI drug dictionary, NCI publications, etc. Available both in English and Spanish.

496   OECD health data. http://www.oecd.org/health/healthdata. Organisation for Economic Co-operation and Development. Paris: Organisation for Economic Co-operation and Development
    Title varies: SourceOECD health data.
Part of SourceOECD, which contains publications (monographs, periodicals, and statistical databases) issued by the OECD.

Interactive database and source of statistics on health and health care systems of the OECD member states. Allows cross-country comparisons of national health care systems. Includes, for example, health status, health care resources, health care utilization, expenditure on health, and health care financing. Available in online and CD-ROM formats.

497   Physician compensation and production survey. Medical Group Management Association, Center for Research in Ambulatory Health Care Administration (U.S.). Englewood, Colo.: Center for Research in Ambulatory Health Care Administration, 1992–. v.
    331 1064-4563   R728.5.P48152
Merger of the production survey of: *Cost and production survey report*, and: *Physician compensation survey report*.

Now published by the Medical Group Management Association (MGMA). Title varies: *MGMA physician compensation and production survey*.

Description based on 2007 report. 2012 report based on 2011 data is the most recent available.

Contents: Section 1, Key findings and demographics; section 2, Physician compensation and benefits; section 3, Physician productivity; section 4, Physician time worked; section 5, Summary tables; section 6, Nonphysician providers; section 7, Physician placement starting salaries.

"Data on compensation for healthcare professionals and on medical group practices and financial operations . . . will assist . . . in evaluating the ranges of compensation and productivity for both . . . physicians and nonphysician providers" (*Publ. notes*). The Bureau of Labor Statistics website "Sector 62—Health Care and Social Assistance" (http://www.bls.gov/oes/current/oessrci.htm#62) also provides extensive information in this area as part of its occupational employment and wage estimates.

Physician socioeconomic statistics (formed by the union of *Physician marketplace statistics* and *Socioeconomic characteristics of medical practice*), publ. by the American Medical Association, was discontinued in 2003.

498   Health statistics (NLM). http://www.nlm.nih.gov/services/Subject_Guides/healthstatistics/. National Library of

Medicine (U. S.), National Institutes of Health (U.S.). Bethesda, Md.: U.S. National Library of Medicine, National Institutes of Health, Dept. of Health and Human Resources. 2000–

Compiled by the User Services Unit of the National Library of Medicine (NLM) Reference and Web Services Section, Public Services Division.

Contents: NLM medical subject headings (MeSH, 858) guide for searching this topic; General statistical resources; general health statistics and vital statistics; specific health conditions and concerns; health economics; Health insurance; health professions and manpower; hospitals and health statistics; health insurance; health professions and manpower; hospitals and health statistics; procedures or therapeutics; special populations; veterinary medicine; international statistics and numerical data.

Part of NLM's subject guides. Topics drawn from the most frequently asked questions the reference and Web services staff encounters in e-mails and onsite. Intended to serve as a non-comprehensive starting point.

Other currently available NLM subject guides:

Conference proceedings http://www.nlm.nih.gov/services/Subject_Guides/conferenceproceedings/

Library statistics http://www.nlm.nih.gov/services/Subject_Guides/librarystatistics/

499   Injury data and resources. http://www.cdc.gov/nchs/injury.htm. National Center for Health Statistics. Atlanta: National Center for Health Statistics

"The purpose of this Web site is to provide an overview of injury morbidity and mortality data and statistics available from the National Center for Health Statistics (NCHS) and other sources and to provide details on injury surveillance methodology and tools to assist in data analysis"—*main page*. Provides links to a variety of resources, including the International Collaborative Effort (ICE) on Injury Statistics (http://www.cdc.gov/nchs/injury/advice.htm), relevant coding schemes, and additional resources (e.g., WISQARS: Web-based Injury Statistics Query and Reporting System (517), CDC WONDER, Faststats, and others).

500   Medical statistics from A to Z. 2nd ed. Brian Everitt. Cambridge, U.K.; New York: Cambridge University Press, 2006.

vi, 248 p., ill. ISBN 0521867630

610.727   RA407.E943

First ed., 2003.

Contains approx. 1,500 terms with definitions and references for further reading. Written in non-technical language. For health professionals and students. Also available as an e-book.

Another more recent title by the same author is *Encyclopaedic companion to medical statistics* (110).

501   National Center for Health Statistics (NCHS). http://www.cdc.gov/nchs/. National Center for Health Statistics (U.S.), Centers for Disease Control and Prevention (U.S.). Hyattsville, Md.: Centers for Disease Control and Prevention. 1990s–

RA409

NCHS is the primary agency for compiling and making available American health and vital statistics and data sets. Searchable website, with topically arranged site index. Its home page provides links to various resources in several categories, including What's new; Health e-stats; Information showcase; Top ten links; surveys and data collection systems (data collected through personal interviews and systems based on records, with data from vital and medical records); and microdata access (including links to NCHS public-use data files and documentation and state data). Surveys and data collection systems include the National health and nutrition examination survey (NHANES), National health care survey (NCHS), National health interview survey (NHIS), National immunization survey (NIS), Longitudinal studies of aging (LSOAs), National vital statistics system (NSS), and Injury statistics query and reporting system. Examples of linked resources include *Faststats a to z* and Health, United States. Details on NCHS publications and information products are provided at http://www.cdc.gov/nchs/products.htm.

NCHS serves as the World Health Organization's (WHO's) Collaborating Center for the Family of International Classifications for North America (North American Collaborating Center [NACC] established in 1976) and is responsible for coordinating all official disease classification activities in the United States, in close cooperation with the Canadian Institute for Health Information

(CIHI), Statistics Canada, and the Pan American Health Organization (941). A portal to the disease classifications in North America (e.g., International classification of diseases, Ninth Revision, Clinical modification: ICD-9-CM and International classification of functioning, disability, and health (ICF)) is provided at http://www.cdc.gov/nchs/icd.htm.

502   National vital statistics system (NVSS). http://www.cdc.gov/nchs/nvss.htm. National Center for Health Statistics (U. S.). Hyattsville, Md.: National Center for Health Statistics. 2000s–

A unit of the National Center for Health Statistics, which is responsible for the official vital statistics of the United States: births, deaths (annual mortality data, monthly provisional mortality data, cause-of-death data by age, race, sex, etc.), marriages, divorces, and fetal deaths. Has contact information for obtaining vital records from states and territories. Provides access to a vital-statistics information sources portal (http://www.cdc.gov/nchs/data_access/VitalStats Online.htm), with links to publications and information products (http://www.cdc.gov/nchs/products.htm), including *Advance data*, *Vital and health statistics reports* (also referred to as "series reports" and "rainbow series"), and many others that can be identified via a NCHS Web search or a helpful site index at http://www.cdc.gov/az/a.html.

503   Physician characteristics and distribution in the U.S. American Medical Association. Chicago: Division of Survey and Data Resources, American Medical Association, 1982–
331.119161069520973
0731-0315   RA410.7.D47
Earlier titles: 1963–69, *Distribution of physicians, hospitals, and hospital beds in the U.S.*; 1970–73, *Distribution of physicians in the U.S.*; 1974–81, *Physician distribution and medical licensure in the U.S.* No issue publ. in 1989. Data derived from the American Medical Association's (AMA) Physician Masterfile, originally established in 1906 as a record-keeping system for physician membership and mailing purposes.—*Foreword*

Description based on 2013 ed. (publ. 2012); 2014 ed. (publ. 2013) is available.

Contents: Six chapters: 1. Physician characteristics (i.e., by age, sex, major professional activity, specialty, and race); 2. Physician distribution (i.e., geographical distribution by state); 3. Analysis of professional activity by self-designated specialty and geographic region; 4. Primary care specialties (including trends, age, sex, board certification, school and year of graduation, state location and metro area); 5. Osteopathic physicians; 6. Physician trends (trend data for specialty, major professional activity, age, and sex); Appendixes A–D (self-designated practice specialties, American specialty boards, Metropolitan statistical areas [MSAs], and Regions, divisions, and states); index.

Current, historical, and comparative data on U.S. physicians, with both summary and detailed statistical information and tabulations. Describes professional and individual characteristics of physicians and provides information on their geographical location. Census summary data by state, age, gender, and specialty. Earlier editions of this resource remain important data sources when researching health care issues and trends in physician supply and physician services.

504   Portrait of health in the United States. 1st ed. Daniel Melnick, Beatrice A. Rouse. Lanham, Md.: Bernan, 2001. xxi, 376 p., ill. ISBN 089059189X
614.4/273   RA410.53.P675
"Major statistical trends & guide to resources" (*Cover*).

"Presents a picture of American health using a variety of measures ranging from self-perceived health status and reported acute and chronic health conditions to more objective measures such as life expectancy, medical diagnosis, hospitalization, and death rates. Data not found easily elsewhere are included. . . ." (*Pref.*). Compiled from results reported by federal and public health agencies. Includes, for example, societal trends, health outcomes, leading chronic and acute health conditions and causes of death, incidence, mortality and survival rates of various illnesses, access to care, insurance and costs, life expectancy, quality of life issues, and other relevant information. Also available as an e-book.

505   ProQuest statistical abstract of the United States. ProQuest. Lanham, Md.:

Bernan Press, 2013. 1025 p.
ISBN 9781598885910
317.3   **HA 202**

Successor to the important federal publication. When the U.S. government cut funding for the Statistical Abstract of the United States published by the Census Bureau, over the objections of librarians and researchers, ProQuest launched this replacement edition as an annual publication beginning with 2013. Intentionally mimics the format, scope and organization of the original resource. Remains an excellent source for the most current possible data on population, government finance, the economy, and even for some international statistics. Original source publications for figures in tables are indicated. Appendixes include a guide to sources of statistics, state statistical abstracts, and foreign statistical abstracts; discussion of metropolitan and micropolitan statistical areas; and a table of weights and measures. Index. Also available in an online edition, from which the data tables can be retrieved in PDF.

506   Secondary data sources for public health: A practical guide. Sarah Boslaugh. Cambridge, [England]; New York: Cambridge University Press, 2007. x, 152 p. ISBN 052169023
362.10727   RA409.B66

Part of Practical guides to biostatistics and epidemiology.

Contents: ch. 1, "An introduction to secondary analysis"; ch. 2, "Health services utilization data"; ch. 3, "Health behaviors and risk factors data"; ch. 4, "Data on multiple health topics"; ch. 5, "Fertility and mortality data"; ch. 6, "Medicare and Medicaid data"; ch. 7, "Other sources of data"; appendixes: I, "Acronyms"; II, "Summary of data sets and years available"; III, "Data import and transfer".

This guide lists the major sources of secondary data for health-related subjects that are important in epidemiology and public health research. They are often stored in different locations and not necessarily easily accessible. Examples include the National hospital discharge survey, the Healthcare cost utilization project, the Behavioral risk factor surveillance system, the National health and nutrition survey, Medicare public use files, Web portals to statistical data, etc. Description of each resource includes title, focus, core section, data collection, and information on accessing data and ancillary

materials. Includes bibliography and index. Also available as an e-book.

507   SEER cancer statistics review 1975-2009. http://seer.cancer.gov/ csr/1975_2009_pops09/index.html. National Cancer Institute (U.S.), National Institutes of Health (U.S.). Bethesda, Md.: National Cancer Institute. 1993–
362.1   RA645.C3.A65

National Cancer Institute (NCI); SEER (Surveillance Epidemiology and End Results).

Titles of print and online products vary, including *Cancer statistics review* (CSR), published annually by the Cancer Statistics Branch of the NCI. Description based on the 1975–2009 online ed.

CSR is "a report of the most recent cancer incidence, mortality, survival, prevalence, and lifetime risk statistics"—*main page*.

NCI's SEER Program (http://seer.cancer.gov) is an authoritative source of information on cancer incidence and survival in the United States. Overview of the SEER program can be found at http:// seer.cancer.gov/about/. The SEER website provides a wide array of additional cancer statistics resources, including a glossary of statistical terms, cancer statistics fact sheets, state cancer profiles, statistical reports and monographs, etc.

508   State medical licensure requirements and statistics. American Medical Association. Chicago: American Medical Association, 1999–
362.172 1549-4055   RA396.A3U2
1999/2000– (publ. 2000)–

1982-98: *U.S. medical licensure statistics and licensure requirements* (title varies). Description based on 2012 ed.; 2013 and 2014 ed. available, also as e-books.

Contents: Ch. 1, "Licensure policies and regulations of state medical/osteopathic boards"; ch. 2, "Licensing board statistics"; ch. 3, "Medical licensing examinations and organizations"; ch. 4, "Information for international medical graduates"; ch. 5, "Federal and national programs and activities"; ch. 6, "Other organizations and programs"; Appendixes A-E, e.g., "Glossary of medical licensure terms" and "AMA policy on medical licensure."

"Presents current information and statistics on medical licensure in the United States and possessions. Data were obtained from a number of sources, including state boards of medical examiners, the Federation of State Medical Boards, National Board of Medical Examiners, National Board of Osteopathic Medical Examiners, Educational Commission for Foreign Graduates, and the United States Medical Licensing Examination,and others."—*Foreword* Includes 54 allopathic and 14 osteopathic boards of medical examiners.

A related Internet resource on medical licensure is provided by the AMA at http://www.ama-assn .org/go/licensure.

509 Statistical abstract. http://www.census .gov/compendia/statab/st_abstracts.html. U.S. Census Bureau. U.S. Census Bureau
Links to most recent statistical abstracts for all 50 states. Includes contact information for publishing agencies and links to other major state statistical publications.

510 Statistical handbook on infectious diseases. Sarah Watstein, John Jovanovic. Westport, Conn.: Greenwood Press, 2003. xxiii, 321 p., ill., maps. ISBN 1573563757
614/.07/27   RA643.W33
Contents: (A) Nationally notifiable diseases; (B) Human Immunoficiency Virus (HIV) and Acquired Immunodeficiency Syndrome (AIDS); (C) Malaria; (D) Sexually transmitted diseases; (E) Tuberculosis; (F) Foodborne diseases; (G) Waterborne diseases; (H) Infectious disease worldwide: present issues, emerging concerns; (I) Vaccine-preventable diseases; (J) Infectious disease elimination and eradication; (K) Bioterrorism and biological warfare; Appendix: World Health Organization (WHO) regions. Glossary.

"Comprehensive statistical overview of the status of infectious disease worldwide . . . often hard to find, or difficult to interpret . . . a carefully selected array of tables and charts of authoritative statistical information, placing valuable statistics into context with introductory text" (*Publ. notes*). Selection from a variety of print and web-based sources. Includes bibliographical references (p. [315]–318) and index. For general readers and students as a good starting point for research. Also available as an e-book.

511 Statistical record of health and medicine. Gale Research Inc. Detroit: Gale Research Inc., c1995–c1998. 2 v. 362.10973021 1078-6961   RA407.3.S732
Description based on 2nd ed., 1998.
Compilation of U.S. national, state, and municipal health and medical statistics from a variety of sources. Provides statistics on health status of Americans, health insurance, health care costs and expenditures, medical professions, international rankings and comparisons, etc. Further detailed notes on scope and coverage in the introduction and the sources from which the information is drawn. Keyword index.

Can be supplemented by more recent resources, for example, *Chronology of public health in the United Sates* (by Wright), which covers events back to 1796, but mainly since 1900, as well as various government websites containing health and medical statistics.

512 United States cancer statistics . . . incidence and mortality. http://purl .access.gpo.gov/GPO/LPS56576. U.S. Cancer Statistics Working Group., Centers for Disease Control and Prevention (U.S.), National Cancer Institute (U.S.), North American Association of Central Cancer Registries. Atlanta: Centers for Disease Control, U.S. Department of Health and Human Services. 1999-
Based on U.S. Cancer Statistics Working Group. *United States cancer statistics: 1999–2009 incidence and mortality Web-based report.* Atlanta: U.S. Department of Health and Human Services, Centers for Disease Control and Prevention and National Cancer Institute; 2013.

Produced by the Centers for Disease Control and Prevention (CDC) and the National Cancer Institute (NCI), in collaboration with the North American Association of Central Cancer Registries (NAACCR).

"Includes the official federal statistics on cancer incidence from registries that have high-quality data and cancer mortality statistics for each year and 2005–2009 combined."—*Website.* Provides statistics by cancer type and for the most commonly diagnosed cancers in the U.S. (e.g., breast cancer; cervical cancer; HPV-associated cancers; lung cancer; ovarian cancer; prostate cancer; skin cancer; uterine cancer). Provides graphs ("top ten cancers"; "state vs. national comparisons"; "selected cancers ranked by state"), tables ("cancer types grouped by race and ethnicity;" "cancers grouped by state and region"; "childhood cancer"; "brain cancers by tumor type"), maps ("interactive cancer atlas" http://apps.nccd.cdc.gov/DCPC_INCA/DCPC_INCA.aspx); and "cancer data by state." Further information about this report at http://www.cdc.gov/cancer/npcr/uscs/about.htm.

Earlier *United States cancer statistics reports* can be accessed at http://www.cdc.gov/cancer/npcr/uscs/archive.htm.

A cancer statistics glossary is found at http://www.cdc.gov/cancer/npcr/uscs/glossary.htm.

513   WHO child growth standards. http://www.who.int/childgrowth/en/index.html. World Health Organization. Geneva, Switzerland: World Health Organization. 2006

Since the late 1970s, the National Center for Health Statistics/WHO growth reference has been in use to chart children's growth. It was based on data from a limited sample of children from the United States and is now considered less adequate for international comparisons. In 1997, WHO, in collaboration with the United Nations University, undertook the Multicentre Growth Reference Study (MGRS), which is a community-based, multicountry project with more than 8,000 children from Brazil, Ghana, India, Norway, Oman, and the United States. The new standards are the result of this study, which had as its goal "to develop a new international standard for assessing the physical growth, nutritional status and motor development in all children from birth to age five"—*press release*. The first new growth charts released (Apr. 2007) include weight-for-age, length/height-for-age, and weight-for-length/height growth indicators as well as a Body Mass Index (BMI) standard for children up to age 5, and standards for sitting, standing, walking, and several other key motor developments.

The title of the print version is *WHO child growth standards: Length/height-for-age, weight-for-age, weight-for-length, weight-for-height and body mass index–for–age: Methods and development.*

514   WHO global infobase. http://www.who.int/infobase. World Health Organization. Geneva, Switzerland: World Health Organization. 2000s?–

Produced by World Health Organization (WHO).

Title varies: also called WHO global infobase online.

"Data warehouse that collects, stores and displays information on chronic diseases and their risk factors for all WHO member states"—*main page*. Provides information on health topics, e.g., alcohol and its relationship to disease and injury, blood pressure, cholesterol, diet, overweight and obesity, physical activity, tobacco, diabetes, oral health, visual impairment, and other topics, such as mortality estimates. Information comes from various national surveys, and WHO collaborates with its regional offices to keep information up to date. Provides individual country pages, allows comparison of countries, and displays comparable risk factor data. Extensive help pages include glossary, FAQ page, definitions of terms used, etc.

515   WHO mortality data and statistics. http://www.who.int/healthinfo/statistics/mortality/en/index.html. World Health Organization. Geneva, Switzerland: World Health Organization. 2005–

Part of WHO's "health statistics and health information systems" http://www.who.int/healthinfo/en/.

The focus of WHO's work in health statistics is in the following areas: "Global Health Observatory (GHO)" (http://www.who.int/gho/en/index.html), described as "gateway to the wealth of WHO data statistics, analysis and reports on key health themes, "standards and tools," and "country monitoring and evaluation guidance" —http://www.who.int/healthinfo/en/. Provides access to a variety of resources and related links. An important resource is, for example, the WHO mortality database (http://www.who.int/healthinfo/mortality_data/en/), a compilation of mortality data by age, sex and cause of death, as officially reported annually by WHO member states from their civil registration systems. It includes cause-of-death statistics coded according to the ninth and tenth revision of the ICD (International statistical classification of diseases and related Health Problems: Tabular List of Inclusions and Four-Character subcategories), i.e., data on registered deaths by age group, sex, year, and cause of death. These files are not considered user-friendly since they consist of raw data files. However, the necessary instructions are provided.

The Human mortality database (HMD) (http://www.mortality.org), a collaborative project by demographers John R. Wilmoth (Univ. of California, Berkeley) and Vladimir Shkolnikov (Max Planck Institute for Demographic Research, Germany),

provides detailed mortality and population data for 37 countries to researchers. Data sets include births, deaths, population size, populations exposed to risk, and life expectancy at birth. Alphabetical list of the countries, with link to data set for that country. The sets can be displayed individually, or users can download complete data sets. Users must create an account (free) in order to access the data sets.

516   WHOSIS. http://www.who.int/whosis/. World Health Organization. Geneva, [Switzerland]: World Health Organization. [1994]–

Published by World Health Organization (WHO).

Provides description and online access to statistical and epidemiological information, data, and tools available from WHO and other sites: mortality and health status, disease statistics, health systems statistics, risk factors and health services, and inequities in health. Provides links to several databases: WHOSIS database, with the latest "core health indicators" from WHO sources (including *The world health report* (519) and *World health statistics*), which make it possible to construct tables for any combination of countries, indicators and years, Causes of death database, WHO global infobase online, Global health atlas, and Reproductive health indicators database.

As of 2011, WHOSIS has been incorporated into WHO's Global health observatory (GHO, 479) which provides additional data & tools, and also more analysis and reports.

517   WISQARS. http://www.cdc.gov/injury/wisqars/index.html. National Center for Injury Prevention and Control. Atlanta: National Center for Injury Prevention and Control. 2000–

HB1323.A2

WISQARS (Web-Based Injury Statistics Query and Reporting System), National Center for Injury

Prevention and Control of the U.S. Centers for Disease Control and Prevention; CDC Injury Center.

Described as "an interactive database system that provides customized reports of injury-related data."—*Main page* Injury statistics presented in two categories, i.e., fatal U.S. injury statistics and national estimates of nonfatal injuries treated in U.S. hospital emergency departments, each with links to tables, charts, tutorials, help, and FAQs. CDC's Injury Center (http://www.cdc.gov/injury/) provides links to a variety of injury related topics, fact sheets, and overviews on injury response, violence prevention, and prevention of unintentional injuries.

The National Center for Health Statistics (NCHS, 63) also makes a variety of injury data and resources available at http://www.cdc.gov/nchs/injury.htm.

518   Women's health USA (WHUSA). http://purl.access.gpo.gov/GPO/LPS21379. U.S. Dept. of Health and Human Services, Maternal and Child Health Bureau. Rockville, Md.: U.S. Dept. of Health and Human Services, Maternal and Child Health Bureau. 2002–

"An illustrated collection of current and historical data"—*main page*.

Part of Health Resources and Services Administration (HRSA, 896), within the U.S. Dept. of Health and Human Services (HHS)

Description based on WHUSA 2012 ed. Online access to previous editions is included.

Contents: Population characteristics; Health status; Health services utilization; HRSA programs women's health.

Collection of current and historical data on health challenges facing women, with information on life expectancy and addressing topics such as postpartum depression, smoking, alcohol, illicit drug use, etc. Brings together the latest available information from various government agencies (HHS, U.S. Dept. of Agriculture, U.S. Dept. of Labor, U.S. Dept. of Justice).

Other notable women's health and policy websites include, for example, Women's health (MedlinePlus) http://www.nlm.nih.gov/medlineplus/womenshealth.html, Women's health resources http://whr.nlm.nih.gov/, Womenshealth.gov (575) http://www.womenshealth.gov/health-topics/; The Kaiser Family Foundation's Women's health policy (488) http://kff.org/womens-health-policy/.

519 **The world health report**. http://www
.who.int/whr/. World Health Organization.
Geneva, [Switzerland]: World Health
Organization. 1995–
614.405 1020-3311   RA8.A265
Pt. of WHOSIS: WHO statistical information
system.

"Every year . . . takes a new and expert look at
global health, focusing on a specific theme, while
assessing the current global situation. Using the
latest data gathered and validated by WHO, each
report paints a picture of the changing world."—
Website Website also provides links to the full-text
reports 1995–2005, each with a focus on a special
theme: 1995, "bridging the gaps"; 1996, "fighting
disease, fostering development"; 1997, "conquering suffering, enriching humanity"; 1998, "life in
the 21st century: a vision for all"; 1999, "making a
difference"; 2000, "health systems: improving performance"; 2001, "mental health: new understanding, new hope"; 2002, "reducing risks, promoting
healthy life"; 2003, "shaping the future"; 2004,
"changing history"; 2005, "make every mother and
child count"; 2006, "working together for health";
2007, "a safer future: global public health security in
the 21st century"; 2008, "primary health care: now
more than ever"; 2010, "health systems financing:
the path to universal coverage"; 2013, "Research
for universal health coverage". No reports for 2009,
2011, or 2012. Also available in print.

520 **World health statistics**. http://www
.who.int/gho/publications/world_health
_statistics/en/index.html. World Health
Organization. Geneva, Switzerland:
World Health Organization. 2005–
RA407.A1
1939/46–96 publ. as *World health statistics
annual = Annuaire de statistiques sanitaires mondiales* (print version).

Part of WHOSIS: WHO statistical information
system.

Provides online access to the 2005-2013 reports.
Description based on 2013 online edition (http://
www.who.int/whosis/whostat/EN_WHS2011
_Full.pdf).

Contents: pt. I, "Health-related millennium
development goals"; pt. II, "Global health indicators"; tables: 1. "Life expectancy and mortality"; 2. "Cause-specific mortality and morbidity";
3. "Selected infectious diseases"; 4. "Health service
coverage"; 5. "Risk factors"; 6. "Health systems";
7. "Health expenditure"; 8. "Health inequities";
9. "Demographic and socioeconomic statistics."

"Annual compilation of health-related data for its
193 Member States . . . includes a summary of the
progress made towards achieving the health-related
Millennium Development Goals (MDGs) and associated targets . . . using publications and databases
produced and maintained by the technical programmes and regional offices of WHO. Indicators
have been included on the basis of their relevance to
global public health; the availability and quality of
the data; and the reliability and comparability of the
resulting estimates. Taken together, these indicators
provide a comprehensive summary of the current
status of national health and health systems."—
Introd. Derived from multiple sources, depending
on each indicator and the availability and quality
of data. Every effort has been made to ensure the
best use of country-reported data – adjusted where
necessary to deal with missing values, to correct for
known biases, and to maximize the comparability
of the statistics across countries and over time (cf.
Introd.) A print version is also available.

Medical illustration and images

521 **Anatomy atlases**. http://www.anatomy
atlases.org/. Ronald A. Bergman, Michael
A. D'Allesandro. 2006–
QM23.2
Pt. of BEN (BioSciEdNet): Digital library portal for
teaching and learning in the biological sciences
http://www.biosciednet.org/portal/, managed by
the American Association for the Advancement
of Science (AAAS) since 1999. In 2005, selected
for the National Science Digital Library (NSDL) as
"pathway for biological sciences education." Further information about BEN at http://www.bio
sciednet.org/portal/about/index.php.

Freely accessible digital anatomy collection,
containing several different anatomy and histology
atlases with images and original plates. One goal
is to "ensure an optimal educational experience
through simplicity and clarity in design.—*About
us*. Also provides links to related digital libraries
in the areas of medicine, radiology, and pediatrics.
Intended to educate medical students, residents,

and fellows, healthcare professionals, also patients and other general readers.

522   The art of medicine: Over 2,000 years of images and imagination.
Julie Anderson, Emma Shackleton, Emm Barnes, Antony Gormley. Chicago; Lewes, U.K.: The University of Chicago Press ; Ilex Press, 2011. 255 p., chiefly col. ill. ISBN 9780226749365
610.22/2   N8223.A53
Contents: Ch. 1, Mapping the body; ch. 2, Medicine in our lives; ch. 3, Understanding illnesses and developing cures; ch. 4, Treating with surgery and healing wounds; ch. 5, The mind and mental illness; ch. 6, Staying well.

Drawn from the holdings of London's Wellcome Collection http://www.wellcomecollection.org/. Includes many images of rare objects and works of art. Extensive bibliography, selected resources for further reading, picture list, and index.

Further information about the Wellcome Collection, the Wellcome Library, and its history http://library.wellcome.ac.uk/about-us/history-of-wellcome-library/ can be found at the respective websites.

523   DermAtlas. http://www.dermatlas.org. Bernard A. Cohen, Christoph U. Lehmann, Johns Hopkins University. Baltimore: Johns Hopkins University. 2000–
International collaborative project providing access to a growing collection of dermatology images. Contains more than 13,000 images in dermatology and skin diseases. Can be browsed by diagnosis, category, or body site. Searchable by keywords, diagnosis, pigmentation, color, body site, morphology, etc. Also provides links to other dermatology websites. Copyright and other disclaimer information at http://www.dermatlas.org/disclaimer. For health care professionals, patients, and other health care consumers.

DermIS (http://www.dermis.net/dermisroot/en/home/index.htm) is another example of an online collection of dermatology images and links to related information from various academic institutions worldwide.

524   Dermatology lexicon project. http://people.rit.edu/grhfad/DLP2/aboutDLP/abtFAQS.htm. Art Papier, Lowell Goldsmith, University of Rochester, Dept. of Dermatology. Rochester, N.Y.: University of Rochester. 2005–
International online open-source project with the goal of creating a standardized and reliable dermatology vocabulary. Provides diagnostic concepts, definitions, morphologic terminology, with illustrations and interactive animations. Includes dermatologic diagnoses and their synonyms, therapies, procedures, lab tests, etc. Also provides links to lexical/medical informatics resources, dermatology research, and organizations as well as patient information.

525   De humani corporis fabrica. http://vesalius.northwestern.edu/. Andreas Vesalius, Daniel Garrison, Malcolm Hast, Northwestern University (Evanston, Ill.), Dept. of Classics. Evanston, Ill.: Northwestern University. 2003–
Collaborative project of faculty members of Northwestern University Weinberg College of Arts and Sciences and Feinberg School of Medicine, library administrators of Galter Health Sciences Library and Northwestern University Library, and Northwestern University Academic Technologies to translate and annotate Vesalius's work *De humani corporis fabrica*. English translation has title *On the fabric of the human body: An annotated translation of the 1543 and 1555 editions of Andreas Vesalius's De humani corporis fabrica libri septem*.

This website provides access to the complete annotated text of the first book of the atlas. The translated text contains many bibliographic citations. The online edition of the atlas includes modern anatomical names (*nomina anatomica*) for all parts of the body and provides the ability to search text, reference figures, and anatomical terms. Also includes 272 anatomical woodcut drawings and diagrams, "applying 21st century computer technology to sixteenth century images, the online Fabrica's illustrations have been edited and enhanced for better viewing"—*press release*. Images can be browsed by name and by body location. Notes on the graphical editing are provided on the website.

Translation of all seven books of the original anatomical atlas and its revisions is in progress and will eventually appear on this website. A listing of the titles of Books 1–7, a fact sheet, and other help pages found on the website provide further detailed information. Information on the new complete translation and Vesalius can be found at http://www.vesalius-fabrica.com. Website also provides information on the the publication for Vesalius' 500th anniversary, *Transforming Vesalius: The 16th -century scientific revolution brought to lifw for the 21st century.*

526 Hardin MD:. http://hardinmd.lib. uiowa.edu/index.html. Hardin Library for the Health Sciences. Iowa City, Iowa: Hardin Library for the Health Sciences, University of Iowa. 1996–
004.67025; 610.02   RC81.H37
Listing of websites from a variety of sources, covering diseases and conditions and, in many cases, providing links to illustrations for diseases. Provides a good starting point for basic medical and health information. A related site by the Hardin Library is Medical/Health Sciences Libraries on the Web.

527 Health on the Net Foundation (HON). http://www.hon.ch/. Health on the Net Foundation. Geneva, Switzerland: Health on the Net Foundation (HON). 1995–
R859.7.E43
Health On the Net Foundation (HON) is a nonprofit, nongovernmental organization known for its HONcode, which defines rules and ethical standards for website developers on how information is provided in terms of the source and data provided. The HONcode is not considered an award or quality rating system for websites.

Provides a "portal to medical information on the Internet" (*Website*). Searchable website provides access to resources for individuals/patients and medical professionals. Includes HON's history and current contact information, access to listservs, newsgroups, and FAQs. For medical and health queries, HON's Search HON (http://www.hon.ch/ HONHunt/AdvHONHunt.html) and HONselect© (http://www.hon.ch/HONselect/) help locate quality websites and support groups, medical terminology, journal articles, and healthcare news. HONmedia (http://www.hon.ch/HONmedia/) is a growing and searchable repository of medical images and videos (currently contains 6,800 medical images and videos, pertaining to 1,700 topics and themes).

528 Historical anatomies on the Web. http://www.nlm.nih.gov/exhibition/

historicalanatomies/home.html. National Library of Medicine (U.S.). Bethesda, Md.: National Library of Medicine. 2003–
NC760
Digital project designed to provide access to selected high-quality images (not the entire books) from important anatomical atlases in NLM's collection, with author and title description, the artist, and illustration technique. Emphasis on the images, not the text. Examples include Albrecht Dürer's *Vier Bücher von menschlicher Proportion* (1528) and Andreas Vesalius's *De humani corporis fabrica libri septem* (1543) (525).

529 History and bibliography of artistic anatomy: Didactics for depicting the human figure. Boris Röhrl. Hildesheim, Germany: Olms, 2000. xx, 493 p., ill. ISBN 3487110741
743.4/9   NC760.R65
Contents: pt. 1, History: ch.1, Introd., ch. 2, Anatomy in the art of the Ancient World and the Middle Ages; ch. 3, From the 13th to the 15th cent.; ch. 4, 16th cent.; ch. 5, 17th cent.; ch. 6, 18th cent.; ch. 7, 19th cent.; ch. 8, 20th cent.; ch. 9, definition of genres; pt. 2, Bibliography: (1) Bibliography and description of books A–Z; (2) Appendices: Selected list of secondary literature; Index of ill.; Index of persons; Index of places and schools of art.

Considered a reference book which contains the didactical structure and content of specific teaching manuals. Presents the different subgroups of medically oriented teaching and how anatomy was taught in schools. Includes, for example, Leonardo da Vinci's anatomical sketchbooks. The bibliography in pt. 2 contains "books on osteology, myology, morphology, and locomotion for artists. Treatises accompanying écorchés and theoretical essays. Manuals on proportions, expression and portrait drawing" (*t.p.*).

530 Human anatomy: From the Renaissance to the digital age. Benjamin A. Rifkin, Michael J. Ackerman. New York: Abrams, 2006. 343 p., ill. (some col.) ISBN 0810955458
743.4/9   NC760.R54
History of artistic anatomy, with anatomic art and ill. from the Middle Ages to the computerized images of modern times. Contains biographies of famous anatomists and reproductions of their

work. For artists, physicians, medical students, and also general readers.

531 MedEdPORTAL. https://www.meded portal.org/. Association of American Medical Colleges. Washington: Association of American Medical Colleges. 2006–

MedEdPORTAL® is a project by the Association of American Medical Colleges (AAMC), in partnership with the American Dental Education Association (ADEA, 797) and other organizations, that provides free access to peer-reviewed teaching resources used in medical education (e.g., tutorials, virtual patients, simulation cases, lab guides, videos, podcasts, assessment tools, etc.). Designed to help faculty publish and share teaching resources. MedEdPORTAL staff review submissions for relevance and appropriateness before they are published on the site. Information about copyright is provided. Further details are provided at https://www.meded portal.org/about, including a video with an overview of MedEdPORTAL.

MedEdPORTAL publications are cataloged using medical subject headings (MeSH: Medical subject headings, 858). To locate these and other resources, MedEdPORTAL can be browsed by discipline (list of subject areas and number of available resources within each category). Also searchable by keyword.

The freely accessible *Directory & repository of educational assessment measures (DREAM)* (http://www.mededportal.org/dream), a collection of tested health professions assessment measures, is part of MedEdPORTAL, including "a copy of the assessment instrument itself and a peer-reviewed critical analysis of the literature surrounding the use of the instrument."—*Publ. description*.

AAMC also participates in Health education assets library (HEAL), a repository of health sciences images, videos, and audio files from different collections.

532 Medical encyclopedia (MedlinePlus). http://www.nlm.nih.gov/medlineplus/ encyclopedia.html. National Library of Medicine (U.S.). Atlanta; Bethesda, Md.: A.D.A.M.; National Library of Medicine. 1999–

RC81.A2

Title varies: A.D.A.M. Medical Encyclopedia; MedlinePlus, Medical Encyclopedia.

Articles about diseases and conditions, injuries, nutrition, poisons, surgeries, symptoms, tests, and other special topics. Contains medical illustrations and images. Editorial processes and policy at http://www.adam.com/editorialGuidelines.aspx.

533 NCI visuals online. http://visualsonline .cancer.gov/. National Cancer Institute. Bethesda, Md.: National Cancer Institute. 200?–

Produced by National Cancer Institute (NCI), Office of Communication and Education; NCI Office of Media Relations.

Contains images from the NCI collections, e.g., general biomedical and science-related images, cancer-specific scientific and patient care–related images, portraits of NCI directors and staff, etc. Can be searched (http://visualsonline.cancer.gov/ search.cfm) and browsed (http://visualsonline .cancer.gov/browse.cfm). All images are in the public domain and may be used, linked, or reproduced without permission, but credit should be given to the listed source and/or author.

534 NetAnatomy. http://www.NetAnatomy. com/. Raymond J. Walsh, Stephen P. Raskin, Scholar Educational Systems, Inc. Crofton, Md.: Scholar Educational Systems, Inc. 2001–

QM23.2

Produced by Scholar Educational Systems (SES). "This website contains content that addresses three of the major anatomical disciplines, including radiographic anatomy, cross-sectional anatomy, and human gross anatomy"—*publ. notes*. For educators and students in the health professions. Available only through institutional subscription.

535 The Netter collection of medical illustrations. Frank H. Netter, Ernst Oppenheimer. Summit, N.J.: Novartis, 1997–. vols., ill. (some col.) ISBN 0914168754 616.07/022/2 RB33.N48 (Netter clinical science)

Anatomical and pathological color ill., with explanatory text, of the major organ systems of the human body as well as diagnostic and surgical procedures. Available in a variety of educational products in various formats, including books, charts, and software (e.g., The Netter Presenter™—Human Anatomy). Individual volumes in this new series are listed at http://www.elsevier.com/books/book -series/netter-clinical-science.

Based on and continues *The Ciba collection of medical illustrations: A compilation of pathological and anatomical paintings,* prepared by Frank H. Netter, publ. 1953–94. Contents: Digestive system: pt. I, Upper digestive tract (1954); pt. II, Lower digestive tract (1959); pt. III, Liver, biliary, tract and pancreas (1964); Endocrine system (1965); Heart (1969); Kidneys, ureters and urinary bladder (1973); Musculoskeletal system: pt. I, Anatomy, physiology, and metabolic disorders (1994); pt. II, Developmental disorders, tumors, rheumatic diseases and joint replacements (1994); pt. III, Trauma, evaluation and management (1988); Nervous system: pt. I, Anatomy and physiology (1984); pt. II, Neurologic and neuromuscular disorders (1987); Respiratory system (1979).

Also avaialable as e-boooks, with newer eds. of several vols.; see http://www.elsevier.com/books/ book-series/netter-clinical-science. Small images are freely available, with options for purchasing larger images, at http://www.netterimages.com/.

536   Public health image library (PHIL). http://phil.cdc.gov/Phil/. Centers for Disease Control and Prevention. Atlanta: Centers for Disease Control and Prevention. [1998]–

Public health image library (PHIL), created by a working group at the Centers for Disease Control and Prevention (CDC); National Library of Medicine (NLM).

Collection of a variety of single images, image sets, multimedia files, etc., with current and historical content about people, places, scientific subjects, etc. FAQ section (http://phil.cdc.gov/Phil/ faq.asp) provides detailed information. Useful for public health professionals, scientists, librarians, teachers, and students.

This website also provides links to other CDC and NLM image libraries (e.g., Images from the history of medicine and Visible Human). Complements other medical image collections such as Health education assets library (HEAL) and Images-MD (http://www.springerimages.com/imagesMD/).

537   The Sourcebook of medical illustration: Over 900 anatomical, medical, and scientific illustrations
available for general re-use and adaptation free of normal copyright restrictions. Peter Cull. Carnforth, U.K.;Park Ridge, N.J: Parthenon Pub. Group, 1989. xxiii, 481 p., chiefly ill. ISBN 0940813726

611/.0022/2   QM25.S677

A collection of line drawings, simple medical illustrations, and graphics designed to assist in the communication of medical and scientific information. Sections include body outlines and all anatomical features, as well as illustrations relating to obstetrics, anesthesia, cells and tissues, bacteria, yeasts, protozoans, helminths, viruses, arthropods, scientific symbols, and maps.

538   Turning the pages online. http:// archive.nlm.nih.gov/proj/ttp/intro.htm. Lister Hill National Center for Biomedical Communications, National Library of Medicine (U.S.). Bethesda, Md.: National Library of Medicine. 2003–

Produced by National Library of Medicine (NLM).

Turning the Pages Information System (TTPI), initially created by the British Library. TTP at NLM is the result of collaboration between the British Library and NLM, with refinement of the original technology. Detailed information about research, design, system development, software, and content available on website.

Web version provides access to the digitized images of rare historic books in the biomedical sciences. Includes many important and influential works in the history of medicine. Provides the ability to browse titles and bibliographic information, to turn the pages, and to use zoom images. Information regarding the mobile version of this resource is part of NLM's Gallery of mobile apps and sites.

539   The Visible Human Project. http:// www.nlm.nih.gov/research/visible/ visible_human.html. National Library of Medicine (U.S.). Bethesda, Md.: U.S. National Library of Medicine. 1994–

The Visible Human Project® (VHP) was established in 1989. The Visible Human male data set was released in Nov. 1994, the Visible Human female data set in Nov. 1995.

Presents "anatomically detailed, three-dimensional representations of the normal male and female human bodies" (*Website*). Consists of MRI (magnetic resonance imaging), CT (computed tomography), and cryosection images of cadavers, intended "as a reference for the study of human anatomy . . . and to serve as test bed and model for the construction of network-accessible image libraries . . . data sets have been applied to a wide range of educational, diagnostic, treatment planning, virtual reality, artistic, mathematical, and industrial uses" (*Website*) and other applications by NLM and by a large number of licensees worldwide. The applications developed by or under the direction of NLM include, for example, "AnatQuest", "Atlas of functional human anatomy," and other projects of electronically representing images in clinical medicine and biomedical research. Useful mainly for graduate students and faculty.

540   Wellcome images: 2000 years of human culture. http://wellcomeimages.org/indexplus/. Wellcome Library. London: Wellcome Library. 2007–

R133

Previously known as the Wellcome Trust Medical Photographic Library. Part of the Wellcome Collection (http://www.wellcomecollection.org/sitemap/index.htm) developed by the Wellcome Trust (http://www.wellcomecollection.org/aboutus/WTD027244.htm), linked from The Wellcome library: The library of the Wellcome collection website.

Allows access to images, manuscripts, and illustrations on the medical and social history of medicine, modern biomedical science, clinical medicine from antiquity to the present, molecular models, portraits, depiction of medical practice, etc. All content made available under a Creative Commons License, which allows users to copy, distribute and display the image, provided the source is fully attributed and it is used for noncommercial purposes. A valuable aid for teachers and researchers.

Another recommended web-resource is the "Royal Society picture library" (https://pictures.royalsociety.org/home), an online database (browsable and searchable/basic and advanced search) of freely available for viewing digital images of paintings, drawings and prints held in the archives of the Royal Society collections. The collections contain, for example, portraits of eminent scientists and physicians, anatomical drawings, images of rare published plates from the16th to 19th century, etc. Further

details at https://pictures.royalsociety.org/about. For researchers in the history of science and medicine.

541   The whole brain atlas. http://www.med.harvard.edu/AANLIB/home.html. Keith A. Johnson, J. Alex Becker, Harvard University School of Medicine. Cambridge, Mass.: Harvard Medical School

RC386.6

Sponsored in part by the "Depts. of Radiology and Neurology at Brigham and Women's Hospital, Harvard Medical School, the Countway Library of Medicine, and the American Academy of Neurology"—*Sponsors*.

Contents: Normal Brain; Cerebrovascular Disease (Stroke or "Brain Attack"); Neoplastic Disease (Brain Tumor); Degenerative Disesae; Inflammatory or Infectious Disease.

Atlas of the human brain in health and disease, providing a resource for central nervous system imaging. Includes magnetic resonance, x-ray computed tomography, and nuclear medicine images. Contains normal and pathologic structure images and multiplanar and vascular anatomy.

Quotations

542   Medicine in quotations: Views of health and disease through the ages. 2nd ed. Edward J. Huth, T. J. Murray. Philadelphia: American College of Physicians, 2006. xvi, 581 p. ISBN 1930513674
610.2   R705.M465
First ed., 2000.

Compilation of 3,521 quotations about "views of health and disease through the ages." Includes quotations submitted by readers of the previous edition. Alphabetical arrangement by topics, presented in chronological order, providing citations to the exact location of the quoted passages. Each entry numbered. Author citation index; subject index. Supplements Maurice B. Strauss' *Familiar medical quotations. Doctor's book of humorous quotations* by Bennett can possibly serve as a reference when preparing a presentation to medical professionals. Another resource in this area, available both in print and as an e-book, is *Medically speaking* by Gaither et al.

The searchable *Medicine in Quotations* system, previously made available with the first edition by the American College of Physicians, is no longer available.

Another resource is *Medical education: A dictionary of quotations* by Walsh et al., with quotations on curriculum, learning, teaching, etc.

543   The quotable Osler. William Osler, Mark E. Silverman, T. J. Murray, Charles S. Bryan, American College of Physicians—American Society of Internal Medicine. Philadelphia, Pa.: American College of Physicians—American Society of Internal Medicine, 2002. xxxv, 283 p., ill. ISBN 1930513348

610   R705.O83

Contents: (1) Personal qualities; (2) The art and practice of medicine; (3) The medical profession; (4) Diagnosis; (5) Disease, specific illnesses, lifestyle, drugs; (6) Medical education; (7) Men and women, aging, history; (8) Science and truth; (9) Faith, religion, melancholy, death.

"Filled with Osler's best sayings and writings, . . . provides a comprehensive view of Osler's wisdom for an audience of the 21st century"— *Publ. notes*. "Brief remarks or aphorisms rather than lengthy quotations" (*Foreword*) and proverbs, organized by topics. Bibliography and index. A rev. 2008 ed. is available.

Sir William Osler: an annotated bibliography with illustrations (407), supplemented by addenda in 1997, provides details on Osler's extensive writings.

544   The Yale book of quotations. Fred R. Shapiro, Joseph Epstein. New Haven, Conn.: Yale University Press, 2006. xxiv, 1067 p., ports. ISBN 0300107986

082   PN6081.Y35

Compiler of the *Oxford dictionary of American legal quotations* and profiled in the *Wall Street journal* (January 22, 1997) for his indefatigable research on legal footnotes, the Yale librarian Fred Shapiro has ascended to the highest ranks of quotation mavens.

Modeled on the *Oxford English dictionary* approach to documenting first word use, this work serves as an outstanding historical dictionary of quotations. Besides including quotations omitted from many classic works, the *Yale book of quotations* includes modern American popular culture, children's literature, sports, and computers among its 12,000 entries. Shapiro used eclectic sources to find and verify entries, including databases, the Internet, hundreds of quotation books, and the American Dialect Society e-mail list.

He relied on the "indispensable" *Oxford dictionary of quotations* for pre-1800 citations; post-1800 quotations were rechecked and verified.

Arranged alphabetically by author or specific category (e.g., modern proverbs, radio and television catchphrases). Keyword index.

Other important sources that involved extensive research on quotation origins include *Quote verifier* and *Brewer's quotations*.

Internet resources

545   AEGiS. http://www.aegis.org/. AEGiS. San Juan Capistrano, Calif.: AEGiS. 1990–

AIDS Education Global Information System (AEGiS) is a nonprofit organization.

This frequently updated resource provides the latest international HIV/AIDS news, clinical information, legal information about HIV-related cases, a conference database, links to relevant U.S. government sites and other websites, and HIV/AIDS-related publications (e.g., activist, general, patient oriented, and professional) available via the Internet. Also provides a timeline and HIV/AIDS statistics.

546   AIDSinfo. http://www.aidsinfo.nih.gov. U.S. Department of Health and Human Services, National Institutes of Health (U.S.), AIDS Clinical Trials Information Service. Bethesda, Md.: National Institutes of Health

RA643.8

Result of merging two previous U.S. Dept. of Health and Human Services (DHHS) projects. Supersedes the AIDS Clinical Trials Information Service (ACTIS) and the HIV/AIDS Treatment Information Service (ATIS).

Resource for current information on federally and privately funded clinical trials for AIDS patients and HIV-infected persons, federally approved HIV treatment and prevention guidelines, and medical practice guidelines. Provides access to a searchable HIV/AIDS drugs database (via "Drugs" tab) that includes approved and investigational anti-HIV medications, including side effects, dosages, and interactions with other drugs or food; also access to brochures, fact sheets, and other Web resources on HIV/AIDS, current and archived versions of DHHS guidelines, and a searchable HIV/AIDS glossary (English and Spanish). For HIV/AIDS patients, the general public, health care providers, and researchers. Information regarding the mobile version of this resource is part of NLM's Gallery of mobile apps and sites.

Additional major HIV/AIDS resources can be accessed via the following sites: Fact sheet, AIDS Information Resources (http://www.nlm.nih.gov/pubs/factsheets/aidsinfs.html), Specialized Information Services: HIV/AIDS Information (http://sis.nlm.nih.gov/hiv.html), CDC National Prevention Information Network (NPIN) (http://www.cdcnpin.org/scripts/hiv/index.asp), UNAIDS: Joint United National Programming on HIV/AIDS (http://www.unaids.org/en/), and AIDS Treatment Data Network (http://www.atdn.org/).

547 American Medical Association. http://www.ama-assn.org/. American Medical Association. Chicago: American Medical Association. 1995–
610.9206   R130.5

This searchable website provides a variety of professional resources and standards for AMA members, including, for example, information sources on medical ethics, public health (e.g., eliminating health disparities, health preparedness, disaster response, obesity), medical science, legal issues, and AMA history (with time line and highlights of AMA history). Also provides information on medical education and licensure as well as online resources and other links for medical school students and residents. Includes a section for patients, with access to patient education resources (e.g., "Health literacy resources," "Atlas of the human body," etc.).

Other useful AMA-related links include, for example, DoctorFinder, *Code of medical ethics, current opinions with annotations*, *Current procedural terminology: CPT* (856), FREIDA (291), *Graduate medical education directory* (292), *Health professions career and education directory*, and *State medical licensure requirements and statistics* (508).

Many of these resources have general reference value in academic and public libraries.

548 amfAR. http://www.amfar.org. American Foundation for AIDS Research. New York; Washington: American Foundation for AIDS Research. 1999–

"amfAR™, the Foundation for AIDS Research, is one of the world's leading nonprofit organizations dedicated to the support of AIDS research, HIV prevention, treatment education, and the advocacy of sound AIDS-related public policy."—*Website*

Provides basic HIV/AIDS facts and statistics, HIV testing, information about various therapies (approved or under development), young people and HIV/AIDS, women and HIV/AIDS, global initiatives, and many other related topics and links.

"amfAR global links," formerly know as *HIV/AIDS treatment directory*, and "HIV/AIDS treatment insider," available 2000-5, have ceased publication. *The AmFAR AIDS handbook: The complete guide to understanding HIV and AIDS*, a comprehensive guide to help readers understand HIV/AIDS, treatment options, and how treatment decisions are made, has not been updated since 1999.

549 AOA American Osteopathic Association. http://www.osteopathic.org/. Chicago: American Osteopathic Association. 2003-

Website contents for professionals and students include About the AOA, Accreditation, Advocacy, Education, Events, News & Publications, Professional Development. Section on "Osteopathic medicine and your health" is geared toward patients and general audiences, and includes a search to "Find a DO."

AOA members have access to many details formerly available in the AOA yearbook and directory.

550 Association of American Medical Colleges (AAMC). http://www.aamc.org/. Association of American Medical Colleges (AAMC). Washington: Association of American Medical Colleges (AAMC). 1995–
610.71106; 610.07

Not-for-profit association representing U.S. and Canadian medical schools; teaching hospitals and health systems; and academic and professional societies. Intends to serve and lead the academic medical community, with its mission, vision, and strategy outlined at https://www.aamc.org/about/. Links to related member groups, e.g., Council of Academic Societies, Council of Deans, Group on Resident Affairs, Group on Student Affairs, Women in Medicine, and others. AAMC publications and projects include *AAMC data book* (460), *Directory of American medical education* (266), *Medical school admission requirements, U.S.A. and Canada* (268), MedEdPORTAL, and others.

551 Cancer.gov. http://www.cancer.gov/.
National Cancer Institute. Bethesda, Md.:
National Cancer Institute. 1990s–

A metasite for cancer information for health care professionals as well as patients. Provides extensive information on all aspects of cancer as a disease and current cancer treatment, including, for example, complementary and alternative medicine, screening, prevention, and genetics. Links for searching the PubMed cancer literature subset and PDQ Query at http://www.cancer.gov/cancertopics/pdq/cancerdatabase.

552 DermAtlas. http://www.dermatlas.org.
Bernard A. Cohen, Christoph U.
Lehmann, Johns Hopkins University.
Baltimore: Johns Hopkins University.
2000–

International collaborative project providing access to a growing collection of dermatology images. Contains more than 13,000 images in dermatology and skin diseases. Can be browsed by diagnosis, category, or body site. Searchable by keywords, diagnosis, pigmentation, color, body site, morphology, etc. Also provides links to other dermatology websites. Copyright and other disclaimer information at http://www.dermatlas.org/disclaimer. For health care professionals, patients, and other health care consumers.

DermIS (http://www.dermis.net/dermisroot/en/home/index.htm) is another example of an online collection of dermatology images and links to related information from various academic institutions worldwide.

553 Digital collections (NLM). http://collections.nlm.nih.gov/muradora/.
National Library of Medicine (U.S.).
Bethesda, Md.: U.S. National Library of

Medicine, National Institutes of Health, Dept. of Health and Human Resources

Repository for access and preservation of biomedical resources from NLM's collections, including books and films & videos. This continually updated resource contains several collections and "featured items from the collection," e.g., "Cholera online: A modern pandemic in text and images," "Medicine in the Americas," and others. This site can be browsed by collections, titles, subjects, authors, years, and languages. Further information can be found on the NLM Digital Repository Project information page (http://www.nlm.nih.gov/digitalrepository/index.html). It complements PMC (PubMed Central), the digital archive of electronic journal articles.

Related sites are "Digital resources" from NLM's historical collections (http://www.nlm.nih.gov/hmd/collections/digital/index.html) and its digital manuscripts program (http://www.nlm.nih.gov/hmd/collections/archives/dmp/index.html).

554 GeneTests. http://www.genetests.org/.
Children's Hospital and Medical Center
(Seattle, Wash.), Univ. of Wash.,
School of Medicine; National Library of
Medicine (U.S.). Seattle, Wash.: Univ. of
Washington. 1993–

Contents: Home page; Disorders; GeneReviews; Panel Directory; Laboratory directory; Clinic directory.

Provides authoritative information on genetic testing and its use in diagnosis, disease management, and genetic counseling. Promotes use of genetic services in patient care and decision making by individuals. GeneReviews and Laboratory directory can be searched by disease, gene symbol, protein name, etc. Contains context-sensitive illustrated glossary, teaching tools, and other resources.

555 Grants.gov. http://www.grants.gov.
United States Dept. of Health and Human
Services. Washington: Dept. of Health
and Human Services

"Grants.gov is a central storehouse for information on over 1,000 grant programs and provides access to approximately $400 billion in annual awards."—*Website* Organizations, local and state government agencies, businesses, and individuals need to register in order to apply for grants from the 26 federal grant-making agencies. Many user guides and help screens. Downloadable instructions and grant application forms.

Related site: Catalog of Federal Domestic Assistance

556   Hardin MD:. http://hardinmd.lib.uiowa
.edu/index.html. Hardin Library for
the Health Sciences. Iowa City, Iowa:
Hardin Library for the Health Sciences,
University of Iowa. 1996–
004.67025; 610.02   RC81.H37

Listing of websites from a variety of sources, covering diseases and conditions and, in many cases, providing links to illustrations for diseases. Provides a good starting point for basic medical and health information. A related site by the Hardin Library is Medical/Health Sciences Libraries on the Web.

**557   Health education assets library
(HEAL) Collection**. http://library.med
.utah.edu/heal/. Sharon E. Dennis,
Chris Candler, Sebastian Uijtdehaage,
University of California, University
of Utah, University of Oklahoma. Los
Angeles; Salt Lake City, Utah; Oklahoma
City, Okla.: University of California;
University of Utah; University of
Oklahoma. 2000–

HEAL is a collaborative multi-institutional project to collect digital materials for health sciences education. It is a repository of health sciences images, videos, and audio files from different authoritative collections. Users can search, browse, download, and contribute their own files. The resources are described with metadata, including medical subject headings (MeSH, 858), for easy and accurate browsing and searching.

The HEAL project was initially funded by the National Science Foundation and the National Library of Medicine.

Another major project, MedEdPortal (AAMC), provides a growing number of online resources for use in medical education.

**558   Human Genome Project information
archive**. http://www.ornl.gov/sci/tech
resources/Human_Genome/home.shtml.
U.S. Department of Energy Office
of Science, Office of Biological and
Environmental Research, Human

Genome Program. Oak Ridge, Tenn.:
Oak Ridge National Laboratory, U.S.
Department of Energy. 1990–2013
                                    QH447

Website sponsored by the U.S. Dept. of Energy Office of Science, Office of Biological and Environmental Research, Human Genome Program; website maintained by the Human Genome Management Information System (HGMIS) at Oak Ridge National Laboratory for the U.S. Department of Energy Human Genome Program.

Contents: About HGP; Research; Publications; Education. Subtopics include Ethical, Legal, and Social Issues (ELSI); Genetics Privacy and Education; and more.

This website provides a multitude of annotated links to resources on all aspects of the HPG. Articles analyzing the genome continue to be published but not necessarily linked in the archive. Information for Genetic Professionals (http://www.kumc.edu/gec/geneinfo.html), a clinical-genetics site by Debra Collins, Genetics Education Center, University of Kansas Medical Center, provides further information in this area.

559   Institute of Medicine (IOM). http://
www.iom.edu/. Institute of Medicine.
Washington: National Academy of
Sciences. 1998–

The Institute of Medicine (IOM), one of the U.S. National Academies, has the mission to "serve as adviser to the nation to improve health" and "provides independent, objective, evidence-based advice to policymakers, health professionals, the private sector, and the public"—*main page*. Offers a list of all publications by the IOM since 1970 (http://www.iom.edu/Reports.aspx), which cover a broad range of topics, including aging, child health, a variety of diseases, global health, health care quality, minority health, nutrition, public health, public policy, preventive medicine, women's health, and many other areas. The National Academies Press (http://www.nap.edu, 31) provides online access to the publications of the four National Academies, i.e., National Academy of Sciences, National Academy of Engineering, IOM, and National Research Council.

560   MedEdPORTAL. https://www.meded
portal.org/. Association of American
Medical Colleges. Washington:

Association of American Medical
Colleges. 2006–

MedEdPORTAL® is a project by the Association of American Medical Colleges (AAMC), in partnership with the American Dental Education Association (ADEA, 797) and other organizations, that provides free access to peer-reviewed teaching resources used in medical education (e.g., tutorials, virtual patients, simulation cases, lab guides, videos, podcasts, assessment tools, etc.). Designed to help faculty publish and share teaching resources. MedEdPORTAL staff review submissions for relevance and appropriateness before they are published on the site. Information about copyright is provided. Further details are provided at https://www.meded portal.org/about, including a video with an overview of MedEdPORTAL.

MedEdPORTAL publications are cataloged using medical subject headings (MeSH: Medical subject headings, 858). To locate these and other resources, MedEdPORTAL can be browsed by discipline (list of subject areas and number of available resources within each category). Also searchable by keyword.

The freely accessible *Directory & repository of educational assessment measures (DREAM)* (http:// www.mededportal.org/dream), a collection of tested health professions assessment measures, is part of MedEdPORTAL, including "a copy of the assessment instrument itself and a peer-reviewed critical analysis of the literature surrounding the use of the instrument."—*Publ. description*.

AAMC also participates in Health education assets library (HEAL), a repository of health sciences images, videos, and audio files from different collections.

561 MedlinePlus. http://medlineplus.gov/.
U.S. National Library of Medicine.
Bethesda, Md.: U.S. Dept. of Health and
Human Services, National Library of
Medicine. 1998–
025.04; 651.504261; 613   RA776.5

A consumer health reference database with free and reliable information from the National Library of Medicine (NLM), the National Institutes of Health (NIH), other government agencies, and various health-related organizations. A continually expanding and updated resource. Information on over 900 diseases and conditions, as well as

drug information (prescription, nonprescription (ASHF—American Society of Health System Pharmacists consumer medication information)), herbs and supplements, with content as of September 2010 from *Natural medicines comprehensive database (NMCD,* 644), no longer from *Natural standard* as was previously the case, an illustrated medical encyclopedia (*A.D.A.M. medical encyclopedia*) and a search box for look-up of medical terms on the English homepage, interactive patient tutorials, anatomy (http://www.nlm.nih. gov/medlineplus/anatomyvideos.html) & surgery videos and other tools by following the "videos & cool tools" tab, lists of hospitals, physicians, and dentists, and health news. Provides preformulated MEDLINE/PubMed® searches for recent articles. Includes *NIH MedlinePlus magazine*, a quarterly publication for patients and their families, providing authoritative medical and healthcare information. "MedlinePlus en español" toggles between English and Spanish. Also provides links to browse selected health information in multiple languages other than English and Spanish at http://www.nlm.nih.gov/medlineplus/languages/ languages.html. Web 2.0 technologies help users share content, e.g., RSS feeds for all health topics. The MedlinePlus search cloud (http://www .nlm.nih.gov/medlineplus/cloud.html)   displays the top 100 search terms typed into the MedlinePlus search box, usually updated every week day. Further detailed descriptive information of MedlinePlus is available at http://www.nlm.nih.gov/ pubs/factsheets/medlineplus.html. For patients, families, and healthcare providers. Information regarding the mobile version of this resource is part of NLM's Gallery of mobile apps and sites.

MedlinePlus Connect, launched in November 2010, is a free service that allows electronic health record (EHR) systems to link users to MedlinePlus. NLM has mapped MedlinePlus health topics to two standard diagnostic coding systems used in EHRs (further description at http://www.nlm.nih.gov/ medlineplus/connect/overview.html).

Also available in a mobile version (m.medline plus.gov).

562 Men's health (MedlinePlus). http://
www.nlm.nih.gov/medlineplus/
menshealth.html. National Library of
Medicine (U.S.). Bethesda, Md.: National

Library of Medicine, National Institutes of Health, Dept. of Health and Human Services. 200?–

RA777.8

A MedlinePlus® health topic. Collection of links for a variety of resources on men's health (e.g., specific conditions, treatments, prevention/screening, etc.) and also related issues and topics.

563 MLANET. http://www.mlanet.org/. Medical Library Association. Chicago: Medical Library Association (MLA). 1998–

Medical Library Association (MLA), since 1889, "a nonprofit, educational organization of more than 1,100 institutions and 3,600 individual members in the health sciences information field, committed to educating health information professionals, supporting health information research, promoting access to the world's health sciences information, and working to ensure that the best health information is available to all" (*MLA website*).

Searchable home page for MLA which provides a variety of resources for its members, such as professional standards and practices, discussion of information issues and policy, career information resources, professional credentialing, publications, etc. Also provides resources for health consumers, e.g., "A User's guide to finding and evaluating health information on the Web" (http://www.mlanet.org/resources/userguide.html), including "Deciphering MedSpeak," and MLA's guidelines on finding quality information on the Internet. Provides links to websites considered quality sites ("top ten") by MLA, such as: Cancer.gov, Centers for Disease Control (CDC), familydoctor.org (http://familydoctor.org)healthfinder®; HIV InSite, Kidshealth® (http://www.kidshealth.org/), Mayo Clinic, MedlinePlus. Some content is restricted to members only.

Currently 23 different MLA sections have their own webpages (http://www.mlanet.org/sections/sections.html). A prominent example of a section website is the Consumer and Patient Information Section of the Medical Library Association (CAPHIS).

564 National academies press. www.nap.edu/. National Academies Press (U.S.), National Academies (U.S.), National Academy of Sciences (U.S.). Washington:

National Academies Press. 1999–

Z1217.N37

Contains free online access to over 3,700 monographs, mainly reports of the academy on issues of importance to the science community and society—for example, future trends in employment opportunities in different fields, analyses of discrepancies in gender/racial makeup of scientists in discplines, as well as the prospects of scientific projects or programs. Overall, it provides a wealth of information on the state of science. The National Academies are made up of the National Academy of Sciences (456), National Academy of Engineering, the Institute of Medicine (24), and the National Research Council.

565 National Cancer Institute. http://www.cancer.gov/. National Cancer Institute, U.S. National Institutes of Health. Bethesda, Md.: National Cancer Institute

Website created by the National Cancer Institute (NCI), a division of the National Institutes of Health (NIH).

Contents: NCI home, Cancer topics, Clinical trials, Cancer statistics, Research and funding, News, About NCI.

Links to cancer-related information for health professionals, medical students, and patients. Provides guidance to searching the cancer literature in PubMed by searching the "cancer subset" and access to already prepared searches on more than 100 different topics. Non-PubMed citations previously found in CANCERLIT, a database no longer being maintained, consist primarily of meeting abstracts from the annual meetings of the American Society of Clinical Oncology (ASCO) and the American Association for Cancer Research (AACR). ASCO abstracts for recent years are available via http://www.asco.org, AACR abstracts at http://aacrmeetingabstracts.org/. Also provides access to PDQ: Physician data query (http://www.cancer.gov/cancertopics/pdq), a database with the latest information about cancer treatment, screening, prevention, genetics, etc.

The NCI website includes descriptions of various types of cancer (A–Z list of cancers: http://www.cancer.gov/cancertopics/alphalist/) and related topics, with links to diagnosis and treatment information and supportive care, information on clinical trials, cancer prevention, cancer statistics (e.g., SEER cancer statistics review), cancer statistics tools, cancer mortality maps and graphs, and related NCI websites. Links to the Dictionary of cancer terms and various cancer vocabulary resources (e.g., NCI thesaurus, NCI metathesaurus, and NCI terminology browser), NCI drug dictionary, NCI publications, etc. Available both in English and Spanish.

566 National Center for Complementary and Alternative Medicine. http:// nccam.nih.gov. National Center for Complementary and Alternative Medicine. Silver Spring, Md.: National Center for Complementary and Alternative Medicine. 2000–

RC271.A62

National Center for Complementary and Alternative Medicine (NCCAM), established in 1998. Part of the National Institutes of Health (NIH).

Explores complementary and alternative medicine (CAM), providing research opportunities in clinical and basic science and research training. Operates an information clearinghouse to answer requests for information and is considered the public's point of contact for scientifically-based information on CAM and for information about NCCAM. Provides a variety of publications and extensive online health information (http://nccam .nih.gov/health/), links to clinical trials, popular health topics, diseases, conditions, treatments, and therapies for both health professionals and consumers. Also provides links to other organizations, including MedlinePlus: Alternative Medicine, MedlinePlus: Herbs and Supplements, NIH Office of Dietary Supplements, and other organizations that provide CAM information. NCCAM and the National Library of Medicine (NLM) have collaborated to create CAM on PubMed.

567 National Human Genome Research Institute. http://genome.gov/. National Human Genome Research Institute (U.S.). Bethesda, Md.: National Human Genome Research Institute, National Institutes of Health, U.S. Department of Health and Human Services. 1995–

QH445.2

National Human Genome Research Institute (NHGRI), previously known as National Center for Human Genome Research (NCHGR), which was established in 1989 because of the Human

Genome Project (HGP), since 1990 is a collaborative project of the U.S. Dept. of Energy (DOE) and National Institutes of Health (NIH) to map the human genome; and since HGP's completion in 1993, to apply genome technologies to the study of specific diseases. In 1996, the Center for Inherited Disease Research (CIDR) was also established (cofunded by eight NIH institutes and centers) to study the genetic components of complex disorders. A timeline, 1988 to the present, provides further details about HPG, its completion in 2003, associated events, research, and relevant publications at http://genome.gov/10001763.

Provides access to information, databases, and links to other resources concerning research, grants, health, policy and ethics, educational resources, etc. Some examples include the Talking glossary of genetic terms http://www.genome.gov/ glossary/, the NHGRI policy and legislation database http://genome.gov/PolicyEthics/LegDatabase/ pubsearch.cfm, Online bioethics resources (625), the Ethical, legal and social implications (ELSI) research program, and Initiatives and resources for minority and special populations (http://genome. gov/10001192), information on current research projects (e.g., the ENCODE project [ENCyclopedia Of DNA Elements], a pilot project for testing and comparing new methods to identify functional sequences in DNA, model organisms, creation of Centers of excellence in genomic science, the Genetic variation program, the Haplotype map, gene discovery and technology development, establishment of the Center for Inherited Disease Research, and much more.

568 National Institutes of Health (NIH). http://www.nih.gov/. National Institutes of Health. Bethesda, Md.: National Institutes of Health. 1995–

Portal to information about NIH's organization, its programs for conducting and supporting medical research, and links to other U.S. government information. Includes information and scientific advances, with listing, descriptions, and quick links to the 27 individual NIH institutes and centers, at http:// www.nih.gov/icd/, including the National Library of Medicine (NLM). Functions as an online medical reference tool to access health-related information of various kinds (for example, Health topics A–Z). Includes, for example, research training and scientific resources at NIH facilities, hospitals, and laboratories supported by NIH; Nobel prize winners among NIH scientists; information resources provided by NLM; information on NIH news and events; health information, research, grants and contracts, scientists, scientific resources, institutes, and offices.

569 National Library of Medicine. http://www.nlm.nih.gov/. National Library of Medicine (U.S.), National Institutes of Health. Bethesda, Md.: National Library of Medicine. 1993–

Homepage of the U.S. National Library of Medicine (NLM). Contains information about NLM's databases and other electronic resources, e.g., PubMed/MEDLINE, ClinicalTrials.gov, LocatorPlus, MedlinePlus, MeSH (858), NLM Catalog, NLM classification, NLM gateway, TOXNET, Unified medical language system (UMLS), and the Visible human project, to name a few of NLM's important resources. An annotated list of NLM databases and electronic resources (http://www.nlm.nih.gov/databases/) provides access to additional resources. Also includes a link to NLM's numerous "retired databases" (http://www.nlm.nih.gov/services/pastdatabases.html). Health information and NLM's products and services are presented for several different user groups: the public, health care professionals, researchers, librarians, and publishers. A listing and link to NIH clinical alerts, which are "provided to expedite the release of findings from the NIH-funded clinical trials where such release could significantly affect morbidity and mortality" (*Clinical Alerts and Advisories page*) are available at http://www.nlm.nih.gov/databases/alerts/clinical_alerts.html. Milestones in NLM history (http://apps.nlm.nih.gov/175/milestones.cfm) and the NLM fact sheets (http://www.nlm.nih.gov/pubs/factsheets/nlm.html) provide further information.

570 National Network of Libraries of Medicine (NN/LM). http://nnlm.gov/. National Library of Medicine (U.S.). Bethesda, Md.: National Library of Medicine. 2001–

Coordinated by the National Library of Medicine (NLM). Searchable website, with informative sections on member services, outreach, resource sharing, document delivery, funding, training, and other educational opportunities. The Health Information on the Web tab provides "links to web resources from the National Library of Medicine that Network members may share with health professionals and the public"—*Health information on the Web page*. Several NN/LM National centers, i.e., National Training Center and Clearinghouse (NTCC), Outreach Evaluation Resource Center (OERC), and Web Services Technology Operations Center (Web STOC), are important components. The National Network of Libraries of Medicine fact sheet (http://www.nlm.nih.gov/pubs/factsheets/nnlm.html) and National Network of Libraries of Medicine membership program fact sheet (http://www.nlm.nih.gov/pubs/factsheets/nnlmem.html) provide additional information.

571 National Organization for Rare Disorders, Inc. http://www.rarediseases.org/. National Organization for Rare Disorders. Danbury, Conn.: National Organization for Rare Disorders. 1999–

RC48

The National Organization for Rare Disorders (NORD) provides alphabetical Index of rare diseases and several searchable databases—namely, Rare disease database, Index of organizations (list of organizations), and Organizational database (patient organizations)—as well as advice on how to interpret search results. Other resources in this area can be located via *NORD guide to rare disorders* and NIH's Office of Rare Diseases.

572 New York Academy of Medicine Library online catalog. http://www.nyam.org/library/search-collections/. New York Academy of Medicine, New York Academy of Medicine Library. New York: New York Academy of Medicine

Z680.3

Contains the library's complete journal collection, and portions of rare books, manuscript collections, and government documents. "Records for some, but not all, of the archival and manuscript collections in the New York Academy of Medicine Library can be found in the Library's online catalog, although many of the small manuscript holdings can only be found at the present time by consulting the printed catalog"—Website. For materials not found in the online catalog, the New York Academy of Medicine's card catalog or printed catalogs (images of all cards filed in the card catalog through approximately 1970) still need to be consulted. They include *Subject catalog of the library* (1969; 34 v. and 4-v. supplement), *Author catalog of the library* (1969; 43 v. and 5-v. supplement), *Illustration catalog* (1976), and *Portrait catalog* (5 v., 1960).

A prominent title published by the New York Academy of Medicine is *Grey literature report* (22). "Resource guide for disaster medicine and public health" (http://disasterlit.nlm.nih.gov/, 1443), developed in collaboration with the National Library of Medicine, is described "gateway to freely available online resources related to disaster medicine and public health . . . resources include expert guidelines, factsheets, websites, research reports, articles, and other tools aimed at the public health community."—Website.

573 Office of Rare Diseases. http://rarediseases.info.nih.gov. National Institutes of Health (U.S.), Office of Rare Diseases. Bethesda, Md.: National Institutes of Health. 2002–

Answers questions about rare diseases for patients and other health consumers, healthcare providers, researchers, educators, students, and others interested in rare diseases. Links to definitions, causes, treatments, and publications about rare diseases, provides resources on genetic information, genetic research, genetic testing laboratories and clinics, genetic counseling services, and patient support groups. Also includes information on rare diseases research and research resources. Other reference sources in this area include, for example, National Organization for Rare Disorders, Inc. and *NORD guide to rare disorders*.

574 OncoLink. http://cancer.med.upenn.edu/. Abramson Cancer Center of the University of Pennsylvania. Philadelphia, Pa.: University of Pennsylvania. 1994–
615.507; 616.992; 616.994

Contents: Cancer types; Cancer treatment; Risk and prevention; Support; Healthcare professionals.

Designed for educational purposes to help cancer patients, families, health care professionals, and the general public to get accurate cancer-related information. Provides comprehensive information about specific types of cancer, updates on cancer treatment, and news about research advances, with information provided at various levels, from introductory to in-depth.

575 Womenshealth.gov. http://www.womenshealth.gov/. National Women's Health Information Center, United States.; Public Health Service.; Office on Women's Health. Fairfax, Va.: U.S. Department of Health and Human Services. 1990s–
613.04240285; 615.507;
305.40285   RA778

A federal government resource for women's health information. Presents reliable information on women's health concerns and issues for health professionals and health consumers. Links to organizations concerned with women's health, health tools, health topics (http://www.womenshealth.gov/health-topics/), publications of interest and concern to women of all ages, and statistics (http://www.womenshealth.gov/statistics/). Includes link to girlshealth.gov with health information for young girls and educators.

Other Internet resources in this subject area with valuable information for health consumers, health professionals, and researchers include, for example, "Women's health resources: Women's health research from NIH" (http://whr.nlm.nih.gov/), a portal that serves as an access point to all NIH sex and gender differences resources and information on priorities for research in women's health, "Women's health (MedlinePlus)" (http://www.nlm.nih.gov/medlineplus/womenshealth.html), and "Women's health (NIH)" (http://health.nih.gov/category/WomensHealth).

2 *Bioethics*

576 **The Cambridge world history of
medical ethics.** Robert B. Baker,
Laurence B. McCullough. Cambridge,
U.K.; New York: Cambridge University
Press, 2009. 876 p. ISBN 9780521888790
174.2   R724.C3274

Contents: Pt. I, An introduction to the history of
medical ethics; pt. II, A chronology of medical ethics; pt. III, Discourses of medical ethics throughout
the life cycle; pt. IV, The discourses of religion on
medical ethics; pt. V, The discourses of philosophy
on medical ethics; pt. VI, The discourses of practitioners on medical ethics; pt. VII, The discourses
of bioethics; pt. VIII, Discourses on medical ethics
and society; Appendix: Biographies: Who was who
in the history of medical ethics.

Influenced by philosopher Jürgen Habermas'
"discourse ethics," the meaning of "discourse" is
extended to include a wide range of discussion
and writings beyond what are generally considered
primary sources. In addition to oaths and codes,
it also includes "oral conversations and traditions,
epithets, pamphlets, letters, discursive texts of
various sorts, statutes, court rulings, and trial transcripts" to better understand the historical background of medical ethics—*Pref.*

The "Chronology of medical ethics," an outline of the history of bioethics, provides reference
value, with a large number of facts regarding bioethics, and listing dates, events, persons, and texts.

Extensive bibliography and index. For bioethics
scholars, students, practicing health care professionals, and general readers. Aslo available as an
e-book.

Guides

577 **The Blackwell guide to medical
ethics.** Rosamond Rhodes, Leslie Francis,
Anita Silvers. Malden, Mass.: Blackwell
Publ., 2007. 435 p.
ISBN 9781405125833
174.2   R724.B515
(Blackwell philosophy guides; 21)

Contents: part I, Individual decisions about clinical
issues: (1) Patient decisions; (2) Individual decisions of physicians and other health care professionals; part II, Legislative and judicial decisions
about social policy: (1) Liberty; (2), Justice.

"Helpful tool for navigating the complex literature and diverse views on the key issues in medical ethics. Employing crucial distinctions between
the personal decisions of patients, the professional
decisions of individual health care providers, and
political decisions about public policy, the chapters
in the volume address the most central and controversial topics in medical ethics" (*Publ. notes*).
Includes bibliographical references and index. Also
available as an e-book.

Bibliography

578 Bibliography of bioethics. LeRoy
Walters, Tamar Joy Kahn, Kennedy
Institute; Center for Bioethics. Detroit;
New York; Washington: Gale Research
Co.; Free Press; Kennedy Institute of
Ethics, 1975–2009
016.1742 0363–0161   Z6675.E8B53;
R724; QH332
"An ongoing research project of the Kennedy
Institute, Center for Bioethics at Georgetown University." Imprint varies: 1975-80, Detroit: Gale
Research; 1981–83, New York: Free Press. 1984–
Washington: Kennedy Institute of Ethics. Vol.
1–10, ed. by LeRoy Walters; v. 10–, LeRoy Walters and Tamar Joy Kahn. Ceased publication with
v. 35, 2009.

Includes in a separate section *Bioethics thesaurus* which is also published independently.

Description based on v. 35 (2009).

Section I: Periodical literature and essays—
subject entries; Section II: Periodical literature and
essays—author index; Section III: Monographs—
subject entries; Section IV: Monographs—title index.

A subject bibliography listing journal and
newspaper articles, books and book chapters, government reports, and reports of international organizations and Web documents selected for indexing
for the bioethics subset of MEDLINE® and for the
National Library of Medicine's NLM catalog. Concerned with ethical and public policy aspects; for
example, assisted suicide, new reproductive technologies, cloning, human experimentation, genetic
engineering, informed consent, organ donation,
and transplantation, managed care, and other concerns in the allocation of health care resources.
Vol. 35 (2009) indexes material acquired by
the Kennedy Institute of Ethics. In addition to
PubMed® and the NLM Catalog and using NLM's
Medical subject headings (MeSH®, 858), citations
are also available via the databases maintained by
the Bioethics research library at Georgetown, i.e.,
ETHXWeb, and GenETHX (583).

579 Medical humanities dissertations.
http://www.hsls.pitt.edu/histmed/
dissertations/. Jonathon Erlen, University

of Pittsburgh Health Sciences Library
System. Pittsburgh: Health Sciences
Library, University of Pittsburgh Medical
Center. 2001–
Provides a monthly current awareness service for
selected recent medical dissertations and theses.
Arranged by topics, currently covers the following
areas: AIDS (social and historical contexts); alternative medicine (social and historical contexts); art and
medicine; biomedical ethics; history of medicine prior
to 1800; history of medicine and health care; history of science and technology; literature/theater and
medicine; nursing history; pharmacy/pharmacology
and history; philosophy and medicine; psychiatry/
psychology and history; public health/international
health; religion and medicine; women's health and
history. To view complete citations, abstracts, and
full-text of dissertations requires a subscription to
Proquest dissertations and theses (PQDT).

**580 Medicine, health, and bioethics:
Essential primary sources.** K. Lee
Lerner, Brenda Wilmoth Lerner. Detroit:
Thomson/Gale, 2006. lvii, 513 p., ill.
ISBN 1414406231
174.2   R724.M313
(Series: Social issues primary sources collection)

Contains complete primary sources or excerpts
of documents and publications published 1823–
2006, illustrating major biomedical issues. Each
entry includes the complete text or an excerpt with
complete original citation, subject area, historical
context, significance. For students, health professionals, and also general readers. Available online
via Gale virtual reference library.

Indexes; Abstract journals; Databases

581 Bibliography of bioethics. LeRoy
Walters, Tamar Joy Kahn, Kennedy
Institute; Center for Bioethics. Detroit;
New York; Washington: Gale Research
Co.; Free Press; Kennedy Institute of
Ethics, 1975–2009
016.1742 0363–0161   Z6675.E8B53;
R724; QH332

"An ongoing research project of the Kennedy Institute, Center for Bioethics at Georgetown University." Imprint varies: 1975-80, Detroit: Gale Research; 1981–83, New York: Free Press. 1984– Washington: Kennedy Institute of Ethics. Vol. 1–10, ed. by LeRoy Walters; v. 10–, LeRoy Walters and Tamar Joy Kahn. Ceased publication with v. 35, 2009.

Includes in a separate section *Bioethics thesaurus* which is also published independently.

Description based on v. 35 (2009).

Section I: Periodical literature and essays— subject entries; Section II: Periodical literature and essays—author index; Section III: Monographs— subject entries; Section IV: Monographs—title index.

A subject bibliography listing journal and newspaper articles, books and book chapters, government reports, and reports of international organizations and Web documents selected for indexing for the bioethics subset of MEDLINE® and for the National Library of Medicine's NLM catalog. Concerned with ethical and public policy aspects; for example, assisted suicide, new reproductive technologies, cloning, human experimentation, genetic engineering, informed consent, organ donation, and transplantation, managed care, and other concerns in the allocation of health care resources. Vol. 35 (2009) indexes material acquired by the Kennedy Institute of Ethics. In addition to PubMed® and the NLM Catalog and using NLM's Medical subject headings (MeSH®), citations are also available via the databases maintained by the Bioethics research library at Georgetown, i.e., ETHXWeb, and GenETHX (583).

582 ETHXWeb. http://bioethics.georgetown .edu/databases/ethxweb/. Bioethics Research Library, Kennedy Institute of Ethics, Georgetown University, Library and Information Services, Kennedy Institute of Ethics, Georgetown University. Washington: Bioethics Research Library, Kennedy Institute of Ethics, Georgetown University. 2000– Bibliographic database on bioethics and professional ethics. Indexes journal articles, books and book chapters, bills, laws, court decisions, reports, news articles, audiovisuals relating to bioethics and professional ethics.—*Website* Allows for basic, advanced,

and Boolean search. Search tips are provided. The same search interface is used for GenETHX (583), another bibliographic database provided by the Bioethics research library at GeorgetownUniversity.

583 GenETHX. http://bioethics.georgetown. edu/databases/genethx/index.html. Bioethics Research Library, Kennedy Institute of Ethics, Georgetown University, Library and Information Services, Kennedy Institute of Ethics, Georgetown University. Washington: Kennedy Institute of Ethics, Georgetown University. 2003– Indexes journal articles, books and book chapters, bills, laws, court decisions, reports, news articles, and audiovisuals relating to ethics and public policy issues in genetics. Allows for basic, advanced, and Boolean searches. The same search interface is used for ETHXWeb, another bibliographic database provided by the Bioethics Research Library at Georgetown. Helpful online searching aids are the comprehensive *Bioethics thesaurus database* http://bioethics.georgetown.edu/databases/bt/ and *Bioethics thesaurus for genetics: Alphabetical list of keyword descriptors and genetics tree* (http://bioethics.georgetown.edu/nirehg/BioethicsThesaurus ForGeneticsSe archersGuide.pdf).

584 PubMed. http://www.ncbi.nlm.nih .gov/pubmed. U.S. National Center for Biotechnology Information, National Library of Medicine, National Institutes of Health. Bethesda, Md.: U.S. National Center for Biotechnology Information. 1996– PubMed®, developed and maintained by the National Center for Biotechnology Information (NCBI) at the National Library of Medicine® (NLM). Provides a search interface for more than 20 million bibliographic citations and abstracts in the fields of medicine, nursing, dentistry, veterinary medicine, health care systems, and preclinical sciences. It provides access to articles indexed for MEDLINE® and for selected life sciences journals. PubMed subsets found under the "Limits" tab are: MEDLINE and PubMed central®, several journal groups (i.e., core clinical journals, dental journals, and nursing journals), and topical subsets (AIDS, bioethics, cancer, complementary medicine, dietary supplements, history of medicine, space life sciences, systematic reviews, toxicology, and veterinary science). "Linkout" provides access to full-text articles.

For detailed information see the PubMed fact sheet at http://www.nlm.nih.gov/pubs/factsheets/pubmed.html and also MEDLINE®/PubMed® resources guide (http://www.nlm.nih.gov/bsd/pmresources.html) which provides detailed information about MEDLINE data and searching PubMed.

Information regarding the mobile version of this resource is part of NLM's Gallery of mobile apps and sites.

Encyclopedias

585   Encyclopedia of bioethics. 3rd ed.
Stephen Garrard Post. New York: Macmillan Reference USA, 2003.
ISBN 0028657748
174.95703   QH332.E52
First ed., 1978; 2nd ed., 1995.

The definition of bioethics as "the systematic study of the moral dimensions—including moral vision, decisions, conduct, and politics—of the life sciences and health care, employing a variety of ethical methodologies in a interdisciplinary setting"—(*Introd.* to the 1995 ed.) also ". . . shapes [this revised edition], which continues the broad topical range of earlier editions."—*Introd.* Approximately 450 original, signed articles focus on the core areas of bioethics. Articles are arranged alphabetically, with numerous cross-references. Most articles have extensive bibliographies. Significant revisions, updates, and new entries (e.g., bioterrorism, cloning, health policy, and stem cell research) since the last edition. Topical outline of entries and index. The appendix, a collection of primary documents, gives the text of codes and various policy and ethical statements related to medical ethics. It also includes an annotated bibliography on literature and medicine and an annotated bibliography on law and medicine. Previous editions are still considered useful for anyone interested in the history of bioethics. For researchers, students, and general readers. Available online via Gale virtual reference library and also as an e-book.

586   Encyclopedia of science, technology, and ethics. Carl Mitcham. Detroit: Macmillan Reference USA, 2005. 4 v.,

cxiv, 2378 p., ill., maps.
ISBN 0028658310
503   Q175.35.E53

Over 670 articles exploring issues, technologies, or other concepts in science and technology. Includes description of the technologies or scienctific principles involved, relevant social institutions and organizations, and social perspectives surrounding the technology. Entries have bibliographies and are referenced in the text. Some entries can be strident and opinionated, but all are well referenced. Available as an e-book.

Dictionaries

587   A handbook of bioethics terms. James B. Tubbs, Jr. Washington: Georgetown University Press, 2009. xiii, 191 p.
ISBN 9781589012592
174.2   R725.5.T83

Glossary-style reference, with brief entries on the multidisciplinary terminology of bioethics. Also included are expressions, titles, and court cases important to bioethics. Useful for students, members of institutional ethics committees, and various health professionals.

Also available as an e-book.

588   Thesaurus ethics in the life sciences.
http://www.drze.de/bioethics-thesaurus?set_language=en. German Reference Centre for Ethics in the Life Sciences (DRZE). Bonn, Germany: Deutsches Referenzzentrum für Ethik in den Biowissenschaften (DRZE). 1999–
                            QH332

Description based on 8th ed., 2012. Publ. in English, German, and French. Joint project of the German Reference Centre for Ethics in the Life Sciences (DRZE), Centre de documentation en éthique des sciences de la vie et de la santé, Information and Documentation Centre for Ethics in Medicine, Interdepartmental Centre for Ethics in the Sciences and Humanities, and Library and Information Services, Kennedy Institute of Ethics (578).

Contents: (I) Ethics, philosophy, theology; (II) Society, politics, economics, law, education, media; (III) Science, research, technology and technology assessment; (IV) Biology; (V) Medicine and care; (VI) Transplantation and transfusion; (VII) Prolongation of life, Dying and death; (VIII) Health care and health economics; (IX) Genetics, human reproduction and sexuality; (X) Environment, landscape and ecosphere; (XI) Agriculture and forestry, animal husbandry and food; (XI General terms; (XIII) Geographic names; (XIV) Personal names.

Controlled indexing and research tool to include established and also new fields of bioethics which previously were treated either marginally or not at all. For researchers (both experts and interested members of the public), librarians, and information specialists indexing bioethical literature and documents.

Handbooks

589   A handbook of bioethics terms. James
    B. Tubbs, Jr. Washington: Georgetown
    University Press, 2009. xiii, 191 p.
    ISBN 9781589012592
    174.2   R725.5.T83
Glossary-style reference, with brief entries on the multidisciplinary terminology of bioethics. Also included are expressions, titles, and court cases important to bioethics. Useful for students, members of institutional ethics committees, and various health professionals.

Also available as an e-book.

**590   International guidelines on HIV/AIDS
    and human rights**. http://www2.ohchr
    .org/english/issues/hiv/docs/consolidated
    _guidelines.pdf. Office of the United
    Nationals High Commissioner for
    Human Rights (OHCHR); UNAIDS Joint
    United Nations Programme on HIV/
    AIDS, UNAIDS Joint United Nations
    Programme on HIV/AIDS. Geneva,
    Switzerland: United Nations OHCHR.
    2006
Organized jointly by the Office of the United Nations High Commissioner for Human Rights (OHCHR) and the UNAIDS Joint United Nations Programme on HIV/AIDS.

2006 consolidated version of the Second (Geneva, 23–25 Sep. 1996) and Third (Geneva, 25–26 Jul. 2002) International Consultation on HIV/AIDS and Human Rights.

Contents: (I) Guidelines for state action: (A) Institutional responsibilities and processes; (B) Law review, reform and support services;

(C) Promotion of a supportive and enabling environment; (II) Recommendations for dissemination and implementation of the guidelines on HIV/AIDS and human right: (A) States; (B) United Nationals system and regional intergovernmental bodies; (C) Nongovernmental organizations; (III) International human rights obligations and HIV: (A) Human rights standards and the nature of State obligations; (B) Restrictions and limitations; (C) The application of specific human rights in the context of the HIV epidemic; Annex 1, History of the recognition of the importance of human rights in the context of HIV; Annex 2, List of participants at the Second International Consultation on HIV/AIDS and Human Rights; Annex 3, List of participants at the Third International Consultation on HIV/AIDS and Human Rights.

"A tool for States in designing, co-ordinating and implementing effective national HIV/AIDS policies and strategies . . . human rights standards apply in the context of HIV/AIDS and translating them into practical measures that should be undertaken at the national level, based on three broad approaches: improvement of government capacity for multisectoral coordination and accountability; reform of laws and legal support services, with a focus on anti-discrimination, protection of public health, and improvement of the status of women, children and marginalized groups; and support and increased private sector and community participation to respond ethically and effectively to HIV/AIDS.

OHCHR encourages governments, national human rights institutions, non-governmental organizations and people living with HIV and AIDS to use the Guidelines for training, policy formulation, advocacy, and the development of legislation on HIV/AIDS-related human rights."—*Website*

591   A companion to bioethics. 2nd ed.
    Helga Kuhse, Peter Singer. Malden,
    Mass.: Wiley-Blackwell, 2009. 622 p.
    ISBN 9781405163316
    174.2   R724.C616
First ed., 1998; (Blackwell companions to philosophy ; 15).

Contents: Pt. I, Introduction; pt. II, Questions about bioethics; pt. III, Ethical approaches; pt. IV, Before birth: issues involving embryos and fetuses; pt. V, Issues in reproduction; pt. VI, The new genetics; pt. VII, Life and death issues; pt. VIII,

Resource allocation; pt. IX, Organ donations; pt. X, Global health-care issues; pt. XI, Experimentation with humans and animals; pt. XII, Ethical issues in the practice of health care; pt. XIII, The teaching and practice of bioethics.

Contains 49 chapters, with essays by different scholars on a variety of issues and concepts in contemporary bioethics. Ch. I is a historical introduction to bioethics. Includes bibliographical references and index. Also available as an e-book.

592 APA ethics office. http://www.apa.org/ ethics/homepage.html. American Psychological Association. Washington: American Psychological Association. 2002

Areas covered include but are not limited to the clinical, counseling, and school practice of psychology; research; teaching; supervision of trainees; public service; policy development; social intervention; development of assessment instruments; conducting assessments; educational counseling; organizational consulting; forensic activities; program design and evaluation; and administration. Provides links to full-text ethics information: "Ethical Principles of Psychologists and Code of Conduct"; "Ethics Committee on Services by Telephone, Teleconferencing, and Internet"; "Guidelines for Ethical Conduct in the Care and Use of Animals"; and more. Available online from APA in HTML, PDF, and MS Word formats.

593 BioLaw: A legal and ethical reporter on medicine, health care, and bioengineering. James F. Childress. Frederick, Md.: University Publications of America, 1986–. v. (loose-leaf)
1983–1985 had title: *Bioethics reporter*.

Editors: 1986– , James F. Childress et al.

Loose-leaf; updated between editions. Has supplement: Biolaw . . . microfiche supplement.

Each annual consists of 2 v.: v.1, Resource manual, contains essays on biological, medical, and health care issues with ethical and legal implications; v.2 includes updates on many previously published topics and special sections on laws, regulations, court cases, etc. Each update comes with a cumulative subject index covering both volumes and a cumulative index to court cases.

594 Code of medical ethics, current opinions with annotations: Including the principles of medical ethics, fundamental elements of the patient-physician relationship and rules of the Council on Ethical and Judicial Affairs. Southern Illinois University at Carbondale, AMA Council on Ethical and Judicial Affairs. Chicago: American Medical Association
174.13 1540-2916   R725.A55a
Since 1847, published every two years, with regular revisions. Description based on 2012–2013 ed.

Ethics guide for physicians and other medical professionals, attorneys, and others, containing AMA's "Principles of Medical Ethics" (rev. 2001) and more than 200 ethical opinions (issued through 2005) on social policy issues, hospital relations, practice, and other matters, with new guidelines and updated or amended guidelines for several contemporary topics and issues (for example, financial relationships with industry in continuing medical education; advance care planning, professionalism in the use of social media; research with stem cells; transplantation of organs from living donors; pediatric decision making; HIV testing, and others). Appendix contains bylaws rules. Table of Cases, Table of Articles, and Index to Opinions. Also available as e-book.

New Opinions issued every six months, available at http://www.ama-assn.org/ama/pub/about-ama/our-people/ama-councils/council-ethical-judicial-affairs .page and the AMA's online policy database, Policy-Finder http://www.ama-assn.org/ama/pub/about-ama/ our-people/house-delegates/policyfinder.page.

595 Contemporary issues in healthcare law and ethics. 3rd ed. Dean M. Harris. Chicago; Washington: Health Administration Press; AUPHA Press, 2007. 377 p. ISBN 9781567932
344.730321   KF3825.Z9.H3
First edition, 1999, had title *Healthcare law and ethics: Issues for the age of managed care*; 2nd ed., 2003.

Contents: (1) "The role of law in the U.S. healthcare system"; (2) "Managing and regulating the healthcare system"; (3) "Patient care issues"; (4) "Legal and ethical issues in health insurance and managed care"; table of cases; table of statutes; table of regulations; index.

This revised and updated edition presents essential information and examines legal and ethical issues in health care. Includes, for example, the U.S. Supreme Court's decisions on physician-assisted suicide, partial-birth abortion, issues in emergency contraception, HIPAA Privacy Rule, medical malpractice, reporting of medical errors, and other topics. Also available as e-book.

596   Ethics resources and standards. http://www.psychiatry.org/practice/ ethics/resources-standards. American Psychiatric Association. Arlington, Va.: American Psychiatric Association
Produced by the American Psychiatric Association (APA).

Provides online access to APA's ethics-related publications, originally published in print version in 2001: *Opinions of the Ethics Committee on the principles of medical ethics: With annotations especially applicable to psychiatry*, which includes the APA's procedures for handling complaints of unethical conduct, and *Ethics primer of the American Psychiatric Association*.

597   Guide to the code of ethics for nurses: Interpretation and application. Marsha Diane Mary Fowler, American Nurses Association. Silver Spring, Md.: American Nurses Association, 2008. 176 p. ISBN 9781558102
174.2   RT85.G85
Produced by American Nurses Association (ANA). Reissued with a new cover in 2010.

Intended as a guide to the *Code of ethics for nurses with interpretive statements* on how to apply ethical standards and values in nursing practice. Discusses a single code provision and provides the text of the code of ethics, the history, purpose, theory, application, case studies, and examples. Includes bibliographical references and index.

Related recent ANA publications include *Essential guide to nursing practice* and *Nursing's social policy statement statement*.

598   Handbook for health care ethics committees. Linda Farber Post, Jeffrey Blustein, Nancy N. Dubler. Baltimore:

Johns Hopkins University Press, 2007. xiii, 327 p. ISBN 0801884489
610   R725.3.P67
Contents: (I) Curriculum for ethics committees; (II) Clinical ethics consultation; (III) White papers, memoranda, guidelines, and protocols; (IV) Sample policies and procedures; (V) Institutional code of ethics; (VI) Key legal cases in bioethics; (VII) An ethics committee meeting. "A handbook . . . that distills the important information and presents basic foundation of bioethical theory and its practical application in clinical and organizational settings" (*Pref.*). Contains chapters on ethical foundations of clinical practice, decision making, informed consent and refusal, truth telling: disclosure and confidentiality, special decision-making concerns of minors, end-of-life issues, palliation, justice, access to care, and organizational ethics, clinical ethics consultation, white papers, memoranda, guidelines and protocols, and sample policies and procedures. Also available as an e-book.

599   Handbook of bioethics: Taking stock of the field from a philosophical perspective. George Khushf. Dordrecht, Netherlands; Boston: Kluwer Academic, 2004. vi, 568 p. ISBN 1402018703
174/.957   R725.5.H36
(Philosophy and medicine; v.78) Contents: section I, The emergence of bioethics; section II, Bioethical theory; section III, Core concepts in clinical ethics; section IV, The public policy context; section V, Foundations of the health professions. "This volume takes stock of bioethics from a philosophical perspective. Twenty-six essays . . . provide a survey of the most important theoretical and practical areas of bioethics. Each essay reviews the extant literature on the topic, identifying the important philosophical themes and resources. Each sketches important areas where future research needs to be conducted and where valuable collaboration can take place with those doing more traditional philosophical research on topics such as personal identity, moral theory, or the nature of scientific judgment" (*Introd.*) Includes bibliographical references and index. Also available as an e-book.

600   Handbook of bioethics and religion. David E. Guinn. Oxford; New York:

Oxford University Press, 2006. xv, 437 p., ill. ISBN 0195178734

174/.957   R725.55.H36

Contents: pt. I, Historical perspectives; pt. II, Religion and the terrain of public discourse; pt. III, Religion and bioethics in the public square; pt. IV, Religion and official discourse; pt. V, Religion an ethical praxis; pt. VI, Instrumentalizing religion; pt. VII, Institutional religion. Presents the "important question of *how* religion plays a role and normatively what *should be* its role in public bioethics" against the background of those who object to any "religious engagement in the formation of public bioethical policy," and who were unwilling to contribute to this publication. Contributors approach "the issue from a non-absolutist position (i.e., that religion should or should not participate in public bioethics)" (*Introd.*). Includes bibliographical references and index. Also available as an e-book from publisher.

601   Handbook of global bioethics. H ten Have, Bert Gordijn. Springer, 2013. xxvi, 1685 pages 9789400725119

Contents: v.1: section I, Introduction; section II, Principles of global bioethics; section III, Cultural perspectives; section IV, Religious perspectives; v.2: section V, Specific issues from a global perspective; section VI, Future perspectives; v.3: section VII, Countries and regions: Argentina-Lithuania; v.4, Countries and regions: Malawi-USA.

Geographic and systematic overview of global bioethics. Discusses existing and emerging bioethics topics. Provides a description and an analysis of the current state of bioethics in approx. 50 different countries worldwide. Addresses cultural diversity and pluralism and the various cultural and religious perspectives. Also available as an e-book.

602   History of AMA ethics. http://www .ama-assn.org/ama/pub/about-ama/ our-history/history-ama-ethics.page. American Medical Association (AMA). Chicago: American Medical Association (AMA). 1995?–

Provides links to various resources such as the *Code of medical ethics history*, the Council on Ethical and Judicial Affairs' *AMA code of medical ethics*, digitized versions of different editions (1847, 1903, 1957, 1980, and 2001 versions), timelines

(1847-1940, 1941-1980, 1981-2009) which trace AMA's work in medical ethics, and more.

603   Law, liability, and ethics for medical office professionals. 5th ed. Myrtle Flight. Clifton Park, N.Y.: Delmar Cengage Learning, 2011. xxiv, 338 p., col. ill. ISBN 9781428359413

KF2905.F58

First ed., 1988; 4th ed., 2004.

Contents: Ch. 1, From examining room to courtroom; ch. 2, Functioning within the legal system; ch. 3, Crime and punishment: Intent makes the difference; ch. 4, Your words may form a contract; ch. 5, Anatomy of a medical malpractice case; ch. 6, Health care is big business; ch. 7, The medical record: The medical assistant's responsibility; ch. 8, Introduction to ethics; ch. 9, Privacy, confidentiality, privileged communication: A nexus of law and ethics; ch. 10, Birth and the beginning of life; ch. 11, Professional ethics and the living; ch. 12, Ethics: Death and dying; Appendixes: (A) The civil and criminal case processes; (B) Answers to cases for discussion; Glossary; Bibliography; Index.

Provides basic information in medical law and ethics for medical professionals and helps with understanding their rights and the rights of the patients.

Another legal resource, designed for dental professionals, is *Law and risk management in dental practice* (806).

604   Legal and ethical issues for health professionals. 2nd ed. George D. Pozgar, Nina M. Santucci, John W. Pinnella. Sudbury, Mass.: Jones and Bartlett Publishers, 2010. xxi, 425 p. ISBN 9780763764739

174.2   KF3821.P68

Contents: ch. 1, Introduction to ethics; ch. 2, Contemporary ethical dilemmas; ch. 3, End-of-life dilemmas; ch. 4, Health care ethics committees; ch. 5, Development of law; ch. 6, Introduction to law; ch. 7, Government, ethics, and the law; ch. 8, Organizational ethics and the law; ch. 9, Health care professionals' ethical and legal issues; ch. 10, Physicians' ethical and legal issues; ch. 11, Employee rights and responsibilities; ch. 12, Patient consent; ch. 13, Patient abuse; ch. 14, Patient rights and responsibilities.

Overview of the ethical and legal issues and their interrelationship in the health care field. Guide to additional resources. Includes glossary, bibliographical references, and index. Also available as an e-book.

605 Medical ethics: Codes, opinions, and statements. Baruch A. Brody. Washington: Bureau of National Affairs, 2000. xxxix, 1074 p., ill. ISBN 1570181004

174/.2   R725.M117

Compilation of documents of medical ethics standards and policy positions of the major medical organizations in the U.S., including both usual and controversial issues. Includes bibliographical references and index. Another title by the same author, Medical ethics: Analysis of the issues raised by the codes, opinions, and statements, complements this resource.

606 Medical records and the law. 4th ed. William H. Roach, American Health Information Management Association. Sudbury, Mass.: Jones and Bartlett Publ., 2006. xix, 591 p. ISBN 0763734454

344.7304/1   KF3827.R4R63

First edition, 1985; 3rd ed., 1998.

Contents: ch. 1, Introduction to the American legal system; ch. 2, Medical records and managed care; ch. 3, Medical record requirements; ch. 4, Medical records entries; ch. 5, Documenting consent to treatment; ch. 6, Access to health information; ch. 7, Reporting and disclosure requirements; ch. 8, Documentation and disclosure: special areas of concern; ch. 9, HIV/AIDS: mandatory reporting and confidentiality; ch. 10, Discovery and admissibility of medical records; ch. 11, Legal theories in improper disclosure cases; ch. 12, Risk management and quality management; ch. 13, Electronic health records; ch. 14, Health information in medical research; Index.

Provides information on the growth of electronic health record systems and electronic data networks. Addresses the issues related to medical research involving human subjects and how patient information can be used. Also available as an e-book.

607 The Oxford handbook of bioethics. Bonnie Steinbock. Oxford: Oxford Univ. Pr., 2007

Contents: pt. I, Theoretical and methodological issues; pt. II, Justice and policy; pt. III, Bodies and bodily parts; pt. IV, End of life; pt. V, Reproduction and cloning; pt. VI, Genetics and enhancement; pt. VII, Research ethics; pt. VIII, Public and global health. Contains a selection and discussion of central issues in contemporary bioethics, with original essays reflective of a particular author's interpretation of a bioethical issue. Includes bibliographical references and index. Also available as an e-book.

608 Source book in bioethics. Albert R. Jonsen, Robert M. Veatch, LeRoy Walters. Washington: Georgetown Univ. Pr., 1998. ix, 510 p. ISBN 0878406832

174/.2/09   R724.S599

Contents: Ethics of research with human subjects; A short history; Ethics of death and dying; Changing attitudes toward death and medicine; Ethical issues in human genetics; Issues in genetics; Ethical issues arising from human reproductive technologies and arrangements; Readings on human reproduction; Ethical issues in the changing health care system; The changing health care scene. Collection of significant documents in bioethics and social ethics, covering the time period from 1947–95, with original text reprinted either in full or abridged format, presenting a historical survey of bioethics and major ethical issues in healthcare and key bioethical decisions. Includes legislative documents and reports by various organizations and governments. Bibliographical references and index.

609 The rights of patients: The authoritative ACLU guide to the rights of patients. 3rd ed. George J. Annas. Carbondale, Ill.: Southern Illinois University Press, 2004. xxi, 387 p. ISBN 0809325152

344.73/03211   KF3823.A96

Title varies: 1st ed., 1975, had title: *The rights of hospital patients: The basic ACLU guide to a hospital patient's rights;* 2nd ed., 1989, had title: *The rights of patients: The basic ACLU guide to patient rights.*

American Civil Liberties Union (ACLU)

(ACLU handbook series)

Contents: (I) Patient rights; (II) The patient rights advocate; (III) Reforming American medicine; (IV) Hospitals; (V) Emergency medicine; (VI) Informed choice; (VII) Choices about surgery and children's care; (VIII) Reproductive health; (IX) Research; (X) Medical records; (XI) Privacy and confidentiality; (XII) Care of the dying; (XIII) Suffering, pain, and suicide; (XIV) Death, organ donation, and autopsy; (XV) Patient safety and medical malpractice. Appendixes: (A) Internet resources; (B) Convention on human rights and biomedicine; (C) Childbearing patient bill of rights. Index.

"Offers fully documented exposition and explanation of the rights of patients from birth to death . . . a resource not only for patients and their families but also for physicians, hospital administrators, medical and nursing students, and other health care workers" (**Publ. notes**). Emphasizes the importance of having a patient rights advocate, with a section "tips for advocates" in most chapters.

610   The SAGE handbook of health care ethics: core and emerging issues. Ruth F. Chadwick, Henk ten Have, Eric M. Meslin. Los Angeles; London: SAGE, 2011. xxi, 454 p., ill. ISBN 9781412945349

Presents a global perspective on health care ethics. Discusses in detail an array of bioethical topics, including international medical research and technological topics. Also includes a discussion of historical aspects of terminology, i.e., medical ethics, bioethics, health care ethics, etc. Intended audience is upper-level undergraduates, graduate students, and health professionals. Extensive bibliographic references; index. Also available as an e-book and via Credo reference.

Histories

611   The Cambridge world history of medical ethics. Robert B. Baker, Laurence B. McCullough. Cambridge, U.K.; New York: Cambridge University Press, 2009. 876 p. ISBN 9780521888790
174.2   R724.C3274

Contents: Pt. I, An introduction to the history of medical ethics; pt. II, A chronology of medical ethics; pt. III, Discourses of medical ethics throughout the life cycle; pt. IV, The discourses of religion on medical ethics; pt. V, The discourses of philosophy on medical ethics; pt. VI, The discourses of

practitioners on medical ethics; pt. VII, The discourses of bioethics; pt. VIII, Discourses on medical ethics and society; Appendix: Biographies: Who was who in the history of medical ethics.

Influenced by philosopher Jürgen Habermas' "discourse ethics," the meaning of "discourse" is extended to include a wide range of discussion and writings beyond what are generally considered primary sources. In addition to oaths and codes, it also includes "oral conversations and traditions, epithets, pamphlets, letters, discursive texts of various sorts, statutes, court rulings, and trial transcripts" to better understand the historical background of medical ethics—*Pref.*

The "Chronology of medical ethics," an outline of the history of bioethics, provides reference value, with a large number of facts regarding bioethics, and listing dates, events, persons, and texts. Extensive bibliography and index. For bioethics scholars, students, practicing health care professionals, and general readers. Aslo available as an e-book.

612   The development of bioethics in the United States. Jeremy R. Garrett, Fabrice Jotterrand, D. Christopher Ralston. Dordrecht, Netherlands; New York: Springer, 2013. viii, 279 p. ISBN 9789400740105
174.2   QH332
(Philosopy and medicine; v.115)

Contents: Pt. I, "The birth of bioethics: Historical analysis"; pt. II, "The nature of bioethics: Cultural and philosophical analysis"; pt. III, "The practice of bioethics: Bringing physician ethics into the moral consensus"; pt. IV, "The future of bioethics: Looking ahead."

Exploration of the past, present, and future of bioethics in the United States, with essays by authors who are considered important to the development of medical ethics/bioethics. Addresses philosophical, professional, and cultural issues. Provides a valuable contribution to the understanding of the history of bioethics and the development of bioethics as a field. Intended for scholars and advanced students. Also available as an e-book.

Internet resources

613   ACP Center for Ethics and Professionalism. http://www.acponline .org/ethics/. American College of

Physicians (ACP). Philadelphia: American College of Physicians. 1996–

As part of the American College of Physicians (ACP), "the nation's largest medical specialty society. Its mission is to enhance the quality and effectiveness of health care by fostering excellence and professionalism in the practice of medicine (http://www.acponline.org/about_acp/who_we_are/mission/) [and] "devoted to policy development and implementation on issues related to medical ethics and professionalism, and is a resource for ACP members and the public" (http://www.acponline.org/running_practice/ethics/). Includes ethics and human rights, end-of-life care, managed care ethics, and other issues. The Center develops position papers on current topics, case studies that explore common ethical dilemmas for patients and physicians, educational programs and resources, and performs advocacy and outreach efforts. Provides online access to its "Ethics manual" (http://www.acponline.org/running_practice/ethics/manual/) and position papers (http://www.acponline.org/running_practice/ethics/issues/policy).

614   American Medical Association. http://www.ama-assn.org/. American Medical Association. Chicago: American Medical Association. 1995–
610.9206   R130.5

This searchable website provides a variety of professional resources and standards for AMA members, including, for example, information sources on medical ethics, public health (e.g., eliminating health disparities, health preparedness, disaster response, obesity), medical science, legal issues, and AMA history (with time line and highlights of AMA history). Also provides information on medical education and licensure as well as online resources and other links for medical school students and residents. Includes a section for patients, with access to patient education resources (e.g., "Health literacy resources," "Atlas of the human body," etc.).

Other useful AMA-related links include, for example, DoctorFinder, *Code of medical ethics, current opinions with annotations*, *Current procedural terminology: CPT*, FREIDA (291), *Graduate medical education directory* (292), *Health professions career and education directory*, and *State medical licensure requirements and statistics* (508). Many of these

resources have general reference value in academic and public libraries.

615   Bioethics information resources. http://www.nlm.nih.gov/bsd/bioethics.html. National Library of Medicine (U.S.). Bethesda, Md.: U.S. National Library of Medicine, National Institutes of Health, Dept. of Health and Human Services. 2007–

Resource to assist users (specialists, researchers, clinicians, and the general public) in finding bioethics information. Provides, for example, bioethics-filtered search boxes for MEDLINE®, PubMed®, NLM catalog, and links to other National Library of Medicine databases or information resources (e.g., Genetics home reference, MedlinePlus®, NLM gateway, NIH's Bioethics resources on the Web and other bioethics-related websites from various academic centers, educational sites, professional bioethics organizations, etc.

616   Bioethics.net. http://bioethics.net/. Alden March Bioethics Institute. Albany, N.Y.: Alden March Bioethics Institute; Albany Medical College

Website content is provided by the Alden March Bioethics Institute at the Albany Medical College in New York, home to the editorial board of the *American Journal of Bioethics* (AJOB), published since 1998. The site offers free access to some full text from the journal and links to many other websites and online publications carefully selected for their relevance to bioethics. Features include RSS feeds to bioethics news, a bioethics blog, and a search engine that covers the entire website, the AJOB, or news sources (retrieves articles from sources such as Reuters, *Wired* magazine, BBC News, *The Scientist*, the *New York Times*, and SciDev.net). Useful for any type of library.

617   Bioethics research library at Georgetown University. http://bioethics.georgetown.edu/. Bioethics Research Library, Kennedy Institute of Ethics, Georgetown University. Washington: Bioethics Research Library, Kennedy Institute of Ethics, Georgetown University

Produced by the Kennedy Institute of Ethics at Georgetown University.

The Bioethics Library at Georgetown University continues the work of the National Reference Center for Bioethics Literature. It is described as an "interdisciplinary and multi-format collection on ethical issues related to health care, biomedical research, biotechnology, and the environment" *(website home page)* and functions both as a reference library for the public and as an in-depth research resource for scholars from the U.S. and abroad. Specialized collection of books, journals, newspaper articles, legal materials, regulations, codes, government publications, and other relevant documents concerned with issues in biomedical and professional ethics. Includes extensive information on Islamic medical and scientific ethics, Jewish medical ethics, and other special collections (http://bioethics.georgetown.edu/collections/index.html).

Specialized databases include ETHXWeb, GenETHX (583), a listing of international bioethics organizations, bioethics syllabi, and several others, including EthicShare, a research and collaboration website (University of Minnesota Center for Bioethics https://www.ethicshare.org/), with access to many full-text materials. Other sources of full-text documents on this site include the digital archives of the Presidential Bioethics Commission, the Office of Research Protections, and the National Information Resource on Ethics and Human Genetics.

618 Bioethics resources on the web. http://purl.access.gpo.gov/GPO/LPS55764. National Institutes of Health (U.S.). [Bethesda, Md.]: National Institutes of Health (NIH), Office of Extramural Research (OER), Inter-Institute Bioethics Groups (BIG). 2000–

Web page sponsored by the NIH Office of Science Policy (OSP) and the NIH Inter-Institute Bioethics Interest Group in cooperation with the NIH Office of Extramural Research (OER).

Annotated list of resources and web links that provide access to NIH and other federal resources, relevant organizations, documents, background information, and various positions on bioethical issues, with emphasis on research ethics, genetics, and medicine and healthcare topics. A link to "Health Law Resources" is provided at http://bioethics.od.nih.gov/legal.html.

619 Ethics and health. http://www.who.int/ethics/en/. World Health Organization (WHO). Geneva, Switzerland: World Health Organization. 2002–

World Health Organization (WHO) Dept. of Ethics, Trade, Human Rights and Health Law (ETH); WHO Dept. Sustainable Development and Environmental Health (SDE); WHO Research Ethics Review Committee; U.N. Inter-Agency Committee on Bioethics; National Bioethics Commissions.

"This site has been created as an aid to persons, both inside and outside WHO, seeking information about bioethics, including the ethical aspects of healthcare delivery and planning as well as the ethics of clinical care, research, and biotechnology . . . [with] information about a range of topics in ethics" (*Website*). Reflects various collaborative projects within WHO and also other agencies and provides links to various bioethics topics, full text of ethics publications, ethical considerations and guidelines for research and good clinical practice.

620 Ethics (World Medical Association). http://www.wma.net/en/20activities/10ethics/index.html. World Medical Association.; Ethics Unit. Ferney-Voltaire, France: World Medical Association. 2003–

Produced by World Medical Association (WMA).

"The purpose of the WMA is to serve humanity by endeavoring to achieve the highest international standards in Medical Education, Medical Science, Medical Art and Medical Ethics, and Health Care for all people in the world."—*About page*. Coordinates the WMA's ethics policies with the goal to establish and promote high standards of ethical behavior and care by physicians. Serves as a clearinghouse of ethics information resources for national medical associations and physicians, develops new resources, and collaborates with other international organizations involved in medical ethics and health and human rights. Makes accessible the online version of *Medical ethics manual* (http://www.wma.net/en/30publications/30ethicsmanual/index.html) in many different languages, a list of codes and declarations of adopted ethics policies and declarations in order of their date of first adoption and amendments, including the International Code of Medical Ethics and Declaration of Helsinki: Ethical Principles for Medical Research Involving Human Subjects, as well as many others. Also provides a list of health and human rights organizations and resources.

621 Genetics and ethics. http://genethx
.georgetown.edu/. Bioethics Research
Library, Kennedy Institute of Ethics,
Georgetown University. Washington:
Kennedy Institute of Ethics, Georgetown
University

Part of the Bioethics research library at Georgetown. Supported by the National Human Genome
Research Institute (NIH, 189) and its predecessor
from 1994 to 2011.

Provides access to topics related to the ethical,
legal, and social implications of research and clinical practice in human genetics. Includes a variety
of information resources, including bibliographic
databases, educational resources, and online bibliographies. Provides custom searches and other
services for researchers upon request.

622 The Hastings Center. http://bibpurl.oclc.
org/web/6093. Hastings Center. Garrison,
N.Y.: The Hastings Center. 1999–

QH332

"The Hastings Center is an independent, non-
partisan, and nonprofit bioethics research institute founded in 1969 to explore fundamental and
emerging questions in health care, biotechnology,
and the environment."—*About page*. Its home page
provides a description of the Hastings Center activities, including biomedical research projects, case
studies, and updates, as well as links to various
scholarly resources (e.g., "Bioethics forum: diverse
commentary on issues in bioethics") and selected
online publications. Selected issues highlighted on
the home page include, for example, animal research
ethics, clinical trials & human subject research, conflict of interest in research, end of life, genetic testing, organ transplantation, stem cells, and others. A
related publication is *Hastings Center guidelines for
decisions on life-sustaining treatment and care near
the end of life*, a recent update of the Center's *Guidelines on the termination of life-sustaining treatment
and the care of the dying* (1987). Site index.

623 Human Genetics programme. http://
www.who.int/genomics/en/. World
Health Organization, Human Genetics
Programme. Geneva, Switzerland: World
Health Organization. 2003–

Addresses the ethical, legal, and social implications
(ELSI) of human genomics.

"WHO's Human Genetics programme aims to
provide information and raises awareness within
health sector, government and the public on the
health challenges and opportunities within the new
and rapidly developing science of human genetics."
(*Website*). Addresses areas of medical genetics,
such as genetic counselling, presymptomatic diagnosis, population genetics, and ethics & genomics. "ELSI genetics resource directory" (http://www
.who.int/genomics/elsi/regulatory_data/en/index.
html) provides online resources on ELSI of human
genetics, ethics organizations, guidelines, codes,
declarations, legislations, etc. For health professionals, policy makers, patients and their families,
and the general public.

**624 Human Genome Project information
archive**. http://www.ornl.gov/sci/tech
resources/Human_Genome/home.
shtml. U.S. Department of Energy
Office of Science, Office of Biological
and Environmental Research, Human
Genome Program. Oak Ridge, Tenn.:
Oak Ridge National Laboratory, U.S.
Department of Energy. 1990–2013

QH447

Website sponsored by the U.S. Dept. of Energy
Office of Science, Office of Biological and Environmental Research, Human Genome Program;
website maintained by the Human Genome Management Information System (HGMIS) at Oak
Ridge National Laboratory for the U.S. Department
of Energy Human Genome Program.

Contents: About HGP; Research; Publications;
Education. Subtopics include Ethical, Legal, and
Social Issues (ELSI); Genetics Privacy and Educa-
tion; and more.

This website provides a multitude of annotated links to resources on all aspects of the HPG.
Articles analyzing the genome continue to be published but not necessairly linked in the archive.
Information for Genetic Professionals (http://www
.kumc.edu/gec/geneinfo.html), a clinical-genetics
site by Debra Collins, Genetics Education Center,
University of Kansas Medical Center, provides further information in this area.

**625 National Human Genome Research
Institute**. http://genome.gov/. National
Human Genome Research Institute

(U.S.). Bethesda, Md.: National Human Genome Research Institute, National Institutes of Health, U.S. Department of Health and Human Services. 1995–

QH445.2

National Human Genome Research Institute (NHGRI), previously known as National Center for Human Genome Research (NCHGR), which was established in 1989 because of the Human Genome Project (HGP), since 1990 is a collaborative project of the U.S. Dept. of Energy (DOE) and National Institutes of Health (NIH) to map the human genome; and since HGP's completion in 1993, to apply genome technologies to the study of specific diseases. In 1996, the Center for Inherited Disease Research (CIDR) was also established (cofunded by eight NIH institutes and centers) to study the genetic components of complex disorders. A timeline, 1988 to the present, provides further details about HPG, its completion in 2003, associated events, research, and relevant publications at http://genome.gov/10001763.

Provides access to information, databases, and links to other resources concerning research, grants, health, policy and ethics, educational resources, etc. Some examples include the Talking glossary of genetic terms http://www.genome.gov/glossary/, the NHGRI policy and legislation database http://genome.gov/PolicyEthics/LegDatabase/pubsearch.cfm, Online bioethics resources, the Ethical, legal and social implications (ELSI) research program, and Initiatives and resources for minority and special populations (http://genome.gov/10001192), information on current research projects (e.g., the ENCODE project [ENCyclopedia Of DNA Elements], a pilot project for testing and comparing new methods to identify functional sequences in DNA, model organisms, creation of Centers of excellence in genomic science, the Genetic variation program, the Haplotype map, gene discovery and technology development, establishment of the Center for Inherited Disease Research, and much more.

626 **National Institute of Environmental Health Sciences**. http://www.niehs.nih.gov. National Institute of Environmental Health Sciences. Research Triangle Park, N.C.: National Institute of Environmental Health Sciences. 1994?–

RA565

Website of National Institute of Environmental Health Sciences (NIEHS).

Contents: Health and Education; Research; Funding Opportunities; Careers and Training; News and Events; About NIEHS.

Presents information and resources for several user groups, including health professionals, research scientists, teachers, children, and the general public. Includes a list of environmental health topics (i.e., A–Z list of conditions and diseases linked to environmental exposures), access to specialized databases and software, resources of the NIEHS library and information services (http://www.niehs.nih.gov/research/resources/library/index.cfm), NIEHS bioethics resources (http://www.niehs.nih.gov/research/resources/bioethics/index.cfm), and other information resources.

627 **NLM gateway**. http://gateway.nlm.nih.gov/. National Library of Medicine (U.S.). Bethesda, Md.: National Library of Medicine. 2000–

RA11

As announced in 2011, "the NLM® gateway has transitioned to a new pilot project from the Lister Hill National Center for Biomedical Communications (LHNCBC, 392)."—*Website* The new site focuses now on two databases: Meeting abstracts and Health services research projects. All of the other resources previously accessed through the NLM gateway are available through their individual sites. For a list of these databases previously available via the NLM gateway see http://gateway.nlm.nih.gov/about.jsp.

The NLM gateway previously allowed simultaneous searching of information resources at the National Library of Medicine (NLM)/National Center for Biotechnology Information (NCBI, 3) with an overview of the search results presented in several categories (bibliographic resources, consumer health resources, and other information), with a listing of the individual databases and the number of results within these categories. Previously included were, for example, MEDLINE/PubMed and the NLM Catalog as well as other resources, including information on current clinical trials and consumer health information (MedlinePlus) and many others.

628 **Online bioethics resources**. http://genome.gov/10001744. National Human

Genome Research Institute (U.S.), National Institutes of Health. Bethesda, Md.: National Institutes of Health. 2000s–

Produced by National Human Genome Research Institute (NHGRI), which includes the Ethical, Legal and Social Issues (ELSI) Program.

Provides information about the ELSI research program (http://genome.gov/10001618) and an extensive collection of selected online bioethics resources, including ELSI websites, programs, and reports from NHGRI, National Institutes of Health (NIH), U.S. Dept. of Health and Human Services (HHS) Bioethics resources on the web, U.S. Dept. of Energy (DOE), and other resources.

629   Presidential commission for the study of bioethical issues. http://www .bioethics.gov. U.S. Executive Office of the President, Presidential Commission for the Study of Bioethical Issues. Washington: [Executive Office of the President, Presidential Commission for the Study of Bioethical Issues]. 2009–

Managed by the U.S. Dept. of Health and Human Services,

"Advises the President on bioethical issues that may emerge from advances in biomedicine and related areas of science and technology. The Commission works with the goal of identifying and promoting policies and practices that ensure scientific research, health care delivery, and technological innovation are conducted in an ethically responsible manner."—*Website home page* Provides access to all former U.S. national bioethics commissions (1974-2009 http://bioethics.gov/former-commissions), their reports, transcripts, and background materials.

Another resource, the Bioethics research library at Georgetown, holds original documents from the earliest U.S. Presidential Commissions about bioethics, as well as archived websites of more recent commissions.

630   Quackwatch. http://www.quackwatch. org. Stephen Barrett. [Allentown, Pa.]: Stephen Barrett, M.D. [1996]–
615.8   R730

Founded in 1969 as the Lehigh Valley Committee Against Health Fraud, incorporated in 1970.

Assumed its current name in 1997. Maintained by Dr. S. Barrett and a network of volunteers and expert advisors. Affiliated with the National Council Against Health Fraud (http://www.ncahf.com/) and Bioethics Watch.

"Nonprofit corporation whose purpose is to combat health-related frauds, myths, fads, fallacies, and misconduct. Its primary focus is on quackery-related information that is difficult or impossible to get elsewhere. Activities include: Investigating questionable claims; Answering inquiries about products and services; Advising quackery victims; Distributing reliable publications; Debunking pseudoscientific claims; Reporting illegal marketing; Assisting or generating consumer-protection lawsuits; Improving the quality of health information on the Internet; Attacking misleading advertising on the Internet."—*Website*

In addition, includes a list of websites that provide access to 24 special areas—e.g., autism, chiropractic, dentistry, diet and nutrition, mental health, and other topics of interest to consumers. Its "Internet Health Pilot" site provides links to many other reliable health sites, its "Casewatch" site contains legal matters and regulatory issues. The contents of all sites can be searched simultaneously or individually (http://www.quackwatch .org/wgsearch.html).

631   Universal declaration on bioethics and human rights. http://www.unesco .org/new/en/social-and-human-sciences/ themes/bioethics/bioethics-and-human -rights/. UNESCO. Paris: UNESCO. 2005

Adopted by the United Nations Educational, Scientific, and Cultural Organization (UNESCO) on 19 Oct. 2005. Website includes full text and brochure in several languages, explanatory memorandum, presentation, and background of the declaration.

"By enshrining bioethics in international human right and by ensuring respect for the life of human beings, the Declaration recognizes the interrelations between ethics and human rights in the specific field of bioethics."—*Brochure fwd. The Universal declaration on bioethics and human rights: Background, principles and application*, provides historical background contributes to the understanding of these principles worldwide.

Other examples of global bioethics codes, declarations, oaths, codes of conduct/professional codes include the following:

CIOMS (Council for International Organizations and Medical Sciences) guidelines:

http://www.cioms.ch/index.php/bioethics

Declaration of Helsinki (World Medical Association, 620):

http://www.wma.net/en/20activities/10ethics/10helsinki/

Hippocratic oath:

http://www.nlm.nih.gov/hmd/greek/greek_oath.html

International code of medical ethics (World Medical Association):

http://www.wma.net/en/30publications/10policies/c8/

Nuremberg code:

http://www.hhs.gov/ohrp/archive/nurcode.html

Consumer Health

632 **Academy of General Dentistry**. http://www.agd.org/. Academy of General Dentistry. Chicago: Academy of General Dentistry. 1996–

Academy of General Dentistry (AGD), a nonprofit organization of more than 35,000 general dentists, founded in 1952.

Provides fee-based services with access to professional resources for dentists and students (e.g., continuing education, professional news, practice management, etc.) Also offers freely accessible patient- and consumer-oriented oral health resources, such as help with finding a dentist; a list of oral health resources ("ABC's of oral health"), an oral health glossary, "life of a tooth-a visual timeline," and others.

633 **Consumer and Patient Health Information Section of the Medical Library Association (CAPHIS)**. http://caphis.mlanet.org. Medical Library Association. Chicago: Medical Library Association. 2001–

RA393

CAPHIS (Consumer and Patient Health Information Section) of the Medical Library Association (MLANET: the Medical Library Association's network of health information professionals).

"Tailored to the professional needs and interests of consumer health information specialists" (*Publ. notes*), the CAPHIS portal provides selected consumer health information sources and practical tools provided for librarians and health care consumers: CAPHIS discussion list, *Consumer connections* (an online newsletter), a consumer health library directory, collection development tools, the official MLA policy statement "The Librarian's Role in the Provision of Consumer Health Information and Patient Education," list of health topics ("CAPHIS top 100 list: Web sites you can trust"), and other useful resources.

634 **DailyMed**. http://dailymed.nlm.nih.gov/. National Library of Medicine (U.S.). Bethesda, Md.: U.S. National Library of Medicine, National Institutes of Health, Health and Human Services. [2005]–

A searchable website with growing content, providing health consumers, students, and health professionals with online information on prescription medications and labeling from FDA-approved medication package inserts. Each entry gives a description of the medication, its clinical pharmacology, indications and usage, warnings and precautions, dosage and administration, adverse reactions, etc. Information regarding the mobile version of this resource is part of NLM's Gallery of mobile apps and sites.

Additional consumer health information about U.S. drugs provided by NLM can be found in *MedlinePlus* under headings such as drugs, supplements, and herbal information, drug safety, medicines, over-the-counter medicines, pain relievers, and possibly others. PubMed and its MEDLINE subset and TOXLINE, can be searched for references to professional journal articles.

635 Drugs in pregnancy and lactation: A reference guide to fetal and neonatal risk. Gerald G. Briggs. Baltimore: Williams and Wilkins, 1983–
618.32071 0897-6112
RG627.6.D79D798
Description based on 9th ed., 2011.
This updated edition summarizes data on specific drugs. Arranged in alphabetical order, each drug monograph provides the U.S. generic name, pharmacologic class, risk factor, fetal risk summary, breast feeding summary, and references, where available. Lists drugs which are contraindicated during breastfeeding, during pregnancy, and also drugs which cause human developmental toxicity. Three changes in format in this edition (cf. *Preface*): The FDA's risk categories, previously included (since 1979 when they first appeared), have been removed. Furthermore, information on drugs that are no longer available has been removed, i.e., drugs are still listed with the notation "withdrawn from the market see 8th edition." Another change is the addition to the index of prescription combination drugs; they are listed by trade name with the names of the individual drugs mentioned in the text. An appendix arranges the drugs by pharmacologic category, allowing comparison of drugs within the same pharmacologic class to determine different risk factors. Written for clinicians caring for pregnant women. Also available as an e-book.

Other resources are *Drugs for pregnant and lactating women* by Weiner, and *Drugs during pregnancy and lactation* by Schaefer. An online resource, LactMed (part of TOXNET) (http://toxnet.nlm.nih .gov/), is a web-based peer-reviewed database with information on drugs and lactation.

636 The 5-minute herb and dietary supplement consult. Adriane Fugh-Berman. Philadelphia: Lippincott Williams & Wilkins, 2003. xv, 475 p.
ISBN 0683302736
615.321
RM666.H33.F835
Ready-reference resource, arranged alphabetically by botanical or dietary supplement, with Latin and biological names. Entries include concise description, appropriate dosage, pharmacokinetics, drug interactions, risks, etc.

For academic medical and public libraries.

637 Food and Nutrition Information Center. http://www.nal.usda.gov/fnic/.
Food and Nutrition Information Center (U. S.). Beltsville, Md.: Food and Nutrition Information Center
351; 640.73;
RA784
371.7; 612.3; 641.3
The Food and Nutrition Information Center (FNIC), located at the National Agricultural Library (NAL, 672) of the U.S. Dept. of Agriculture (USDA), provides online global nutrition information and links to nutrition-related resources provided by the National Agricultural Library, federal and state governments, professional organizations, universities, and others. The FNIC website contains multiple links to reliable food and nutrition and metabolism information for consumers and nutrition professionals. The a–z list (http://fnic.nal.usda .gov/topics-z) includes important topics (e.g., infant nutrition, childhood & adolescent obesity, weight control, etc.), or a browse by subject section for dietary guidance, lifecycle nutrition, diet & disease, weight & obesity , food safety, and many other subject areas. Also included are links to resource lists for specific nutrition topics (http://fnic.nal .usda.gov/resource-lists-0) and to FNIC and other nutrition-related databases (http://fnic.nal.usda .gov/databases).

638 The Gale encyclopedia of neurological disorders. 2nd ed. Brigham Narins. Detroit: Gale Cengage Learning, 2012. 2 v. (xxii, 1330 p.), ill. (some col.)
ISBN 9781414490083
616.8003
RC334.G34
First ed., 2005.
Contents: v.1, A–L; v.2, M–Z, glossary, index.

Includes 400 alphabetically arranged entries on disorders of the nervous system, with articles on neurological diseases, disorders and syndromes, tests, treatments, diagnostic equipment, and medications. Also includes articles on the brain and nervous system anatomy. A typical entry for a disease includes, e.g., definition, description, demographics, causes and symptoms, diagnosis, treatment team, treatment, recovery and rehabilitation, clinical trials, prognosis, special concerns, resources, and key terms. Also included are resource lists of books, periodical articles, organizations, and websites. Both volumes include a complete list of entries. Intended for patients, their families, allied health students, and general readers. Drug and treatment data also provide structured entries, with definition, purpose, description, recommended dosage, precautions, side effects, interactions, resources, and key terms. Available online in the Gale Virtual Reference Library.

639 Health and wellness resource center.
http://www.gale.com/HealthRC/. Gale Group. Farmington Hills, Mich.: Gale; Cengage Learning. 2001–

Also called *Gale®'s health & wellness resource center*.

Provides access to a collection of Gale reference titles (e.g., *Gale encyclopedia of cancer*, *Gale encyclopedia of childhood and adolescence*, *Gale encyclopedia of genetic disorders*, *Gale encyclopedia of medicine*, *Medical and health information directory*, and others; access to full-text articles from the periodical literature; pamphlets; news; and other content, such as access to selected health websites. Also makes available add-on modules (e.g., Alternative Health Module with, for example, the *Gale encyclopedia of alternative medicine*, and the Disease Profiler Module with health statistics). "Ever-growing electronic resource center for all levels of health research" (*Publ. notes*), particularly for nursing and allied health professionals and consumer health, public, and health science libraries.

Other Gale resources include Health reference center—academic and Gale virtual reference library.

640 Health information for international travel. http://purl.access.gpo.gov/GPO/LPS3580. Phyllis E. Kozarsky, Paul M. Arguin, Ava W. Navin, U.S. Centers for Disease Control and Prevention. Atlanta: U.S. Dept. of Health and Human Services, Centers for Disease Control and Prevention. 1974–

Part of the Centers for Disease Control (CDC) Travelers' health website (http://wwwnc.cdc.gov/travel/default.aspx). Also called "Yellow book" or "CDC yellow book." Description based on the 2014 ed., also issued in print with title *CDC health information for international travel: The yellow book*. Previous print editions issued since 1989 as a serial, *International travel health guide*.

Contents: Ch. 1, "Introduction"; ch. 2, "The Pre-travel consultation"; ch. 3, "Infectious diseases related to travel"; ch. 4, "Select destinations"; ch. 5, "Post-travel evaluation"; ch. 6, "Conveyance and transportation issues"; ch. 7, "International travel with infants and children"; ch. 8, "Advising travelers with specific needs"; ch. 9, "Health considerations for newly arrived immigrants and refugees". Appendix (A), "Promotion of quality in the practice of travel medicine"; (B), "Essential electronic resources for the travel medicine practitioner"; (C), Travel vaccine summary table; (D), "The Health-Map (923) system." Also contains separate lists of tables, maps, boxes, and figures.

Provides comprehensive information on vaccination requirements and recommendations for international travelers concerning health risks.

The World Health Organization's website, International travel and health, also offers extensive travel information.

641 Health on the Net Foundation (HON).
http://www.hon.ch/. Health on the Net Foundation. Geneva, Switzerland: Health on the Net Foundation (HON). 1995–
R859.7.E43

Health On the Net Foundation (HON) is a nonprofit, nongovernmental organization known for its HONcode, which defines rules and ethical standards for website developers on how information is provided in terms of the source and data provided. The HONcode is not considered an award or quality rating system for websites.

Provides a "portal to medical information on the Internet" (*Website*). Searchable website provides access to resources for individuals/patients and medical professionals. Includes HON's history and current contact information, access to listservs, newsgroups, and FAQs. For medical and health queries, HON's Search HON (http://www.hon.ch/HONHunt/AdvHONHunt.html) and HONselect© (http://www.hon.ch/HONselect/) help locate quality websites and support groups, medical terminology, journal articles, and healthcare news.

HONmedia (http://www.hon.ch/HONmedia/) is a growing and searchable repository of medical images and videos (currently contains 6,800 medical images and videos, pertaining to 1,700 topics and themes).

642 **Household products database**. http:// householdproducts.nlm.nih.gov/. Specialized Information Services, National Library of Medicine (U.S.). Bethesda, Md.: Specialized Information Services, U.S. National Library of Medicine, National Institutes of Health, Dept. of Health & Human Services
TS175

Part of TOXNET®.

Provides information on potential health effects and composition of chemicals contained in common household products. Includes reference to health effects information contained in Material Safety Data Sheets (MSDS). Products can also be searched by type, manufacturer, product ingredient/chemical name and by health effects. Additional details concerning this resource can be found via TOXNET fact sheet at http://www.nlm.nih.gov/ pubs/factsheets/toxnetfs.html.

643 **MLANET**. http://www.mlanet.org/. Medical Library Association. Chicago: Medical Library Association (MLA). 1998–

Medical Library Association (MLA), since 1889, "a nonprofit, educational organization of more than 1,100 institutions and 3,600 individual members in the health sciences information field, committed to educating health information professionals, supporting health information research, promoting access to the world's health sciences information, and working to ensure that the best health information is available to all" (*MLA website*).

Searchable home page for MLA which provides a variety of resources for its members, such as professional standards and practices, discussion of information issues and policy, career information resources, professional credentialing, publications, etc. Also provides resources for health consumers, e.g., "A User's guide to finding and evaluating health information on the Web" (http://www.mlanet.org/ resources/userguide.html), including "Deciphering MedSpeak," and MLA's guidelines on finding

quality information on the Internet. Provides links to websites considered quality sites ("top ten") by MLA, such as: Cancer.gov, Centers for Disease Control (CDC), familydoctor.org (http://familydoctor .org)healthfinder®; HIV InSite, Kidshealth® (http://www.kidshealth.org/), Mayo Clinic, MedlinePlus. Some content is restricted to members only.

Currently 23 different MLA sections have their own webpages (http://www.mlanet.org/sections/ sections.html). A prominent example of a section website is the Consumer and Patient Information Section of the Medical Library Association (CAPHIS).

644 **Natural medicines comprehensive database**. http://www.naturaldatabase .com/. Jeff M. Jellin, Therapeutic Research Faculty. Stockton, Calif.: Therapeutic Research Faculty. 1995–
RM258.5

Available in a professional and a consumer version. Publication varies.

Compilation of natural medicines distributed in the U.S. Contains up-to-date clinical and research information for natural (i.e., herbal and and nonherbal) medicines and dietary supplements distributed in the U.S. Products can be found by most commonly used name, brand name (with editor's comments as appropriate or necessary), ingredient names, scientific names (botanical names), or popular names, with search features to find the safe use (with safety ratings based on evidence: likely safe; possibly safe; possibly unsafe; likely unsafe; unsafe), adverse effects (between natural and pharmaceutical products), interactions ("natural product/drug interaction checker"); also a "natural product effectiveness checker" for each natural medicine. Suitable for pharmacists, physicians, and students in the healthcare field, all types of medical libraries, and also for consumers. Also available in print version since 1999 (13th ed., 2013). Everything in the book is also contained in the web version, which has important added features, such as daily updates, additional search capabilities, patient education handouts, and hyperlinked references, to name a few.

Since 2010, many English and Spanish monographs dietary supplements and herbal remedies from the consumer version of this database have been added to MedlinePlus. This new content replaces the Natural standard monographs previously included in MedlinePlus.

645 NLM gateway. http://gateway.nlm.nih
.gov/. National Library of Medicine
(U.S.). Bethesda, Md.: National Library of
Medicine. 2000–

RA11

As announced in 2011, "the NLM® gateway has transitioned to a new pilot project from the Lister Hill National Center for Biomedical Communications (LHNCBC)."—*Website* The new site focuses now on two databases: Meeting abstracts and Health services research projects. All of the other resources previously accessed through the NLM gateway are available through their individual sites. For a list of these databases previously available via the NLM gateway see http://gateway.nlm.nih.gov/about.jsp.

The NLM gateway previously allowed simultaneous searching of information resources at the National Library of Medicine (NLM)/National Center for Biotechnology Information (NCBI) with an overview of the search results presented in several categories (bibliographic resources, consumer health resources, and other information), with a listing of the individual databases and the number of results within these categories. Previously included were, for example, MEDLINE/PubMed and the NLM Catalog as well as other resources, including information on current clinical trials and consumer health information (MedlinePlus) and many others.

646 patientINFORM. http://www.patient
inform.org/. patientINFORM. [s.l.]:
patientINFORM. 2005–

Online service that provides patients and their caregivers access to the latest research findings and important advances in regard to the diagnosis and treatment of specific diseases, with initial focus on cancer, diabetes, and heart disease. Current participants are the American Cancer Society (ACS), American Diabetes Organization (ADA), American Heart Association (AHA), and the National Organization for Rare Disorders (NORD), approximately 20 publishers, the International Association of STM Publishers, MedlinePlus, the Welch Medical Library at Johns Hopkins, and others. Publishers provide these organizations with online access to

their peer-reviewed biomedical journals of newly published articles and also to the backfiles of these journals. These organizations, in turn, provide consumers with links to the full text of selected journal articles and create additional patient-oriented information on their own websites.

**647 Tyler's honest herbal: A sensible
guide to the use of herbs and related
remedies. 4th ed.** Steven Foster,
Varro E. Tyler. New York: Haworth
Herbal Press, 1999. xxi, 442 p.
ISBN 0789007053

615.321   RM666.H33T94

Title varies: 1st ed. (1981) had title *The honest herbal;* 2nd ed. (1987), *The new honest herbal;* 3rd ed., 1993. Provides references and peer-reviewed scientific data on the uses of herbs and herbal remedies. Includes approx. 100 herbs. Arranged in alphabetical order by common name, each entry describes the plant with the appropriate nomenclature, botanical information, the chemistry and pharmacology of its active ingredients, its traditional uses, positive and negative features when used for therapeutic purposes, folklore, and other facts. An evaluation by the author based on available evidence follows for each herb. Mentions possible safety concerns. Includes a chapter on laws and regulations. References to the literature. For general readers and as a starting point for scientists; index. Also available as an e-book.

Tyler's *Herbs of choice* (re-issued in 1999 as *Tyler's herbs of choice: The therapeutic use of phytomedicinals* and now in its third edition) provides related information.

Guides

648 AIDSinfo. http://www.aidsinfo.nih.gov.
U.S. Department of Health and Human
Services, National Institutes of Health
(U.S.), AIDS Clinical Trials Information
Service. Bethesda, Md.: National
Institutes of Health

RA643.8

Result of merging two previous U.S. Dept. of Health and Human Services (DHHS) projects. Supersedes the AIDS Clinical Trials Information Service (ACTIS) and the HIV/AIDS Treatment Information Service (ATIS).

Resource for current information on federally and privately funded clinical trials for AIDS patients and HIV-infected persons, federally approved HIV treatment and prevention guidelines, and medical practice guidelines. Provides access to a searchable HIV/AIDS drugs database (via "Drugs" tab) that includes approved and investigational anti-HIV medications, including side effects, dosages, and interactions with other drugs or food; also access to brochures, fact sheets, and other Web resources on HIV/AIDS, current and archived versions of DHHS guidelines, and a searchable HIV/AIDS glossary (English and Spanish). For HIV/AIDS patients, the general public, health care providers, and researchers. Information regarding the mobile version of this resource is part of NLM's Gallery of mobile apps and sites.

Additional major HIV/AIDS resources can be accessed via the following sites: Fact sheet, AIDS Information Resources (http://www.nlm.nih.gov/pubs/factsheets/aidsinfs.html), Specialized Information Services: HIV/AIDS Information (http://sis.nlm.nih.gov/hiv.html), CDC National Prevention Information Network (NPIN) (http://www.cdcnpin.org/scripts/hiv/index.asp), UNAIDS: Joint United National Programming on HIV/AIDS (http://www.unaids.org/en/), and AIDS Treatment Data Network (http://www.atdn.org/).

649 Alternative medicine. Christine A. Larson. Westport, Conn.: Greenwood Press, 2007. xv, 215 p. ISBN 0313337187
610   R733.L37

Contents: "The origins of alternative medicine"; "The theories underlying alternative medicine"; "The business of alternative medicine"; "Why consumers seek alternative treatments"; "Do alternative therapies work?"; "Should alternative medicine be regulated by the government?"; "Should managed care provide coverage for alternative therapies?"; "Pharmaceuticals versus alternative therapies"; "Culture and health: Who bears responsibility for health and healthcare?"; "The future of health and healthcare."

Guide to alternative medicine, covering practical and also controversial issues, with recommendations on using safe alternative medicine practices together with Western medicine. Annotated primary source documents, alternative medicine timeline, and glossary. Includes bibliographical references

(p. [201]–208) and index. For researchers, clinicians, consumers, and academic and medical libraries. Also available as an e-book.

The Medical Library Association guide to finding out about complementary and alternative medicine by Crawford provides an overview of resources, with emphasis on consumer health resources.

650 Alternative medicine resource guide. Francine Feuerman, Marsha J. Handel. Lanham, Md.: Medical Library Association, 1997. 335 p. ISBN 0810832844
615.5   R733.F48

Provides information on alternative systems of medicine—Ayurvedic, Chinese, and herbal medicine, homeopathy, naturopathy—and various manipulative (e.g., chiropractic and osteopathy) and other therapies, such as biofeedback and sensory therapies. Organized into two main sections: pt. I, a resource guide with reference information on specific services and products, organizations, and companies; pt. II, a selective, evaluative, annotated bibliography of books, journals, and newsletters, limited to English-language print sources published in the U.S. since 1988. Appendix lists book publishers. Index.

A more recent resource, *The Medical Library Association guide to finding out about complementary and alternative medicine* provides an overview of resources, with emphasis on consumer health resources. Includes books, periodicals, and websites.

651 American Medical Association family medical guide. 4th ed., completely rev. and updated ed. American Medical Association. Hoboken, N.J.: John Wiley and Sons, 2004. xiv, 1184 p., ill. (some col.) ISBN 0471269115
613   RC81.A543

First ed., 1982; 2nd ed., 1987; 3rd ed. (print), 1994; computer disk, 1995. Aimed at general readers, this guide presents a general discussion of the healthy body, self-diagnosis symptom charts with visual aids to diagnosis, diseases and other disorders and problems, preventive health care practices, and caring for the sick. Includes a section on accidents and emergencies. Glossary and subject index. Also available as an e-book.

Another consumer resource, *American Medical Association complete guide to prevention and wellness: What you need to know about preventing illness, staying healthy, and living longer* offers guidance to prevent illness and to promote health.

652   The complementary and alternative medicine information source book.
Alan M. Rees. [Phoenix, Ariz.]: Oryx Press, 2001. x, 229 p., ill.
ISBN 1573563889
615.5   R733.C65285
Contents: (1) Complementary and alternative medicine: a new dimension in medical consumerism; (2) The best of complementary and alternative medicine information resources; (3) Complementary and alternative medicine organizations; (4) Complementary and alternative medicine magazines and newsletters; (5) Pamphlet materials; (6) Professional literature; (7) CD-ROM information products; (8) Complementary and alternative medicine sources on the Internet (Tom Flemming); (9) Popular books on complementary and alternative medicine. Appendixes: (1) General information about CAM and the NCCAM; (2) Major domains of complementary and alternative medical practices; (3) Frequently asked questions (about CAM); (4) Considering CAM?; (5) NCCAM CAM research centers; (6) Want information about alternative medicine?; (7) MEDLINE and related databases (and alternative medicine). Author, title, and subject indexes. Also available as an e-book.

Intended as a companion volume to the *Consumer health information source book* (654) and as a "supplement . . . by providing in depth access to the growing literature relating to complementary and alternative medicine" (*Pref.*). For patients, other health consumers, and librarians in both public and academic libraries.

Available online via Gale's Health and Wellness Resource Center.

653   Consumer health: A guide to Internet information resources. 2nd rev. ed.
Jana Liebermann, Cecilia Durkin, Medical Library Association. Chicago, Ill.: Medical Library Association, 2004. 213+ p.
ISBN 9780912176529
0912176520;   RA773.6
First ed., 2001; (MLA BibKit; no. 7). Contents: ch. 1, Quality matters; ch. 2, Gateways to health

information on the Internet; ch. 3, Electronic libraries; ch. 4, Diseases and conditions; ch. 5, Family health issues; ch. 6, Special populations; ch. 7, Drug information sources; ch. 8, Mental health and substance abuse; ch. 9, Complementary and alternative therapies; ch. 10, Wellness and prevention; ch. 11, Health care providers; ch. 12, Hot health topics—medical news sites; Conclusion: surviving Internet overload. Designed to assist librarians in identifying quality consumer-oriented websites which are considered to be useful for patients, caregivers, and other health care consumers to better understand diseases, treatments, and healthcare issues. Includes annotated entries for a variety of resources (e.g., online guides and tutorials, medical search engines, quality filters, international gateways, electronic libraries, subject-specific websites, medical news, etc.). A chapter focuses on special populations (e.g., senior citizens, minorities, and disabled individuals). Eight appendixes: (1) Savvy health surfing; (2) Quality filters for medical websites; (3) Medical and health information databases and directories; (4) Medical dictionaries and glossaries; (5) Selected health books and pamphlets; (6) Health materials in multiple languages; (7) Easy-to-read/easy-to-understand/low literacy consumer health materials; (8) Quick guide to Internet drug information sources. Includes bibliographical references (p. 182–206) and index.

Additional information in this area can be found, for example, via the website of the *Consumer and Patient Health Information Section of the Medical Library Association (CAPHIS)*.

654   Consumer health information source book. 7th ed. Alan M. Rees. Westport, Conn.: Greenwood Press, 2003. p. cm.
ISBN 1573565091
016.613   Z6673.R43; RA766
A guide to popular health information in both print and electronic format on a wide variety of topics. Provides brief annotations and evaluations of approx. 2,000 selected consumer health publications in a variety of formats: books, home medical guides, popular health magazines, and newsletters. English- and Spanish-language pamphlets, and websites. Also includes information on clearinghouses and centers, toll-free hotlines, and health organizations that provide information to the general public. Contains chapters on recent

developments in consumer health information on the Internet with a ranking of websites, and a description of 12 innovative libraries considered "models of excellence." Author, title, and subject indexes. Has a companion volume, The complementary and alternative medicine information source book. Intended for consumers and reference and collection development librarians. Also available as an e-book.

655 A consumer's guide to dentistry.
2nd ed. Gordon J. Christensen. St. Louis: Mosby, 2002. x, 214 p., col. ill.
ISBN 0323014836
617.6   RK61.C57
First ed., 1994.

Contents: Ch. 1 "How to use this book," finding solutions to your oral problems; ch. 2 "Divisions in dentistry," types of dentists; ch. 3 "Finding the right dentist," what to consider in your choice of dentists; ch. 4 "Managed care," managed care programs in dentistry; ch. 5 "Pain control," controlling pain in dentistry; ch. 6 "Infection control," infection control in the dental office; ch. 7 "Endodontics," root canals, dead teeth, inside of teeth; ch. 8 "Esthetic dentistry," cosmetic dentistry, improving your smile; ch. 9 "Geriatric dentistry," dentistry for mature people; ch. 10 "Implant dentistry," substitutes for tooth roots placed into your jaw; ch. 11 "Occlusion," your bite, the way your teeth come together, temporomandibular joints, temporomandibular dysfunction; ch. 12 "Oral and maxillofacial surgery," oral pathology, oral medicine diseases, and surgery related to the oral and facial areas; ch. 13 "Orthodontics," straightening teeth; ch. 14 "Pediatric dentistry," dentistry for children; ch. 15 "Periodontics," gums and bone surrounding teeth, ch. 16 "Prosthodontics," fixed crowns or bridges cemented onto teeth; ch. 17 "Prosthodontics," removable dentures replacing all or some teeth; ch. 18 "Restorative or operative dentistry," fillings for teeth; ch. 19. "Preventing the need for dental treatment"; ch. 20 "Additional sources of information."

Written for the dental patient, provides information about dental health and various treatment options for dental problems. Illustrations.

656 Dietary guidelines for Americans,
2010. http://www.cnpp.usda.gov/ Publications/DietaryGuidelines/2010/ PolicyDoc/PolicyDoc.pdf. U.S.

Department of Health and Human Services, U.S. Department of Agriculture. Washington: U.S. Department of Health and Human Services; U.S. Department of Agriculture. 2010
613.25   RA784

Published jointly every five years by the Department of Health and Human Services, Office of Disease Prevention and Health Promotion, the Department of Agriculture, Center for Nutrition Policy and Promotion, and the Agricultural Research Service.

First five editions, 1980–2000, had title, Nutrition and your health: Dietary guidelines for Americans. Print equivalents for these editions published in Home and garden bulletin (U.S. Dept. of Agriculture) no. 232. Current and earlier online editions linked from http://www.health.gov/ DietaryGuidelines/.

Description based on the 2010 Web edition.

Contents: Ch. 1, "Introduction"; ch. 2, "Balancing calories to manage weight"; ch. 3, "Foods and food components to reduce"; ch. 4, "Foods and nutrients to increase"; ch. 5, "Building healthy eating patterns"; ch. 6, "Helping Americans make healthy choices"; Appendixes (1) "Guidance for specific population groups"; (2) "Key consumer behaviors and potential strategies for professionals to use in implementing the 2010 Dietary Guidelines"; (3) "Food safety principles and guidance for consumers"; (4) "Using the food label to track calories, nutrients, and ingredients"; (5) "Nutritional goals for age-gender groups based on dietary reference intakes and dietary guidelines recommendations"; (6) Estimated calorie needs per day by age, gender, and physical activity level (detailed)"; (7) "USDA food patterns"; (8) "Lacto-ovo vegetarian adaptation of the USDA food patterns"; (9) "Vegan adaptation of the USDA food patterns"; (10) "The DASH eating plan at various calorie levels"; (11) "Estimated EPA and DHA and mercury content in 4 ounces of selected seafood varieties"; (12) "Selected food sources ranked by amounts of potassium and calories per standard food portion"; (13) "Selected food sources ranked by amounts of dietary, fiber and calories per standard food portion"; (14) "Selected food sources ranked by amounts of calcium and calories per standard food portion"; (15) "Selected food sources ranked by amounts of

169

vitamin D and calories per standard food portion"; (16), "Glossary of terms".

These guidelines provide authoritative advice for people two years old and older about how good dietary habits can promote health and reduce risk for major chronic diseases. Additional information and access to related documents and resources can be found at http://teamnutrition.usda.gov/library.html.

Choose My Plate (http://www.choosemyplate.gov), launched in June 2011, is based on these dietary guidelines. This new food icon is intended to assist consumers in visualizing and preparing a plate with healthy proportions of fruits, vegetables, grains, protein, and dairy during mealtimes. These food choices are considered to lead to healthier lifestyles.

657 Finding health and wellness @ the library: A consumer health toolkit for library staff. http://bibpurl.oclc.org/web/40791. Kelli Ham, Suzanne Flint, Meredith Bloom, California State Library.; Library Development Services Bureau., National Network of Libraries of Medicine (U.S.).; Pacific Southwest Region. Sacramento, Calif.: California State Library, Library Development Services Bureau. 2013 610

A project of California State Library and the National Network of Libraries of Medicine/Pacific Southwest Region.

First ed., 2010.

Assists libraries to "become providers of reliable health promotion and wellness information . . . [and] develop effective partnerships with health professionals and community agencies."*Foreword*

Includes sections on "core competencies," "health resources," "consumer health information services," "technology & health 2.0," "workplace wellness," "resources for serving health care professionals," and also an "acronyms reference list." Table of contents helps to navigate through the different sections. No index. Website links in PDF are live. Icons indicate the type of format, i.e., book, PDF document, video, audio, DVD, or online training materials. Also indicated are language and reading level. Provides guidelines and tips on handling medical questions and providing health reference to the public. For updates and new

resources, follow this toolkit on Twitter (twitter.com/healthtoolkit). Also available in print.

658 Genetics home reference. http://purl.access.gpo.gov/GPO/LPS74916. Lister Hill National Center for Biomedical Communications, National Library of Medicine, National Institutes of Health, Department of Health and Human Services. Bethesda, Md.: National Library of Medicine. 2003–

Aims to make genetics and its relationship to disease accessible to the general public. Information is presented in a question and answer format, with explanation on how a disease is inherited, the symptoms, and what treatments are available. Provides general information on genes, gene maps, genetic markers, chromosomes, DNA, and details on the specific genes related to a particular disease. Includes a "help me understand genetics page," a glossary of genetics terms, links to clinical trials, etc. Updated as new information becomes available. A detailed description at http://www.nlm.nih.gov/pubs/factsheets/ghr.html.

GeneEd (http://geneed.nlm.nih.gov), a new educational resource developed by the National Library of Medicine in collaboration with the National Human Genome Research Institute and also teachers and genetics & genetics counseling professionals. Intended as a resource for students and teachers in grades 9 - 12, it also is useful for health consumers, providing valuable information about genetic conditions and related topics.

659 Health care almanac: Every person's guide to the thoughtful and practical sides of medicine. 2nd ed. Lorri A. Zipperer, American Medical Association. Chicago, Ill.: American Medical Association, 1998. xiv, 546 p. ISBN 0899709001
362.1/0973/03   R104.H43

First ed. (1993) had title: *The healthcare resource and reference guide;* rev. 1995 ed. had title: *Health care almanac: a resource guide to the medical field.* Addresses common queries by physicians and patients, including health and medical practice-related issues. In three sections: (1) Dictionary-style directory arranged alphabetically by subject, with the names of organizations that may be able to provide information on specific subjects; (2) Outlines major administrative units of the American Medical Association (AMA), with an historical overview since 1846;(3) Tools to help navigate the almanac: listing of sources and index which is also intended to serve cross-referencing needs. Includes "Principles of Medical Ethics," "The Hippocrat Oath," and "Patient Bill of Rights." Provides information and glossaries on managed care, tort reform, Medicare, background on terminal care and advanced directives and end-of-life issues, patient safety, home health care, etc. This print resource can be supplemented with web-based, possibly more up-to-date information found on the AMA website (American Medical Association [homepage]) with its professional resources section, including online ethics resources; DoctorFinder; and other links.

660   Health care resources on the Internet: A guide for librarians and health care consumers. M. Sandra Wood. New York: Haworth Information Press, 2000. xxi, 205 p. ISBN 0789006324

025.0661   R119.9.H39

Contents: ch. 1, Use of the Internet at the reference desk (Nancy Calabretta); ch. 2, Natural language and beyond: tips for search services (Eric P. Delozier); ch. 3, Megasites for health care information (Cindy A. Gruwell, Scott Marsalis); ch. 4, MEDLINE on the Internet (Helen-Ann Brown, Valerie G. Rankow); ch. 5, Searching the Internet for diseases (Alexa Mayo, Cynthia R. Phyillaier); ch. 6, Consumer health information on the Internet (Janet M. Coggan); ch. 7, Alternative medicine on the Net (Suzanne M. Shultz, Nancy I. Henry, Esther Y. Dell); ch. 8, Government resources on the Net (Nancy J. Allee, 9); Health-related statistical information on the Net (Dawn M. Littleton, Kathryn Robbins); ch. 10, Electronic journals on the Internet (Virginia A. Lingle); ch. 11, Searching international medical resources on the World Wide Web (Jeri Ann Risin). Provides a list of of selected websites and also general information on developing skills and techniques for Internet searching for health-related information, including evidence-based medicine. Includes a "Comparative Chart of MEDLINE Searching Systems." A practical resource, useful for librarians, health care professionals, and general readers.

Finding and using health and medical information on the Internet by Sue Welsh et al. and Sydney S. Chellen's *Essential guide to the Internet for health professionals* are other guides on how to locate biomedical information effectively. Even though some of the content in these three resources needs updating, they nevertheless remain useful guides.

661   Healthfinder.gov. http://purl.access.gpo .gov/GPO/LPS45861. Office of Disease Prevention and Health Promotion (U.S.), National Health Information Center. Washington: U.S. Department of Health and Human Services. 1997–

Z6673

Healthfinder® is a project coordinated by the Office of Disease Prevention and Health Promotion (ODPHP) and its National Health Information Center.

Gateway and search engine to help locate health-related information from federal and state government agencies, clearinghouses, nonprofit organizations, and universities. Provides links to selected resources on diseases, conditions, and injuries. Tabs for an A–Z "health library" and "consumer guides" (e.g., medical errors, patient privacy, Medicare, Medicaid), with links to online publications, databases, medical dictionaries. For consumers and health professionals. Selected by the Medical Library Association (MLA) as one of its "'Top Ten' Most Useful Websites" (http://www .mlanet.org/resources/medspeak/topten.html).

662   Health reference series (Omnigraphics, Inc.). Karen Bellenir. Detroit: Omnigraphics, Inc., 1990–. Vol. 1-, ill.

sn 92-33485

See description and titles at http://omnigraphics .com/shop/category/health-reference-series/ #description.

Volumes in this series provide information on a wide variety of medical topics, including diseases, treatments, and related topics. Includes sourcebooks on adolescent health, adult health, alcoholism, allergies, Alzheimer's disease, arthritis, asthma, autism and developmental disorders, blood and circulatory disorders, brain disorders, cancer, cancer in women, cardiovascular disorders, child abuse, childhood diseases & disorders, complementary and alternative medicine, congenital disorders, contagious diseases, cosmetic and reconstructive surgery, death and dying, dental care & oral health, depression, diet & nutrition, disabilities, drug abuse, ear, nose, and throat disorders, eating disorders, endocrine and metabolic disorders, environmental health, eye care, genetic disorders, HIV/AIDS, fitness and exercise, learning disabilities, medical tests, men's health, mental health, movement disorders, pain, podiatry, pregnancy & birth, respiratory disorders, sexually transmitted diseases, sports injuries, sleep disorders, stress-related disorders, surgery, women's health, and others. Individual volumes contain materials and information issued by different government agencies, professional associations, research centers, journals, and other sources. Another series appropriate for consumer health collections by the same publisher is *Teen health series*. Also available online.

663 International travel and health. http://www.who.int/ith/en/. World Health Organization. Geneva, Switzerland: World Health Organization. 2005–

RA638.I58

Description based on the 2011 online edition. Also available as a print edition. Selected chapters of 2012 are free online.

Contents: ch. 1, "Health risks and precautions: General considerations"; ch. 2, "Mode of travel: Health considerations"; ch. 3, "Environmental health risks"; ch. 4, "Injuries and violence"; ch. 5, "Infectious diseases of potential risk for travellers"; ch. 6, "Vaccine-preventable diseases and vaccines"; ch. 7, "Malaria"; ch. 8, "Exposure to blood and body fluids"; ch. 9, "Special groups of travelers"; ch. 10, "Psychological health"; ITH 2011 country list: 1. "Yellow fever vaccination requirements and recommendations"; 2. "Malaria situation"; ITH Annexes: 1. "Countries with risk of yellow fever transmission and countries requiring yellow fever vaccination"; 2. "International health regulations (935)."

Provides information on the main health risks for travelers at specific destinations with different modes of travel. Website also provides related links on, for example, disease outbreaks (e.g., avian influenza, drug-resistant tuberculosis, etc.), International health regulations (2005) and others. Intended for medical professionals; also useful to consumers.

Health information for international travel (640) is another resource for travel information.

664 MayoClinic.com. http://www.mayoclinic.com/. Mayo Foundation for Medical Education and Research, Mayo Clinic. [Rochester, Minn.]: Mayo Foundation for Medical Education and Research. 1998–

RA776.5

Formerly had title: Mayo health oasis.

Searchable website. Separate pages for diseases and conditions A–Z and first aid, drugs (prescription and over-the-counter drug information from Micromedex) and supplements (with information from Natural standard), treatment decisions, healthy living (i.e., collection of information and tools to provide help to stay healthy). "Ask a specialist" (i.e., Mayo Clinic specialists answer select questions from readers).

In addition to MedlinePlus and this website, there are many other sites that receive excellent reviews and are frequently used by consumers. Some prominent examples include Familydoctor.org (http://familydoctor.org/), Hardin MD, NetWellness (http://www.netwellness.org/), Healthfinder.gov, and WebMD (http://www.webmd.com/) and its Medscape site (http://www.medscape.com/) which has freely accessible auhoritative medical information (both original content and links to other sources), but requires registration.

665 The Medical Library Association consumer health reference service handbook. Donald A. Barclay, Deborah D. Halsted, Medical Library Association. New York: Neal-Schuman Publ., 2001. xxv, 197 p., ill. ISBN 1555704182

025.06/61   RA776.B234

Contents: pt. 1, Consumer health essentials for librarians; pt. 2, Consumer health resources for librarians; pt. 3, Consumer health services for libraries. Information for librarians providing consumer health services. Includes standard sources for answering questions, selected consumer health websites, and also methods that can be used to establish consumer health information services. CD-ROM includes templates for developing a consumer health website. Includes bibliographical references and index.

Answering consumer health questions: The Medical Library Association guide for reference librarians by Spatz offers guidelines and tips, including both verbal and nonverbal communication skills, for reference librarians in support of providing consumer health information.

666 The Medical Library Association encyclopedic guide to searching and finding health information on the Web. P. F. Anderson, Nancy J. Allee. New York: Neal-Schuman Publ., 2004. 3 v.
ISBN 1555704948
025.06/61   R859.7.I58M436
Contents: v.1, Search strategies/quick reference guide; v. 2, Diseases and disorders/mental health and mental disorders; v. 3, Health and wellness/life stages and reproduction, and cumulative index. A comprehensive guide written by experienced health sciences librarians. Recommends search terms, search strategies, and search engines for checking the Internet for answers to health-related questions. Useful for both health care consumers and librarians involved in teaching health information literacy. Companion website at http://www-personal.umich.edu/~pfa/mlaguide/indextest.html. Also available on CD-ROM, with search capability and links to over 11,000 web sites.

667 The Medical Library Association guide to cancer information: Authoritative, patient-friendly print and electronic resources. Ruti Malis Volk, Medical Library Association. New York: Neal-Schuman, 2007. p. cm.
ISBN 9781555705855
616.99/40025   RC262.M427
Contents: pt. I: Key resources for finding cancer information; pt. II, Key resources for finding information on specific types of cancer. A guide for medical, academic, and public libraries to help in the provision of reliable cancer information for patients, caregivers, and other healthcare consumers. May also prove to be helpful for building consumer health collections. Includes "concepts and terminology followed by in-depth descriptions of twenty-five specific types of adult cancer and ten childhood cancers" (*Publ. notes*) and cancer-related

topics (e.g., chemotherapy, radiation, nutrition, fertility, cancer prevention, cancer quality-of-life issues and supportive care), with a detailed list of authoritative resources in various formats (print, audiovisuals, electronic) and for different users. Index.

668 MedlinePlus. http://medlineplus.gov/. U.S. National Library of Medicine. Bethesda, Md.: U.S. Dept. of Health and Human Services, National Library of Medicine. 1998–
025.04; 651.504261; 613   RA776.5
A consumer health reference database with free and reliable information from the National Library of Medicine (NLM), the National Institutes of Health (NIH), other government agencies, and various health-related organizations. A continually expanding and updated resource. Information on over 900 diseases and conditions, as well as drug information (prescription, nonprescription (ASHF—American Society of Health System Pharmacists consumer medication information)), herbs and supplements, with content as of September 2010 from *Natural medicines comprehensive database (NMCD)*, no longer from *Natural standard* as was previously the case, an illustrated medical encyclopedia (*A.D.A.M. medical encyclopedia*) and a search box for look-up of medical terms on the English homepage, interactive patient tutorials, anatomy (http://www.nlm.nih.gov/medlineplus/anatomyvideos.html) & surgery videos and other tools by following the "videos & cool tools" tab, lists of hospitals, physicians, and dentists, and health news. Provides preformulated MEDLINE/PubMed® searches for recent articles. Includes *NIH MedlinePlus magazine*, a quarterly publication for patients and their families, providing authoritative medical and healthcare information. "MedlinePlus en español" toggles between English and Spanish. Also provides links to browse selected health information in multiple languages other than English and Spanish at http://www.nlm.nih.gov/medlineplus/languages/languages.html. Web 2.0 technologies help users share content, e.g., RSS feeds for all health topics. The MedlinePlus search cloud (http://www.nlm.nih.gov/medlineplus/cloud.html) displays the top 100 search terms typed into the MedlinePlus search box, usually updated every week day. Further detailed descriptive information of MedlinePlus

is available at http://www.nlm.nih.gov/pubs/fact sheets/medlineplus.html. For patients, families, and healthcare providers. Information regarding the mobile version of this resource is part of NLM's Gallery of mobile apps and sites.

MedlinePlus Connect, launched in November 2010, is a free service that allows electronic health record (EHR) systems to link users to MedlinePlus. NLM has mapped MedlinePlus health topics to two standard diagnostic coding systems used in EHRs (further description at http://www.nlm.nih.gov/medlineplus/connect/overview.html).

Also available in a mobile version (m.medline plus.gov).

669 National guideline clearinghouse.
http://www.guideline.gov/. Agency for Healthcare Research and Quality, American Medical Association, American Association of Health Plans. Rockville, Md.: Agency for Healthcare Research and Quality. 1998–

R723.7

Originally created by Agency for Healthcare Research and Quality (AHQR), American Medical Association (AMA), and American Association of Health Plans (now America's Health Insurance Plans [AHIP], http://www.ahip.org/).

Contains evidence-based clinical practice guidelines, protocols, and related documents, with searching and browsing options. Searchable by keyword, disease/condition, treatment/intervention, guideline category, organization and organization type, intended user, clinical specialty, methods to assess and analyze evidence, etc. Related resources (http://www.guideline.gov/resources/index.aspx) include annotated bibliographies, bioterrorism resources, a glossary, guideline archive (lists withdrawn or superseded guidelines), guideline index (complete listing of the guideline summaries available on the website), National Library of Medicine (NLM) and National Center for Biotechnology Information (NCBI, 3) links (PubMed, Health services technology assessment texts (HSTAT), part of the NCBI bookshelf http://www.ncbi.nlm.nih.gov/books?itool=toolbar), patient resources links, and others.

A related site is National Quality Measures Clearinghouse (NQMC).

670 National Library of Medicine guide to finding health information. http://www.nlm.nih.gov/services/guide.html. National Library of Medicine. Bethesda, Md.: National Institutes of Health. 2001–

Contents: How can the National Library of Medicine help me with my research?; Why should I go to a public library, and what can I find there?; What other resources can I find at a medical library, and how do I find one that is open to me?; How can I get information from other government or health-related organizations?; How do I search for other medical information on the Web?; How do I evaluate the information I find?

Overview and starting points for researchers concerning services provided by the National Library of Medicine, other government agencies, and health-related organizations. Provides links to consumer health information resources and professional health literature resources.

671 NORD guide to rare disorders.
National Organization for Rare Disorders. Philadelphia: Lippincott, Williams & Wilkins, 2003. lxiv, 895 p., [16] p. of plates, ill. (some col.) ISBN 0781730635
616   RC48.8.N385

NORD (National Organization for Rare Disorders) is "a non-profit voluntary health agency dedicated to the identification, treatment, and cure of all orphan diseases" (*Pref.*).

Contents: ch. 1, Autoimmune & connective tissue disorders; ch. 2, Cardiovascular disorders; ch. 3, Chromosomal disorders; ch. 4, Dermatologic disorders; ch. 5, Dysmorphic disorders; ch. 6, Emerging/infectious diseases; ch. 7, Endocrine disorders; ch. 8, Gastroenterologic disorders; ch. 9, Hematologic/oncologic disorders; ch. 10, Inborn errors of metabolism; ch. 11, Neurologic disorders; ch. 12, Neuromuscular disorders; ch. 13, Ophthalmologic disorders; ch. 14, Pulmonary disorders; ch. 15, Renal disorders; ch. 16, Skeletal disorders.

At what point a disease is considered rare differs among countries. In the U.S., a disease is considered a rare or an "orphan" disease if it is a low-incidence disease that affects fewer than 200,000 people. This resource "covers about 800 of the estimated 6,000 rare diseases . . . [and] presents many of the sign and symptoms that can be an aid in the diagnosis and differentiation of rare diseases in addition to possible treatment" (*Foreword*). Lists resources which provide help to patients and families affected by a rare disorder. Includes a "List of orphan products approved for marketing." Index. For physicians and other health professionals, patients, and students. Other resources in this area can be located via National Organization for Rare Disorders, Inc. and NIH's Office of Rare Diseases.

NORD compendium of rare diseases and disorders provides updated quick-reference information and data.

672 Nutrition.gov. http://www.nutrition.gov. Food and Nutrition Information Center, United States.; Dept. of Agriculture., National Agricultural Library (U.S.). Beltsville, Md.: National Agricultural Library. 2004-
613.71; 011.53; 612.3; 641.3;   RA784
Maintained by Food and Nutrition Information Center (FNIC).

Access to information from across the federal government on food, food safety, nutrition, weight management, dietary supplements, and food assistance programs. Includes specialized nutrition information for life stages: infants, children, teens, adult women and men, and seniors, as well as the latest nutrition-related news. Provides search capabilities and resource lists.

Healthfinder.gov provides access to consumer resources concerning nutrition, physical fitness, and disease.

673 Quackwatch. http://www.quackwatch. org. Stephen Barrett. [Allentown, Pa.]: Stephen Barrett, M.D. [1996]–
615.8   R730
Founded in 1969 as the Lehigh Valley Committee Against Health Fraud, incorporated in 1970. Assumed its current name in 1997. Maintained by Dr. S. Barrett and a network of volunteers and expert advisors. Affiliated with the National Council Against Health Fraud (http://www.ncahf.com/) and Bioethics Watch.

"Nonprofit corporation whose purpose is to combat health-related frauds, myths, fads, fallacies, and misconduct. Its primary focus is on quackery-related information that is difficult or impossible to get elsewhere. Activities include: Investigating

questionable claims; Answering inquiries about products and services; Advising quackery victims; Distributing reliable publications; Debunking pseudoscientific claims; Reporting illegal marketing; Assisting or generating consumer-protection lawsuits; Improving the quality of health information on the Internet; Attacking misleading advertising on the Internet."—*Website*

In addition, includes a list of websites that provide access to 24 special areas—e.g., autism, chiropractic, dentistry, diet and nutrition, mental health, and other topics of interest to consumers. Its "Internet Health Pilot" site provides links to many other reliable health sites, its "Casewatch" site contains legal matters and regulatory issues. The contents of all sites can be searched simultaneously or individually (http://www.quackwatch .org/wgsearch.html).

674 The rights of patients: The authoritative ACLU guide to the rights of patients. 3rd ed. George J. Annas. Carbondale, Ill.: Southern Illinois University Press, 2004. xxi, 387 p. ISBN 0809325152
344.73/03211   KF3823.A96
Title varies: 1st ed., 1975, had title: *The rights of hospital patients: The basic ACLU guide to a hospital patient's rights;* 2nd ed., 1989, had title: *The rights of patients: The basic ACLU guide to patient rights.*

American Civil Liberties Union (ACLU)
(ACLU handbook series)

Contents: (I) Patient rights; (II) The patient rights advocate; (III) Reforming American medicine; (IV) Hospitals; (V) Emergency medicine; (VI) Informed choice; (VII) Choices about surgery and children's care; (VIII) Reproductive health; (IX) Research; (X) Medical records; (XI) Privacy and confidentiality; (XII) Care of the dying; (XIII) Suffering, pain, and suicide; (XIV) Death, organ donation, and autopsy; (XV) Patient safety and medical malpractice. Appendixes: (A) Internet resources; (B) Convention on human rights and biomedicine; (C) Childbearing patient bill of rights. Index.

"Offers fully documented exposition and explanation of the rights of patients from birth to death . . . a resource not only for patients and their families but also for physicians, hospital administrators, medical and nursing students, and other health care workers" (*Publ. notes*). Emphasizes the importance of having a patient rights advocate, with a section "tips for advocates" in most chapters.

675   Wallach's interpretation of diagnostic tests. 9th ed. Mary A. Williamson, L. Michael. Snyder, Jacques B. Wallach. Philadelphia: Wolters Kluwer/Lippincott Williams & Wilkins Health, 2011. xvi, 1143 p, ill. ISBN 9781605476674
616.07/56   RB38.2.W35
First ed., 1970; 8th ed., 2007. Previous editions had title: *Interpretation of diagnostic tests*.

Provides information about tests and diseases, also new technologies and techniques used in testing. Includes sections on normal values, specific laboratory examinations, diseases of organ systems, and drugs and laboratory test values. This revised edition has been reorganized into two sections: (1) Listing of laboratory tests in alphabetical order, with indication of their sensitivity, specificity, and positive and negative probabilities (cf. *Pref.*). Separate listing for microbiology tests. (2) Disease states (infectious diseases; cardiovascular disorders; central nervous system disorders; digestive diseases; endocrine diseases; renal and urinary tract diseases). Appendixes include a list of abbreviations and acronyms and a glossary. Subject index. Designed for clinicians, but also useful for health consumers. Also available as an e-book.

Similar print titles include *Laboratory tests and diagnostic procedures*, *Manual of laboratory and diagnostic tests* (by Fischbach, et al.), *Mosby's manual of diagnostic and laboratory tests*, and *Tietz clinical guide to laboratory tests*; a web-based resource is *Lab tests online: A public resource on clinical lab testing from the laboratory professionals who do the testing* (327).

676   What your patients need to know about psychiatric medications. 2nd ed. Robert H. Chew, Robert E. Hales, Stuart C. Yudofsky. Washington: American Psychiatric Pub., 2009. xix, 421 p. ISBN 9781585623563
615.788   RM315.H328
Contents: "Medications in pregnancy"; "Antianxiety medication"; "Medications for treatment of insomnia"; "Antidepressants: Selective serotonin

reuptake inhibitors and mixed-action antidepressants"; "Tricyclic antidepressants"; "Monoamine oxidase inhibitors"; "Mood stabilizers"; "First-generation antipsychotics"; "Second-generation antipsychotics"; "Treatment of attention-deficit/hyperactivity disorder in adults"; "Stimulants and nonstimulants for ADHD"; "Cognitive enhancers for treatment of Alzheimer's disease and other forms of dementia"; "Methods for treatment of alcohol dependence"; Index.

Provides relevant and easy-to-understand information about commonly asked questions regarding psychotropic medications. Information about each medication presented in a standard format: brand name; generic name; available strengths; available in generic; medication class; general information; dosing information; common side effects; adverse reactions and precautions; use in pregnancy and breastfeeding; possible drug interactions; overdose; special considerations. Accompanied by CD-ROM that contains PDF files of the pages as they appear in the book. Also available as an e-book via PsychiatryOnline.

Another well-regarded resource in this area is *Handbook of psychiatric drug therapy* (by Labbate).

Encyclopedias

677   American Medical Association complete medical encyclopedia. Jerrold B. Leikin, Lipsky S. Martin, American Medical Association. New York: Random House Reference, 2003. 1408 p., ill. (some col.) ISBN 9780812991000
610.3   RC81.A2A497
Organized in A–Z format, includes medical terms for diseases and disorders, explanations for tests, surgical procedures and imaging techniques, drugs, drug treatments and their potential side effects, preventive medicine, and food and nutrition. Includes information on various issues of current concern and interest, such as alternative medicine and bioterrorism, and a chapter on "Twenty-First Century Medicine" that describes advances in genetic research, stem cell research, biomedical imaging, bionic people, and virtual surgery. Supplemented by symptom charts (p. 12–64), an atlas of the body (p. 65–72), first aid treatment (p. 1312–1333), sample legal forms (p. 1335–43),

a list of self-help organizations (p. 1344–46), HIPAA (Health Insurance Portability and Accountability Act,) and confidentiality of patients' health information. Cross-references. General index.

Other AMA consumer health publications are, for example, "AMA resources for patients" (accessible from the "Patients" tab of the AMA homepage, *American Medical Association complete guide to prevention and wellness*, *American Medical Association handbook of first aid and emergency care*, and *American Medical Association Family medical guide*.

678 The complete reference guide to medicine and health. Richard J. Wagman. New York: Facts on File, 2005. 4 v., ill. (some col.) ISBN 0816061440
610   RC81.C7174

Encyclopedic set, with information on the human body and how to keep it healthy. Addresses physical and mental illnesses and disorders, their causes, symptoms, and treatment, and surgical operations and procedures. Contains sections on drug addiction and alcohol abuse, nutrition, health, physical fitness, and the different stages of life and death. Photographs, illustrations, and diagrams. Glossary and general index in v. 4. Written for general readers, students, and medical and health practitioners. For public library collections.

679 Current medical diagnosis and treatment. Marcus A. Krupp, Milton J. Chatton, Lawrence M. Tierney, Stephen J. McPhee, Maxine A. Papadakis. New York: McGraw-Hill, 1974–. ill.
616.07505 0092-8682   RC71.A14

Imprint varies: 1962–86 publ. by Lange Medical Publ.; 1987–2003, Appleton and Lange. Supersedes: *Current diagnosis and treatment* (1962–73). Also known as *CMDT*.

Description based on 51st ed., 2012, edited by Stephen J. McPhee, Maxine A. Papadakis, and Michael W. Rabow. Also available online through multiple services. 52nd ed., 2013 is available.

Provides concise and up-to-date information on diseases and disorders and widely accepted methods currently available for diagnosis and treatment. Covers internal medicine, gynecology/obstetrics, dermatology, ophthalmology, otolaryngology, psychiatry, neurology, and imaging

procedures. Includes information on nutrition, medical genetics, and an annual update on HIV infection and AIDS. Several chapters are available only online: "Anti-infective chemotherapeutic & antibiotic agents"; "Basic genetics"; "Complementary & alternative medicine"; "Information technology in patient care"; and "Women's health issues." An appendix provides therapeutic drug monitoring and laboratory reference ranges. Index. For health professionals and also general readers seeking information on specific diseases and their diagnosis and treatment.

680 The encyclopedia of addictive drugs. Richard Lawrence Miller. Westport, Conn.: Greenwood Press, 2002. 491 p. ISBN 0313318077
615/.78   RM316.M555

Contents: Introduction; Drug types; Alphabetical listing of drugs; Sources for more information; Drug name index; Subject index. Provides nontechnical description of approx. 130 addictive drugs, including both pharmaceutical and natural products and aspects of drug abuse. Alphabetical listing of substances, with pronunciation, alternative names (including street names), legal status (federal schedule status; discussion of schedules and scheduling), historical and present uses and misuses, abuse factors, interactions with other drugs, and findings of cancer risks and birth defects. Also includes a section on drug types in general categories. List of print and electronic sources with further information. For general readers. Also available as e-book.

Encyclopedia of addictions by Hollen, *Encyclopedia of drugs, alcohol & addictive behavior*, and *Encyclopedia of substance abuse prevention, treatment, and recovery* are additional well-regarded resources in this area. A valuable Internet resource is Substance Abuse and Mental Health Services Administration (SAMHSA).

681 Encyclopedia of aging. David J. Ekerdt. New York: Macmillan Reference USA, 2002. 4 v., ill. ISBN 0028654722
305.2603   HQ1061.E534

A basic, interdisciplinary gerontology encyclopedia for general readers. Entries cover a broad range of sociological, psychological, legal, economic, medical, biological, and public policy subjects. Includes source documents, cross-references, bibliographies at the end of each article, and a list of articles grouped by topical areas. Not so comprehensive as to be overwhelming, this is a basic resource which can serve as a good starting point for some researchers, even for middle and high school students, as well as for older levels. Available as an e-book.

682 **The encyclopedia of Alzheimer's disease. 2nd ed.** Carol Turkington, Deborah R. Mitchell, James E. Galvin. New York: Facts On File, 2010. xvi, 302 p. ISBN 9780816077663
616.831003   RC523

Part of Facts on File library of health and living series; also available online via Health Reference Center (Facts on File, Inc., 712) and others. Alphabetically-arranged entries discuss Alzheimer's disease, its causes, symptoms, treatments, related conditions, both physical and emotional, sufferers, and more. Several appendixes list resources, international associations and agencies, legal and financial issues, clinical trials, etc. Includes cross-references, glossary, bibliography, and index. For general readers, but also useful for health professionals. Another encyclopedia on Alzheimer's disease is Elaine A. Moore's *Encyclopedia of Alzheimer's disease: With directories of research, treatment, and care facilities.*

683 **Encyclopedia of Alzheimer's disease: with directories of research, treatment and care facilities. 2nd ed.** Elaine A. Moore, Lisa Moore. Jefferson, N.C.: McFarland, 2012. viii, 447 p, ill. ISBN 9780786464586
616.8/31003   RC523.M665

"Comprehensive reference work intended for anyone involved in the care, treatment, and day-to-day concerns of patients with Alzheimer's disease and related disorders . . . for anyone who is interested in learning more about the genetic and environmental factors that contribute to both early onset and late onset Alzheimer's disease" (*Pref.*). Entries on the different basic science and medical aspects of this disease, research and treatment, caregiving, and many other topics. Contains sections on long-term and day-care treatment centers, arranged by state and city, research facilities by state, listing of resources (books, booklets, pamphlets, caregiver

resources, legal assistance, Internet support groups, etc.). This updated edition includes more nursing home facilities, also more information regarding prevention, alternative & novel therapies, environmental triggers, and clinical drugs & vaccines trials. Also available as an e-book. For public, academic, and medical libraries. Another encyclopedia on Alzheimer's disease is Carol Turkington's *The encyclopedia of Alzheimer's disease.*

684 **The encyclopedia of complementary and alternative medicine.** Tova Navarra, Adam Perlman. New York: Facts On File, 2004. xxiii, 276 p., ill. ISBN 0816049971
615.503   R733.N38

Provides information concerning medicines and treatments that may supplement Western medical practices. Approx. 400 entries and appendixes, with lists of organizations, herbs, and a historic time line of complementary and alternative therapies. Glossary, bibliography, and index.

Pt. of Facts on file library of health and living series (137); also available online via Health reference center (Facts on File, Inc.) and netLibrary.

685 **Encyclopedia of complementary health practice.** Carolyn Chambers Clark, Rena J. Gordon, Barbara Harris, Carl O. Helvie. New York: Springer, 1999. xxi, 638 p., ill. ISBN 0826112390
615.503   R733.E525

"Comprehensive, authoritative, and concise information in the application of complementary health practices that supplement traditional medical procedure . . . as a vehicle for communication across traditional and complementary disciplines . . ."—*Pref.* Divided into four parts: pt. I, Contemporary issues in complementary health practices; pt. II, Conditions; pt. III, Influential substances; pt. IV, Practices and treatments. Cross-references, contributor directory, resource directory, and extensive references. Subject index and contributor index.

686 **Encyclopedia of dietary supplements. 2nd ed.** Paul M. Coates. New York: Informa Healthcare, 2010. xix, 898 p., ill. ISBN 9781439819289
615/.103 22   RM258.5

"The goal . . . is to provide readers with

comprehensive yet accessible, information on the current state of science for individual supplement ingredients and extracts"—*Pref.* Includes commonly used supplements, including vitamins, minerals, and other ingredients found in foods, and also natural products, such as herb extracts. Alphabetically arranged entries include basic information about each substance and its regulatory status. References to the scientific literature or evidence to support claims of benefit are provided. For clinicians, researchers, health care professionals, and possibly for consumers with a chemistry background. Available both in print and online. Other titles, for example, *Guide to understanding dietary supplements* by Talbott, *Mosby's handbook of herbs and natural supplements* by Skidmore-Roth, and *PDR for nutritional supplements*, may also be useful to health professionals and consumers.

687 Encyclopedia of diet fads. Marjolijn Bijlefeld, Sharon K. Zoumbaris. Westport, Conn.: Greenwood Press, 2003. xv, 242 p., ill. ISBN 0313322236
613.2503   RM222.2.B535

Entries for various kinds of diets and major weight loss programs, with appropriate comments, criticisms, and suggested dietary guidelines. Additional entries and information on nutrition in health and illness, vitamins, etc. Introduction includes a brief history of dieting and fad diets. Annotated list of websites and several other appendixes. For general readers and allied health professionals. Also available as an e-book.

688 The encyclopedia of elder care: The comprehensive resource on geriatric and social care. 2nd ed. Liz Capezuti, Eugenia L. Siegler, Mathy Doval Mezey, Joan Dunbar. New York: Springer, 2008. xxxvii, 860 p.
ISBN 9780826102
362.19897003   RC954.E53

First edition, 2001.

"Designed to encapsulate all aspects of care for an aging population: a comprehensive, multidisciplinary compilation of topics that reflects the breadth and depth of issues of concerns to those who care for older individuals—from individual to society, from patient to professional, from symptom to treatment"—*Pref.* Entries address elder care in the areas of society,

community, caregiving, and the individual. Intended for professionals from a variety of health professions and for students. Organized alphabetically by topic, with listing of Internet resources and bibliographic references. Also available as an e-book.

689 Encyclopedia of family health. 3rd ed. David B. Jacoby, R. M. Youngson, Marshall Cavendish Corporation. Tarrytown, N.Y: Marshall Cavendish, 2005. p. cm.
ISBN 0761474862
610/.3   RC81.A2E5

First ed., 1998. Covers general health topics, physical and mental diseases and their treatment, etc. List of organizations; index. Intended for general readers and useful for undergraduate students.

690 Encyclopedia of foods: A guide to healthy nutrition. Mayo Clinic, University of California, Los Angeles, Dole Food Company. San Diego, Calif.: Academic Press, 2002. xi, 516 p., col. ill.
ISBN 0122198034
641.3003   TX349.E475

Contents: pt. 1, "A guide to healthy nutrition: Optimizing health"; "Nutrients and other food substances"; "Food-health connection"; "Planning meals: Selecting healthful foods, plus two weeks of menus"; "Preparing healthful meals"; pt. 2, "Encyclopedia of foods"; "Fruits"; "Vegetables"; "Grains"; "Dairy goods"; "Meat and other high-protein foods"; "Fats, oils, and sweets"; "Others."

Contains discussion of dietary guidelines and the relationship between diet and various diseases. Appendix includes reading list, selected websites, charts of dietary reference intakes, and information about nutrients in foods, vitamins, and minerals. Color photographs, diagrams, and other illustrations. Useful for public and academic libraries. Also available as an e-book.

691 The encyclopedia of genetic disorders and birth defects. 3rd ed. James Wynbrandt, Mark D. Ludman. New York: Facts On File, 2008. xix, 682 p.
ISBN 9780816063963
616.04203   RB155.5.W96

First ed., 1991; 2nd ed., 2000.

With many entries revised or updated in this edition, presents some 1,000 articles written for both health care professionals and general readers. Entries for disorders, selected on the basis of incidence and historical and clinical importance, discuss prognosis, prevalence, mode of inheritance, and the availability of both carrier screening and prenatal diagnosis; many include addresses of private organizations that can provide further information. Also included are brief discussions of subjects and terminology related to genetic disorders and congenital anomalies. If known, the biochemical and molecular basis of a disease is given. The introduction provides a brief history of human genetics. Numerous cross-references. Appendixes provide statistics and tables on congenital malformations and infant mortality, directory information for private and state, regional, and federal government organizations, and selected Web resources. Bibliography; subject and name index.

Part of Facts on File library of health and living series. Also available online via Health Reference Center (Facts on File, Inc., 712).

692   Encyclopedia of health and aging.
Kyriakos S. Markides. Thousand Oaks, Calif.: Sage Publications, 2007. 650 p.
ISBN 9781412909495
613.043803   RA777.6.E534

Resource on health and aging in the United States and abroad. "Reader's Guide" lists entries by key themes and topics, with entries contributed from different disciplines (e.g., biology, epidemiology, health psychology, public policy, sociology, and others) related to health and aging: aging and the brain; diseases and medical conditions; drug-related issues; function and syndromes; mental health and psychology; nutritional issues; physical status; prevention and health behaviors; sociodemographic and cultural issues; studies of aging and systems of care. Also addresses economic issues and provides recent research results and facts on health and aging. Includes further readings, bibliographical references, a list of online resources, and index. Appropriate for academic, various types of health sciences libraries, and public libraries. Also available as an e-book.

693   The encyclopedia of HIV and AIDS.
3rd ed. Stephen E. Stratton, Evelyn J. Fisher, Sarah Watstein. New York: Facts On File, 2012. xiii, 414 p.
ISBN 9780816077236
362.196/9792003   RC606.6.W385

First ed. (1998) had title: *The AIDS dictionary.*; 2nd ed., 2003.

While the previous edition also included general medical terminology not specifically related to HIV and AIDS, the focus in this edition is on HIV and AIDS, with many new and revised entries from the previous edition, covering the medical conditions and drugs associated with HIV/AIDS, its science aspects, and vaccine development in greater depth. Also includes cultural and social sciences topics. Revised appendixes with frequently used abbreviations, HIV/AIDS statistics in the U.S. (recent data from the Centers for Disease Control and Prevention's 2007 *HIV/AIDS surveillance report* http://www.cdc.gov/hiv/topics/surveillance/resources/reports/2007report/pdf/2007surveillancereport.pdf) and worldwide by country (2010 United Nations *UNAIDS Report on the global AIDS epidemic* http://www.unaids.org/globalreport/), and other selected resources. Includes bibliography and index. For students and general readers.

Part of the Facts on File library of health and living series. Available online via Health reference center (Facts on File, Inc.) and also as an e-book.

Another resource in this subject area for general readers is *Encyclopedia of AIDS: a social, political, cultural, and scientific record of the HIV epidemic* (111).

694   Encyclopedia of mental health.
Howard S. Friedman. San Diego, Calif.: Academic Press, 1998. 3 v., ill.
ISBN 0122266757
616.89/003   RA790.5.E53

Contents: v. 1, A–Di; v. 2, Do–N; v. 3, O–Z, index. "Taking into account new knowledge about the genetic, biological, developmental, social, societal and cultural nature of human beings, . . . bring[s] together . . . emerging trends . . . of mental health . . . validity (or invalidity) of psychiatric diagnosis (and DSM IV), including standards for psychotherapy, models of normality, and psychiatric epidemiology" (*Pref.*). Each article contains an outline, a glossary, cross-references, and a bibliography. Aimed at a wide range of users, including students, researchers, and allied health professionals.

More recent titles in this subject area include, for example, *Gale encyclopedia of mental health* and *Encyclopedia of mental health* by Kahn et al., part of the Facts on File Library of health and living series, a collection of titles on medical subjects for general readers which is also available online via Health Reference Center (Facts on File, Inc., 712).

695 Encyclopedia of obesity. Kathleen Keller. Los Angeles: Sage, 2008. 2 v., ill., port. ISBN 9781412952385
362.196398003   RC628.E53

"Reader's guide" topics: biological or genetic contributions to obesity; children and obesity; dietary interventions to treat obesity; disordered eating and obesity; environmental contributions to obesity; health implications of obesity; medical treatments for obesity; new research frontiers on obesity; obesity and ethnicity/race; obesity and the brain or obesity and behavior; obesity as a public health crisis; psychological influences and outcomes of obesity; societal influences and outcomes of obesity; women and obesity; worldwide prevalence of obesity.

This interdisciplinary resource explores a variety of topics on obesity, health conditions, and issues related to obesity. Written in nontechnical language and intended as a starting point for different audiences, from scholars to the general public. References at the end of each entry. Glossary and index in both volumes. Available online via Sage eReference.

696 Encyclopedia of obesity and eating disorders. 3rd ed. Dana K. Cassell, David H. Gleaves. New York: Facts on File, 2006. 362 p. ISBN 0816061971
616.8526003   RC552.E18.C37

First edition, 1994; 2nd ed., 2000.

Provides concise entries on the causes, symptoms, and treatments, including pharmacotherapy, of obesity and the various eating disorders (e.g., anorexia nervosa, bulimia, etc.). Lists sources of information, websites, audiovisuals, and other resources. Bibliography and index. For general readers and health professionals.

Part of *Facts on File library of health and living* series. Available online via Health Reference Center (712).

697 Encyclopedia of sports medicine. Lyle J. Micheli. Thousand Oaks, Calif.: SAGE Publications, 2011. 4 v. (xliii, 1758 p.), ill. ISBN 9781412961158
617.1/02703   RC1206.E53

Authoritative entries of varying length and depth on the diagnosis and treatment of various health conditions related to sports medicine, including the psychological needs of the injured athlete. Alphabetical list of entries and a reader's guide, illustrations, see-also references, further readings, glossary, and index. Also includes an annotated list of sports medicine organizations and step-by-step instructions and images for various taping and bracing techniques. Written for medical students and various health professionals & practitioners. Also considered useful to health consumers. Also available as an e-book.

Two other encyclopedias, *Encyclopedia of exercise, sport and health* by Brukner et al. and *Encyclopedia of sports medicine* by Oakes et al., are both written for general readers.

698 The encyclopedia of the brain and brain disorders. 3rd ed. Carol Turkington, Joseph R. Harris. New York: Facts On File, 2009. xi, 434 p. ISBN 9780816063956
612.8203   QP376.T87

First ed., 2006, has title: *The brain encyclopedia*; 2nd ed., 2002.

Accessible reference about the brain and brain disorders for general readers. Clear and concise entries on elements and functions of the brain and its various disorders and diseases. Increased amount of material on memory in this edition. Also includes three directories (of self-help, professional, and governmental organizations), helpful websites, a glossary, an extensive list of references, and an index to a wide range of terms.

Part of the *Facts on File library of health and living series*. Available online via Health Reference Center (712) and other providers.

699 The encyclopedia of women's health. 6th ed. Christine Ammer. New York: Facts On File, 2009. xiii, 480 p., ill. ISBN 9780816074075
613/.0424403   RA778.A494

First ed. (1983) has title *A to Z of women's health*; [2nd] ed. (1989) through 4th ed. (2000) have title *The new A to Z of women's health*. Title for 5th ed.

varies; issued both as *The new A to Z of women's health: A concise encyclopedia* and *The encyclopedia of women's health* (160). Pt. of *Facts on file library of health and living series* (137).

Some revised and a few new entries in this edition. Entries cover a broad range of women's health issues and changing health needs during the different stages of their lives. Also gives attention to social and emotional issues. Appendix, topically arranged, provides contact information for associations and organizations. Alphabetical arrangement, cross-references, and index. Also available as an e-book.

700 Encyclopedia of women's health issues. Kathlyn Gay. Westport, Conn.: Oryx Press, 2002. xvii, 300 p., ill.
ISBN 157356303X
613.0424403   RA778.G39

Goes beyond the description of the various health problems and diseases that women experience and also includes social, political, legal, economic, and ethical aspects of women's health. Treats contemporary issues and also provides a historical perspective when appropriate. Can serve as a starting point for research on gender issues in health care policy and politics. Alphabetical arrangement, bibliography, and a selection of websites. Index. For an academic audience and also general readers.

701 The Facts on File encyclopedia of health and medicine. Glenn S. Rothfeld, Deborah S. Romaine, Facts on File, Inc. New York: Facts On File, 2006. p.
ISBN 0816060630
610.3   R125.R68

Provides health and medical information in a concise format, intended for general readers. Body systems and general health problems and topics are interconnected; e.g., each section begins with an overview of a system, related medical breakthroughs, and an A-to-Z listing of disorders and topics relating to the particular system. Index is essential for any topic not commonly known to relate to a particular body system. Vol. 4 provides a cumulative bibliography. A resource section lists URLs for various healthcare organizations; several appendixes, with medical abbreviations and symbols, a listing of Nobel prize winners for physiology or medicine, and recommended immunization and routine exam schedules. Also available as an e-book.

Another resource for general readers by the same publisher is *The complete reference guide to medicine and health.*

702 Facts on File library of health and living series. Facts On File. New York: Facts On File, 1999– ISBN 0816074364

This series is a growing collection of titles on medical subjects that provide an overview and help for understanding specific health conditions and health care issues. Contains different encyclopedias on a variety of diseases, conditions, and health issues. Each typically contains an A-to-Z section that defines the causes, cures, key research, medical terms, symptoms, treatments, and trends; appendixes with statistical information; bibliographies for further research; directory of organizations, associations, support groups, etc. Written for general readers but also useful to health professionals.

Encyclopedias for the following subjects are available: addictions and addictive behaviors; adoption; allergies; Alzheimer's disease (*The encyclopedia of Alzheimer's disease*); arthritis; asthma and respiratory disorders; autism spectrum disorders; autoimmune diseases; back and spine systems and disorders; blindness and vision impairment; brain and brain disorders (*The encyclopedia of the brain and brain disorders* [702]); breast cancer; cancer; child abuse; children's health and wellness; complementary and alternative medicine (*The encyclopedia of complementary and alternative medicine*); deafness and hearing disorders; death and dying; digestive system and digestive disorders; endocrine diseases and disorders; genetic disorders & birth defects (*The encyclopedia of genetic disorders and birth defects*); heart and heart disease; hepatitis and other liver diseases; HIV and AIDS (*The encyclopedia of HIV and AIDS*); infectious diseases; kidney diseases; learning disabilities; memory and memory disorders; men's health; mental health; multiple sclerosis; muscle and skeletal systems and disorders; nutrition and good health; obesity and eating disorders (*The encyclopedia of obesity and eating disorders*); Parkinson's disease; schizophrenia and other psychotic disorders; senior health and well-being; sexually transmitted diseases; skin and skin disorders; sleep disorders; sports medicine; stress and stress-related diseases; suicide; vitamins, minerals, and supplements; women's health (*The encyclopedia of women's health* [160]); women's reproductive cancer; work-related illnesses, injuries, and health.

Available online via Health reference center.

703 **The Gale encyclopedia of alternative medicine. 3rd ed.** Laurie J. Fundukian. Detroit: Gale, Cengage Learning, 2009. 4 v. (xxii, 2688 p.), ill. (some col.) ISBN 9781414448725
615.503   R733.G34
First ed., 2001; 2nd ed., 2005.

Contents: v. 1, A–C; v. 2, D–K; v. 3, L–R; v. 4, S–Z.

This expanded edition presents information and covers all aspects of alternative and complementary practices, therapies, and remedies, and their effect on various diseases and disorders. Entries also include conventional treatments.

Alphabetically arranged entries, sidebar glossary of key terms, websites, suggestions for further readings, list of selected organizations, etc. Each volume contains a list of all entries in the set. Color illustrations and photographs. Bibliography. General index. Available online in the Gale Virtual Reference Library. Intended for general readers and nonspecialist professionals.

704 **The Gale encyclopedia of cancer: A guide to cancer and its treatments. 3rd ed.** Jacqueline L. Longe. Detroit: Gale, Cengage Learning, 2010. 2 v. (xxxvii, xxxvii, 1724 p.), color ill. ISBN 9781414475981
616.994003   RC254.5.G353
First ed., 2002; 2nd ed., 2005.

Contents: v. 1, A–K; v. 2, L–Z.

This updated ed. provides a detailed guide to cancer topics and issues. Following a standardized format, entries on a variety of cancers, treatments, diagnostic procedures, cancer drugs and their side effects, also on cancer biology, carcinogenesis, and cancer genetics. Entries for cancer types include definition, description, demographics, causes and symptoms, diagnosis, clinical staging, treatments and treatment team, prognosis, coping with cancer treatment, clinical trials, prevention, special concerns, and resources. For cancer drugs: definition, purpose, description, recommended dosage, precautions, side effects, and drug interactions are included, also traditional and alternative

treatments and information on clinical trials. A resources section provides additional information. Contact information for organizations, support groups, government agencies, and research groups in an appendix at the back of v. 2. Alphabetical arrangement, cross-references, color images for many malignancies, and anatomical illustrations of the major body systems affected by cancers. List of contents; general index.

Also available as an e-book as part of Gale Virtual Reference Library. Intended for general readers and nonspecialist professionals.

705 **Gale encyclopedia of children's health: Infancy through adolescence. 2nd ed.** Jacqueline L. Longe. Detroit: Gale, 2011. 4 v., col. ill. ISBN 9781414486413
618.920003   RJ26.G35
V. 1, A–C; v.2, D–K; v.3, L–R; v.4, S–Z.

Includes approximately 600 articles, presented in a standardized format. Covers common medical conditions and also rare diseases, developmental issues, immunizations, drugs, and various procedures. Each entry provides definition and description of various diseases, disorders and other problems, their causes, symptoms, diagnosis, treatment, prognosis, etc. Glossary, color photos, illustrations, charts (growth charts), tables, childhood medications, and resources for further reading and study. General index. For use by general readers and health professionals. Also available as an e-book.

706 **The Gale encyclopedia of genetic disorders. 3rd ed.** Laurie J. Fundukian. Farmington Hills, Mich.: Gale, 2010. 2 v., ill. (chiefly color). ISBN 9781414476025
616.04203   RB155.5.G35
First ed., 2002; 2nd ed., 2005.

Contents: v. 1, A–L; v. 2, M–Z.

Signed entries with detailed information for genetic or congenital diseases, disorders, and conditions. A standardized format provides for each entry as appropriate: Definitions, description, genetic profile, demographics, signs and symptoms, tests, diagnosis, treatment and management, prognosis, resources, and key terms. Written for the non-specialist. Available as an e-book as part of the Gale virtual reference library.

707   The Gale encyclopedia of medicine. 4th ed. Laurie J. Fundukian, Gale Group. Detroit: Gale, 2011. 6 v., col. ill. ISBN 9781414486468

616.003   RC41.G35

First ed., 1999; 2nd ed., 2002; 3rd ed., 2006. Revised edition, with comprehensive coverage of basic medical information, with articles on diseases, common conditions and disorders, various treatments, including alternative treatments, and tests. Diets and preventive measures are also covered. Includes sidebars with biographical information of prominent individuals in medicine. Articles are written in a standardized format, in alphabetical arrangement, with definitions of key terms, contact information for organizations and support groups, resources section for additional information, full-color illustrations, photographs, and tables. General index.

Encyclopedias in other medical subjects published by Gale also following this type of arrangement and a standardized format include *The Gale encyclopedia of alternative medicine* (164), *The Gale encyclopedia of cancer: A guide to cancer and its treatments* (165), *The Gale encyclopedia of genetic disorders*, *The Gale encyclopedia of mental health*, and *The Gale encyclopedia of nursing and allied health* by Longe. Also available as an e-book.

708   The Gale encyclopedia of mental health. 3rd ed. Kristin Key. Detroit: Gale Cengage Learning, 2012. 2 v. (xix, 1828 p.), ill. (chiefly col.) ISBN 9781414490120

616.89/003   RC437.G36

First ed., 2003, had title *The Gale encyclopedia of mental disorders*; 2nd ed., 2008.

Provides a comprehensive overview of mental health and illness, diagnostic procedures, psychotherapy, and various other treatments, including drugs, herbal preparations, and alternative therapies. Includes mostly disorders recognized by the American Psychiatric Association, but also mentions some not formally recognized as distinct disorders. This revised edition contains 500 entries, with 65 new entries to this edition, with color illustrations, graphs, charts, tables, and sidebars of key terms and references for further reading. Also includes a list of organizations, a glossary, and index. Disease and medication entries are in a standardized format. Entries for diseases include definition, description, causes and symptoms, demographics, diagnosis, treatment, prognosis, prevention, and resources. Entries for medications include definition, purpose, description, recommended dosage, precautions, side effects, interactions, and resources. Considered a highly useful resource for mental health professionals and health consumers.

Available electronically through Gale Virtual Reference Library.

709   The Gale encyclopedia of senior health: A guide for seniors and their caregivers. Jacqueline L. Longe. Detroit: Gale, c2009. 5 v. (2120 p.), ill. (chiefly col.) ISBN 9781414403830

618.97003 22   RC952.5.G3485 2009

Comprehensive encyclopedia, alphabetically organized, with approx. 600 illustrated entries and arranged in five categories: diseases and conditions; treatment, rehabilitation, recovery; aging, general health, death and dying; healthy living: nutrition, exercise, prevention; and community care giving. A typical entry provides definition, description, causes and symptoms, diagnosis, treatment, various resources, etc. Glossary of key terms, appendix listing organizations, and general index. Intended as a resource for senior patients/health consumers to educate themselves about their condition. It is not intended to replace a doctor's visit. It is also considered a useful reference source for librarians. Also available online through Gale virtual reference library.

Some overlap of content with other Gale encyclopedias, e.g., *Gale encyclopedia of medicine* and *Gale encyclopedia of nursing*, can be expected.

Encyclopedia of aging and *Encyclopedia of health and aging* address the biological, psychological, social, and economic aspects of health and aging and are intended for health care professionals who work with an aging population.

710   The Gale encyclopedia of surgery and medical tests: A guide for patients and caregivers. 2nd ed. Brigham Narins. Detroit: Gale, 2009. 4 v., color ill. ISBN 9781414448848

617.003   RD17.G342

Contents: v. 1, A–C; v. 2, D–K; v. 3, L–P; v. 4, Q-Z, organizations, glossary, index.

Approx. 500 alphabetically arranged entries, with definitions of key terms and articles of varying length. Explains surgical procedures, medical tests, and laboratory procedures. Information is presented in a consistent format (definition, description, purpose, diagnosis/preparation, aftercare, precautions, risks, etc.), with step-by-step illustrations for many procedures. Appendixes list centers for specific surgical specialties, national organizations, and support groups for patients. Bibliographies for further reading. Intended for nursing and allied health professionals and general readers. Also available as an e-book.

711 The Harvard Medical School family health guide. 1st Free Press trade paperback ed. Anthony L. Komaroff, Harvard Medical School. New York: Free Press, 2005. 1312 p., ill. (some col.) ISBN 0684863731

610   RC81.H38

[First ed.], 1999. Contents: Navigating the health care system; Taking charge of your health; How your body works; Diagnosing disease; Symptom charts; Brain and nervous system; Behavioral and emotional disorders; Eyes; Ears, nose, and throat; Teeth, mouth, and gums; Lungs; Skin, hair, and nails; Color guide to visual diagnosis; Cosmetic and reconstructive surgery; Bones, joints, and muscles; Blood disorders; Digestive system; Urinary system; Hormonal disorders; Infections and immune system diseases; Infertility, pregnancy, and childbirth; Health of infants and children; Health of adolescents; Health of women; Health of men; Health of seniors; Caregiving and eldercare; Death and dying; Medicines; First aid and emergency care; Replaceable parts of irreplaceable you. Updated edition. Comprehensive, easy-to-understand guide to information about the diagnosis, treatment, and prevention of disease. Helpful to health consumers in finding good medical care and in evaluating the care they receive. Kept up-to-date by an associated searchable website.

712 Health reference center (Facts on File, Inc.). http://www.infobase publishing.com/Bookdetail.aspx?ISBN =0816046964&Ebooks=0. Facts on File, Inc. New York: Facts on File. 2005–

Database containing full-text encyclopedic information (drawn from titles in the Facts on file library of health and living series [137]) on a wide variety of health topics and related social issues, mental health, health and wellness, and topics about body systems and related diseases and conditions. Written in nontechnical language. Hyperlinked entries. Glossary.

713 Magill's medical guide. 6th ed. Brandon P. Brown. Pasadena, Calif.: Salem Press, 2011. 6 v., ill. ISBN 9781587656774

610.3   RC41.M34

First edition, 1995–96; 5th ed., 2008.

Contents: v. 1. Abdomen–Childbirth complications; v. 2. Childhood infectious diseases-Flat feet; v. 3. Fluids and electrolytes-Kidneys; v. 4. Kinesiology-Parasitic diseases; v.5. Parathyroidectomy-Subdural hematoma; 6. Substance abuse-Zoonoses; Appendixes; Indexes.

This revised edition includes 1,178 articles, with 161 new topics since the last edition. Arranged alphabetically, with cross-references, describes diseases and disorders, also surgical and non-surgical procedures, and also the medical/surgical specialties involved. Entries include information on human genetics, human anatomy, human physiology, and microbiology as appropriate. Bibliographies, including references to websites. Several appendixes, for example, "Diseases and Other Medical Conditions," with a listing of approx. 900 diseases, disorders, symptoms, etc., with definitions, medical journal titles, websites, and health-care associations. Alphabetical list of contents, lists of entries arranged by anatomy or system affected, and entries arranged by specialties and related fields at the end of each volume. Includes a three-year subscription to the e-version.

Other health sciences titles published by Salem Press include, for example, *Cancer* by Knight et al., *Genetics & inherited conditions* by Knight, and *Infectious diseases & conditions* by Hawley.

714 Mayo Clinic family health book. 4th ed. Karen Wallevand, Scott Litin. New York: Time Inc. Home Entertainment, 2009. 1423 p., ill. (some color). ISBN 9781603200776

613.M473m4   RC81

First ed., 1990; 3rd ed., 2003.

Contents: pt. I, Injuries and symptoms; pt. II, Pregnancy and healthy children; pt. III, Healthy adults; pt. IV, Diseases and disorders; pt. V, Tests and treatments.

Described as "a classic home medical reference. with a strong emphasis on self-care".—*Publ. notes* Another title, *Mayo Clinic book of alternative medicine* (2nd ed., 2010), provides information on using natural therapies in conjunction with conventional medicine. A related web resource is MayoClinic.com: Reliable information for a healthier life.

715 Medical encyclopedia (MedlinePlus). http://www.nlm.nih.gov/medlineplus/ encyclopedia.html. National Library of Medicine (U.S.). Atlanta; Bethesda, Md.: A.D.A.M.; National Library of Medicine. 1999–

RC81.A2

Title varies: A.D.A.M. Medical Encyclopedia; MedlinePlus, Medical Encyclopedia.

Articles about diseases and conditions, injuries, nutrition, poisons, surgeries, symptoms, tests, and other special topics. Contains medical illustrations and images. Editorial processes and policy at http://www.adam.com/editorialGuidelines.aspx.

716 World of health. Brigham Narins. Detroit: Gale Group, 2000. viii, 1424 p., ill. ISBN 0787636495

610   R130.5.W67

Overview of the medical sciences and health-related disciplines, covering significant discoveries and brief biographies of important persons related to these discoveries and other historical events, disorders, therapies, procedures, devices, etc. Alphabetical arrangement, cross-references, bibliographical references (p. 1277–1281), a chronology 5000 BCE–1999, and index. Written in concise language for students and general readers. Useful for public libraries.

Dictionaries

717 The American Heritage medical dictionary. Boston: Houghton Mifflin, 2007. xxxii, 909 p., ill. ISBN 0618824359

610.3   R121.A4446

First ed., 1995, to 2nd ed., 2004, had title *The American Heritage Stedman's medical dictionary*; 2007 ed. is rev. ed. of the 2nd ed. Provides clear definitions for approx. 45,000 medical words and phrases, including tests, diseases, treatments, technology, and prescription and nonprescription drugs. Also includes health policy terms. Intended for health care consumers, students, and health professionals. Also available online via Credo reference (http://corp.credoreference.com/).

718 The cancer dictionary. 3rd ed. Michael J. Sarg, Ann D. Gross, Roberta Altman. New York: Facts On File, 2007. xv, 416 p., ill. ISBN 0816064113

616.994003   RC262

First ed., 1992; [2nd] rev. ed., 2000. Designed for general readers, attempts to provide definitions for every term connected with cancer, with many new terms, drugs, and treatments since the previous edition. Includes many cross-references, and capitalized terms within a definition have their own entry. Appendixes include websites of national cancer and AIDS organizations, and listings of both comprehensive and clinical cancer centers by state. Includes bibliographic references and index. Also available as an e-book.

719 Dictionary of cancer terms. http://www.cancer.gov/dictionary/. National Cancer Institute, National Institutes of Health. Bethesda, Md.: National Cancer Institute

Contains more than 4,000 terms related to cancer and medicine. Available in both English and Spanish. Detailed instructions on how to search this dictionary are available on the website. Other cancer vocabulary resources include the NCI Thesaurus, NCI Metathesaurus, and NCI Terminology Browser, made available via NCI Enterprise Vocabulary Services (EVS) at http://evs.nci.nih.gov.

720 Medical dictionary (MedlinePlus). http://www.nlm.nih.gov/medlineplus/ mplusdictionary.html. National Library of Medicine (U.S.). Bethesda, Md.: National Library of Medicine. 2002–

R121

Part of MedlinePlus. This online dictionary, based on *Merriam-Webster's medical dictionary*, can be searched from the MedlinePlus home page (via

"Dictionary" tab). Contains definitions for words and phrases used by health care professionals, a pronunciation guide, and brief biographies of individuals (after whom particular diseases are named). Most MedlinePlus Health Topics pages contain a link or links to additional online dictionaries and/or glossaries from various sources.

Numerous online medical dictionaries and glossaries are also available from many other sources. They include titles made available from various government agencies, organizations, and commercial publishers. Some examples include online medical dictionaries accessible via Credo reference (currently 24 titles), Deciphering medspeak (http://www.mlanet.org/resources/medspeak/; MLANET), Diabetes dictionary (http://diabetes.niddk.nih.gov/dm/pubs/dictionary/index.htm; National Institute of Diabetes and Digestive and Kidney Diseases), Dictionary of cancer terms (National Cancer Institute), mediLexicon tools (http://www.medilexicon.com/), Talking glossary of genetics terms (http://www.nhgri.nih.gov/glossary.cfm; National Human Genome Research Institute), and many others.

721 Webster's new world medical dictionary. 3rd ed. William C. Shiel, Melissa Conrad Stöppler. Hoboken, N.J.: Wiley, 2008. 470 p.
ISBN 9780470189283
610.3   R121
First ed., 2000; 2nd ed., 2003.
"From the doctors and experts at WebMD."

This new "fully revised, updated" edition provides definitions of 8,500 medical terms, including diseases, treatments, scientific terms, abbreviations and acronyms, pharmaceuticals, herbal supplements, etc. Intended to support clear communication of health consumers with their physicians. Online access via Credo reference, MedicineNet.com's MedTerms dictionary (http://www.medterms.com/), and also available as an e-book.

Directories

722 AOA American Osteopathic Association. http://www.osteopathic.org/. Chicago: American Osteopathic Association. 2003-
Website contents for professionals and students

include About the AOA, Accreditation, Advocacy, Education, Events, News & Publications, Professional Development. Section on "Osteopathic medicine and your health" is geared toward patients and general audiences, and includes a search to "Find a DO."

AOA members have access to many details formerly available in the AOA yearbook and directory.

723 ClinicalTrials.gov. http://clinicaltrials.gov. National Institutes of Health, National Library of Medicine (U.S.), United States. Bethesda, Md.: National Institutes of Health. 2000–
                                       R853.C55
Provides information about federally and privately funded research in human volunteers for patients, their families and other consumers, and health care professionals. Contents include clinical trials, experimental treatments, experimental and new diagnostic procedures, patient enrollment and recruitment, and all study phases. Explains who may participate, location (U.S. and other countries), and contact information. Searchable by key terms, disease, location, treatment, age group, study phase, etc. Trial listings by condition, sponsor, and status. For additional information and various links to related websites, consult the NLM fact sheet on ClinicalTrials.gov at http://www.nlm.nih.gov/pubs/factsheets/clintrial.html.

As of 2012, new homepage and graphic design, with core functions of the site remaining unchanged. Recent enhancement introduced and described in detail in "New style and new content for ClinicalTrials.gov" http://www.nlm.nih.gov/pubs/techbull/ja12/ja12_clinicaltrials.html.

724 Directories (MedlinePlus). http://www.nlm.nih.gov/medlineplus/directories.html. National Library of Medicine (U.S.), National Institutes of Health (U.S.). Bethesda, Md.: U.S. National Library of Medicine, National Institutes of Health, Dept. of Health and Human Services. 200?–
                                       RC48
Pt. of MedlinePlus.
Contents: Doctors and dentists—general; Hospital and clinics—general; Doctors and dentists—specialists; Other healthcare providers; Hospitals

and clinics—specialized; Other healthcare facilities and services; Libraries.

Links to directories to help find health professionals, services, and facilities. Includes, for example, access to the American Medical Association's DoctorFinder, how to find a dentist, a Medicare participants physicians directory, and many others.

725 DoctorFinder. https://extapps.ama-assn .org/doctorfinder/home.jsp. American Medical Association. Chicago: American Medical Association. 1997–

R712.A1

Also called AMA Doctor Finder; earlier title was AMA Physician Select: On-Line Doctor Finder.

Tool for locating licensed physicians (doctors of medicine [M.D.] and doctors of osteopathy [D.O.]) in the United States and information about them. Can be searched by physician name or medical specialty. Listings include address, medical school and year of graduation, residency training, primary practice, specialty, and indication of AMA membership. AMA member listings generally include more information.

Other sites to find doctors include, for example, a search engine created by the Administrators In Medicine (AIM) National Organization for State Medical and Osteopathic Board Executive Directors, entitled Docfinder Searches (http://www.docboard.org/) and links identified through Healthfinder.gov.

Handbooks

726 American Medical Association handbook of first aid and emergency care. Rev. & updated ed ed. Italo. Subbarao, Jim. Lyznicki, James J James, American Medical Association. New York: Random House Reference, c2009. xix, 396 p., ill. ISBN 9781400007127
616.02/52 22   RC86.8.A426 2009
First ed., 1980; rev. ed., 1990; rev. ed., 2000.

Contents: pt. I, Prevention; pt. II, Being prepared for injuries and emergencies; pt. III, Alphabetical listing of illnesses, injuries, and other medical emergencies; pt. IV, Sports first aid; pt. V,

Environmental injuries and illnesses; pt. VI, Disaster preparedness; Medical chart; Index.

This illustrated handbook provides guidance on how to respond to medical problems and what to do in a medical emergency. Intended for general readers as a "guidebook for household use."—*Publisher description*. Most of the information included in this edition can also be found on the Internet (e.g., following the health topics link "first aid" in MedlinePlus) will lead to reliable, up-to-date online information.

727 First aid manual. 4th ed. Gina M. Piazza, American College of Emergency Physicians. London; New York: DK Pub, 2011. 288 p., col. ill. ISBN 9780756672355
616.0252   RC86.8.F565
Published by American College of Emergency Physicians® (ACEP)

Contents: (1) Becoming a first aider; (2) Managing an incident; (3) Assessing a victim; (4) The unconscious victim; (5) Respiratory problems; (6) Wounds and circulation; (7) Bone, joint, and muscle injuries; (8) Nervous system problems; (9) Effects of heat and cold; (10) Foreign objects, poisoning, bites, & stings; (11) Medical problems; (12) Techniques and equipment; (13) Emergency first aid; First aid regulations; Index.

"A comprehensive guide to treating emergency victims of all ages in any situation" (*Cover*). Step-by-step explanation and color photographs of life-saving procedures (e.g., cardiopulmonary resuscitation, treatment of blocked airway, etc.), treatments and techniques, following current first-aid guidelines. Section for the most critical emergencies at the end of the book.

728 Handbook of non-prescription drugs. American Pharmaceutical Association. Washington: American Pharmaceutical Association, 1967–. ill.
615.105 0889-7816   RS250.N66
Title varies: *Handbook of nonprescription drugs: An interactive approach to self-care*. Description based on 17th ed., 2012.

Contents: sec. I, "The practitioner's role in self-care"; sec. II, "Pain and fever disorders"; sec. III, "Reproductive and genital disorders"; sec. IV, "Respiratory disorders"; sec. V, "Gastrointestinal disorders"; sec. VI, "Nutrition and nutritional supplementation"; sec. VII, "Ophthalmic, otic, and oral disorders"; sec. VIII, "Dermatologic disorders"; sec. IX, "Other medical disorders"; sec. X "Home medical equipment"; sec. XI, "Complementary therapies"; appendix I, "Pregnancy and lactation risk categories for selected nonprescription medications and nutritional supplements"; appendix II, "Safety issues with the use of selected natural products in pregnancy."

A compilation of facts on home remedies in 52 chapters with broad headings, such as asthma, diabetes mellitus, headache, musculoskeletal injuries and disorders, sexually transmitted infections, multicultural aspects of self-care, etc. Each chapter discusses the etiology of the condition; the anatomy, physiology, and pathophysiology of the affected systems; the signs and symptoms; the treatment and adjunctive measures; an evaluation of ingredients in over-the-counter products; and important patient and product considerations. Bibliographic references at the end of each chapter. Subject index. Useful for pharmacists, other health professionals, and consumers. Online content for the 17th edition is available through the subscription-based PhamacyLibrary portal (http://www.pharmacylibrary.com).

729   The Medical Library Association guide to health literacy. Marge Kars, Lynda M. Baker, Feleta L. Wilson. New York: Neal-Schuman Publ., 2008. xiv, 314 p., ill. ISBN 9781555706258
026/.610973   Z675.M4; M497

Overviews issues related to health literacy and approaches to effective health communication. A practical guide, including best practices for librarians working in hospital and consumer health settings and providing health/patient education and appropriate services for persons with low literacy or illiterate persons. Intends to empower patients to understand their health care information. Explains different types of health literacy. Includes reference interview techniques, collaboration between libraries, exploration of the role of the librarian in promoting health literacy, etc. Addresses the special needs of senior citizens and adolescents.

Each chapter has a thorough list of current references. Resources for health professionals; upper-level and graduate-level health care students.

Useful for librarians working in hospital and consumer health settings.

730   Medicare handbook. Center for Medicare Advocacy. New York: Aspen Publishers, 2000–. v.
368 1530-8979   KF3608.A4M436

Description based on 2014 ed. Contents: Important enrollment information; sect.1, Learn how Medicare works; sect. 2, Signing up for Medicare Part A & Part B; sect. 3, Find out if Medicare covers your test, service, or item; sect. 4, Choose your health & prescription drug coverage; sect. 5, Get information about your Medicare health coverage choices; sect.6, Get information about prescription drug coverage; sect. 7, Get help paying your health & prescription drug costs; sect. 8, Know your rights & how to protect yourself from fraud; sect. 9, Plan ahead for long-term care; sect. 10, Get more information ; sect. 11, Definitions.

PDF version of 2014 ed. available at http://www.medicare.gov/pubs/pdf/10050.pdf

Resource to help understand Medicare's rules and regulations. Further helpful, detailed information can also be found on the Medicare website (Medicare: the official U.S. government site for people with Medicare at http://www.medicare.gov), part of the Centers for Medicare & Medicaid Services.

731   The Merck manuals. http://www.merck manuals.com//. Merck and Co. Whitehouse Station, N.J.: Merck and Co. 1995–

"A trusted source for medical information . . . ." —*Website*

Overview of the various titles and editions of the Merck manuals, organized in categories by user group, with information about online availability, online in other languages, as printed book or PDA download, and appropriate links. Under "patients and caregivers" lists the *Merck manual of medical information—home edition* (available online, online in other languages, and also as printed book) and the *Merck manual of health and aging* (available online and as printed book). Under "healthcare professionals" lists the *Merck manual of diagnosis and therapy* (available online, online in other languages, as PDA download, and as printed book); *Merck manual of geriatrics* (available online, online in other languages, and as printed book. The listing also includes under "chemists" the *Merck index* (available online and as printed book) and the *Merck veterinary manual* (available online, as PDA download, and as printed book).

MerckEngage® http://www.merckengage.com/, (formerly Mercksource), is a related website intended for healthcare consumers as a good starting point, together with MedlinePlus. It provides information concerning medical conditions, health news, searches topics in Spanish. Its "resource library" and "health tool" tabs provide additional useful information.

732   Mosby's dental drug reference. Tommy
W. Gage, Frieda Atherton Pickett. St.
Louis: Mosby, 1994–
615.10246176   RK701.M58
Description based on 9th ed., 2010; 10th ed., 2012, is available both in print and also as en e-book.

Contents: Therapeutic management of common oral lesions; Medically compromised patients; Individual drug monographs; Appendixes: (A) Abbreviations; (B) Aesthetics; (C) Combination drugs by trade names; (D) Controlled substances chart; (E) Disorders and conditions; (F) Drugs associated with dry mouth; (G) Drugs that affect taste; (H) Complementary and alternative medications and dietary supplements; (I) Pregnancy and pediatrics; (J) Preventing medication errors and improving medication safety; (K) Oral contraceptives; Generic and trade name index.

Alphabetical arrangement of drugs that dental patients may be taking, listed by generic name and indexed by brand name, with drug monograph information presented in a consistent format. Provides information on side effects, precautions, contraindications, and drug interactions. Also includes alternative therapies. Therapeutic and pharmacologic index. Accompanied by CD-ROM that contains color images of conditions resulting from drugs patients are taking, and also customizable patient handouts. The 9th ed. includes 33 new drugs approved by the FDA since the last edition. Intended for dental professionals, but also useful for health consumers. Ready-reference appendixes provide additional drug-related information. Also available as an e-book.

733   The nutrition desk reference. 3rd ed.
Robert H. Garrison, Elizabeth Somer.
New Canaan, Conn.: Keats, 1995. xxii,
663 p., ill. ISBN 0879836652

613.2   QP141.G33
First edition, 1985; 2nd ed., 1990.
Contents: pt. 1, Dietary factors; pt. 2, Nutrition and cancer; pt. 3, Nutrition and cardiovascular disease; pt. 4, Nutrition and disease; pt. 5, Dietary recommendations.

Presents basic nutrition information, biochemical explanations, and important nutrition-related topics in concise format and readable style. For health professionals and general readers. Figures, tables, glossary, and index. Also available as an e-book. Information found in this desk reference can be updated with online publications, for example, via PubMed and Nutrition (MedlinePlus) and other nutrition-related pages in MedlinePlus.

**734   Patients' rights in the age of managed
health care.** Lisa Yount. New York: Facts
on File, 2001. 280 p. ISBN 0816042586
344.73041   KF3823.Y68
Provides overview of the issues in health care delivery, patients' rights and applicable laws, a chronology of significant events, and also a guide to further research in patients' rights issues. Glossary, index, and annotated bibliography. *The rights of patients: The authoritative ACLU guide to the rights of patients* provides further information. Also available as an e-book.

Internet resources

**735   Agency for Healthcare Research and
Quality (AHRQ).** http://www.ahrq.gov.
Agency for Healthcare Research and
Quality (U.S.). Rockville, Md.: Agency for
Healthcare Research and Quality. 1990s
Searchable website ("search AHRQ" and "A–Z Quick Menu") provides access to a variety of resources, with links to clinical and consumer health information, research findings, funding opportunities, data and surveys, quality assessment, specific populations (minorities, women, elderly, and others), and public health preparedness (bioterrorism and response). Links to a large number of full-text documents, including links to the tools, literature, and news in patient safety (e.g., *AHRQ patient safety network*) and tips on how to prevent medical errors.

736   AHRQ Patient safety network. http://psnet.ahrq.gov/. United States. Agency for Healthcare Research and Quality. Rockville, Md.: Agency for Healthcare Research and Quality. 2005-

Also referred to as AHRQ PSNet; Patient safety network PSNet; PSNet: Patient safety network.

Described as a searchable and customizable web-based resource, featuring the latest news and essential resources on patient safety, with weekly updates of patient safety literature, annotated links to important research on patient safety, patient safety primers, patient safety classics (i.e., articles that serve as a basis for safe, high-quality patient care), and a glossary. A related website is *AHRQ WebM&M* (http://webmm.ahrq.gov/) with cases of medical errors submitted by users, expert commentaries, perspectives on patient safety, and links to related information. "About AHRQ PSNet" (http://psnet.ahrq.gov/about.aspx) provides further explanation.

737   AIDSinfo. http://www.aidsinfo.nih.gov. U.S. Department of Health and Human Services, National Institutes of Health (U.S.), AIDS Clinical Trials Information Service. Bethesda, Md.: National Institutes of Health

RA643.8

Result of merging two previous U.S. Dept. of Health and Human Services (DHHS) projects. Supersedes the AIDS Clinical Trials Information Service (ACTIS) and the HIV/AIDS Treatment Information Service (ATIS).

Resource for current information on federally and privately funded clinical trials for AIDS patients and HIV-infected persons, federally approved HIV treatment and prevention guidelines, and medical practice guidelines. Provides access to a searchable HIV/AIDS drugs database (via "Drugs" tab) that includes approved and investigational anti-HIV medications, including side effects, dosages, and interactions with other drugs or food; also access to brochures, fact sheets, and other Web resources on HIV/AIDS, current and archived versions of DHHS guidelines, and a searchable HIV/AIDS glossary (English and Spanish). For HIV/AIDS patients, the general public, health care providers, and researchers. Information regarding the mobile version of this resource is part of NLM's Gallery of mobile apps and sites.

Additional major HIV/AIDS resources can be accessed via the following sites: Fact sheet, AIDS Information Resources (http://www.nlm.nih.gov/pubs/factsheets/aidsinfs.html), Specialized Information Services: HIV/AIDS Information (http://sis.nlm.nih.gov/hiv.html), CDC National Prevention Information Network (NPIN) (http://www.cdcnpin.org/scripts/hiv/index.asp), UNAIDS: Joint United National Programming on HIV/AIDS (http://www.unaids.org/en/), and AIDS Treatment Data Network (http://www.atdn.org/).

738   American Dental Association. http://www.ada.org/. American Dental Association. Chicago: American Dental Association. 1995– 617.6

Official website of the American Dental Association (ADA), founded in 1859.

Provides information for dental professionals concerning education and testing, practice management, and patient care. Includes a list of all accredited dental programs in the U.S. (http://www.ada.org/103.aspx) and Canada, and links to national dental organizations. Resources for consumers include, for example, "Oral Health Topics A–Z" (http://www.ada.org/286.aspx), "Find a dentist" (http://www.mouthhealthy.org/en/find-a-dentist.aspx), and other helpful resources. Also includes "ADA timeline" (http://www.ada.org/adatimeline.aspx), a list of presidents (1860 to the present), and links to various other dental history resources. Some of the resources are restricted to ADA members.

Another ADA web resource, ADA Center for Evidence-Based Dentistry™ http://ebd.ada.org/about.aspx is a useful resource for clinicians to identify systematic reviews and critical summaries. It also provides links to further resources and educational tutorials as well as links to patient resources.

The American Academy of Pediatric Dentistry (AAPD) http://www.aapd.org/ provides a variety of dental health resources, policies & guidelines, etc.

739   American Medical Association. http://www.ama-assn.org/. American Medical Association. Chicago: American Medical Association. 1995–
610.9206   R130.5

This searchable website provides a variety of professional resources and standards for AMA members, including, for example, information sources on medical ethics, public health (e.g., eliminating health disparities, health preparedness, disaster response, obesity), medical science, legal issues, and AMA history (with time line and highlights of AMA history). Also provides information on medical education and licensure as well as online resources and other links for medical school students and residents. Includes a section for patients, with access to patient education resources (e.g., "Health literacy resources," "Atlas of the human body," etc.).

Other useful AMA-related links include, for example, DoctorFinder, *Code of medical ethics, current opinions with annotations, Current procedural terminology: CPT* (856), FREIDA (291), *Graduate medical education directory, Health professions career and education directory*, and *State medical licensure requirements and statistics*. Many of these resources have general reference value in academic and public libraries.

740   Anatomy videos (MedlinePlus).
http://www.nlm.nih.gov/medlineplus/anatomyvideos.html. Bethesda, Md.: U.S. Dept. of Health and Human Services, National Library of Medicine. 2008-
Produced by A.D.A.M.

This site contains brief animated videos (in QuickTime format, with narration & closed-captioning) of varying length and structure which show the anatomy of body parts and organ systems and how they are affected by various conditions and diseases. Alphabetical listing by title. These videos are also integrated in the MedlinePlus encyclopedia. Intended for health consumers.

741   Association of Cancer Online Resources (ACOR). http://acor.org/.
Association of Cancer Online Resources (ACOR). New York: Association of Cancer Online Resources, Inc. 1995–
Contents: Mailing lists; Support & resources; Types of cancer; Treatment options; Clinical trials; Publications; Partnerships; Help ACOR.

"ACOR is a unique collection of online communities designed to provide timely and accurate information in a supportive environment" (*Website*), developing and hosting Internet-based knowledge systems to make it possible to find and use relevant cancer information and oncology

resources. ACOR publications include a bibliography of cancer books, a series of cancer fact sheets, and the latest scientific abstracts relating to cancer. Contains links to the National Cancer Institute.

742   Biodefense and bioterrorism (MedlinePlus). http://www.nlm.nih.gov/medlineplus/biodefenseandbioterrorism.html. National Library of Medicine (U.S.), National Institutes of Health (U.S.). Washington: U.S. National Library of Medicine, National Institutes of Health, Dept. of Health and Human Services. 2000–
A Health Topic within MedlinePlus. Contents: Overviews; Treatment; Prevention/Screening; Alternative medicine; Coping; Specific conditions; Related issues; Pictures and photographs; Research; Journal articles; Dictionaries/Glossaries; Directories; Organizations; Law and policy; Children.

Collection of links from a variety of government agencies, professional associations, and organizations, with representative bioterrorism resources selections from the Centers for Disease Control and Prevention (CDC), National Institute of Allergy and Infectious Diseases, American Medical Association, American Academy of Family Physicians, American Psychiatric Association, Dept. of Homeland Security, and others. Related information also at Disaster preparation and recovery (MedlinePlus) and Emergency preparedness and response (CDC), for example.

743   CAM resources project. http://camresources.pbworks.com/. CAM Special Interest Group, Medical Library Association. Chicago: Medical Library Association. 2008-
Complementary and Alternative Medicine (CAM) Special Interest Group (SIG), Medical Library Association (MLA)

"The goal of the project is to have members. contribute to a bibliography of authoritative and informative books, databases, and websites that libraries can use to build their collections and to recommend to their users."—*Home page*. Arranged by subject categories (e.g., acupuncture, Ayurveda, energy medicine, herbal medicine, homeopathy, naturopathic medicine, osteopathic medicine, etc.).

Presented in wiki format which allow participants to contribute directly. Website contains criteria for inclusion and instructions on how to contribute to the wiki. Includes both professional and consumer health titles.

744 Cancer.gov. http://www.cancer.gov/. National Cancer Institute. Bethesda, Md.: National Cancer Institute. 1990s–

A metasite for cancer information for health care professionals as well as patients. Provides extensive information on all aspects of cancer as a disease and current cancer treatment, including, for example, complementary and alternative medicine, screening, prevention, and genetics. Links for searching the PubMed cancer literature subset and PDQ Query at http://www.cancer.gov/cancertopics/pdq/cancerdatabase.

745 Centers for Medicare and Medicaid services (U.S.). http://cms.hhs.gov/. Centers for Medicare and Medicaid Services (U.S.), U.S. Health Care Financing Administration. Baltimore: Centers for Medicare and Medicaid Services, U.S. Dept. of Health and Human Services. 2001–

RA395.A3

Centers for Medicare and Medicaid Services (CMS), formerly Health Care Financing Administration.

Detailed information on Medicare, the federal health insurance program for people 65 years and older and for younger people with certain disabilities, providing details on enrollment, benefits, and other data; Medicaid, a joint federal and state program (state programs vary from state to state) that helps with medical costs for people with low income and limited means; SCHIP (State Children's Health Insurance Program); regulation and guidance manuals and Health Insurance Portability and Accountability Act (HIPAA), research, statistics, data and systems. Also provides various tools and resources helpful in navigating this website, for example a "glossary tool," an "acronym lookup tool," "FAQs," and others.

Includes information on the electronic health record (EHR) (http://www.cms.gov/Medicare/E-Health/EHealthRecords/index.html), sometimes also called electronic medical record (EMR) which "allows healthcare providers to record patient information electronically instead of using paper records" and furthermore "the ability to support other care-related activities directly or indirectly through various interfaces, including evidence-based decision support, quality management, and outcomes reporting."—*Website*. Also provides related links, for example, to the "EHR Incentive Program" and "Health Level Seven International (HL7)" standards for interoperability.

746 Dental health (MedlinePlus). http://www.nlm.nih.gov/medlineplus/dentalhealth.html. National Library of Medicine (U.S.), National Institutes of Health (U.S.). Bethesda, Md.: U.S. National Library of Medicine, National Institutes of Health, Dept. of Health and Human Services. 2000?–

A Health Topic within MedlinePlus. Collection of links to information from government agencies and professional associations and organizations, with access to selected oral health resources. Provides basic information, research findings, a "reference shelf" with dental dictionaries/glossaries, directories, organizations, statistics, etc.

747 DermAtlas. http://www.dermatlas.org. Bernard A. Cohen, Christoph U. Lehmann, Johns Hopkins University. Baltimore: Johns Hopkins University. 2000–

International collaborative project providing access to a growing collection of dermatology images. Contains more than 13,000 images in dermatology and skin diseases. Can be browsed by diagnosis, category, or body site. Searchable by keywords, diagnosis, pigmentation, color, body site, morphology, etc. Also provides links to other dermatology websites. Copyright and other disclaimer information at http://www.dermatlas.org/disclaimer. For health care professionals, patients, and other health care consumers.

DermIS (http://www.dermis.net/dermisroot/en/home/index.htm) is another example of an online collection of dermatology images and links to related information from various academic institutions worldwide.

748 Directories (MedlinePlus). http://www.nlm.nih.gov/medlineplus/directories.html. National Library of Medicine

(U.S.), National Institutes of Health (U.S.). Bethesda, Md.: U.S. National Library of Medicine, National Institutes of Health, Dept. of Health and Human Services. 200?–

RC48

Pt. of MedlinePlus.

Contents: Doctors and dentists—general; Hospital and clinics—general; Doctors and dentists—specialists; Other healthcare providers; Hospitals and clinics—specialized; Other healthcare facilities and services; Libraries.

Links to directories to help find health professionals, services, and facilities. Includes, for example, access to the American Medical Association's DoctorFinder, how to find a dentist, a Medicare participants physicians directory, and many others.

749 Disaster preparation and recovery (MedlinePlus). http://www.nlm.nih .gov/medlineplus/disasterpreparation andrecovery.html. National Library of Medicine (U.S.), National Institutes of Health (U.S.). Washington: National Library of Medicine. 2000–

Disaster preparation and recovery guides for the public from various organizations including the Dept. of Homeland Security, Federal Emergency Management Agency, American Red Cross, and Centers for Disease Control and Prevention. Listing of MedlinePlus "related topics" pages and links, e.g., Biodefense and Bioterrorism (MedlinePlus), coping with disasters, posttraumatic stress disorder, safety issues, and others.

750 Drug abuse (MedlinePlus). http://www. nlm.nih.gov/medlineplus/drugabuse. html. National Library of Medicine (U.S.). Bethesda, Md.: National Library of Medicine. 2000?–

A health topic in MedlinePlus.

Contents: Overviews; Latest news; Diagnosis/symptoms; Treatment; Prevention/screening; Specific conditions; Related sssues; Pictures and photographs; Games; Clinical trials; Research; Journal articles; Dictionaries/glossaries; Directories; Organizations; Newsletters/print publications; Law and policy; Statistics; Children; Teenagers; Men; Women; Seniors; Other languages.

Collection of links on substance abuse from a variety of government agencies, professional associations, and organizations, such as the National Institute on Drug Abuse, the Office of National Drug Control, Substance Abuse and Mental Health Services Administration (SAMHSA), National Library of Medicine, American Medical Association, American Academy of Family Physicians, and others. Also links to related MedlinePlus topics, e.g., alcoholism, prescription drug abuse, and substance abuse, to name a few.

751 Drug information portal. http:// druginfo.nlm.nih.gov/. National Library of Medicine (U.S.). Bethesda, Md.: National Library of Medicine. 2008–

"Gateway to selected drug information from the National Library of Medicine and other key government agencies . . . [with] access to over 12,000 selected drugs"—*About This Portal*. Can be searched by a drug's trade or generic name. Provides a summary of the information about the drug, and links to further related information, such as MedlinePlus, AIDSinfo (648), MEDLINE/PubMed®, LactMed, HSDB, Dietary supplements labels database, TOXLINE, DailyMed, Clinical Trials.gov, PubChem, ChemIDplus, Drugs@FDA, and others. For the public, health care professionals, and researchers. Information regarding the mobile version of this resource is part of NLM's Gallery of mobile apps and sites.

752 Drugs, supplements, and herbal information (MedlinePlus). http:// www.nlm.nih.gov/medlineplus/ druginformation.html. National Library of Medicine (U.S.). Bethesda, Md: National Library of Medicine, National Institutes of Health, U.S. Dept. of Health and Human Services. 2003?–

Pt. of MedlinePlus®.

Generic or brand name drugs, arranged A–Z, with prescription and over-the-counter medication information from MedMaster™ (American Society of Health-System Pharmacists [ASHP]). For additional drug information, see the MedlinePlus Drug Therapy topic pages (http://www.nlm.nih .gov/medlineplus/drugtherapy.html). Also provides access to information on herbs and supplements from Natural Standard©. Additional herb and supplement information can be found via MedlinePlus Complementary and Alternative Therapies topics (http://www.nlm.nih.gov/medlineplus/complementary andalternativetherapie s.html).

753   Genetics home reference. http://purl .access.gpo.gov/GPO/LPS74916. Lister Hill National Center for Biomedical Communications, National Library of Medicine, National Institutes of Health, Department of Health and Human Services. Bethesda, Md.: National Library of Medicine. 2003–

Aims to make genetics and its relationship to disease accessible to the general public. Information is presented in a question and answer format, with explanation on how a disease is inherited, the symptoms, and what treatments are available. Provides general information on genes, gene maps, genetic markers, chromosomes, DNA, and details on the specific genes related to a particular disease. Includes a "help me understand genetics page," a glossary of genetics terms, links to clinical trials, etc. Updated as new information becomes available. A detailed description at http://www.nlm.nih.gov/pubs/factsheets/ghr.html.

GeneEd (http://geneed.nlm.nih.gov), a new educational resource developed by the National Library of Medicine in collaboration with the National Human Genome Research Institute and also teachers and genetics & genetics counseling professionals. Intended as a resource for students and teachers in grades 9 - 12, it also is useful for health consumers, providing valuable information about genetic conditions and related topics.

754   Health facilities (MedlinePlus). http://www.nlm.nih.gov/medlineplus/healthfacilities.html. National Library of Medicine (U.S.), National Institutes of Health (U.S.). Bethesda, Md.: U.S. National Library of Medicine, National Institutes of Health, Dept. of Health and Human Services. 2000-

Provides useful starting points (sections: "start here" and a "reference shelf" with "directories" and "statistics"), with online publications from government agencies and organizations (e.g., AHA, Joint Commission, National Institute of Aging) and statistics concerning health care facilities. Aimed at helping the general public choose an appropriate facility.

For example, "Guide to choosing a hospital" at http://www.medicare.gov/Pubs/pdf/10181.pdf is a useful introduction.

755   Health fraud (MedlinePlus). http://www.nlm.nih.gov/medlineplus/health fraud.html. National Library of Medicine (U.S.), National Institutes of Health (U.S.). Bethesda, Md: U.S. National Library of Medicine, National Institutes of Health, Dept. of Health & Human Services. 2000?–

A "health topic" in MedlinePlus.

Contents: Overviews; Related issues; Journal articles; Organizations; Law and policy; Seniors.

Collection of links on health scams and quackery, how to detect health fraud, how to report unlawful sales of medical products, etc. Quackwatch provides additional information in this area.

756   Health system (MedlinePlus). http://www.nlm.nih.gov/medlineplus/healthsystem.html. National Library of Medicine (U.S.), National Institutes of Health (U.S.). Bethesda, Md.: U.S. National Library of Medicine, National Institutes of Health, Dept. of Health and Human Services. 200?–

List of links to a wide variety of healthcare-related topics, with each link leading to a separate page within MedlinePlus. Provides extensive reference information on the particular topic. Examples include assisted living, health occupations, caregivers, personal medical records, home care services, emergency medical services, health facilities, health insurance, managed care, home care services, hospice care, nursing homes, patients rights, patient safety, veterans and military health, and many others.

757   Lab tests online. http://www.labtests online.org. American Association for Clinical Chemistry. Washington: American Association for Clinical Chemistry. 2001–

Produced and maintained by the American Association for Clinical Chemistry, in collaboration with several other professional societies.

Provides patients and other health consumers with reliable information on clinical laboratory tests that are commonly used to diagnose various diseases and conditions and their interpretation. Also provides links to additional resources and websites.

Print titles containing information about lab tests include *Interpretation of diagnostic tests* by Wallach, *Laboratory tests and diagnostic procedures* by Chernecky et al.,*Manual of laboratory and diagnostic tests*by Fischbach et al., *Mosby's manual of diagnostic and laboratory tests* by Pagana et al., and *Tietz clinical guide to laboratory tests*.

758   MedlinePlus. http://medlineplus.gov/.
U.S. National Library of Medicine.
Bethesda, Md.: U.S. Dept. of Health and
Human Services, National Library of
Medicine. 1998–
025.04; 651.504261; 613   RA776.5

A consumer health reference database with free and reliable information from the National Library of Medicine (NLM), the National Institutes of Health (NIH), other government agencies, and various health-related organizations. A continually expanding and updated resource. Information on over 900 diseases and conditions, as well as drug information (prescription, nonprescription (ASHF—American Society of Health System Pharmacists consumer medication information)), herbs and supplements, with content as of September 2010 from *Natural medicines comprehensive database (NMCD)*, no longer from *Natural standard* as was previously the case, an illustrated medical encyclopedia (*A.D.A.M. medical encyclopedia*) and a search box for lookup of medical terms on the English homepage, interactive patient tutorials, anatomy (http://www .nlm.nih.gov/medlineplus/anatomyvideos.html) & surgery videos and other tools by following the "videos & cool tools" tab, lists of hospitals, physicians, and dentists, and health news. Provides preformulated MEDLINE/PubMed® searches for recent articles. Includes *NIH MedlinePlus magazine*, a quarterly publication for patients and their families, providing authoritative medical and healthcare information. "MedlinePlus en español" toggles between English and Spanish. Also provides links to browse

selected health information in multiple languages other than English and Spanish at http://www.nlm .nih.gov/medlineplus/languages/languages.html. Web 2.0 technologies help users share content, e.g., RSS feeds for all health topics. The Medline Plus search cloud (http://www.nlm.nih.gov/medline plus/cloud.html) displays the top 100 search terms typed into the MedlinePlus search box, usually updated every week day. Further detailed descriptive information of MedlinePlus is available at http://www.nlm.nih .gov/pubs/factsheets/medlineplus.html. For patients, families, and healthcare providers. Information regarding the mobile version of this resource is part of NLM's Gallery of mobile apps and sites.

MedlinePlus Connect, launched in November 2010, is a free service that allows electronic health record (EHR) systems to link users to MedlinePlus. NLM has mapped MedlinePlus health topics to two standard diagnostic coding systems used in EHRs (further description at http://www.nlm.nih.gov/ medlineplus/connect/overview.html).

Also available in a mobile version (m.medline plus.gov).

759   MedWatch. http://purl.access.gpo.gov/
GPO/LPS81698. United States; Food and
Drug Administration. Rockville, Md.:
U.S. Food and Drug Administration
344.73041   HE20.4058

Produced by Food and Drug Administration (FDA).

"FDA gateway for clinically important safety information and reporting serious problems with human medical products."—*Home page*. Considered a valuable resource for consumers, pharmacists, physicians, and other health professionals regarding recalls and other news of drugs; medical devices; radiation-emitting products; vaccines, blood and biologics; animal and veterinary; cosmentics; and tobacco products. Online video discusses information available on site. Searchable or browsable for recalls by date, brand, or type of recalled products, with information available in a variety of formats (e.g., e-mail alerts, RSS feeds, adding a widget to Web pages, etc.).

760   Men's health (MedlinePlus). http://
www.nlm.nih.gov/medlineplus/mens
health.html. National Library of Medicine
(U.S.). Bethesda, Md.: National Library of
Medicine, National Institutes of Health,

Dept. of Health and Human Services. 200?–

RA777.8

A MedlinePlus® health topic. Collection of links for a variety of resources on men's health (e.g., specific conditions, treatments, prevention/screening, etc.) and also related issues and topics.

761   National Cancer Institute. http://www .cancer.gov/. National Cancer Institute, U.S. National Institutes of Health.

Bethesda, Md.: National Cancer Institute Website created by the National Cancer Institute (NCI), a division of the National Institutes of Health (NIH).

Contents: NCI home, Cancer topics, Clinical trials, Cancer statistics, Research and funding, News, About NCI.

Links to cancer-related information for health professionals, medical students, and patients. Provides guidance to searching the cancer literature in PubMed by searching the "cancer subset" and access to already prepared searches on more than 100 different topics. Non-PubMed citations previously found in CANCERLIT, a database no longer being maintained, consist primarily of meeting abstracts from the annual meetings of the American Society of Clinical Oncology (ASCO) and the American Association for Cancer Research (AACR). ASCO abstracts for recent years are available via http://www.asco.org, AACR abstracts at http:// aacrmeetingabstracts.org/. Also provides access to PDQ: Physician data query (http://www.cancer .gov/cancertopics/pdq), a database with the latest information about cancer treatment, screening, prevention, genetics, etc.

The NCI website includes descriptions of various types of cancer (A–Z list of cancers: http:// www.cancer.gov/cancertopics/alphalist/) and related topics, with links to diagnosis and treatment information and supportive care, information on clinical trials, cancer prevention, cancer statistics (e.g., SEER cancer statistics review), cancer statistics tools, cancer mortality maps and graphs, and related NCI websites. Links to the Dictionary of cancer terms and various cancer vocabulary resources (e.g., NCI thesaurus, NCI metathesaurus, and NCI terminology browser), NCI drug dictionary, NCI publications, etc. Available both in English and Spanish.

762   National Organization for Rare Disorders, Inc. http://www.rarediseases .org/. National Organization for Rare Disorders. Danbury, Conn.: National Organization for Rare Disorders. 1999–

RC48

The National Organization for Rare Disorders (NORD) provides alphabetical Index of rare diseases and several searchable databases—namely, Rare disease database, Index of organizations (list of organizations), and Organizational database (patient organizations)—as well as advice on how to interpret search results. Other resources in this area can be located via *NORD guide to rare disorders* and NIH's Office of Rare Diseases.

763   National Patient Safety Foundation (NPFS). http://www.npsf.org. National Patient Safety Foundation. North Adams, Mass.: National Patient Safety Foundation

Independent, not-for-profit organization, with the mission to "measurably improve patient safety"— *main page*. Searchable website, with links to online patient safety resources and organizations. Information is presented in different categories (e.g., health care quality and safety, medication safety, surgical safety, cancer treatment safety, and others) for different user groups, such as health professionals, patients and families, and researchers.

764   Nursing home compare. http://www .medicare.gov/nhcompare/home.asp. Centers for Medicare and Medicaid Services, U.S. Dept. of Health and Human Services. Baltimore: Centers for Medicare and Medicaid Services. 1990s–

Produced by Centers for Medicare and Medicaid Services (U.S.)

Includes nursing homes that are Medicare or Medicaid certified and provide a full range of skilled nursing care, but also other types of facilities with different levels of care and possibly licensed only at the state level. Searchable by geography (state, county), by proximity (city, zip code), or by name. Part of the Medicare website at http://www.medicare.gov/, which also provides access to additional search tools to compare, for example, prescription drug plans, health plans, and hospitals; information on finding a physician; and answers to other health care questions.

765   Nutrition (MedlinePlus). http://www
.nlm.nih.gov/medlineplus/nutrition
.html. National Library of Medicine
(U.S.), National Institutes of Health
(U.S.). Bethesda, Md.: U.S. National
Library of Medicine, National Institutes
of Health, Dept. of Health and Human
Services. 2000?–
A health topic within MedlinePlus®.
Contents: Overviews; Latest news; Related issues; Health check tools; Tutorials; Clinical trials; Research; Journal articles; Directories; Organizations; Law and policy; Teenagers; Women.

Selected links to a wide range of nutrition-related information provided by government agencies, societies, professional associations, organizations, and foundations. Also provides links to related topics with separate pages in MedlinePlus, e.g., breast feeding, child nutrition, dietary fats, fiber, and protein, eating disorders, food safety, infant and toddler nutrition, obesity, vegetarian diets, and others.

766   The nutrition source. http://www.hsph
.harvard.edu/nutritionsource/. Harvard
School of Public Health. Boston: Harvard
School of Public Health. 2002–
Contents: Nutrition in the news; What Should I Eat?; Healthy Drinks; Salt and Sodium; Carbohydrates; Healthy Weight; Preventing Diabetes; Recipes; Healthy Food Service; Your Nutrition Questions Answered; Index: Nutrition A to Z; Additional Resources; About Us; FAQ; Contact Us.

"The Nutrition Source provides evidence-based diet & nutrition information for clinicians, health professionals and the public." —*main page*.

767   Office of Dietary Supplements. http://
dietary-supplements.info.nih.gov/index.
aspx. National Institutes of Health Office
of Dietary Supplements. Bethesda, Md.:
National Institutes of Health Office of
Dietary Supplements. 1990s–
615.854   RM258.5
National Institutes of Health (NIH) Office of Dietary Supplements (ODS); U.S. Dept. of Agriculture (USDA).

ODS homepage includes extensive health information on dietary supplement use and safety and nutrient recommendations. Provides access to NIH and USDA databases and research resources, such as dietary supplement databases, product integrity resources, and the USDA food composition database. Another resource for researchers is the CARDS (Computer access to research on dietary supplements) database (http://ods.od.nih
.gov/research/cards_database.aspx) which includes records of research projects pertaining to dietary supplements funded by various government agencies, centers, and institutes. For health professionals, researchers, students, and health consumers.

768   Office of Rare Diseases. http://rare
diseases.info.nih.gov. National Institutes
of Health (U.S.), Office of Rare Diseases.
Bethesda, Md.: National Institutes of
Health. 2002–
Answers questions about rare diseases for patients and other health consumers, healthcare providers, researchers, educators, students, and others interested in rare diseases. Links to definitions, causes, treatments, and publications about rare diseases, provides resources on genetic information, genetic research, genetic testing laboratories and clinics, genetic counseling services, and patient support groups. Also includes information on rare diseases research and research resources. Other reference sources in this area include, for example, National Organization for Rare Disorders, Inc. and *NORD guide to rare disorders*.

769   OncoLink. http://cancer.med.upenn.
edu/. Abramson Cancer Center of the
University of Pennsylvania. Philadelphia,
Pa.: University of Pennsylvania. 1994–
615.507; 616.992; 616.994
Contents: Cancer types; Cancer treatment; Risk and prevention; Support; Healthcare professionals.

Designed for educational purposes to help cancer patients, families, health care professionals, and the general public to get accurate cancer-related information. Provides comprehensive information about specific types of cancer, updates on cancer treatment, and news about research advances, with information provided at various levels, from introductory to in-depth.

770   PDRhealth. http://www.pdrhealth.com/
home/home.aspx. Thomson Healthcare.

Montvale, N.J.: Thomson Healthcare. 2008–

Launched as PDRhealth.com in Nov. 2007, now called PDRhealth, which is a revised Thomson website, previously also called PDRhealth or PDR health.

Provides prescription drug and supplement information (based on information found in *Physicians' desk reference: PDR*, including drug interactions (e.g., "interaction checker"), side effects, dosages, alternative therapies for brand-name and generic prescription drugs, over-the-counter drugs, herbals, and supplements. Also provides information on diseases and conditions, treatment options, online health tools (e.g., HDL and LDL cholesterol level risk factor analyzer), clinical trials, and surgery.

771 Smoking and health resource library (CDC). http://nccd.cdc.gov/ shrl/QuickSearch.aspx. Centers for Disease Control and Prevention (U.S.). Atlanta: Centers for Disease Control and Prevention. 1990s-

Pt. of CDC's "Smoking & tobacco use" site http:// www.cdc.gov/tobacco/.

Continually updated database. Indexes and abstracts tobacco-related "articles from medical and professional journals; books and book chapters; dissertations; reports; conference proceedings and papers; government documents from federal, state, local, and foreign entities; fact sheets and policy documents from U.S. and international non-profit organizations, and other documents. New citations include recently published tobacco-related articles from peer-reviewed journals of behavioral, scientific, and medical literature."—*Publ. description*.

Examples of other resources are "Tobacco, smoking and health" http://sis.nlm.nih.gov/enviro/ tobacco.html (pt. of Enviro-Health Links, Smoking (MedlinePlus) (http://www.nlm.nih.gov/medline plus/smoking.html), and other smoking-related entries in MedlinePlus.

772 Substance Abuse and Mental Health Services Administration (SAMHSA). http://www.samhsa.gov. Substance Abuse and Mental Health Services Administration. Rockville, Md.: Substance Abuse and Mental Health Services Administration

362.21; 362.29   RA790.6

Substance Abuse and Mental Health Services Administration (SAMHSA), part of U.S. Dept. of Health and Human Services (HHS).

SAMHSA has as its mission "building resilience and facilitating recovery for people with or at risk for mental or substance use disorders . . . gearing all of its resources . . . toward that outcome."—*About Us* Searchable website. Provides resources for prevention, treatment, and rehabilitation services for patients with various forms of mental illness and addictions. Includes three centers: SAMHSA's Center for Mental Health Services (CMHS), Center for Substance Abuse Prevention (CSAP), and Center for Substance Abuse Treatment (CSAT). Examples of SAMHSA resources include "Find substance abuse and mental health treatment" (http://www.samhsa .gov/treatment/) with clickable maps to locate different programs throughout the United States, and links to various related publications (http://store.samhsa .gov/home). Provides the latest data (http://www .samhsa.gov/data/) on alcohol, tobacco, and illegal drugs as well as other statistical data and resources.

773 U.S. Food and Drug Administration. http://www.fda.gov. Food and Drug Administration. Washington: Food and Drug Administration

The Food and Drug Administration (FDA) regulates foods, drugs, medical devices, biologics (vaccines, blood products, etc.), and radiation-emitting products (e.g., cell phones, lasers, microwaves, etc.). Searchable website with A–Z index (http:// www.fda.gov/SiteIndex/default).

Major links include Drugs (http://www.fda .gov/Drugs/default.htm) which evaluates drugs before they can be sold and provides resources such as Drugs@FDA, Electronic orange book, and National drug code directory. Another FDA center is Food (http://www.fda.gov/Food/default .htm), with resources on foods and food safety, such as the GRAS (Generally Recognized as Safe) list of substances (http://www.fda.gov/Food/Ingredients PackagingLabeling/GRAS/SCOGS/default.htm), the "bad bug book" (http://www.fda.gov/food/ foodborneillnesscontaminants/causesofillness badbugbook/default.htm) and publications on food-borne illness, FDA food code, allergens, dietary supplements, etc. Additional FDA centers provide information on biologics, cosmetics, medical devices, radiological health, toxicological research, and veterinary medicine.

Other examples of resources provided at the FDA site include access to the "blue book" (i.e., *Requirements of laws and regulations enforced by the U.S. Food and Drug Administration*), oncology tools, patient safety portal, special health issues, and information on bioterrorism, trans fats, vaccines, xenotransplantation, and many other subjects and topics relating to human and animal drugs and biologics, foods, and medical devices. Information is tailored to the needs of different user groups, with separate pages for consumers, patients, health professionals, state/local officials, industry, press, women, and children. Frequently requested FDA documents can be accessed via an "electronic reading room" (http://www.fda.gov/foi/electrr.htm). Milestones in U.S. Food and Drug Law History 1820–2005 is available at http://www.fda.gov/AboutFDA/WhatWeDo/History/Milestones/default.htm.

774   Videos of surgical procedures (MedlinePlus). http://www.nlm.nih.gov/medlineplus/surgeryvideos.html. National Library of Medicine (U.S.). Bethesda, Md: National Library of Medicine, National Institutes of Health, U.S. Dept. of Health and Human Services. 2004?–

Pt. of MedlinePlus®. Provides links to prerecorded webcasts of surgical procedures, that is, actual operations performed at medical centers in the U.S. since Jan. 2004. Intended for educational purposes.

775   Womenshealth.gov. http://www.womenshealth.gov/. National Women's Health Information Center, United States.; Public Health Service.; Office on Women's Health. Fairfax, Va.: U.S. Department of Health and Human Services. 1990s–
613.04240285; 615.507; 305.40285
RA778

A federal government resource for women's health information. Presents reliable information on women's health concerns and issues for health professionals and health consumers. Links to organizations concerned with women's health, health tools, health topics (http://www.womenshealth.gov/health-topics/), publications of interest and concern to women of all ages, and statistics (http://www.womenshealth.gov/statistics/). Includes link to girlshealth.gov with health information for young girls and educators.

Other Internet resources in this subject area with valuable information for health consumers, health professionals, and researchers include, for example, "Women's health resources: Women's health research from NIH" (http://whr.nlm.nih.gov/), a portal that serves as an access point to all NIH sex and gender differences resources and information on priorities for research in women's health, "Women's health (MedlinePlus)" (http://www.nlm.nih.gov/medlineplus/womenshealth.html), and "Women's health (NIH)" (http://health.nih.gov/category/WomensHealth).

Dentistry

776 Academy of General Dentistry. http://www.agd.org/. Academy of General Dentistry. Chicago: Academy of General Dentistry. 1996–

Academy of General Dentistry (AGD), a nonprofit organization of more than 35,000 general dentists, founded in 1952.

Provides fee-based services with access to professional resources for dentists and students (e.g., continuing education, professional news, practice management, etc.) Also offers freely accessible patient- and consumer-oriented oral health resources, such as help with finding a dentist; a list of oral health resources ("ABC's of oral health"), an oral health glossary, "life of a tooth-a visual timeline," and others.

Guides

777 A consumer's guide to dentistry.
2nd ed. Gordon J. Christensen. St. Louis: Mosby, 2002. x, 214 p., col. ill.
ISBN 0323014836
617.6   RK61.C57
First ed., 1994.

Contents: Ch. 1 "How to use this book," finding solutions to your oral problems; ch. 2 "Divisions in dentistry," types of dentists; ch. 3 "Finding the right dentist," what to consider in your choice of dentists; ch. 4 "Managed care," managed care programs in dentistry; ch. 5 "Pain control," controlling pain in dentistry; ch. 6 "Infection control," infection control in the dental office; ch. 7 "Endodontics," root canals, dead teeth, inside of teeth; ch. 8 "Esthetic dentistry," cosmetic dentistry, improving your smile; ch. 9 "Geriatric dentistry," dentistry for mature people; ch. 10 "Implant dentistry," substitutes for tooth roots placed into your jaw; ch. 11 "Occlusion," your bite, the way your teeth come together, temporomandibular joints, temporomandibular dysfunction; ch. 12 "Oral and maxillofacial surgery," oral pathology, oral medicine diseases, and surgery related to the oral and facial areas; ch. 13 "Orthodontics," straightening teeth; ch. 14 "Pediatric dentistry," dentistry for children; ch. 15 "Periodontics," gums and bone surrounding teeth, ch. 16 "Prosthodontics," fixed crowns or bridges cemented onto teeth; ch. 17 "Prosthodontics," removable dentures replacing all or some teeth; ch. 18 "Restorative or operative dentistry," fillings for teeth; ch. 19. "Preventing the need for dental treatment"; ch. 20 "Additional sources of information."

Written for the dental patient, provides information about dental health and various treatment options for dental problems. Illustrations.

Bibliography

778 Dental bibliography: Literature of dental science and art as found in the libraries of the New York academy

of medicine and Bernhard Wolf Weinberger. 2nd ed. Bernhard Wolf Weinberger, First District Dental Society of the State of New York. [New York]: First District Dental Society, State of New York, [1929]–1932. 2 v. in 1

Z6668.N53

First ed., 1916.

Repr. 1998, 1929, 2 v. in 1 (Mansfield Centre, Conn.: Martino Fine Books).

Contents: [pt. I], A reference index; pt. II, A subject index, with additional reference index.

"Though far from a complete dental bibliography, it contains every important dental publication that has been published, thereby enabling those who are interested in dental research and study to fulfill their needs."—*Pref.* Subject index covers only dental books, not dental periodicals. Includes sections on "Medical classics containing dental citations" (p. 178–83) and "Earliest dental books published, 1530–1810" (p. 220–22). Pt. 2 updates the previous volume.

Available online at http://www.hathitrust.org.

Indexes; Abstract journals; Databases

779   Dental abstracts. American Dental Association. Chicago: American Dental Association, 1956–. v., ill.

617.6082 0011-8486   RK1.A5416

Bimonthly. Imprint varies. Abstracts of state-of-the-art articles from selected English-language dental and medical journals published worldwide. Each issue currently contains approx. 50 abstracts, with developments and advances in general dentistry and dental specialties, including graphs, tables, and figures from the original articles. Author and subject indexes since 1990 in the November/December issue. Available online via Elsevier ScienceDirect.

An earlier title, also titled *Dental abstracts*, publ. 1941–50 by Columbia University School of Dental and Oral Surgery, provides access to some of the earlier dental literature as an index of "dental progress . . . valuable to the research worker . . . as a comprehensive guide to the literature" (*Pref.*) of this time period.

780   Index to dental literature. American Dental Association; National Library of Medicine (U.S.). Chicago: American Dental Association, 1962–1999. ISBN 00193992

016.60016   Z6668.I45; RK51

1839/75–1936/38 (publ. 1921–39) had title: *Index of the periodical dental literature published in the English language;* 1939–61, *Index to dental periodical literature in the English language;* 1962–99 (print version discontinued). Continued as part of MEDLINE/PubMed. An author and subject index to dental periodical literature. Since 1962, includes periodicals in foreign languages. Contains lists of dental books, and theses and dissertations that have been accepted for degrees by schools of dentistry. Since 1965, coverage has been expanded to include articles in nondental journals. Relevant content can be found in MEDLINE/PubMed. A search in PubMed can be limited to "dental journals" subset.

781   Lexi-Comp online. http://www.lexi.com/. Lexi-Comp, Inc. Hudson, Ohio: Lexi-Comp, Inc. 1978–

Point-of-care drug and clinical information resource, with links to primary literature. Contains 15 clinical databases (e.g., Lexi-Drugs Online, AHFS, Lexi-Natural Products Online, Nursing Lexi-Drugs Online, Pharmacogenomics, Poisoning and Toxicology, Lab Tests and Diagnosis, and several others) and provides drug information and treatment recommendation for diseases and conditions. Also includes other features, e.g., an online interaction tool (Lexi-Interact) and medical calculator (Lexi-CALC). For pharmacists, physicians, nurses, and dentists. Detailed information available at the Lexi-Comp website "tour portal" (http://www.lexi.com/web/toursol.jsp).

782   MEDLINE. http://purl.access.gpo.gov/GPO/LPS4708. National Library of Medicine (U.S.). Bethesda, Md.: National Library of Medicine (U.S.). 1900s–

MEDLINE®—Medical literature analysis and retrieval system online (National Library of Medicine®—NLM), primary subset of PubMed® (48) and part of the databases provided by the National Center for Biotechnology Information (NCBI). Coverage extends back to 1946, with some older material.

Bibliographic database, providing comprehensive access to the international biomedical literature from the fields of medicine, nursing, dentistry, veterinary medicine, allied health, and the preclinical sciences. It is also a primary source of information from the international literature on biomedicine, including the following topics as they relate to biomedicine and health care: Biology, environmental science, marine biology, plant and animal science, biophysics, and chemistry. For indexing articles, NLM uses MeSH: Medical subject headings® (858), a controlled vocabulary of biomedical terms. An increasing number of MEDLINE citations contain a link to the free full-text articles.

The MEDLINE database is the electronic counterpart of *Index medicus®*, *Index to dental literature*, and the *International nursing index*. The databases is offered at no additional cost on a variety of indexing platforms.

For detailed information, see the MEDLINE fact sheet at http://www.nlm.nih.gov/pubs/factsheets/medline.html, which also includes a list of related fact sheets (e.g., "MEDLINE, PubMed, and PMC (PubMed Centeral): How are they different?").

783 NLM gateway. http://gateway.nlm.nih.gov/. National Library of Medicine (U.S.). Bethesda, Md.: National Library of Medicine. 2000–

RA11

As announced in 2011, "the NLM® gateway has transitioned to a new pilot project from the Lister Hill National Center for Biomedical Communications (LHNCBC)."—*Website* The new site focuses now on two databases: Meeting abstracts and Health services research projects. All of the other resources previously accessed through the NLM gateway are available through their individual sites. For a list of these databases previously available via the NLM gateway see http://gateway.nlm.nih.gov/about.jsp.

The NLM gateway previously allowed simultaneous searching of information resources at the National Library of Medicine (NLM)/National Center for Biotechnology Information (NCBI) with an overview of the search results presented in several categories (bibliographic resources, consumer health resources, and other information), with a listing of the individual databases and the number of results within these categories. Previously

included were, for example, MEDLINE/PubMed and the NLM Catalog as well as other resources, including information on current clinical trials and consumer health information (MedlinePlus) and many others.

784 PubMed. http://www.ncbi.nlm.nih.gov/pubmed. U.S. National Center for Biotechnology Information, National Library of Medicine, National Institutes of Health. Bethesda, Md.: U.S. National Center for Biotechnology Information. 1996–

PubMed®, developed and maintained by the National Center for Biotechnology Information (NCBI) at the National Library of Medicine® (NLM). Provides a search interface for more than 20 million bibliographic citations and abstracts in the fields of medicine, nursing, dentistry, veterinary medicine, health care systems, and preclinical sciences. It provides access to articles indexed for MEDLINE® and for selected life sciences journals. PubMed subsets found under the "Limits" tab are: MEDLINE and PubMed central®, several journal groups (i.e., core clinical journals, dental journals, and nursing journals), and topical subsets (AIDS, bioethics, cancer, complementary medicine, dietary supplements, history of medicine, space life sciences, systematic reviews, toxicology, and veterinary science). "Linkout" provides access to full-text articles.

For detailed information see the PubMed fact sheet at http://www.nlm.nih.gov/pubs/factsheets/pubmed.html and also MEDLINE®/PubMed® resources guide (http://www.nlm.nih.gov/bsd/pmresources.html) which provides detailed information about MEDLINE data and searching PubMed.

Information regarding the mobile version of this resource is part of NLM's Gallery of mobile apps and sites.

Classification

785 Application of the international classification of diseases to dentistry and stomatology: ICD-DA. 3rd ed. World Health Organization. Geneva, Switzerland: World Health Organization,

1995. v., 238 p. ISBN 9241544678

617.5220012   RK51.5.W67

First ed. (WHO), 1973 (companion to the *International classification of disease* [ICD], 8th rev.); 2nd ed., 1978 (companion to the ICD 9th rev.). Derived from the 1992–94 print version of the ICD-10 (*International statistical classification of diseases and related health problems*) and prepared as a companion volume to the ICD-10.

Contents: "The International Classification of Diseases—ICD-DA"; "Recommended use of ICD-DA"; "ICD-DA tabular list"; "Extract from numerical index of morphology of neoplasms (ICD-O)"; "Annex 1. Histological typing of odontogenic tumours"; "Annex 2. Histological typing of salivary gland tumors."

Provides "a comprehensive and consistent classification of oral diseases and oral manifestations of other diseases, standard recording system for all oral diseases and conditions, . . . [and] by means of the recording system, to make possible the collection of data that will allow the prevalence of oral diseases and conditions to be compared at an international level"—*Introd.*

Includes a tabular section and a comprehensive alphabetical index. Neoplasm section includes both malignant and benign tumors. Use of ICD-DA is recommended "at the national, regional, institutional, or individual practice level." Includes bibliographical references and index. Related publications are *International classification of diseases for oncology: ICD-O, Histological typing of odontogenic tumours*, and *Histological typing of salivary gland tumours*. Also available as an e-book.

Encyclopedias

786   Encyclopedia of biomaterials and biomedical engineering. 2nd ed.
Gary E. Wnek, Gary L. Bowlin.
New York: Informa Healthcare USA,
2008. 4 v. (various pagings), ill.
ISBN 9781420078022
610.28403   R857.M3E53

Provides an "important and continual resource for the many individuals whose work touches, and is touched by, biomaterials and biomedical engineering in order to further stimulate, create, and deliver improvements in quality of life" (*Pref.* Topics

include facets of biosensors, implants, orthopedic devices, and tissue engineering. Intended to be multidisciplinary and comprehensive. Second edition has doubled in size and contains nearly 300 articles averaging about ten pages in length. Articles are signed. Contributors (more than 500, largely from the U.S.) are predominantly from academia, but some are from industry. Arranged alphabetically. Includes brief contents (inside front cover), table of contents, cross-references, article references, and index. Published in print and online formats.

Dictionaries

787   Academy of General Dentistry. http://www.agd.org/. Academy of General Dentistry. Chicago: Academy of General Dentistry. 1996–

Academy of General Dentistry (AGD), a nonprofit organization of more than 35,000 general dentists, founded in 1952.

Provides fee-based services with access to professional resources for dentists and students (e.g., continuing education, professional news, practice management, etc.) Also offers freely accessible patient- and consumer-oriented oral health resources, such as help with finding a dentist; a list of oral health resources ("ABC's of oral health"), an oral health glossary, "life of a tooth-a visual timeline," and others.

788   American Dental Association.
http://www.ada.org/. American Dental Association. Chicago: American Dental Association. 1995– 617.6

Official website of the American Dental Association (ADA), founded in 1859.

Provides information for dental professionals concerning education and testing, practice management, and patient care. Includes a list of all accredited dental programs in the U.S. (http://www.ada.org/103.aspx) and Canada, and links to national dental organizations. Resources for consumers include, for example, "Oral Health Topics A–Z" (http://www.ada.org/286.aspx), "Find a dentist" (http://www.mouthhealthy.org/en/find-a-dentist.aspx), and other helpful resources. Also includes "ADA timeline" (http://www.ada.org/adatimeline.aspx), a list of presidents (1860 to the present), and links to various other dental history resources. Some of the resources are restricted to ADA members.

Another ADA web resource, ADA Center for Evidence-Based Dentistry™ http://ebd.ada.org/about.aspx is a useful resource for clinicians to identify systematic reviews and critical summaries. It also provides links to further resources and educational tutorials as well as links to patient resources.

The American Academy of Pediatric Dentistry (AAPD) http://www.aapd.org/ provides a variety of dental health resources, policies & guidelines, etc.

789 CDT: Current dental terminology.
American Dental Association. Chicago: American Dental Association, 1991–
RK28

American Dental Association (ADA). Description based on 2011-12 ed. (publ. 2010). Subtitle: "The ADA practical guide to dental procedure codes."

Provides the latest dental procedure codes, dental terminology, nomenclature and descriptors, and tooth numbering systems. Described as a "standardized coding system to document and to communicate accurate information about dental treatment procedures and services to agencies involved in adjudicating insurance claims."— *ADA Website* Organized into 12 categories (e.g., diagnostic, preventive, restorative, endodontics, etc.), with each category having a series of five-digit alphanumeric codes. Also available as an e-book.

790 A dictionary of dentistry. Robert Ireland. Oxford; New York: Oxford University Press, 2010. 410 p., ill.
ISBN 9780199533015
617.6003   RK27.I745
(Oxford paperback reference)

Also called *Oxford dictionary of dentistry*

Covers approx. 4,000 terms and concepts used in dentistry & dental specialties and related basic sciences areas. Emphasis is on British terminology. Cross-references are provided. Included are some entries with line drawings and "further readings." Appendixes cover various aspects of head & neck anatomy, diseases, biographies of important historical figures, organizations, general terms relevant in dentistry, etc. For selected entries, additional information and color images are accessible from a companion website.

Mosby's dental dictionary may be a more appropriate resource for U.S. dental professionals. Also available online via Credo reference (http://corp. credoreference.com/).

791 Dictionary of dentistry English-Spanish, Spanish-English = Diccionario de odontologia Ingles-Espanol, Espanol-Ingles. Ana Veronica Franscini-Paiva. Barcelona, Spain: Editorial Quintessence, 2005. 421 p.
ISBN 8489873364
RK27.F73

Dental terms and biomedical terms associated with dentistry, with translations in both English and Spanish.

792 Drug dictionary for dentistry. J. G. Meechan, R. A. Seymour. Oxford; New York: Oxford University Press, 2002. 434 p.
ISBN 0192632744
617.606103   RK701.M44

Includes drugs prescribed by dentists and drugs that a dental patient may already be taking, describing use, dosage, drug-drug interactions, and reasons why they shouldn't be used. Drugs are listed by their approved name. An appendix lists trade names and cross-references to the approved name of the drug. Written for dental practitioners and students. Available as an e-book.

A recent addition to the dental reference literature is *Dictionary of dentistry*.

793 Harty's dental dictionary. 3rd ed.
Peter A. Heasman, Giles McCracken, F. J. Harty. Edinburgh; New York: Churchill Livingstone, 2007. p. ISBN 9780443102
617.6003   RK27.H37

First ed., 1987 and 2nd ed., 1994 had title: *Concise illustrated dental dictionary*. Updated edition. Offers brief definitions for a comprehensive range of dental terminology, including both common and more exotic terms. Includes cross-references and line drawings illustrating anatomical features and dental instruments. Appendixes include a chronological table of the development and eruption of the teeth and information about dental schools and dental organizations. Useful to dental practitioners and dental students, however "directed primarily towards health care professionals outside of the United States" (*Publ. notes*).

794   Heinemann dental dictionary. 4th ed.
Jenifer E. H. Fairpo, C. Gavin Fairpo.
Oxford; Boston: Butterworth Heinemann,
1997. xvi, 347 p. ISBN 0750622083
617.6/003   RK27.F35

First ed., 1962, had title: *Heinemann modern dictionary for dental students;* 3rd ed., 1987. A major revision. Provides brief definitions of terms, including many obsolete terms from the early dental literature. Cross-references from the older terminology to the preferred term. American terms are included, although the clinical terminology is based on British and ISO standard vocabulary (cf. *Pref.*). Anatomical charts of the head and neck show arteries, veins, muscles, and nerves; an appendix lists dental periodicals, with country of origin and frequency of publication. List of commonly used abbreviations for dental institutions, degrees, etc.

795   Mosby's dental dictionary. 2nd ed.
Charles A. Babbush, Margaret J.
Fehrenback, Mary Emmons. St. Louis;
London: Mosby, Inc., 2007
ISBN 9780323049634

First ed., 1998, ed. by Thomas J. Zwemer; also a 2004 ed., by Scott Stocking and Jyothimai Gubili (ed. consultants: Thomas Zwemer, Margaret J. Fehrenbach, Mary Emmons, and Mary Ann Tiedemann).

Includes approx. 9,500 terms related to dentistry and related sciences, dental office management, and medical terms in common use. Ill. with diagrams, photographs, and line drawings. Contains several appendixes; e.g., American Dental Association dental codes, an overview of the Health Insurance Portability and Accountability Act, symbols and abbreviations used in dentistry, tooth numbering systems. Online access via Credo Reference.

**796   Stedman's dental dictionary:
Illustrated. 2nd ed.** Thomas Lathrop
Stedman, Wolters Kluwer Health.
Philadelphia: Wolters Kluwer Health/
Lippincott Williams & Wilkins, 2011.
xxx, 606, 82 p., ill. (some col.)
ISBN 9781608311460
617.6003   RK27.S744

First ed., 2005 had title: *Stedman's medical dictionary for the dental professions: illustrated,* also called *Medical dictionary for the dental professions.*

Title varies: *Dental dictionary; Stedman's medical dictionary for the dental professions.*

Revised edition. A to Z listing, with 16,000 terms, approximately 500 color and black and white images and illustrations. Icons are used to identify images, common medical prefixes, suffixes, and combining forms. Contains tooth numbering systems, dental imaging errors, guidelines for infection control, weights and measures, and information about the different dental professions and professional organizations. Also indicates the Mendelian Inheritance in Man number (OMIM: Online Mendelian Inheritance in Man) and Terminologia Anatomica Latin term.

Available to subscribers is *Stedman's online: Stedman's medical dictionary for the dental professions*, which includes "all the content from the print dictionary, as well as access to 5,600 images, more than 8,500 audio pronunciations, 42 live action videos, and a customizable section, My Stedman's, which allows users to add terms, add notes, add definitions, save searches and illustrations, and include outside links."—*Publ. description.*

Directories

797   ADEA official guide to dental schools.
American Dental Education Association.
Washington: American Dental Education
Association, 2001–
617.6007117 2152-5196   RK91.A582a;
Q617.6A

Continues: *Admission requirements of American dental schools,* 1963–74 (published in cooperation with the Council on Dental Education) and *Admission requirements of U.S. and Canadian dental schools,* [10th]–38th ed., 1974/75–2001 (published by American Association of Dental Schools). 2001– published by the American Dental Education Association (ADEA).

Description based on 2012 ed. "for students entering in Fall 2013."

Contents: ch. 1, "Exploring a world of opportunities," ch.2, "Applying to dental schools," ch. 3, "Deciding where to apply," ch. 4, "Financing a dental education," ch. 5, "Getting more information."

Provides an extensive range of information for each school: general information, description of programs, admission requirements, application processes and timetables, costs, financing options and scholarships for dental education, etc. Information is based on data collected from ADEA, ADA, and data provided by the dental schools. Familiarizes the reader with the dental profession. Additional information about dental education and the ADEA at http://www.adea.org/.

798 American dental directory. American Dental Association. Chicago: American Dental Association, 1947–2001. v., ill.
617.6002573 0065-8073   RK37.A25
American dentists are listed by state and city, with an alphabetical index of names. Gives address and indicates specialization and dental school, with year of graduation. Additional sections on affiliate members of the American Dental Association (ADA), i.e., foreign dental graduates who are practicing in a country other than the U.S., and associate and honorary members. Also includes national dental organizations and dental organizations outside the U.S. Since 2001, no longer publ. in print format. Continued by an online directory, ADA member directory (http://www.ada.org/).

799 Barron's guide to medical and dental schools. Barron's Educational Series, Inc. Woodbury, N.Y.: Barron's Educational Series, Inc., 1982–
610 1935-7559   R735.A4B37
Based on *Barron's guide to medical, dental, and allied health science careers* [1974], and its updated versions, published in 1975 and 1977. 13th ed., 2012. Description based on 12th ed., 2009.

Contents: pt. 1. Medicine; pt. 2. Dentistry; Appendixes A-K.

Intended as a guidance manual for pre-professional students. Presents basic data and detailed information for accredited medical, dental, and osteopathic schools in the U.S. and Canada, such as admissions requirements, curriculum, grading and promotion policies, facilities, and special features of an institution, etc. Includes a full-length model Medical College Admission Test (MCAT) with answers, and selected questions from recent Dental College Admission Tests (DAT), sample essays for medical student applications, and other advice for students considering a medical or dental career. Includes a chapter on "physicians and medicine in the twenty-first century," addressing many issues facing physicians today, including cybermedicine

and medical informatics. Bibliography and indexes (index of medical school profiles; subject index).

800 Directories (MedlinePlus). http://www.nlm.nih.gov/medlineplus/directories.html. National Library of Medicine (U.S.), National Institutes of Health (U.S.). Bethesda, Md.: U.S. National Library of Medicine, National Institutes of Health, Dept. of Health and Human Services. 200?–
RC48
Pt. of MedlinePlus.

Contents: Doctors and dentists—general; Hospital and clinics—general; Doctors and dentists—specialists; Other healthcare providers; Hospitals and clinics—specialized; Other healthcare facilities and services; Libraries.

Links to directories to help find health professionals, services, and facilities. Includes, for example, access to the American Medical Association's DoctorFinder, how to find a dentist, a Medicare participants physicians directory, and many others.

Handbooks

801 ADA/PDR guide to dental therapeutics. 5th ed. American Dental Association. Chicago: American Dental Association, 2009. xii, 1164 p. ISBN 1563637693
615   RK701
First (1998)–3rd (2003) ed. had title: *ADA guide to dental therapeutics*. The 4th (2006) edition and this edition produced by the American Dental Association (ADA) in partnership with the Physicians' Desk Reference.

Authoritative guide to dental therapeutics, covering brand names and generic drugs. Contains sections on drugs used in dentistry, drugs used in medicine, with treatment considerations for dental patients, and drug issues in dental practice, including oral manifestations of systemic agents. Appendix includes U.S. controlled substances, smoking cessation, and related products.

Other PDR-related titles include *Physicians' desk reference: PDR, PDR drug guide for mental health professionals, PDR guide to drug interactions, side effects, and indications, PDR for herbal medicines, PDR for nonprescription drugs, PDR for nutritional supplements, PDR nurse's drug handbook, Physicians' desk reference for ophthalmic medicines, PDR guide to biological and chemical warfare response, PDR guide to terrorism response,* and other titles. PDR and its major companion volumes are also found in the PDR® Electronic Library.

802 CDT: Current dental terminology.
American Dental Association. Chicago: American Dental Association, 1991–
RK28
American Dental Association (ADA). Description based on 2011-12 ed. (publ. 2010). Subtitle: "The ADA practical guide to dental procedure codes."

Provides the latest dental procedure codes, dental terminology, nomenclature and descriptors, and tooth numbering systems. Described as a "standardized coding system to document and to communicate accurate information about dental treatment procedures and services to agencies involved in adjudicating insurance claims."—*ADA Website* Organized into 12 categories (e.g., diagnostic, preventive, restorative, endodontics, etc.), with each category having a series of five-digit alphanumeric codes. Also available as an e-book.

803 Dental materials: Properties and manipulation. 10th ed. John M. Powers, John C. Wataha. St. Louis: Elsevier/Mosby, 2013. x, 236 p., ill. (chiefly col.) ISBN 9780323078368
617.695   RK652.5
First ed., 1975; 8th ed., 2004; 9th ed., 2008.

Contents: (1) "Introduction to restorative dental materials," (2) "Properties of materials," (3) "Preventive dental materials," (4) "Direct esthetic restorative materials," (5) "Dental amalgam," (6) "Finishing, polishing, and cleansing materials," (7) "Cements," (8) "Impression materials," (9) "Model and die materials," (10) "Waxes," (11) "Casting alloys, wrought alloys, and solders," (12) "Casting and soldering," (13) "Polymers in prosthodontics," (14) "Dental ceramics," (15) "Dental implants."

This revised edition describes materials commonly used by dentists, dental hygienists, and dental assistants. Contains photographs, drawings, tables, and glossary. Associated website, intended for students and instructors, provides instructional video

clips and various other aids useful in teaching and learning. Intended as an introductory text but also useful as a reference tool. Also available as an e-book.

804 Dental terminology. 3rd ed.
Charline M. Dofka. Clifton Park, N.Y.: Delmar, Cengage Learning, 2013. xvi, 464 p., ill (chiefly col.)
ISBN 9781133019718
617.60014   RK28.D64
First ed., 2000; 2nd ed., 2007.

Contents: ch. 1, "Introduction to dental terminology"; ch. 2, "Anatomy and oral structures"; ch. 3, "Tooth origin and formation"; ch. 4, "Practice and facility setups"; ch. 5, "Infection control"; ch. 6, "Emergency care"; ch. 7, "Examination and prevention"; ch. 8, "Pain management and pharmacology"; ch. 9, "Radiography"; ch. 10, "Tooth restorations"; ch. 11, "Cosmetic dentistry"; ch. 12, "Prosthodontics"; ch. 13, "Endodontics"; ch. 14, "Oral and maxillofacial surgery"; ch. 15, "Orthodontics"; ch. 16, "Periodontics"; ch. 17, "Pediatric dentistry"; ch. 18, "Dental laboratory procedures"; ch. 19, "Business procedures." Appendixes :(A) Word elements ; (B) Answers to chapter 1 exercises; Glossary; Glossary of acronyms; Glossary of insurance terms. Index.

This revised edition contains common dental terms used in dental practice and in the various dental specialties. Includes pronunciations guide.

805 Drug information handbook. North American ed. Charles F. Lacy, Laura Armstron, Morton Goldman, Leonard Lance, Lexi-Comp, Inc., American Pharmaceutical Association. Hudson, Ohio; Washington: Lexi-Comp, Inc.; American Pharmaceutical Association, 1994–
615 1533-4511   RM301.12.D783
Publ. in cooperation with the Amer. Pharmacists Assoc. (APhA).

First ed., 1993/94. Available in North Amer. and internat. editions. Description based on 19th ed., 2010. Subtitle: A comprehensive resource for all clinicians and healthcare professionals. The 22nd ed.(2013) is the most recent edition available.

(Lexi-Comp's clinical reference library).

Concise, comprehensive, and user-friendly drug reference. Alphabetical listing of drug monographs, with new drugs and updates to monographs since the last edition. Includes detailed information in consistent format, such as dosage, drug interactions, adverse reactions (by occurrence, overdose, and toxicology), etc., with warnings highlighted. Appendix. Pharmacologic category index. For clinicians and healthcare professionals.

Several other comprehensive print pharmacology handbooks, also published by Lexi-Comp and frequently updated, include *Anesthesiology and critical care drug handbook* (1999– ; 10th ed., 2011); *Drug information handbook for nursing* (1998-; 14th ed., 2012); *Drug information handbook for advanced practice nursing* (1990– , 11th ed., 2010); *Drug information handbook for dentistry* (1996- ; 18th ed., 2012); *Drug information handbook for oncology* (2000- ; 11th ed., 2013); *Drug information handbook for psychiatry: A comprehensive reference of psychotropic, nonpsychotropic, and herbal agents* (1999- ; 7th ed., 2009); *Drug information handbook for the allied health professional* (1995- ; 12th ed., 2005); *Drug information handbook with international trade names index* (21st ed., 2012); *Geriatric dosage handbook* (1993- ; 18th ed., 2012); *Infectious diseases handbook: Including antimicrobial therapy & diagnostic test/procedures* (1994- ; 6th ed., 2006); *Natural therapeutics pocket guide* (2000- , 2nd ed., 2003); *Pediatric dosage handbook* (1992- ; 18th ed., 2011); and *Pharmacogenomics handbook* (2003- ; 2nd ed., 2006). Also available online as pt. of Lexi-Comp Online™ (http://webstore.lexi.com/Store/ONLINE).

806 Law and risk management in dental practice. Burton R. Pollack. Chicago: Quintessence Publ. Co., 2002. xii, 284 p. ISBN 0867154160
617.6/0068   RK58.P65

Contents: (1) Introduction to the judicial system of the United States; (2)The regulation of dental practice; (3) The dentist-patient relationship: contract law; (4) Is it negligence, malpractice, or breach of contract?; (5) Statute of limitations and statute of repose: how long the patient has to sue; (6) Experts and the standards of care; (7) Vicarious liability and respondeat superior; (8) Does the dentist have to treat?; (9) Consent, informed consent, and informed refusal; (10) Abandonment and dismissal of a patient; (11) Taking the medical-dental history; (12) Patient records; (13) Trial of a suit in malpractice: res ipsa loquitur, hearsay evidence, and

contributory negligence; (14) What to do and what not to do if you are sued; (15) Dentist as witness; (16) Reports on jury trials and disciplinary proceedings; (17) Risk management in dental practice; (18) Office audit risk assessment for the general dentist; (19) Insuring a dental practice; Appendix: Legal terms with dental applications.

Information on the U.S. judicial system and basic legal information for dental professionals. Another legal resource, *Law, liability, and ethics for medical office professionals* provides additional information.

807 Mosby's dental drug reference. Tommy W. Gage, Frieda Atherton Pickett. St. Louis: Mosby, 1994–
615.10246176   RK701.M58

Description based on 9th ed., 2010; 10th ed., 2012, is available both in print and also as en e-book.

Contents: Therapeutic management of common oral lesions; Medically compromised patients; Individual drug monographs; Appendixes: (A) Abbreviations; (B) Aesthetics; (C) Combination drugs by trade names; (D) Controlled substances chart; (E) Disorders and conditions; (F) Drugs associated with dry mouth; (G) Drugs that affect taste; (H) Complementary and alternative medications and dietary supplements; (I) Pregnancy and pediatrics; (J) Preventing medication errors and improving medication safety; (K) Oral contraceptives; Generic and trade name index.

Alphabetical arrangement of drugs that dental patients may be taking, listed by generic name and indexed by brand name, with drug monograph information presented in a consistent format. Provides information on side effects, precautions, contraindications, and drug interactions. Also includes alternative therapies. Therapeutic and pharmacologic index. Accompanied by CD-ROM that contains color images of conditions resulting from drugs patients are taking, and also customizable patient handouts. The 9th ed. includes 33 new drugs approved by the FDA since the last edition. Intended for dental professionals, but also useful for health consumers. Ready-reference appendixes provide additional drug-related information. Also available as an e-book.

808 Woelfel's dental anatomy. 8th ed. Rickne C. Scheid, Julian B. Woelfel.

Philadelphia: Wolters Kluwer/Lippincott Williams & Wilkins Health, 2012. viii, 504 p., col. ill. ISBN 9781608317462

611/.314   QM311.W64

Title varies: 1st ed., 1974: *An outline for dental anatomy*, Dorothy Permar; 2nd ed., 1979: *Permar's outline for dental anatomy*; 3rd ed., 1984: *Dental anatomy and its correlation with dental health service*, Julian B. Woelfel and Dorothy Permar; 6th ed., 2002: *Dental anatomy: Its relevance to dentistry*; 7th ed., 2007: *Woelfel's dental anatomy*.

While intended as a study guide for dental, dental hygiene and dental assisting students, it can also serve as a reference book for dental anatomy and dental terminology. Includes an overview of teeth, description of each adult tooth, roots, root morphology, normal oral structures, and also dental anomalies. Illustrated with drawings, photographs, and charts. Includes techniques to draw, sketch, and carve teeth. Index. A companion website offers various resources for both students and instructors.

Histories

809 American Dental Association.
http://www.ada.org/. American Dental Association. Chicago: American Dental Association. 1995– 617.6

Official website of the American Dental Association (ADA), founded in 1859.

Provides information for dental professionals concerning education and testing, practice management, and patient care. Includes a list of all accredited dental programs in the U.S. (http://www.ada.org/103.aspx) and Canada, and links to national dental organizations. Resources for consumers include, for example, "Oral Health Topics A–Z" (http://www.ada.org/286.aspx), "Find a dentist" (http://www.mouthhealthy.org/en/find-a-dentist.aspx), and other helpful resources. Also includes "ADA timeline" (http://www.ada.org/adatimeline.aspx), a list of presidents (1860 to the present), and links to various other dental history resources. Some of the resources are restricted to ADA members.

Another ADA web resource, ADA Center for Evidence-Based Dentistry™ http://ebd.ada.org/about.aspx is a useful resource for clinicians to identify systematic reviews and critical summaries. It also

provides links to further resources and educational tutorials as well as links to patient resources.

The American Academy of Pediatric Dentistry (AAPD) http://www.aapd.org/ provides a variety of dental health resources, policies & guidelines, etc.

810 The American dentist: A pictorial history with a presentation of early dental photography in America.
Richard A. Glenner, Audrey B. Davis, Stanley B. Burns. Missoula, Mont.: Pictorial Histories Publ. Co., 1990. viii, 194 p., ill. ISBN 0929521056

MLCM9301439(R)

History of American dentistry as represented by dental photography, considered an important part of the development of dentistry as a "scientifically based practice with specific educational standards . . . intended to introduce the reader to major components of a dentist's career and how it grew out of American society, as well as contributing to this society over the past century and a half."— *Pref.* Twenty-one chapters, including early dental equipment, dental education in America, women becoming dentists, military dentistry in World War I and World War II, and more. Notes and index.

811 Dentistry: An illustrated history.
Malvin E. Ring. New York; St. Louis: Abrams; C.V. Mosby, 1985. 12, 319 p., ill., ports. (some col.) ISBN 0810911000

617.6009   RK29.R54

Contents: (I) The primitive world; (II) The ancient Near East; (III) The classical world; (IV) The early Middle Ages; (V) The Islamic world; (VI) The Far East; (VII) The late Middle Ages in Western Europe; (VIII) The Renaissance; (IX) The 17th century in Europe; (X) The 18th century in Europe; (XI) America: from the earliest times to the mid-19th century; (XII) The late 19th century in the U.S. and Europe; (XIII) The 20th century. Overview of the history of dentistry, from the earliest times to the 20th century. Illustrations, bibliography, and index.

812 A history of dentistry from the most ancient times until the end of the eighteenth century. Vincenzo Guerini, National Dental Association. Philadelphia; New York: Lea & Febiger,

1909. x, [17]–355 p., illus., plates, ports., facsims.

RK29.G8

Frequently reprinted. Published under the auspices of the National Dental Assoc. of the United States of America. A classic in this field, well documented by footnotes to sources. Includes name and subject index. Also available as an e-book.

Other resource in this area are, for example, *History of dentistry: A practical treatise for the use of dental students and practitioners* by Taylor and *An introduction to the history of dentistry: With medical & dental chronology & bibliographic data.*

813 **History of periodontology.** Fermin A. Carranza, Gerald Shklar. Chicago: Quintessence Publ., 2003. ix, 214 p., ill. ISBN 0867154241

617.6/32   RK361.C373

Contents: pt. I, The prehistoric era and early civilizations; pt. II, Classical and medieval ages; pt. III, The modern era; pt. IV, The nineteenth century; pt. V, The twentieth century. Covers the history of periodontology from prehistoric times to the present. Includes the important contributions from the basic biological and medical sciences and also from technology. Describes the accomplishments of many individuals, past and present, and their contributions to the development of the specialty of periodontics. Illustrations, index of persons, and subject index.

814 **An introduction to the history of dentistry: With medical & dental chronology & bibliographic data.** Bernhard Wolf Weinberger. St. Louis: C.V. Mosby Co., 1948. 2 v., ill., ports., facsims.

617.609   RK29.W39

Vol. 2 has title: *An introduction to the history of dentistry in America.* Describes the origin, evolution, and growth of knowledge of dentistry through the 19th century; presents the history of dentistry "graphically and biographically" (*Pref.*). Includes bibliography of important literature in the history of dentistry; chronology of important related events in history, medicine, and dentistry. Index of personal names; subject index. Based in part on the author's earlier work, *Orthodontics: an historical review of its origin and evolution* by Weinberger. Vol 2 available as an e-book through Hathi Trust.

815 **A sourcebook of dental medicine: Being a documentary history of dentistry and stomatology from the earliest times to the middle of the twentieth century.** Gerald Shklar, David A. Chernin. Waban, Mass.: Maro Publ., 2002. xxi, 839 p., ill. 0971748004

(Dental classics in perspective; 3) Contents: pt. I, Knowledge of dental medicine in primitive times and early ages of civilization (seven chapters); pt. II, The classical and middle ages—ancient and medieval times (four chapters); pt. III, The Renaissance and its influence (seven chapters); pt. IV, The modern era (four chapters). This documentary history presents, in English translation, the major existing primary sources and original texts dealing with tooth and oral diseases. Presented in 22 chapters, starting with prehistoric times and ending with the 20th century. Each chapter begins with a introductory description of the particular era. Includes bibliographical references and indexes.

Biography

816 **African American firsts in science and technology.** Raymond B. Webster. Detroit: Gale Group, 1999. xiii, 461 p., ill. ISBN 0787638765

508.996073   Q141.W43

Chronology of firsts in various fields: Agriculture and Everyday Life, Dentistry and Nursing, Life Science, Math and Engineering, Medicine, Physical Science, and Transportation. Includes bibliography, index by year, occupational index, general index, and citations for first achievents. Over 1200 entries, 100 illustrations.

Atlases

817 **Netter's head and neck anatomy for dentistry. 2nd ed.** Neil Scott Norton, Frank H. Netter. Philadelphia: Elsevier/ Saunders, 2012. xii, 659 p., ill. (chiefly col.) ISBN 9781437726633

611/.91   RK280

First ed., 2007.

Contents: ch.1, Development of the head and neck; ch. 2, Osteology; ch. 3, Basic neuroanatomy and cranial nerves; ch. 4, The neck; ch. 5, Scalp and muscles of facial expression; ch. 6, Parotid bed and gland; ch. 7, Temporal and infratemporal fossae; ch. 8, Muscles of mastication; ch. 9, Temporomandibular joint; ch. 10, Pterygopalatine fossa; ch. 11, Nose and nasal cavity; ch. 12, Paranasal sinuses; ch. 13, Oral cavity; ch. 14, Tongue; ch. 15, Pharynx; ch. 16, Larynx; ch. 17. Cervical fascia; ch. 18, Ear; ch. 19, Eye and orbit; ch. 20, Autonomics of the head and neck; ch. 21, Intraoral injections; ch. 22, Introduction to the upper limb, back, thorax, and abdomen. Appx. A: Questions and answers; Appx. B: Lymphatics. Index

Contains important images from the Netter collection and also new art by a team of medical illustrators to complement the anatomical illustrations of Dr. Frank H. Netter. Includes many clinical images, also radiographic images, and concise factual information, mostly in outline and tabular format, with a clinical correlation section at the end of each chapter. Intended "for those in all stages of the dental profession."—*Pref.* Useful for preparation for the national boards for dental students, dental hygiene students, and also for medical students. Also available as an e-book.

Internet resources

818 American Dental Association.
http://www.ada.org/. American Dental Association. Chicago: American Dental Association. 1995– 617.6

Official website of the American Dental Association (ADA), founded in 1859.

Provides information for dental professionals concerning education and testing, practice management, and patient care. Includes a list of all accredited dental programs in the U.S. (http://www.ada.org/103.aspx) and Canada, and links to national dental organizations. Resources for consumers include, for example, "Oral Health Topics A–Z" (http://www.ada.org/286.aspx), "Find a dentist" (http://www.mouthhealthy.org/en/find-a-dentist.aspx), and other helpful resources. Also includes "ADA timeline" (http://www.ada.org/adatimeline.aspx), a list of presidents (1860 to the present), and links to various other dental history resources. Some of the resources are restricted to ADA members.

Another ADA web resource, ADA Center for Evidence-Based Dentistry™ http://ebd.ada.org/about.aspx is a useful resource for clinicians to identify systematic reviews and critical summaries. It also provides links to further resources and educational tutorials as well as links to patient resources.

The American Academy of Pediatric Dentistry (AAPD) http://www.aapd.org/ provides a variety of dental health resources, policies & guidelines, etc.

819 Dental health (MedlinePlus). http://www.nlm.nih.gov/medlineplus/dentalhealth.html. National Library of Medicine (U.S.), National Institutes of Health (U.S.). Bethesda, Md.: U.S. National Library of Medicine, National Institutes of Health, Dept. of Health and Human Services. 2000?–

A Health Topic within MedlinePlus. Collection of links to information from government agencies and professional associations and organizations, with access to selected oral health resources. Provides basic information, research findings, a "reference shelf" with dental dictionaries/glossaries, directories, organizations, statistics, etc.

820 General Dental Council. http://www.gdc-uk.org/. General Dental Council. London: General Dental Council. 2005– (?)

General Dental Council (GDC) is a regulatory body which provides patient protection and maintains statutory responsibilities for education and professional conduct and development of the dentists and dental auxiliaries in the U.K. Provides extensive web-based information and links for the public, including news, publications, and events, with an A–Z index and a list of links, including professional organizations (e.g., link to the British Dental Association (BDA) "Find a Dentist" http://www.bda-findadentist.org.uk/), dental education, U.K. regulatory bodies, various government health departments, and information for patients. Makes available, for example, "Dentists Register or Dental Care Professionals Register" database (http://www.gdc-uk.org/Pages/SearchRegisters.aspx) to check if a dentist, dental hygienist, or dental therapist is registered to practice in the U.K. *The dentists register* is available as a print resource, 1879 to the present.

821 MedEdPORTAL. https://www.meded
portal.org/. Association of American
Medical Colleges. Washington:
Association of American Medical
Colleges. 2006–

MedEdPORTAL® is a project by the Association of American Medical Colleges (AAMC), in partnership with the American Dental Education Association (ADEA) and other organizations, that provides free access to peer-reviewed teaching resources used in medical education (e.g., tutorials, virtual patients, simulation cases, lab guides, videos, podcasts, assessment tools, etc.). Designed to help faculty publish and share teaching resources. MedEdPORTAL staff review submissions for relevance and appropriateness before they are published on the site. Information about copyright is provided. Further details are provided at https://www.mededportal.org/about, including a video with an overview of MedEdPORTAL.

MedEdPORTAL publications are cataloged using medical subject headings (MeSH: Medical subject headings, 858). To locate these and other resources, MedEdPORTAL can be browsed by discipline (list of subject areas and number of available resources within each category). Also searchable by keyword.

The freely accessible *Directory & repository of educational assessment measures (DREAM)* (http://www.mededportal.org/dream), a collection of tested health professions assessment measures, is part of MedEdPORTAL, including "a copy of the assessment instrument itself and a peer-reviewed critical analysis of the literature surrounding the use of the instrument."—*Publ. description.*

AAMC also participates in Health education assets library (HEAL), a repository of health sciences images, videos, and audio files from different collections.

5 *Health Care*

822 Dictionary of health economics and finance. David E. Marcinko, Hope R. Hetico. New York: Springer Publ., 2006. 436 p. ISBN 0826102549

338.47362103   RA410.A3D53

Definitions, abbreviations and acronyms, and eponyms of medical economics and health care sector terminology. Bibliography. A similar title is *The dictionary of health economics*.

823 Health services research and public health information programs. http://www.nlm.nih.gov/hsrph.html. National Library of Medicine (U.S.). Bethesda, Md.: National Library of Medicine, U.S. National Institutes of Health, Dept. of Health and Human Services

Lists resources from multiple National Library of Medicine (NLM) programs, including collaborative projects (e.g., HSR information central), links to several databases, e.g., HSRProj (Health Services Research Projects in Progress), HSRR (Health Services and Sciences Research Resources), Health Services/Technology Assessment Text (HSTAT), American Indian and Asian American Health, and others. Provides preformulated PubMed search filters and search strategies. Its outreach and training resources, with links to their full text, include "Finding and using health statistics," "Health economics: information resources," Health technology assessment

101 (HTA 101), "Public health information and data tutorial," publications, and informatics. Also provides access various online publications, informatics resources, and links to additional information and related products.

824 Introduction to health services. 7th ed. Stephen J. Williams, Paul R. Torrens. Clifton Park, N.Y.: Thomson Delmar Learning, 2008. vii, 384 p., ill. (some color). ISBN 9781418012892

362.10973   RA395.A3I495

First ed., 1980; 6th ed., 2001.

Contents: Understanding health systems: The organization of health care in the United States; Technology in the U.S. health care system; Population and disease patterns and trends; Financing health systems; Private health insurance and managed care; Public health: Joint public-private responsibility in an era of new threats; Ambulatory health care services and organizations; Hospitals and health systems; The continuum of long-term care; Mental and behavioral health services; The pharmaceutical industry; Health care professionals; Understanding health policy; The quality of health care; Ethical issues in public health and health services; The future of health services.

This revised edition "builds on a well-established format written by nationally recognized authors with updated research and statistics."—*Publ. notes*

Provides a description of the structure and function of the U.S. healthcare system, including the healthcare industry and healthcare provider organizations. Includes historical and current perspectives and recent changes in healthcare delivery. Also available as an e-book.

Guides

825   **A brief guide to the U.S. health care delivery system: Facts, definitions, and statistics. 2nd ed.** Sara A. Beazley. Chicago: AHA Press/Health Forum, 2010. xi, 178 p., ill. ISBN 9781556483684

362.1   RA395.A3B75

Contents: ch. 1, Patient care; ch. 2, Caregivers; ch. 3, Facilities; ch. 4, Finance; ch. 5, Government and other types of oversight. "Organized for quick answers and easy understanding"—Publ. notes.

This rev. ed. presents an overview of the U.S. healthcare system, the practice of healthcare management, and delivery of healthcare. Contains industry data and research findings and selected trends in medical practice. Glossary, bibliographical references, and index.

826   **Health care almanac: Every person's guide to the thoughtful and practical sides of medicine. 2nd ed.** Lorri A. Zipperer, American Medical Association. Chicago, Ill.: American Medical Association, 1998. xiv, 546 p. ISBN 0899709001

362.1/0973/03   R104.H43

First ed. (1993) had title: *The healthcare resource and reference guide;* rev. 1995 ed. had title: *Health care almanac: a resource guide to the medical field.* Addresses common queries by physicians and patients, including health and medical practice-related issues. In three sections: (1) Dictionary-style directory arranged alphabetically by subject, with the names of organizations that may be able to provide information on specific subjects; (2) Outlines major administrative units of the American Medical Association (AMA), with an historical overview since 1846;(3) Tools to help navigate the almanac: listing of sources and index which is also intended to serve cross-referencing

needs. Includes "Principles of Medical Ethics," "The Hippocratic Oath," and "Patient Bill of Rights." Provides information and glossaries on managed care, tort reform, Medicare, background on terminal care and advanced directives and end-of-life issues, patient safety, home health care, etc. This print resource can be supplemented with web-based, possibly more up-to-date information found on the AMA website (American Medical Association [homepage]) with its professional resources section, including online ethics resources; DoctorFinder; and other links.

827   **Health care resources on the Internet: A guide for librarians and health care consumers.** M. Sandra Wood. New York: Haworth Information Press, 2000. xxi, 205 p. ISBN 0789006324

025.0661   R119.9.H39

Contents: ch. 1, Use of the Internet at the reference desk (Nancy Calabretta); ch. 2, Natural language and beyond: tips for search services (Eric P. Delozier); ch. 3, Megasites for health care information (Cindy A. Gruwell, Scott Marsalis); ch. 4, MEDLINE on the Internet (Helen-Ann Brown, Valerie G. Rankow); ch. 5, Searching the Internet for diseases (Alexa Mayo, Cynthia R. Phyillaier); ch. 6, Consumer health information on the Internet (Janet M. Coggan); ch. 7, Alternative medicine on the Net (Suzanne M. Shultz, Nancy I. Henry, Esther Y. Dell); ch. 8, Government resources on the Net (Nancy J. Allee); Health-related statistical information on the Net (Dawn M. Littleton, Kathryn Robbins); ch. 10, Electronic journals on the Internet (Virginia A. Lingle); ch. 11, Searching international medical resources on the World Wide Web (Jeri Ann Risin). Provides a list of of selected websites and also general information on developing skills and techniques for Internet searching for health-related information, including evidence-based medicine. Includes a "Comparative Chart of MEDLINE Searching Systems." A practical resource, useful for librarians, health care professionals, and general readers.

Finding and using health and medical information on the Internet by Sue Welsh et al. and Sydney S. Chellen's *Essential guide to the Internet for health professionals* are other guides on how to locate biomedical information effectively. Even though some of the content in these three resources needs updating, they nevertheless remain useful guides.

828   The new Blackwell companion to medical sociology. William C. Cockerham. Malden, Mass.: Wiley-Blackwell, 2010. xvii, 596 p., ill. ISBN 9781405188685

362.1/042   RA418

Global and comprehensive survey of the emerging field of medical sociology, or the study of the impact of cultural constructs on medical understanding and practice. Provides a definition of the field and its importance for health care research. This new edition offers 24 articles grouped around major themes such as Health and Social Inequalities, Health and Social Relationships, Health and Disease, and Health Care Delivery. The 2001 edition, *The Blackwell companion to medical sociology* by the same author, remains useful for the 17 summaries of regional or national health care practices around the world. Each chapter has bibliographical references. Indexes by author and subject. Available as an e-book.

Bibliography

829   American health care in transition: A guide to the literature. Barbara A. Haley, Brian Deevey. Westport, Conn.: Greenwood Press, 1997. xii, 336 p. ISBN 0313273235

362.1/0973   RA395.A3H3426

(Bibliographies and indexes in medical studies ; no. 14). This annotated bibliography includes periodical articles and government publications, covering the literature 1979–1996. Index.

830   The health care crisis in the United States: A bibliography. Joan Nordquist. Santa Cruz, Calif.: Reference and Research Services, 1997. 72 p. ISBN 0937855901

016.3621/0973   Z6675.E2N67;
                                          RA395.A3

(Contemporary social issues ; no. 46)

Entries are organized under broad topics and covers areas such as medical care, cost of medical care, right to health care, and delivery of health care. Provides a good starting point for further research. Includes books, journals, dissertations, congressional hearings, and other publications. HealthSTAR (Ovid, 103), MEDLINE®/PubMed®, NLM gateway, and

CINAHL (101), for example, could be used to update information found in this bibliography.

831   Health services research methodology core library recommendations, 2007. http://www.nlm.nih.gov/nichsr/corelib/hsrmethods.html. AcademyHealth, National Library of Medicine (U.S.). Bethesda, Md.: National Library of Medicine. 2007

Produced by AcademyHealth; National Library of Medicine (NLM); National Information Center on Health Services Research and Health Care (NICHSR). Although dated 2007, website is reviewed and updated regularly.

List of books, journals, bibliographic databases, websites, and other media; useful for collection development librarians and researchers interested in health services research methods. Lists both "core" materials and "desired" materials in areas such as general health policy, health economics, health services research, public health, and several others. The NICHSR website (http://www.nlm.nih.gov/nichsr/outreach.html) lists links to several other recommended lists, including Health economics core library recommendations (2011), Health outcomes core library recommendations (2011), Health policy core library recommendations 2011 (also called Core health policy library recommendations), and other information.

832   Health services technology assessment texts (HSTAT). http://hstat.nlm.nih.gov. National Library of Medicine (U.S.). Bethesda, Md.: National Library of Medicine (U.S.), National Institutes of Health, Dept. of Health and Human Services. 1994?–

Coordinated by the National Library of Medicine's National Information Center on Health Services Research and Health Care Technology (NICHSR). Part of the "NCBI Bookshelf" (http://www.ncbi.nlm.nih.gov/books).

Searchable collection of full-text documents containing results of health services research, evidence reports and technology assessments, consensus conference reports, clinical practice guidelines (e.g., HIV/AIDS approved guidelines and information), reports of the Surgeon General, and other health information in support of health care decision making. Intended for health care providers, health service researchers, policymakers, payers, consumers, and information professionals. Further details in the *HSTAT fact sheet* (http://www.nlm.nih.gov/pubs/factsheets/hstat.html).

833 Introduction to health services research. http://www.nlm.nih.gov/ nichsr/ihcm/index.html. National Library of Medicine (U.S.). Bethesda, Md.: National Library of Medicine. 2007–

Produced by National Information Center on Health Services Research (NICHSR) of the National Library of Medicine (NLM).

Contents: Introduction and purpose; Course objectives; Modules: (1) What Is health services sesearch? (HSR); (2) Brief history of health services research and key projects and milestones; (3) Selected players (federal and private); (4) Search the literature of HSR: Databases; (5) Quality filtering and evidence-based medicine and health; (6) Basic components of a study; (7) Librarians' role in health services research; Selected HSR Internet sites; Essential concepts; Bibliography; Glossaries; Review sections.

Provides extensive information on health services issues, health services research, study design, bibliography of articles and books, databases, and literature analysis.

834 Medical humanities dissertations. http://www.hsls.pitt.edu/histmed/ dissertations/. Jonathon Erlen, University of Pittsburgh Health Sciences Library System. Pittsburgh: Health Sciences Library, University of Pittsburgh Medical Center. 2001–

Provides a monthly current awareness service for selected recent medical dissertations and theses. Arranged by topics, currently covers the following areas: AIDS (social and historical contexts); alternative medicine (social and historical contexts); art and medicine; biomedical ethics; history of medicine prior to 1800; history of medicine and health care; history of science and technology; literature/theater and medicine; nursing history; pharmacy/pharmacology and history; philosophy and medicine; psychiatry/ psychology and history; public health/international health; religion and medicine; women's health and history. To view complete citations, abstracts, and full-text of dissertations requires a subscription to Proquest dissertations and theses (PQDT).

835 U.S. health law and policy, 2001: A guide to the current literature. Donald H. Caldwell, American Health Lawyers Association. San Francisco; Chicago: Jossey-Bass; Health Forum, 2001. xxi, 593 p. ISBN 0787955043
016.34473/041   KF3821.A1C35

Earlier edition had title: *U.S. health law and policy 1999: A guide to the current literature,* 1998.

Contents: pt. 1, Medical facilities and organizations; pt. 2, Regulatory matters; pt. 3, Licensure, liability, and labor issues; pt. 4, Selected health care policy topics. Appendixes: (A) Health law periodicals, digests, and newsletters; (B) Reference sources and government serials; (C) Computer databases and Internet sites; (D) State-by-state synopsis of selected statutes of limitation laws; (E) Table of acronyms and abbreviations; (F) Glossary; (G) Relevant federal agencies; (H) Selected nongovernmental agencies; (I) State laws governing medical records; (J) Health Care Financing Administration regional offices. Subject, name, title indexes.

This revised edition is a comprehensive annotated bibliographic guide to the healthcare law and policy literature and related legal issues. Sources are books, journals, government documents, and websites. Entries provide publication information and a brief synopsis of the content of the citation. A future edition is planned.

Indexes; Abstract journals; Databases

836 AgeLine. http://www.ebscohost.com/ academic/ageline. EBSCO Publishing (Firm), AARP (Organization). Washington; Ipswich, Mass.: AARP; EBSCO Pub. 2004–
                                    HQ1061

Previously produced as a free database by the American Association of Retired Persons (AARP), now available via subscription through EBSCO.

A comprehensive online index with abstracts, providing coverage of the scholarly and professional literature on aging and age-related matters, including the delivery of health care to the older population and its costs, and various public policy issues.

Covers 1978 to the present, with selected coverage from 1966–77. Includes journal and magazine articles, books & book chapters, dissertations, videos, and selected grey literature. Cross-searchable with other subscribed EBSCO databases, with basic and advanced search options. Publications indexed in this database use *Thesaurus of aging terminology*, a controlled vocabulary of subject terms, currently in its 8th ed. For researchers at institutions with gerontology/aging and public policy programs and also for consumers. Useful for health professionals, psychologists, social workers, sociologists and other researchers, and also consumers.

837   CINAHL. http://www.ebscohost.com/
cinahl/. Cinahl Information Systems,
EBSCO. Ipswich, Mass.: EBSCO. 1982–

CINAHL® [database]. Title varies. Online version: 1984–1992 (with coverage 1982–), publ. by Cinahl Information Systems; 1993– , publ. jointly by EBSCO and Cinahl Information Systems. Also available in different enhanced versions: CINAHL® with Full Text, CINAHL® Plus™, and CINAHL® Plus with Full Text. Comparisons of the different versions at http://www.ebscohost.com/uploads/thisTopic-dbTopic-592.pdf.

Print version: 1956–76 entitled: *Cumulative index to nursing and allied health literature*; 1977– *Cumulative index to nursing and allied health literature*® (continues to be published in print).

Authoritative database for the professional literature of nursing and allied health. Provides references to journal articles, books, book chapters, pamphlets, audiovisual materials, dissertations, educational software, selected conference proceedings, standards of professional practice, and more. Some full-text material is included. Currently indexes a large number of journals, as well as publications from the American Nurses' Association and the National League for Nursing. Allows for application of specific interest category filter, e.g., evidence-based practice, informatics, patient safety, public health, women's health, and others. Subject access is provided by *CINAHL . . . subject heading list: Alphabetic list, tree structures, permuted list*. Complements *International nursing index*, publ. 1966–2000.

838   The Cochrane Library. http://www
.thecochranelibrary.com/. Cochrane

Collaboration. Hoboken, N.J.: Wiley Interscience. 1996–

1465-1858   R723.7

Acronyms: Evidence-based medicine (EBM); Evidence-based health care (EBHC).

Imprint varies: 1996–2003, Update Software Ltd., Oxford, U.K.; publ. by Wiley Interscience 2004–. Produced by contributors to the Cochrane Collaboration (founded in 1993 and named after the British epidemiologist, Archie Cochrane) and consists of a group of experts in the various clinical specialties who apply EBM criteria to the review and selection of studies, perform meta-analyses, and then write detailed topical reviews.

The Cochrane Library consists of several online databases that provide systematic reviews, meta-analyses of the literature, and randomized clinical trials: Cochrane database of systematic reviews (CDSR)—Cochrane reviews and protocols; Database of abstracts of reviews of effectiveness (DARE)—Other Reviews; Cochrane central register of controlled trials (CENTRAL)—Clinical trials; Cochrane methodology register (CMR)—Methods studies; Health technology assessment database (HT)—Health technology; and NHS economic evaluation database (NHSEED).

The major product of the Cochrane Collaboration is the *Cochrane database of systematic reviews*, prepared mostly by healthcare professionals who work as volunteers in one of the many Cochrane Review Groups. Editorial teams oversee the preparation and updating of the reviews and applying quality standards. Provides access to full-text articles that review the effects of health care.

Other examples of EBM and EBHC resources include ACP journal club and ACP PIER (American College of Physicians), Clinical evidence (BMJ), DynaMed (EBSCO), Evidence matters, PubMed/PubMed clinical queries (systematic reviews and meta-analyses) (http://www.ncbi.nlm.nih.gov/pubmed/clinical), Turning research into practice (TRIP) database, Health services technology assessment text (HSTAT), NLM gateway, National guideline clearinghouse, and others.

Many websites from various organizations and universities provide EBM and EBHC-related subject guides, e.g., EBM Resource Center, New York Academy of Medicine (http://www.ebmny.org/), "Evidence-based practice" subject guide (Hardin Library for the Health Sciences, The University of

Iowa, http://guides.lib.uiowa.edu/ebp), "Evidence based medicine," Johns Hopkins University (http://www.hopkinsmedicine.org/gim/research/method/ebm.html), and many others.

Print EBM/EBHC resources are, for example, *Evidence-based medicine: How to practice and teach EBM* and *Clinical epidemiology: How to do clinical practice research.*

839 HealthSTAR (Ovid). http://www.ovid
.com/site/products/ovidguide/hstrdb.
htm. National Library of Medicine (U.S.).
Sandy, Utah: Ovid Technologies. 2000–
Ovid HealthSTAR (HSTR); HealthSTAR (Health Services Technology, Administration, and Research).

"Comprised of data from the National Library of Medicine's (NLM) MEDLINE and former Health-STAR (103) databases . . . contains citations to the published literature on health services, technology, administration, and research. It focuses on both the clinical and non-clinical aspects of health care delivery. . . . Offered by Ovid as a continuation of NLM's now-defunct HealthSTAR database. Retains all existing backfile citations and is updated with new journal citations culled from MEDLINE. Contains citations and abstracts (when available) to journal articles, monographs, technical reports, meeting abstracts and papers, book chapters, government documents, and newspaper articles from 1975 to the present." —*Publ. notes.* A list of NLM's retired databases, including the original Health-STAR database, can be found at http://www.nlm
.nih.gov/services/pastdatabases.html.

Relevant content on health services research, health technology, health administration, health policy, health economics, etc., can also be found in MEDLINE®/PubMed®, NLM® Gateway, and also CINAHL® (101).

**840 Hospital and health administration
index.** American Hospital Association.,
American Hospital Association.; Resource
Center., National Library of Medicine
(U.S.). Chicago: American Hospital
Association, 1995–1999
016.36211 1077-1719   Z6675.H75H67;
RA963
1945–54, *Index of current hospital literature;*
1955–57, *Hospital periodical literature index;*
1957–94, *Hospital literature index,* cumulated

at five-year intervals for the 1945–77 volumes as *Cumulative index of hospital literature.* Discontinued; last published in 1999. Described as a "primary guide to literature on hospital and other health care facility administration, including multi-institutional systems, health policy and planning, and the administrative aspects of health care delivery . . . Special emphasis is given to the theory of health care systems in general; health care in industrialized countries, primarily in the United States; and provision of health care both inside and outside of health care facilities" (*Introd.*). A separate online database, HealthSTAR (Health Services Technology, Administration, and Research) for this literature, previously maintained by NLM, is no longer available (cf. list of NLM's retired databases at http://www.nlm.nih.gov/services/pastdatabases.html). Relevant content is available via MEDLINE/PubMed or HealthSTAR (Ovid, 103), and also CINAHL (101)

841 PubMed. http://www.ncbi.nlm.nih.
gov/pubmed. U.S. National Center for
Biotechnology Information, National
Library of Medicine, National Institutes
of Health. Bethesda, Md.: U.S. National
Center for Biotechnology Information.
1996–
PubMed®, developed and maintained by the National Center for Biotechnology Information (NCBI) at the National Library of Medicine® (NLM). Provides a search interface for more than 20 million bibliographic citations and abstracts in the fields of medicine, nursing, dentistry, veterinary medicine, health care systems, and preclinical sciences. It provides access to articles indexed for MEDLINE® and for selected life sciences journals. PubMed subsets found under the "Limits" tab are: MEDLINE and PubMed central®, several journal groups (i.e., core clinical journals, dental journals, and nursing journals), and topical subsets (AIDS, bioethics, cancer, complementary medicine, dietary supplements, history of medicine, space life sciences, systematic reviews, toxicology, and veterinary science). "Linkout" provides access to full-text articles.

For detailed information see the PubMed fact sheet at http://www.nlm.nih.gov/pubs/factsheets/pubmed.html and also MEDLINE®/PubMed® resources guide (http://www.nlm.nih.gov/bsd/pmresources.html)

which provides detailed information about MEDLINE data and searching PubMed.

Information regarding the mobile version of this resource is part of NLM's Gallery of mobile apps and sites.

Encyclopedias

842   Encyclopedia of cancer and society.
Graham A. Colditz. Thousand Oaks,
Calif.: Sage, 2007. 3 v., ill. (some col.)
ISBN 9781412949
616.994003   RC254.5.E48

Addresses the issues surrounding cancer and its effects on society. Describes the different types of cancer; possible causes; suspected carcinogens; cancer treatments, including alternative treatments and diets; and controversies in treatment and research. Contains information on the relationship between race and ethnicity and cancer risk, socioeconomic factors, cancer researchers, cancer associations, hospitals and treatment centers, health and medical policy issues, cancer incidence rates for other countries, and many other related topics. Includes a chronology of cancer from 3000 BCE to the present as well as an "Atlas of cancer" (p. A1–A16). Intended for students, practitioners, and researchers. Also available as an e-book and via Credo reference.

**843   Encyclopedia of health care
management.** Michael J. Stahl.
Thousand Oaks, Calif.: Sage, 2004.
xxxvii, 621 p., ill. ISBN 0761926747
362.1068   RA971.E52

Alphabetical list of entries at the beginning of the book provides an overview of the terminology and variety of subject areas covered in this resource including business and economics, statistics, law, clinical research, informatics, and others. A reader's guide with the following major headings is provided: Accounting and activity-based costing, Economics, Finance, Health policy, Human resources, Information technology, Institutions and organizations, International health care issues, Legal and regulatory issues, Managed care, Marketing and customer value, Operations and decision making, Pharmaceuticals and clinical trials, Quality, Statistics and data mining, and Strategy. The main section, consisting of approximately 650 entries, is alphabetically arranged. Each entry contains the term's definition, background, and other relevant information. Includes tables on health care acronyms, medical degrees, medical legislation, and others. Cross-references, list of further readings, and websites. Index. Also available as an e-book.

**844   Encyclopedia of health services
research.** Ross M. Mullner. Los Angeles:
Sage, 2009. 2 v. (xxx, 1409 p.), ill.
ISBN 9781412951791
362.103   RA440.85.E63
Vol. 1, A-K; v. 2, L-Z.

Provides information, written in non-technical language, on the major concepts and topics of the multidisciplinary field of health services research, such as health administration, health economics, medical sociology; as well as entries on accessibility, cost, quality, outcomes, etc. Also contains biographies of current and past leaders, associations, foundations, and research organizations. Signed entries, with further suggested readings, are alphabetically arranged.

"Reader's guide" in v. 1, extensive annotated bibliography and list of web resources in v. 2. Index. For undergraduate and graduate students, health professionals, and also general readers. Also available as an e-book.

**845   Encyclopedia of medical decision
making.** Michael W. Kattan, Mark E.
Cowen. Thousand Oaks, Calif.: SAGE
Publications, 2009. 2 v. (xxxvi, 1229 p.), ill.
ISBN 9781412953726
610.3   R723.5.E53

Approx. 300 signed essays on concepts and methods in the patient-care decision-making process. Entries cover topics such as mathematical and statistical aspects of decision-making, biostatistics, clinical decision-making and analysis, clinical epidemiology, and outcome measures. Also includes essays on process and technology in medical decision-making. Contains a reader's guide, bibliographical references, "see also" references, tables, charts, and further readings. Index. Useful for graduate students, physicians, and other health professionals. Also available as an e-book.

**846   Health care policy and politics A to Z.
3rd ed.** Julie Rovner. Washington: CQ
Press, 2009. xiii, 314 p., ill.

ISBN 9780872897762
362.1/042 22   RA395.A3 R685 2009
First ed., 2000; 2nd ed., 2003.

Concise entries and definitions important in understanding health care, health policy, and related areas and issues. Focus is on health policy issues. Includes health policy timeline (1796-2007), a list of key health care policy acronyms, a list of house and senate congressional committees responsible for health care policy, suggested readings, sources for further information, and index. Also available as an e-book.

Dictionaries

847   The dictionary of health economics. 2nd ed. A. J. Culyer. Chelthenham, U.K.; Northampton, Mass.: Edward Elgar, 2010. xix, 694 p., ill. ISBN 9781849800419
362.103   RA410.A3C85

Concise definitions of terms, concepts, and methods from the field of health economics and related fields, such as epidemiology, pharmacoeconomics, medical sociology, medical statistics, and others. Expanded number of words and phrases relating to health economics of poor and middle-income countries (cf. *Pref.*). Increased number of entries in this edition (from 1,586 in the previous edition to 2,130). Many cross-references. An appendix contains "100 economic studies of health interventions." For health services researchers and professionals. Also available as an e-book. A similar title is *Dictionary of health economics and finance*.

848   Dictionary of health insurance and managed care. David Edward Marcinko. New York: Springer Pub. Co., 2006. ISBN 0826149944
368.382003   RA413.D53

Health insurance, managed care plans and programs, health care industry terminology and definitions, abbreviatons, and acronyms. Also available as e-book.

849   Dictionary of medical sociology. William C. Cockerham, Ferris Joseph Ritchey. Westport, Conn.: Greenwood Press, 1997. xxvi, 169 p.

ISBN 0313292698
306.46103   RA418.C655

Positioned at the intersection of arguably the softest of the soft sciences (sociology) and the hardest of the hard sciences (medicine), medical sociology has developed at a rapid pace over the last two decades to richly inform both of its parent disciplines. This dictionary from 1997 defines key terms from the newly-emerging field at that time, but also demonstrates how each discipline informs and expands the other. A useful reference tool, and also an informal guide to the newly-created field. Includes bibliographical references and index.

850   Health care defined: A glossary of current terms. Bruce Goldfarb. Baltimore: Williams & Wilkins, 1997. xi, 347 p. ISBN 0683036157
362.1/03   RA423.G65

Scholarly resource. Explains the terminology used in the healthcare field, e.g., medical care, delivery of health care, and health services terminology. Contains approx. 3,000 essential terms and explains them in non-medical terminology. Includes bibliographical references (p. 313–315). Useful for insurance and legal professionals.

851   Health services cyclopedic dictionary: A compendium of health-care and public health terminology. 3rd ed. Thomas C. Timmreck. Sudbury, Mass.: Jones and Bartlett Publishers, 1997. xii, 860 p., col. ill. ISBN 0867205156
362.1/068   RA393.T56

First ed. (1982) and 2nd ed. (1987) had title: *Dictionary of health services management*.

(The Jones and Bartlett series in health sciences)
   This rev. and exp. ed. contains terminology and definitions from the fields of health services and medical care, health administration, health care reform, public health, environmental health, epidemiology, managed care, and other related areas.

852   The managed health care dictionary. 2nd ed. Richard Rognehaugh. Gaithersburg, Md.: Aspen Publ., 1998. xii, 261 p. ISBN 0834211440
362.1/04258/03   RA413.R58

Forst ed., 1996.

Includes over 1,000 terms with definitions, including slang, acronyms, etc., many with cross-references. Does not include medical specialties and health professions. Intended for health professionals, patients, and others. Another more recent title is Dictionary of health insurance and managed care.

853 The progressive era's health reform movement: A historical dictionary.
Ruth C. Engs. Westport, Conn.: Praeger, 2003. xxii, 419 p. ISBN 0275979326
362.1/0973/03   RA395.A3E547
Covers 1880–1925, the time period labeled the Progressive era of the United States. Entries cover individuals (biographical information/assessment of historical importance), events, crusades (e.g., exercise, vegetarian diets, alternative health care), legislation, publications, and terms. Includes entries on the health reform movement and campaigns against alcohol, tobacco, drugs, and sexuality. For scholars, students, and general readers. "Selected chronology" (p. [371]–407), bibliographical references, and index. Also available as an e-book.

854 Slee's health care terms. 5th ed.
Debora A. Slee, Vergil N. Slee, H. Joachim Schmidt. Sudbury, Mass.: Jones and Bartlett Publ., 2007. 700 p. ISBN 9780763746155
362.103   RA423.S55
First ed., 1986; 4th ed., 2001. Also called *Health care terms*.

Provides concise definitions for terms from a wide range of disciplines in the healthcare field, including administration, organization, finance, statistics, law, and governmental regulation. Many cross-references. Pays particular attention to acronyms. Terms used in definitions are italicized to indicate the term is defined elsewhere in the dictionary; related terms may be grouped together under one term, such as the many entries under the term "hospital." Intended for all types of healthcare consumers.

Directories

855 AHA guide to the health care field.
American Hospital Association. Chicago:

Healthcare Infosource, Inc., 1997-98 –
RA977.A1
Title varies: 1949–71, pt. 2 of Aug. issue (called "Guide issue," 1956–70) of *Hospitals*, which superseded *American hospital directory* (1945–48); 1972–73, *The AHA guide to the health care field*; 1974–96, *American Hospital Association guide to the health care field*.

Description based on 2011-2012 ed.; 2014 ed. available.

"Provides basic data reflecting the delivery of health care in the United States and associated areas, and is not to serve as an official and all-inclusive list of services offered by individual hospitals."—*Acknowledgements and Advisements*. Four major sections, each with table of contents and explanatory information: (A) Hospitals, institutional, and associate members; (B) networks, health care systems, and alliances; (C) lists of health organizations, agencies, and providers; and (D) indexes. Also available in CD-ROM format. Additional information about this resource is available at http://www.AHAdata.com. Statistical information concerning hospitals is published in AHA hospital statistics.

A web-based resource, American hospital directory® (AHD®) http://www.ahd.com/ (by a Kentucky Company) provides data for over 6,000 hospitals, with data derived from Medicare claims, hospital cost reports, Centers for Medicare and Medicaid Services, and other sources (further details at http://www.ahd.com/data_sources.html). While most features of this website are only available to subscribers, free access is provided to "hospital profiles."

856 Current procedural terminology: CPT. Standard ed. American Medical Association. Chicago: American Medical Association, 1999–
616.0014   RB115.C17
First ed., 1966 and 2nd ed., 1970 had title: *Current procedural terminology*. Vols. for 1999–publ. as a revision of the 4th ed. of *Physicians' current procedural terminology*, originally publ. in 1977. Description based on "CPT 2013 Standard Edition," publ. 2012.

"A listing of descriptive terms and identifying codes for reporting medical services and procedures performed by physicians . . . to accurately describe

medical, surgical, and diagnostic services."—
Foreword Each procedure or service is identified
with a five-digit CPT® code. Sections: Evaluation
and management; Anesthesia; Surgery; Radiology
(including nuclear medicine and diagnostic ultrasound); Pathology and laboratory; Medicine. CPT
2010 procedure codes and descriptions are also
available on CD-ROM as data files and electronic
software, as are CPT changes from previous and
current editions.

857 EMTREE thesaurus. Excerpta Medica
(Firm). Amsterdam, Netherlands; New
York: Excerpta Medica, 1991–. v.
09293299   Z699.5.M39E49
Developed from 1974–90, *Master list of medical
indexing terms (MALIMET)*; EMTAGS (discont.
in 1998) and EMCLAS (i.e., the original subject
classification system for EMBASE) integration into
EMTREE (1988–91). Annual updates.

Description based on 2008 ed.

Cover title: *EMTREE: the life science thesaurus.*
Contents: v. 1, Alphabetical index; v. 2, Tree structure; v. 3, Permuted term index.

Hierarchically structured drug and disease
controlled vocabulary used for subject indexing
and for searching the biomedical literature (e.g.,
EMBASE, with "preferred terms" [i.e., drug and
medical terms]), synonyms, and MeSH®: Medical
Subject Headings (858). Contains a list of EMBASE
section headings which, with a few exceptions, correspond to the titles of the Excerpta Medica abstract
journals, published since 1947, and searchable in
EMBASE since 1974. Also available online.

858 MeSH: medical subject headings.
http://www.nlm.nih.gov/mesh/MBrowser
.html. National Library of Medicine
(U.S.). Bethesda, Md.: U.S. National
Library of Medicine. 1975–
                          Z695.1.M48
MeSH®; MeSH Browser; National Library of Medicine (NLM).

"MeSH is the National Library of Medicine's
controlled vocabulary thesaurus. It consists of
sets of terms naming descriptors in a hierarchical
structure that permits searching at various levels of
specificity. MeSH descriptors are arranged in both
an alphabetic and a hierarchical structure. 26,853
descriptors in 2013 MeSH. 213,000 entry terms.

214,000 headings called 'Supplementary concept records' (formerly 'Supplementary chemical
records') within a separate thesaurus." -*MeSH fact
sheet*   (http://www.nlm.nih.gov/pubs/factsheets/
mesh.html). Many cross-references help in locating the most appropriate MeSH heading. MeSH
is used for indexing, cataloging, and searching
biomedical and health-related information and
documents.

Access points to MeSH are available via the
MeSH browser, which contains the full contents of
the vocabulary and the MeSH website (http://www
.nlm.nih.gov/mesh), which provides additional
information about MeSH and for obtaining MeSH
in different electronic formats.

MeSH subject descriptors appear in MED-
LINE®/PubMed®, the NLM catalog, and elsewhere.
Related pages are the Unified medical language sys-
tem (UMLS®) and the NLM classification.

Supplement to index medicus®, commonly
known as "black and white" MeSH, combines the
alphabetic arrangement and the tree structures in
a single publication. It was published in print format each Jan. through 2007. Other separate MeSH
publications (*Annotated alphabetic MeSH*, the *MeSH
trees structures*, and the *Permuted MeSH*) ceased
publication in 2004. A brief history of MeSH and
other introductory material can be found at http://
www.nlm.nih.gov/mesh/intro_preface2007.html.
"MeSH is 50 years old http://ojs.med.utah.edu/
index.php/esynapse/article/view/166/278 (*eSynapse*
v.26 (1), 2011), includes links to historical information about MeSH, i.e., a videocast and presentation
remarks by Robert M. Braude ("50 years of medical
subject headings: Past, present, and future impact
on biomedical information").

**859 Who's who in medicine and
healthcare.** New Providence, N.J.:
Marquis Who's Who, 1996–
0000-1708   R153.W43
Description based on 2011–12 edition. Compilation of biographical information on medical professionals, including administrators, educators,
researchers, clinicians, and other medical and
healthcare personnel. This edition contains 27,150
biographical profiles. Listings include full name,
occupation, date/place of birth, family background,
education summary, writings, and association
memberships and awards.

The biographical profiles included in this resource are also available online as part of Marquis biographies online through a subscription.

Handbooks

860 Health care reform around the world. Andrew C. Twaddle. Westport, Conn.: Auburn House, 2002. xiii, 419 p., ill. ISBN 0865692882

362.1 RA394.H4145

Describes health care reform efforts and trends in different countries, with roughly comparable information for the countries included. Ch. 1 is an international comparison of health care system reforms—United Kingdom, Eastern and Western Europe, United States, the Middle East, Latin America, Asia, and Oceania. Also available as an e-book.

861 Health care systems around the world: Characteristics, issues, reforms. Marie L. Lassey, William R. Lassey, Martin J. Jinks. Upper Saddle River, N.J.: Prentice Hall, 1997. xiii, 370 p., ill., maps. ISBN 0131042335

362.1 RA393.L328

Contents: Introduction, basic issues and concepts; The countries and their characteristics; The United States, high-technology and limited access; Canada, challenges to public payment for universal care; Japan, preventive health care as cultural norm; Germany, a tradition of universal health care; France, centrally controlled and locally managed; The Netherlands, gradual adaptation; Sweden, decentralized comprehensive care; The United Kingdom, the economy model; The Czech Republic, a new mixture of public and private services; Hungary, creating a remodeled system; Russia, transition to market and consumer orientation; China, privatizing socialist health care; Mexico, modernizing structure and expanded rural services; Organization variations and reforms; Economic organization of health care, comparative perspectives; Expectations for reform, a glimpse at the future. Description and analysis of health care systems in different countries, addressing demographic, social, and economic characteristics, also health promotion, prevention of disease, and health care. Includes bibliographical references and index.

A 2013 publication, *Health care systems around the world: A comparative guide* by Boslaugh, describes health care systems for a large number of countries. Arranged in alphabetical order by country, with content for each country presented in a standardized format, allowing for comparison from country to country.

862 Health care systems of the developed world: How the United States' system remains an outlier. Duane A. Matcha. Westport, Conn.: Praeger, 2003. x, 198 p., ill. ISBN 027597992X

362.1/0973 RA441.M38

Contents: ch. 1, Introduction; ch. 2, The United States; ch. 3, Canada; ch. 4, United Kingdom; ch. 5, Germany; ch. 6, Sweden; ch. 7, Japan; ch. 8, Conclusion. Provides an introduction to selected major healthcare systems, with consideration of their historical and political basis. Provides a framework for analysis and comparison of the different systems. Various tables and figures related to health insurance, personal health care expenditures, self-rated health status, future concerns, and others. Includes bibliographical references and index. Also available as an e-book.

World health systems: challenges and perspectives presents profiles of health systems in 28 countries. *Health care systems around the world: Characteristics, issues, reforms*, provides additional information in this area. Milton I Roemer's *National health systems of the world* remains an important title. It consists of a comprehensive study and analysis of national health systems in 68 industrialized, middle-income, and very poor countries, with a cross-national analysis of the major health care issues within different systems.

863 Contemporary issues in healthcare law and ethics. 3rd ed. Dean M. Harris. Chicago; Washington: Health Administration Press; AUPHA Press, 2007. 377 p. ISBN 9781567932

344.730321 KF3825.Z9.H3

First edition, 1999, had title *Healthcare law and ethics: Issues for the age of managed care*; 2nd ed., 2003.

Contents: (1) "The role of law in the U.S. healthcare system"; (2) "Managing and regulating the healthcare system"; (3) "Patient care issues"; (4) "Legal and ethical issues in health insurance and managed care"; table of cases; table of statutes; table of regulations; index.

This revised and updated edition presents essential information and examines legal and ethical issues in health care. Includes, for example, the U.S. Supreme Court's decisions on physician-assisted suicide, partial-birth abortion, issues in emergency contraception, HIPAA Privacy Rule, medical malpractice, reporting of medical errors, and other topics. Also available as e-book.

864 Delivering health care in America: A systems approach. 5th ed. Leiyu Shi, Douglas A. Singh. Sudbury, Mass.: Jones & Bartlett Learning, 2012. 634 p., ill. ISBN 9781449626501
362.10973   RA395.A3S485
First ed., 1998; 4th ed., 2008.

An abbreviated version of this book is *Essentials of the U.S. health care system*.

Contents: ch. 1, A distinctive system of health care delivery; ch. 2, Beliefs, values, and health; ch. 3, The evolution of health services in the United States; ch. 4, Health services professionals; ch. 5, Medical technology; ch. 6, Health services financing; ch. 7, Outpatient and primary care services; ch. 8, Inpatient facilities and services; ch. 9, Managed care and integrated organizations; ch. 10, Long-term care; ch. 11, Health services for special populations; ch. 12, Cost, access, and quality; ch. 13, Health policy; ch. 14, The future of health services delivery.

While layout and structure of this work remain the same, there have been some major revisions in this edition, mainly due to current developments in health reform. Provides a basic introduction and overview of the U.S. healthcare system, with coverage of all aspects of healthcare delivery, including quality, cost, and health and medical policy, with the latest data, trends, and research findings. Includes information on health care reform in several other countries, bibliographical references, and index. Also available as an e-book.

Another recent title in this area, intended for general readers, is *United States health caresystem: Combining business, health, and delivery* by Austin et al. provides an overview of the U.S. healthcare

system, including the 2010 healthcare reform legislation and recent statistics.

865 Doing a literature review in nursing, health, and social care. 1st ed. Michael Coughlan, Patricia Cronin, Francis Ryan. Thousand Oaks, Calif.: SAGE Publications, Ltd., 2013. 153 p., ill. ISBN 9781446249604
610.73072   RT81.5

Contents: ch. 1, What is a literature review; ch. 2, Types of literature review; ch. 3, Systematic review; ch. 4, Selecting a review topic and searching the literature; ch. 5, Reading and organising the literature; ch. 6, Critically analysing the literature; ch. 7, Synthesizing the literature; ch.8, Writing up your literature review; ch. 8, Referencing and plagiarism; ch. 10, What comes next.

Provides an overview of the literature review process, with basic information on the review process, on types of reviews, searching and analyzing the literature, etc. Glossary, references, and index. Intended audience is nursing and social work professionals, but also considered useful for other health professionals.

866 Essentials of managed health care. 6th ed. Peter R. Kongstvedt. Burlington, Mass.: Jones and Bartlett Learning, 2013. xxv, 688 p., ill.
9781449653316   RA413.E87

First ed., 1989; 4th ed., 2001 had title *The managed health care handbook*. 5th ed., 2007 is the rev. ed. of two different titles by the same author: *The managed health care handbook*, 4th ed., 2001, and rev. ed. of *Essentials of managed health care*, 4th ed., 2001.

Contents: Pt I, Introduction to health insurance and managed health care (ch. 1–3); pt. II, Network contracting and provider payment (ch. 4-6); pt. III, Management of utilization and quality (ch. 7–15); pt. IV, Sales, finance, and administration (ch. 16–23); pt. V, Special markets (ch. 24–27); pt. VI, Laws and regulations (ch. 28–30); glossary; index.

Intended as a guide and a resource to the managed health care system, with information on types of managed care plans and integrated healthcare delivery systems, physician networks in managed health care, prescription drug benefits in managed health care, etc.

Handbook of health delivery systems by Yih, available in print and also as an e-book, provides related information.

867   Handbook of research on informatics in healthcare and biomedicine. Athina A. Lazakidou. Hershey, Pa.: Idea Group Reference, 2006. xxx, 437, 11 p., ill. ISBN 1591409829

610/.285   R853.D37H36

Contents: section 1, Medical data and health information systems; section 2, Standardization and classification systems in medicine; section 3, Virtual reality applications in medicine; section 4, Virtual learning environments in healthcare and biomedicine; section 5, Computer assisted diagnosis; section 6, Data mining and medical decision making; section 7, Current aspects of knowledge management in medicine; section 8, Telemedicine and e-health services; section 9, Image processing and archiving systems; section 10, Signal processing techniques; section 11, Use of new technologies in biomedicine; section 12, Ergonomic and safety issues in computerized medical equipment; section 13, Health economics and health services research. Provides information on new trends, computer applications, and advanced technologies in health care and biomedicine. Key terms and their definitions; cross-referencing of key terms; index. Available online via netLibrary.

868   Jonas & Kovner's health care delivery in the United States. 10th ed. Anthony R. Kovner, James R. Knickman, Steven Jonas, Victoria D. Weisfeld. New York: Springer Pub., 2011. 405 p., ill., maps. ISBN 9780826108920

36210973   RA395.A3H395

First ed., 1977–5th ed., 1995, *Health care delivery in the United States*; 6th ed., 1999 to the present, *Jonas and Kovner's health care delivery in the United States*; 9th ed., 2008.

Contents: Part I, Health policy; part II, Population health; part III, Medical care delivery; part IV, Support for medical care delivery; part V, The future of health care delivery. Appendix, "Major provisions of the Patient Protection Affordable Care Act of 2010"; Glossary.

Examines the state of health care delivery in the U.S. and answers questions regarding health policy.

Describes (and helps to understand) the characteristics of U.S. health care, its complexities, and its provision. Examines how changes in the healthcare system affect the health of the population, the cost of health care, access to care, and related issues. Also provides answers to policy questions. Includes a chapter on "new five-year trend forecast." Bibliographical references and index. Also available as an e-book.

869   The law and the public's health.
7th ed. Kenneth R. Wing, Benjamin Gilbert. Chicago: Health Administration Press, 2007. xiii, 391 p.

344.7304   KF3775.W5

Contents: ch. 1, "The law and the legal system"; ch. 2, "The power of the state governments in matters affecting health care"; ch. 3, "Government power and the right to privacy"; ch. 4, "The constitutional discretion of the state and federal governments to limit or condition social welfare benefits"; ch. 5, "Government regulation of health care providers and payers"; ch. 6, "The scope of discretion of administrative agencies in matters affecting health and health care"; ch. 7, "The fraud and abuse laws"; ch. 8, "The antitrust laws: Government enforcement of competition"; ch. 9, "Malpractice: Liability for negligence in the delivery and financing of health care"; ch. 10, "Health care business law: Legal considerations in the structuring of health care entities and their transactions."

Intended as an introductory text for schools of public health and law-related courses, this book can also serve as a reference book in the health care field. Provides an introduction to the law, the legal system, and principles applicable to the delivery and financing of health care but is not considered a treatise on health law. Includes bibliographical references and index. Also available as an e-book.

870   Medical records and the law. 4th ed.
William H. Roach, American Health Information Management Association. Sudbury, Mass.: Jones and Bartlett Publ., 2006. xix, 591 p. ISBN 0763734454

344.7304/1   KF3827.R4R63

First edition, 1985; 3rd ed., 1998.

Contents: ch. 1, Introduction to the American legal system; ch. 2, Medical records and managed care;

ch. 3, Medical record requirements; ch. 4, Medical records entries; ch. 5, Documenting consent to treatment; ch. 6, Access to health information; ch. 7, Reporting and disclosure requirements; ch. 8, Documentation and disclosure: special areas of concern; ch. 9, HIV/AIDS: mandatory reporting and confidentiality; ch. 10, Discovery and admissibility of medical records; ch. 11, Legal theories in improper disclosure cases; ch. 12, Risk management and quality management; ch. 13, Electronic health records; ch. 14, Health information in medical research; Index.

Provides information on the growth of electronic health record systems and electronic data networks. Addresses the issues related to medical research involving human subjects and how patient information can be used. Also available as an e-book.

871 Medicare handbook. Center for Medicare Advocacy. New York: Aspen Publishers, 2000–. v.
368 1530-8979   KF3608.A4M436
Description based on 2014 ed. Contents: Important enrollment information; sect.1, Learn how Medicare works; sect. 2, Signing up for Medicare Part A & Part B; sect. 3, Find out if Medicare covers your test, service, or item; sect. 4, Choose your health & prescription drug coverage; sect. 5, Get information about your Medicare health coverage choices; sect.6, Get information about prescription drug coverage; sect. 7, Get help paying your health & prescription drug costs; sect. 8, Know your rights & how to protect yourself from fraud; sect. 9, Plan ahead for long-term care; sect. 10, Get more information ; sect. 11, Definitions.

PDF version of 2014 ed. available at http://www.medicare.gov/pubs/pdf/10050.pdf

Resource to help understand Medicare's rules and regulations. Further helpful, detailed information can also be found on the Medicare website (Medicare: the official U.S. government site for people with Medicare at http://www.medicare.gov), part of the Centers for Medicare & Medicaid Services.

872 Patients' rights in the age of managed health care. Lisa Yount. New York: Facts on File, 2001. 280 p. ISBN 0816042586
344.73041   KF3823.Y68

Provides overview of the issues in health care delivery, patients' rights and applicable laws, a chronology of significant events, and also a guide to further research in patients' rights issues. Glossary, index, and annotated bibliography. *The rights of patients: The authoritative ACLU guide to the rights of patients* provides further information. Also available as an e-book.

873 Procedure coding handbook for psychiatrists. 4th ed. Chester W. Schmidt, Rebecca K. Yowell, Ellen Jaffe. Washington: American Psychiatric Pub., 2011. xiii, 192 p. ISBN 9781585623747
616.890012   RC465.6.S36
First ed., 1993; 3rd ed., 2004. CPT (Current Procedural Terminology, 856).

Contents: ch. 1, "Basics of CPT"; ch. 2, "Introduction to documentation of psychiatric services"; ch. 3, "Codes and documentation for psychiatric services"; ch. 4, "Codes and documentation for other mental health services"; ch. 5, "Codes and documentation for evaluation and management services"; ch. 6, "Medicare"; ch. 7, "Commercial insurance issues"; ch. 8, "Putting it all together for accurate coding"; ch. 9, "FAQs and problem scenarios." Appendixes: A, "The CPT coding system: How it came to be, how it changed"; B, "The Health Insurance Portability and Accountability Act (HIPPA)"; C, "Modifier"; D, "Place of service codes for Medicare"; E, "1997 CMS documentation guidelines for evaluation and management services (abridged and modified for psychiatric services"; F, "Vignettes for evaluation and management codes"; G, "Most frequently missed items in evaluation and management (E/M) documentation"; H, "Documentation templates"; I, "ECT patient information, consent form, and record template"; J, "Examples of Relative Value Units (RVUs) (2010)"; K, "National distribution of evaluation and management code selection by psychiatrists"; L, "American Psychiatric Association CPT coding service and additional resources"; M, "Medicare carriers and administrative contractors"; N, "Centers for Medicare and Medicaid services regional offices."

Explains the structure and function of CPT, how to use the psychiatric therapeutic procedure codes, and how CPT affects the practice of psychiatry. Also available as an e-book.

874   World health systems: Challenges and perspectives. 2nd ed. Bruce Fried, Laura M. Gaydos. Chicago: Health Administration Press, 2012. xxx, 780 p. ISBN 9781567934205
362.1   RA441.W676
Contents: Pt. I, Current issues facing global health systems; pt. II, Profiled countries: The low income countries (ch. 7-11); The middle-income countries (ch. 12–18); The high-income countries (ch. 19-31); glossary; index.

This revised edition presents new introductory chapters on health systems (e.g., defining a health system, health system strengthening, health system regulation, and the politics of health system reform) and profiles of 26 health systems from around the world. Organized in three categories by the wealth of each nation: low-, middle-, and high-income countries. Addresses the various challenges health services face, how they are organized, and how they are financed. Each chapter includes disease patterns and health system financing, also past, present status, and future health policy issues and various challenges of the individual health systems.

Histories

875   U.S. health policy and politics: A documentary history. Kevin Hillstrom. Washington: CQ Press, 2012. xxiii, 717 p. ISBN 9781608710263
362.10973   RA395.A3; H555
Contents: ch. 1, Health care and medical practice in the new world, 1600-1800; ch. 2, Health care and regulation in antebellum America, 1800-1860; ch. 3, The professionalization of American medicine, 1860-1890; ch. 4, Health care in the progressive era, 1890-1920; ch. 5, The struggle over health insurance between the wars, 1920-1940; ch. 6, Partisan jousting over health care in the postwar era, 1940-1960; ch. 7, Medicare changes the health care landscape, 1960-1980; ch. 8, Restraining health care costs in the age of Reagan, 1980-1990; ch. 9, The Clinton health plan and scorched-earth politics, 1990-2000; ch. 10, Controversial policy prescriptions for American health care, 2000-2010.

Authoritative text supplemented by primary source materials. Includes topics of both historic and current interest regarding the American health care system and policy. Contains the complete or excerpted essential portion of text of 150 selected primary historic source documents (e.g., congressional and courtroom testimony, speeches, letters, classified documents, etc) to help explain and understand U.S. health policy. Each chapter has an introduction that "puts the primary documents in a lager social, political, economic, and scientific content.—*Introd.* Chronology (major health care laws and events in U.S. history), bibliography, subject index.

Statistics

876   AHA hospital statistics. American Hospital Association, Health Forum (Organization). Chicago: Healthcare InfoSource, 2005–
0090-6662   RA981.A2A6234
Title varies: Prior to 1971 issued as part 1 of the annual guide issue of *Hospitals*; 1971–90, *Hospital statistics*; 1991–97, *American Hospital Association hospital statistics*; 1998–2004, *Hospital statistics*. Editions starting in 1998 draw data from the 1996–*AHA annual survey of hospitals*. Statistical complement to the AHA guide to the health care field.

Description based on 2012 ed. Subtitle: *The comprehensive reference source for analysis and comparison of hospital trends.*

Compilation of data on trends, including emerging trends, in the hospital field through 2010. Additions in recent years include community health indicators, utilization, personnel, and finance by all metropolitan statistical areas (MSAs), five-year trend data, breakdowns between inpatient and outpatient care, and facilities and services information. Includes "Historical trends in utilization, personnel, and finances for selected years from 1946-2010." Includes section on "Statistics for multihospital health care systems and their hospitals." A glossary explains specific terms used in the tables and text of this volume. Hospitals included are not necessarily identical to those included in the *AHA guide to the health care field.*

877   American health: Demographics and spending of health care consumers. New Strategist Publications, Inc. Ithaca, N.Y.: New Strategist Publications, 2005–.

xvi, 504 p., ill. ISBN 1885070748
614.4273   RA445.A442
Publ. 1998–2000 as *Best of health: demographics of health care consumers.*

(American consumer series)

1st, 2005 ed.; 2nd ed., 2007. Description based on 3rd ed., 2010.

Contents: ch. 1, Addictions; ch. 2, Aging; ch. 3, Alternative medicine; ch. 4, Attitudes towards health care; ch. 5, Births; ch. 6, Coverage and cost; ch. 7, Deaths; ch. 8, Disability; ch. 9, Diseases and conditions; ch. 10, Health care visits; ch. 11, Hospital care; ch. 12, Mental health; ch. 13, Sexual attitudes and behavior; ch. 14, Weight and exercise.

Data on health care consumers from many different sources, including information from the federal government (e.g., National Center for Health Statistics, incl. *Health, United States,* Consumer Expenditure Survey (http://www.bls.gov/cex/), MEPS Medical Expenditure Panel Survey, to name a few). Contains more than 300 tables, graphs, a glossary, bibliographical references, and index. Also available as an e-book.

878   A brief guide to the U.S. health care delivery system: Facts, definitions, and statistics. 2nd ed. Sara A. Beazley. Chicago: AHA Press/Health Forum, 2010. xi, 178 p., ill. ISBN 9781556483684
362.1   RA395.A3B75

Contents: ch. 1, Patient care; ch. 2, Caregivers; ch. 3, Facilities; ch. 4, Finance; ch. 5, Government and other types of oversight. "Organized for quick answers and easy understanding"—Publ. notes.

This rev. ed. presents an overview of the U.S. healthcare system, the practice of healthcare management, and delivery of healthcare. Contains industry data and research findings and selected trends in medical practice. Glossary, bibliographical references, and index.

879   Faststats A to Z. http://www.cdc.gov/nchs/fastats/Default.htm. National Center for Health Statistics (NCHS). Hyattsville, Md: U.S. Dept. of Health and Human Services, Centers for Disease Control and Prevention, National Center for Health Statistics

Provides topic-appropriate public health statistics (e.g., birth data, morbidity and mortality statistics, and health care use) and relevant links to further information and publications. Includes state and territorial data, with clickable map for individual state data. Also includes data derived from the "Behavioral Risk Factor Surveillance System (BRFSS)," which compiles data for 16 negative behaviors.

880   Health, United States. http://purl.access.gpo.gov/GPO/LPS2649. National Center for Health Statistics, National Center for Health Services Research. Rockville, Md.: National Center for Health Statistics. 1975–

An annual report on trends in health statistics.

The report consists of several main sections: complete report; "at a glance" table; highlights; a chartbook containing text and figures that illustrate major trends in the health of Americans; and a trend tables section that contains 150 detailed data tables. Includes extensive appendixes and an index. Hyperlinks to tables and graphs, which are available in formats such as Excel, PowerPoint, and PDF.

New for the 2012 edition is a special feature on emergency care.

Easy access to related online resources provided by the National Center for Health Statistics (NCHS).

881   Health and healthcare in the United States: County and metro area data. Richard K. Thomas, NationsHealth Corporation. Lanham, Md.: Bernan Press, c1999–c2001. 2 v., maps
362 1526-1573   RA407.3.H415

First ed., 1999–2nd ed., 2000; 2nd ed. technical consultant, Russell G. Bruce. Compendium of health-related statistics and reference maps for each of the 3,000 counties and the 80 metropolitan areas in the U.S.—demographics, vital statistics, healthcare resources, and Medicare data. Based on information from the National Center for Health Statistics and the U.S. Bureau of the Census. Accompanying CD-ROMs make it possible to manipulate the data. Also available as an e-book.

882   Health and medical care archive. http://www.icpsr.umich.edu/icpsrweb/HMCA/. Robert Wood Johnson

Foundation, Inter-University Consortium for Political and Social Research. Ann Arbor, Mich.: Inter-University Consortium for Political and Social Research

Data archive of the Robert Wood Johnson Foundation (RWJF), operated by the Inter-university Consortium for Political and Social Research (ICPSR) at the University of Michigan.

"Preserves and disseminates data collected by selected research projects funded by the Foundation and facilitates secondary analyses of the data . . . surveys of health care professionals and organizations, investigations of access to medical care, surveys on substance abuse, and evaluations of innovative programs for the delivery of health care. Our goal is to increase understanding of health and health care in the United States through secondary analysis of RWJF-supported data collections."— *About page*. Data collections can be searched by keyword or browsed by the following subjects: health care providers; cost/access to health care; substance abuse and health; chronic health conditions; other. Details about RWJF's "community tracking study" at https://www.icpsr.umich.edu/icpsrweb/content/HMCA/community-tracking-study.html.

883   Health care state rankings. Morgan Quitno Corporation. Lawrence, Kans.: Morgan Quitno Corp., 1993–
362.10973 1065-1403   RA407.3.H423

Description based on 2011 ed. Subtitle: *Health care across America*. Contains data relating to medical care, delivery of health care, and health status indicators, which are derived from federal and state government sources, and from professional and private organizations. Presented in tabular form, with tables arranged in seven categories: Birth and reproductive health; Deaths; Facilities (hospitals, nursing homes, etc.); Finance; Incidence of disease; Providers; Physical fitness. Appendix (with 2008 and 2009 charts), sources, and index. Another title, *Health care state perspectives*, includes state-specific reports for each of the 50 states.

884   Health data tools and statistics from PHPartners. http://phpartners.org/health_stats.html. Partners in Information Access for the Public Health

Workforce, National Library of Medicine (U.S.). Bethesda, Md.: U.S. National Library of Medicine, National Institutes of Health, Dept. of Health and Human Services

Contents: County and local health data; State health data; Individual state data; National health data; Global health data; Statistical reports; Demographic data; Geographic information systems (GIS); Training and education; Health information technology and standards; Tools for data collection and planning.

Provides lists of selected links with brief annotations to assist in locating public health data and statistics. Part of The Partners in Information Access for the Public Health Workforce (PHPartners) website (http://phpartners.org/index.html) which is described as "a collaboration of U.S. government agencies, public health organizations and health sciences libraries, with the mission of helping the public health workforce find and use information effectively to improve and protect the public's health."—*About page*. Its topics pages include, for example, bioterrorism, dental public health, HIV/AIDS, nutrition, obesity, public health genomics, and other relevant information for public health professionals and researchers.

Additional highly useful sites in this area are, for example, Health services research and public health information, HSR information central, and National Information Center on Health Services Research and Health Care Technology.

885   Healthy people. http://www.cdc.gov/nchs/healthy_people.htm. National Center for Health Statistics (NCHS). Hyattsville, Md.: Centers for Disease Control (U.S.), National Center for Health Statistics

RA395.A3

Contents: Healthy people 2000; Healthy People 2010; Healthy People 2020; Progress Reviews; Publications.

"Healthy People provides science-based, national goals and objectives with 10-year targets designed to guide national health promotion and disease prevention efforts to improve the health of all people in the United States." —*Home Page*. Previous reports include *Healthy people 2000* (http://purl.access.gpo.gov/GPO/LPS3745) and *Healthy people: The Surgeon General's report on health promotion and disease prevention: Background papers: Report to the Surgeon General on health promotion and disease prevention.* "Healthy People DATA 2010," an interactive database system accessible via CDC WONDER provides various reports and data. A search interface providing searches for published literature related to Healthy People 2010 was added to the "special queries" section of PubMed.

Also available in print format: *Tracking healthy people 2010.* Progress Reviews and publications are added to the website regularly.

886 Healthy women. http://www.cdc.gov/ nchs/data/healthywomen/womenschart book_aug2004.pdf. Centers for Disease Control and Prevention (U.S.); National Center for Health Statistics (U.S.). Hyattsville, Md.: National Center for Health Statistics, Centers for Disease Control and Prevention, U.S. Dept. of Health and Human Services. 2004

RA408.W65

Title varies: Suggested title for website: *Healthy women: State trends in health and mortality;* suggested citation for print version, publ. in 2004 as *Women's health and mortality chartbook* by K. M. Brett and Suzanne G. Hayes.

PDF of *Women's Health and Mortality Chartbook,* developed by NCHS with support from the Office on Women's Health. It describes the health of people in each state in the U.S. by sex, race, and age by reporting current data on critical issues of relevance to women.

Other publications in this area include *Women's health data book: A profile of women's health in the United States,* ed. by D. Misra, a collaborative publication by the Jacobs Institute of Women's Health and the Henry J. Kaiser Family Foundation (Kaiser Family Foundation) since 1992, complemented by *State profiles on women's health: Women's health issues,* publ. since 1998.

887 HHS Data Council. http://aspe.hhs.gov/ datacncl/. United States.; Dept. of Health and Human Services.; Data Council. Washington: U.S. Department of Health and Human Services. 200?–

RA407.3

"The HHS Data Council coordinates all health and human services data collection and analysis activities of the Department of Health and Human Services, including an integrated data collection strategy, coordination of health data standards and health and human services and privacy policy activities."—*Website.*

Provides access to key health and human services data and statistics. Covers information sponsored by federal, state, and local governments. Complements other government resources such as USA.gov and FedStats. Links to health and human services surveys and data systems sponsored by federal agencies and leads to websites and other key resources that contain statistics and data. Additionally, HealthData.gov http://www.hhs .gov/open/datasets/index.html provides access to datasets, various tools, and applications using data about health and healthcare.

888 Mental health, United States. National Institute of Mental Health (U.S.). Rockville, Md.: U.S. Dept. of Health and Human Services, Public Health Service, Alcohol, Drug Abuse, and Mental Health Administration, National Institute of Mental Health, Div. of Biometry and Epidemiology, 1983–. v.

362.2/0973 0892-0664   RA790.6.M463

Substance Abuse and Mental Health Services Administration (SAMSHA).

Description based on *Mental health, United States, 2010* (Substance Abuse and Mental Health Services Administration), publ. 2012.

Contents: Section (1), Introduction; (2) Mental health of the population; (3) Providers and settings for mental health services; (4) Payers and payment mechanisms; (5) States: People, providers, and payers; (6) Data gaps; (7) Tables; Appendix (A), Data source descriptions; (B), Glossary; (C) Medication lists.

Contains statistical reports and data on trends in mental health services, derived to a large extent from national surveys conducted by SAMSHA (Substance Abuse and Mental Health Services Administration) Center for Mental Health Services in collaboration with various major national, state, and professional associations. Three new sections in this edition: Section 1 contains an editorial on likely future directions and an overview of the mental health field over the past 100 years; Section 2 reports on the current status of mental health statistics, and Section 3 on the current status of mental health services. Section 4, as in previous editions, provides current mental health statistics. Electronic full-text of several recent volumes available from the SAMSHA National Mental Health Information Center website at http://purl .access.gpo.gov/GPO/LPS24728.

889 MEPS Medical Expenditure Panel Survey. http://www.meps.ahrq.gov/ mepsweb/. U.S. Agency for Healthcare Research and Quality. Bethesda, Md.: Agency for Healthcare Research and Quality. 1996–

RA408.5

Produced by Agency for Health Care Research and Quality (AHRQ).

"Set of large-scale surveys of families and individuals, their medical providers (doctors, hospitals, pharmacies, etc.), and employers across the United States. MEPS collects data on the specific health services that Americans use, how frequently they use them, the cost of these services, and how they are paid for, as well as data on the cost, scope, and breadth of health insurance held by and available to U.S. workers" (*Website*). Provides information on health expenditures, utilization of health services, health insurance, and nursing homes, and reimbursement mechanisms. MEPS topics include access to health care, children's health, children's insurance coverage, health care disparities, mental health, minority health, the uninsured, and other topics. Further details concerning the survey background, data overview, and frequently asked questions are provided at the website. Provides full-text access to MEPS publications: highlights, research findings, statistical briefs, etc.

890 Munro's statistical methods for health care research. 6th ed.
Stacey Beth Plichta, Elizabeth A. Kelvin, Barbara Hazard Munro. Philadelphia: Wolters Kluwer Health/Lippincott Williams & Wilkins, 2012. vii, 567 p., ill. ISBN 9781451115611

610.72/7   RT81.5.M86

First edition, 1986 to 5th ed. 2005 had title: *Statistical methods for health care research*.

Explains statistical methods and techniques frequently used in the health care literature. Includes charts, graphs, and examples from the literature. Contains, for example, principles underlying statistical inference, material on statistical model building and logistic regression, structural equation modeling, writing and presenting for publication, and other areas. Written for students and teachers.

891 OECD health data. http://www.oecd .org/health/healthdata. Organisation for Economic Co-operation and Development. Paris: Organisation for Economic Co-operation and Development

Title varies: SourceOECD health data.

Part of SourceOECD, which contains publications (monographs, periodicals, and statistical databases) issued by the OECD.

Interactive database and source of statistics on health and health care systems of the OECD member states. Allows cross-country comparisons of national health care systems. Includes, for example, health status, health care resources, health care utilization, expenditure on health, and health care financing. Available in online and CD-ROM formats.

892 Physician compensation and production survey. Medical Group Management Association, Center for Research in Ambulatory Health Care Administration (U.S.). Englewood, Colo.: Center for Research in Ambulatory Health Care Administration, 1992–. v.

331 1064-4563   R728.5.P48152

Merger of the production survey of: *Cost and production survey report*, and: *Physician compensation survey report*.

Now published by the Medical Group Management Association (MGMA). Title varies: *MGMA physician compensation and production survey*.

Description based on 2007 report. 2012 report based on 2011 data is the most recent available.

Contents: Section 1, Key findings and demographics; section 2, Physician compensation and benefits; section 3, Physician productivity; section 4, Physician time worked; section 5, Summary tables; section 6, Nonphysician providers; section 7, Physician placement starting salaries.

"Data on compensation for healthcare professionals and on medical group practices and financial operations . . . will assist . . . in evaluating the ranges of compensation and productivity for both . . . physicians and nonphysician providers" (*Publ. notes*). The Bureau of Labor Statistics website "Sector 62—Health Care and Social Assistance" (http://www.bls.gov/oes/current/oessrci.htm#62) also provides extensive information in this area as part of its occupational employment and wage estimates.

Physician socioeconomic statistics (formed by the union of *Physician marketplace statistics* and *Socioeconomic characteristics of medical practice*), publ. by the American Medical Association, was discontinued in 2003.

893   Portrait of health in the United States. 1st ed. Daniel Melnick, Beatrice A. Rouse. Lanham, Md.: Bernan, 2001. xxi, 376 p., ill.
614.4/273   RA410.53.P675
089059189X

"Major statistical trends & guide to resources" (*Cover*).

"Presents a picture of American health using a variety of measures ranging from self-perceived health status and reported acute and chronic health conditions to more objective measures such as life expectancy, medical diagnosis, hospitalization, and death rates. Data not found easily elsewhere are included. . . ." (*Pref.*). Compiled from results reported by federal and public health agencies. Includes, for example, societal trends, health outcomes, leading chronic and acute health conditions and causes of death, incidence, mortality and survival rates of various illnesses, access to care, insurance and costs, life expectancy, quality of life issues, and other relevant information. Also available as an e-book.

894   ProQuest statistical abstract of the United States. ProQuest. Lanham, Md.: Bernan Press, 2013. 1025 p.
ISBN 9781598885910
317.3   HA 202

Successor to the important federal publication. When the U.S. government cut funding for the Statistical Abstract of the United States published by the Census Bureau, over the objections of librarians and researchers, ProQuest launched this replacement edition as an annual publication beginning with 2013. Intentionally mimics the format, scope and organization of the original resource. Remains an excellent source for the most current possible data on population, government finance, the economy, and even for some international statistics. Original source publications for figures in tables are indicated. Appendixes include a guide to sources of statistics, state statistical abstracts, and foreign statistical abstracts; discussion of metropolitan and micropolitan statistical areas; and a table of weights and measures. Index. Also available in an online edition, from which the data tables can be retrieved in PDF.

895   Secondary data sources for public health: A practical guide. Sarah Boslaugh. Cambridge, [England]; New York: Cambridge University Press, 2007. x, 152 p. ISBN 052169023
362.10727   RA409.B66

Part of Practical guides to biostatistics and epidemiology.

Contents: ch. 1, "An introduction to secondary analysis"; ch. 2, "Health services utilization data"; ch. 3, "Health behaviors and risk factors data"; ch. 4, "Data on multiple health topics"; ch. 5, "Fertility and mortality data"; ch. 6, "Medicare and Medicaid data"; ch. 7, "Other sources of data"; appendixes: I, "Acronyms"; II, "Summary of data sets and years available"; III, "Data import and transfer".

This guide lists the major sources of secondary data for health-related subjects that are important in epidemiology and public health research. They are often stored in different locations and not necessarily easily accessible. Examples include the National hospital discharge survey, the Healthcare cost utilization project, the Behavioral risk factor surveillance system, the National health and nutrition survey, Medicare public use files, Web portals to statistical data, etc. Description of each resource includes title, focus, core section, data collection, and information on accessing data and ancillary materials. Includes bibliography and index. Also available as an e-book.

896   Women's health USA (WHUSA). http://purl.access.gpo.gov/GPO/ LPS21379. U.S. Dept. of Health and

Human Services, Maternal and Child Health Bureau. Rockville, Md.: U.S. Dept. of Health and Human Services, Maternal and Child Health Bureau. 2002–

"An illustrated collection of current and historical data"—*main page*.

Part of Health Resources and Services Administration (HRSA), within the U.S. Dept. of Health and Human Services (HHS)

Description based on WHUSA 2012 ed. Online access to previous editions is included.

Contents: Population characteristics; Health status; Health services utilization; HRSA programs women's health.

Collection of current and historical data on health challenges facing women, with information on life expectancy and addressing topics such as postpartum depression, smoking, alcohol, illicit drug use, etc. Brings together the latest available information from various government agencies (HHS, U.S. Dept. of Agriculture, U.S. Dept. of Labor, U.S. Dept. of Justice).

Other notable women's health and policy websites include, for example, Women's health (MedlinePlus) http://www.nlm.nih.gov/medlineplus/womenshealth .html , Women's health resources http://whr.nlm.nih .gov/, Womenshealth.gov http://www.womenshealth .gov/health-topics/; The Kaiser Family Foundation's Women's health policy http://kff.org/womens -health-policy/.

Internet resources

897   Agency for Healthcare Research and Quality (AHRQ). http://www.ahrq.gov. Agency for Healthcare Research and Quality (U.S.). Rockville, Md.: Agency for Healthcare Research and Quality. 1990s

Searchable website ("search AHRQ" and "A–Z Quick Menu") provides access to a variety of resources, with links to clinical and consumer health information, research findings, funding opportunities, data and surveys, quality assessment, specific populations (minorities, women, elderly, and others), and public health preparedness (bioterrorism and response). Links to a large number of full-text documents, including links to the tools, literature, and news in patient safety (e.g., *AHRQ patient safety network*) and tips on how to prevent medical errors.

898   AHRQ health care innovations exchange. http://www.innovations.ahrq .gov/index.aspx. Agency for Healthcare Research and Quality (AHRQ). Rockville, Md: Agency for Healthcare Research and Quality

"Innovations and tools to improve quality and reduce disparities."—*Website*.

Clearinghouse for practical tools for measuring and possibly improving the quality of health care. Provides a list of tools, with the newest listed first (http:// www.innovations.ahrq.gov/innovations_qualitytools .aspx). Allows to browse by subject (http://www .innovations.ahrq.gov/browse.aspx) to find tools "relevant to a specific disease, clinical specialty, or type of clinical care."—*Website*. Also provides an A-Z index of diseases. Each entry contains several elements as appropriate, such as summary, tool availability, URL, description, tool category, audience, key features, target population, target population age, association with vulnerable populations, and other elements.

Related sites are Agency for Healthcare Research and Quality (AHRQ, 335), National Guideline Clearinghouse™ (NGC, 335), and National Quality Measures Clearinghouse™ (NQMC).

899   American hospital association. http://www.aha.org/aha_app/index.jsp. American Hospital Association. Chicago: American Hospital Association

Founded in 1898, the association represents hospitals, health care networks, and their consumers. The website provides "Fast Facts on U.S. Hospitals," reports and studies, trends, testimony, regulations, and a section for members only. Some information is only available for a fee.

900   Centers for Medicare and Medicaid services (U.S.). http://cms.hhs.gov/. Centers for Medicare and Medicaid Services (U.S.), U.S. Health Care Financing Administration. Baltimore: Centers for Medicare and Medicaid Services, U.S. Dept. of Health and Human Services. 2001–

RA395.A3

Centers for Medicare and Medicaid Services (CMS), formerly Health Care Financing Administration.

Detailed information on Medicare, the federal health insurance program for people 65 years and older and for younger people with certain disabilities, providing details on enrollment, benefits, and other data; Medicaid, a joint federal and state program (state programs vary from state to state) that helps with medical costs for people with low income and limited means; SCHIP (State Children's Health Insurance Program); regulation and guidance manuals and Health Insurance Portability and Accountability Act (HIPAA), research, statistics, data and systems. Also provides various tools and resources helpful in navigating this website, for example a "glossary tool," an "acronym lookup tool," "FAQs," and others.

Includes information on the electronic health record (EHR) (http://www.cms.gov/Medicare/E-Health/EHealthRecords/index.html), sometimes also called electronic medical record (EMR) which "allows healthcare providers to record patient information electronically instead of using paper records" and furthermore "the ability to support other care-related activities directly or indirectly through various interfaces, including evidence-based decision support, quality management, and outcomes reporting."—*Website*. Also provides related links, for example, to the "EHR Incentive Program" and "Health Level Seven International (HL7)" standards for interoperability.

901 County health rankings & roadmaps.
http://www.countyhealthrankings.org/.
Robert Wood Johnson Foundation,
University of Wisconsin Population
Health Institute. Madison, Wisc.:
University of Wisconsin Population
Health Institute. 2010–

RA407.3

Part of the County Health Rankings & Roadmaps program, a collaboration between the Robert Wood Johnson Foundation and the University of Wisconsin Population Health Institute. Further information at http://www.countyhealthrankings.org/about-project.

A map of the U.S. allows to click on individual states to show county-by-county health data and the rank of the health of "nearly every county in the nation."—*Website*. Provides data of the overall health of each county and helps with understanding the factors that affect health (e.g., income, limited access to health foods, air and water quality, smoking, obesity, etc.) Offers various display options

for data. FAQs (http://www.countyhealthrankings.org/faq-page) answer general and methodology questions. For all audiences.

902 The Dartmouth atlas of health care.
http://www.dartmouthatlas.org/atlases.shtm. Dartmouth Institute for Health Policy and Clinical Practice, Dartmouth Medical School, American Hospital Association. Lebanon, N.H.: Dartmouth Institute for Health Policy and Clinical Practice

The Dartmouth Atlas Project started as a series of books and is now accessible via a web-based resource, providing access to the *Dartmouth atlas of health care* series (national editions, specialty-specific editions, state editions, and regional editions). Describes and illustrates quality, cost, and delivery of healthcare services in the U.S. and geographic variations in practice patterns, with description of the physician workforce and distribution of resources. Written for health policy analysts and other health professionals. The home page at http://www.dartmouthatlas.org/index.shtm provides additional information.

903 Health and medical care archive.
http://www.icpsr.umich.edu/icpsrweb/HMCA/. Robert Wood Johnson Foundation, Inter-University Consortium for Political and Social Research. Ann Arbor, Mich.: Inter-University Consortium for Political and Social Research

Data archive of the Robert Wood Johnson Foundation (RWJF), operated by the Inter-university Consortium for Political and Social Research (ICPSR) at the University of Michigan.

"Preserves and disseminates data collected by selected research projects funded by the Foundation and facilitates secondary analyses of the data. surveys of health care professionals and organizations, investigations of access to medical care, surveys on substance abuse, and evaluations of innovative programs for the delivery of health care. Our goal is to increase understanding of health and health care in the United States through secondary analysis of RWJF-supported data collections."—*About page*. Data collections can be searched by keyword or browsed by the following subjects: health care providers; cost/access to health care; substance abuse and health; chronic health conditions; other. Details about RWJF's "community tracking study" at https://www.icpsr.umich.edu/icpsrweb/content/HMCA/community-tracking-study.html.

904 Healthcare cost and utilization project (HCUP). http://www.hcup-us.ahrq.gov/home.jsp. Agency for Healthcare Research and Quality (AHRQ). Rockville, Md.: Agency for Healthcare Research and Quality, U.S. Dept. of Health and Human Services

"Family of health care databases and related software tools and products . . . made possible by a Federal-State-Industry partnership sponsored by the Agency for Healthcare Research and Quality (AHRQ)" (*Website*).

Website designed to answer HCUP-related questions. Provides information on HCUP databases (e.g., Nationwide Inpatient Sample, State Inpatient Databases, State Ambulatory Surgery Databases, and others), tools and software products (e.g., HCUPnet, an interactive tool for identifying, tracking, analyzing, and comparing statistics on hospital care (e.g.,*HCUP statistical briefs* http://www.hcup-us.ahrq.gov/reports/statbriefs/statbriefs.jsp); Clinical classifications software, and others), and offers technical assistance to HCUP users.

905 HealthCare.gov. http://www.healthcare.gov. United States.; Department of Health and Human Services., U.S. Centers for Medicare & Medicaid Services. Baltimore: U.S. Centers for Medicare & Medicaid Services. 2010-

RA395.A3

Also available in Spanish http://www.CuidadoDeSalud.gov; other language resources available at https://www.healthcare.gov/language-resource/

The new health care law, the Patient Protection and Affordable Care Act (also referred to as Affordable Care Act, ACA, and "Obamacare"), changes the American health care system in many ways, with significant impact on individuals and families, and on small businesses. ACA is designed to expand access to more affordable health insurance, to improve quality of healthcare services, to increase consumer protection, to emphasize prevention and wellness, to improve healthcare system performance, to curb healthcare costs, etc.

Guaranteed coverage, individual mandate, and financial assistance are important features of ACA. The law is administered by the Center for Consumer Information & Insurance Oversight, and creates public health insurance exchanges, i.e., online marketplaces in all U.S. states. Different levels of plans are available as well as cost assistance for qualified persons. U.S. citizens and legal residents are eligible to apply for coverage. Starting 1 Oct 2013, Americans who don't have insurance can choose from quality, affordable health insurance plans in the Marketplace for coverage that begins 1 Jan 2014. Open enrollment starts 1 Oct 2013 and closes on 31 Mar 2014. Applicants must enroll by 15 Dec 2013 for coverage effective 1 Jan 2014.

HealthCare.gov tabs: Learn; Get insurance; Individuals & families; Small businesses; All topics: Health insurance marketplace; Using the marketplace; Getting lower costs on coverage; Young adults; Businesses; Health insurance basics; Other health insurance programs; If you have health insurance; Rights, protections, and the law; Prevention.

The federal website for the new health law information, managed by the Centers for Medicare & Medicaid Services (U.S.). Provides access to official resources to help health consumers learn about and get ready for changes, with information about ACA and the opening of the new health insurance Marketplace in every state. These resources provide answers to questions about health coverage options, private health plans and comparison of private health plans, status of a particular state's Marketplace, how to get help enrolling in the Marketplace, pre-existing conditions, how to get an estimate of costs and savings on Marketplace insurance, etc.

Selected links to ACA resources from government/organizations websites:

Healthcare.gov:

"Contact us (Affordable Care Act)"—https://www.healthcare.gov/contact-us/

"Find local help (Affordable Care Act)"—https://localhelp.healthcare.gov/

"Read the law" http://www.hhs.gov/healthcare/rights/law/index.html

"What's the marketplace in my state"? http://www.healthcare.gov/what-is-the-marketplace-in-my-state

Finder.HealthCare.gov http://finder.healthcare.gov/: This tool can help with finding health insurance coverage if needed before 2014.

HealthCare.gov Archive https://www.healthcare.gov/archive/: Includes all material formerly found on HealthCare.gov, captured at weekly intervals.

Marketplace social media channels to share stories: http://Facebook.com/HealthCare.gov; http://Facebook.com/CuidadoDeSalud.gov; @HealthCare Gov; @CuidadoDeSalud

Centers for Medicare & Medicaid Services CMS.gov selected links:

Affordable Care Act in Action at CMS http://cms.gov/about-cms/aca/affordable-care-act-in-action-at-cms.html

Marketplace.CMS.gov http://marketplace.cms.gov/

Marketplace.CMS.gov "Get official resources" http://marketplace.cms.gov/getofficialresources/get-official-resources.html

Glossary https://www.healthcare.gov/glossary/

HHS(U.S. Dept. of Health and Human Services)selected links:

Healthcare.gov sitemap https://www.healthcare.gov/sitemap/

HHSgov/HealthCarehttp://www.hhs.gov/healthcare/

Affordable Care Act http://www.hhs.gov/opa/affordable-care-act/index.html

Affordable Care Act fact sheets http://www.hhs.gov/healthcare/facts/factsheets/index.html

Key features of the health care law http://www.hhs.gov/healthcare/facts/timeline/index.html

Key features of the Affordable Care Act by year http://www.hhs.gov/healthcare/facts/timeline/timeline-text.html

State by state: "Click on your state to learn about health care where you live" http://www.hhs.gov/healthcare/facts/bystate/statebystate.html

Blog: Join social media channels to keep up with the latest developments http://www.hhs.gov/healthcare/facts/blog/index.html

National Library of Medicine (NLM)

Health insurance (MedlinePlus) http://www.nlm.nih.gov/medlineplus/healthinsurance.html

National Network of Libraries of Medicine (NN/LM)

Greater Midwest Region http://nnlm.gov/gmr/outreach/aca.html

MidContinental Region http://nnlm.gov/mcr/resources/aca.html

Middle Atlantic Region http://guides.nnlm.gov/mar_aca

New England Region http://nnlm.gov/ner/training/aca.html

Pacific Northwest Region http://nnlm.gov/pnr/ACA.html

Pacific Southwest Region http://guides.nnlm.gov/psr/aca

South Central Region http://nnlm.gov/scr/outreach/aca.html

Southeastern/Atlantic Region http://guides.nnlm.gov/sea/ACA

Substance Abuse and Mental Health Services Administration (SAMHSA)

"Getting ready for the health insurance marketplace toolkits" for various user groups (e.g., general audience, community-based prevention, consumer, family, peer & recovery community organizations, and others http://marketplace.cms.gov/getofficialresources/other-partner-resources/other-partner-resources.html

Related websites:

AARP http://www.aarp.org/

American Library Association (ALA) http://www.ala.org/tools/affordable-care-act

American Medical Association (AMA) "Some facts about ACA implementation" http://www.ama-assn.org/resources/doc/washington/aca-implementation-fa cts.pdf

Kaiser Family Foundation

"Understanding health reform: Resources for consumers" http://kff.org/health-reform/

"State health insurance marketplace profiles" http://kff.org/state-health-marketplace-profiles/

"Summary of the Affordable Care Act" http://kff.org/health-reform/fact-sheet/summary-of-new-health-reform-l aw/

WebJunction (Partnership between WebJunction and ZeroDivide, funded by the Institute of Museum and Library Services [IMLS] to provide the library community with training and information about patron requests for health insurance-related resources, with the "mission to promote learning for all library staff providing an open, affordable online learning community" (*Website*):

"Health happens in libraries" http://www.webjunction.org/explore-topics/ehealth.html

"Preparing libraries for the Affordable Care Act" http://www.webjunction.org/news/webjunction/preparing-libraries-afford able-care-act.html

906   **Health Resources and Services Administration (HRSA)**. http://www.hrsa.gov/. Health Resources and Services Administration. Washington: Department of Health and Human Services. 1999–

Health Resources and Services Administration (HSRA), pt. of U.S. Dept. of Health and Human Services (HHS).

HRSA provides leadership and direction for various major national programs, such as organ donation and transplantation, HIV/AIDS, drug pricing, programs related to rural health, health information technology, telehealth, emergency preparedness, and bioterrorism. Also provides information and data on the health professions, a "geospatial data warehouse," health workforce analysis and other reports, and a variety of other topics and links to related sites both within the HRSA and other agencies and programs.

907   **Health services research methodology core library recommendations, 2007**. http://www.nlm.nih.gov/nichsr/corelib/hsrmethods.html. AcademyHealth, National Library of Medicine (U.S.). Bethesda, Md.: National Library of Medicine. 2007

Produced by AcademyHealth; National Library of Medicine (NLM); National Information Center on Health Services Research and Health Care (NICHSR). Although dated 2007, website is reviewed and updated regularly.

List of books, journals, bibliographic databases, websites, and other media; useful for collection development librarians and researchers interested in health services research methods. Lists both "core" materials and "desired" materials in areas such as general health policy, health economics, health services research, public health, and several others. The NICHSR website (http://www.nlm.nih.gov/nichsr/outreach.html) lists links to several other recommended lists, including Health economics core library recommendations (2011), Health outcomes core library recommendations (2011), Health policy core library recommendations 2011 (also called Core health policy library recommendations), and other information.

908   **Healthy people**. http://www.cdc.gov/nchs/healthy_people.htm. National

Center for Health Statistics (NCHS). Hyattsville, Md.: Centers for Disease Control (U.S.), National Center for Health Statistics

RA395.A3

Contents: Healthy people 2000; Healthy People 2010; Healthy People 2020; Progress Reviews; Publications.

"Healthy People provides science-based, national goals and objectives with 10-year targets designed to guide national health promotion and disease prevention efforts to improve the health of all people in the United States." —*Home Page*. Previous reports include *Healthy people 2000* (http://purl.access.gpo.gov/GPO/LPS3745) and *Healthy people: The Surgeon General's report on health promotion and disease prevention: Background papers: Report to the Surgeon General on health promotion and disease prevention*. "Healthy People DATA 2010," an interactive database system accessible via CDC WONDER provides various reports and data. A search interface providing searches for published literature related to Healthy People 2010 was added to the "special queries" section of PubMed.

Also available in print format: *Tracking healthy people 2010*. Progress Reviews and publications are added to the website regularly.

909   **Health system (MedlinePlus)**. http://www.nlm.nih.gov/medlineplus/healthsystem.html. National Library of Medicine (U.S.), National Institutes of Health (U.S.). Bethesda, Md.: U.S. National Library of Medicine, National Institutes of Health, Dept. of Health and Human Services. 200?–

List of links to a wide variety of healthcare-related topics, with each link leading to a separate page within MedlinePlus. Provides extensive reference information on the particular topic. Examples include assisted living, health occupations, caregivers, personal medical records, home care services, emergency medical services, health facilities, health insurance, managed care, home care services, hospice care, nursing homes, patients rights, patient safety, veterans and military health, and many others.

910   **Healthy women**. http://www.cdc.gov/nchs/data/healthywomen/womens

chartbook_aug2004.pdf. Centers for Disease Control and Prevention (U.S.); National Center for Health Statistics (U.S.). Hyattsville, Md.: National Center for Health Statistics, Centers for Disease Control and Prevention, U.S. Dept. of Health and Human Services. 2004

RA408.W65

Title varies: Suggested title for website: *Healthy women: State trends in health and mortality;* suggested citation for print version, publ. in 2004 as *Women's health and mortality chartbook* by K. M. Brett and Suzanne G. Hayes.

PDF of *Women's Health and Mortality Chartbook,* developed by NCHS with support from the Office on Women's Health. It describes the health of people in each state in the U.S. by sex, race, and age by reporting current data on critical issues of relevance to women.

Other publications in this area include *Women's health data book: A profile of women's health in the United States,* ed. by D. Misra, a collaborative publication by the Jacobs Institute of Women's Health and the Henry J. Kaiser Family Foundation (Kaiser Family Foundation) since 1992, complemented by *State profiles on women's health: Women's health issues,* publ. since 1998.

911   HSR information central. http://www.nlm.nih.gov/hsrinfo/. Bethesda, Md.: National Library of Medicine (U.S.), National Institutes of Health, Dept. of Health and Human Services. 1993–

HSRIC = Health Services Research Information Central

Contents: HSR general resources: Data, tools, and statistics; HSR social media resources; Education and training; Grants, funding, and fellowships; Guidelines, journals, other publications; Key organizations; Legislation; Meetings and conferences; State resources. HSR topics: Aging Population Issues; Comparative effectiveness research (CER); Child health services research; Evidence-based practice and health; Technology assessment; Health care reform, health economics, and health policy; Health disparities; Health informatics; Public health systems and services research; Quality; Rural health. Alphabetic index (all websites in alphabetic order).

Developed by the National Library of Medicine

to serve the information needs of the health services research community, in partnership with other government agencies and institutes (e.g., Agency for Healthcare Research and Quality (AHRQ, 335), National Cancer Institute, the Cecil C. Sheps Center for Health Services Research, and the Health Services Research and Development Service [HSR&D] at the Veterans Administration, and others). Provides selected links which are intended to represent a sample of available information.

912   Introduction to health services research. http://www.nlm.nih.gov/nichsr/ihcm/index.html. National Library of Medicine (U.S.). Bethesda, Md.: National Library of Medicine. 2007–

Produced by National Information Center on Health Services Research (NICHSR) of the National Library of Medicine (NLM).

Contents: Introduction and purpose; Course objectives; Modules: (1) What Is health services sesearch? (HSR); (2) Brief history of health services research and key projects and milestones; (3) Selected players (federal and private); (4) Search the literature of HSR: Databases; (5) Quality filtering and evidence-based medicine and health; (6) Basic components of a study; (7) Librarians' role in health services research; Selected HSR Internet sites; Essential concepts; Bibliography; Glossaries; Review sections.

Provides extensive information on health services issues, health services research, study design, bibliography of articles and books, databases, and literature analysis.

913   Kaiser Family Foundation. http://www.kff.org/. Henry J. Kaiser Family Foundation. Menlo Park, Calif.: Henry J. Kaiser Family Foundation. 2000– 362.1; 361.7

The Henry J. Kaiser Family Foundation is an independent philanthropy focusing on major health care issues. Website contains statistics on Medicare, Medicaid, the uninsured in each state of the United States, minority health, etc. Links to resources on health policy covering such topics as women's health policy, HIV/AIDS, and media programs. A wide variety of resources are accessible via the following tabs found on the website: (1) Kaiser Health News(http://www.kaiserhealthnews.org/): search for recent daily reports and webcasts; (2) State-HealthFacts (http://kff.org/statedata/): source for state health data; (3) Global Health Facts (http://kff.org/globaldata/); (4) Perspectives; and more.

914   MEPS Medical Expenditure Panel Survey. http://www.meps.ahrq.gov/mepsweb/. U.S. Agency for Healthcare Research and Quality. Bethesda, Md.: Agency for Healthcare Research and Quality. 1996–

RA408.5

Produced by Agency for Health Care Research and Quality (AHRQ).

"Set of large-scale surveys of families and individuals, their medical providers (doctors, hospitals, pharmacies, etc.), and employers across the United States. MEPS collects data on the specific health services that Americans use, how frequently they use them, the cost of these services, and how they are paid for, as well as data on the cost, scope, and breadth of health insurance held by and available to U.S. workers" (*Website*). Provides information on health expenditures, utilization of health services, health insurance, and nursing homes, and reimbursement mechanisms. MEPS topics include access to health care, children's health, children's insurance coverage, health care disparities, mental health, minority health, the uninsured, and other topics. Further details concerning the survey background, data overview, and frequently asked questions are provided at the website. Provides full-text access to MEPS publications: highlights, research findings, statistical briefs, etc.

915   National Information Center on Health Services Research and Health Care Technology (NICHSR). http://www.nlm.nih.gov/nichsr/. National Library of Medicine (U.S.). Bethesda, Md.: National Library of Medicine, National Institutes of Health, U.S. Department of Health and Human Services. 2002–

Health services research (HSR); NICHSR; National Library of Medicine® (NLM®).

NICHSR coordinates NLM's HSR information programs, with links to databases and retrieval services, HSR information central, presentations, publications, and other information. An alphabetic list

(http://www.nlm.nih.gov/hsrinfo/alphahsre.html) of related websites provides a large number of HSR-related links: Federal agencies; associations; data sets and data sources; epidemiology and health statistics; evidence-based medicine and health technology assessment; funding; health policy and health economics; informatics; public health; rural health; state resources; disparities, and others.

A related page is NLM's Health Services Research & Public Health Information Programs, a website that lists resources from multiple NLM programs.

916   National Patient Safety Foundation (NPFS). http://www.npsf.org. National Patient Safety Foundation. North Adams, Mass.: National Patient Safety Foundation

Independent, not-for-profit organization, with the mission to "measurably improve patient safety"—*main page*. Searchable website, with links to online patient safety resources and organizations. Information is presented in different categories (e.g., health care quality and safety, medication safety, surgical safety, cancer treatment safety, and others) for different user groups, such as health professionals, patients and families, and researchers.

917   National quality measures clearinghouse (NQMC). http://www.qualitymeasures.ahrq.gov/. National Quality Measures Clearinghouse (U.S.), Agency for Healthcare Research and Quality (U.S.), U.S. Department of Health & Human Services. Rockville, Md.: U.S. Agency for Healthcare Research and Quality. 2002–

Originally created by Agency for Healthcare Research and Quality (AHQR), American Medical Association (AMA), and American Association of Health Plans (now America's Health Insurance Plans [AHIP]).

Contains evidence-based clinical practice guidelines, protocols, and related documents, with searching and browsing options. Searchable by keyword, disease/condition, treatment/intervention, guideline category, organization and organization type, intended user, clinical specialty, methods to assess and analyze evidence, etc. Related resources (http://www.guideline.gov/resources/index.aspx) includes annotated bibliographies, bioterrorism resources, a glossary, guideline archive (lists withdrawn or superseded guidelines), guideline index (complete listing of the guideline summaries available on the website), National Library of Medicine (NLM) and National Center for Biotechnology Information (NCBI) links (PubMed, Health services technology assessment texts (HSTAT), part of the NCBI bookshelf (http://www.ncbi.nlm.nih.gov/books), patient resources links, and others.

A related site is National guideline clearinghouse (NQMC).

918 NLM gateway. http://gateway.nlm.nih .gov/. National Library of Medicine (U.S.). Bethesda, Md.: National Library of Medicine. 2000–

RA11

As announced in 2011, "the NLM® gateway has transitioned to a new pilot project from the Lister Hill National Center for Biomedical Communications (LHNCBC)."—*Website* The new site focuses now on two databases: Meeting abstracts and Health services research projects. All of the other resources previously accessed through the NLM gateway are available through their individual sites. For a list of these databases previously available via the NLM gateway see http://gateway.nlm.nih.gov/ about.jsp.

The NLM gateway previously allowed simultaneous searching of information resources at the National Library of Medicine (NLM)/National Center for Biotechnology Information (NCBI) with an overview of the search results presented in several categories (bibliographic resources, consumer health resources, and other information), with a listing of the individual databases and the number of results within these categories. Previously included were, for example, MEDLINE/PubMed and the NLM Catalog as well as other resources, including information on current clinical trials and consumer health information (MedlinePlus) and many others.

919   Partners in information access for the public health workforce. http:// phpartners.org/. U.S. National Library of Medicine. Bethesda, Md.: U.S. National Library of Medicine, National Institutes of Health, Dept. of Health and Human Services. 2003–

"Collaboration of U.S. government agencies, public health organizations, and health sciences libraries which provides timely, convenient access to selected public health resources on the Internet . . . [with the mission of] helping the public health workforce find and use information effectively to improve and protect the public's health."—*Website*

Provides links to the individual partner websites, such as Agency for Healthcare Research and Quality (AHRQ, 335), American Public Health Association (APHA), Association of Schools of Public Health (ASPH), Association of State and Territorial Health Officials (ASTHO), Centers for Disease Control and Prevention (CDC), MLANET: Medical Library Association, National Library of Medicine, and several other organizations. Provides extensive information on several public health topics (currently to bioterrorism, environmental health, and HIV/AIDS). For additional information and links see the Partners in Information Access for the Public Health Workforce fact sheet at http://www.nlm .nih.gov/nno/partners.html.

920   State snapshots. http://statesnapshots. ahrq.gov/snaps11/. Agency for Healthcare Research and Quality. Rockville, Md.: Agency for Healthcare Research and Quality. 2007–

Based on data collected from the *National healthcare quality report* (http://purl.access.gpo.gov/ GPO/LPS62498). Also called *NHRQ state snapshots*. Linked Agency for Healthcare Research and Quality Web site.

Provides "state-specific health care quality information including strengths, weaknesses, and opportunity for improvement . . . [to] better understand healthcare quality and disparities" (*Website*). A "state selection map" (http://statesnapshots .ahrq.gov/snaps11/map.jsp?menuId=2&state=) allows users to choose a particular state and compare it to other states in terms of healthcare quality, types of care (preventive, acute, and chronic), settings of care (hospitals, ambulatory care, nursing home, and home health), several specific conditions, and clinical preventive services. Provides help with interpretation of results and a methods section.

The Kaiser Family Foundation makes a comparable website available: "State Health Facts" (http:// www.statehealthfacts.org). Provides statistical data and health policy information on various health topics, with a standardized menu for information about each state ("individual state profiles" tab) and to find out how it compares to the U.S. overall ("50 state comparisons" tab). Categories include demography and the economy, health status, health coverage & the uninsured, Medicaid and SCHIP, health costs & budgets, Medicare, managed care and health insurance, providers and service use, minority health, women's health, and HIV/AIDS.

921   U.S. Dept. of Health and Human Services (HHS.gov). http://www.hhs .gov/. U.S. Dept. of Health and Human Services (HHS). Washington: U.S. Dept. of Health and Human Services. 1997–

HV85

"United States government's principal agency for protecting the health of all Americans and providing essential human services, especially for those who are least able to help themselves."— *About page*

HHS works closely with state and local governments. The Department's approx. 300 programs are administered by 11 operating divisions, including eight agencies in the U.S. Public Health Service and three human services agencies. A guide to information resources, i.e. "HHS information resources directory," is available at http:// www.hhs.gov/about/referlst.html. This site also provides, for example, information on key initiatives (e.g., HealthCare.gov, FoodSafety.gov, InsureKidsNow.gov, for example), news and a news archive, information on prevention of diseases and a healthy lifestyle and on diseases and conditions, health information privacy, human research protections, health information technology standards, laws and regulations, and policies and guidelines. The current HHS website is searchable at http:// www.hhs.gov/. Archival access to older materials (e.g., speeches, materials of historical or research interest, etc.) is available at http://archive.hhs.gov/. Historical Highlights and Past Secretaries, from 1798-2009, can be found at http://www.hhs.gov/ about/hhshist.html.

International and Global Health

922 Circumpolar health atlas. T. Kue
Young, Rajiv Rawat. Toronto; Buffalo,
N.Y.: University of Toronto Press, 2012.
ix, 190 p., ill. (chiefly col.), maps.
ISBN 9781442644564
614.4/21130223   RC957.3.C57

Contents: Pt. 1, The circumpolar world; pt. 2,
Circumpolar peoples; pt. 3, Health status; pt.
4, Health determinants; pt. 5, Health systems;
Bibliography.

Description of the circumpolar regions in the
Northern Hemisphere and explanation of this particular physical environment's influence on the
health of the different populations and their cultures & languages. The five sections of this atlas are
color-coded and include full-color charts, maps,
tables, and photos. It is a reference guide for health
researchers, and general and professional readers.
This atlas is an outgrowth of *Health transitions in
Arctic populations* by Young et al.

Another resource in this area is the information
provided by the Circumpolar Health Observatory
(CircHOB) at http://circhob.circumpolarhealth.
org/, located at the Institute for Circumpolar
Health Research Data Centre, Yellowknife, Northwest Territories, Canada. It is described as an
"international collaborative health information
system, involved in systematic, standardized, and
consistent data collection and analysis. In addition to aggregating online and print resources,
CircHOB is population-based, and produces

data for all northern regions in all circumpolar
countries."—*About page*.

**923 Health information for international
travel**. http://purl.access.gpo.gov/GPO/
LPS3580. Phyllis E. Kozarsky, Paul M.
Arguin, Ava W. Navin, U.S. Centers
for Disease Control and Prevention.
Atlanta: U.S. Dept. of Health and Human
Services, Centers for Disease Control and
Prevention. 1974–

Part of the Centers for Disease Control (CDC)
Travelers' health website (http://wwwnc.cdc.gov/
travel/default.aspx). Also called "Yellow book"
or "CDC yellow book." Description based on the
2014 ed., also issued in print with title *CDC health
information for international travel: The yellow
book*. Previous print editions issued since 1989 as
a serial, *International travel health guide*.

Contents: Ch. 1, "Introduction"; ch. 2, "The
Pre-travel consultation"; ch. 3, "Infectious diseases
related to travel"; ch. 4, "Select destinations"; ch.
5, "Post-travel evaluation"; ch. 6, "Conveyance and
transportation issues"; ch. 7, "International travel
with infants and children"; ch. 8, "Advising travelers with specific needs"; ch. 9, "Health considerations for newly arrived immigrants and refugees".
Appendix (A), "Promotion of quality in the practice of travel medicine"; (B), "Essential electronic
resources for the travel medicine practitioner";
(C), Travel vaccine summary table; (D), "The

HealthMap system." Also contains separate lists of tables, maps, boxes, and figures.

Provides comprehensive information on vaccination requirements and recommendations for international travelers concerning health risks.

The World Health Organization's website, International travel and health, also offers extensive travel information.

924 World atlas of epidemic diseases.
A. D. Cliff, Peter Haggett, Matthew Smallman-Raynor. London; New York: Arnold; Distributed in the U.S. of America by Oxford University Press, 2004. 1 atlas (ix, 212 p.), ill. (some col.), maps (some col.) ISBN 9780340761717

614.4/2/0223   G1046.E51 C57

Contents: Ch. 1, "Introduction"; ch. 2, "The classic plagues, I"; ch. 3, "The classic plagues, II"; ch. 4, "Persistent scourges"; ch. 5, "Childrens' diseases"; ch. 6, "Winter and seasonal ailments"; ch. 7, "Tropical diseases, I"; ch. 8. "Tropical diseases, II"; ch. 9, "Vaccine-preventable diseases"; ch. 10, "Newly-emergent diseases, I"; ch. 11, "Newly-emergent diseases, II"; ch. 12, "Future patterns of disease."

"Collection of maps, illustrations, and commentary offers an authoritative overview of the global distribution of major epidemic diseases on a variety of spatial scales from the local to the global. Arranged in a historical sequence, beginning with the classic plagues such as the Black Death and moving on through smallpox and measles to modern diseases such as AIDS and Legionnaires disease. The text for each disease includes discussion of its nature and epidemiological features, its origin (where known) and historical impacts, and its global status at the start of the twenty-first century."—*Publ. description*. Glossary, bibliography, further readings, and index. This atlas complements an earlier title by the same authors, *Atlas of disease distributions: Analytic approaches to epidemiological data*.

Indexes; Abstract journals; Databases

925 Food Safety Research Information Office at the National Agricultural

Library. http://fsrio.nal.usda.gov/index. php. National Agricultural Library (U.S.), Food Safety Research Information Office. Beltsville, Md.: National Agricultural Library, Food Safety Research Information Office. 2002–

TX537

Produced by National Agricultural Library (NAL); Food Service Research Information Office (FSRIO).

A major component of this searchable website is its "Research Projects Database" for locating information on food safety and related research. Categories currently in use in this database include food and food products, food composition and characteristics, food quality characteristics, food handling and processing, on-farm food safety, diseases and poisonings, sanitation and pathogen control, contaminants and contamination, government policy and regulations, methodology and quality standards, human health and epidemiology, education and training, facilities and sites, and pathogen biology.

Complements information found, for example, in *Food safety handbook*, *Food safety: A reference handbook* by Redman, *Foodborne disease handbook* by Hui, and two books with the same title, but different authors, i.e., *Foodborne diseases* by Cliver et al., and *Foodborne diseases* by Simjee.

926 Global health. http://www.cabi.org/ publishing-products/online-information-resources/global-health/. C.A.B. International., Great Britain. Wallingford, Oxfordshire, U.K.: CABI. 1973–

RA441

Formerly known as *CAB health*.

Global health, 1973– (derived from *CAB abstracts* and *Public health and tropical medicine* databases; *Global health archive*, 1910–83 (derived from six former print abstracting sources). Includes records from the Bureau of Hygiene and Tropical Diseases to 1983.

Online databases available through CAB Direct, OvidSP, EBSCO, Dialog, and others. Indexes journals, books, book chapters, conference proceedings, and other resources, mostly English-language publications, but also in other languages. Useful databases for searching the international health and public health literature, in addition to searching MEDLINE and EMBASE.

For researchers, health professionals, policy makers, and students.

927 International clinical trials registry platform search portal (ICTRP).
http://www.who.int/trialsearch/.
World Health Organization. Geneva, Switzerland: World Health Organization. 200?–

Produced by World Health Organization (WHO).

Database to locate information about clinical trials. Described by Tim Evans (WHO) as a "collaborative international initiative led by WHO that facilitates the identification of all clinical trials, regardless of whether or not they have been published." For health care researchers.

928 POPLINE. http://www.popline.org/.
Johns Hopkins University Bloomberg School of Public Health, Information and Knowledge for Optimal Health Project. Baltimore: Johns Hopkins University Bloomberg School of Public Health

HQ766

A free resource, maintained by the Knowledge for Health Project http://www.k4health.org/ at the Johns Hopkins Bloomberg School of Public Health/Center for Communication Programs and funded by the United States Agency for International Development (USAID) http://www.usaid.gov/.

Database on reproductive health with international coverage. Provides bibliographic citations with abstracts to English-language published and unpublished biomedical and social science literature, with links to full-text documents, RSS feeds for topical searches, and other special features. POPLINE subjects (http://www.popline.org/poplinesubjects) in 12 main categories: Adolescent reproductive health; family planning methods; family planning programs; gender; health communication; HIV/AIDS; maternal and child health; population dynamics; population law and policy; population, health, and environment; reproductive health; sexually transmitted infections.

929 PubMed. http://www.ncbi.nlm.nih.gov/pubmed. U.S. National Center for Biotechnology Information, National Library of Medicine, National Institutes of Health. Bethesda, Md.: U.S. National Center for Biotechnology Information. 1996–

PubMed®, developed and maintained by the National Center for Biotechnology Information (NCBI) at the National Library of Medicine® (NLM). Provides a search interface for more than 20 million bibliographic citations and abstracts in the fields of medicine, nursing, dentistry, veterinary medicine, health care systems, and preclinical sciences. It provides access to articles indexed for MEDLINE® and for selected life sciences journals. PubMed subsets found under the "Limits" tab are: MEDLINE and PubMed central®, several journal groups (i.e., core clinical journals, dental journals, and nursing journals), and topical subsets (AIDS, bioethics, cancer, complementary medicine, dietary supplements, history of medicine, space life sciences, systematic reviews, toxicology, and veterinary science). "Link-out" provides access to full-text articles.

For detailed information see the PubMed fact sheet at http://www.nlm.nih.gov/pubs/factsheets/pubmed.html and also MEDLINE®/PubMed® resources guide (http://www.nlm.nih.gov/bsd/pmresources.html) which provides detailed information about MEDLINE data and searching PubMed.

Information regarding the mobile version of this resource is part of NLM's Gallery of mobile apps and sites.

Dictionaries

930 Historical dictionary of the World Health Organization. 2nd ed.
ed. Kelley Lee, Jennifer Fang.
Lanham, Md.: Scarecrow Press, 2013.
ISBN 9780810878587
362.1   RA8
First ed., 1998.

(Historical dictionaries of international organizations series)

Provides information on the history of the World Health Organization (WHO) and its contributions to international health cooperation, with emphasis on the last 20 years. Includes a new introduction to WHO agencies & programs, an extensive bibliography on WHO documents and writings about WHO, and a chronology of selected major events in the history of international health organizations. Includes appendixes, for example, constitution of WHO, chronological list of member states, and WHO directors. Related information available on the World Health Organization (WHO) home page.

Handbooks

931 Health care reform around the world.
Andrew C. Twaddle. Westport, Conn.: Auburn House, 2002. xiii, 419 p., ill.
ISBN 0865692882

362.1   RA394.H4145

Describes health care reform efforts and trends in different countries, with roughly comparable information for the countries included. Ch. 1 is an international comparison of health care system reforms—United Kingdom, Eastern and Western Europe, United States, the Middle East, Latin America, Asia, and Oceania. Also available as an e-book.

932 Health care systems around the world: Characteristics, issues, reforms. Marie L. Lassey, William R. Lassey, Martin J. Jinks. Upper Saddle River, N.J.: Prentice Hall, 1997. xiii, 370 p., ill., maps.
ISBN 0131042335

362.1   RA393.L328

Contents: Introduction, basic issues and concepts; The countries and their characteristics; The United States, high-technology and limited access; Canada, challenges to public payment for universal care; Japan, preventive health care as cultural norm; Germany, a tradition of universal health care; France, centrally controlled and locally managed; The Netherlands, gradual adaptation; Sweden, decentralized comprehensive care; The United Kingdom, the economy model; The Czech Republic, a new mixture of public and private services; Hungary, creating a remodeled system; Russia, transition to market and consumer orientation; China, privatizing socialist health care; Mexico, modernizing structure and expanded rural services; Organization variations and reforms; Economic organization of health care, comparative perspectives; Expectations for reform, a glimpse at the future. Description and analysis of health care systems in different countries, addressing demographic, social, and economic characteristics, also health promotion,

prevention of disease, and health care. Includes bibliographical references and index.

A 2013 publication, *Health care systems around the world: A comparative guide* by Boslaugh, describes health care systems for a large number of countries. Arranged in alphabetical order by country, with content for each country presented in a standardized format, allowing for comparison from country to country.

933 Health care systems of the developed world: How the United States' system remains an outlier. Duane A. Matcha. Westport, Conn.: Praeger, 2003. x, 198 p., ill. ISBN 027597992X

362.1/0973   RA441.M38

Contents: ch. 1, Introduction; ch. 2, The United States; ch. 3, Canada; ch. 4, United Kingdom; ch. 5, Germany; ch. 6, Sweden; ch. 7, Japan; ch. 8, Conclusion. Provides an introduction to selected major healthcare systems, with consideration of their historical and political basis. Provides a framework for analysis and comparison of the different systems. Various tables and figures related to health insurance, personal health care expenditures, self-rated health status, future concerns, and others. Includes bibliographical references and index. Also available as an e-book.

World health systems: challenges and perspectives presents profiles of health systems in 28 countries. *Health care systems around the world: Characteristics, issues, reforms,* provides additional information in this area. Milton I Roemer's *National health systems of the world* remains an important title. It consists of a comprehensive study and analysis of national health systems in 68 industrialized, middle-income, and very poor countries, with a cross-national analysis of the major health care issues within different systems.

934 International guidelines on HIV/AIDS and human rights. http://www2 .ohchr.org/english/issues/hiv/docs/ consolidated_guidelines.pdf. Office of the United Nationals High Commissioner for Human Rights (OHCHR); UNAIDS Joint United Nations Programme on HIV/AIDS, UNAIDS Joint United Nations Programme on HIV/AIDS. Geneva, Switzerland: United Nations OHCHR. 2006

Organized jointly by the Office of the United Nations High Commissioner for Human Rights (OHCHR) and the UNAIDS Joint United Nations Programme on HIV/AIDS.

2006 consolidated version of the Second (Geneva, 23–25 Sep. 1996) and Third (Geneva, 25–26 Jul. 2002) International Consultation on HIV/AIDS and Human Rights.

Contents: (I) Guidelines for state action: (A) Institutional responsibilities and processes; (B) Law review, reform and support services; (C) Promotion of a supportive and enabling environment; (II) Recommendations for dissemination and implementation of the guidelines on HIV/AIDS and human right: (A) States; (B) United Nationals system and regional intergovernmental bodies; (C) Nongovernmental organizations; (III) International human rights obligations and HIV: (A) Human rights standards and the nature of State obligations; (B) Restrictions and limitations; (C) The application of specific human rights in the context of the HIV epidemic; Annex 1, History of the recognition of the importance of human rights in the context of HIV; Annex 2, List of participants at the Second International Consultation on HIV/AIDS and Human Rights; Annex 3, List of participants at the Third International Consultation on HIV/AIDS and Human Rights.

"A tool for States in designing, co-ordinating and implementing effective national HIV/AIDS policies and strategies . . . human rights standards apply in the context of HIV/AIDS and translating them into practical measures that should be undertaken at the national level, based on three broad approaches: improvement of government capacity for multi-sectoral coordination and accountability; reform of laws and legal support services, with a focus on anti-discrimination, protection of public health, and improvement of the status of women, children and marginalized groups; and support and increased private sector and community participation to respond ethically and effectively to HIV/AIDS.

OHCHR encourages governments, national human rights institutions, non-governmental organizations and people living with HIV and AIDS to use the Guidelines for training, policy formulation, advocacy, and the development of legislation on HIV/AIDS-related human rights."—*Website*

935   International health regulations (2005). http://www.who.int/ihr/publications/9789241596664/en/index.html. World Health Organization. Geneva, Switzerland: World Health Organization. 2007
IHR

Rev. ed., with the new regulations in force on June 15, 2007. Also publ. as a print edition. Supersedes *International health regulations (1969)*, publ. in several different print editions. Title varies: previously called *International sanitary regulations*.

Part of WHO's Global Alert and Response http://www.who.int/csr/en/

Considered a code of practices and procedures for the prevention of the spread of disease, "in consideration of the increases in international travel and trade, and emergence and re-emergence of new international disease threats" (*Publ. notes*), with the goal of preventing and protecting against the international spread of disease. Related WHO websites are "International health regulations"(http://www.who.int/topics/international_health_regulations/en/) and "Alert, response, and capacity building under the international health regulation news" (http://www.who.int/ihr/en/).

936   The new Blackwell companion to medical sociology. William C. Cockerham. Malden, Mass.: Wiley-Blackwell, 2010. xvii, 596 p., ill.
ISBN 9781405188685
362.1/042   RA418

Global and comprehensive survey of the emerging field of medical sociology, or the study of the impact of cultural constructs on medical understanding and practice. Provides a definition of the field and its importance for health care research. This new edition offers 24 articles grouped around major themes such as Health and Social Inequalities, Health and Social Relationships, Health and Disease, and Health Care Delivery. The 2001 edition, *The Blackwell companion to medical sociology* by the same author, remains useful for the 17 summaries of regional or national health care practices around the world. Each chapter has bibliographical references. Indexes by author and subject. Available as an e-book.

937   A practical guide to global health service. Edward O'Neil, American

Medical Association. Chicago: American Medical Association, 2006. xxxv, 402 p. ISBN 1579476732

610.73/7   RA390.U5O54

OMNI Med ("loosely translated from the Latin meaning 'health care for all'" [*Pref.*]) is a nongovernmental organization founded by the author in 1998.

Contents: ch. 1, Overcoming obstacles: cultural and practical guidelines; ch. 2, Travel, health, and safety guidelines; ch. 3, The Omni Med database of international health service opportunities; ch. 4, Cross-referencing guide to the database; ch. 5, Other relevant organizations; Appendix A, Useful web sites; Appendix B, About Omni Med.

"A health providers guide to the practical aspects of serving internationally, including data on more than 300 organizations that send health providers overseas" (*Publ. notes*). Organization profiles include concise descriptions, contact information, and practical information about length of service terms, personnel sought, areas served, and availability of funding, training, room and board, and other essential information (e.g., trip planning, travel and safety guidelines, commonly encountered illnesses, information about the culture of a particular country, etc.). Written for persons interested in medical volunteering. Glossary; bibliography.

Caring for the world: A guidebook to global health opportunities, also available as an e-book, is a resource for finding out about health opportunities abroad, with a directory of relevant government and non-government organizations, educational opportunities, funding resources, and trip planning.

938   Routledge handbook of global public health. Richard G. Parker, Marni Sommer. Abingdon, Oxon, U.K.: Routledge, 2011. xxvi, 521 p., ill. ISBN 9780415778480

362.1   RA441.R68

Contents: pt. I, The transition from international health to global health; pt. II, Structural inequalities and global public health; pt. III, Ecological transformation and environmental health in the global system; pt. IV, Population and reproductive health; pt. V, Conflict, violence, and emergencies in global public health; pt. VI, Global public health policy and practice; pt. VII, Global public health and development; pt. VIII, Global mental health; pt. IX, Global access to essential medicines; pt. X, Health

systems, health capacity, and the politics of global public health.

Addresses complex issues important in global health, with contributions from international public health experts. Recommended. Considered a useful resource for graduate students in both the health sciences and also social sciences (e.g., medical sociology, public policy). An important resource for students in public health, nursing, medicine, medical sociology, international public policy studies. Index. Available as an e-book.

939   World health systems: Challenges and perspectives. 2nd ed. Bruce Fried, Laura M. Gaydos. Chicago: Health Administration Press, 2012. xxx, 780 p. ISBN 9781567934205

362.1   RA441.W676

Contents: Pt. I, Current issues facing global health systems; pt. II, Profiled countries: The low income countries (ch. 7-11); The middle-income countries (ch. 12–18); The high-income countries (ch. 19-31); glossary; index.

This revised edition presents new introductory chapters on health systems (e.g., defining a health system, health system strengthening, health system regulation, and the politics of health system reform) and profiles of 26 health systems from around the world. Organized in three categories by the wealth of each nation: low-, middle-, and high-income countries. Addresses the various challenges health services face, how they are organized, and how they are financed. Each chapter includes disease patterns and health system financing, also past, present status, and future health policy issues and various challenges of the individual health systems.

Histories

940   Encyclopedia of pestilence, pandemics, and plagues. Joseph Patrick Byrne, Anthony S. Fauci. Westport, Conn.: Greenwood Press, 2008. 2 v. (xxv, 872 p.), ill., maps. ISBN 9780313341014

614.4003   RA652.E535

Contents: v. 1. A-M — v. 2. N-Z.

Covers both historical and modern infectious diseases (e.g., HIV/AIDS; SARS; influenza epidemics, etc.) and historical epidemics (e.g., black death;

bubonic plague; great plague of London; public health in the Islamic world 1000-1600; syphilis during the 16th century, etc.), including social, economic, and political factors. Sidebars within entries contain information from primary sources. Also includes entries on persons considered important in historical epidemiology. List of all entries and a guide to related topics in front of v. 1. Glossary, bibliography of both print and electronic resources, and index in v. 2. For students, health professionals, and also general readers. Also available as an e-book.

By the same author, *Encyclopedia of black death*, is "a collection of 300 interdisciplinary entries covering plague and its effects on Western society across four centuries" (*Introd.*), with main focus on the second plague pandemic for the years 1340-1840. However, also includes some pre-1340s and post-1840s subjects, a timeline of events, glossary, cross-references, and a bibliography. Considered a useful resource for undergraduates and above and also for general readers. *Encyclopedia of plague and pestilence: From ancient times to the present* is another resource in this area.

The following two Internet resources provide details on the influenza epidemic of 1918-1919: *The Great pandemic: The United States in 1918-1919* http://www.flu.gov/pandemic/history/1918, with historical details (and also a link to current information http://www.flu.gov/index.html) and *Influenza encyclopedia* (University of Michigan Center for the History of Medicine) http://www.influenzaarchive.org/, an excellent, comprehensive searchable collection of primary source documents, images, timelines, reference lists, etc. which provides details of the impact of the epidemic on 50 U.S. cities.

The Centers for Disease Control and Prevention (CDC) provides maps and statistics of cases of human plague in the U.S. and worldwide at http://www.cdc.gov/plague/maps/.

941 **The value of health: A history of the Pan American Health Organization.**
Marcos Cueto. Washington: Pan American Health Organization, 2007. 239 p.
ISBN 9781580462631
362.1   RA10.C8413
(Scientific and technical publication; 600) Pan American Health Organization (PAHO)

Contents: ch. 1, The origins of international public health in the Americas; ch. 2, The birth of a new organization; ch. 3, The consolidation of an identity; ch. 4, For a continent free of disease; ch. 5, Health, development, and community participation; v. 6, Validity and renewal.

History of PAHO, contributions of individuals in PAHO, and also contemporary issues. Endnotes, bibliography, and index.

942 **WHO historical collection**. http://www.who.int/library/collections/historical/en/print.html. World Health Organization. Geneva, Switzerland: World Health Organization. 2000s–
Produced by World Health Organization (WHO); part of WHO Library and Information Networks for Knowledge (LNK).

Covers conferences before the founding of the WHO, WHO official records, International Sanitary Conventions (since 1851), and official records, reports, and other published materials from the Office International d'Hygiène Publique (OIHP), the health organization of the League of Nations (UNRRA). Includes materials on plague, cholera, and yellow fever, and also more recent epidemics; international classifications and nomenclatures of diseases; and public health and medicine monographs on public health in different countries and languages. Related links are, for example, WHOLIS: World Health Organization library database and WHO archives (http://www.who.int/archives/en/index.html). The distinctions between the WHO library, the WHO archives, and WHO records are described at http://www.who.int/archives/fonds_collections/partners/en/index.html.

Statistics

943 **European health for all database (HFA-DB)**. http://data.euro.who.int/hfadb/. World Health Organization Regional Office for Europe. Copenhagen, Denmark: World Health Organization Regional Office for Europe. 2000s–
Description based on Jan. 2013 version.

Provides basic health statistics and health trends for the member states of the WHO European Region, with approximately 600 health indicators, including basic demographic and socioeconomic indicators; some lifestyle- and environment-related indicators; mortality, morbidity, and disability; hospital discharges; and health care resources, utilization, and expenditures. Can be used as a tool for international comparison and for assessing the health situation and trends in any European country. Help available at https://euro.sharefile .com/d-sb7422ab51e54f20b.

944 Finding and using health statistics.
http://www.nlm.nih.gov/nichsr/usestats/. National Information Center on Health Services Research and Health Care Technology, National Library of Medicine (U.S.). Bethesda, Md.: National Library of Medicine. 2008–

Contents: "Introduction"; "About health statistics" ("Importance"; "Uses"; "Sources"; "Health statistics enterprise"); "Finding health statistics" ("Challenges"; "Natural structure"; "Strategies"; "Internet strategies"); "Supporting material" (including a glossary, exercises, and examples).

"This course describes the range of available health statistics, identifies their sources and helps you understand how to use information about their structure as you search."—*Main page*

Reviews various approaches to finding health statistics and provides help with developing search strategies. Links to numerous relevant examples of statistical web resources and portals from federal and state governments, universities, and private organizations. Provides a good introduction and overviews for health professionals, students, and reference librarians.

945 The global burden of disease: A comprehensive assessment of mortality and disability from diseases, injuries, and risk factors in 1990 and projected to 2020.
Christopher J. L. Murray, Alan D. Lopez, Harvard School of Public Health., World Health Organization., World Bank. Cambridge, Mass.: Publ. by the Harvard School of Public Health on behalf of the World Health Organization and the World Bank, 1996. xxxii, 990 p. ISBN 0674354486

614.4/2   RA441.G56
(Global burden of disease and injury series; v. 1)
"The Global Burden of Disease Series provides, on a global and regional level, a detailed and internally consistent approach to meeting . . . information needs . . . concerning epidemiological conditions and disease burden" (*Foreword*). GDB is considered to have set new standards for measuring population health. It also attempts to provide a comparative index of the burden of each disease or injury, i.e., the number of disability-adjusted life years lost as a result of either premature death or years lived with disability. The findings attempt to provide a comprehensive assessment of the health of populations. Results are only approximate, with the reliability of data considered poor for some regions of the world; with estimates of causes of death, incidence and prevalence of disease, injury, and disability, measures and projections of disease burden, and measures of risk factors. Other titles in this series include, e.g., Global health statistics: a compendium of incidence, prevalence, and mortality estimates for over 200 conditions, *Health dimensions of sex and reproduction: the global burden of sexually transmitted diseases, HIV, maternal conditions, perinatal disorders, and congenital anomalies*, and *The global epidemiology of infectious diseases*. Another related title is Global burden of disease and risk factors and the World Health Organization's "Global burden of disease estimates" website (http://www.who.int/healthinfo/ bodestimates/en/index.html), with recent results and links.

946 Global burden of disease and risk factors. Alan D. Lopez, Disease Control Priorities Project. New York; Washington: Oxford University Press; World Bank, 2006. xxix, 475 p., ill. ISBN 9780821362

362.1   RA441.G5613
Disease Control Priorities Project is a partnership of the Fogarty International Center (U.S. National Institutes of Health), the World Bank, The World Health Organization, and the Population Reference Bureau).

Contents: ch. 1, Measuring the Global Burden of Disease and risk factors, 1990–2001; ch. 2, Demographic and epidemiological characteristics of major regions, 1990–2001; ch. 3, The burden of disease and mortality by condition: data, methods, and results for 2001; ch. 4, Comparative quantification of mortality and burden of disease attributable to selected risk factors; ch. 5, Sensitivity and uncertainty analyses for burden of disease and risk factor estimates; ch. 6, Incorporating deaths near the time of birth into estimates of the Global Burden of Disease.

Presents the results of the "Global Burden of Disease Study" (quantification of the impact of diseases, injuries, and risk factors on population health) and the CEA (Cost-Effectiveness Analysis) Study and a description of the global epidemiology of diseases, injuries, and risk factors. Resource for researchers interested in the development of methods to measure disease burden and in global and regional health policy.

Related titles are, e.g., The global burden of disease: A comprehensive assessment of mortality and disability from diseases, injuries, and risk factors, Global health statistics: A compendium of incidence, prevalence, and mortality estimates for over 200 conditions, and the World Health Organization's "Global burden of disease estimates" website(http://www.who.int/healthinfo/bod estimates/en/index.html), with recent results and links.

Available online at http://bibpurl.oclc.org/web/13502.

947 Global health atlas. http://apps. who.int/globalatlas/. World Health Organization. Geneva, Switzerland: World Health Organization. 2003–

RA441

Title varies: WHO's *Communicable disease global atlas*; *Global atlas of infectious disease*; *Global atlas of infectious diseases: An interactive information and mapping system.*

World Health Organization Internet resource "bringing together for analysis and comparison standardized data and statistics for infectious diseases at country, regional, and global levels. The analysis and interpretation of data are further supported through information on demography, socioeconomic conditions, and environmental factors."—*Website*. Searchable database which allows users to create reports, charts, and maps (e.g., geographic areas can be selected to create maps of diseases). Links to related sites, e.g., *Global atlas of the health workforce* and others.

948 Global health observatory (GHO). http://www.who.int/gho/en/. World

Health Organization. Geneva, Switzerland: World Health Organization

RA427

Pt. of the World Health Organization (WHO).

Provides access to data and analysis for monitoring the global health situation. Serves as a health statistics repository. Includes major statistical reports (e.g. *World health statistics*, *Global health risks*; *Women and health*; *Global burden of disease: 2004 update*) by Mathers et al. and links to other reports on a variety of topics from various WHO programs. Also provides access to "country statistics" with health data and statistics for each country, a "map gallery" with an extensive list of maps on major health topics (e.g., environmental health, global influenza virology surveillance, mortality and global burden of disease, violence against women, and others).

949 Global health statistics: A compendium of incidence, prevalence, and mortality estimates for over 200 conditions. Christopher J. L. Murray, Alan D. Lopez, World Health Organization., World Bank., Harvard School of Public Health. Boston; Cambridge, Mass.: Publ. by The Harvard School of Public Health on behalf of the World Health Organization and the World Bank ; Distributed by Harvard University Press, 1996. vii, 906 p. ISBN 0674354494

614.4/2   RA407.M87

(Global burden of disease and injury series; 2)

Provides information on the underlying epidemiological statistics for over 200 conditions and several chapters with detailed data for each condition.

Part of the Global burden of disease series which "provides, on a global and regional level, a detailed and internally consistent approach to meeting . . . information needs . . . concerning epidemiological conditions and disease burden . . . volumes summarize epidemiological knowledge about all major conditions and most risk factors" (*Foreword*).

Other titles in this series include, for example, The global burden of disease: A comprehensive assessment of mortality and disability from diseases, injuries, and risk factors in 1990 and projected to 2020, *Health dimensions of sex and reproduction: the global burden of sexually transmitted diseases,*

HIV, maternal conditions, perinatal disorders, and congenital anomalies, and *The global epidemiology of infectious diseases.* Other related titles are Global burden of disease and risk factors and the World Health Organization's "Global burden of disease estimates" website (http://www.who.int/healthinfo/global_burden_disease/en/index.html), with recent results and links.

950 Health in the Americas. Pan American Sanitary Bureau. Washington: Pan American Health Organization, Pan American Sanitary Bureau, Regional Office of the World Health Organization, 1998–. v., ill.

610/.8s; 362.1/09181/2   RA10.P252

Published by Pan American Health Organization (PAHO); "Salud en las Américas."

Title varies: Previously had title *Summary of reports on the health conditions in the Americas* and *Health conditions in the Americas.* Description based on 2007 ed. (2 v.): v. 1, Regional analysis; v. 2, Country-by-country assessment.

Health data, facts, health trends, and related information for Central and South America, with emphasis on health disparities. Provides a vision for the future of health and health challenges in the Americas. Also available online through net Library; both print and online versions in English or Spanish.

A complement to this publication is *Health statistics from the Americas,* publ. in print format 1991–98, and now online (2003 ed. http://www.paho.org/english/dd/pub/SP_591.htm and 2006 ed. http://www.paho.org/English/DD/AIS/HSA2006.htm).

951 Health statistics (MedlinePlus). http://www.nlm.nih.gov/medlineplus/healthstatistics.html. National Library of Medicine (U.S.). Bethesda, Md.: National Library of Medicine. 2000–

Part of MedlinePlus; National Library of Medicine (NLM).

Contents: Overviews; Latest News; Related Issues; Research; Journal Articles; Directories; Organizations; Newsletters/Print Publications; Law and Policy; Children; Teenagers; Men; Women; Seniors.

Provides helpful links to various types of health and vital statistics for consumers and health professionals. FAQ Statistics (http://www.nlm.nih.gov/services/statistics.html) is another website made available by NLM that answers questions on how to find statistics for U.S. and global health and medicine topics.

952 OECD health data. http://www.oecd.org/health/healthdata. Organisation for Economic Co-operation and Development. Paris: Organisation for Economic Co-operation and Development

Title varies: SourceOECD health data.

Part of SourceOECD, which contains publications (monographs, periodicals, and statistical databases) issued by the OECD.

Interactive database and source of statistics on health and health care systems of the OECD member states. Allows cross-country comparisons of national health care systems. Includes, for example, health status, health care resources, health care utilization, expenditure on health, and health care financing. Available in online and CD-ROM formats.

953 WHO global infobase. http://www.who.int/infobase. World Health Organization. Geneva, Switzerland: World Health Organization. 2000s?–

Produced by World Health Organization (WHO).

Title varies: also called WHO global infobase online.

"Data warehouse that collects, stores and displays information on chronic diseases and their risk factors for all WHO member states"—*main page.* Provides information on health topics, e.g., alcohol and its relationship to disease and injury, blood pressure, cholesterol, diet, overweight and obesity, physical activity, tobacco, diabetes, oral health, visual impairment, and other topics, such as mortality estimates. Information comes from various national surveys, and WHO collaborates with its regional offices to keep information up to date. Provides individual country pages, allows comparison of countries, and displays comparable risk factor data. Extensive help pages include glossary, FAQ page, definitions of terms used, etc.

954 WHOSIS. http://www.who.int/whosis/. World Health Organization. Geneva,

[Switzerland]: World Health Organization. [1994]–

Published by World Health Organization (WHO).

Provides description and online access to statistical and epidemiological information, data, and tools available from WHO and other sites: mortality and health status, disease statistics, health systems statistics, risk factors and health services, and inequities in health. Provides links to several databases: WHOSIS database, with the latest "core health indicators" from WHO sources (including *The world health report* (519) and *World health statistics*), which make it possible to construct tables for any combination of countries, indicators and years, Causes of death database, WHO global infobase online, Global health atlas, and Reproductive health indicators database.

As of 2011, WHOSIS has been incorporated into WHO's Global health observatory(GHO) which provides additional data & tools, and also more analysis and reports.

955   The world health report. http://www .who.int/whr/. World Health Organization. Geneva, [Switzerland]: World Health Organization. 1995–

614.405 1020-3311   RA8.A265

Pt. of WHOSIS: WHO statistical information system.

"Every year . . . takes a new and expert look at global health, focusing on a specific theme, while assessing the current global situation. Using the latest data gathered and validated by WHO, each report paints a picture of the changing world."— *Website* Website also provides links to the full-text reports 1995–2005, each with a focus on a special theme: 1995, "bridging the gaps"; 1996, "fighting disease, fostering development"; 1997, "conquering suffering, enriching humanity"; 1998, "life in the 21st century: a vision for all"; 1999, "making a difference"; 2000, "health systems: improving performance"; 2001, "mental health: new understanding, new hope"; 2002, "reducing risks, promoting healthy life"; 2003, "shaping the future"; 2004, "changing history"; 2005, "make every mother and child count"; 2006, "working together for health"; 2007, "a safer future: global public health security in the 21st century"; 2008, "primary health care: now more than ever"; 2010, "health

systems financing: the path to universal coverage"; 2013, "Research for universal health coverage". No reports for 2009, 2011, or 2012. Also available in print.

956   World health statistics. http://www .who.int/gho/publications/world_health _statistics/en/index.html. World Health Organization. Geneva, Switzerland: World Health Organization. 2005–

RA407.A1

1939/46–96 publ. as *World health statistics annual = Annuaire de statistiques sanitaires mondiales* (print version).

Part of WHOSIS: WHO statistical information system.

Provides online access to the 2005-2013 reports. Description based on 2013 online edition (http://www.who.int/whosis/whostat/EN_WHS 2011_Full.pdf).

Contents: pt. I, "Health-related millennium development goals"; pt. II, "Global health indicators"; tables: 1. "Life expectancy and mortality"; 2. "Cause-specific mortality and morbidity"; 3. "Selected infectious diseases"; 4. "Health service coverage"; 5. "Risk factors"; 6. "Health systems"; 7. "Health expenditure"; 8. "Health inequities"; 9. "Demographic and socioeconomic statistics."

"Annual compilation of health-related data for its 193 Member States . . . includes a summary of the progress made towards achieving the health-related Millennium Development Goals (MDGs) and associated targets . . . using publications and databases produced and maintained by the technical programmes and regional offices of WHO. Indicators have been included on the basis of their relevance to global public health; the availability and quality of the data; and the reliability and comparability of the resulting estimates. Taken together, these indicators provide a comprehensive summary of the current status of national health and health systems."—*Introd.* Derived from multiple sources, depending on each indicator and the availability and quality of data. Every effort has been made to ensure the best use of country-reported data – adjusted where necessary to deal with missing values, to correct for known biases, and to maximize the comparability of the statistics across countries and over time (cf. Introd.) A print version is also available.

Internet resources

957 amfAR. http://www.amfar.org. American Foundation for AIDS Research. New York; Washington: American Foundation for AIDS Research. 1999–

"amfAR™, the Foundation for AIDS Research, is one of the world's leading nonprofit organizations dedicated to the support of AIDS research, HIV prevention, treatment education, and the advocacy of sound AIDS-related public policy."—*Website*

Provides basic HIV/AIDS facts and statistics, HIV testing, information about various therapies (approved or under development), young people and HIV/AIDS, women and HIV/AIDS, global initiatives, and many other related topics and links.

"amfAR global links," formerly know as *HIV/ AIDS treatment directory*, and "HIV/AIDS treatment insider," available 2000-5, have ceased publication. *The AmFAR AIDS handbook: The complete guide to understanding HIV and AIDS*, a comprehensive guide to help readers understand HIV/ AIDS, treatment options, and how treatment decisions are made, has not been updated since 1999.

958 Centers for Disease Control and Prevention (U.S.). http://www.cdc. gov/. Centers for Disease Control and Prevention (U.S.). Atlanta: Centers for Disease Control and Prevention, U.S. Dept. of Health and Human Services. 1998–

The Centers for Disease Control and Prevention (CDC), part of the Dept. of Health and Human Services (HHS), is considered "the principal agency in the United States government for protecting the health and safety of all Americans and for providing essential human services" (*Website*). Involved in public health efforts to monitor health, to prevent and control infectious and chronic diseases, injury, workplace hazards, disability, and environmental health threats. Works with partners in the U.S. and worldwide, such as the World Health Organization.

"About CDC" (http://www.cdc.gov/about/ organization/cio.htm) provides information about the centers, institutes, and offices associated with the CDC, linking each to its own website and associated information resources. Examples include

the National Center for Health Statistics [NCHS], National Center for Environmental Health (NCEH), National Center for Injury Prevention and Control (NCIPC) "Injury Center" (http://www.cdc.gov/ ncipc/), National Office of Public Health Genomics, Coordinating Office for Global Health (http://www .cdc.gov/cogh/index.htm), Coordinating Office for Emergency Preparedness and Response (http:// www.bt.cdc.gov/), to name a few. An A–Z index (http://www.cdc.gov/az/a.html) provides information on many diseases and other health topics found on the CDC website, with new topics frequently added. CDC WONDER provides a search interface to a variety of health-related topics and statistics. For health professionals and general users.

CDC: Emergency preparedness and response is CDC's primary source of information for responding to public health emergencies.

"MMWR: the first 30 years" http://stacks.cdc .gov/mmwr is a recent addition to the CDC website. It contains the first 30 years of *Morbidity and mortality weekly report (MMWR)* issues in digital format and is considered an important resource for public health professionals, historians, researchers, and others. For current editions of *MMWR*, see http://www.cdc.gov/MMWR.

959 Ethics (World Medical Association). http://www.wma.net/ en/20activities/10ethics/index.html. World Medical Association.; Ethics Unit. Ferney-Voltaire, France: World Medical Association. 2003–

Produced by World Medical Association (WMA).

"The purpose of the WMA is to serve humanity by endeavoring to achieve the highest international standards in Medical Education, Medical Science, Medical Art and Medical Ethics, and Health Care for all people in the world."—*About page*. Coordinates the WMA's ethics policies with the goal to establish and promote high standards of ethical behavior and care by physicians. Serves as a clearinghouse of ethics information resources for national medical associations and physicians, develops new resources, and collaborates with other international organizations involved in medical ethics and health and human rights. Makes accessible the online version of *Medical ethics manual* (http://www.wma.net/en/30 publications/30ethicsmanual/index.html) in many different languages, a list of codes and declarations of adopted ethics policies and declarations in order of their date of first adoption and amendments, including the International Code of Medical Ethics and Declaration of Helsinki: Ethical Principles for Medical Research Involving Human Subjects, as well as many others. Also provides a list of health and human rights organizations and resources.

960   Global alert and response (GAR). http://www.who.int/csr/en/. World Health Organiztion. Geneva, Switzerland: World Health Organization. 2000s?-

GAR, one of WHO's many programs and projects list of all "programmes and projects" at http://www.who.int/csr/en/ is described as "an effective international system for coordinated response" (*Website*). It informs the public about epidemics and other public health emergencies, with emphasis on the global impact of epidemic preparedness and response. The pandemic and epidemic diseases of concern are listed in alphabetical order http://www.who.int/csr/disease/en/. GAR's focus is on a coordinated international effort to respond to epidemics to prevent outbreaks from spreading. It provides authoritative information on disease outbreaks and also on biorisk reduction, the latest news, official statements, press briefings, and documents for developing standardized approaches to responding to epidemic-prone diseases. Quick links are provided for publications, films, and outbreak news (i.e., Disease outbreak news (http://www.who.int/csr/don/en/). The "Global Alert and Response Network" is fully described at http://www.who.int/csr/outbreaknetwork/en/.

961   Global health atlas. http://apps.who.int/globalatlas/. World Health Organization. Geneva, Switzerland: World Health Organization. 2003–

RA441

Title varies: WHO's *Communicable disease global atlas*; *Global atlas of infectious disease*; *Global atlas of infectious diseases: An interactive information and mapping system*.

World Health Organization Internet resource "bringing together for analysis and comparison standardized data and statistics for infectious diseases at country, regional, and global levels. The analysis and interpretation of data are further supported through information on demography, socioeconomic conditions, and environmental factors."—*Website*. Searchable database which allows users to create reports, charts, and maps (e.g., geographic areas can be selected to create maps of diseases). Links to related sites, e.g., *Global atlas of the health workforce* and others.

962   Globalhealth.gov. http://globalhealth.gov/index.html. U.S. Dept. of Health and Human Services. Washington: U.S. Dept. of Health and Human Services. 1990s–

Produced by HHS Office of Global Health Affairs (OGHA). Title varies: Global Health.gov; GlobalHealth.

Provides access to information about major global health topics, such as avian influenza, HIV/AIDS, malaria, etc. and links to partner organizations (e.g., WHO, PAHO, and others) and information on international travel, health regulation, refugee health, and related areas. CDC's Coordinating Office for Global Health (http://www.cdc.gov/cogh/) provides additional information and resources.

963   Global health library. http://www.globalhealthlibrary.net/php/index.php. World Health Organization. Geneva, Switzerland: World Health Organization. 2005–

Produced by Global Health Library (GHL); World Health Organization (WHO); the Knowledge Management and Sharing Department of WHO (WHO/KMS).

A WHO collaborative project with many partners worldwide, such as U.N. bodies, national libraries of medicine, various public health institutes, academic and special libraries, and others. Points to reliable health information from various providers and in various formats. Provides access to the international scientific and technical literature and links to further information and access to global and regional indexes and international agencies (e.g., PAHO, WHOLIS, various directories, and other information via its Global Health Library Virtual Platform. Designed for different users and user groups, including health professionals, patients, their families, and the general public.

964   HealthMap. http://www.healthmap.org/. Clark Freifeld, John Brownstein,

Children's Hospital [Boston] Informatics Program, Harvard-MIT Division of Health Sciences and Technology. [New Haven, Conn.]: Clark Freifeld and John Brownstein. [2006–]

616.9   RA643; RA566

Title varies: HEALTHmap: Global disease alert mapping system.

"Brings together disparate data sources, including online news aggregators, eyewitness reports, expert-curated discussions and validated official reports, to achieve a unified and comprehensive view of the current global state of infectious diseases and their effect on human and animal health."— *About page.* Official alerts from WHO are available via *Disease outbreak news,* which is part of WHO's "Epidemic and pandemic alert and response (EPR)" website (http://www.who.int/csr/don/en). EuroSurveillance (http://www.eurosurveillance.org/), a program of the European Centre for Disease Prevention and Control (http://www.ecdc.europa.eu), is another data source. Uses marker icons (square-shaped: Country-level marker; round: state, province, and local) and low or high "heat index". Provides links for information on particular diseases to Wikipedia, the World Health Organization (WHO), the Centers for Disease Control and Prevention (CDC), PubMed, and Google trends. Available in different views, i.e., as map, satellite, or hybrid map.

A detailed overview of the HealthMap system is available as part of Health information for international travel in "*Yellow book*: Appendix D: The HealthMap system."

965 International health (MedlinePlus). http://www.nlm.nih.gov/medlineplus/internationalhealth.html. National Library of Medicine (U.S.). Bethesda, Md.: National Library of Medicine. 2000?–

A Health Topic within MedlinePlus. Provides extensive global health information, with access to various online reference resources, links to major organizations (e.g., Centers for Disease Control, World Health Organization), foundations (e.g., Henry J. Kaiser Family Foundation), research, journal articles, law and policy information (e.g., International Health Regulations [2005]), WHO and UNICEF statistics, etc. Links to related MedlinePlus topics, such as Traveler's Health and Health system (MedlinePlus).

966 Kaiser Family Foundation. http://www.kff.org/. Henry J. Kaiser Family Foundation. Menlo Park, Calif.: Henry J. Kaiser Family Foundation. 2000– 362.1; 361.7

The Henry J. Kaiser Family Foundation is an independent philanthropy focusing on major health care issues. Website contains statistics on Medicare, Medicaid, the uninsured in each state of the United States, minority health, etc. Links to resources on health policy covering such topics as women's health policy, HIV/AIDS, and media programs. A wide variety of resources are accessible via the following tabs found on the website: (1) Kaiser Health News (http://www.kaiserhealthnews.org/): search for recent daily reports and webcasts; (2) State-HealthFacts (http://kff.org/statedata/): source for state health data; (3) Global Health Facts (http://kff.org/globaldata/); (4) Perspectives; and more.

967 Malaria atlas project (MAP). http://www.map.ox.ac.uk/. Malaria Public Health and Epidemiology Group, Centre for Geographic Medicine, Kenya, Spatial Ecology & Epidemiology Group, University of Oxford, UK. Nairobi, Kenya; Oxford, U.K.: Centre for Geographic Medicine, Kenya; University of Oxford. 2006–

Funded by the Wellcome Trust, United Kingdom.

Provides an overview of the MAP project and enables viewers to browse worldwide malaria and malaria-control data and also allows the submission of new data. Offers health links (e.g., malaria, general health, and food security and health), global and regional links, and links to malaria-related organizations. Also provides research-related links, including libraries, a listing of online resources, databases for literature searching, tutorials, and information about various software tools. Further details about this project and its future plans can be found on the MAP website.

968 NLM gateway. http://gateway.nlm.nih.gov/. National Library of Medicine (U.S.). Bethesda, Md.: National Library of Medicine. 2000–

RA11

As announced in 2011, "the NLM® gateway has transitioned to a new pilot project from the Lister

Hill National Center for Biomedical Communications (LHNCBC)."—*Website* The new site focuses now on two databases: Meeting abstracts and Health services research projects. All of the other resources previously accessed through the NLM gateway are available through their individual sites. For a list of these databases previously available via the NLM gateway see http://gateway.nlm.nih.gov/about.jsp.

The NLM gateway previously allowed simultaneous searching of information resources at the National Library of Medicine (NLM)/National Center for Biotechnology Information (NCBI) with an overview of the search results presented in several categories (bibliographic resources, consumer health resources, and other information), with a listing of the individual databases and the number of results within these categories. Previously included were, for example, MEDLINE/PubMed and the NLM Catalog as well as other resources, including information on current clinical trials and consumer health information (MedlinePlus) and many others.

969 Pan American Health Organization (PAHO). http://www.paho.org/. Pan American Health Organization, World Health Organization. Washington: Pan American Health Organization. 1990s–
RA438.A45

Published by World Health Organization (WHO); United Nations.

PAHO is WHO's regional office for the Americas, an international public health agency with the mission to improve health and living standards of the countries of the Americas.

Searchable website, with detailed information about PAHO's governance and mission, links to basic health indicators, core health data, country health profiles, trends and situation analysis, information products, and other related information. Includes, for example, Regional core health data initiative (http://www.paho.org/english/dd/ais/coredata.htm), including access to PAHO's Basic country health profiles for the Americas (http://www.paho.org/English/DD/AIS/cp_index.htm), which provides mortality statistics for the Americas and health profiles for all countries in North and South America.

Provides access to PAHO electronic books (English and Spanish) at http://www.paho.org/Project.asp?SEL=PR&LNG=ENG&ID=360.

A related title is *Health in the Americas*.

970 World Health Organization (WHO). http://www.who.int/en/. World Health Organization (WHO). Geneva, [Switzerland]: World Health Organization. 1995–

The World Health Organization is the United Nations' specialized agency for health, "the directing and coordinating authority for health within the United Nations system. It is responsible for providing leadership on global health matters, shaping the health research agenda, setting norms and standards, articulating evidence-based policy options, providing technical support to countries and monitoring and assessing health trends. In the 21st century, health is a shared responsibility, involving equitable access to essential care and collective defence against transnational threats."—*About WHO*. WHO was established on 7 April 1948. Its objective, as set out in its Constitution, is the attainment by all peoples of the highest possible level of health. Health is defined in WHO's Constitution as a state of complete physical, mental and social well-being and not merely the absence of disease or infirmity" (*WHO Constitution*). WHO is governed by 193 Member States through the World Health Assembly, composed of representatives from WHO's member states. Since 2005, this website is available in WHO's six official languages: Arabic, Chinese, English, French, Russian, and Spanish. Separate pages for WHO regions, i.e., Africa, The Americas, Eastern Mediterranean, Europe, Southeast Asia, and Western Pacific.

Portal on international health, with basic and advanced search options. Information is arranged under the following tabs: Home; Health topics index (alphabetically organized, accidents through zoonoses), with related links, sites, and topics, publications and other information resources (http://www.who.int/topics/en/); Data & statistics with analyses of situations and trends for various diseases and with links to WHO's Global health observatory (GHO) with its data repository, country statistics, and other relevant statistical information; Media centre, with new releases concerning current international health issues and disease outbreaks, information about upcoming WHO-sponsored events worldwide and videos and photographs, fact sheets, etc.; Publications, with easy access to the most recent WHO reports and links to WHO regional publications; Countries, with country list of member states; Programmes and projects, with lists of WHO programs, partnerships and other projects in alphabetical order; About WHO provides further details about the organization and its functions.

WHO publications can be accessed at http://www.who.int/publications/en/. Examples of WHO online publications and databases include "Basic documents" (http://apps.who.int/gb/bd/), International pharmacopoeia and information on policy and quality and safety standards, essential drugs, and traditional medicine ("Medicines Home" http://www.who.int/medicines/en/), International travel and health, and vaccination requirements; bioethics topics (Ethics and health); epidemiological and statistical information ("Guide to statistical information at WHO," http://www.who.int/whosis/en); law-related publications (e.g., International health regulations (2005) and International digest of health legislation; research tools such as WHO's library database WHOLIS; WHOSIS (WHO statistical information system); Burden of disease statistics (http://www.who.int/topics/global_burden_of_disease/en/); mortality data; statistics by disease or condition; the WHO family of international classifications; and many other important internal and external links. Links to social media accounts, such as Facebook, YouTube, and Google+. Useful to researchers, professionals, students, and the general public.

Medical Jurisprudence

**971 Clinical manual of psychiatry and
law. 1st ed.** Robert I. Simon, Daniel
W. Shuman. Washington: American
Psychiatric Publ., 2007. p.
614/.15   RA1151.S56
Contents: (1) Psychiatry and the law; (2) The
doctor-patient relationship; (3) Confidentiality and
testimonial privilege; (4) Informed consent and the
right to refuse treatment; (5) Psychiatric treatment:
tort liability; (6) Seclusion and restraint; (7) Involuntary hospitalization; (8) The suicidal patient;
(9) Psychiatric responsibility and the violent patient;
(10) Maintaining treatment boundaries: clinical
and legal issues. Appendix A: Suggested readings;
Appendix B: Glossary of legal terms; Index.

Covers a variety of topics concerning the
requirements and legal regulations of psychiatric
practice, including treatment issues that may lead
to liability and malpractice law suits.

Clinical handbook of psychiatry and law covers
topics such as confidentiality and privilege, legal
issues in emergency psychiatry and inpatient psychiatry, forensic evaluations, the clinician in court,
and others.

Guides

**972 The Blackwell guide to medical
ethics.** Rosamond Rhodes, Leslie Francis,
Anita Silvers. Malden, Mass.: Blackwell

Publ., 2007. 435 p.
ISBN 9781405125833
174.2   R724.B515
(Blackwell philosophy guides; 21)

Contents: part I, Individual decisions about
clinical issues: (1) Patient decisions; (2) Individual decisions of physicians and other health
care professionals; part II, Legislative and judicial decisions about social policy: (1) Liberty;
(2), Justice.

"Helpful tool for navigating the complex literature and diverse views on the key issues in medical ethics. Employing crucial distinctions between
the personal decisions of patients, the professional
decisions of individual health care providers, and
political decisions about public policy, the chapters
in the volume address the most central and controversial topics in medical ethics" (*Publ. notes*).
Includes bibliographical references and index. Also
available as an e-book.

Bibliography

**973 U.S. health law and policy, 2001: A
guide to the current literature.** Donald
H. Caldwell, American Health Lawyers
Association. San Francisco; Chicago:
Jossey-Bass; Health Forum, 2001. xxi,
593 p. ISBN 0787955043
016.34473/041   KF3821.A1C35

Earlier edition had title: *U.S. health law and policy 1999: A guide to the current literature,* 1998.

Contents: pt. 1, Medical facilities and organizations; pt. 2, Regulatory matters; pt. 3, Licensure, liability, and labor issues; pt. 4, Selected health care policy topics. Appendixes: (A) Health law periodicals, digests, and newsletters; (B) Reference sources and government serials; (C) Computer databases and Internet sites; (D) State-by-state synopsis of selected statutes of limitation laws; (E) Table of acronyms and abbreviations; (F) Glossary; (G) Relevant federal agencies; (H) Selected nongovernmental agencies; (I) State laws governing medical records; (J) Health Care Financing Administration regional offices. Subject, name, title indexes.

This revised edition is a comprehensive annotated bibliographic guide to the healthcare law and policy literature and related legal issues. Sources are books, journals, government documents, and websites. Entries provide publication information and a brief synopsis of the content of the citation. A future edition is planned.

Indexes; Abstract journals; Databases

974 POPLINE. http://www.popline.org/. Johns Hopkins University Bloomberg School of Public Health, Information and Knowledge for Optimal Health Project. Baltimore: Johns Hopkins University Bloomberg School of Public Health
HQ766

A free resource, maintained by the Knowledge for Health Project http://www.k4health.org/ at the Johns Hopkins Bloomberg School of Public Health/ Center for Communication Programs and funded by the United States Agency for International Development (USAID) http://www.usaid.gov/.

Database on reproductive health with international coverage. Provides bibliographic citations with abstracts to English-language published and unpublished biomedical and social science literature, with links to full-text documents, RSS feeds for topical searches, and other special features. POPLINE subjects (http://www.popline.org/ poplinesubjects) in 12 main categories: Adolescent reproductive health; family planning methods; family planning programs; gender; health communication; HIV/AIDS; maternal and child health; population dynamics; population law and policy; population, health, and environment; reproductive health; sexually transmitted infections.

975 PubMed. http://www.ncbi.nlm.nih.gov/ pubmed. U.S. National Center for Biotechnology Information, National Library of Medicine, National Institutes of Health. Bethesda, Md.: U.S. National Center for Biotechnology Information. 1996–

PubMed®, developed and maintained by the National Center for Biotechnology Information (NCBI) at the National Library of Medicine® (NLM). Provides a search interface for more than 20 million bibliographic citations and abstracts in the fields of medicine, nursing, dentistry, veterinary medicine, health care systems, and preclinical sciences. It provides access to articles indexed for MEDLINE® and for selected life sciences journals. PubMed subsets found under the "Limits" tab are: MEDLINE and PubMed central®, several journal groups (i.e., core clinical journals, dental journals, and nursing journals), and topical subsets (AIDS, bioethics, cancer, complementary medicine, dietary supplements, history of medicine, space life sciences, systematic reviews, toxicology, and veterinary science). "Linkout" provides access to full-text articles.

For detailed information see the PubMed fact sheet at http://www.nlm.nih.gov/pubs/factsheets/ pubmed.html and also MEDLINE®/PubMed® resources guide (http://www.nlm.nih.gov/bsd/pm resources.html) which provides detailed information about MEDLINE data and searching PubMed.

Information regarding the mobile version of this resource is part of NLM's Gallery of mobile apps and sites.

976 State cancer legislative database program (SCLD). http://www.scld-nci .net/mtcindex.cfm. National Cancer Institute. Bethesda, Md.: National Cancer Institute, National Institutes of Health

Databases providing summaries of state laws and resolutions on the major cancers and cancer-related topics. Considered a resource for a variety of audiences, including universities and research centers, professional organizations, and the public.

977   THOMAS. http://thomas.loc.gov/home/
thomas.php. Edward F. Willett, Library of
Congress, United States. [Washington]:
Library of Congress. [1995–]
025.06   KF49.T56

Search for bills by keyword, status, bill number, or
sponsor for the current Congress. Search bills from
multiple congresses for the 101st Congress (1989)
forward; separate search interfaces are provided
for Public Laws, Congressional Record, presidential nominations, committee reports, roll call votes,
and treaties. Table of appropriations bills available
for FY 1998 forward. Links to current activity in
Congress, educational materials, and to a detailed
explanation of the legislative process. In late 2014,
THOMAS is slated to be replaced by a new Con-
gress.gov site.

Encyclopedias

978   Comprehensive clinical psychology.
Alan S. Bellack, Michel Hersen.
Amsterdam, Netherlands; New York:
Pergamon, 1998. 11 v., ill.
ISBN 0080427073
616.89   RC467.C597

Contents: v. 1, *Foundations*, ed. Eugene Walker;
v. 2, *Professional issues*, ed. Arthur N. Wiens; v. 3,
Research methods, ed. Nina R. Schooler; v. 4, *Assess-
ment*, ed. Cecil R. Reynolds; v. 5, *Children and ado-
lescents*, ed. Thomas Ollendick; v. 6, *Adults*, ed.
Paul Salkovskis; v. 7, *Clinical geropsychology*, ed.
Barry Edelstein; v. 8, *Health psychology*, ed. Derek
W. Johnston and Marie Johnston; v. 9, *Applications
in diverse populations*, ed. Nirbhay N. Singh; v. 10,
Sociocultural and individual differences, ed. Cynthia
D. Belar; v. 11, *Indexes*.

Review of the field of clinical psychology,
including its historical, theoretical, and scientific
foundations. Scholarly reviews of clinical topics
and professional issues. Bibliographical references.
Also available online via Elsevier Science Direct.

Encyclopedia of behavioral medicine is a more
recent resource in this area.

**979   The Corsini encyclopedia of
psychology. 4th ed ed.** Irving B. Weiner,
W. Edward Craighead. Hoboken, N.J.:
Wiley, 2010. 4 v. (xxii, 1961 p.), ill.

ISBN 9780470170243
150.3   BF31

Updated since the 2001 edition. More than 1,200
signed entries in alphabetical order, with suggestions for further reading. Intended for students and
researchers. Topics, methods, significant individuals. Covers disorders in the DSM-IV-TR. Appendix
of 543 brief biographical entries. Bibliography.
Expanded index. Available as an e-book.

980   Encyclopedia of adolescence.
http://www.springer.com/psychology/
child+%26+school+psychology/
book/978-1-4419-1694-5. Roger J. R.
Levesque. New York: Springer. 2011.
ISBN 9781441916952
155.5   HQ796

More than 600 signed articles in alphabetical order
with suggestions for further reading. Covers biological, cognitive and social development; types of
identity; relationships with family, peers, and nonpa-
rental adults; the influence of educational, religious,
legal, medical, cultural and economic institutions;
and mental health including normalcy, deviance and
disability. Bibliography. Also available in print format, in five volumes.

981   Encyclopedia of behavioral medicine.
Marc D. Gellman, J. Rick Turner. New
York: Springer, 2013. Four vols., ill.
(some color)
616.89003   R726.5.E495

The interdisciplinary field of behavioral medicine is
based on the understanding of relationships among
behavior, psychosocial processes, and sociocultural
contexts. Includes 1,200 entries on behavioral medicine concepts and topics, behavioral (e.g., lifestyle:
diet, physical activity, smoking; medication adherence), psychosocial (e.g., temperament and personality, marital and work stressors, social support),
and sociocultural variables as potential risk factors
for chronic diseases. Includes, for example, articles
on alcohol consumption, psychosocial treatment
of cancer, gene-environment interaction, history
of behavioral medicine, evidence-based behavioral
medicine (EBBM) and practice, lipid abnormalities, translational behavioral medicine, etc. Entries
include definition, synonym(s), cross-references,
references, and citations for further reading. Available as an e-book.

982 Encyclopedia of behavior modification and cognitive behavior therapy. Michel Hersen, Johan Rosqvist. Thousand Oaks, Calif.: Sage, 2005. 3 v.; xx, 1637 p., ill. ISBN 0761927476

616.89142003   RC489.B4E485

Broader in scope than the *Encyclopedia of cognitive behavior therapy*, this set brings together the expertise of both researchers and practitioners. Includes a volume each on adult and child clinical applications. A third volume on educational applications is particularly valuable for classroom and school contexts. Five anchor articles in each volume summarize current trends and treatment directions. Each volume includes an alphabetical list of its entries, an extensive general bibliography, and a comprehensive index. Each entry contains brief background, description of the treatment strategy, discussion of potential complications, a case illustration, a brief list of recent publications, and, if appropriate, a summary of research. Entries for prominent contributors to the field chronicle their professional careers.

983 Encyclopedia of cognitive science. Lynn Nadel. Hoboken, N.J.: John Wiley, 2005. 4 v., ill. ISBN 0470016191

BF311.E53

A massive encyclopedia which aims to capture current thinking about the relatively new field of cognitive science. An excellent overview article, "What is cognitive science?" is followed by more than 400 topical entries written by experts in their field. Essays are clearly laid out and well illustrated, suggesting further readings. Extensive subject index provides easy access to related materials. Glossary. Available as an online database.

984 Encyclopedia of depression. Linda Wasmer Andrews. Santa Barbara, Calif.: Greenwood Press, 2010. 2 v. (xlii, 570 p.) ISBN 9780313353789

616.85/27003   RC537

Over 300 articles with suggestions for further reading, written in non-technical terms for a general audience. Covers risk factors, causes, symptoms, diagnosis, treatment and prevention. Biographical entries for key figures. Topical guide and quick reference outline point to related concepts. Timeline of opinions and research findings since antiquity. Index. Available as an e-book.

985 Encyclopedia of drugs, alcohol and addictive behavior. http://www.gale .cengage.com/. Pamela Korsmeyer, Henry R. Kranzler. Detroit: Macmillan Reference USA. 2009. ISBN 9780028660646

362.2903   HV5804

Third ed. with 133 new articles and extensive revision of more than 200 others. New coverage of the Internet as a factor in addictions; drugs and alcohol in the media and in sports and fashion industries; and connections between terrorist groups and the drug trade. Wider regional and international coverage, and updated content on medical, chemical and physiological aspects of addiction. Includes addictive behaviors such as eating disorders and compulsive gambling. Over 500 signed entries, with bibliographies. Multidisciplinary perspective includes legal, behavioral and pharmacological aspects; extensive listings of organizations that deal with various aspects of alcoholism, drug abuse, and addictive behaviors. The sweeping coverage and certain authority of the 1st ed. has been preserved and enhanced. Also available in print format.

986 Encyclopedia of forensic and legal medicine. Jason Payne-James. Amsterdam; Boston: Elsevier Academic Press, 2005. 4 v., ill., ports. ISBN 0125479700

614.103   RA1017.E53

Contents: v. 1, A–Co; v. 2. Cr–H; v. 3, I–Ri; v. 4, Ro–Z, index.

Comprehensive overview of forensic and legal medicine and related specialties and issues. Detailed table of contents, glossary, cross-references, further reading, and index. Includes diagrams, tables, and color images. Online edition available from Elsevier Science Direct.

987 Encyclopedia of forensic sciences. Jay A. Siegel, Pekka J. Saukko, Geoffrey C. Knupfer. San Diego, Calif.: Academic Press, 2000. 3 v. (xxxviii, 1440, lxv, lvii p.), ill. (some col.) ISBN 0122272153

363.2503   HV8073.E517

Considers basic principles of forensic science and a wide range of topics, including theories, methods, and techniques used by forensic scientists. Covers, for example, accident investigation, crime scene investigation, clinical forensic medicine (e.g., overview, defense wounds, self-inflicted injury, child abuse, sexual assault, gunshot wounds, etc.), autopsy, "psychologial autopsies," medicolegal causes of death, DNA data banks, alcohol and drug analysis, ethical aspects, etc. Also available online via Elsevier Science Direct.

988   Encyclopedia of mental health.
Howard S. Friedman. San Diego, Calif.: Academic Press, 1998. 3 v., ill.
ISBN 0122266757
616.89/003   RA790.5.E53

Contents: v. 1, A–Di; v. 2, Do–N; v. 3, O–Z, index. "Taking into account new knowledge about the genetic, biological, developmental, social, societal and cultural nature of human beings, . . . bring[s] together . . . emerging trends . . . of mental health . . . validity (or invalidity) of psychiatric diagnosis (and DSM IV), including standards for psychotherapy, models of normality, and psychiatric epidemiology" (*Pref.*). Each article contains an outline, a glossary, cross-references, and a bibliography. Aimed at a wide range of users, including students, researchers, and allied health professionals.

More recent titles in this subject area include, for example, *Gale encyclopedia of mental health* and *Encyclopedia of mental health* by Kahn et al., part of the Facts on File Library of health and living series, a collection of titles on medical subjects for general readers which is also available online via Health Reference Center (Facts on File, Inc. [712]).

989   Encyclopedia of obesity and eating disorders. 3rd ed. Dana K. Cassell, David H. Gleaves. New York: Facts on File, 2006. 362 p. ISBN 0816061971
616.8526003   RC552.E18.C37

First edition, 1994; 2nd ed., 2000.
Provides concise entries on the causes, symptoms, and treatments, including pharmacotherapy, of obesity and the various eating disorders (e.g., anorexia nervosa, bulimia, etc.). Lists sources of information, websites, audiovisuals, and other resources. Bibliography and index. For general readers and health professionals.

Part of *Facts on File library of health and living* series. Available online via Health Reference Center (712).

990   Encyclopedia of psychology. Alan E. Kazdin. Washington; Oxford; New York:

American Psychological Association; Oxford University Press, 2000. 8 v.; 29 cm. ISBN 1557986509
150.3   BF31.E52

Covers methods, findings, advances, and applications in the broad field of psychology from historical topics to new areas of development. Extensive cross-references guide users to related topics among the eight volumes. Each signed entry includes alternate spellings and synonyms, as well as bibliographies and further references.

991   Encyclopedia of psychotherapy.
Michel Hersen, William H. Sledge. Amsterdam, Netherlands; Boston: Academic Press, 2002. 2 v., ill.
ISBN 0123430100
616.891403   RC475.7.E55

Vol. 1, A–H; v. 2, I–Z.
Broad coverage of the field, with detailed information on the major psychotherapies currently practiced and also the classical treatments previously in use. The 233 alphabetically arranged topics address "clinical, theoretical, cultural, historical, and administrative and policy issues" (*Pref.*), including contemporary schools, approaches and techniques, and measurement of outcomes. Most articles follow a similar format: description of treatment, theoretical basis, applications and exclusions, empirical studies, case illustration, and summary. Each article also contains an outline, a glossary of relevant terms, cross-references, and a list of further readings. Each volume has separate pagination. Index includes subjects but no names. For an academic audience. Also available as an e-book and via *Credo reference*.

992   Encyclopedia of statistics in behavioral science. Brian S. Everitt, David C. Howell. Hoboken, N.J.: John Wiley & Sons, 2005. 4 v., 2208 p., ill.
ISBN 0470860804
150.15195   BF39.E498

Essential reference work for researchers, educators, and students in the fields of applied psychology, sociology, market research, consumer behavior, management science, decision making, and human resource management and a valuable addition to both the psychological and statistical literature. Contains over 600 articles; contributions from eminent psychologists and statisticians worldwide.

Emphasizes practical, nontechnical methods with wide-ranging applications. Extensively cross-referenced. Available in print and online.

993   Encyclopedia of stress. 2nd ed.
George Fink. Boston: Elsevier, 2007. p.
cm 0120885034
First ed., 2000.

"Comprehensive reference source on stressors, the biological mechanisms involved in the stress response, the effects of activating the stress response mechanisms, and the disorders that may arise as a consequence of acute or chronic stress . . . includes a wide range of related topics such as neuroimmune interactions, cytokines, enzymatic disorders, effects on the cardiovascular system, immunity and inflammation, and physical illnesses. It also goes beyond the biological aspects of stress to cover topics such as stress and behavior, psychiatric and psychosomatic disorders, workplace stress, post-traumatic stress, stress-reduction techniques, and current therapies" (*Publ. notes*). For researchers, clinicians, professionals, and students. Available online via Elsevier ScienceDirect.

The encyclopedia of stress and stress-related diseases by Kahn et al., part of the Facts on File Library of health and living series and available online via Health reference center (Facts on File, Inc.), provides accessible content on stress and stress-related diseases for all types of readers and libraries.

994   Encyclopedia of the neurological sciences. 1st ed. Michael J. Aminoff, Robert B. Daroff. Amsterdam; Boston: Academic Press, 2003. 4 v., ill. (some col.) ISBN 0122268709
612.8/03   RC334.E535
v. 1, A–De; v. 2, Di–L; v. 3, M–Ph; v. 4, Pi–Z, index.

Approx. 1,000 concise entries in 32 subject areas deal with basic science aspects and clinical issues of the neurological sciences, including neurology, neuroanatomy, neurobiology, neurosurgery, psychiatry, and other related areas. Alphabetical sequence by title, with groupings according to specific discipline. Suggestions for further reading at the end of each entry. Includes biographies of famous neuroscientists. Some graphics. Outline of contents in v. 4. Extensive cross-references. Subject index. Written for readers from other disciplines, not necessarily for the specialist. Also available online via ScienceDirect.

A second edition is planned to be published in 2014.

995   The Freud encyclopedia: Theory, therapy, and culture. Edward Erwin.
New York: Routledge, 2002. xxvii, 641 p.
ISBN 0415936772
150.1952092   BF173.F6176

More than 250 signed entries reflect much of the recent international scholarship on Freud's largely unproven theories, which continue to provide insights and exert tremendous influence. Each entry contains a list of references, and ample cross-references are provided. Available as an e-book.

996   Gabbard's treatments of psychiatric disorders. 4th ed. Glen O. Gabbard.
Washington: American Psychiatric, 2007.
xxvi, 960 p., ill. ISBN 9781585622
616.891   RC480.T69

First edition, 1989, had title *Treatments of psychiatric disorders: A task force report of the American Psychiatric Association,* 4 v.; 2nd ed., 1995 (2 v.), and 3rd ed., 2001 (2 v.), had title *Treatments of psychiatric disorders.*

Contents: pt. 1, "Disorders usually first diagnosed in infancy, childhood, or adolescence" (ed. E. B. Weller and J.F. McDermott); pt. 2, "Delirium, dementia, and amnestic and other cognitive disorders" (ed. S.C. Yudofsky and R.E. Hales); pt. 3, "Substance-related disorders" (ed. H. D. Kleber and M. Galanter); pt. 4, "Schizophrenia and other psychotic disorders" (ed. R. L. Munich and C.A. Tamminga); pt. 5, "Mood disorders" (ed. A. J. Rush); pt. 6, "Anxiety disorders, dissociative disorders, and adjustment disorders" (ed. F. R. Schneier, L.A. Mellman, and D. Spiegel); pt. 7, "Somatoform and factitious disorders" (ed. K.A. Phillips); pt. 8, "Sexual and gender identity disorders" (ed. S. B. Levine and R. T. Segraves); pt. 9, "Eating disorders" (ed. A. S. Kaplan and K. A Halmi); pt. 10, "Personality disorders" (ed. J.G. Gunderson); pt. 11, "Sleep disorders" (ed. K. Doghramji and Anna Ivanenko); pt. 12, "Disorders of impulse control" (ed. Susan L. McElroy).

Current approaches, treatments, and therapies for common psychiatric disorders and mental illnesses. Provides comprehensive descriptions of the disorders and covers multiple approaches, including pharmacologic, psychodynamic, behavioral, cognitive, family, individual, and group treatments, recognizing evolving knowledge and preferred treatments as well as acceptable alternatives. Includes data from new and controlled studies. Includes bibliographical references and index. Useful for graduate research and health professionals. Available in electronic format as part of PsychiatryOnline.

997 The Gale encyclopedia of childhood and adolescence. Jerome Kagan, Susan B. Gall. Detroit: Gale, 1998. xiii, 752 p., ill. ISBN 0810398842

305.23103   HQ772.G27

More than 700 signed essays by experts in the field cover key theories and issues in child development and offer suggestions for further reading. Provides detailed name and subject indexes. Available online as part of Health and Wellness Resource Center.

998 The Gale encyclopedia of mental health. 3rd ed. Kristin Key. Detroit: Gale Cengage Learning, 2012. 2 v. (xix, 1828 p.), ill. (chiefly col.)
ISBN 9781414490120

616.89/003   RC437.G36

First ed., 2003, had title *The Gale encyclopedia of mental disorders*; 2nd ed., 2008.

Provides a comprehensive overview of mental health and illness, diagnostic procedures, psychotherapy, and various other treatments, including drugs, herbal preparations, and alternative therapies. Includes mostly disorders recognized by the American Psychiatric Association, but also mentions some not formally recognized as distinct disorders. This revised edition contains 500 entries, with 65 new entries to this edition, with color illustrations, graphs, charts, tables, and sidebars of key terms and references for further reading. Also includes a list of organizations, a glossary, and index. Disease and medication entries are in a standardized format. Entries for diseases include definition, description, causes and symptoms, demographics, diagnosis, treatment, prognosis, prevention, and resources. Entries for medications include definition, purpose, description, recommended dosage, precautions, side effects, interactions, and resources. Considered a highly useful resource for mental health professionals and health consumers.

Available electronically through Gale Virtual Reference Library.

999 The Gale encyclopedia of psychology. 2nd ed. Bonnie B. Strickland. Detroit: Gale Group, 2001. xiii, 701 p., ill. ISBN 0787647861

150.3   BF31.G35

Covers the entire spectrum of psychological terms, theories, personalities, and experiments. Designed to be of use to both students and the general public, with signed entries ranging from 25 to 1,000 words. Provides suggestions for further reading and a subject index. Available as an e-book.

1000 The international encyclopedia of depression. Rick E. Ingram. New York: Springer Publ., 2009. xxv, 613 p., ill., ports. ISBN 9780826137937

616.85/27003   RC537.I573

Covers the psychological, psychiatric, and medical aspects of depression and its various treatments in depth. Topics are arranged alphabetically, with extensive bibliographies. Written for clinicians, researchers, nurses, and also general readers. Also available as an e-book.

1001 Lawyers' medical cyclopedia of personal injuries and allied specialties. 5th ed. Richard M. Patterson. Newark, N.J.: LexisNexis, c2002–c2005. v. , ill.

1558340378   RA1022.U6L38

First ed., 1958–62; 4th ed., 1977–99 (10 v.). Publication of the current (5th) ed. in progress.

"Authoritative reference for attorneys involved in personal injury, medical malpractice, workers' compensation, social security, disability income, and health insurance cases . . . Offers in-depth information and caselaw on hundreds of medical and surgical specialties.written by physicians skilled at translating complex anatomy, physiology, and medical treatment into clear language" (*Publ. notes*). Kept up to date by pocket parts and revised volumes. Includes bibliographical references and indexes.

1002 Mental disorders of the new millennium. Thomas G. Plante.

Westport, Conn.: Praeger, 2006. 3 v.
ISBN 0275987817
616.89   RC454.M462
Praeger Perspectives series.
Contents: v. 1, *Behavioral issues*; v. 2, *Public and social problems*; v. 3, *Biology and function*.

Provides an overview of mental disorders. Vol. 1 includes articles on behavioral issues such as narcissism, anger disorders, pathological gambling, kleptomania, mood disorders in children and adolescents, adult depression, suicide, self-injurious behavior, etc. Vol. 2 includes, for example, articles discussing post-traumatic stress disorder among U.S. veterans, family violence, homicide-suicide, social and developmental issues of youth gangs, adolescent substance abuse, workaholism, psychopathology in culture, etc. Vol. 3 includes aspects of psychobiology, with articles on postpartum depression, mental retardation, autism, attention deficit/hyperactivity disorder, obsessive-compulsive disorder, eating disorders, body dysmorphic disorder, gender identity disorders, etc. Bibliographical references and index. For health professionals, graduate students, and general readers. Also available as an e-book.

1003 The MIT encyclopedia of the cognitive sciences. Robert W. Wilson, Frank C. Keil. Cambridge, Mass.: MIT Press, 1999. cxxxvii, 964 p. 0262232006
MITECS represents the methodological and theoretical diversity of this changing field. With 471 concise entries written by leading researchers in the field, providing accessible introductions to important concepts in the cognitive sciences, as well as references or further readings. Six extended essays collectively serve as a road map to the articles and provide overviews of six major areas: philosophy; psychology; neurosciences; computational intelligence; linguistics and language; and culture, cognition, and evolution. Available online via MIT CogNet as an e-book at http://cognet.mit.edu/library/erefs/mitecs/.

1004 The Oxford companion to the mind. 2nd ed. R. L. Gregory. Oxford; New York: Oxford University Press, 2004. xx, 1004 p., ill. ISBN 0198662246
128.2   BF31.O94
Part dictionary and part encyclopedia, it features entries ranging from a few sentences to several pages. Its purpose is to teach a wide range of users about the mind, and topics covered include brain imaging, children's drawings of human figures, hypnosis, delirium, free association, and illusions. Biographical entries are also included, along with many helpful ill. The signed entries include *see* and *see also* references, and most of the longer articles provide brief bibliographies. List of contributors, glossary, and index. Available electronically from Oxford reference online and also as an e-book.

1005 Psychology & mental health. 3rd rev. ed. Nancy A. Piotrowski. Pasadena, Calif.: Salem Press, 2010. 5 v. (c, 2208, clxxvi p.), ill. ISBN 9781587655562
150.3   BF636
Covers all aspects of psychology and mental health, including biographies of key persons, physiological elements, theories and conditions. Nearly 600 entries in alphabetical order with suggestions for further reading, on a wide range of theoretical, experimental, applied and physiological topics. All entries have been reviewed and updated as needed, with over 150 new articles since the earlier edition, which was published as *Magill's encyclopedia of social science: Psychology*. Intended for lay readers and students. Glossary. Bibliography, list of relevant films, and directory of Web sites. Appendices cover helpful organizations, a biographical roster, and a list of court cases. Indexes by category, person and subject. Also known as *Salem health: Psychology & mental health*. Available as an e-book.

Dictionaries

1006 Attorney's illustrated medical dictionary. Ida Dox. St. Paul, Minn.: West Group, 2002. 1 v. (various pagings), ill. (some col.)
                         KF8933.A44
First ed., 1997. At head of title: American jurisprudence proof of facts, 3rd series. Includes index of illustrations. ".replaces Am. Jur. Proof of Facts Taber's Cyclopedic Medical Dictionary" (*insert from West Group*). Kept up-to-date with supplements. Concise definitions of approx. 30,000 terms, synonyms, pronunciations, 3,500 illustrations, index of illustrations, and references to further information.

Other dictionaries are J. E. Schmidt's *Attorneys' dictionary of medicine* or Schmidt's *Attorneys' dictionary of medicine illustrated,* a loose-leaf publication also referred to as *Attorney's dictionary of medicine and word finder.*

1007 The concise dictionary of medical-legal terms: A general guide to interpretation and usage. Joseph A. Bailey. New York: Parthenon Publ., 1998. 148 p., ill. ISBN 1850706808

614/.1/03   RA1017.B35

As used in this dictionary, medical-legal covers the regulation and utilization of medicine by the legal profession (cf. *Foreword*). Designed as a guide to common words and phrases used in medicine and law, it is "particularly designed to help those just entering the medical-legal field. For more detailed specific knowledge the reader should consult more comprehensive references that are specific to his or her legal system . . ." (*Pref.*). Illustrations, tables, and diagrams.

1008 Dictionary of ethical and legal terms and issues: The essential guide for mental health professionals. Len Sperry. New York: Routledge, 2007. xi, 277 p. ISBN 0415953219

174.2   RC455.2.E8.S655

Contents: pt. 1, Dictionary of ethical and legal terms; pt. 2, Ethical issues and considerations; pt. 3, Legal issues and considerations; appendix: Key legal cases and legislation impacting mental health practice; index.

Concise guide to the key ethical and legal issues and considerations; codes and statutes; and key legal opinions, legislation, and regulations relevant to everyday mental health practice in the United States. Pt. 2 and 3 present particular topics in some detail, with definitions of key terms. Intended for graduate and undergraduate students and as a ready-reference source for mental health practitioners. Also available as an e-book.

Legal and ethical dictionary for mental health professionals by Ahia is another resource in this area, containing definitions provided in a legal context. Also includes mental health acronyms and codes of ethics of several professional associations (e.g., American Counseling Association, American Psychological Association, and others).

1009 Health care defined: A glossary of current terms. Bruce Goldfarb. Baltimore: Williams & Wilkins, 1997. xi, 347 p. ISBN 0683036157

362.1/03   RA423.G65

Scholarly resource. Explains the terminology used in the healthcare field, e.g., medical care, delivery of health care, and health services terminology. Contains approx. 3,000 essential terms and explains them in non-medical terminology. Includes bibliographical references (p. 313–315). Useful for insurance and legal professionals.

1010 Health services cyclopedic dictionary: A compendium of health-care and public health terminology. 3rd ed. Thomas C. Timmreck. Sudbury, Mass.: Jones and Bartlett Publishers, 1997. xii, 860 p., col. ill. ISBN 0867205156

362.1/068   RA393.T56

First ed. (1982) and 2nd ed. (1987) had title: *Dictionary of health services management.*

(The Jones and Bartlett series in health sciences)

This rev. and exp. ed. contains terminology and definitions from the fields of health services and medical care, health administration, health care reform, public health, environmental health, epidemiology, managed care, and other related areas.

Handbooks

1011 BioLaw: A legal and ethical reporter on medicine, health care, and bioengineering. James F. Childress. Frederick, Md.: University Publications of America, 1986–. v. (loose-leaf)

1983–1985 had title: *Bioethics reporter.*

Editors: 1986– , James F. Childress et al.

Loose-leaf; updated between editions. Has supplement: Biolaw . . . microfiche supplement.

Each annual consists of 2 v.: v. 1, Resource manual, contains essays on biological, medical, and health care issues with ethical and legal implications; v. 2 includes updates on many previously published topics and special sections on laws, regulations, court cases, etc. Each update comes with a cumulative subject index covering both volumes and a cumulative index to court cases.

1012 Clinical handbook of psychiatry and the law. 4th ed. Paul S. Appelbaum, Thomas G. Gutheil. Philadelphia: Wolters Kluwer Health/Lippincott, Williams and Wilkins, 2007. xiii, 322 p.
ISBN 0781778913
344.73041   KF2910.P75G87
First ed., 1982; 3rd ed., 2000.

Contents: ch. 1, "Confidentiality and privilege"; ch. 2, "Legal issues in emergency psychiatry"; ch. 3, "Legal issues in inpatient psychiatry"; ch. 4, "Malpractice and other forms of liability"; ch. 5, "Competence and substitute decision making"; ch. 6, "Forensic evaluations"; ch. 7, "Clinicians and lawyers"; ch. 8, "The clinician in court"; index.

Provides up-to-date information for clinicians on "how law affects practice, and how psychiatry can contribute to the law" (*Pref.*) and discussion of its interrelated clinical and legal aspects. Each chapter has the following seven sections: Case examples, legal issues, clinical issues, pitfalls, case example epilogues, action guide, and suggested readings. Available online to subscribers via Books@Ovid.

1013 Code of medical ethics, current opinions with annotations: Including the principles of medical ethics, fundamental elements of the patient-physician relationship and rules of the Council on Ethical and Judicial Affairs. Southern Illinois University at Carbondale, AMA Council on Ethical and Judicial Affairs. Chicago: American Medical Association
174.13 1540-2916   R725.A55a
Since 1847, published every two years, with regular revisions. Description based on 2012–2013 ed.

Ethics guide for physicians and other medical professionals, attorneys, and others, containing AMA's "Principles of Medical Ethics" (rev. 2001) and more than 200 ethical opinions (issued through 2005) on social policy issues, hospital relations, practice, and other matters, with new guidelines and updated or amended guidelines for several contemporary topics and issues (for example, financial relationships with industry in continuing medical education; advance care planning, professionalism in the use of social media; research with stem cells; transplantation of organs

from living donors; pediatric decision making; HIV testing, and others). Appendix contains bylaws rules. Table of Cases, Table of Articles, and Index to Opinions. Also available as e-book.

New Opinions issued every six months, available at http://www.ama-assn.org/ama/pub/about-ama/our-people/ama-councils/council-ethical-judicial -affairs.page and the AMA's online policy database, PolicyFinder http://www.ama-assn.org/ama/pub/about-ama-our-people/house-delegates/policyfinder .page.

1014 Contemporary issues in healthcare law and ethics. 3rd ed. Dean M. Harris. Chicago; Washington: Health Administration Press; AUPHA Press, 2007. 377 p. ISBN 9781567932
344.730321   KF3825.Z9.H3
First edition, 1999, had title *Healthcare law and ethics: Issues for the age of managed care*; 2nd ed., 2003.

Contents: (1) "The role of law in the U.S. healthcare system"; (2) "Managing and regulating the healthcare system"; (3) "Patient care issues"; (4) "Legal and ethical issues in health insurance and managed care"; table of cases; table of statutes; table of regulations; index.

This revised and updated edition presents essential information and examines legal and ethical issues in health care. Includes, for example, the U.S. Supreme Court's decisions on physician-assisted suicide, partial-birth abortion, issues in emergency contraception, HIPAA Privacy Rule, medical malpractice, reporting of medical errors, and other topics. Also available as e-book.

1015 Health and human rights: Basic international documents. 2nd ed. Stephen P. Marks, Francois-Xavier Bagnoud Center for Health and Human Rights. Cambridge, Mass.: Francois-Xavier Bagnoud Center for Health and Human Rights, 2006. xiii, 392 p.
ISBN 0674023773
                              RA418.H3872
First ed., c2004.
(Harvard series on health and human rights)

"Updated and expanded from the previous edition to provide the practitioner, scholar, and advocate with access to the most basic instruments of international law and policy that express the values of human rights for advancing health. The topics covered include professional ethics; research and experimentation; treatment of prisoners and detainees; patients' rights; right to health; right to life; freedom from torture, war crimes, crimes against humanity, and genocide; the right to an adequate standard of living; women and reproductive health; children; persons with disabilities; rights of older persons; infectious diseases; business, trade, and intellectual property; occupational health and safety; biotechnology; and protection of the environment" (*Publ. notes*). Sample documents include a selection of previously published documents: Universal declaration of human rights, Declaration of Geneva (Geneva Convention), Nuremberg code, Convention on the elimination of all forms of discrimination against women, Convention on the rights of the child, and others. A new edition (3rd, 2012) is available.

1016 International guidelines on HIV/AIDS and human rights. http://www2 .ohchr.org/english/issues/hiv/docs/ consolidated_guidelines.pdf. Office of the United Nationals High Commissioner for Human Rights (OHCHR); UNAIDS Joint United Nations Programme on HIV/ AIDS, UNAIDS Joint United Nations Programme on HIV/AIDS. Geneva, Switzerland: United Nations OHCHR. 2006

Organized jointly by the Office of the United Nations High Commissioner for Human Rights (OHCHR) and the UNAIDS Joint United Nations Programme on HIV/AIDS.

2006 consolidated version of the Second (Geneva, 23–25 Sep. 1996) and Third (Geneva, 25–26 Jul. 2002) International Consultation on HIV/AIDS and Human Rights.

Contents: (I) Guidelines for state action: (A) Institutional responsibilities and processes; (B) Law review, reform and support services; (C) Promotion of a supportive and enabling environment; (II) Recommendations for dissemination and implementation of the guidelines on HIV/AIDS and human right: (A) States; (B) United Nationals system and regional intergovernmental bodies; (C) Nongovernmental organizations; (III) International human rights obligations and HIV:

(A) Human rights standards and the nature of State obligations; (B) Restrictions and limitations; (C) The application of specific human rights in the context of the HIV epidemic; Annex 1, History of the recognition of the importance of human rights in the context of HIV; Annex 2, List of participants at the Second International Consultation on HIV/AIDS and Human Rights; Annex 3, List of participants at the Third International Consultation on HIV/AIDS and Human Rights.

"A tool for States in designing, co-ordinating and implementing effective national HIV/AIDS policies and strategies . . . human rights standards apply in the context of HIV/AIDS and translating them into practical measures that should be undertaken at the national level, based on three broad approaches: improvement of government capacity for multi-sectoral coordination and accountability; reform of laws and legal support services, with a focus on anti-discrimination, protection of public health, and improvement of the status of women, children and marginalized groups; and support and increased private sector and community participation to respond ethically and effectively to HIV/AIDS.

OHCHR encourages governments, national human rights institutions, non-governmental organizations and people living with HIV and AIDS to use the Guidelines for training, policy formulation, advocacy, and the development of legislation on HIV/AIDS-related human rights."—*Website*

1017 International health regulations (2005). http://www.who.int/ihr/ publications/9789241596664/en/index. html. World Health Organization. Geneva, Switzerland: World Health Organization. 2007
IHR

Rev. ed., with the new regulations in force on June 15, 2007. Also publ. as a print edition. Supersedes *International health regulations (1969)*, publ. in several different print editions. Title varies: previously called *International sanitary regulations*.

Part of WHO's Global Alert and Response http://www.who.int/csr/en/

Considered a code of practices and procedures for the prevention of the spread of disease, "in consideration of the increases in international travel and trade, and emergence and re-emergence of new international disease threats" (*Publ. notes*), with the goal of preventing and protecting against the international spread of disease. Related WHO websites are "International health regulations"(http://www .who.int/topics/international_health_regulations/ en/) and "Alert, response, and capacity building under the international health regulation news" (http://www.who.int/ihr/en/).

1018 Law and risk management in dental practice. Burton R. Pollack. Chicago: Quintessence Publ. Co., 2002. xii, 284 p. ISBN 0867154160

617.6/0068   RK58.P65

Contents: (1) Introduction to the judicial system of the United States; (2)The regulation of dental practice; (3) The dentist-patient relationship: contract law; (4) Is it negligence, malpractice, or breach of contract?; (5) Statute of limitations and statute of repose: how long the patient has to sue; (6) Experts and the standards of care; (7) Vicarious liability and respondeat superior; (8) Does the dentist have to treat?; (9) Consent, informed consent, and informed refusal; (10) Abandonment and dismissal of a patient; (11) Taking the medical-dental history; (12) Patient records; (13) Trial of a suit in malpractice: res ipsa loquitur, hearsay evidence, and contributory negligence; (14) What to do and what not to do if you are sued; (15) Dentist as witness; (16) Reports on jury trials and disciplinary proceedings; (17) Risk management in dental practice; (18) Office audit risk assessment for the general dentist; (19) Insuring a dental practice; Appendix: Legal terms with dental applications.

Information on the U.S. judicial system and basic legal information for dental professionals. Another legal resource, *Law, liability, and ethics for medical office professionals* provides additional information.

1019 The law and the public's health. 7th ed. Kenneth R. Wing, Benjamin Gilbert. Chicago: Health Administration Press, 2007. xiii, 391 p.

344.7304   KF3775.W5

Contents: ch. 1, "The law and the legal system"; ch. 2, "The power of the state governments in matters affecting health care"; ch. 3, "Government power and the right to privacy"; ch. 4, "The constitutional discretion of the state and federal governments to limit or condition social welfare benefits";

ch. 5, "Government regulation of health care providers and payers"; ch. 6, "The scope of discretion of administrative agencies in matters affecting health and health care"; ch. 7, "The fraud and abuse laws"; ch. 8, "The antitrust laws: Government enforcement of competition"; ch. 9, "Malpractice: Liability for negligence in the delivery and financing of health care"; ch. 10, "Health care business law: Legal considerations in the structuring of health care entities and their transactions."

Intended as an introductory text for schools of public health and law-related courses, this book can also serve as a reference book in the health care field. Provides an introduction to the law, the legal system, and principles applicable to the delivery and financing of health care but is not considered a treatise on health law. Includes bibliographical references and index. Also available as an e-book.

1020 Law, liability, and ethics for medical office professionals. 5th ed. Myrtle Flight. Clifton Park, N.Y.: Delmar Cengage Learning, 2011. xxiv, 338 p., col. ill. ISBN 9781428359413

KF2905.F58

First ed., 1988; 4th ed., 2004.

Contents: Ch. 1, From examining room to courtroom; ch. 2, Functioning within the legal system; ch. 3, Crime and punishment: Intent makes the difference; ch. 4, Your words may form a contract; ch. 5, Anatomy of a medical malpractice case; ch. 6, Health care is big business; ch. 7, The medical record: The medical assistant's responsibility; ch. 8, Introduction to ethics; ch. 9, Privacy, confidentiality, privileged communication: A nexus of law and ethics; ch. 10, Birth and the beginning of life; ch. 11, Professional ethics and the living; ch. 12, Ethics: Death and dying; Appendixes: (A) The civil and criminal case processes; (B) Answers to cases for discussion; Glossary; Bibliography; Index.

Provides basic information in medical law and ethics for medical professionals and helps with understanding their rights and the rights of the patients.

Another legal resource, designed for dental professionals, is *Law and risk management in dental practice*.

1021 Legal and ethical issues for health professionals. 2nd ed.

George D. Pozgar, Nina M. Santucci, John W. Pinnella. Sudbury, Mass.: Jones and Bartlett Publishers, 2010. xxi, 425 p.

174.2   KF3821.P68

         9780763764739

Contents: ch. 1, Introduction to ethics; ch. 2, Contemporary ethical dilemmas; ch. 3, End-of-life dilemmas; ch. 4, Health care ethics committees; ch. 5, Development of law; ch. 6, Introduction to law; ch. 7, Government, ethics, and the law; ch. 8, Organizational ethics and the law; ch. 9, Health care professionals' ethical and legal issues; ch. 10, Physicians' ethical and legal issues; ch. 11, Employee rights and responsibilities; ch. 12, Patient consent; ch. 13, Patient abuse; ch. 14, Patient rights and responsibilities.

Overview of the ethical and legal issues and their interrelationship in the health care field. Guide to additional resources. Includes glossary, bibliographical references, and index. Also available as an e-book.

1022 Legal medicine. 7th ed. American College of Legal Medicine. Philadelphia; London: Elsevier Mosby, 2007. xv, 748 p., ill. ISBN 9780323037532

344.73041   KF3821.L44

First ed., 1988, had title *Legal medicine: Legal dynamics of medical encounters*; 6th ed., 2004.

Contents: pt. 1, "Medical licensure, credentialing and privileging, profiling, and impairment"; pt. 2, "Business aspects of medical practice"; pt. 3, "Medicolegal and ethical encounters"; pt. 4, "Professional medical liability"; pt. 5, "Care of special patients"; pt. 6, "Forensic science and medicine"; pt. 7, "Legal aspects of public health"; pt. 8, "International contributions"; glossary: "Selected health care and legal terminology"; case index; subject index.

This updated and expanded edition explores the legal issues and problems of medical practice and provides answers to health care–related legal questions. Contains new chapters on patient safety, medication errors, apology to patients, medical malpractice overview, liability of pharmacists, and no-fault liability. Useful as a reference for health professionals. Also available as an e-book.

1023 Medical records and the law. 4th ed. William H. Roach, American Health Information Management Association.

Sudbury, Mass.: Jones and Bartlett Publ., 2006. xix, 591 p. ISBN 0763734454

344.7304/1   KF3827.R4R63

First edition, 1985; 3rd ed., 1998.

Contents: ch. 1, Introduction to the American legal system; ch. 2, Medical records and managed care; ch. 3, Medical record requirements; ch. 4, Medical records entries; ch. 5, Documenting consent to treatment; ch. 6, Access to health information; ch. 7, Reporting and disclosure requirements; ch. 8, Documentation and disclosure: special areas of concern; ch. 9, HIV/AIDS: mandatory reporting and confidentiality; ch. 10, Discovery and admissibility of medical records; ch. 11, Legal theories in improper disclosure cases; ch. 12, Risk management and quality management; ch. 13, Electronic health records; ch. 14, Health information in medical research; Index.

Provides information on the growth of electronic health record systems and electronic data networks. Addresses the issues related to medical research involving human subjects and how patient information can be used. Also available as an e-book.

1024 Medicare handbook. Center for Medicare Advocacy. New York: Aspen Publishers, 2000–. v.

368 1530-8979   KF3608.A4M436

Description based on 2014 ed. Contents: Important enrollment information; sect.1, Learn how Medicare works; sect. 2, Signing up for Medicare Part A & Part B; sect. 3, Find out if Medicare covers your test, service, or item; sect. 4, Choose your health & prescription drug coverage; sect. 5, Get information about your Medicare health coverage choices; sect.6, Get information about prescription drug coverage; sect. 7, Get help paying your health & prescription drug costs; sect. 8, Know your rights & how to protect yourself from fraud; sect. 9, Plan ahead for long-term care; sect. 10, Get more information ; sect. 11, Definitions.

PDF version of 2014 ed. available at http://www.medicare.gov/pubs/pdf/10050.pdf

Resource to help understand Medicare's rules and regulations. Further helpful, detailed information can also be found on the Medicare website (Medicare: the official U.S. government site for people with Medicare at http://www.medicare.gov), part of the Centers for Medicare & Medicaid Services.

1025 Nurse practitioner's legal reference.
Springhouse Corp. Springhouse, Pa.:
Springhouse Corp., 2001. xii, 361 p., ill.
ISBN 1582550972
344.73/0414   RT82.8.N8646
Contents: ch. 1, Nurse practitioner practice and
the law; ch. 2, Legal risks and responsibilities on
the job; ch. 3, Legal issues on the job; ch. 4, Legal
risks while off duty; ch. 5, Malpractice liability;
ch. 6, Legal aspects of documentation; ch. 7, Ethical decision making; ch. 8, Ethical conflicts in clinical practice; ch. 9, Ethical conflicts in professional
practice; ch. 10, Patients' rights; ch. 11, NPs in a
changing health care marketplace.

Provides coverage of legal issues affecting nurses and the nursing profession, including issues
currently facing legislative and judicial review.
Contains several appendixes: "Understanding the
judicial process," "Interpreting legal citations," and
"Types of law." Court case citation index and a general index.

**1026 Patients' rights in the age of managed
health care.** Lisa Yount. New York: Facts
on File, 2001. 280 p. ISBN 0816042586
344.73041   KF3823.Y68
Provides overview of the issues in health care delivery, patients' rights and applicable laws, a chronology of significant events, and also a guide to further
research in patients' rights issues. Glossary, index,
and annotated bibliography. *The rights of patients:
The authoritative ACLU guide to the rights of
patients* provides further information. Also available
as an e-book.

1027 The public health law manual.
3rd ed. Frank P. Grad, American
Public Health Association. Washington:
American Public Health Association,
2005. ISBN 0875530427
First edition, 1965, had title *Public health manual:
A handbook on the legal aspects of public health
administration and enforcement;* 2nd ed., 1990,
had title *Public health law manual: A handbook on
the legal aspects of public health administration and
enforcement.*

"The purpose of this manual: Achieving the
most effective use of legal powers; recognition
of legal problems and their management; effective use of available legal assistance; improving

communication between the public health and
legal professions; continuing dialogue"—*Foreword*.
Intended for use by health care professionals and
public health administrators in planning, developing, and implementing public health programs.
Deals with basic legal procedures in public health
enforcement—restrictions of persons; permits,
licenses, and registration; searches and inspections;
embargo, seizure, etc.—and with legal administrative techniques of public health administration.
This edition emphasizes issues in environmental
health law, legal aspects of personal health services,
right to privacy, "right to die" issues, and discussion of various related issues. Provides an overview
of public health policies and public health law and
a summary of international responses to SARS, bioterrorism, global warming, etc.

**1028 The rights of patients: The
authoritative ACLU guide to the
rights of patients. 3rd ed.** George J.
Annas. Carbondale, Ill.: Southern Illinois
University Press, 2004. xxi, 387 p.
ISBN 0809325152
344.73/03211   KF3823.A96
Title varies: 1st ed., 1975, had title: *The rights
of hospital patients: The basic ACLU guide to a
hospital patient's rights;* 2nd ed., 1989, had title:
*The rights of patients: The basic ACLU guide to
patient rights.*

American Civil Liberties Union (ACLU)
(ACLU handbook series)

Contents: (I) Patient rights; (II) The patient
rights advocate; (III) Reforming American medicine; (IV) Hospitals; (V) Emergency medicine;
(VI) Informed choice; (VII) Choices about surgery
and children's care; (VIII) Reproductive health;
(IX) Research; (X) Medical records; (XI) Privacy and
confidentiality; (XII) Care of the dying; (XIII) Suffering, pain, and suicide; (XIV) Death, organ donation, and autopsy; (XV) Patient safety and medical
malpractice. Appendixes: (A) Internet resources;
(B) Convention on human rights and biomedicine;
(C) Childbearing patient bill of rights. Index.

"Offers fully documented exposition and
explanation of the rights of patients from birth to
death . . . a resource not only for patients and their
families but also for physicians, hospital administrators, medical and nursing students, and other
health care workers" (*Publ. notes*). Emphasizes the

importance of having a patient rights advocate, with a section "tips for advocates" in most chapters.

1029 Source book in bioethics. Albert R. Jonsen, Robert M. Veatch, LeRoy Walters. Washington: Georgetown Univ. Pr., 1998. ix, 510 p. ISBN 0878406832
174/.2/09   R724.S599
Contents: Ethics of research with human subjects; A short history; Ethics of death and dying; Changing attitudes toward death and medicine; Ethical issues in human genetics; Issues in genetics; Ethical issues arising from human reproductive technologies and arrangements; Readings on human reproduction; Ethical issues in the changing health care system; The changing health care scene. Collection of significant documents in bioethics and social ethics, covering the time period from 1947–95, with original text reprinted either in full or abridged format, presenting a historical survey of bioethics and major ethical issues in healthcare and key bioethical decisions. Includes legislative documents and reports by various organizations and governments. Bibliographical references and index.

Statistics

1030 State medical licensure requirements and statistics. American Medical Association. Chicago: American Medical Association, 1999–
362.172 1549-4055   RA396.A3U2
1999/2000– (publ. 2000)–
1982-98: *U.S. medical licensure statistics and licensure requirements* (title varies). Description based on 2012 ed.; 2013 and 2014 ed. available, also as e-books.
Contents: Ch. 1, "Licensure policies and regulations of state medical/osteopathic boards"; ch. 2, "Licensing board statistics"; ch. 3, "Medical licensing examinations and organizations"; ch. 4, "Information for international medical graduates"; ch. 5, "Federal and national programs and activities"; ch. 6, "Other organizations and programs"; Appendixes A-E, e.g., "Glossary of medical licensure terms" and "AMA policy on medical licensure."
"Presents current information and statistics on medical licensure in the United States and possessions. Data were obtained from a number of sources, including state boards of medical examiners, the Federation of State Medical Boards, National Board of Medical Examiners, National Board of Osteopathic Medical Examiners, Educational Commission for Foreign Graduates, and the United States Medical Licensing Examination,and others."—*Foreword* Includes 54 allopathic and 14 osteopathic boards of medical examiners.

A related Internet resource on medical licensure is provided by the AMA at http://www.ama-assn.org/go/licensure.

Internet resources

1031 American Health Lawyers Association (AHLA). http://www.healthlawyers.org/. American Health Lawyers Association. Washington: American Health Lawyers Association
"Educational organization devoted to legal issues in the healthcare field" (*Website*). Provides a list of suggested websites as a starting point for conducting research, links to government agencies and original materials, healthcare and health law websites, documents, and other law-related materials. Access to full-text documents may be restricted to members.

Another website, the Health Law section of the American Bar Association (ABA)(http://www.abanet.org/health/), also provides a variety of links.

1032 American Medical Association. http://www.ama-assn.org/. American Medical Association. Chicago: American Medical Association. 1995–
610.9206   R130.5
This searchable website provides a variety of professional resources and standards for AMA members, including, for example, information sources on medical ethics, public health (e.g., eliminating health disparities, health preparedness, disaster response, obesity), medical science, legal issues, and AMA history (with time line and highlights of AMA history). Also provides information on medical education and licensure as well as online resources and other links for medical school students and residents. Includes a section for patients, with access to patient education resources (e.g., "Health literacy resources," "Atlas of the human body," etc.).

Other useful AMA-related links include, for example, DoctorFinder, *Code of medical ethics, current opinions with annotations*, *Current procedural terminology: CPT* (856), FREIDA (291), *Graduate medical education directory*, *Health professions career and education directory*, and *State medical licensure requirements and statistics*. Many of these resources have general reference value in academic and public libraries.

1033 Bioethics resources on the web. http://purl.access.gpo.gov/GPO/LPS55764. National Institutes of Health (U.S.). [Bethesda, Md.]: National Institutes of Health (NIH), Office of Extramural Research (OER), Inter-Institute Bioethics Groups (BIG). 2000–

Web page sponsored by the NIH Office of Science Policy (OSP) and the NIH Inter-Institute Bioethics Interest Group in cooperation with the NIH Office of Extramural Research (OER).

Annotated list of resources and web links that provide access to NIH and other federal resources, relevant organizations, documents, background information, and various positions on bioethical issues, with emphasis on research ethics, genetics, and medicine and healthcare topics. A link to "Health Law Resources" is provided at http://bioethics.od.nih.gov/legal.html.

1034 Drug abuse (MedlinePlus). http://www.nlm.nih.gov/medlineplus/drugabuse.html. National Library of Medicine (U.S.). Bethesda, Md.: National Library of Medicine. 2000?–

A health topic in MedlinePlus.

Contents: Overviews; Latest news; Diagnosis/symptoms; Treatment; Prevention/screening; Specific conditions; Related sssues; Pictures and photographs; Games; Clinical trials; Research; Journal articles; Dictionaries/glossaries; Directories; Organizations; Newsletters/print publications; Law and policy; Statistics; Children; Teenagers; Men; Women; Seniors; Other languages.

Collection of links on substance abuse from a variety of government agencies, professional associations, and organizations, such as the National Institute on Drug Abuse, the Office of National Drug Control, Substance Abuse and Mental Health Services Administration (SAMHSA), National

Library of Medicine, American Medical Association, American Academy of Family Physicians, and others. Also links to related MedlinePlus topics, e.g., alcoholism, prescription drug abuse, and substance abuse, to name a few.

1035 Ethics and health. http://www.who.int/ethics/en/. World Health Organization (WHO). Geneva, Switzerland: World Health Organization. 2002–

World Health Organization (WHO) Dept. of Ethics, Trade, Human Rights and Health Law (ETH); WHO Dept. Sustainable Development and Environmental Health (SDE); WHO Research Ethics Review Committee; U.N. Inter-Agency Committee on Bioethics; National Bioethics Commissions.

"This site has been created as an aid to persons, both inside and outside WHO, seeking information about bioethics, including the ethical aspects of healthcare delivery and planning as well as the ethics of clinical care, research, and biotechnology . . . [with] information about a range of topics in ethics" (*Website*). Reflects various collaborative projects within WHO and also other agencies and provides links to various bioethics topics, full text of ethics publications, ethical considerations and guidelines for research and good clinical practice.

1036 Health fraud (MedlinePlus). http://www.nlm.nih.gov/medlineplus/healthfraud.html. National Library of Medicine (U.S.), National Institutes of Health (U.S.). Bethesda, Md: U.S. National Library of Medicine, National Institutes of Health, Dept. of Health & Human Services. 2000?–

A "health topic" in MedlinePlus.

Contents: Overviews; Related issues; Journal articles; Organizations; Law and policy; Seniors.

Collection of links on health scams and quackery, how to detect health fraud, how to report unlawful sales of medical products, etc. Quackwatch provides additional information in this area.

1037 Human Genetics programme. http://www.who.int/genomics/en/. World Health Organization, Human Genetics Programme. Geneva, Switzerland: World Health Organization. 2003–

Addresses the ethical, legal, and social implications (ELSI) of human genomics.

"WHO's Human Genetics programme aims to provide information and raises awareness within health sector, government and the public on the health challenges and opportunities within the new and rapidly developing science of human genetics." (*Website*). Addresses areas of medical genetics, such as genetic counselling, presymptomatic diagnosis, population genetics, and ethics & genomics. "ELSI genetics resource directory" (http://www.who.int/genomics/elsi/regulatory_data/en/index.html) provides online resources on ELSI of human genetics, ethics organizations, guidelines, codes, declarations, legislations, etc. For health professionals, policy makers, patients and their families, and the general public.

1038 International health (MedlinePlus).
> http://www.nlm.nih.gov/medlineplus/internationalhealth.html. National Library of Medicine (U.S.). Bethesda, Md.: National Library of Medicine. 2000?–

A Health Topic within MedlinePlus. Provides extensive global health information, with access to various online reference resources, links to major organizations (e.g., Centers for Disease Control, World Health Organization), foundations (e.g., Henry J. Kaiser Family Foundation), research, journal articles, law and policy information (e.g., International Health Regulations [2005]), WHO and UNICEF statistics, etc. Links to related MedlinePlus topics, such as Traveler's Health and Health system (MedlinePlus).

1039 National Human Genome Research Institute. http://genome.gov/. National Human Genome Research Institute (U.S.). Bethesda, Md.: National Human Genome Research Institute, National Institutes of Health, U.S. Department of Health and Human Services. 1995–
> QH445.2

National Human Genome Research Institute (NHGRI), previously known as National Center for Human Genome Research (NCHGR), which was established in 1989 because of the Human Genome Project (HGP), since 1990 is a collaborative project of the U.S. Dept. of Energy (DOE) and National Institutes of Health (NIH) to map the human genome; and since HGP's completion in 1993, to apply genome technologies to the study of specific diseases. In 1996, the Center for Inherited Disease Research (CIDR) was also established (cofunded by eight NIH institutes and centers) to study the genetic components of complex disorders. A timeline, 1988 to the present, provides further details about HPG, its completion in 2003, associated events, research, and relevant publications at http://genome.gov/10001763.

Provides access to information, databases, and links to other resources concerning research, grants, health, policy and ethics, educational resources, etc. Some examples include the Talking glossary of genetic terms http://www.genome.gov/glossary/, the NHGRI policy and legislation database http://genome.gov/PolicyEthics/LegDatabase/pubsearch.cfm, Online bioethics resources, the Ethical, legal and social implications (ELSI) research program, and Initiatives and resources for minority and special populations (http://genome.gov/10001192), information on current research projects (e.g., the ENCODE project [ENCyclopedia Of DNA Elements], a pilot project for testing and comparing new methods to identify functional sequences in DNA, model organisms, creation of Centers of excellence in genomic science, the Genetic variation program, the Haplotype map, gene discovery and technology development, establishment of the Center for Inherited Disease Research, and much more.

1040 NLM gateway. http://gateway.nlm.nih.gov/. National Library of Medicine (U.S.). Bethesda, Md.: National Library of Medicine. 2000–
> RA11

As announced in 2011, "the NLM® gateway has transitioned to a new pilot project from the Lister Hill National Center for Biomedical Communications (LHNCBC)."—*Website* The new site focuses now on two databases: Meeting abstracts and Health services research projects. All of the other resources previously accessed through the NLM gateway are available through their individual sites. For a list of these databases previously available via the NLM gateway see http://gateway.nlm.nih.gov/about.jsp.

The NLM gateway previously allowed simultaneous searching of information resources at the

National Library of Medicine (NLM)/National Center for Biotechnology Information (NCBI) with an overview of the search results presented in several categories (bibliographic resources, consumer health resources, and other information), with a listing of the individual databases and the number of results within these categories. Previously included were, for example, MEDLINE/PubMed and the NLM Catalog as well as other resources, including information on current clinical trials and consumer health information (MedlinePlus) and many others.

1041 Online bioethics resources. http://genome.gov/10001744. National Human Genome Research Institute (U.S.), National Institutes of Health. Bethesda, Md.: National Institutes of Health. 2000s–

Produced by National Human Genome Research Institute (NHGRI), which includes the Ethical, Legal and Social Issues (ELSI) Program.

Provides information about the ELSI research program (http://genome.gov/10001618) and an extensive collection of selected online bioethics resources, including ELSI websites, programs, and reports from NHGRI, National Institutes of Health (NIH), U.S. Dept. of Health and Human Services (HHS) Bioethics resources on the web, U.S. Dept. of Energy (DOE), and other resources.

1042 Public health law program. http://www2a.cdc.gov/phlp/lawmat.asp. Centers for Disease Control and Prevention (U.S.), Dept. of Health and Human Services. Atlanta, Ga.: Centers for Disease Control and Prevention, Dept. of Health and Human Services. 200?–

Pt. of the (CDC) website with information on a variety of areas and subjects related to public health law and legal issues, including a list of state public health departments.

Includes emergency preparedness-related statutes, regulations, orders, reports, and legal tools; publications such as bench books, winnable battles, and public health concerns; and directories to counsel at state, selected local, and bodering countries.

1043 Quackwatch. http://www.quackwatch.org. Stephen Barrett. [Allentown, Pa.]:

Stephen Barrett, M.D. [1996]–
615.8   R730

Founded in 1969 as the Lehigh Valley Committee Against Health Fraud, incorporated in 1970. Assumed its current name in 1997. Maintained by Dr. S. Barrett and a network of volunteers and expert advisors. Affiliated with the National Council Against Health Fraud (http://www.ncahf.com/) and Bioethics Watch.

"Nonprofit corporation whose purpose is to combat health-related frauds, myths, fads, fallacies, and misconduct. Its primary focus is on quackery-related information that is difficult or impossible to get elsewhere. Activities include: Investigating questionable claims; Answering inquiries about products and services; Advising quackery victims; Distributing reliable publications; Debunking pseudoscientific claims; Reporting illegal marketing; Assisting or generating consumer-protection lawsuits; Improving the quality of health information on the Internet; Attacking misleading advertising on the Internet."—*Website*

In addition, includes a list of websites that provide access to 24 special areas—e.g., autism, chiropractic, dentistry, diet and nutrition, mental health, and other topics of interest to consumers. Its "Internet Health Pilot" site provides links to many other reliable health sites, its "Casewatch" site contains legal matters and regulatory issues. The contents of all sites can be searched simultaneously or individually (http://www.quackwatch.org/wgsearch.html).

1044 U.S. Dept. of Health and Human Services (HHS.gov). http://www.hhs.gov/. U.S. Dept. of Health and Human Services (HHS). Washington: U.S. Dept. of Health and Human Services. 1997–
                                              HV85

"United States government's principal agency for protecting the health of all Americans and providing essential human services, especially for those who are least able to help themselves."—*About page*

HHS works closely with state and local governments. The Department's approx. 300 programs are administered by 11 operating divisions, including eight agencies in the U.S. Public Health Service and three human services agencies. A guide to information resources, i.e. "HHS information resources directory," is available at http://www.hhs.gov/about/ referlst.html. This site also provides, for example, information on key initiatives (e.g., HealthCare.gov, FoodSafety.gov, InsureKidsNow.gov, for example), news and a news archive, information on prevention of diseases and a healthy lifestyle and on diseases and conditions, health information privacy, human research protections, health information technology standards, laws and regulations, and policies and guidelines. The current HHS website is searchable at http://www.hhs.gov/. Archival access to older materials (e.g., speeches, materials of historical or research interest, etc.) is available at http://archive.hhs.gov/. Historical Highlights and Past Secretaries, from 1798-2009, can be found at http://www.hhs.gov/about/hhshist.html.

8 *Nursing*

Bibliography

1045 Celebrating nursing history. http://nahrs.mlanet.org/home/weeding. Margaret Allen, Medical Library Association. Chicago: Medical Library Association. 1994–

Produced by Medical Library Association (MLA), Nursing and Allied Health Resources Section (NAHRS). Reprint of article originally publ. in *NAHRS newsletter*, Apr. 1994, updated Oct. 2005.

Contents: What to Keep; Significant Nursing Books to Find and Keep; Periodicals to Keep; Sources Used for Some of These Comments and Selections; Reprints; Films and Videos; How and Where to Search; Other Sources for Historical Research; Why Go to Historical Sources?; Other Articles of Interest.

Provides an annotated bibliography of nursing books, reports, landmark studies, periodicals, films, videos, and other resources for historical research in nursing and related allied health literature. Chronological arrangement under the different headings. Intended to answer questions on archives, weeding, and other collection management issues posed by nursing librarians and others interested in the history of nursing.

1046 Essential nursing resources. http://www.icirn.org/Homepage/Essential-Nursing-Resources/Essential-Nursing-Resources-PDF.aspx. Janet Schnall, Susan Fowler, Interagency Council on Information Resources for Nursing (ICIRN). New York: Interagency Council on Information Resources for Nursing. 1967–

Produced by Interagency Council on Information Resources in Nursing (ICIRN).

Previous editions had title: *Essential nursing references*.

Description based on 26th ed., 2012. Collaborative project, compiled from contributions by representatives from ICIRN member agencies. Previously also published biennially in print issue of *Nursing education perspectives*. Starting in 2012, only available online in either PDF or HTML format.

Contents: Alerting services/RSS; Bibliographies/book and serial lists; Bioethics; Blogs, forums, and discussion lists; Complementary and alternative medicine; Consumer health and patient education; Cultural competency; Databases and indexes; Dictionaries; Evidence-based nursing; Drugs; Education and career directories; Grants resources; History of nursing and archives; Informatics; Management; Meta-sites for nursing information; Patient safety and quality assurance; Public health/disaster preparedness; Statistics; Writers' manuals and guides.

"Presented as a resource for locating nursing information and for collection development . . . includes print, electronic sources, and web sources to support nursing practice, education, administration, and research activities"—*Introd.*

Well-regarded and helpful research tool for nurses and librarians. Provides a listing of important and useful references and resources. Format of resource (via mobile, online or print) is indicated. Further information at: http://icirn.org/Homepage/Essential-Nursing-Resources/default.aspx

1047 IndexCat. http://www.nlm.nih.gov/hmd/indexcat/ichome.html. U.S. National Library of Medicine, Library of the Surgeon-General's Office, Army Medical Library, Armed Forces Medical Library, National Library of Medicine. Bethesda, Md.: U.S. National Library of Medicine, National Institutes of Health, Health and Human Services. 2004-

Z6676

IndexCat™ is the digitized version of the *Index-catalogue of the library of the Surgeon General's office* (Army Medical Library), ser. 1–5, 61 v. Washington: U.S. Govt. Printing Office (16), 1880–1961. Ser. 1, A–Z (1880–95); ser. 2, A–Z (1896–1916); ser. 3, A–Z (1918–32); ser. 4. v. 1–11, A–Mn (1936–55); ser. 4 is incomplete, last half was never published; 5th series (1959–61).

"A collaborative project initiated by the American Association for the History of Medicine with support from the Wellcome Trust, the Burroughs Wellcome Fund, and the U.S. National Library of Medicine."—*Website*

Content and coverage is the same as the printed catalog, e.g., from early times through 1950 imprints, including books, journal articles, dissertations, pamphlets, reports, newspaper clippings, case studies, obituary notices, letters, and portraits, as well as rare books and manuscripts. Recently, two new collections, involving medieval scientific English and Latin texts, were made available through IndexCat. Further detailed information about content and coverage of *IndexCat* is at http://www.nlm.nih.gov/hmd/indexcat/aboutic.html and http://www.nlm.nih.gov/services/faqic.html.

Subject headings in IndexCat do not conform to the Medical subject headings (MeSH®, 858). Searchable by keywords (subject, author, title, journal title, note content, and by year of publication).

IndexCat and LocatorPlus™ (52), NLM's online public catalog, may be searched at the same time. LocatorPlus contains NLM holdings and current information for books, pamphlets, dissertations, and journal titles.

1048 Medical humanities dissertations. http://www.hsls.pitt.edu/histmed/dissertations/. Jonathon Erlen, University of Pittsburgh Health Sciences Library System. Pittsburgh: Health Sciences Library, University of Pittsburgh Medical Center. 2001–

Provides a monthly current awareness service for selected recent medical dissertations and theses. Arranged by topics, currently covers the following areas: AIDS (social and historical contexts); alternative medicine (social and historical contexts); art and medicine; biomedical ethics; history of medicine prior to 1800; history of medicine and health care; history of science and technology; literature/theater and medicine; nursing history; pharmacy/pharmacology and history; philosophy and medicine; psychiatry/psychology and history; public health/international health; religion and medicine; women's health and history. To view complete citations, abstracts, and full-text of dissertations requires a subscription to Proquest dissertations and theses (PQDT).

1049 Nursing history research resources. http://www.aahn.org/resource.html. American Association for the History of Nursing. Wheat Ridge, Colo.: American Association for the History of Nursing. 2005?–

Produced by American Association for the History of Nursing (AAHN; http://www.aahn.org).

Contents: Archives and history centers; Conferences, exhibits and celebrations; Funding; Internet resources; Journals; New books and publications; Organizations; Videos.

Listing of selected available nursing resources, including Internet resources, for the history of nursing. Provides links to other nursing history organizations, nursing education, and related government websites. Includes, for example, a link to nursing history centers, museums, and archives (http://www.aahn.org/resources/centers.html) and a page entitled "Black nurses in history: A bibliography and guide to Web resources" (http://libguides.rowan.edu/blacknurses), prepared by the University of Medicine and Dentistry of New Jersey.

Indexes; Abstract journals; Databases

1050 CINAHL. http://www.ebscohost.com/
cinahl/. Cinahl Information Systems,
EBSCO. Ipswich, Mass.: EBSCO. 1982–
CINAHL® [database]. Title varies. Online version: 1984–1992 (with coverage 1982–), publ. by Cinahl Information Systems; 1993– , publ. jointly by EBSCO and Cinahl Information Systems. Also available in different enhanced versions: CINAHL® with Full Text, CINAHL® Plus™, and CINAHL® Plus with Full Text. Comparisons of the different versions at http://www.ebscohost.com/uploads/thisTopic-dbTopic-592.pdf.

Print version: 1956–76 entitled: *Cumulative index to nursing and allied health literature*; 1977– *Cumulative index to nursing and allied health literature®* (continues to be published in print).

Authoritative database for the professional literature of nursing and allied health. Provides references to journal articles, books, book chapters, pamphlets, audiovisual materials, dissertations, educational software, selected conference proceedings, standards of professional practice, and more. Some full-text material is included. Currently indexes a large number of journals, as well as publications from the American Nurses' Association and the National League for Nursing. Allows for application of specific interest category filter, e.g., evidence-based practice, informatics, patient safety, public health, women's health, and others. Subject access is provided by *CINAHL* (101) . . . *subject heading list: Alphabetic list, tree structures, permuted list*. Complements *International nursing index*, publ. 1966–2000.

1051 Health and wellness resource center.
http://www.gale.com/HealthRC/. Gale
Group. Farmington Hills, Mich.: Gale;
Cengage Learning. 2001–
Also called *Gale®'s health & wellness resource center*.

Provides access to a collection of Gale reference titles (e.g., *Gale encyclopedia of cancer*, *Gale encyclopedia of childhood and adolescence*, *Gale encyclopedia of genetic disorders*, *Gale encyclopedia of medicine*, *Medical and health information directory*, and others; access to full-text articles from the periodical literature; pamphlets; news; and other content, such as access to selected health websites. Also makes available add-on modules (e.g., Alternative Health Module with, for example, the *Gale encyclopedia of alternative medicine*, and the Disease Profiler Module with health statistics). "Ever-growing electronic resource center for all levels of health research" (*Publ. notes*), particularly for nursing and allied health professionals and consumer health, public, and health science libraries.

Other Gale resources include Health reference center—academic and Gale virtual reference library.

1052 International nursing index. American
Journal of Nursing Company, Institute
for Scientific Information., National
Library of Medicine (U.S.), American
Nurses' Association., National League for
Nursing. New York: American Journal of
Nursing Company, 1966–2000
610.73016 0020-8124   Z6675.N7.I5
Print version discontinued in 2000. Currently searchable in MEDLINE/PubMed. Relevant content can also be found in CINAHL (101).

A computer-produced index using MEDLARS (Medical Literature Analysis and Retrieval System) facilities. Because subject headings were originally chosen for a medical index, a "Nursing thesaurus," included in the annual cumulation, gives commonly used nursing terms as cross-references to the subject headings used in the index. Cross-references from MeSH: Medical subject headings (858) are included in each annual cumulation since 1972. Also includes brief sections listing nursing publications of organizations and agencies as well as books published by or for nurses. A list of doctoral dissertations by nurses appears in the annual cumulative volume.

1053 Lexi-Comp online. http://www.lexi.com/.
Lexi-Comp, Inc. Hudson, Ohio: Lexi-
Comp, Inc. 1978–
Point-of-care drug and clinical information resource, with links to primary literature. Contains 15 clinical databases (e.g., Lexi-Drugs Online, AHFS, Lexi-Natural Products Online, Nursing Lexi-Drugs Online, Pharmacogenomics, Poisoning and Toxicology, Lab Tests and Diagnosis, and several others) and provides drug information and treatment recommendation for

diseases and conditions. Also includes other features, e.g., an online interaction tool (Lexi-Interact) and medical calculator (Lexi-CALC). For pharmacists, physicians, nurses, and dentists. Detailed information available at the Lexi-Comp website "tour portal" (http://www.lexi.com/web/toursol.jsp).

1054 MEDLINE. http://purl.access.gpo.gov/ GPO/LPS4708. National Library of Medicine (U.S.). Bethesda, Md.: National Library of Medicine (U.S.). 1900s–
MEDLINE®—Medical literature analysis and retrieval system online (National Library of Medicine®—NLM), primary subset of PubMed® and part of the databases provided by the National Center for Biotechnology Information (NCBI). Coverage extends back to 1946, with some older material.

Bibliographic database, providing comprehensive access to the international biomedical literature from the fields of medicine, nursing, dentistry, veterinary medicine, allied health, and the preclinical sciences. It is also a primary source of information from the international literature on biomedicine, including the following topics as they relate to biomedicine and health care: Biology, environmental science, marine biology, plant and animal science, biophysics, and chemistry. For indexing articles, NLM uses MeSH: Medical subject headings® (858), a controlled vocabulary of biomedical terms. An increasing number of MEDLINE citations contain a link to the free full-text articles.

The MEDLINE database is the electronic counterpart of *Index medicus®*, *Index to dental literature*, and the *International nursing index*. The databases is offered at no additional cost on a variety of indexing platforms.

For detailed information, see the MEDLINE fact sheet at http://www.nlm.nih.gov/pubs/factsheets/ medline.html, which also includes a list of related fact sheets (e.g., "MEDLINE, PubMed, and PMC (PubMed Central): How are they different?").

1055 Micromedex products. http://www .micromedex.com/products/index.html. Truven Health Analytics. Ann Arbor, Mich.: Truven Health Analytics. [199?–]
Produced by Truven Health Analytics, formerly known as Thomson Reuters (Healthcare) Inc.

Intended for clinicians; academic program available. Includes a variety of resources for finding information on drugs, toxicology, emergency, acute care, and disease data as well as alternative medicine information. Drug resources include DRUG-DEX, DRUG-REAX, IDENTIDEX, IV Index, *Index nominum*, *Martindale: The complete drug reference*, POISINDEX, *Red book*, and REPRORISK. Emergency and disease data can be found, for example, in DISEASEDEX and alternative therapies in AltMed-Dex and other Thomson products. Searchable across either all databases, by specific database(s), and by groups of databases. Drugs can be searched by trade or generic drug name. Specific drug database search and drug topic search provide, for example, a drug evaluation overview, dosing information, pharmacokinetics, contraindications, precautions, adverse reactions, single and multiple drug interactions, IV compatibility, teratogenicity, therapeutic uses, and comparative efficacy.

A matrix of all Micromedex products and versions in this series, with listing of the individual titles, various format options, and indication of whether a particular title is also available in print can be found at http://www.micromedex.com/ support/faqs/plat_matrix.html. Help with citing the various Micromedex versions is provided at http://www.micromedex.com/about_us/legal/cite/.

1056 NLM gateway. http://gateway.nlm.nih .gov/. National Library of Medicine (U.S.). Bethesda, Md.: National Library of Medicine. 2000–

RA11

As announced in 2011, "the NLM® gateway has transitioned to a new pilot project from the Lister Hill National Center for Biomedical Communications (LHNCBC)."—*Website* The new site focuses now on two databases: Meeting abstracts and Health services research projects. All of the other resources previously accessed through the NLM gateway are available through their individual sites. For a list of these databases previously available via the NLM gateway see http://gateway.nlm.nih.gov/ about.jsp.

The NLM gateway previously allowed simultaneous searching of information resources at the National Library of Medicine (NLM)/National Center for Biotechnology Information (NCBI) with an overview of the search results presented in several categories (bibliographic resources, consumer health resources, and other information), with a listing of the individual databases and the number of results within these categories. Previously included were, for example, MEDLINE/PubMed and the NLM Catalog as well as other resources, including information on current clinical trials and consumer health information (MedlinePlus) and many others.

1057 Nursing studies index. Virginia Henderson, Yale University. New York: Garland, 1984. 4 v. ISBN 0824065158

016.61073   Z6675.N7.N869; RT41

Contents: v. 1, 1900–29 (publ. 1972); v. 2, 1930–49 (publ. 1970); v. 3, 1950–56 (publ. 1966); v. 4, 1957–59 (publ. 1963).

Subtitle: *An annotated guide to reported studies, research in progress, research methods and historical materials, in periodicals, books, and pamphlets published in English.*

Provides retrospective coverage for a wide range of materials not treated elsewhere. The number of journals covered varies from 110 in v. 1 to 239 in v. 4, according to availability at the time of publication. Annotations note study methods used and nature and scope of the investigation, and they frequently indicate the author's qualifications and the auspices under which the work was done. Includes unpublished doctoral dissertations but not master's theses. Subject arrangement with author index.

1058 PubMed. http://www.ncbi.nlm.nih. gov/pubmed. U.S. National Center for Biotechnology Information, National Library of Medicine, National Institutes of Health. Bethesda, Md.: U.S. National Center for Biotechnology Information. 1996–

PubMed®, developed and maintained by the National Center for Biotechnology Information (NCBI) at the National Library of Medicine® (NLM). Provides a search interface for more than 20 million bibliographic citations and abstracts in the fields of medicine, nursing, dentistry, veterinary medicine, health care systems, and preclinical sciences. It provides access to articles indexed for MEDLINE® and for selected life sciences journals. PubMed subsets found under the "Limits" tab are: MEDLINE and PubMed central®, several journal groups (i.e., core clinical journals, dental journals, and nursing journals), and topical subsets (AIDS, bioethics, cancer,

complementary medicine, dietary supplements, history of medicine, space life sciences, systematic reviews, toxicology, and veterinary science). "Linkout" provides access to full-text articles.

For detailed information see the PubMed fact sheet at http://www.nlm.nih.gov/pubs/factsheets/pubmed.html and also MEDLINE®/PubMed® resources guide (http://www.nlm.nih.gov/bsd/pm resources.html) which provides detailed information about MEDLINE data and searching PubMed.

Information regarding the mobile version of this resource is part of NLM's Gallery of mobile apps and sites.

1059 PubMed health. http://www.ncbi.nlm .nih.gov/pubmedhealth/. National Center for Biotechnology Information (U.S.); National Library of Meidcine (U.S.). Bethesda, Md.: National Center for Biotechnology Information U.S.); National Library of Medicine (U.S.). 2011-

Based on systematic reviews of clinical trials which help to determine which treatments and preventive measures work. Searchable database which allows access to clinical effectiveness research and reviews (CER). Easy-to-read summaries as well as full-text reviews & reports can help consumers and clinicians understand and use clinical research results. Information is drawn, for example, from NCBI bookshelf (http://www.ncbi.nlm.nih.gov/sites/entrez?db=books), PubMed, and published systematic reviews from the Agency for Health Care Research and Quality, National Cancer Institute, The Cochrane Collaboration (see related entry Cochrane Library, and many others. A comprehensive listing of collaborators and other information about this resource at http://www.ncbi .nlm.nih.gov/pubmedhealth/about/.

Encyclopedias

1060 Encyclopedia of aging. 4th ed. Richard Schulz. New York: Springer, 2006. 2 v., 720 p. ISBN 0826148433

305.2603   HQ1061.E53

From the 1st ed. in 1987, this encyclopedia has provided a thorough presentation of a wide range of items, issues, and facts dealing with aging. Now in its 4th ed., it documents in thoughtful essays many aspects of the lives of older persons, as well as issues and services for the elderly. Made up of some 600 essays, including 200 that are entirely new, with others significantly updated. Multidisciplinary, covering relevant materials from biology, physiology, genetics, medicine, psychology, nursing, social services, sociology, economics, technology, and political science. Extensive listing of further resources, cross-references, and thorough index. Definitive work on gerontology and geriatrics. A must-have reference title for general and research collections. Available as an e-book.

1061 The encyclopedia of elder care: The comprehensive resource on geriatric and social care. 2nd ed.
Liz Capezuti, Eugenia L. Siegler, Mathy Doval Mezey, Joan Dunbar. New York: Springer, 2008. xxxvii, 860 p.
ISBN 9780826102
362.19897003   RC954.E53
First edition, 2001.

"Designed to encapsulate all aspects of care for an aging population: a comprehensive, multidisciplinary compilation of topics that reflects the breadth and depth of issues of concerns to those who care for older individuals—from individual to society, from patient to professional, from symptom to treatment"—*Pref.* Entries address elder care in the areas of society, community, caregiving, and the individual. Intended for professionals from a variety of health professions and for students. Organized alphabetically by topic, with listing of Internet resources and bibliographic references. Also available as an e-book.

1062 Encyclopedia of nursing research.
3rd ed. Joyce J. Fitzpatrick, Meredith Wallace Kazer. New York: Springer Publ., 2012. xxxi, 699 p. ISBN 9780826107503
610.73072   RT81.5.E53
First ed., 1998; 2nd ed., 2006. Based on *Annual review of nursing research* (ARNR): 1st ed., (ARNR v. 1-15); 2nd ed. (ARNR v.22); 3rd ed., 2012 (ARNR v.1-30).

Provides key terms and concepts in nursing research. A "comprehensive, authoritative, yet concise guide to current nursing research literature . . .

cognizant of the current depth of nursing research in some areas . . . and a timely source of the most relevant and recent research."—*Pref.* Also incorporates topics from the first and second editions. Includes topics such as nursing care; services; education; specialties; historical, philosophical, and cultural issues; geriatric nursing; cancer survivorship; disparities in minority mental health; and formal nursing languages. Offers cross-references. Written for nursing researchers and graduate students in nursing. Subject index. Available as an e-book. A companion volume is Dictionary of nursing theory and research.

1063 The Gale encyclopedia of nursing and allied health. 3rd ed. Brigham Narins. Detroit: Gale Cengage Learning, 2013.
6 v. (xxvi, 3784 p.), ill. (some col.)
ISBN 9781414498881
610.7303   RT21
First edition, 2002; 2nd ed., 2006.
Contents: v. 1, A-C; v. 2, D-F; v. 3, G-K; v. 5, O-S; v. 5, T-Z.

Contains articles on various aspects of nursing and allied health, with lists of resources. Covers nursing, physical therapy, occupational therapy, respiratory therapy and other health professions. Alphabetically arranged entries are written in a standardized format, with definitions, descriptions, key terms, print and non-print resources, and information specific to the subject treated. Covered, for example, are various diseases and disorders, treatments, tests and procedures, equipment/tools, current health issues, human biology/body systems, education, training, work settings for the different health professions, etc. Cross-references, color illustrations, and sketches. Bibliographical references and comprehensive index. An online edition will be made available through Gale virtual reference library.

1064 The Gale encyclopedia of senior health: A guide for seniors and their caregivers. Jacqueline L. Longe. Detroit: Gale, c2009. 5 v. (2120 p.), ill. (chiefly col.) ISBN 9781414403830
2009 618.97003 22   RC952.5.G3485
Comprehensive encyclopedia, alphabetically organized, with approx. 600 illustrated entries and arranged in five categories: diseases and conditions; treatment, rehabilitation, recovery; aging, general

health, death and dying; healthy living: nutrition, exercise, prevention; and community care giving. A typical entry provides definition, description, causes and symptoms, diagnosis, treatment, various resources, etc. Glossary of key terms, appendix listing organizations, and general index. Intended as a resource for senior patients/health consumers to educate themselves about their condition. It is not intended to replace a doctor's visit. It is also considered a useful reference source for librarians. Also available online through Gale virtual reference library.

Some overlap of content with other Gale encyclopedias, e.g., *Gale encyclopedia of medicine* and *Gale encyclopedia of nursing*, can be expected.

Encyclopedia of aging and *Encyclopedia of health and aging* address the biological, psychological, social, and economic aspects of health and aging and are intended for health care professionals who work with an aging population.

1065 The Gale encyclopedia of surgery and medical tests: A guide for patients and caregivers. 2nd ed. Brigham
　　Narins. Detroit: Gale, 2009. 4 v., color ill.
　　ISBN 9781414448848
　　617.003　　　　　　　　　RD17.G342
Contents: v. 1, A–C; v. 2, D–K; v. 3, L–P; v. 4, Q-Z, organizations, glossary, index.

Approx. 500 alphabetically arranged entries, with definitions of key terms and articles of varying length. Explains surgical procedures, medical tests, and laboratory procedures. Information is presented in a consistent format (definition, description, purpose, diagnosis/preparation, aftercare, precautions, risks, etc.), with step-by-step illustrations for many procedures. Appendixes list centers for specific surgical specialties, national organizations, and support groups for patients. Bibliographies for further reading. Intended for nursing and allied health professionals and general readers. Also available as an e-book.

1066 Historical encyclopedia of nursing.
　　Mary Ellen Snodgrass. Santa Barbara,
　　Calif.: ABC-CLIO, 1999. xvii, 354 p., ill.
　　610.7309　　　　　　　　　RT31.S66
Covers the history of nursing and healing from ancient times to the present. Includes key nursing concepts and individuals, medical topics, organizations, wars, etc. Articles list sources, including websites. Black-and-white illustrations and "see also" references.

"Timeline of landmarks in nursing" (p. 297–310), "Works by and about healers" (p. 311–13), bibliographical references (p. 315–33), and index.

Dictionaries

1067 Black's medical dictionary. 42nd ed.
　　Harvey Marcovitch. London: A. & C.
　　Black, 2010. viii, 764 p., 16 p. of plates, ill.
　　ISBN 9780713689020
　　610.3　　　　　　　　　R121
First ed., 1906. 40th ed., 2002; 41st ed., 2005.

A standard dictionary of British terminology, with clear explanation of medical terms. This revised edition contains approximately 5,000 medical terms, including new terms and concepts (e.g., new diagnostic imaging techniques, minimally invasive surgery, gene therapy) and revisions. Many cross-references. Several appendixes provide information on subjects such as basic first aid, travel and health, measurements in medicine, health policy organizations, and others. Intended for nurses, healthcare professionals, students, and consumers. Available online via Credo reference.

1068 Churchill Livingstone's dictionary of nursing. 19th ed. Christine Brooker.
　　Edinburgh, U.K.: Churchill Livingstone,
　　2006. x, 293 p., ill. ISBN 0443101752
　　610.7303　　　　　　　　　RT21.C487
A–Z entries, covering of a variety of nursing topics. Appendixes have been completely updated with many new words and illustrations. Supplemented by Elsevier's Evolve website (https://evolve.elsevier .com/productPages/s_894.html), free with purchase of print testbook, with approximately 7,500 selected dictionary entries, nursing abbreviations, and a spellchecker. An icon indicates the availability of additional material on the website. Primarily intended for health professionals and students "outside of the U.S." (*Publ. notes*). Online edition available via Credo Reference.

1069 Concise dictionary of modern medicine. Joseph C. Segen. New York:
　　McGraw-Hill, 2006. xix, 765 p. ISBN
　　0838515355
　　　　　　　　　　　　　　　R121.S42
A revision of *Current med talk: A dictionary of medical terms, slang, and jargon.*

Illustrated dictionary, with 20,000 current medical terms, covering clinical and basic science aspects, also jargon and casual speech not necessarily found in other reference sources. Intended to supplement standard medical dictionaries. Also available in a 2002 ed. with the same title and as *Dictionary of modern medicine* which contains 40,000 entries.

1070 Dictionary of nursing. 5th ed.

E. A. Martin, Tanya A. McFerran. Oxford; New York: Oxford University Press, 2008. 584 p. ISBN 9780199211784
610.7303; 610.3   RT21

First ed., 1990; 4th ed., 2003. Description based on 5th ed., 2008. Also called *Oxford dictionary of nursing*.

Vocabulary of the nursing profession and related terminology. Concise definitions of approx. 10,000 terms, pronunciation guide, some black-and-white illustrations and tables. Appendixes include, for example, reference values of biochemical and hematologic data, standard values for body weight, immunization schedule, nutritional guidelines, the nursing code of conduct, and healthcare website addresses. Many entries in the fields of medicine, surgery, anatomy, physiology, psychiatry, nutrition, and pharmacology have been adapted from the *Concise medical dictionary* by Martin. Available in electronic format as part of Oxford reference online.

1071 Dictionary of nursing theory and research. 4th ed. Bethel Ann Powers, Thomas R. Knapp. New York: Springer Publ. Co., 2011. xv, 228 p., ill. ISBN 9780826106650
610.73/03   RT81.5.P69

First ed., 1990; 3rd ed., 2006.

Provides terminology and definitions, with notes, comments, and examples commonly found in nursing literature. Reflects the changes in the clinical health sciences, with entries in the areas of inter-professionalism, communication, areas of research (e.g., translational research, health services research, comparative effectiveness research, biobehavioral research) and evidence-based practice, theory development, etc. Includes cross-references and bibliographical references. Also available as an e-book.

Considered a companion volume to *Encyclopedia of nursing research*.

1072 Dorland's illustrated medical dictionary. 32nd ed. W. A. Newman Dorland. Philadelphia: Saunders/Elsevier, 2012. xxvii, 2147 p., ill. (chiefly color). ISBN 9781416062578
R121.D73

First–22nd ed., 1900–51 had title: *The American illustrated medical dictionary*; 31st ed., c2007.

Designed to satisfy the conventional use of a dictionary; that is, to discover spelling, meaning, and derivation of specific terms and to assist in the creation of words by defining prefixes, suffixes, and stems. Includes a section on "Fundamentals of medical etymology." Reflects standard and current terminology, with official nomenclatures from various fields, e.g., for anatomy, *Terminologia Anatomica* (Federative International Committee on Anatomical Terminology), for enzymology (Nomenclature Committee of the International Union of Biochemistry and Molecular Biology on the Nomenclature and Classification of Enzymes), and several others as listed in the preface. Also includes eponyms, acronyms, abbreviations, pronunciation, cross-references, etc. 1,525 illustrations in this edition. Eight appendixes include, for example, selected abbreviations used in medicine, symbols, phobias, table of elements, units of measurements, and others. Accompanying CD-ROM contains supplementary appendixes, e.g., selected terms in anatomy, a listing of surgical equipment not covered in the main section (A-Z) of the dictionary, also audio phonetics for over 35,000 terms. Internet access to this dictionary is available for subscribers at http://www.dorlands.com. For health professionals and students in medicine, nursing, and allied health. Index to tables; Index to plates; Index to appendixes; extensive "notes on the use of this dictionary" in the beginning pages of the dictionary.

1073 Encyclopedia and dictionary of medicine, nursing, and allied health. 7th ed. Benjamin Frank Miller. Philadelphia: Saunders, 2003. xxxi, 2262 p., [40] p. of plates, ill. (chiefly col.) ISBN 0721697917
610.3   R121.M65

First ed. (1972) had title *Encyclopedia and dictionary of medicine and nursing*; 6th ed. (1997) had title *Miller-Keane encyclopedia and dictionary of medicine, nursing, and allied health*.

A concise work intended for students and

workers in the nursing and allied health fields. Clear definitions and explanations of the current multidisciplinary terminology. This edition has 3,900 new terms, including the "latest changes for diagnosis-related groups, nursing diagnoses, and key nursing taxonomies."—*Foreword*; for example, definitions are provided for the complete vocabulary of the Unified Nursing Language System. Pronunciation guides; a list of stems, prefixes, and suffixes; and a 32-page color atlas of human anatomy.

The print resource is supplemented by a CD-ROM that contains spellchecker software, derived from *Dorland's medical speller*.

1074 Medical dictionary (MedlinePlus). http://www.nlm.nih.gov/medlineplus/ mplusdictionary.html. National Library of Medicine (U.S.). Bethesda, Md.: National Library of Medicine. 2002–

R121

Part of MedlinePlus. This online dictionary, based on *Merriam-Webster's medical dictionary*, can be searched from the MedlinePlus home page (via "Dictionary" tab). Contains definitions for words and phrases used by health care professionals, a pronunciation guide, and brief biographies of individuals (after whom particular diseases are named). Most MedlinePlus Health Topics pages contain a link or links to additional online dictionaries and/ or glossaries from various sources.

Numerous online medical dictionaries and glossaries are also available from many other sources. They include titles made available from various government agencies, organizations, and commercial publishers. Some examples include online medical dictionaries accessible via Credo reference (currently 24 titles), Deciphering medspeak (http:// www.mlanet.org/resources/medspeak/; MLANET), Diabetes dictionary (http://diabetes.niddk.nih.gov/ dm/pubs/dictionary/index.htm; National Institute of Diabetes and Digestive and Kidney Diseases), Dictionary of cancer terms (National Cancer Institute), mediLexicon tools (http://www.medilexicon.com/), Talking glossary of genetics terms (http://www.nhgri .nih.gov/glossary.cfm; National Human Genome Research Institute), and many others.

1075 Melloni's illustrated dictionary of medical abbreviations. Biagio John Melloni, June L. Melloni. New York:

Parthenon Publ. Group, 1998. 485 p., ill. ISBN 1850707081

610/.1/48 R121.M539

Abbreviations compiled from recent medical texts and journals. Approx. 15,000 entries and 150 ill. A–Z arrangement.

1076 Melloni's illustrated dictionary of obstetrics and gynecology. June L. Melloni, Ida Dox, Harrison H. Sheld. New York: Parthenon Publ. Group, 2000. 401 p., ill. (some col.) ISBN 1850707103

618/.03 RG45.M45

Contains over 15,000 concise definitions, including terms from other disciplines that are related to female health. Includes 280 ill., with color correlation of a defined term and its illustration. Cross-references, pronunciation guide, and relevant abbreviations. For health professionals and students.

1077 Mosby's dictionary of medicine, nursing & health professions. 9th ed. Mosby, Inc. St. Louis: Elsevier/Mosby, 2013. xiv, A-43, 1989 p., ill. (chiefly col.) ISBN 9780323074032

610.3 R121

First ed., 1982 and 2nd ed., 1986, had title: *Mosby's medical and nursing dictionary*; 3rd ed., 1990 and 4th ed., 2002, had title: *Mosby's medical, nursing, and allied health dictionary*; 5th ed., 1998 and 6th ed., 2001, had title: *Mosby's medical, nursing, and allied health dictionary*; 7th ed., 2006; 8th ed., 2009.

Reflects recent developments in medical and healthcare terminology. Encyclopedic-style definitions and approx. 2,450 color illustrations, photographs, and a "color atlas of human anatomy," organized by organ system. Numerous appendixes include, for example, reference information such as normal laboratory values for children and adults, units of measurement, dietary guide and U.S. dietary reference intakes, complementary and alternative medicine, herbs and natural supplements, American sign language guidelines, major nursing classifications, online resources, etc. Available online via Credo reference.

1078 Mosby's medical dictionary. 9th ed. Marie T. O'Toole. St. Louis: Elsevier/Mosby, 2013. xiv, A1-A43, 1921 p., col. ill. ISBN 9780323085410

610.3   R121
First ed., 1982; 8th ed., 2009.

Contains over 56,000 terms and over 2,450 color illustrations. Includes a color atlas of human anatomy and other ready-reference information, such as "American sign language and manual communication;" "Common abbreviations used in writing prescriptions;" "Spanish-French-English equivalents of commonly used medical terms and phrases;" "Commonly used abbreviations;" "Joint Commission do not use list." For physicians, nurses, and allied health professionals. Also useful for health consumers.

1079 Say it in Spanish: A guide for health care professionals. 3rd ed.

Esperanza Villanueva Joyce, Maria Elena Villanueva. St. Louis: Saunders, 2004. xiii, 440 p., ill. ISBN 0721604242

468.2/421/02461   R121.J69
First ed., 1996; [2nd ed.], 1999.

Contains commonly used English words and phrases in healthcare settings, with their Spanish translation and pronunciation. Includes information on Hispanic culture and popular health beliefs. For health-care workers who communicate with Spanish-speaking patients. Alphabetical word index; phrase and sentence index. Includes audio CD.

1080 Stedman's medical abbreviations, acronyms & symbols. 5th ed.

Thomas Lathrop Stedman. Philadelphia: Wolters Kluwer Health/Lippincott Williams & Wilkins, 2013. 1 v. (various pagings). ISBN 9781608316991

610.1/48   R123.S69
Title varies: First ed., 1992, had title *Stedman's abbrev.: Abbreviations, acronyms and symbols*; 2nd ed., 1999, *Stedman's abbreviations, acronyms, and symbols*; 3rd ed., 2003, *Stedman's abbrev.: Abbreviations, acronyms and symbols*.

Contains abbreviations, acronyms, and symbols for medical, health, and nursing professionals; and medical transcriptionists, medical editors, and copy editors; and others. Includes professional titles and degrees, hospital abbreviations, abbreviations for specialties, and professional organizations & associations. Also includes abbreviations for viruses, medical informatics, molecular biology, and other subject areas. Abbreviations in boldface; multiple meanings listed alphabetically,

with explanatory material in parentheses. Includes "do not use" abbreviations and slang terms. Nine appendixes. Also comes with three months of free access to *Stedman's online*.

Recent editions of other Stedman's dictionaries include *Stedman's medical dictionary* (28th ed., 2006), *Stedman's medical dictionary for the health professions and nursing* (7th ed., 2012), and *The American heritage medical dictionary* (2007 ed.), formerly titled *The American heritage Stedman's medical dictionary*.

1081 Stedman's medical dictionary for the health professions and nursing. Illustrated 7th ed.

Thomas L. Stedman. Philadelphia: Wolters Kluwer Health/ Lippincott Williams & Wilkins, 2012. xxxix, 512 p., 59 p. of plates, ill. (chiefly col.) ISBN 9781608316922

610.3   R121.S8
Title varies. 1st ed., 1986, had title *Stedman's pocket medical dictionary*; 2nd ed., 1994, *Stedman's concise medical dictionary*; 3rd ed., 1997, *Stedman's concise medical dictionary: Illustrated*; 4th ed., 2001, *Stedman's concise medical dictionary for the health professions*; 5th ed., 2005, *Stedman's medical dictionary for the health professions and nursing*; 6th ed., 2008.

Provides concise definitions with pronunciation keys. Contains 56,000 entries, 68 appendixes with extensive information (e.g., nursing classifications), and many color and black-and-white illustrations. CD-ROM contains the full text of the print edition, with audio-pronunciation, anatomy animations, various images, and medical/pharmaceutical spellchecker. Also available as an online edition: Stedman's Online: Stedman's medical dictionary for the health professions and nursing includes all the content from the print dictionary, audio pronunciations, and 48 videos; along with a free version of Stedman's Plus Medical/Pharmaceutical Spellchecker.—Cf. *publ. description.*

Recent editions of other Stedman's dictionaries include, for example, *Stedman's medical dictionary* (28th ed., 2006); *The American Heritage medical dictionary* (2007 ed.), formerly titled *The American Heritage Stedman's medical dictionary*; and *Stedman's medical abbreviations, acronyms and symbols* (4th ed., 2008). Also available via Credo reference.

Thesauruses

1082 CINAHL . . . subject heading list: Alphabetic list, tree structures, permuted list. CINAHL Information Systems. Glendale, Calif.: Cinahl Information Systems, 1994–2007

025.4961073 1522-1156   Z695.1.N8.N87

Published in 1984 as *CINAHL subject headings*; 1986–93 had title *Nursing and allied health (CINAHL) . . . subject heading list*. Annual. No longer published in print.

The subject thesaurus to CINAHL (101) and its print version, *Cumulative index to nursing and allied health literature*. Includes more than 11,000 CINAHL subject headings specifically for nursing and allied health and also many from the National Library of Medicine's MeSH (858).

The CINAHL search system provides help with translating terms into searchable subject headings. CINAHL subject headings follow the structure of MeSH. This structure has been used to develop CINAHL subject headings which reflect the terminology used by nursing and allied health sciences professionals. An online tutorial video ("Using CINAHL/MeSH headings") at http://support.ebsco.com/training/flash_videos/cinahl_mesh/cinahl_mesh.html and a visual user guide at http://support.ebsco.com/knowledge_base/detail.php?id=4256, explain options such as "explode feature," "subheadings feature," etc.

Directories

1083 Official guide to graduate nursing programs. National League for Nursing. Sudbury, Mass.: Jones and Bartlett, 2004–. v.

RT75.O345

First ed. (2000) had title: *Official guide to graduate nursing schools*.

(Guide to graduate nursing programs)

Comprehensive directory of graduate nursing programs (master's and doctoral), with reliable data collected by the NLN. Provides help in retrieving information about each school and comparing different programs, with basic information and facts on every school and program presented in a consistent format. In three main parts: (1) Introductory section; (2) School profiles; (3) Expanded school profiles, with information provided directly by the different schools. Includes two indexes: listing of schools by graduate specialty programs, and an alphabetical listing of schools.

Other directories related to nursing programs published by the NLN include the *Official guide to undergraduate and graduate nursing programs*, *Guide to state-approved schools of nursing, LPN/LVN*, and *Guide to state-approved schools of nursing, RN*.

1084 Official guide to undergraduate and graduate nursing programs. 2nd ed. National League for Nursing. Sudbury, Mass.: Jones and Bartlett Publ., 2004. v, 1268 p. ISBN 0763718076

610.73/071/173   RT73.O34

First ed., 2000 has title: *Official guide to undergraduate and graduate nursing schools*.

(Guide to undergraduate and graduate nursing programs)

Provides information on accredited undergraduate and graduate nursing schools and nursing programs. In three parts: (1) Introductory section; (2) School profiles; (3) Expanded school profiles. Includes two indexes: listing of schools by graduate specialty programs, and an alphabetical listing of schools.

Other directories related to nursing programs published by the NLN include *Official guide to graduate nursing programs*, *Guide to state-approved schools of nursing, LPN/LVN*, and *Guide to state-approved schools of nursing, RN*.

1085 Peterson's nursing programs. 10th ed. Peterson's (Firm); American Association of Colleges of Nursing. Lawrenceville, N.J.: Thomson/Peterson's, 2005–. v., ill.

610.73071173   RT79

Publ. in cooperation with the American Association of Colleges of Nursing.

1994–2002 had title: *Peterson's guide to nursing programs*; 2003–04: *Nursing programs*. Description based on 18th ed., 2012 (Subtitle: "Nursing programs 2013"); 19th ed., 2013 (print and also as e-book) is available.

Profiles more than 3,500 undergraduate, graduate, and postdoctoral nursing programs in the U.S.

and Canada, degree programs, and full-time, part-time, and distance learning options, also continuing education programs. Includes entrance requirements, research-facility descriptions, tuition, financial aid programs, and also a section ("Nursing school adviser") with articles and advice from school deans and professors.

Additional nursing programs resources can be found in *Essential nursing resources* under Education/Careers.

Handbooks

**1086 Anatomy of writing for publication
for nurses.** Cynthia Saver, Sigma Theta
Tau International. Indianapolis, Ind.:
Sigma Theta Tau International, c2011.
xx, 342 p., ill. ISBN 9781930538757
610.73   RT24.S28

Contents: pt. I, A primer on writing and publishing; pt. II, Writing for different styles and platforms; Appendixes: (A) Parts of speech; (B) Additional resources; (C) Ten tips for editing checklists; (D) Proofing checklist.

Explains the publishing and submission process, how to write effectively, and how to give a formal presentation. Includes, for example, chapters on writing clinical articles, writing articles for scholarly & research journals, books & book chapters, online publications, blogs, and others. A chapter addresses compliance with copyright law & other legal issues, and ethics of publishing issues. Bibliographical references; index. Also available as an e-book. For upper-level nursing students and nursing professionals at all levels.

**1087 Bates' guide to physical examination
and history-taking. 11th ed.** Lynn S.
Bickley, Peter G. Szilagyi, Barbara Bates.
Philadelphia: Wolters Kluwer Health/
Lippincott Williams & Wilkins, 2013.
xxv, 994 p., ill. (chiefly col.)
ISBN 9781609137625
616.07/54   RC76.B38

Covers the essential process of obtaining a patient history and performing a comprehensive physical examination, with the goal of providing the best care for patients. Imparts basic knowledge of human anatomy and physiology. Includes case studies, examples of evidence-based practice, with step-by-step techniques. Intended for medical and advanced nursing students. Also a useful resource for health professionals. *Bates' nursing guide to physical examination and history taking* by Hogan-Quigley et al. is intended for beginning nursing students.

Also available as a set of DVDs or in a streaming video version: *Bates' visual guide to physical examination* (4th ed., 2005) is currently the only edition which includes the complete set of videos. A new edition/online product is under development: *Bates' visual guide to physical examination* or *Bates' visual guide* for short, with new video content will be available and include the following modules: Approach to the patient; Head to toe assessment (adult); Pediatric head-to-toe assessment (infant); Pediatric head-to-toe assessment (child); Head-to-toe assessment (Older adult); General survey and vital signs; Examination of the skin; Head, eyes, and ears; Nose, mouth , and neck; Thorax and lungs; Cardiovascular system; Peripheral vascular system; Breasts and axillae; Abdomen; Male genitalia, hernias, rectum, and prostate; Female genitalia, anus, and rectum; Musculoskeletal system; Nervous system: cranial nerves and motor system; Nervous system: sensory system and reflexes. Further information at http://www.batesvisualguide.com/.

**1088 Clinical Care Classification (CCC)
system manual: A guide to nursing
documentation.** Virginia K. Saba. New
York: Springer, 2006. ISBN 0826102689
651.504261   RT50.S23

Clinical Care Classification (CCC); Clinical Care Classification System (CCCS), formerly known as Home Health Care Classification System; Clinical Care Costing Methods (CCCM).

Contents: pt. 1, "Overview"; pt. 2, "Research, integration, and evaluation"; pt. 3, "Terminology uses; appendixes".

The CCCS consists of two interrelated terminologies—the CCCS of nursing diagnoses and outcomes, and the CCCS of nursing interventions, both of which are classified by 21 care components. "The Clinical Care Classification (CCC) System . . . is the only standard coded nursing terminology that is based on sound research using the nursing process model framework and that meets the Patient Medical Record Information (PMRI) comparability requirement. The CCC System allows patient care data generated by nurses to be incorporated into the PMRI database, and enables nurses' contributions to patient outcomes to be studied and acknowledged."—*Foreword*

Includes bibliography of major CCCS articles published 1991–2006 and a chapter on the CCC framework and terminology tables. Also available as an e-book.

Other nursing terminologies (and links to information about them) include, for example, Nursing Diagnoses, Definitions, and Classification International (NANDA-I; http://www.nanda.org), Nursing Interventions Classification System (NIC; http://www.ncvhs.hhs.gov/970416w4.htm), Nursing Outcomes Classification (NOC; http://www.ncvhs.hhs.gov/970416w5.htm), Omaha System (http://www.omahasystem.org), and others. Several of these and additional nursing terminologies are also included in the Unified Medical Language System (UMLS) metathesaurus and are mapped partly or completely to SNOMED International: Systematized Nomenclature of Medicine.

1089 Clinical research manual: Practical tools and templates for managing clinical research. R. Jennifer Cavalieri, Mark E. Rupp, Sigma Theta Tau International. Indianapolis, Ind.: Sigma Theta Tau International, 2013.
ISBN 9781937554637
610.72/4   R853.C55

Contents: ch. 1, Introduction to clinical research operations; ch. 2, Site administration; ch. 3, Managing financial processes; ch. 4, Managing regulating activities and documents; ch. 5, Working with institutional review boards (ethics committees); ch. 6, Managing clinical trial activities and processes; ch. 7, Managing data and research records; ch. 8, Professional development; Appx. A, Your go-to regulatory reference tool; Appx. B, Keeping track of things; Index.

Explains the research process, answers questions about the details of conducting clinical research/clinical trial research, and offers practical advice on how to carry out study activities effectively and efficiently. Covers all important aspects and provides a comprehensive description of all steps, various forms, and tips. Useful for a wide variety of professionals involved in clinical research. Also available as an e-book.

1090 Doing a literature review in nursing, health, and social care. 1st ed.
Michael Coughlan, Patricia Cronin, Francis Ryan. Thousand Oaks, Calif.: SAGE Publications, Ltd., 2013. 153 p., ill.
ISBN 9781446249604
610.73072   RT81.5

Contents: ch. 1, What is a literature review; ch. 2, Types of literature review; ch. 3, Systematic review; ch. 4, Selecting a review topic and searching the literature; ch. 5, Reading and organising the literature; ch. 6, Critically analysing the literature; ch. 7, Synthesizing the literature; ch.8, Writing up your literature review; ch. 8, Referencing and plagiarism; ch. 10, What comes next.

Provides an overview of the literature review process, with basic information on the review process, on types of reviews, searching and analyzing the literature, etc. Glossary, references, and index. Intended audience is nursing and social work professionals, but also considered useful for other health professionals.

1091 Drug information handbook. North American ed. Charles F. Lacy, Laura Armstron, Morton Goldman, Leonard Lance, Lexi-Comp, Inc., American Pharmaceutical Association. Hudson, Ohio; Washington: Lexi-Comp, Inc.; American Pharmaceutical Association, 1994–
615 1533-4511   RM301.12.D783

Publ. in cooperation with the Amer. Pharmacists Assoc. (APhA).

First ed., 1993/94. Available in North Amer. and internat. editions. Description based on 19th ed., 2010. Subtitle: A comprehensive resource for all clinicians and healthcare professionals. The 22nd ed.(2013) is the most recent edition available. (Lexi-Comp's clinical reference library).

Concise, comprehensive, and user-friendly drug reference. Alphabetical listing of drug monographs, with new drugs and updates to monographs since the last edition. Includes detailed information in consistent format, such as dosage, drug interactions, adverse reactions (by occurrence, overdose, and toxicology), etc., with warnings highlighted. Appendix. Pharmacologic category index. For clinicians and healthcare professionals.

Several other comprehensive print pharmacology handbooks, also published by Lexi-Comp and frequently updated, include *Anesthesiology and critical care drug handbook* (1999– ; 10th ed., 2011); *Drug information handbook for nursing* (1998-; 14th ed., 2012); *Drug information handbook for advanced practice nursing* (1990– , 11th ed., 2010); *Drug information handbook for dentistry* (1996- ; 18th ed., 2012); *Drug information handbook for oncology* (2000- ; 11th ed., 2013); *Drug information handbook for psychiatry: A comprehensive reference of psychotropic, nonpsychotropic, and herbal agents* (1999- ; 7th ed., 2009); *Drug information handbook for the allied health professional* (1995- ; 12th ed., 2005); *Drug information handbook with international trade names index* (21st ed., 2012); *Geriatric dosage handbook* (1993- ; 18th ed., 2012); *Infectious diseases handbook: Including antimicrobial therapy & diagnostic test/procedures* (1994- ; 6th ed., 2006); *Natural therapeutics pocket guide* (2000- , 2nd ed., 2003); *Pediatric dosage handbook* (1992- ; 18th ed., 2011); and *Pharmacogenomics handbook* (2003- ; 2nd ed., 2006). Also available online as pt. of Lexi-Comp Online™ (http://webstore.lexi.com/Store/ONLINE).

1092 The family practice desk reference.
   4th ed. Charles E. Driscoll, Edward T. Bope. Chicago: AMA Press, 2003. xi, 1035 p., ill. ISBN 1579471900
   610   RC55.F22
First ed., 1986 had title: *Handbook of family practice*; 3rd ed., 1996.

Includes aspects of health and illness management for common conditions and diseases encountered by family physicians. Organized by "life-cycle approach" (*Pref.*), e.g., care of children, maternity care, women's health, men's health, and by body system (e.g., cardiovascular, respiratory, gastrointestinal, etc.). Entries in standardized format, each with a table of contents and list of references, and organized by conditions. Each chapter presents symptoms using differential diagnosis tables, laboratory values, and diagnostics.

1093 Guide to the code of ethics for nurses: Interpretation and application. Marsha Diane Mary Fowler, American Nurses Association. Silver Spring, Md.: American Nurses Association, 2008. 176 p. ISBN 9781558102
   174.2   RT85.G85

Produced by American Nurses Association (ANA). Reissued with a new cover in 2010.

Intended as a guide to the *Code of ethics for nurses with interpretive statements* on how to apply ethical standards and values in nursing practice. Discusses a single code provision and provides the text of the code of ethics, the history, purpose, theory, application, case studies, and examples. Includes bibliographical references and index.

Related recent ANA publications include *Essential guide to nursing practice* and *Nursing's social policy statement statement*.

1094 Health professionals style manual.
   Shirley H. Fondiller, Barbara J. Nerone. New York: Springer, 2006. ISBN 0826102077
   808.06661   R119.F66
Rev. ed. of *Health professionals stylebook*, 1993.

Contents: ch. 1, "Style and substance: The dynamic duo"; ch. 2, "From principles to practice: The art of effective writing"; ch. 3, "Understanding usage: An alphabetical guide to specific writing tips and pitfalls"; ch. 4, "Be clear and direct: How to avoid redundancies, euphemisms, and cliches"; ch. 5, "Harness the potential of computers and the Internet." Appendixes: A, "Common abbreviations and acronyms in health care"; B, "Commonly misspelled words"; C, "Using prefixes and suffixes"; D, "Common proofreader's marks"; E, "Electronic resources"; F, "Referencing." Includes references for further reading and index.

Provides guidelines about writing clearly and effectively, covering American usage only. Addresses style, style errors, English grammar, composition techniques, and other areas of technical writing. Can be used as a supplement to other style manuals. For researchers and students in the various health professions. Also available as an e-book.

1095 Interpreting the medical literature.
   5th ed. Stephen H. Gehlbach. New York: McGraw-Hill, 2006. x, 293 p., ill. ISBN 0071437894
   610.7222   R118.6.G43
   First edition, 1982; 4th ed., 2002.
Contents: ch. 1, "Tasting an article"; ch. 2, "Study design: General considerations"; ch. 3, "Study design: The case-control approach"; ch. 4, "Study design: The cross-sectional and follow-up approaches"; ch. 5, "Study design: The experimental approach";

ch. 6, "Study design: Variations"; ch. 7, "Making measurements"; ch. 8, "Analysis: Statistical significance"; ch. 9, "Analysis: Some statistical tests"; ch. 10, "Interpretation: Sensitivity, specificity, and predictive value"; ch. 11, "Interpretation: Risk"; ch. 12, "Interpretation: Causes"; ch. 13, "Cases series, editorials, and reviews"; ch. 14, "A final word"; Index.

Assists with understanding and utilizing the information presented in medical studies and reports and also with the critical reading and interpretation of conflicting studies. Provides clinical examples from the published medical and public health literature. Also available as an e-book.—CM

1096 Legal, ethical, and political issues in nursing. 2nd ed. Tonia D. Aiken. Philadelphia: F.A. Davis, 2004. xxii, 458 p., ill., map. ISBN 0803605714

362.17321   RT86.5.A37

Contents: pt. 1, "Nursing practice"; pt. 2, "Nursing and the law"; pt. 3, "Nursing ethics"; pt. 4, "Liability in professional practice"; pt. 5, "Professional issues".

Provides an overview of the responsibilities of nurses, with focus on legal and ethical issues and considerations a nurse may encounter in clinical practice. List of resources at the end of each chapter. For nursing educators and students. Also available as an e-book.

1097 The Medical Library Association guide to health literacy. Marge Kars, Lynda M. Baker, Feleta L. Wilson. New York: Neal-Schuman Publ., 2008. xiv, 314 p., ill. ISBN 9781555706258

026/.610973   Z675.M4; M497

Overviews issues related to health literacy and approaches to effective health communication. A practical guide, including best practices for librarians working in hospital and consumer health settings and providing health/patient education and appropriate services for persons with low literacy or illiterate persons. Intends to empower patients to understand their health care information. Explains different types of health literacy. Includes reference interview techniques, collaboration between libraries, exploration of the role of the librarian in promoting health literacy, etc. Addresses the special needs of senior citizens and adolescents.

Each chapter has a thorough list of current references. Resources for health professionals; upper-level

and graduate-level health care students. Useful for librarians working in hospital and consumer health settings.

1098 Mosby's manual of diagnostic and laboratory tests. 4th ed. Kathleen Deska Pagana, Timothy James Pagana. St. Louis: Mosby/Elsevier, 2010. xi, 1245 p., col. ill. ISBN 9780323057479

RB38.2.P34

First edition, 1998; 3rd ed., 2006.

Contents: "Guidelines for proper test preparation and performance"; "Blood studies"; "Electrodiagnostic tests"; "Endoscopic studies"; "Fluid analysis studies"; "Manometric studies"; "Microscopic studies"; "Nuclear scanning"; "Stool tests"; "Ultrasound studies"; "Urine studies"; "X-ray studies"; "Miscellaneous studies"; bibliography; appendixes: (A) "Alphabetical list of tests"; (B) "List of tests by body systems"; (C) "Disease and organ panels"; (D) "Abbreviations for diagnostic and laboratory tests." Index, with names of all tests and their synonyms and other terms within tests.

Provides information and explanation on clinically relevant laboratory and diagnostic tests, including procedures and patient care before, during, and after a particular test, contraindications, and potential complications. Includes bibliographical references (p. 1215-17) and index. Another publication by the same author, is *Mosby's diagnostic and laboratory test reference* (11th ed., 2012).

Similar print titles include *Interpretation of diagnostic tests* by Wallach, *Laboratory tests and diagnostic procedures* by Chernecky et al., *Tietz clinical guide to laboratory tests*; a Web-based resource is *Lab tests online: A public resource on clinical lab testing from the laboratory professionals who do the testing* (327).

1099 NOC and NIC linkages to NANDA-I and clinical conditions: Supporting critical thinking and quality care. 3rd ed. Marion Johnson, Sue Moorhead, Gloria M. Bulechek, Howard Karl. Butcher, Meridean. Maas, Elizabeth A Swanson, North American Nursing Diagnosis Association. Maryland Heights, Mo.: Elsevier Mosby, 2012. ix, 422 p. ISBN 9780323077033

RT48.6.N63

Title varies: 1st ed., 2001, had title *Nursing diagnoses, outcomes, and interventions*; 2nd ed.,

2006: *NANDA, NOC, and NIC linkages: Nursing diagnoses.*

Contents: pt. I, "Languages and applications"; pt. II, "NOC and NIC linked to NANDA-I diagnoses"; pt III, "NOC and NIC linked to clinical conditions"; pt. IV, Appendixes: (A) "NOC outcomes labels and definitions"; (B) "NIC intervention labels and definitions."

Three standardized languages recognized by the American Nurses Association: NANDA (North American Diagnosis Association) International, NOC (Nursing Outcomes Classification), NIC (Nursing Interventions Classification).

This revised edition describes the common nursing classification system languages and terminology related to nursing diagnoses, the nursing process, nursing care methods and standards, and outcome assessment and their linkages to NANDA. Mostly in tabular format. Reference to help with the development of a care plan. New to this edition are links to ten clinical conditions commonly encountered by nurses, e.g., asthma, diabetes, colon cancer, stroke, and several others. Also available as an e-book.

1100 Nurse practitioner's legal reference.

Springhouse Corp. Springhouse, Pa.:
Springhouse Corp., 2001. xii, 361 p., ill.
ISBN 1582550972
344.73/0414   RT82.8.N8646

Contents: ch. 1, Nurse practitioner practice and the law; ch. 2, Legal risks and responsibilities on the job; ch. 3, Legal issues on the job; ch. 4, Legal risks while off duty; ch. 5, Malpractice liability; ch. 6, Legal aspects of documentation; ch. 7, Ethical decision making; ch. 8, Ethical conflicts in clinical practice; ch. 9, Ethical conflicts in professional practice; ch. 10, Patients' rights; ch. 11, NPs in a changing health care marketplace.

Provides coverage of legal issues affecting nurses and the nursing profession, including issues currently facing legislative and judicial review. Contains several appendixes: "Understanding the judicial process," "Interpreting legal citations," and "Types of law." Court case citation index and a general index.

1101 Nursing interventions classification (NIC). 6th ed. Gloria M. Bulechek.

St. Louis: Elsevier/Mosby, 2013. xxviii,
608 p. ISBN 9780323100113
610.7301/2   RT42
First edition, 1992; 5th ed., 2008.

Contents: pt. 1, Overview and use of the classification; pt. 2, Taxonomy of nursing interventions; pt.3, The classification; pt. 4, Core interventions for nursing specialties areas; pt. 5, Estimated time and education level necessary to perform NIC intervention; pt. 6, NIC interventions linked to NANDA-I diagnosis; pt. 7, Appendixes: (A) Interventions: New revised and retired since the fifth edition; (B) Guidelines for submission of a new and revised intervention; (C) Timeline and highlights for NIC; (D) Abbreviations; (E) Previous editions and translations.

Provides an overview of the interventions performed by all nurses and of the NIC taxonomy, with different groupings representing the areas of nursing practice and coding guidelines. Includes 554 interventions. Interventions can be used with diagnostic classifications, e.g., NANDA (North American Nursing Diagnosis Association), ICD (International Classification of Diseases), DSM (*Diagnostic and statistical manual*), and those included in clinical information systems (e.g., SNOMED International). Interventions are listed alphabetically, and each intervention has been assigned a unique number. Appendixes include new, revised, and retired interventions since the last edition, selected publications, abbreviations, and several other resources. Has associated website and companion book, *NANDA, NOC, and NIC linkages: Nursing diagnoses, outcomes, and interventions* by Johnson.

1102 Nursing procedures and protocols.

Lippincott Williams & Wilkins.
Philadelphia: Lippincott Williams &
Wilkins, 2003. x, 661 p., ill.
ISBN 1582552371
610.73   RT49.N88

Contents: ch. 1, "Fundamentals"; ch. 2, "Infection control"; ch. 3, "Medication administration"; ch. 4, "Intravascular therapy"; ch. 5, "Cardiovascular care"; ch. 6, "Pulmonary care"; ch. 7, "Neurologic care"; ch. 8, "Gastrointestinal care"; ch. 9, "Renal and urologic care"; ch. 10, "Musculoskeletal care"; ch. 11, "Skin care"; ch. 12, "Endocrine and hematologic care."

Presents a wide range of research-based protocols and procedures for application in clinical settings, including patient information tips. Describes various procedures and medical equipment and provides step-by-step instructions and explanations, with cross-references to related information. Includes illustrations, checklists, tables, and flowcharts and uses several logos (evidence-base logo, troubleshooting logo, alert logo) to draw attention to certain information.

1103 PDR nurse's drug handbook. Delmar Cengage Learning. Clifton Park, N.Y.: Delmar Cengage Learning, 2000–. ill.
615 1535-4601   RM125

Title varies: *PDR nurse's handbook*; *Physician's desk reference nurse's drug handbook*; *Nurse's drug handbook*. Description based on 2007 ed. of *PDR nurse's drug handbook*; 2013 ed. is available.

Description of the major prescription drugs, with phonetic pronunciation of drug name, drug classification, drug interactions, FDA warnings, etc. Includes various aids to prevent medication errors (e.g., listing of drug names that sound alike, administration and storage of drugs, etc.). Includes a visual identification guide. For nursing students, nurses, and other health care professionals.

Related titles include *Physicians' desk reference: PDR*, *ADA/PDR guide to dental therapeutics* (American Dental Association), *PDR drug guide for mental health professionals*, *PDR guide to drug interactions, side effects, and indications*, *PDR for herbal medicines*, *PDR for nonprescription drugs*, *PDR for nutritional supplements*, *Physicians' desk reference for ophthalmic medicines*, also *PDR guide to biological and chemical warfare response*, and *PDR guide to terrorism response*, and other titles.

PDR and its major companion volumes are available online in the PDR electronic library.

1104 Professional guide to signs & symptoms. 6th ed. Lippincott Williams & Wilkins. Philadelphia: Wolters Kluwer/ Lippincott Williams & Wilkins, 2011. ix, 801 p., color ill.
ISBN 9781608310982
616.047   RC69.P77

First ed., 1993; 5th ed., 2007.

Alphabetically-organized reference tool helpful for identification and interpretation of selected signs and symptoms of various diseases, agents of bioterrorism, signs and symptoms associated with herbs, and laboratory test results. Includes a table of English-Spanish translations (on inside front and back cover). Selected references and index. Also available as an e-book. A related title, *Professional guide to diseases*, has been regularly updated since 1981. Also available as an e-book.

1105 Resources for nursing research: An annotated bibliography. 4th ed. Cynthia G. L. Clamp, Stephen Gough, Lucy Land. London; Thousand Oaks, Calif.: Sage, 2004. xi, 419 p.
ISBN 0761949917
016.61073   Z6675.N7.C53; RT81.5

First ed., 1991; 3rd ed., 1999.

Contents: pt. 1, "Sources of literature"; pt. 2, "Methods of inquiry"; pt. 3, "The background to research in nursing."

Bibliography of sources for nursing research, with approximately 3,000 entries with brief annotations, including literature (papers, books, and Internet resources) published since 1998. Expanded section on electronic resources in this edition. Cross-references, several appendixes (for example, "Computer programs for design and analysis"), author and subject indexes. "Intended for all those with an interest in nursing research—students, teachers, librarians, practitioners and researchers"—*Introd.* Also available as an e-book.

Also available as an e-book.

1106 Saunders nursing drug handbook. Barbara B. Hodgson, Robert J. Kizior. Philadelphia; St. Louis: Saunders, Saunders Elsevier, 1998–
615 1098-8661   RM125.N82

Title varies: 1993–97 had title *Nurse's drug handbook*; 1998– titled *Saunders nursing drug handbook*. Description based on 2012 ed.; 2013 ed., publ. 2012; 2014 ed. will appear in 2013.

"Designed as an easy-to-use source of current drug information."—*Pref.* Contains generic and brand names of drugs, pharmacokinetics, action, therapeutic effect, interactions, adverse reactions, toxic effects, etc., and their nursing implications. Several appendixes. Similar specialized nursing drug references include, for example, *Mosby's nursing drug reference*, *Intravenous medications: A handbook for nurses and allied health professionals*, and *Mosby's pediatric drug consult*. Also available as an e-book.

1107 Writing for publication in nursing. 2nd ed. Marilyn H. Oermann, Judith C. Hays. New York: Springer Publ., 2010. xiii, 361 p., ill. ISBN 9780826118028
808/.06661   RT24.O35

First ed., 2002

Contents: I, Preparing to write; II, Writing research, evidence-based practice, and clinical practice articles; III, Chapters, books, and other forms of writing; IV, The writing process; V, Final paper through publication; Appendix 1, Selected statistical symbols and abbreviations; 2, Unnecessary words in writing; 3, Guidelines and resources for preparing manuscripts; Index.

Helps to simplify the process of developing and submitting a manuscript for publication of journal articles, book chapters, or a book. Explains the writing process, outlining, drafting, revision, and eliminating unnecessary words. Explains peer review and scholarly publishing. Provides specific examples. Intended for nursing students at all levels. Available as an e-book.

Histories

1108 American nursing: A history. 4th ed.
Philip Arthur Kalisch, Beatrice J. Kalisch. Philadelphia: Lippincott Williams & Wilkins, 2004. ix, 500 p., ill. ISBN 9780781739696
362.1730973   RT4.K34
First three editions (1978–95) had title *The advance of American nursing*.

"The purpose of this book is to place nursing's past in a broader social, cultural, and economic context. . . . While . . . largely a history of nursing in the United States, it explores the impact of the profession on American society . . . helps students appreciate the history and complexity of nursing and the U.S. health care system; develops a framework, past and present, for assessing current and emerging issues in health care"—*Pref.* Divided into 22 chapters on subjects including the founding of early schools of nursing, public health nursing, nursing during the different wars, the hospital industry, minorities in nursing, health care reform and nursing, and a look toward the future. Index.

Another title, available both in print and as an e-book, *A history of American nursing: Trends and eras*, provides a "streamlined yet inclusive approach, focusing on historical trends in nursing that emerged in the United States from the 1600s to the present."—*Pref.*

1109 Capturing nursing history: A guide to historical methods in research.

Sandra Lewenson, Eleanor Krohn Herrmann. New York: Springer Pub, 2008. xx, 236 p. ISBN 9780826115669
610.73   RT31.C37
Helps to "develop the skills needed to capture nursing history."—*Pref.* Provides guidance and a framework for nurses doing historical research—e.g., biographical research, oral histories, research in international settings, how to use artifacts, conducting research in primary sources, etc. Provides standards and ethical guidelines. Appendixes include information on artifacts, nursing histories centers, museums, and archives, also nursing histories internet sites. Also available as an e-book.

1110 Celebrating nursing history. http:// nahrs.mlanet.org/home/weeding. Margaret Allen, Medical Library Association. Chicago: Medical Library Association. 1994–
Produced by Medical Library Association (MLA), Nursing and Allied Health Resources Section (NAHRS). Reprint of article originally publ. in *NAHRS newsletter*, Apr. 1994, updated Oct. 2005.

Contents: What to Keep; Significant Nursing Books to Find and Keep; Periodicals to Keep; Sources Used for Some of These Comments and Selections; Reprints; Films and Videos; How and Where to Search; Other Sources for Historical Research; Why Go to Historical Sources?; Other Articles of Interest.

Provides an annotated bibliography of nursing books, reports, landmark studies, periodicals, films, videos, and other resources for historical research in nursing and related allied health literature. Chronological arrangement under the different headings. Intended to answer questions on archives, weeding, and other collection management issues posed by nursing librarians and others interested in the history of nursing.

1111 Doctors, nurses, and medical practitioners: A bio-bibliographical sourcebook. Lois N. Magner. Westport, Conn.: Greenwood Press, 1997. xiii, 371 p. ISBN 0313294526
610/.92/2B   R153.D63
Biographical information on 56 "significant but lesser known individuals . . . outside their own country . . . extraordinary . . . yet unsung" (*Introd.*), covering the time period 1710–1924, with essays focusing on

the life and career. Bibliographic references include archival materials and works written by and about the particular individual. Appendixes: (A), Listing by occupations and special interests; (B), Listing by date of birth; (C), Listing by place of birth; (D), Listing of women practitioners. Intended for students and scholars.

1112 Historical encyclopedia of nursing.
Mary Ellen Snodgrass. Santa Barbara, Calif.: ABC-CLIO, 1999. xvii, 354 p., ill.
610.7309   RT31.S66

Covers the history of nursing and healing from ancient times to the present. Includes key nursing concepts and individuals, medical topics, organizations, wars, etc. Articles list sources, including websites. Black-and-white illustrations and "see also" references. "Timeline of landmarks in nursing" (p. 297–310), "Works by and about healers" (p. 311–13), bibliographical references (p. 315–33), and index.

1113 A history of nursing, from ancient to modern times: A world view.
5th ed. Isabel Maitland Stewart, Anne L. Austin. New York: Putnam, [1962]. 516 p., ill.
610.7309   RT31.S7

First edition, 1920, by L. L. Dock and I. M. Stewart, had title *A short history of nursing* and was based on Dock and M. Adelaide Nutting, *A history of nursing: The evolution of nursing systems from the earliest times to the foundation of the first English and American training schools for nurses*.

Intended especially for student nurses. Pt. 1 consists of eight chapters sketching the history of nursing from ancient to modern times; pt. 2, 11 chapters on nursing today in various countries throughout the world. Includes a general classified bibliography and selected bibliographies for each chapter. Subject and name index.

1114 Nurse-midwifery: The birth of a new American profession. Laura Elizabeth Ettinger. Columbus, Ohio: Ohio State University Press, 2006. xvi, 269 p., ill. ISBN 0814210236
618.2   RG950.E77

Contents: ch. 1, "Conception: Nurse-midwives and the professionalization of childbirth"; ch. 2, "Eastern Kentucky's frontier nursing service: Mary Breckinridge's mission, survival strategies, and race"; ch. 3, "New York City's Maternity Center Association: Educational opportunities and urban constraints"; ch. 4, "Transitions: New directions, new limitations"; ch. 5, "Traditions: Home birth in a high-tech age"; ch. 6, "Don't push: Struggling to create a political strategy and professional identity"; Epilogue, "Afterbirth: Learning from the past, looking to the future."

Historical study of the emergence and rise of nurse-midwifery as a profession and barriers experienced by nurse-midwives today. Notes, bibliography, and index.

An earlier title, *American midwives, 1860 to the present*, is a historical study of the changing role of the midwife in American society between 1860 and 1978, with explanation of the use of the terms midwifery and obstetrics, and chapters devoted to the early 20th-century midwife debate and its proponents, along with other relevant topics. Bibliography: p. [153]-91.

1115 Nursing, a historical bibliography.
Bonnie Bullough, Vern L. Bullough, Barrett Elcano. New York: Garland, 1981. xxiv, 408 p. ISBN 0824095111
016.6107309   Z6675.N7.B84; RT31
(Garland reference library of social science; v. 66)

A bibliography of some 3,500 references collected from major sources. The cutoff date is 1978. Includes index.

1116 Nursing history research resources.
http://www.aahn.org/resource.html.
American Association for the History of Nursing. Wheat Ridge, Colo.: American Association for the History of Nursing. 2005?–

Produced by American Association for the History of Nursing (AAHN; http://www.aahn.org).

Contents: Archives and history centers; Conferences, exhibits and celebrations; Funding; Internet resources; Journals; New books and publications; Organizations; Videos.

Listing of selected available nursing resources, including Internet resources, for the history of nursing. Provides links to other nursing history organizations, nursing education, and related government websites. Includes, for example, a link to nursing history centers, museums, and archives (http://www.aahn.org/resources/centers.html) and a page entitled "Black nurses in history: A bibliography and guide to Web resources" (http://libguides. rowan.edu/blacknurses), prepared by the University of Medicine and Dentistry of New Jersey.

1117 Nursing, the finest art: An illustrated history. 3rd ed. M. Patricia Donahue. Maryland Heights, Mo.: Mosby Elsevier, 2011. xviii, 390 p., ill. (some color), color maps. ISBN 9780323053051

610.73   RT31.D66

First ed., 1985; 2nd ed., 1996.

Contents: Unit 1, "The origin of nursing"; unit 2, "Nursing in a Christian world"; unit 3, "Nursing in transition"; unit 4, "The development of nursing in America"; unit 5, "Nurses during war"; unit 6, "Nursing in an era of change and challenge"; unit 7, "The nursing transformation"; unit 8, "The healing spirit of nursing"; unit 9, "A global view of nursing and healthcare"; unit 10, "Epilogue."

The content of the previous edition has been reorganized and new content and artwork has been added regarding the current status of the nursing profession, with emphasis on a global view of nursing. "This combination of visual representation and the written word has proven to be a significant and valuable means to facilitate an understanding of all types of knowledge and phenomena."—*Pref.* Timelines in each unit, containing major global and nursing events, have been updated. Presentation is not entirely chronological, but more thematic. Color and halftone illustrations and artwork. Includes list of plates, bibliographical references (p. 356-374), and index.

Nursing, the finest art: Master prints is a related title by the same author.

Biography

1118 African American firsts in science and technology. Raymond B. Webster. Detroit: Gale Group, 1999. xiii, 461 p., ill. ISBN 0787638765

508.996073   Q141.W43

Chronology of firsts in various fields: Agriculture and Everyday Life, Dentistry and Nursing, Life Science, Math and Engineering, Medicine, Physical Science, and Transportation. Includes bibliography, index by year, occupational index, general index, and citations for first achievents. Over 1200 entries, 100 illustrations.

1119 American nursing: A biographical dictionary. Vern L. Bullough, Olga Maranjian Church, Alice P. Stein, Lilli Sentz. New York: Garland, 1988–2000. 3 v., ill. ISBN 082408540X

610.73/092/2B   RT34.A44

Vol. 2 ed. by Vern L. Bullough, Lilli Sentz, and Alice P. Stein; v. 3 ed. by Vern L. Bullough and Lilli Sentz, and publ. by Springer Publ.

Contains long entries for those who "made a significant contributions to nursing" (*Introd.*). Vol. 1 contains entries for those who were born prior to 1890 or deceased, v. 2 includes those born before 1915 or deceased, v. 3 includes notable women in American and Canadian nursing in the 20th century. Entries include bibliographies. Vols. 1 and 2 are indexed separately by decade of birth, first nursing school attended, area of special interest or accomplishment, and state and country of birth. Covers much of the same ground as Dictionary of American nursing biography. Of the individuals in these sources, 109 appear in both, but each provides unique information. Vol. 3 also available as an e-book.

1120 Dictionary of American nursing biography. Martin Kaufman, Joellen Watson Hawkins, Loretta P. Higgins, Alice Howell Friedman. New York: Greenwood Press, 1988. x, 462 p. ISBN 0313245207

610.73/092/2B   RT34.D53

Companion to *Dictionary of American medical biography*.

Contains "196 biographical sketches of persons who were important in the history of American nursing" (*Pref.*) and who died prior to Jan. 31, 1987. For each individual, includes biographical data, summary of contributions to nursing, and a list of writings and references. Appendixes list persons by place of birth, state where prominent, and specialty or occupation. Indexed by personal name, organization, place, and special subject.

Covers much of the same ground as *American nursing: a biographical dictionary,* but each provides unique information.

1121 Doctors, nurses, and medical practitioners: A bio-bibliographical sourcebook. Lois N. Magner. Westport,

Conn.: Greenwood Press, 1997. xiii, 371 p.
ISBN 0313294526

610/.92/2B   R153.D63

Biographical information on 56 "significant but
lesser known individuals . . . outside their own
country . . . extraordinary . . . yet unsung" (*Introd.*),
covering the time period 1710–1924, with essays
focusing on the life and career. Bibliographic references include archival materials and works written
by and about the particular individual. Appendixes: (A), Listing by occupations and special interests; (B), Listing by date of birth; (C), Listing by
place of birth; (D), Listing of women practitioners.
Intended for students and scholars.

Statistics

**1122 Munro's statistical methods for health
care research. 6th ed.** Stacey Beth Plichta,
Elizabeth A. Kelvin, Barbara Hazard Munro.
Philadelphia: Wolters Kluwer Health/
Lippincott Williams & Wilkins, 2012. vii,
567 p., ill. ISBN 9781451115611

610.72/7   RT81.5.M86

First edition, 1986 to 5th ed. 2005 had title: *Statistical methods for health care research.*

Explains statistical methods and techniques frequently used in the health care literature. Includes
charts, graphs, and examples from the literature.
Contains, for example, principles underlying statistical inference, material on statistical model building and logistic regression, structural equation
modeling, writing and presenting for publication,
and other areas. Written for students and teachers.

Internet resources

**1123 National Institute of Nursing
Research.** http://www.ninr.nih.gov/.
National Institute of Nursing Research.
Bethesda, Md.: National Institute of
Nursing Research. 1997–

RT81.5

The mission of the National Institute of Nursing
Research (NINR) is "to promote and improve the
health of individuals, families, communities, and
populations. This mission is accomplished through
support of research in a number of science areas.

Among those areas of research are chronic and acute
diseases, health promotion and maintenance, symptom management, health disparities, caregiving,
self-management, and the end of life"—*About/direc-
tor's page.* Links to NINR publications and meeting
reports; information on nursing, minority/ethnic
nurses, regional nursing research, and professional
nurses and practice organizations; federal government
links, links to search engines; and other resources.

**1124 National Patient Safety Foundation
(NPFS).** http://www.npsf.org. National
Patient Safety Foundation. North Adams,
Mass.: National Patient Safety Foundation

Independent, not-for-profit organization, with the
mission to "measurably improve patient safety"—
main page. Searchable website, with links to online
patient safety resources and organizations. Information is presented in different categories (e.g.,
health care quality and safety, medication safety,
surgical safety, cancer treatment safety, and others) for different user groups, such as health professionals, patients and families, and researchers.

1125 Nursing history research resources.
http://www.aahn.org/resource.html.
American Association for the History of
Nursing. Wheat Ridge, Colo.: American
Association for the History of Nursing.
2005?–

Produced by American Association for the History
of Nursing (AAHN; http://www.aahn.org).

Contents: Archives and history centers; Conferences, exhibits and celebrations; Funding; Internet
resources; Journals; New books and publications;
Organizations; Videos.

Listing of selected available nursing resources,
including Internet resources, for the history of nursing.
Provides links to other nursing history organizations,
nursing education, and related government websites.
Includes, for example, a link to nursing history centers,
museums, and archives (http://www.aahn.org/resourc-
es/centers.html) and a page entitled "Black nurses in
history: A bibliography and guide to Web resources"
(http://libguides.rowan.edu/blacknurses), prepared by
the University of Medicine and Dentistry of New Jersey.

1126 OncoLink. http://cancer.med.upenn.
edu/. Abramson Cancer Center of the
University of Pennsylvania. Philadelphia,

Pa.: University of Pennsylvania. 1994–
615.507; 616.992; 616.994

Contents: Cancer types; Cancer treatment; Risk
and prevention; Support; Healthcare professionals.

Designed for educational purposes to help cancer patients, families, health care professionals, and
the general public to get accurate cancer-related
information. Provides comprehensive information
about specific types of cancer, updates on cancer
treatment, and news about research advances, with
information provided at various levels, from introductory to in-depth.

9 *Nutrition*

1127 Codex alimentarius. http://www
.codexalimentarius.net/web/index
_en.jsp#/. Joint FAO/WHO Food
Standards Programme; Codex Alimentarius
Commission. Rome, Italy; Geneva,
Switzerland: Food and Agriculture
Organization of the United Nations; World
Health Organization. [200?]

The *Codex alimentarius* (Latin for "Food Law" or
Code) is a collection of international food standards
adopted by the Codex Alimentarius Commission
and presented in a uniform manner. These standards
include raw, semiprocessed, and processed foods.

**1128 Food and Nutrition Information
Center**. http://www.nal.usda.gov/
fnic/. Food and Nutrition Information
Center (U. S.). Beltsville, Md.: Food and
Nutrition Information Center
351; 640.73; 371.7;   RA784
612.3; 641.3

The Food and Nutrition Information Center (FNIC),
located at the National Agricultural Library (NAL)
of the U.S. Dept. of Agriculture (USDA), provides
online global nutrition information and links to
nutrition-related resources provided by the National
Agricultural Library, federal and state governments,
professional organizations, universities, and others.
The FNIC website contains multiple links to reliable
food and nutrition and metabolism information for
consumers and nutrition professionals. The a–z list

(http://fnic.nal.usda.gov/topics-z) includes important topics (e.g., infant nutrition, childhood & adolescent obesity, weight control, etc.), or a browse
by subject section for dietary guidance, lifecycle
nutrition, diet & disease, weight & obesity , food
safety, and many other subject areas. Also included
are links to resource lists for specific nutrition topics (http://fnic.nal.usda.gov/resource-lists-0) and to
FNIC and other nutrition-related databases (http://
fnic.nal.usda.gov/databases).

Guides

**1129 The food safety hazard guidebook.
2nd ed.** Richard Lawley, Laurie Curtis,
Judy Davis, Royal Society of Chemistry
(Great Britain). Cambridge, U.K.: RSC
Pub, 2012. xi, 533 p.
ISBN 9781849733816
664.001579   RA601.L39
First ed., 2008.

Contents: Sect. 1, Biological hazards; sect. 2, Chemical hazards; sect. 3, Allergens; sect. 4, HACCP
(hazard analysis critical control point) and food
safety management systems; sect. 5, Food safety
legislation; sect. 6, Sources of further information;
Abbreviations and acronyms; Subject index.

Concise, accessible reference which supplies
the technical and scientific information that food
safety professionals require. It is "intended as a

guidebook rather than an encyclopedia, and has been conceived as a portal for the immense and ever expanding body of scientific knowledge that exists for food."—*Pref.* Covers a wide range of biological and chemical food safety hazards, including potential and emerging food safety hazards. Also available as an e-book.

Current authoritative updates and reports concerning issues of food safety can be found at "Food safety" (Centers for Disease Control and Prevention) http://www.cdc.gov/foodsafety/ and Food-Safety.gov http://www.foodsafety.gov/.

1130 Nutrition.gov. http://www.nutrition.gov. Food and Nutrition Information Center, United States.; Dept. of Agriculture., National Agricultural Library (U.S.). Beltsville, Md.: National Agricultural Library. 2004-
613.71; 011.53;   RA784
612.3; 641.3;

Maintained by Food and Nutrition Information Center (FNIC).

Access to information from across the federal government on food, food safety, nutrition, weight management, dietary supplements, and food assistance programs. Includes specialized nutrition information for life stages: infants, children, teens, adult women and men, and seniors, as well as the latest nutrition-related news. Provides search capabilities and resource lists.

Healthfinder.gov provides access to consumer resources concerning nutrition, physical fitness, and disease.

Bibliography

1131 Annual bibliography of significant advances in dietary supplement research. http://purl.access.gpo.gov/ GPO/LPS78261. National Institutes of Health Office of Dietary Supplements, Consumer Healthcare Products Association. Bethesda, Md.: National Institutes of Health Office of Dietary Supplements. 1999–2007 1940-0926

Annual bibliography presenting significant research on dietary supplements, selected each year by an international team of expert reviewers; National Institutes of Health (NIH) Office of Dietary

Supplements (ODS) selects the top 25 for publication in this bibliography. Useful for students, nutrition and health professionals, and others conducting nutrition-related research. ODS is no longer producing these publications, but the nine issues published between 1999-2007 are still accessible. ODS and the National Library of Medicine have created the "dietary supplement" subset for PubMed. The International bibliographic information on dietary supplements (IBIDS) database and several other dietary supplement–related NIH and USDA databases can be accessed from the ODS website.

Indexes; Abstract journals; Databases

1132 AGRICOLA. http://agricola.nal.usda. gov. National Agricultural Library (U.S.). Washington: National Agricultural Library (U.S.). [1970–]
025.0663   S494.5.A8

"AGRICOLA (AGRICultural OnLine Access) serves as the catalog and index to the collections of the National Agricultural Library, as well as a primary public source for world-wide access to agricultural information. The database covers materials in all formats and periods, including printed works from as far back as the 15th century. The records describe publications and resources encompassing all aspects of agriculture and allied disciplines, including animal and veterinary sciences, entomology, plant sciences, forestry, aquaculture and fisheries, farming and farming systems, agricultural economics, extension and education, food and human nutrition, and earth and environmental sciences."—*National Agricultural Library Website*

In the 1990s, AGRICOLA was the definitive index for domestic agricultural information. Unfortunately, continuous funding cuts to the NAL budget have severely diminished AGRICOLA's scope and usefulness. AGRICOLA remains a very good index for pre-2000 agricultural publications. The researcher may wish to consult CAB Abstracts for a more comprehensive review of the agricultural literature since 2000.

1133 Annual bibliography of significant advances in dietary supplement

research. http://purl.access.gpo.gov/
GPO/LPS78261. National Institutes of
Health Office of Dietary Supplements,
Consumer Healthcare Products
Association. Bethesda, Md.: National
Institutes of Health Office of Dietary
Supplements. 1999–2007 1940-0926

Annual bibliography presenting significant research
on dietary supplements, selected each year by an
international team of expert reviewers; National
Institutes of Health (NIH) Office of Dietary Supplements (ODS) selects the top 25 for publication in
this bibliography. Useful for students, nutrition
and health professionals, and others conducting
nutrition-related research. ODS is no longer producing these publications, but the nine issues published between 1999-2007 are still accessible. ODS
and the National Library of Medicine have created
the "dietary supplement" subset for PubMed. The
International bibliographic information on dietary
supplements (IBIDS) database and several other
dietary supplement–related NIH and USDA databases can be accessed from the ODS website.

1134 CAB abstracts. http://cabi.org. CAB
International. Wallingford, Oxfordshire,
U.K.: CABI. 1990s-

Z699.5.A5

A major bibliographic, abstracting, and indexing
database in the applied life sciences. CABI subject
scope is broad and deep, including all aspects of
agriculture, forestry, human nutrition, veterinary
medicine, and the environment from 150 countries
and more than 50 languages. The database contains
more than 6.3 million records from 1973 onwards,
with some 300,000 abstracts added annually, and
nearly all records have an abstract. The records,
which include not only journal articles, but books/
book chapters, conference proceedings, newsletters, handbooks, and other forms of grey literature are indexed using the CAB thesaurus. CABI
Full Text option includes 120,000 full-text journal
articles,conference papers, and reports, 80 percent
of which are not available elsewhere. The *CAB
Abstracts Archive*, available for an additional fee,
includes over 1.8 million records covering the literature from 1913 to 1972. *CAB abstracts* is available online from numerous distributors including
CAB Direct, Dialog, EBSCO, Web of Science, and
OvidSP.

1135 Dietary supplement label database.
http://www.dsld.nlm.nih.gov/dsld/. NIH
Office of Dietary Supplements, National
Library of Medicine (U.S.). Bethesda,
Md.: National Library of Medicine.
2013–

Joint project of the National Institutes of Health
(NIH) Office of Dietary Supplements (ODS) and
National Library of Medicine (NLM) Division
of Specialized Information Services (SIS). Also
referred to as DSLD.

DSLD, a document repository database, captures
information on dietary supplement labels. Contains
the full label contents from 17,000 dietary supplement products marketed in the U.S. and will eventually include 55,000 products available in the U.S.
Obtained from the manufacturers' labels. Includes
image of the product label, both "DSLD on market"
(i.e., label information from dietary supplement
products that are currently on the U.S. market)
and "DSLD off-market "(i.e., label information from
dietary supplement products that have been discontinued or are no longer on the U.S. market). Allows
for searching, browsing, sorting, and filtering; and
data can be saved and analyzed. Answers many
questions researchers and users of dietary supplements might have concerning ingredients shown
on labels of specific brands, chemical ingredients,
animal products, proven medical benefits, toxicity
of specific ingredients, etc. Includes reference links
leading to further explanation (e.g., unit conversion, daily value, dietary reference intakes, etc.),
definitions (A-Z), also a frequently asked questions
section and links to reference sources.

An earlier database, "Dietary supplements labels
database: Brands, ingredients, and references," has
been retired.

1136 NLM gateway. http://gateway.nlm.nih
.gov/. National Library of Medicine
(U.S.). Bethesda, Md.: National Library of
Medicine. 2000–

RA11

As announced in 2011, "the NLM® gateway has
transitioned to a new pilot project from the Lister
Hill National Center for Biomedical Communications (LHNCBC)."—*Website* The new site focuses
now on two databases: Meeting abstracts and
Health services research projects. All of the other
resources previously accessed through the NLM

gateway are available through their individual sites. For a list of these databases previously available via the NLM gateway see http://gateway.nlm.nih.gov/about.jsp.

The NLM gateway previously allowed simultaneous searching of information resources at the National Library of Medicine (NLM)/National Center for Biotechnology Information (NCBI) with an overview of the search results presented in several categories (bibliographic resources, consumer health resources, and other information), with a listing of the individual databases and the number of results within these categories. Previously included were, for example, MEDLINE/PubMed and the NLM Catalog as well as other resources, including information on current clinical trials and consumer health information (MedlinePlus) and many others.

1137 Nutrition abstracts and reviews series A. http://www.cabi.org/publishing-products/online-information-resources/nutrition-abstracts-and-reviews-series-ahuman-and-experimental/. CAB International. Wallingford, U.K: CAB International. 1990–

Vol. 1 (Oct. 1931) through v. 46 (1976), *Nutrition abstracts and reviews* (NARA), Commonwealth Agricultural Bureau (CAB) International (CABI). Split into ser. A (Human and experimental) and ser. B (Livestock feeds and feeding). Since 1977, available in print. A searchable online back file, derived from *CAB abstracts*, is available going back to 1990; also included in the full CAB abstracts database, available though multiple vendors.

A searchable international abstract database that includes a variety of biomedical and agricultural subject areas, with papers relevant to all aspects of human nutrition selected from approximately 1,000 journals, books, reports, and conferences. Covers techniques (analytical methodologies for carbohydrates, fiber, lipids, proteins, etc.); foods (functional foods, food additives, supplements; beverages, food processing, food contamination, etc.); physiological and biochemical aspects (endocrinology and nutritional immunology, fasting, vitamins, phytochemicals, minerals, etc.); nutrition and health (diet studies, infant feeding, sports nutrition, nutritional status, etc.); clinical nutrition

(e.g., malnutrition, obesity, food allergies, cancer, etc.); and many other subjects.

1138 PubMed. http://www.ncbi.nlm.nih.gov/pubmed. U.S. National Center for Biotechnology Information, National Library of Medicine, National Institutes of Health. Bethesda, Md.: U.S. National Center for Biotechnology Information. 1996–

PubMed®, developed and maintained by the National Center for Biotechnology Information (NCBI) at the National Library of Medicine® (NLM). Provides a search interface for more than 20 million bibliographic citations and abstracts in the fields of medicine, nursing, dentistry, veterinary medicine, health care systems, and preclinical sciences. It provides access to articles indexed for MEDLINE® and for selected life sciences journals. PubMed subsets found under the "Limits" tab are: MEDLINE and PubMed central®, several journal groups (i.e., core clinical journals, dental journals, and nursing journals), and topical subsets (AIDS, bioethics, cancer, complementary medicine, dietary supplements, history of medicine, space life sciences, systematic reviews, toxicology, and veterinary science). "Linkout" provides access to full-text articles.

For detailed information see the PubMed fact sheet at http://www.nlm.nih.gov/pubs/factsheets/pubmed.html and also MEDLINE®/PubMed® resources guide (http://www.nlm.nih.gov/bsd/pmresources.html) which provides detailed information about MEDLINE data and searching PubMed.

Information regarding the mobile version of this resource is part of NLM's Gallery of mobile apps and sites.

1139 PubMed dietary supplement subset. http://ods.od.nih.gov/Research/PubMed_Dietary_Supplement_Subset.aspx. National Institutes of Health, Office of Dietary Supplements , National Library of Medicine. Bethesda, Md. 2011-
RM258.5

Database produced by the Office of Dietary Supplements (ODS) of the National Institutes of Health. Contains journal articles related to a broad spectrum of dietary supplement-related literature, including articles on vitamins, minerals, phytochemicals, ergogenics, botanical, and herbal supplements in human nutrition and animal models.

Replaces International bibliographic information on dietary supplements (IBIDS) database.

1140 USDA nutrient data laboratory. http://
www.ars.usda.gov/ba/bhnrc/ndl. Nutrient
Data Laboratory, U.S. Department of
Agriculture. Beltsville, Md.: Nutrient
Data Laboratory, U.S. Department of
Agriculture. [199?]– 612.3641.3

Its mission is "to develop authoritative food composition databases and state of the art methods to acquire, evaluate, compile and disseminate composition data on foods available in the United States."—*Main page* Contains links to historical information of 115 years of USDA food composition tables (http://www.ars.usda.gov/Aboutus/docs.htm?docid=9418). Currently, the National Nutrient Data Bank contains information for approx. 130 nutrients for more than 7,000 foods. Its major database is USDA national nutrient database for standard reference (SR), release 24 (http://www.ars.usda.gov/Services/docs.htm?docid=8964); also online via Knovel), for determining the nutrient content of foods (published previously in print format in *Agriculture handbook* no. 8 and supplements and *Home and garden bulletin* no. 72). Also provides links to food composition information from other countries (e.g., Canada, Australia, New Zealand, and others), food consumption surveys, food labeling, general nutrition information (e.g., Nutrition.gov, Dietary Guidelines for Americans 2010), dietary supplements databases (USDA is working with the Office of Dietary Supplements and other federal agencies to develop a Dietary supplement ingredient database [DSID] at http://www.ars.usda.gov/dsid), and other resources.

Encyclopedias

1141 Cultural encyclopedia of vegetarianism.
Margaret Puskar-Pasewicz. Santa Barbara,
Calif.: Greenwood, 2010. xxxv, 290 p., ill.
ISBN 9780313375569
641.5/636   TX392

Some 100 entries in alphabetical order, covering influential individuals and sociological, anthropological, historical, philosophical, religious, nutritional and medical aspects. Chronology from antiquity to the present. Bibliography. Index. Available as an e-book.

**1142 Diets and dieting: A cultural
encyclopedia.** Sander L. Gilman. New
York: Routledge, 2008. xii, 308 p., ill.
ISBN 9780415974
613.2503   RM214.5.G55

Cultural history of diets and dieting, covering the period from ancient Greece and Rome to the present. Background information on various diets, dieting, and weight loss. Includes biographies of historical and contemporary figures association with dieting. Alphabetical arrangement. Each article provides a list of references and further reading. Useful as a resource for students and researchers. Also available as an e-book.

1143 Encyclopedia of diet fads. Marjolijn
Bijlefeld, Sharon K. Zoumbaris. Westport,
Conn.: Greenwood Press, 2003. xv, 242
p., ill. ISBN 0313322236
613.2503   RM222.2.B535

Entries for various kinds of diets and major weight loss programs, with appropriate comments, criticisms, and suggested dietary guidelines. Additional entries and information on nutrition in health and illness, vitamins, etc. Introduction includes a brief history of dieting and fad diets. Annotated list of websites and several other appendixes. For general readers and allied health professionals. Also available as an e-book.

**1144 Encyclopedia of foods: A guide
to healthy nutrition.** Mayo Clinic,
University of California, Los Angeles,
Dole Food Company. San Diego, Calif.:
Academic Press, 2002. xi, 516 p., col. ill.
ISBN 0122198034
641.3003   TX349.E475

Contents: pt. 1, "A guide to healthy nutrition: Optimizing health"; "Nutrients and other food substances"; "Food-health connection"; "Planning meals: Selecting healthful foods, plus two weeks of menus"; "Preparing healthful meals"; pt. 2, "Encyclopedia of foods"; "Fruits"; "Vegetables"; "Grains"; "Dairy goods"; "Meat and other high-protein foods"; "Fats, oils, and sweets"; "Others."

Contains discussion of dietary guidelines and the relationship between diet and various diseases. Appendix includes reading list, selected websites, charts of dietary reference intakes, and information about nutrients in foods, vitamins, and minerals. Color photographs, diagrams, and other illustrations. Useful for public and academic libraries. Also available as an e-book.

1145 Encyclopedia of food and culture.
Solomon H. Katz, William Woys Weaver. New York: Scribner, 2003. 3 v., ill. (some color). ISBN 0684805685

394.1203   GT2850.E53

Nimbly covers an enormous scope of no less than food and nutrition and their place in history and culture on a global basis. Some 600 signed articles in three volumes range in length from 250 to 10,000 words. As an example of coverage, the 75 entries under the letter "C" begin with Cabbage, include Julia Child, and then move on to Civilization and Food; Social Class; Climate and Food; Cocktail Party; Cocktails; Codex Alimentarius; Coffee; Food Coloring; and finish with Cucumbers, Melons and Other Cucurbits; Evolution of Cuisine; Curds; Curry; Custard and Puddings; and Cutlery. Throughout, content is enriched by 450 photos and other illustrations, recipes, menus, especially useful timelines, many bibliographic and cross-references, and a necessary navigation device: a thorough index. Food cultures of the world encyclopedia provides similar information on a geographical basis. Available as an e-book.

1146 Encyclopedia of food science and technology. 2nd ed. F. J. Francis. New York: Wiley, 2000. 4 v. (xxi, 2768 p.), ill. ISBN 0471192856

664.003   TP368.2.E62

"This encyclopedia features A-to-Z coverage of all aspects of food science, including: the properties, analysis, and processing of foods; genetic engineering of new food products; and nutrition. Contains information useful to food engineers, chemists, biologists, ingredient suppliers, and other professionals involved in the food chain."—*Publisher Description*. See details at http://www.wiley.com/WileyCDA/WileyTitle/productCd-0471192856.html.

Comprehensive work with approx. 400 articles. Contains black-and-white photographs, illustrations, charts, and tables. Each article has a detailed bibliography. Vol. 1 has front section with conversion factors, abbreviations, and unit symbols; v. 4 has an extensive index. A reviewer in the *Journal of food biochemistry* (27(1):83-89) suggests this work

is most suitable for a readership with a background in food science or a related field.

1147 Encyclopedia of food sciences and nutrition. 2nd ed. Benjamin Caballero, Luiz C. Trugo, Paul M. Finglas. Amsterdam [Netherlands]; New York: Academic Press, 2003. 10 v., ill. ISBN 9999901271

664.003   TX349.E47

First edition, 1993, had title *Encyclopaedia of food science, food technology and nutrition.*

Contents: v. 1, A–Bro; v. 2, Bro–Cla; v. 3, Cle–End; v. 4, Ene–Fru; v. 5, Fru–; v. 6, J–M; v. 7, N–Pre; v. 8, Pre–Soy; v. 9, Soy–V; v. 10, W–Z ; Index.

This revised, expanded, and updated edition contains articles covering a wide variety of topics in food science, food technology, and nutrition. International in scope. For food scientists and technologists, nutritionists, public health researchers, and others. Also available online via the Elsevier ScienceDirect platform.

1148 Encyclopedia of human nutrition. 3rd ed. Benjamin Caballero, Lindsay Allen, Andrew Prentice. Oxford; Academic Press, 2013. 4 volumes, illustrations (some color). ISBN 9780123750839

613.203   QP141

First edition, 1999; 2nd ed., 2005. Volume 1, A-C; v. 2, D-H; v. 3, I-O; v. 4, P-Z.

This revised edition, with many new entries and extensive updates, satisfies "the need to provide accurate, succinct, and up-to-date information on a wide range of topics."—*Foreword*. Topics are listed alphabetically and presented in a rigorous but concise way. Each entry contains a contents list for the particular article in addition to the contents list at the beginning of each volume. Many entries reflect the recognition of the importance of diet and lifestyle as well as reduction of risk. Synonyms, cross-references, graphs, and diagrams. Bibliographical references and comprehensive index. Intended for general readers and also for health professionals. Also available as an e-book.

1149 Food cultures of the world encyclopedia. Ken Albala. Santa Barbara, Calif.: Greenwood, 2011. 4 v., ill. ISBN 9780313376269

394.1   GT2850

Over 150 signed articles identify food practices on a geographical basis, supporting comparison across countries and societies. Four volumes divide the world into regions: Africa and the Middle East, the Americas, Asia and Oceania, and Europe. The United States is broken down into six regions: New England, the South, the Mid-Atlantic, the Midwest, the Southwest, and the Pacific Northwest. Entries for each nation or nationality typically include historical, cultural, environmental and technological influences on food choices. Describes typical foodstuffs and meals, information about cooking practices and diet and health, eating out and special occasions. Illustrations and some recipes. Bibliographic references and suggestions for further reading. Index. Available as an e-book.

Based on the multi-volume series *Food culture around the world* http://www.abc-clio.com/series .aspx?id=51941. *Encyclopedia of food and culture* presents similar information by topic, rather than place.

1150 Leung's encyclopedia of common natural ingredients used in food, drugs, and cosmetics. 3rd ed.
Ikhlas A. Khan, Ehab A. Abourashed. Hoboken, N.J.: John Wiley & Sons, 2010. xxix, 810 p., ill. ISBN 9780471467434
660.6/3   QD415.A25 L48
First ed., 1980, 2nd ed., 1996 (also rev. & exp., 2003) had title: *Encyclopedia of common natural ingredients: Used in food, drugs, and cosmetics.*

This updated and revised edition updates all entries of the previous edition and includes a new section on traditional Indian medicine. Arrangement is by common name. Entries give Latin name, synonyms, general description, chemical composition, pharmacology or biological activities, uses, commercial preparations, and references. Includes an English-language classification for Chinese medicinal herbs and a glossary of commonly encountered terms used in the botanical industry. Excludes prescription drugs and medicinal herbs not readily available in commerce. Indexed. Available as an e-book.

1151 Nutrition and well-being A to Z.
Delores C. S. James. Detroit: Macmillan Reference USA, 2004. 2 v., ill. ISBN 0028657071

613.203   RA784.N838
Contents: v. 1, A–H; v. 2, I–Z.
Provides information on the effects of nutrition and diet on diseases and on quality of life. Covers nutritional concepts, dietary habits, nutritional research, legislation, influential persons in nutrition and medicine, and health organizations. Explores historical aspects of nutrition and well-being in different countries. Alphabetical arrangement, with definitions of major terms in sidebars, related references, and bibliography at the end of each article. Illustrations, photographs, tables, glossary, and index. For students, researchers, and health professionals. Also available as an e-book.

Dictionaries

1152 Benders' dictionary of nutrition and food technology. 8th ed. David A. Bender, Arnold E. Bender. Boca Raton, Fla.; Cambridge, England: CRC Press; Woodhead, 2006. vii, 539 p. ISBN 0849376017
First ed., 1960; 7th ed., 1999.
Revised edition. Designed to define the broad range of words used by individuals involved in nutrition and food technology. Includes 6,100 terms, covering a wide range of disciplines, many cross-references, nutrient composition data, and U.S.-recommended daily amounts of nutrients, for example. Bibliography. Also available online via Knovel.

1153 A dictionary of food and nutrition. 3rd ed. David A. Bender. Oxford; New York: Oxford University Press, 2009. 596 p. ISBN 9780199234875
641.3003   TX349.B4115
First edition, 1995; 2nd ed., 2005.
Revised edition. Nontechnical guide to terms found on "food labels, in advertising, or in the media"— *Publ. note.* Contains more than 6,000 entries with clear definitions on various aspects of food, food groups, nutrition, and diet in relation to health. International in scope. Expanded appendixes list food additives, nutrients, vitamins & minerals, and other useful information. A companion website provides additional information via web links. Also available as an e-book.

1154 Dictionary of food ingredients. 5th ed.
Robert S. Igoe. New York: Springer, 2011.
viii, 255 p. ISBN 9781441997128

TX551.I26

First ed., 1983; 4th ed., 2001.
Contents: pt. I, Ingredients dictionary; pt. II, Ingredient categories; pt. III, Food definitions and formulations; pt. IV, Additives/substances for use in food; pt. V, Food additives E numbers in the European Union; Bibliography.

Clearly written definitions for more than 1,000 food ingredients: "currently used additives, including natural ingredients, FDA-approved artificial ingredients, and compounds used in food processing"—*Pref.* Intended for professionals and students; also appropriate for general use. Also available as an e-book.

1155 Dictionary of food science and technology. 2nd ed. International Food Information Service. Chichester, U.K. ; Ames, Iowa : Reading, U.K.: Wiley-Blackwell ; IFIS, 2009. xii, 473 p. ISBN 9781405187404

664.003   TP368.2.D58

The 7,852 entries found in the first edition have been reviewed and updated as appropriate and "over 750 new terms have been defined for the second edition, many of which are nutrition-related reflecting recent increases in the importance and emphasis placed on nutrition and health by the food industry, academia and the general public."—*Pref.* Entries organized alphabetically letter by letter, not by whole word. Definitions are sufficiently detailed for research but most useful for students of food science and nutrition and the general public. Three appendixes: (A) "Greek alphabet"; (B)"Scientific societies and organisations in the food sciences";

(C)"Web resources in the food sciences." Also available as an e-book.

1156 Dictionary of nutraceuticals and functional foods. N. A. M. Eskin, Snait Tamir. Boca Raton, Fla.: Taylor & Francis/CRC Press, 2006. 507 p., ill. ISBN 0849315727

613.203   QP144.F85.E85

(Functional foods and nutraceuticals series, no. 8).

Concise, science-based information on nutraceutical and functional food products and compounds, with mention of their roles in the promotion of health and the prevention of disease. Includes chemical structures and other illustrations, figures, tables, and literature references. Arranged alphabetically. Based on peer-reviewed literature. No index. For researchers, teachers, students. Also available as an e-book and via FOODnetBASE, part of CRCnetBASE.

1157 Elsevier's dictionary of nutrition and food processing: In English, German, French, and Portuguese. H. E. Philippsborn. Boston: Elsevier, 2002. ISBN 0444510176

613.203   QP141.P515

Includes indexes.

Brief definitions of approx. 6,000 English words or phrases translated into the three languages and identified with the discipline in which it they are predominantly used, e.g, agriculture (Agr.), products and production terminology (Prod.), biochemistry (Biochem.), and medical terms (Med.). The alphabetically arranged English words and phrases in the "Basic table" are numbered. Words in the other three languages are listed in separate sections and are keyed to the number assigned to the English term in the basic table. For researchers.

1158 International dietetics and nutrition terminology (IDNT) reference manual: standardized language for the nutrition care process. 4th ed.
Academy of Nutrition and Dietetics. Chicago: Academy of Nutrition and Dietetics, 2013. iv, 427 p. ISBN 9780880914673

RM216

First edition, 2007 had title: *Nutrition diagnosis and intervention: Standardized language for the nutrition care process*; 2nd ed., 2009; 3rd ed., 2011.

Publ. by the Academy of Nutrition and Dietetics (formerly American Dietetic Association)

The *IDNT reference manual* is a comprehensive guide to implementing the "nutrition care process," described by the publisher at http://www.eatright.org/HealthProfessionals/content.aspx?id=7077. This manual provides the terminology and definitions of the three steps of the nutrition care process, i.e., nutrition assessment, nutrition diagnosis, and nutrition intervention. Also available online.

1159 Nutrition and diet therapy reference dictionary. 5th ed. Rosalinda T. Lagua, Virginia Serraon Claudio. Ames, Iowa: Blackwell, 2004. ix, 407 p., ill.
ISBN 0813810027
613.203   RM217.L34
First edition, 1969; 4th ed., 1996.

Covers all aspects of nutrition. Entries include definition, suggested nutrition therapy, and dietary guidelines. Includes different diets, nutrition therapy for various disorders, and drugs and their effects on nutrition. Also includes brand names of nutritional products. The 50 appendixes cover topics including Dietary Reference Intakes, body mass index, national nutrition objectives for 2010, dietary guidelines for Americans, biochemical assessment of nutritional status, and websites for public health nutrition. For both health professionals and general readers.

1160 Nutrients A to Z: A user's guide to foods, herbs, vitamins, minerals and supplements. 3rd rev. ed. Michael Sharon. London: Carlton Books, 2004. viii, 344 p. ISBN1853755265
613.203

[First edition], 1998; [new ed.], 1999. Imprint varies.

Ready reference, with useful descriptions and definitions for various foods, vitamins, minerals, herbs, and supplements. Written in nontechnical language. For general readers and health professionals and useful in both public and academic libraries. Contains list for herbal associations and herb suppliers in the United States and the United Kingdom. Index lists common and alternative names. A new edition was published in 2009.

Handbooks

1161 ABC of nutrition. 4th ed. A. Stewart Truswell, Patrick G. Wall. London: BMJ, 2003. vii, 140 p., ill.
ISBN 0727916645
613.2   QP141.T785
First ed., 1986; 3rd ed., 1999.

Guidelines for appropriate nutrition and diet therapy for heart disease, blood pressure, various chronic diseases, and cancer. Includes nutritional recommendations for women who are pregnant or nursing, children, and adults. Also covers eating disorders and obesity and nutritional deficiencies in both developing and affluent countries. Illustrations, charts. Includes bibliographical references and index. Also available as an e-book.

1162 Anthropometric standards: An interactive nutritional reference of body size and body composition for children and adults. A. Roberto Frisancho. Ann Arbor, Mich.: University of Michigan Press, 2008. viii, 335 p., ill.
ISBN 047211591X
613.2   TX359.F75
1990 edition had title: Anthropometric standards for the assessment of growth and nutritional status.

Accompanying CD with Excel spreadsheets allows for computer-assisted evaluation of nutritional anthropometry based on NHANES (National Helath and Nutrition Examination Survey) III, CDC (Centers for Disease Control), and WHO (World Health Organization) data.

Contains contemporary standardized noninvasive methods & measurement techniques and data evaluation to assess individuals' health and nutritional status at various ages (from 2 to over 90 years old) and for various ethnic groups. Included, for example, are methods for anthropometric measurements such as height, weight, head circumference, etc., charts with recommended pregnancy weight gain and prenatal growth and birth weights, and other relevant tables and charts. Recommended for graduate students and health professionals. Also available as an e-book via Hathi Trust.

1163 The biochemistry of human nutrition: A desk reference. 2nd ed. Sareen Annora Stepnick Gropper, Eva May Nunnelley Hamilton. Belmont, Calif.: Wadsworth/Thomson Learning, 2000. xxiii, 263 p., ill. ISBN 0534515436
QP141.G76
Rev. ed. of *The biochemistry of human nutrition*, 1987.

Alphabetically arranged definitions and descriptions of nutrition-related biochemical terminology and concepts, with illustrations of structural formulas and biochemical pathways. Includes nutrition-related diseases and nutrient deficiencies.

Biochemical, physiological and molecular aspects of human nutrition by Stipanuk et al. provides more up-to-date information in this subject area.

**1164 Bowes and Church's food values
of portions commonly used.** Anna
De Planter Bowes, Charles Frederick
Church, Helen Nichols Church, Jean A.
Thompson Pennington. Philadelphia:
Lippincott, 1980–. tables.
ISBN 0781744296
641.10212   TX551.B64

Title varies. Earlier editions by Anna De Planter
Bowes and Helen Nichols Church; 1st ed., 1937,
had title *Food values of portions commonly served*;
2nd–12th ed., 1939–75, *Food values of portions
commonly used*; 13th–19th ed., 1980–2010, *Bowes
and Church's food values of portions commonly
used*. Description based on 18th ed., 2005. 20th
ed. due in 2014.

This ready reference provides data on food
composition and the nutritional value of foods, listing 8,500 common foods. The main section provides tables of nutrient contents of foods; foods are
arranged in 32 sections by food type. Includes brand-
name products, prepared and restaurant foods, conversion tables, DRI (dietary reference intake) tables,
estimated energy requirements, acceptable macro-
nutrient distribution ranges, and heat, weight, and
volume conversions. Bibliography, general index,
and various other supplementary tables, including a
list of scientific names for plants and animals used
in food, food name synonyms, bibliography for food
composition data, and index of food names. Considered a classic work. Intended for dietitians, nutritionists, and students of nutrition and dietetics.

**1165 The Cambridge world history of
food.** Kenneth F. Kiple, Kriemhild Coneè
Ornelas. Cambridge, U.K.; New York:
Cambridge University Press, 2000. 2 v.
(xlii, 2153 p.), ill. ISBN 9780521402163
641.309   TX353.C255

Multidisciplinary scholarly work, with sections on
prehistoric and historic food patterns of various
peoples, major animal and vegetable staple foods
and beverages, past and present diets, nutritional
science to evaluate the quality of diets, and the
relationship of nutrition and health. Pt. 8, "A
historical dictionary of the world's plant foods,"
provides brief histories of fruits and vegetables
and also contains synonyms. Tables, graphs, and
black-and-white pictures. Subject index; Latin
name index; Personal name index. Available

online to subscribers via Gale virtual reference
library.

**1166 DRI, dietary reference intakes:
The essential guide to nutrient
requirements.** Jennifer J. Otten,
Jennifer Pitzi Hellwig, Linda D. Meyers.
Washington: National Academies Press,
2006. xiii, 543 p., ill. ISBN 0309100917
612.3   QP141.D75

Summarizes *Recommended dietary allowances*
(U.S. National Research Council), 1943–.

Recommended Dietary Allowances (RDAs) have
been renamed and are now called Dietary Reference
Intakes (DRIs). Eight separate volumes of DRIs,
published between 1998 and 2005 by National
Academies Press, are summarized in this reference
volume. Reviews function of each nutrient in the
human body, food sources, usual dietary intakes,
and effects of deficiencies and excessive intakes.
Information provided includes estimated average
requirement, recommended dietary allowance,
adequate intake level, and tolerable upper intake.
Provides recommendations for health maintenance
and the reduction of chronic disease risk. Other
related areas are also addressed, such as nutrition
labeling, dietary planning, etc. Index, summary
tables, and references. A free online version is available at http://www.nap.edu/catalog/11537.html.

Dietary reference intakes: calcium, vitamin D by
Ross, freely available at http://www.nap.edu/catalog.
php?record_id=13050, supplements this resource.

**1167 Fenaroli's handbook of flavor
ingredients. 6th ed.** George A. Burdock,
Giovanni Fenaroli. Boca Raton, Fla.: CRC
Press/Taylor & Francis Group, 2010.
xxiv, 2135 p., ill.
ISBN 9781420090772
664/.5   TP418.B86

Standard reference for flavor ingredients, prepared
for food engineers and scientists who require data
about the toxicology of flavor-related chemicals
and ingredients. Alphabetical entries for either
chemical or common name. For each entry, the
handbook lists (where appropriate) primary name,
synonyms, CAS number, FEMA number, NAS
number, EINECS number, EEC number, CoE
number, JECFA number, description, sensory
thresholds, molecular structure, empirical formula/

MW, specifications, natural occurrence, synthesis, consumption, food functions, regulations/guidelines. This edition has 200 new entries, including, for example, botanicals and natural substances recognized as safe (GRAS). The difference between GRAS status and approval for use as a dietary supplement are explained in the preface. Glossary, CAS number index, FEMA (Flavor and Extract Manufacturers' Association) index, and general index. Also available as an e-book.

1168 Fennema's food chemistry. 4th ed.
Srinivasan Damodaran, Kirk Parkin, Owen R. Fennema. Boca Raton, Fla.: CRC Press/Taylor & Francis, 2008. 1144 p., ill.
664 0824723457   TX541.F65
First (1976) through third (1996) editions had title *Food chemistry*. Third edition also available online via netLibrary.

Contents: pt. 1, "Major food components"; pt. 2, "Minor food components"; pt. 3, "Food systems"; pt. 4, appendixes: (A) "International system of units (SI): The modernized metric system"; (B) "Conversion factors" (non-SI units to SI units); (C) "Greek alphabet"; (D) "Calculating relative polarities of compounds using the fragmental constant approach to predict log P values."

Rev. ed., with coverage of food analysis and food composition, and topics such as carbohydrates, lipids, proteins, enzymes, vitamins and minerals, colorants, flavors, food additives, nutraceuticals, toxicants, etc., and their role in human health. Contains, for example, a chapter entitled "Introduction to food chemistry" and a new chapter entitled "Impact of biotechnology on food supply and quality."

1169 Food additives data book. 2nd ed.
Jim Smith, Lily Hong-Shum. Chichester, West Sussex, U.K.; Ames, Iowa: Wiley-Blackwell, 2011. xvi, 1107 p., ill.
ISBN 9781405195430
664/.06   TX553.A3 F562
First ed., 2003.
This edition reflects the changes due to improved analytical methods and new & alternative additives, ingredients, etc. Provides concise technical data summary for food additives, organized by category: acidulants, antioxidants, emulsifiers,

enzymes, flavor enhancers, flour additives, gases, nutritive additives, polysaccharides, preservatives, sequestrants, solvents, and sweeteners. Each entry includes, as appropriate, category, food use, synonyms, formula, molecular mass, alternative forms, properties and appearance, boiling point, melting range, flash point, ionization constant, density, heat of combustion, vapor pressure, purity, water content, heavy metal content maximum, arsenic content, ash, solubility, function in foods, alternatives, technology of use in foods, synergists, food safety issues, legislation, and references. Includes list of contributors. Index. Also available as an e-book.

1170 Food chemicals codex. Assembly of Life Sciences (U.S.)., National Research Council (U.S.)., Institute of Medicine (U.S.)., United States Pharmacopeial Convention. Washington: Rockville, Md.: National Academy Press, United States Pharmacopeial Convention, 1966-. v., ill.
664 2153-1412   TP455.F66
First ed., 1966; 7th ed., 2010. Description based on 8th ed., 2012.

Since 2006 publ. by USP, previously by the National Academy of Sciences (NAS, 456) Food and Nutrition Board of the Institute of Medicine (IOM, 24). "Because of its regulatory status in countries other than the United States, and its worldwide use, the *Food Chemicals Codex* contains some monographs for chemicals not currently allowed in foods in the United States."—Pref.

This comprehensive compendium of standards for food ingredients is mandated by the U.S. Food and Drug Administration. The work is divided into the following sections: Front matter, including general provisions and requirements; monograph specifications; general tests and assays; solutions and indicators; general information tables. This edition contains over 1,100 monographs with descriptions of food additives or chemicals. Descriptions usually include a common name, a chemical name, a drawing of chemical structure, chemical formula, formula weight, CAS number, a short description, food function, and assay tests and requirements. Flavor chemicals descriptions include name, formula, physical form, solubility, refractive index, and specific gravity. Includes illustrations, charts. Index. Also contains information on method validation and various analytical techniques, reference tables, and information on current good manufacturing practices. For food technologists, quality control specialists, research investigators, teachers, students, and others involved in the technical aspects of food safety. A brief history of the FCC after it began in 1966 is found in the preface of this edition.

FCC revisions are published biennially in new editions, in supplements published in intervening years and, when circumstances warrant, as "expedited standards" or "immediate standards." Also available as an e-book.

1171 Food safety handbook. Ronald
H. Schmidt, Gary Eugene Rodrick.
Hoboken, N.J.: Wiley-Interscience, 2003.
xiii, 850 p., ill. ISBN 0471210641
363.192   TP373.5.F67
"The intent of this book is to define and categorize the real and perceived safety issues surrounding food, to provide scientifically non-biased perspectives on these issues, and to provide assistance to the reader in understanding these issues. While the primary professional audience for the book includes food technologists and scientists in the industry and regulatory sector, the book should provide useful information for many other audiences."—*Pref*.

Thirty-eight chapters written by specialists are divided into eight sections: characteristics of food safety and risk; biological food hazards; chemical and physical food hazards; systems for food safety surveillance and risk prevention; food safety operations in food processing, handling, and distribution; food safety in retail foods; diet, health, and food safety; and worldwide food safety issues. Chapters have bibliographies. Index. Also available as an e-book.

Current authoritative updates and reports concerning issues of food safety can be found at "Food safety" (Centers for Disease Control and Prevention) http://www.cdc.gov/foodsafety/ and Food-Safety.gov http://www.foodsafety.gov/.

**1172 Food Safety Research Information
Office at the National Agricultural
Library**. http://fsrio.nal.usda.gov/index.
php. National Agricultural Library (U.S.),
Food Safety Research Information Office.
Beltsville, Md.: National Agricultural
Library, Food Safety Research

Information Office. 2002–

                           TX537
Produced by National Agricultural Library (NAL); Food Service Research Information Office (FSRIO).

A major component of this searchable website is its "Research Projects Database" for locating information on food safety and related research. Categories currently in use in this database include food and food products, food composition and characteristics, food quality characteristics, food handling and processing, on-farm food safety, diseases and poisonings, sanitation and pathogen control, contaminants and contamination, government policy and regulations, methodology and quality standards, human health and epidemiology, education and training, facilities and sites, and pathogen biology.

Complements information found, for example, in *Food safety handbook*, *Food safety: A reference handbook* by Redman, *Foodborne disease handbook* by Hui, and two books with the same title, but different authors, i.e., *Foodborne diseases* by Cliver et al., and *Foodborne diseases* by Simjee.

**1173 Handbook of nutraceuticals and
functional foods. 2nd ed.**
Robert E. C. Wildman. Boca Raton, Fla.:
CRC Press/Taylor & Francis, 2007. 541
p., ill. ISBN 0849364094
613.2   QP144.F85.H36
First edition, 2001.
Collection of current topics and data on nutraceutical compounds and functional foods, with new and revised chapters in this edition that reflect the scientific advances in this field. For professionals and students in food chemistry and engineering as well as in the nutritional, pharmaceutical, and biomedical sciences. Includes bibliographical figures, tables, references, and index. Also available as an e-book.

**1174 Handbook of nutrition and food.
2nd ed.** Carolyn D. Berdanier, Johanna
T. Dwyer, Elaine B Feldman. Boca Raton,
Fla.: Taylor & Francis, 2008. 1265 p., [8]
p. of plates, ill. (some col.)
ISBN 9780849392
612.3   QP141.H345
First edition, 2002.
Contents: pt. 1, "Food" (ch. 1-5); pt. 2, "Nutrition science" (ch. 6-12); pt. 3, "Nutrition throughout life" (ch. 13-20); pt. 4, "Nutrition assessment

(ch. 21-37); pt. 5, "Clinical nutrition" (ch. 38-75); Index.

Contains information on food composition, nutrient data, and nutrient needs throughout the human life cycle, nutritional status assessment, SI conversion factors, etc. Chapters on such topics as clinical nutrition, various diets, and sports nutrition include references and bibliographies for further reading. Much of the information is presented in tables, charts, and graphs. Tables on food additives; food contaminants; toxins and food-borne illness; edible, toxic, and medicinal plants; chemical and physical properties of vitamins and minerals; etc. Many of the large data sets found in the previous edition have been placed on the Web, resulting in many more listings of Web addresses in this edition. Web addresses to USDA food composition data are provided. In addition to human nutrition, contains a section on animal nutrition. Electronic version of 2nd ed. available via net Library; 1st ed. as pt. of CRCnetBASE.

Complements B. B. Desai's *Handbook of nutrition and diet* (online version via netLibrary), which discusses the effects of nutrition and diet on the human body and the nutritional management of diseases.

1175 Handbook of vitamins. 5th ed.

Janos Zempleni, J. W. Suttie, Jesse F. Gregory, Patrick J. Stover. xii, 593 p., ill. ISBN 9781466515567

612.3/99   QP771.H35

First edition, 1984, had title *Handbook of vitamins: Nutrition, biochemical, and clinical aspects*; 4th ed., 2007.

Provides new information on the importance of maintaining optimal vitamin status and includes examples of vitamin-related deficiencies. Provides information on particular vitamins, their history, chemistry, structure, nomenclature, content in food, metabolism, biochemical function, deficiency sign, nutritional requirements, safe levels of intake, etc. Bibliographic references with each chapter. Subject index. Intends to "maintain the clinical focus of previous editions, while addressing important concepts that have evolved in recent years owing to the advances in molecular and cellular biology as well as those in analytical chemistry and nanotechnology."—*Pref.* Also available as an e-book.

Another recommended resource in this area, available both in print and also as an e-book, is

Vitamin discoveries and disasters: History, science and controversies by Frankenburg. It describes the research and discovery of vitamin A (retinol), vitamin B1 (thiamine), vitamin B3 (niacin), vitamins B9 (folate) and B12 (cobalamin), vitamin C (ascorbic acid), and vitamin D (calcitriol). Also addresses vitamin deficiencies and vitamin toxicity. For health professionals and general readers.

1176 The health professional's guide to popular dietary supplements. 3rd ed.

Allison Sarubin-Fragakis, Cynthia Thomson, American Dietetic Association. Chicago: American Dietetic Association, 2007. 682 p. ISBN 088091363

613.28   RM258.5.S27

First edition, 2000; 2nd ed., 2002.

Alphabetical guide to supplements, with comments on their safety and literature references concerning scientific evidence. Summary table for each supplement lists media and marketing claims, efficacy, drug/supplement interactions, key points, food sources, dosage and bioavailability research, and safety. Appendixes include information on government regulation of dietary supplements, dietary intake tables and intake assessment, and additional resources. Includes bibliographical references and index. Similarly, *The health professional's guide to dietary supplements* covers 120 dietary supplements, including Web resources.

Available as an e-book from new publisher name at http://www.eatright.org/.

Information in these books can be supplemented with resources such as MEDLINE, the International bibliographic information on dietary supplements (IBIDS) database, Natural medicines comprehensive database, and Natural standard.

1177 International dietetics and nutrition terminology (IDNT) reference manual: standardized language for the nutrition care process. 4th ed.

Academy of Nutrition and Dietetics. Chicago: Academy of Nutrition and Dietetics, 2013. iv, 427 p. ISBN 9780880914673

RM216

First edition, 2007 had title: *Nutrition diagnosis and intervention: Standardized language for the nutrition care process*; 2nd ed., 2009; 3rd ed., 2011.

Publ. by the Academy of Nutrition and Dietetics (formerly American Dietetic Association)

The *IDNT reference manual* is a comprehensive guide to implementing the "nutrition care process," described by the publisher at http://www.eatright.org/HealthProfessionals/content.aspx?id=7077. This manual provides the terminology and definitions of the three steps of the nutrition care process, i.e., nutrition assessment, nutrition diagnosis, and nutrition intervention. Also available online.

1178 Krause's food & the nutrition care process. 13th ed. L. Kathleen. Mahan, Sylvia. Escott-Stump, Janice L. Raymond, Marie V. Krause. St. Louis: Elsevier/Saunders, 2012. xix, 1227 p., col. ill.

615.8/54   RM216.M285

Title varies: 1st ed., 1952, had title *Nutrition and diet therapy in relation to nursing*; 2nd ed., 1957, through 7th ed., 1984, had title *Nutrition and diet therapy*; 11th ed., 2004, had title *Krause's food, nutrition and diet therapy*; 12th ed., 2008, had title *Krause's food and nutrition therapy*.

Contents: pt. 1, "Nutrition assessment"; pt. 2, "Nutrition diagnosis and intervention"; pt. 3, "Nutrition in the life cycle"; pt. 4, "Nutrition for health and fitness"; pt. 5, "Medical nutrition therapy"; pt. 6, "Pediatric specialties."

This revised edition includes chapters on, e.g., nutritional genomics, weight management, eating disorders, and medical nutrition therapy (e.g., expanded "Nutrition in aging" chapter, new chapters on nutrition therapy for thyroid disorders, new calcium and vitamin D dietary recommended intakes (DRIs)), with reference to physiologic and metabolic background and pathophysiology as it relates to nutrition care. Includes the latest recommendations of the Dietary Guidelines for Americans 2010, list of relevant websites at the end of each chapter and a large number of appendixes, including information on exchange lists for meal planning, glycemic index, glycemic load for different carbohydrates, and many others.

1179 Modern nutrition in health and disease. 10th ed. Maurice E. Shils, Moshe Shike. Philadelphia: Lippincott Williams & Wilkins, 2006. xxv, 2069

p., ill. (some col.) ISBN 0781741335

613.2   QP141.M64

First edition, 1955; 9th ed., 1999.

This is the "50th anniversary" edition.

Contents: pt. 1, "Historical landmarks in nutrition"; pt. 2, "Proteins and amino acids"; pt.3, "Nutrition in integrated biologic systems"; pt. 4, "Nutrition needs and assessment during the life cycle"; pt. 5, "Prevention and management of disease"; pt. 6, "Diet and nutrition in health of populations"; pt. 7, "Adequacy, safety, and oversight in the food supply"; pt. 8, appendixes.

Major textbook and reference source, with comprehensive coverage of basic and clinical nutrition and its role in medicine, public health, dietetics, and nursing. Provides extensive information on nutrition's role in disease prevention, covers genetics as it applies to nutrition, and describes major scientific advances in nutrition research. Addresses public health concerns and international nutrition issues. Detailed table of contents, index, and appendixes (text and tables). Appendixes include, for example, information on conversion factors, weights and measures, national and international recommended dietary reference values, energy and protein needs, anthropometric data, therapeutic diets, and websites of interest to health professionals. Includes bibliographical references and index. Electronic full text available via Books@Ovid.

A new edition is planned.

1180 Nutrition: A reference handbook. David A. Bender, Arnold E. Bender. Oxford; New York: Oxford University Press, 1997. xxxvii, 573 p. ISBN 0192623680

613.2   TX353.B45

Contents: ch. 1, "The historical development of nutritional concepts"; ch. 2, "Body composition"; ch. 3, "Growth and development"; ch. 4, "Reference intakes, dietary goals and nutrition labelling of foods"; ch. 5, "Energy balance and overview of metabolism"; ch. 6, "Physiology of feeding and digestion"; ch. 7, "Carbohydrates"; ch. 8, "Lipids: Fats and oils"; ch. 9, "Alcohol and alcoholic beverages"; ch. 10, "Protein nutrition"; ch. 11, "Overnutrition: Problems of overweight and obesity"; ch. 12, "World food supplies and protein-energy malnutrition"; ch. 13, "Vitamin A and carotenes"; ch. 14, "Vitamin D, calcium and phosphorus";

ch. 15, "Vitamin E and selenium"; ch. 16, "Vitamin K"; ch. 17, "Thiamin (vitamin B1)"; ch. 18, "Riboflavin (vitamin B2)"; ch. 19, "Niacin"; ch. 20, "Vitamin B6"; ch. 21, "Folate and vitamin B12; ch. 22, "Vitamin C"; ch. 23, "Biotin, pantothenic acid and other organic compounds"; ch. 24, "Iron"; ch. 25, "Mineral nutrition"; ch. 26, "Food processing"; ch. 27, "Adverse reactions to foods"; ch. 28, "Systematic classification of foods"; ch. 29, "Miscellaneous tables."

Encyclopedic dictionary with tables of data, references to the original sources, cross-references, bibliography, and index. "For anyone working in the broad fields of diet and health, food and nutrition"—*Pref.*

1181 The nutrition desk reference. 3rd ed.
Robert H. Garrison, Elizabeth Somer.
New Canaan, Conn.: Keats, 1995. xxii,
663 p., ill. ISBN 0879836652
613.2   QP141.G33
First edition, 1985; 2nd ed., 1990.

Contents: pt. 1, Dietary factors; pt. 2, Nutrition and cancer; pt. 3, Nutrition and cardiovascular disease; pt. 4, Nutrition and disease; pt. 5, Dietary recommendations.

Presents basic nutrition information, biochemical explanations, and important nutrition-related topics in concise format and readable style. For health professionals and general readers. Figures, tables, glossary, and index. Also available as an e-book. Information found in this desk reference can be updated with online publications, for example, via PubMed and Nutrition (MedlinePlus) and other nutrition-related pages in MedlinePlus.

1182 USDA nutrient data laboratory. http://
www.ars.usda.gov/ba/bhnrc/ndl. Nutrient
Data Laboratory, U.S. Department of
Agriculture. Beltsville, Md.: Nutrient
Data Laboratory, U.S. Department of
Agriculture. [199?]– 612.3641.3

Its mission is "to develop authoritative food composition databases and state of the art methods to acquire, evaluate, compile and disseminate composition data on foods available in the United States."—*Main page* Contains links to historical information of 115 years of USDA food composition tables (http://www.ars.usda.gov/Aboutus/docs.htm?docid=9418). Currently, the National

Nutrient Data Bank contains information for approx. 130 nutrients for more than 7,000 foods. Its major database is USDA national nutrient database for standard reference (SR), release 24 (http://www.ars.usda.gov/Services/docs.htm?docid=8964); also online via Knovel), for determining the nutrient content of foods (published previously in print format in *Agriculture handbook* no. 8 and supplements and *Home and garden bulletin* no. 72). Also provides links to food composition information from other countries (e.g., Canada, Australia, New Zealand, and others), food consumption surveys, food labeling, general nutrition information (e.g., Nutrition.gov, Dietary Guidelines for Americans 2010), dietary supplements databases (USDA is working with the Office of Dietary Supplements and other federal agencies to develop a Dietary supplement ingredient database [DSID] at http://www.ars.usda.gov/dsid), and other resources.

1183 WHO child growth standards. http://
www.who.int/childgrowth/en/index.html.
World Health Organization. Geneva,
Switzerland: World Health Organization.
2006

Since the late 1970s, the National Center for Health Statistics/WHO growth reference has been in use to chart children's growth. It was based on data from a limited sample of children from the United States and is now considered less adequate for international comparisons. In 1997, WHO, in collaboration with the United Nations University, undertook the Multicentre Growth Reference Study (MGRS), which is a community-based, multicountry project with more than 8,000 children from Brazil, Ghana, India, Norway, Oman, and the United States. The new standards are the result of this study, which had as its goal "to develop a new international standard for assessing the physical growth, nutritional status and motor development in all children from birth to age five"—*press release*. The first new growth charts released (Apr. 2007) include weight-for-age, length/height-for-age, and weight-for-length/height growth indicators as well as a Body Mass Index (BMI) standard for children up to age 5, and standards for sitting, standing, walking, and several other key motor developments.

The title of the print version is *WHO child growth standards: Length/height-for-age, weight-for-age, weight-for-length, weight-for-height and body mass index–for–age: Methods and development.*

Tables

1184 USDA nutrient data laboratory. http://www.ars.usda.gov/ba/bhnrc/ndl. Nutrient Data Laboratory, U.S. Department of Agriculture. Beltsville, Md.: Nutrient Data Laboratory, U.S. Department of Agriculture. [199?]– 612.3641.3

Its mission is "to develop authoritative food composition databases and state of the art methods to acquire, evaluate, compile and disseminate composition data on foods available in the United States."—*Main page* Contains links to historical information of 115 years of USDA food composition tables (http://www.ars.usda.gov/Aboutus/docs.htm?docid=9418). Currently, the National Nutrient Data Bank contains information for approx. 130 nutrients for more than 7,000 foods. Its major database is USDA national nutrient database for standard reference (SR), release 24 (http://www.ars.usda.gov/Services/docs.htm?docid=8964); also online via Knovel), for determining the nutrient content of foods (published previously in print format in *Agriculture handbook* no. 8 and supplements and *Home and garden bulletin* no. 72). Also provides links to food composition information from other countries (e.g., Canada, Australia, New Zealand, and others), food consumption surveys, food labeling, general nutrition information (e.g., Nutrition.gov, Dietary Guidelines for Americans 2010), dietary supplements databases (USDA is working with the Office of Dietary Supplements and other federal agencies to develop a Dietary supplement ingredient database [DSID] at http://www.ars.usda.gov/dsid), and other resources.

Internet resources

1185 Dietary guidelines for Americans, 2010. http://www.cnpp.usda.gov/Publications/DietaryGuidelines/2010/PolicyDoc/PolicyDoc.pdf. U.S. Department of Health and Human Services, U.S. Department of Agriculture. Washington: U.S. Department of Health and Human Services; U.S. Department of Agriculture. 2010
613.25   RA784

Published jointly every five years by the Department of Health and Human Services, Office of Disease Prevention and Health Promotion, the Department of Agriculture, Center for Nutrition Policy and Promotion, and the Agricultural Research Service.

First five editions, 1980–2000, had title, Nutrition and your health: Dietary guidelines for Americans. Print equivalents for these editions published in Home and garden bulletin (U.S. Dept. of Agriculture) no. 232. Current and earlier online editions linked from http://www.health.gov/DietaryGuidelines/.

Description based on the 2010 Web edition.

Contents: Ch. 1, "Introduction"; ch. 2, "Balancing calories to manage weight"; ch. 3, "Foods and food components to reduce"; ch. 4, "Foods and nutrients to increase"; ch. 5, "Building healthy eating patterns"; ch. 6, "Helping Americans make healthy choices"; Appendixes (1) "Guidance for specific population groups"; (2) "Key consumer behaviors and potential strategies for professionals to use in implementing the 2010 Dietary Guidelines"; (3) "Food safety principles and guidance for consumers"; (4) "Using the food label to track calories, nutrients, and ingredients"; (5) "Nutritional goals for age-gender groups based on dietary reference intakes and dietary guidelines recommendations"; (6) Estimated calorie needs per day by age, gender, and physical activity level (detailed)"; (7) "USDA food patterns"; (8) "Lacto-ovo vegetarian adaptation of the USDA food patterns"; (9) "Vegan adaptation of the USDA food patterns"; (10) "The DASH eating plan at various calorie levels"; (11) "Estimated EPA and DHA and mercury content in 4 ounces of selected seafood varieties"; (12) "Selected food sources ranked by amounts of potassium and calories per standard food portion"; (13) "Selected food sources ranked by amounts of dietary, fiber and calories per standard food portion"; (14) "Selected food sources ranked by amounts of calcium and calories per standard food portion"; (15) "Selected food sources ranked by amounts of vitamin D and calories per standard food portion"; (16), "Glossary of terms".

These guidelines provide authoritative advice for people two years old and older about how good dietary habits can promote health and reduce risk for major chronic diseases. Additional information and access to related documents and resources can be found at http://teamnutrition .usda.gov/library.html.

Choose My Plate (http://www.choosemyplate .gov), launched in June 2011, is based on these dietary guidelines. This new food icon is intended to assist consumers in visualizing and preparing a plate with healthy proportions of fruits, vegetables, grains, protein, and dairy during mealtimes. These food choices are considered to lead to healthier lifestyles.

1186 Nutrition.gov. http://www.nutrition.gov. Food and Nutrition Information Center, United States.; Dept. of Agriculture., National Agricultural Library (U.S.). Beltsville, Md.: National Agricultural Library. 2004-
  613.71; 011.53; 612.3; 641.3;   RA784
Maintained by Food and Nutrition Information Center (FNIC).

Access to information from across the federal government on food, food safety, nutrition, weight management, dietary supplements, and food assistance programs. Includes specialized nutrition information for life stages: infants, children, teens, adult women and men, and seniors, as well as the latest nutrition-related news. Provides search capabilities and resource lists.

Healthfinder.gov provides access to consumer resources concerning nutrition, physical fitness, and disease.

1187 Nutrition (MedlinePlus). http://www .nlm.nih.gov/medlineplus/nutrition.html. National Library of Medicine (U.S.), National Institutes of Health (U.S.). Bethesda, Md.: U.S. National Library of Medicine, National Institutes of Health, Dept. of Health and Human Services. 2000?–
  A health topic within MedlinePlus®.
Contents: Overviews; Latest news; Related issues; Health check tools; Tutorials; Clinical trials; Research; Journal articles; Directories; Organizations; Law and policy; Teenagers; Women.

Selected links to a wide range of nutrition-related information provided by government agencies, societies, professional associations, organizations, and foundations. Also provides links to related topics with separate pages in MedlinePlus, e.g., breast feeding, child nutrition, dietary fats, fiber, and protein, eating disorders, food safety, infant and toddler nutrition, obesity, vegetarian diets, and others.

1188 The nutrition source. http://www.hsph .harvard.edu/nutritionsource/. Harvard School of Public Health. Boston: Harvard School of Public Health. 2002–
Contents: Nutrition in the news; What Should I Eat?; Healthy Drinks; Salt and Sodium; Carbohydrates; Healthy Weight; Preventing Diabetes; Recipes; Healthy Food Service; Your Nutrition Questions Answered; Index: Nutrition A to Z; Additional Resources; About Us; FAQ; Contact Us.

"The Nutrition Source provides evidence-based diet & nutrition information for clinicians, health professionals and the public." —*main page*.

1189 Office of Dietary Supplements. http:// dietary-supplements.info.nih.gov/index. aspx. National Institutes of Health Office of Dietary Supplements. Bethesda, Md.: National Institutes of Health Office of Dietary Supplements. 1990s–
  RM258.5 615.854
National Institutes of Health (NIH) Office of Dietary Supplements (ODS); U.S. Dept. of Agriculture (USDA).

ODS homepage includes extensive health information on dietary supplement use and safety and nutrient recommendations. Provides access to NIH and USDA databases and research resources, such as dietary supplement databases, product integrity resources, and the USDA food composition database. Another resource for researchers is the CARDS (Computer access to research on dietary supplements) database (http://ods .od.nih.gov/research/cards_database.aspx) which includes records of research projects pertaining to dietary supplements funded by various government agencies, centers, and institutes. For health professionals, researchers, students, and health consumers.

1190 USDA nutrient data laboratory. http:// www.ars.usda.gov/ba/bhnrc/ndl. Nutrient Data Laboratory, U.S. Department of Agriculture. Beltsville, Md.: Nutrient Data Laboratory, U.S. Department of Agriculture. [199?]– 612.3641.3

Its mission is "to develop authoritative food composition databases and state of the art methods to acquire, evaluate, compile and disseminate composition data on foods available in the United States."—*Main page* Contains links to historical information of 115 years of USDA food composition tables (http://www.ars.usda.gov/Aboutus/docs.htm?docid=9418). Currently, the National Nutrient Data Bank contains information for approx. 130 nutrients for more than 7,000 foods. Its major database is USDA national nutrient database for standard reference (SR), release 24 (http://www.ars.usda.gov/Services/docs.htm?docid=8964); also online via Knovel), for determining the nutrient content of foods (published previously in print format in *Agriculture handbook* no. 8 and supplements and *Home and garden bulletin* no. 72). Also provides links to food composition information from other countries (e.g., Canada, Australia, New Zealand, and others), food consumption surveys, food labeling, general nutrition information (e.g., Nutrition.gov, Dietary Guidelines for Americans 2010), dietary supplements databases (USDA is working with the Office of Dietary Supplements and other federal agencies to develop a Dietary supplement ingredient database [DSID] at http://www.ars.usda.gov/dsid), and other resources.

10 *Pharmacology and Pharmaceutical Sciences*

1191 DailyMed. http://dailymed.nlm.nih.gov/. National Library of Medicine (U.S.). Bethesda, Md.: U.S. National Library of Medicine, National Institutes of Health, Health and Human Services. [2005]–

A searchable website with growing content, providing health consumers, students, and health professionals with online information on prescription medications and labeling from FDA-approved medication package inserts. Each entry gives a description of the medication, its clinical pharmacology, indications and usage, warnings and precautions, dosage and administration, adverse reactions, etc. Information regarding the mobile version of this resource is part of NLM's Gallery of mobile apps and sites.

Additional consumer health information about U.S. drugs provided by NLM can be found in *MedlinePlus* under headings such as drugs, supplements, and herbal information, drug safety, medicines, over-the-counter medicines, pain relievers, and possibly others. PubMed and its MEDLINE subset and TOXLINE, can be searched for references to professional journal articles.

1192 Drug abuse (MedlinePlus). http://www.nlm.nih.gov/medlineplus/drugabuse.html. National Library of Medicine (U.S.). Bethesda, Md.: National Library of Medicine. 2000?–

A health topic in MedlinePlus.

Contents: Overviews; Latest news; Diagnosis/symptoms; Treatment; Prevention/screening; Specific conditions; Related sssues; Pictures and photographs; Games; Clinical trials; Research; Journal articles; Dictionaries/glossaries; Directories; Organizations; Newsletters/print publications; Law and policy; Statistics; Children; Teenagers; Men; Women; Seniors; Other languages.

Collection of links on substance abuse from a variety of government agencies, professional associations, and organizations, such as the National Institute on Drug Abuse, the Office of National Drug Control, Substance Abuse and Mental Health Services Administration (SAMHSA), National Library of Medicine, American Medical Association, American Academy of Family Physicians, and others. Also links to related MedlinePlus topics, e.g., alcoholism, prescription drug abuse, and substance abuse, to name a few.

1193 Electronic orange book. http://purl.access.gpo.gov/GPO/LPS1445. Center for Drug Evaluation and Research. Rockville, Md.: U.S. Deptartment of Health and Human Services; Food and Drug Administration. 1999– 615.10285

Title varies: Approved Drug Products with Therapeutic Equivalence Evaluation Orange Book.

"Since the 25th edition, the Annual Edition and monthly Cumulative Supplements are published in electronic Portable Document Format (PDF). The PDF annual and cumulative supplements duplicate previous paper formats. Over time, there will be an archive page of Annual Editions and each year's December Cumulative Supplement that will provide a history of approved drug products' approvals and changes"—"*Publications*" *page.*

Directory of approved drug products with therapeutic equivalence evaluations. Searchable by active ingredient, proprietary name, patents, applicant holder, and application number. Identifies drugs on the market that meet safety and efficacy requirements. Provides information to states about generic drugs that are acceptable for substitution of drug products. "Frequently asked qustions on the *Orange book*" (http://www.fda.gov/Drugs/InformationOnDrugs/ucm114166.htm) provides further information.

1194 Facts and comparisons eAnswers.
http://www.factsandcomparisons.com/facts-comparisons-online/. Facts and Comparisons (Firm). Philadelphia, Pa.: Wolters Kluwer Health. 2001–

RM300

Detailed product information at http://www.factsandcomparisons.com/products.aspx.

Provides access to several drug information resources and the ability to search across the different publications : *A to Z drug facts*, *Drug facts and comparisons*, *Drug identifier*, *Drug interaction facts*, *Drug interaction facts: Herbal supplements and food*, "Investigational drugs" from *Drug facts and comparisons*, *MedFacts* (patient information), *Nonprescription drug therapy*, *Review of natural products*, and several other resources.

1195 Medicinal plants of the world: Chemical constituents, traditional and modern medicinal uses. 2nd ed.
Ivan A. Ross. Totowa, N.J.: Humana Press, 2003–2005. ill. (some col.) ISBN 1588292819
615.32   RS164.R676
First edition, 1999–2001.

This revised edition provides information on traditional medicinal uses, chemical constituents, pharmacological activities, clinical trials, color illustrations, Latin names, botanical descriptions, and how each medicinal plant is used around the world. Cross-references common names to country and scientific name. Index includes terms, symptoms, and treatments as well as bibliographies. Also available as an e-book.

Guides

1196 Drug information: A guide for pharmacists. 4th ed. Patrick M. Malone, Karen L. Kier, John E. Stanovich. New York: McGraw-Hill Medical, 2012. xxiv, 1192 p., ill. ISBN 9780071624954
615.1   RS56.2.D78
First ed., 1996; 2nd ed., 2001; 3rd ed., 2006.

Contents: ch. 1, "Introduction to the concept of medication information"; ch. 2, "Formulating effective responses and recommendations: a structured approach"; ch. 3, "Drug information resources"; ch. 4, "Literature evaluation I: controlled clinical trial evaluation"; ch. 5, "Literature evaluation II: beyond the basics"; ch. 6, "Pharmacoeconomics"; ch. 7, "Evidence-based clinical practice guidelines"; ch. 8, "The application of statistical analysis in the biomedical sciences"; ch. 9, "Professional writing"; ch. 10, "Legal aspects of drug information practice"; ch. 11, "Ethical aspects of drug information practice"; ch. 12, "Pharmacy and therapeutics committee"; ch. 13, "Drug evaluation monographs"; ch. 14, "Quality improvement and the medication use process"; ch. 15, "Medication misadventures I: Adverse drug reactions"; ch. 16, "Medication misadventures II: Medication and patient safety"; ch. 17, "Investigational drugs"; ch. 18, "Policy development, project design, and implementation"; ch. 19, "Drug information in ambulatory care"; ch. 20, "Drug information and contemporary community pharmacy practice"; ch. 21, "Drug information education and training"; ch. 22, "Pharmaceutical industry and regulatory affairs." Appendixes, glossary, index.

This updated and expanded informatics resource, intended for pharmacists and pharmacy students, is a guide to researching, interpreting, organizing, and using drug information. Most chapters in this edition contain case studies. Also available as an e-book.

1197 Drug information: Guide to current resources. 3rd ed. Bonnie Snow, Medical Library Association. New York: Neal-Schuman, 2008. xvii, 546 p., ill. ISBN 9781555706166
016.6151   Z6675.P5S64; RS91
First ed., 1989; 2nd ed., 1999.

Provides an introduction to a wide selection of relevant print and online pharmacology and therapeutics reference sources and discusses common problems in the provision of information concerning drugs. Contains background information on pharmacological terminology, legal and regulatory issues, and marketing and business data. Chapters on industrial pharmacy and market research and competitive intelligence resources. Also included are a detailed contents listing, a keyword index, a glossary that defines pharmaceutical and information science terminology used in the text, practicum exercises, and other useful appendixes.

1198 Herbal medicines: A guide for healthcare professionals. 3rd ed.
Joanne Barnes, Linda Anderson, J. Phillipson, Carol A. Newall. London; Chicago: Pharmaceutical Press, 2007. 710 p. ISBN 0853696233
615.321   RM666.H33
First edition, 1996; 2nd ed., 2002.

This revised and rewritten edition includes 152 herbal monographs. Describes phytochemical, pharmacological, and clinical aspects of each herb. Each monograph provides species, family, synonym(s), part(s) used, pharmacopeial and other monograph references, etc. Includes chemical structure drawings, color photographs, and a directory of product names and suppliers. Quality, safety, and legal requirements are addressed. Includes an overview of U.K. and European legislation concerning herbal products. Appendixes group herbs by their specific actions. Bibliographical references and index. Also available as a book and CD-ROM package and online as part of MedicinesComplete. A new edition (4th ed., 2013, print and onine access) is available.

1199 Using the pharmaceutical literature.
Sharon Srodin. New York: Taylor & Francis, 2006. xiv, 323 p., ill. ISBN 0824729668
615.19   RS56.U85
Contents: ch. 1, "Introduction: The drug discovery and development process"; ch. 2, "Chemistry"; ch. 3, "Genomics, proteomics, and bioinformatics"; ch. 4, "Toxicology"; ch. 5. "Pharmacology"; ch. 6, "Drug regulation"; ch. 7, "Sales and marketing"; ch. 8,

"Competitive intelligence"; ch. 9, "Pharmacoeconomics"; ch. 10, "Intellectual property"; ch. 11, "Medical devices and combination products."

"The chapters in this book correspond to a key stage or components of the drug development process and cover the types of information typically required at each point"—*Pref.* Intended as a guide and collection development tool for pharmaceutical and medical information professionals. Provides an overview of key resources such as databases, online directories, websites, reports, and periodicals. Special attention is given to devices and drug delivery systems. Includes definitions of industry terminology. Also available as an e-book.

Bibliography

1200 Basic resources for pharmacy education. http://www.aacp.org/governance/SECTIONS/library informationscience/Documents/2013 JanBasicResourcesforPharmacyEducation. pdf. Leslie Ann Bowman, Barbara Nanstiel, American Association of Colleges of Pharmacy. Alexandria, Va.: American Association of Colleges of Pharmacy. 2013
A guide for those developing or maintaining the "library collections that serve colleges of pharmacy. . . . The books and other works recommended in the *Basic Resources* are suitable for all pharmacy college libraries, but all pharmacy college libraries need not purchase every title in the list."—*Introd.*

A service project of the Libraries/Educational Resources Section of the American Association of Colleges of Pharmacy. This bibliography and other reference resources for pharmacy faculty, students, and librarians are accessible via the AACP website (http://www.aacp.org/).

Copies of previous editions of this list may be obtained by contacting one of the editors.

1201 Medical humanities dissertations. http://www.hsls.pitt.edu/histmed/dissertations/. Jonathon Erlen, University of Pittsburgh Health Sciences Library System. Pittsburgh: Health Sciences Library, University of Pittsburgh Medical Center. 2001–

Provides a monthly current awareness service for selected recent medical dissertations and theses. Arranged by topics, currently covers the following areas: AIDS (social and historical contexts); alternative medicine (social and historical contexts); art and medicine; biomedical ethics; history of medicine prior to 1800; history of medicine and health care; history of science and technology; literature/theater and medicine; nursing history; pharmacy/pharmacology and history; philosophy and medicine; psychiatry/psychology and history; public health/international health; religion and medicine; women's health and history. To view complete citations, abstracts, and full-text of dissertations requires a subscription to Proquest dissertations and theses (PQDT).

Indexes; Abstract journals; Databases

1202 Dietary supplement label database. http://www.dsld.nlm.nih.gov/dsld/. NIH Office of Dietary Supplements, National Library of Medicine (U.S.). Bethesda, Md.: National Library of Medicine. 2013–

Joint project of the National Institutes of Health (NIH) Office of Dietary Supplements (ODS) and National Library of Medicine (NLM) Division of Specialized Information Services (SIS). Also referred to as DSLD.

DSLD, a document repository database, captures information on dietary supplement labels. Contains the full label contents from 17,000 dietary supplement products marketed in the U.S. and will eventually include 55,000 products available in the U.S. Obtained from the manufacturers' labels. Includes image of the product label, both "DSLD on market" (i.e., label information from dietary supplement products that are currently on the U.S. market) and "DSLD off-market "(i.e., label information from dietary supplement products that have been discontinued or are no longer on the U.S. market). Allows for searching, browsing, sorting, and filtering; and data can be saved and analyzed. Answers many questions researchers and users of dietary supplements might have concerning ingredients shown on labels of specific

brands, chemical ingredients, animal products, proven medical benefits, toxicity of specific ingredients, etc. Includes reference links leading to further explanation (e.g., unit conversion, daily value, dietary reference intakes, etc.), definitions (A-Z), also a frequently asked questions section and links to reference sources.

An earlier database, "Dietary supplements labels database: Brands, ingredients, and references," has been retired.

1203 Drug information portal. http://drug info.nlm.nih.gov/. National Library of Medicine (U.S.). Bethesda, Md.: National Library of Medicine. 2008–

"Gateway to selected drug information from the National Library of Medicine and other key government agencies . . . [with] access to over 12,000 selected drugs"—*About This Portal*. Can be searched by a drug's trade or generic name. Provides a summary of the information about the drug, and links to further related information, such as MedlinePlus, AIDSinfo (648), MEDLINE/PubMed®, LactMed, HSDB, Dietary supplements labels database, TOX-LINE, DailyMed, ClinicalTrials.gov, PubChem, ChemIDplus, Drugs@FDA, and others. For the public, health care professionals, and researchers. Information regarding the mobile version of this resource is part of NLM's Gallery of mobile apps and sites.

1204 Lexi-Comp online. http://www.lexi.com/. Lexi-Comp, Inc. Hudson, Ohio: Lexi-Comp, Inc. 1978–

Point-of-care drug and clinical information resource, with links to primary literature. Contains 15 clinical databases (e.g., Lexi-Drugs Online, AHFS, Lexi-Natural Products Online, Nursing Lexi-Drugs Online, Pharmacogenomics, Poisoning and Toxicology, Lab Tests and Diagnosis, and several others) and provides drug information and treatment recommendation for diseases and conditions. Also includes other features, e.g., an online interaction tool (Lexi-Interact) and medical calculator (Lexi-CALC). For pharmacists, physicians, nurses, and dentists. Detailed information available at the Lexi-Comp website "tour portal" (http://www.lexi.com/web/toursol.jsp).

1205 Micromedex products. http://www.micromedex.com/products/index.html.

Truven Health Analytics. Ann Arbor, Mich.: Truven Health Analytics. [199?–] Produced by Truven Health Analytics, formerly known as Thomson Reuters (Healthcare) Inc.

Intended for clinicians; academic program available. Includes a variety of resources for finding information on drugs, toxicology, emergency, acute care, and disease data as well as alternative medicine information. Drug resources include DRUGDEX, DRUG-REAX, IDENTIDEX, IV Index, *Index nominum*, *Martindale: The complete drug reference*, POISINDEX, *Red book*, and REPROR-ISK. Emergency and disease data can be found, for example, in DISEASEDEX and alternative therapies in AltMedDex and other Thomson products. Searchable across either all databases, by specific database(s), and by groups of databases. Drugs can be searched by trade or generic drug name. Specific drug database search and drug topic search provide, for example, a drug evaluation overview, dosing information, pharmacokinetics, contraindications, precautions, adverse reactions, single and multiple drug interactions, IV compatibility, teratogenicity, therapeutic uses, and comparative efficacy.

A matrix of all Micromedex products and versions in this series, with listing of the individual titles, various format options, and indication of whether a particular title is also available in print can be found at http://www.micromedex.com/support/faqs/plat_matrix.html. Help with citing the various Micromedex versions is provided at http://www.micromedex.com/about_us/legal/cite/.

1206 Natural standard. http://www.natural standard.com. Natural Standard. Cambridge, Mass.: Natural Standard. 2003–

R733

International collaboration, with contributors from academic institutions. Provides evidence-based information and expert opinions about complementary and alternative therapies. Individual monographs provide information in support of clinical decision making. Contains several databases: Herbs and supplements, Condition center, Health and wellness, Dictionary, Interactions, and Brand Names. Individual entries provide an overview of clinically oriented research and historical background of various herbal products. A typical entry, such as that for peppermint oil, includes related terms, essential-oil constituents, leaf constituents, selected brand names (e.g., Ben-Gay), combination products, and a note on a different species of mint with similar appearances. Also provides detailed background information on its medicinal use, including historical information dating back to ancient Egypt, Greece, and Rome. Furthermore, includes information about use for different medical conditions and illnesses, contraindications, safety rating, tradition/theory (i.e., proposed uses that have not been tested in humans and for which safety and effectiveness may not have been scientifically proven), dosing (recommendations for adults and children), safety (allergies, side effects and warnings, pregnancy and breast feeding), interactions (with drugs, herbs, and supplements), author information, and bibliographical references and links to PubMed abstracts.

Content on herbs and supplements in MedlinePlus, previously taken from Natural standard, is now provided by the consumer version of Natural Medicines comprehensive database.

Related print titles include *Natural standard herb & supplement guide: An evidence-based reference* by Ulbricht, *Natural standard herbal pharmacotherpay* by Ulbricht et al., and *Natural standard medical conditions reference* by Ulbricht.

1207 NLM gateway. http://gateway.nlm.nih.gov/. National Library of Medicine (U.S.). Bethesda, Md.: National Library of Medicine. 2000–

RA11

As announced in 2011, "the NLM® gateway has transitioned to a new pilot project from the Lister Hill National Center for Biomedical Communications (LHNCBC)."—*Website* The new site focuses now on two databases: Meeting abstracts and Health services research projects. All of the other resources previously accessed through the NLM gateway are available through their individual sites. For a list of these databases previously available via the NLM gateway see http://gateway.nlm.nih.gov/about.jsp.

The NLM gateway previously allowed simultaneous searching of information resources at the National Library of Medicine (NLM)/National Center for Biotechnology Information (NCBI) with an overview of the search results presented in several categories (bibliographic resources, consumer health resources, and other information), with a listing of the individual databases and the number of results within these categories. Previously included were, for example, MEDLINE/PubMed and the NLM Catalog as well as other resources, including information on current clinical trials and consumer health information (MedlinePlus) and many others.

1208 PubMed. http://www.ncbi.nlm.nih.gov/
pubmed. U.S. National Center for
Biotechnology Information, National
Library of Medicine, National Institutes
of Health. Bethesda, Md.: U.S. National
Center for Biotechnology Information.
1996–

PubMed®, developed and maintained by the National Center for Biotechnology Information (NCBI) at the National Library of Medicine® (NLM). Provides a search interface for more than 20 million bibliographic citations and abstracts in the fields of medicine, nursing, dentistry, veterinary medicine, health care systems, and preclinical sciences. It provides access to articles indexed for MEDLINE® and for selected life sciences journals. PubMed subsets found under the "Limits" tab are: MEDLINE and PubMed central®, several journal groups (i.e., core clinical journals, dental journals, and nursing journals), and topical subsets (AIDS, bioethics, cancer, complementary medicine, dietary supplements, history of medicine, space life sciences, systematic reviews, toxicology, and veterinary science). "Linkout" provides access to full-text articles.

For detailed information see the PubMed fact sheet at http://www.nlm.nih.gov/pubs/factsheets/pubmed.html and also MEDLINE®/PubMed® resources guide (http://www.nlm.nih.gov/bsd/pmresources.html) which provides detailed information about MEDLINE data and searching PubMed.

Information regarding the mobile version of this resource is part of NLM's Gallery of mobile apps and sites.

1209 U.S. Food and Drug Administration.
http://www.fda.gov. Food and Drug
Administration. Washington: Food and
Drug Administration

The Food and Drug Administration (FDA) regulates foods, drugs, medical devices, biologics (vaccines, blood products, etc.), and radiation-emitting products (e.g., cell phones, lasers, microwaves, etc.). Searchable website with A–Z index (http://www.fda.gov/SiteIndex/default).

Major links include Drugs (http://www.fda.gov/Drugs/default.htm) which evaluates drugs before they can be sold and provides resources such as Drugs@FDA, Electronic orange book, and National drug code directory. Another FDA center is Food (http://www.fda.gov/Food/default.htm), with resources on foods and food safety, such as the GRAS (Generally Recognized as Safe) list of substances (http://www.fda.gov/IngredientsPackagingLabeling/GRAS/SCOGS/default.htm), the "bad bug book" (http://www.fda.gov/food/foodborneillnesscontaminants/causesofillnessba dbugbook/default.htm) and publications on food-borne illness, FDA food code, allergens, dietary supplements, etc. Additional FDA centers provide information on biologics, cosmetics, medical devices, radiological health, toxicological research, and veterinary medicine.

Other examples of resources provided at the FDA site include access to the "blue book" (i.e., *Requirements of laws and regulations enforced by the U.S. Food and Drug Administration*), oncology tools, patient safety portal, special health issues, and information on bioterrorism, trans fats, vaccines, xenotransplantation, and many other subjects and topics relating to human and animal drugs and biologics, foods, and medical devices. Information is tailored to the needs of different user groups, with separate pages for consumers, patients, health professionals, state/local officials, industry, press, women, and children. Frequently requested FDA documents can be accessed via an "electronic reading room" (http://www.fda.gov/foi/electrr.htm). Milestones in U.S. Food and Drug Law History 1820–2005 is available at http://www.fda.gov/AboutFDA/WhatWeDo/History/Milestones/default.htm.

**1210 WISER (Wireless Information System
for Emergency Responders)**. http://
wiser.nlm.nih.gov. National Library of
Medicine (U.S.). Bethesda, Md.: U.S.
National Library of Medicine. 2005–

"A system designed to assist first responders in hazardous materials incidents . . . including substance identification support, physical characteristics, human health information, and advice on containment and suppression guidance."—*Home page.* "Information is presented to the emergency responder, Hazmat Specialist, and EMS Specialist in the order that is most relevant to their respective roles."—*About page.* Content from HSDB (Hazardous substance data bank) and from CHEMM (Chemical hazards emergency medical management) http://chemm.nlm.nih .gov. Further information on other data sources and about applications available (for phone, tablet, and desktop) on the About page. This resource is also listed on NLM's Gallery of mobile apps and sites.

Encyclopedias

1211 The encyclopedia of addictive drugs.
Richard Lawrence Miller. Westport, Conn.: Greenwood Press, 2002. 491 p. ISBN 0313318077

615/.78   RM316.M555

Contents: Introduction; Drug types; Alphabetical listing of drugs; Sources for more information; Drug name index; Subject index. Provides nontechnical description of approx. 130 addictive drugs, including both pharmaceutical and natural products and aspects of drug abuse. Alphabetical listing of substances, with pronunciation, alternative names (including street names), legal status (federal schedule status; discussion of schedules and scheduling), historical and present uses and misuses, abuse factors, interactions with other drugs, and findings of cancer risks and birth defects. Also includes a section on drug types in general categories. List of print and electronic sources with further information. For general readers. Also available as e-book.

Encyclopedia of addictions by Hollen, *Encyclopedia of drugs, alcohol & addictive behavior,* and *Encyclopedia of substance abuse prevention, treatment, and recovery* are additional well-regarded resources in this area. A valuable Internet resource is Substance Abuse and Mental Health Services Administration (SAMHSA).

1212 Encyclopedia of biopharmaceutical statistics. 3rd ed. Informa Healthcare: New York, 2010. xvii, 2 v. (1474 p.), ill. ISBN 9781439822456

RM301.25

This revised and expanded edition reflects recent changes in regulatory requirements for drug review and approval processes and also recently developed statistical methods in biopharmaceutical research and development. Includes current standards and best practices in the clinical, laboratory, manufacturing fields, statistical design, investigation, and analysis. Includes bibliographical references and index. Also available as an e-book.

Contents: v. 1. A-L; v. 2. M-Z.

1st ed., 2000; 2nd ed., 2003.

1213 Encyclopedia of clinical toxicology: A comprehensive guide and reference to the toxicology of prescription and OTC drugs, chemicals, herbals, plants, fungi, marine life, reptiles and insect venoms, food ingredients, clothing, and environmental toxins.
Irving S. Rossoff. Boca Raton, Fla.: Parthenon, 2002. xiv, 1507 p. ISBN 1842141015

615.9003   RA1193.R67

Approximately 6,000 alphabetically arranged entries on toxic substances that adversely affect or destroy health or cause death. Mainly human data, with data on animals where insufficient data on human toxicity are available. Entries mention synonyms and use, toxic effects, and treatment, where appropriate. An appendix, "Alternative nomenclature," functions as an index.

1214 Encyclopedia of clinical pharmacy.
Joseph T. DiPiro, American College of Clinical Pharmacy, American Society of Health-System Pharmacists. New York: M. Dekker, 2003. x, 933 p., ill., port. ISBN 0824707524

RS51.E48

Collaboration of the American College of Clinical Pharmacy (ACCP) and the American Society of Health-System Pharmacists (ASHP).

Contains procedures, consensus statements; practice guidelines; regulatory standards for pharmaceutical care; health service delivery models; ethical and legal issues and controversies related to clinical pharmacy; and information on electronic prescription, educational and training programs, and other relevant topics relating to clinical pharmaceutical practice. Each article contains references. Also available in an online version.

For pharmacists, other health professionals, and students. Appropriate for academic libraries and drug information centers. Also available as an e-book.

1215 Encyclopedia of dietary supplements. 2nd ed. Paul M. Coates. New York: Informa Healthcare, 2010. xix, 898 p., ill. ISBN 9781439819289

615/.103 22   RM258.5

"The goal . . . is to provide readers with comprehensive yet accessible, information on the current state of science for individual supplement ingredients and extracts"—*Pref.* Includes commonly used supplements, including vitamins, minerals, and other ingredients found in foods, and also natural products, such as herb extracts. Alphabetically arranged entries include basic information about each substance and its regulatory status. References to the scientific literature or evidence to support claims of benefit are provided. For clinicians, researchers, health care professionals, and possibly for consumers with a chemistry background. Available both in print and online. Other titles, for example, *Guide to understanding dietary supplements* by Talbott, *Mosby's handbook of herbs and natural supplements* by Skidmore-Roth, and *PDR for nutritional supplements*, may also be useful to health professionals and consumers.

1216 Encyclopedic reference of molecular pharmacology. Stefan Offermanns, Walter Rosenthal. Berlin; New York: Springer, 2004. xxii, 1115 p., ill. (some col.)

615.703   RM301.65.E53

With continually expanding knowledge of the molecular basis of drug actions, pharmacogenomics, and pharmacogenetics, this reference book provides up-to-date information on the molecular mechanisms of drug action. Alphabetically arranged entries, with essays describing groups of drugs and drug targets, cellular processes, and pathological conditions and how they can be influenced by drugs. Complemented by 1,600 keywords, tables, color figures, and cross-references. Drugs are listed in an appendix, not in the entries. Also listed in the appendix are, for example, tables listing proteins (such as receptors and transporters) and ion channels. Accompanied by a CD-ROM

that provides the full text and facilitates searching. Written for scientists, advanced students, and informed laypeople. Available online via Springer eReference.

1217 Leung's encyclopedia of common natural ingredients used in food, drugs, and cosmetics. 3rd ed. Ikhlas A. Khan, Ehab A. Abourashed. Hoboken, N.J.: John Wiley & Sons, 2010. xxix, 810 p., ill. ISBN 9780471467434

660.6/3   QD415.A25 L48

First ed., 1980, 2nd ed., 1996 (also rev. & exp., 2003) had title: *Encyclopedia of common natural ingredients: Used in food, drugs, and cosmetics.*

This updated and revised edition updates all entries of the previous edition and includes a new section on traditional Indian medicine. Arrangement is by common name. Entries give Latin name, synonyms, general description, chemical composition, pharmacology or biological activities, uses, commercial preparations, and references. Includes an English-language classification for Chinese medicinal herbs and a glossary of commonly encountered terms used in the botanical industry. Excludes prescription drugs and medicinal herbs not readily available in commerce. Indexed. Available as an e-book.

1218 Meyler's side effects of drugs: The international encyclopedia of adverse drug reactions and interactions. M. N. G. Dukes. Amsterdam, Netherlands; New York: Elsevier Science B.V., 1975–. ill.

0376-7396   RM302.5.S52

Description based on 15th ed., 2006. 6 v. Ed. Jeffrey K. Aronson. Includes most of the content of *Side effects of drugs annual*, 23rd to 27th ed. Referred to as SED (*Meyler's side effects of drugs*) and SEDA (*Side effects of drugs annual*).

Includes approximately 1,500 articles on drugs. Drug monographs in alphabetical order, with information within each monograph in the following sections: general information, organs and systems, long-term effects, second-generation effects, susceptibility factors (patient specific), drug administration, drug interactions, interference with diagnostic tests, diagnosis of adverse drug reactions, and managements of adverse drug reactions.

Classification of adverse drug reactions according to the DoTS system (based on "dose" at which adverse reactions occur relative to the beneficial dose, the "time-course" of the reaction, and individual "susceptibility" factors (*Pref.*); drug names: recommended or proposed international nonproprietary names (rINN or pINN) when available (when not available, chemical names or brand names are used); cross-references; index of drugs, with listing of all references to a drug for which adverse effects and drug interactions have been reported. Also an index of drugs that are covered in the individual monographs. Bibliographic references. Available online via ScienceDirect at: http://www.science direct.com/science/referenceworks/9780444510051

The material for the following related titles, i.e., separate publication and available in both print and also as e-books, has been collected from the 15th edition of this resource:

Meyler's side effects of analgesics and anti-inflammatory drugs; *Meyler's side effects of anti-microbial drugs*; *Meyler's side effects of drugs used in anesthesia*; *Meyler's side effects of drugs used in cancer and immunology*; *Meyler's side effects of cardiovascular drugs*; *Meyler's side effects of endocrine and metabolic drugs*; *Meyler's side effects of herbal medicines*; *Meyler's side effects of psychiatric drugs*.

1219 Remington: The science and practice of pharmacy. Joseph P. Remington. [Philadelphia]: Lippincott Williams and Wilkins, 1995–. ill.
615 13 1558-2922   RS91.R4
First–6th ed. had title: *The practice of pharmacy*; 7th-12th ed., *Remington's practice of pharmacy*; 13th-18th ed., *Remington's pharmaceutical sciences*. Quinquennial.

Description based on 22nd ed., 2013, published by Pharmaceutical Press in collaboration with the Philadelphia College of Pharmacy at University of the Sciences.

Two vols: Vol.1, The science of pharmacy (pts. 1-6); v.2, The practice of pharmacy (pts. 7-10): Pt. 1, "Introduction"; pt. 2, "Pharmaceutical chemistry; pt. 3, "Pharmaceutical analysis and quality control"; pt. 4, "Pharmaceutics"; pt. 5, "Pharmaceutical dosage forms: manufacturing and compounding"; pt. 6, "Pharmacokinetics and pharmacodynamics—Monographs: Pharmaceutical and medicinal agents"; pt. 7, " Fundamentals of pharmacy practice; pt. 8,

"The scope of pharmacy practice "; pt. 9, "Social, behavioral, economic, and administrative sciences"; pt. 10, "Patient care"; Index.

Chapters on history of pharmacy, application of ethical principles to practice dilemmas, medication errors, pharmacogenomics, re-engineering pharmacy practice, specialization in pharmacy practice, emergency patient care, complementary and alternative medical health, and many others. Contains selected Martindale content. Also available as an e-book and online via MedicinesComplete.

Dictionaries

1220 Concise dictionary of pharmacological agents: Properties and synonyms. Ian Morton, Judith Hall. Boston: Kluwer Academic, 1999. viii, 342 p. ISBN 0751404993
615.103   RS51.M67
Based on the three-volume *Dictionary of pharmacological agents*, publ. 1997, it is "a volume encompassing material that hitherto could only be gathered from a well-stocked library"—*Introd.* Provides an A–Z listing of drug names (details on drug names, their alternative names, alternative spellings, alternative chemical forms, with cross-references) and families of pharmacologically active agents. "Appendix A: Glossary" contains approximately 3,000 terms and acronyms; Appendix B consists of tables: (1) amino acid abbreviations (common natural); (2) amino acid abbreviations (found in literature—related and unnatural), and (3) Greek and Latin prefixes. Main articles listed alphabetically in brackets under British Approved Names (BAN), with United States Adopted Name (USAN), Japanese Accepted Name (JAN), and International Nonproprietary Name (INN). Other agents also include standard names in brackets, such as American National Standards Institute (ANSI), British Standards Institution (BSI), and International Standards Organization (ISO). For pharmacologists, medicinal chemists, and graduate students in these areas of research and study and also others in related biomedical sciences. Also available as an e-book.

1221 Dictionary for clinical trials. 2nd ed. Simon Day. Chichester, U.K.; Hoboken,

N.J.: John Wiley & Sons, 2007. xii, 249
p., ill. ISBN 0470058161
610.72/4   R853.C55D39
First ed., 1999.

This rev. and expanded ed. includes definitions for terms and short phrases from a variety of fields (e.g., medicine, statistics, epidemiology, ethics, and others) and from publications related to clinical trials, such as trial protocols, regulatory guidelines, reports, etc. Cross-references, line figures, and graphs. Also available as an e-book.

A more recently published dictionary, available both in print and as an e-book, *Clinical trials dictionary: Terminology and usage recommendations* by Meinert, provides precise terms and clear definitions for the large vocabulary needed to describe the methods and results of clinical trials.

1222 Dictionary of pharmaceutical medicine. http://dx.doi.org/10.1007/978-3-7091-1523-7. Gerhard Nahler, Annette Mollet. Vienna, Austria; New York: Sprigner-Verlag. 2013. 9783709115237
615/.103   RS51
First ed., 1994, 2nd ed., 2009.

"Combines dictionary and lexicon and provides the translational understanding of the complex drug development process."—Foreword. Provides terms and concepts important in pharmaceutical medicine, clinical pharmacology, pharmacotherapy and related areas, such as toxicology, statistics, drug-regulatory & legal affairs and others, including marketing and financial areas. Includes new terms and subtle changes from previous eds. Appendices for acronyms, recommended reading, and useful websites. Considered useful for graduate students, physicians, pharmacists, biologists, chemists, and other professionals. Also available as a print book.

1223 Dictionary of pharmacoepidemiology. Bernard Bégaud. Chichester [England]; New York: Wiley, 2000. x, 171 p. ISBN 0471803618
615.103   RM302.5.B443
English translation of Bernard Bégaud's *Dictionnaire de pharmaco-épidémiologie*, 1998.

Online access available from WileyInterScience Online Books (http://onlinelibrary.wiley.com/book/10.1002/0470842547) and also via netLibrary.

As defined in this dictionary, pharmacoepidemiology is the "study of interactions between drugs and populations, or more specifically, the study of the therapeutic effect(s), risk and use of drugs, usually in large populations, using epidemiology and methods of reasoning," and the work is written for "regulatory authorities, pharmaceutical physicians, lawyers, pharmacists, researchers, evaluators and students"—*Foreword*. Complements epidemiology dictionaries.

1224 A dictionary of pharmacology and allied topics. 2nd ed. D. R. Laurence, John Carpenter. Amsterdam [Netherlands]; New York: Elsevier, 1998. xi, 373 p.
615.103   RS51.L38
First edition, 1994, had title *A dictionary of pharmacology and clinical drug evaluation*.

Includes currently accepted usage for pharmacological terms and relevant terminology from other disciplines (e.g., ethics, law, social policy, statistics), with etymology for most terms, as well as terms used by official regulatory authorities. Does not include individual drugs. Intended for basic and clinical pharmacologists and others involved in clinical drug evaluation.

1225 Dictionary of pharmacovigilance. Amer Alghabban. London; Chicago: Pharmaceutical Press, 2004. ix, 527 p.
615.7042 0853695164   RM302.5.A43
Compilation of the clinical, technical, and regulatory terminology related to pharmacovigilance (or drug monitoring), which can be defined as the detection, assessment, understanding, and prevention of adverse effects of medicines and efforts to minimize risks posed by drugs to patients. International in scope. Entries include drugs, regulatory bodies, and pharmaceutical legislation.

1226 Dictionary of pharmacy. Dennis B. Worthen, Julian H. Fincher. New York: Pharmaceutical Products Press, 2004. xiii, 528 p. ISBN 0789023288
615.103   RS51.D482
Comprehensive list of terms from pharmacy and also terminology relevant to pharmacy from several other disciplines. A–Z arrangement; cross-references

(see, see also, contrast, and compare). In separate sections, includes abbreviations; Latin and Greek terms; weights and measures; practice standards; the code of ethics for pharmacists; and lists of professional associations, organizations, and colleges and schools of pharmacy in the United States and Canada. Resource for pharmacy students, faculty, and practicing pharmacists.

1227 Drugs: Synonyms and properties. 2nd ed.
G. W. A. Milne. Aldershot [England]: Ashgate, 2002. xxi, 1108 p.
ISBN 0566084910

First edition, 2000. "An international guide to 10,000 drugs"—*cover*.

Provides basic drug information. Organized by therapeutic categories, includes drugs, drug synonyms, and trade names. Under each therapeutic category, drugs are listed alphabetically by the U.S. Adopted Names (USAN). For each drug, the following information is included: chemical name, trade name, generic name, synonyms, registry and *Merck index* number, molecular formula, melting and boiling points, various physical properties, manufacturer, and supplier directory. Three indexes: Chemical Abstracts Service (CAS) registry number, European Inventory of Existing Commercial Substances (EINECS) number, and a master index of chemical and proprietary names. Similar in content to other important drug information resources, such as the *Merck index*, *Physicians' desk reference*, and *Organic-chemical drugs and their synonyms*, for example.

1228 Organic-chemical drugs and their synonyms. 9th ed. Martin Negwer, Hans-Georg Scharnow. Weinheim, Germany: Wiley-VCH, 2007. 7 v. (xvii, 5656 p.) 615.19 3527319395

Sixth edition, 1987, is the revised and enlarged ed. and first English translation of *Organisch-chemische Arzneimittel und ihre Synonyme*, 5th ed., 1978; 8th ed., 2001.

The 9th ed. is described by the publisher as a completely revised and extensively enlarged edition.

Contents: v. 1–5, organic-chemical drugs and their synonyms; v. 6, synonym index (pt. 1: A–S); v. 7, synonym index (pt. 2: T–Z); group index; CAS number index.

This edition compiles data on 20,000 drugs, with many newly developed drugs and biopharmaceuticals.

Entries include CAS registry number, structural formula, references, synonyms, and use. Also available as an online database.

1229 Pharmaceutical medicine dictionary.
Amer Alghabban. Edinburgh [Scotland]; New York: Churchill Livingstone, 2001. 390 p. ISBN 044306475X
618.103   RS192.A445

Contains terminology related to pharmaceutical medicine and the drug development and marketing process. Available online via Credo reference.

1230 USP dictionary of USAN and international drug names. United States Pharmacopeial Convention, United States Adopted Names Council. Rockville, Md.: United States Pharmacopeial Convention, 1995–
615.1014 1076-4275   RS55.U54

The United States Adopted Names (USAN) Council, sponsored by the American Medical Association (AMA), the United States Pharmacopeial Convention (USP), and the American Pharmacists Association (APhA), selects appropriate and unique names for drugs. "FDA-recognized, cumulative source of drug USANs."—*Publ. description*. "Prepared under the aegis of the USP Nomenclature, Safety and Labeling Expert Committee."—*Foreword*.

1961–93 had title: *USAN and the USP dictionary of drug names*. 49th ed., 2013 has been published; description based on 48th ed., 2012, "the authorized list of established names for drugs in the United States of America" (*t.p.*), which supersedes the 2011 edition and all earlier editions. Supplements are published bimonthly in the "Nomenclature" section of the *Pharmacopeial forum* (PF), accessible via the USP website at http://www.usp.org/.

A compilation of the United States Adopted Names (USAN) selected and released from June 15, 1961 through January 31, 2012, current USP and NF names for drugs, and other nonproprietary drug names for drugs. It also includes the text previously published in *USAN and the dictionary of drug names*. Comprehensive source of generic and brand drug names. A list of the 177 new proprietary names in this edition is provided on p. 29-31. Arranged alphabetically by generic, trade, or chemical name or drug code designated number. Entries give USAN, year published as USAN, pronunciation, official compendium in which title occurs, molecular formula and weight, chemical names, CAS registry number(s), international nonproprietary name (INN), pharmacologic and/or therapeutic category, brand name(s), manufacturer, drug code designations, and graphic formula. Appendixes include, for example, listings of drugs of brand names for USAN and other nonproprietary names, categories of pharmacological activity, molecular formulas, code designations, and other relevant information. All INNs published by the World Health Organization from the start of the INN program in 1953 through 2012 are included. "Historical note" on p. 1837.

Thesauruses

1231 EMTREE thesaurus. Excerpta Medica (Firm). Amsterdam, Netherlands; New York: Excerpta Medica, 1991–. v. ISBN 09293299

Z699.5.M39E49

Developed from 1974–90, *Master list of medical indexing terms (MALIMET)*; EMTAGS (discont. in 1998) and EMCLAS (i.e., the original subject classification system for EMBASE) integration into EMTREE (1988–91). Annual updates.

Description based on 2008 ed.

Cover title: *EMTREE: the life science thesaurus.* Contents: v. 1, Alphabetical index; v. 2, Tree structure; v. 3, Permuted term index.

Hierarchically structured drug and disease controlled vocabulary used for subject indexing and for searching the biomedical literature (e.g., EMBASE, with "preferred terms" [i.e., drug and medical terms]), synonyms, and MeSH®: Medical Subject Headings (858). Contains a list of EMBASE section headings which, with a few exceptions, correspond to the titles of the Excerpta Medica abstract journals, published since 1947, and searchable in EMBASE since 1974. Also available online.

Directories

1232 World list of pharmacy schools. http://aim.fip.org/world-list-of-pharmacy -schools/. International Pharmaceutical Federation, International Pharmaceutical

Federation (FIP). The Hague: International Pharmaceutical Federation. 2001-

RS103

Also called *Official world list of pharmacy schools*

Publ. by International Pharmaceutical Federation (FIP). Previously maintained and published as a public service by the editor, Dr. David Temple, with the support of the Welsh School of Pharmacy at Cardiff University. Previously published in print, now only published online.

Contains address and other contact information of approximately 120 schools of pharmacy worldwide, listed by country. Entries contain hyperlinks for pharmacy schools that have their own websites.

Handbooks

1233 The ABC clinical guide to herbs. Mark Blumenthal, Josef Brinckmann, Bernd Wollschlaeger. Austin, Tex.: American Botanical Council, 2003. xxx, 480 p., ill. ISBN 1588901572

615.321   RM666.H33.A175

Comprehensive information on 29 popular drugs available in the United States. Each monograph contains primary (supported by clinical trials) and potential uses, dosage, duration of use, pregnancy and lactation guidelines, adverse effects, etc. Also provides background information on herbal medicine, with a brief history of medicinal herbs in North America, legal and regulatory status of herbs and phytomedicines, consumer use, herb safety, etc. Includes bibliographical references and index. Resource for clinicians, researchers, educators, and general readers.

1234 ADA/PDR guide to dental therapeutics. 5th ed. American Dental Association. Chicago: American Dental Association, 2009. xii, 1164 p. ISBN 1563637693

615   RK701

First (1998)–3rd (2003) ed. had title: *ADA guide to dental therapeutics*. The 4th (2006) edition and this edition produced by the American Dental Association (ADA) in partnership with the Physicians' Desk Reference.

Authoritative guide to dental therapeutics, covering brand names and generic drugs. Contains sections on drugs used in dentistry, drugs used in medicine, with treatment considerations for dental patients, and drug issues in dental practice, including oral manifestations of systemic agents. Appendix includes U.S. controlled substances, smoking cessation, and related products.

Other PDR-related titles include *Physicians' desk reference: PDR, PDR drug guide for mental health professionals, PDR guide to drug interactions, side effects, and indications, PDR for herbal medicines, PDR for nonprescription drugs, PDR for nutritional supplements, PDR nurse's drug handbook, Physicians' desk reference for ophthalmic medicines, PDR guide to biological and chemical warfare response, PDR guide to terrorism response,* and other titles. PDR and its major companion volumes are also found in the PDR® Electronic Library.

1235 American Herbal Products Association's botanical safety handbook. 2nd ed. Z. E. Gardner, Michael McGuffin, American Herbal Products Association. Boca Raton, Fla.: American Herbal Products Association, CRC Press, 2013. xxix, 1042 p.
ISBN 9781466516946
615.3/21   RA1250.A45
American Herbal Products Association (AHPA)

This revised edition contains significant modifications from the previous edition. Provides information about botanical products/dietary supplements and their safe use. Medicinal herbs are arranged A-Z by scientific name (*abies balsamea* through *Zanthoxylum spp*), but each record also includes botanical family name, synonym(s), common name(s), also Ayurvedic and pinyin name, and plant part(s) used, summaries and reference lists, safety and interaction classifications, etc. Further details can be found in the "organization of data" chapter. Five appendixes: "Herbal constituent profiles," "Herbal action profiles," "Herbal interaction profiles," "Safety of botanicals in pregnancy and lactation," and "Herb listings by classification." For health care professionals, members of the public, and others interested in the safety and potential interactions of herbal products. For graduate students, faculty, researchers; and also general readers. Also available as an e-book.

First ed., 1997

Since this handbook does not cover the uses of herbal preparations, other resources would need to be consulted. Recommended resources are, for example, *Handbook of medicinal herbs, Weiss's herbal medicine,* and *Principles and practice of phytotherapy{/record}* (2012).

1236 APhA's immunization handbook. 2nd ed. Lauren B. Angelo, American Pharmacists Association. Washington: American Pharmacists Association, 2012. xi, 253 p.
ISBN 9781582121659
614.4/70973   RA638.A54
APhA (American Pharmacists Association).
First ed., 2010.

Contents: Program development and management; Immunization administration and deliver options; Safety measures; Enhanced roles and responsibility; Immunization and vaccine product information

Comprehensive handbook/guide on immunization, considered a requisite for pharmacists involved in immunizations. Includes, for example, a complete vaccine product listing and suggested schedule for administration, vaccine reminder systems, travel health and vaccination clinics, management of emergencies, etc. Online content for this edition is available through APhA's subscription-based Pharmacy Library portal at http://www.pharmacylibrary.com/resource/25.

See also "Healthy people 2020 summary of objectives re immunization and infectious diseases" at http://www.healthypeople.gov/2020/topicsobjectives2020/pdfs/Immunizati on.pdf.

1237 A to Z drug facts. St. Louis: Facts and Comparisons, 1999–
                                              RM301.12.A2
      Eighth ed., 2007.

Alphabetically organized drug reference. Drug monographs with pharmacological and patient care information. Includes action of the drug, indications, dosage, adverse reactions, interactions, side effects, laboratory test interference, etc. No longer published in print. The online version, "A-Z drug facts™ module," is part of {record}Facts & comparisons eAnswers.

1238 Botanical medicines: The desk reference for major herbal supplements. 2nd ed. Dennis J. McKenna, Kenneth Jones, Kerry Hughes, Sheila Humphrey. New York: Haworth

Herbal Press, 2002. xx, 1138 p., ill.
ISBN 0789012650
615.32   RM258.5.M38
Rev. ed. of *Natural dietary supplements*, 1998.

Comprehensive coverage of 34 commonly used herbal products. Each herb monograph covers scientific name, family name, common name, historical perspective, traditional uses, therapeutic applications, clinical studies, recommended doses, safety concerns, contraindications, drug interactions, and pregnancy and lactation. Two appendixes review the quality of herbal supplements and the key provisions of the Dietary Supplement Health and Education Act (DSHEA). Index. Written for health care professionals and also useful to consumers. Also available as an e-book.

1239 Burger's medicinal chemistry, drug discovery and development. 7th ed.
Donald J. Abraham, David P. Rotella, Alfred Burger. Hoboken, N.J.: Wiley, 2010. 8 v., ill. (some col.)
ISBN 9780470278154
615/.19   RS403.B8
First ed., 1951, to 4th ed., 1980–1, had title *Medicinal chemistry*. 5th ed., 1995–7; 6th ed., 2003.

Contents: v. 1 and 2, "Drug discovery"; v. 3, "Drug development"; v. 4, "Cardiovascular, endocrine and metabolic diseases"; v. 5, "Pulmonary, bone, vitamins and autocoid therapeutic agents"; v. 6, "Cancer"; v. 7, "Antiinfectives"; v. 8, "Central nervous systems disorders."

Updated and expanded edition. Comprehensive resource for information on drug studies and drug research, with the latest developments in medicinal drug research and drug development. Includes high priority areas and subjects, such as molecular modeling in drug design, virtual screening, bioinformatics, chemical information computing systems in drug discovery, structural biology of drug action, etc. Bibliographical references and index. For libraries serving medicinal chemists, pharmaceutical professionals, and other scientists. Also available as an e-book.

1240 Catalog of teratogenic agents. 13th ed.
Thomas H Shepard. Baltimore: Johns Hopkins University Press, 2010. xxvii, 576 p. ISBN 9780801897849
616/.043   QM691.S53

First edition, [1973]; 11th ed., 2004; 12th ed., 2007.

Title varies. Also referred to as *Shepard's catalog of teratogenic agents*; *Shepard's catalog*.

Teratology can be defined as the study of the adverse effects of drugs on the fetus. This scholarly and professional resource covers information on chemicals, food additives, household products, environmental pollutants, pharmaceuticals, and viruses as well as fetal exposure to these various agents. Also includes gene mutations that can cause congenital defects. Alphabetically arranged by chemical name, lists synonyms and CAS registry numbers. Author index; agent index.

1241 Clarke's analysis of drugs and poisons: In pharmaceuticals, body fluids and postmortem material.
4th ed. Anthony C. Moffat, M. David Osselton, B. Widdop, Jo Watts. London: Pharmaceutical Press, 2011. 2 v., ill.
ISBN 97808536697
First edition, 1969–75, 2nd ed., 1986, 3rd ed., 2004.

Contents: v. 1, pt. 1: 44 chapters (methodology and analytical techniques); Subject index; v. 2, pt. 2: 2,100 monographs (physical properties, analytical methods, pharmacokinetic data, ultraviolet, infrared and mass spectra, therapeutic and toxicity data of drugs and poisons); pt. 3: Indexes of analytical data; Subject index.

This revised and expanded edition, with more than 350 additional monographs since the last edition, provides analytical procedures used in analytical toxicology and data for drugs and poisons as well as applications of these techniques in areas such as forensic toxicology, workplace drug testing, drug abuse in sports, pesticide poisoning, and others. Drug and poison monographs provide physical properties, analytical methods, pharmacokinetic data, and toxicity data. Ultraviolet, infrared and mass spectra are included within the monographs, as well as therapeutic and toxicity data of drugs and poisons. Indexes of analytical data include, for example, CAS numbers, molecular formulas, therapeutic classes, color tests, molecular weights, melting points, thin-layer chromatographic data, gas chromatographic (GC) data, high-performance liquid chromatographic (HPLC) data, ultraviolet absorption maxima, infrared peaks, mass spectral data of drugs and pesticides, reagents, and pharmacological terms. Subject index covering both volumes at the end of v. 1 as well as v. 2. An essential resource, intended for use primarily by forensic toxicologists, pathologists, and other scientists and students in these areas of study. Available online as part of MedicinesComplete.

Clarke's analytical forensic toxicology (2nd ed., 2013) is based on the content of v.1 of *Clarke's analysis of drugs and poisons*. It is intended as a text for undergraduate and graduate student use, *Clarke's analysis of drugs and poisons* is a reference resource for professional toxicologists.

1242 Clinical pharmacology. http://www .clinicalpharmacology.com/. Elsevier/ Gold Standard. Tampa, Fla.: Gold Standard. 199?–

RM301.28

Produced by Elsevier/Gold Standard (http://www .goldstandard.com/).

Provides concise drug monographs for U.S. prescription drugs, herbal and nutritional supplements, over-the-counter products, and new and investigational drugs; overviews of various drug classes; and various search capabilities (e.g., by generic name, indication, contraindication, and therapeutic classification). Allows for the creation of a variety of customized reports. Includes patient handouts written by pharmacists. Considered a helpful tool for pharmacists, physicians, and other health professionals.

1243 The complete German Commission E monographs. Mark. Blumenthal, Werner R. Busse, Bundesinstitut für Arzneimittel und Medizinprodukte (Germany). Austin, Tex.; Boston: American Botanical Council; Integrative Medicine Communications, 1998. xxii, 685 p. ISBN 096555550X
615.321   RM666.H33.C67

Commissioned by the American Botanical Council (ABC), English translation of the monographs from the original German monographs of the Commission E, a German government special expert committee established in 1978 to evaluate the safety and efficacy of herbs and herbal products on the market in Germany.

Contents: pt. 1, "Introduction"; pt.2, "Monographs"; pt. 3, "Therapeutic indexes"; pt. 4,

"Chemical and taxonomic indexes"; pt. 5, "European regulatory literature"; pt. 6, appendix.

Contains a lists of monographs by approval status, approved and unapproved herbs and herbal combinations. A typical entry contains the name, composition, and actions of the drug and its uses, contraindications, side effects, interactions with other drugs, dosage, and mode of administration. Chemical glossary and index; taxonomic cross-reference by English common name, botanical name, and pharmacopoeial name; excerpts for the German and European pharmacopoeias; and the European Economic Community (EEC) standards for quality of of herbal remedies. Appendix includes, for example, abbreviations and symbols, weights and measures, publication dates of Commission E monographs, list of European Scientific Cooperative on Phytotherapy (ESCOP) monographs, and list of World Health Organization (WHO) monographs. For use by pharmacists, physicians, and other health professionals; researchers; and health consumers. A related title, also edited by Mark Blumenthal, is *Herbal medicine: Expanded Commission E monographs.*

1244 The complete guide to medical writing. Mark Stuart. London; Chicago: Pharmaceutical Press, 2007. 491 p. ISBN 0853696675
808.06661   R119

Contents: sec. 1, "Medical writing essentials"; sec. 2, "Reviews and reports"; sec. 3, "Medical journalism and mass media"; sec. 4, "Medical writing in education"; sec. 5, "Medical writing for medical professionals"; sec. 6, "Medical publishing"; appendixes: (1) "Common medical abbreviations"; (2) "Measurements"; (3) "Normal values for common laboratory tests"; (4) "Proof correction marks"; (5) "A to Z of medical terms in plain English."

Covers aspects of scientific and medical writing, medical journalism, and medical publishing. Resource for medical professionals and students to provide help with writing, communicating, and presenting scientific and medical information clearly and accurately, with examples from the pharmaceutical sciences. Covers copyright and patient confidentiality. For authors and editors. Also available as an e-book.

1245 Comprehensive medicinal chemistry II. David J . . . Triggle, John Taylor.

Amsterdam, Netherlands: Elsevier, 2007.
8 v., ill. (some col.), ports. (some col.)
ISBN 0080445136
First edition, 1990.

Description based on rev. and expanded edition.

Contents: v. 1, *Global perspective* (P. Kennewell); v. 2, *Research and development* (W.H. Moos); v. 3, *Technologies* (H. Kubinyi); v. 4, *Computer-assisted drug design* (J.S. Mason); v. 5, *ADME-Tox approaches* (B. Testa and H. van de Waterbeemd); v. 6, *Therapeutic areas I* (M. Williams); v. 7, *Therapeutic areas II* (J. Plattner and M.C. Desai); v. 8, *Case histories and cumulative subject index* (J.B. Taylor and D.J. Triggle).

Comprehensive reference resource on medicinal chemistry and drug research. Includes recent changes in genomics, proteomics, bioinformatics, combinatorial chemistry, high-throughput technologies, computer-assisted design, and other areas of high current interest. Intended mainly for scientists in the pharmaceutical sciences and biotechnology and for science and medical libraries. Also available online via ScienceDirect at http://www.sciencedirect.com/science/referenceworks/9780080450445.

1246 Desk reference to nature's medicine.
Steven Foster, Rebecca L. Johnson.
Washington: National Geographic
Society, 2006. 416 p., col. ill.
ISBN 0792236661
615.321   RS164.F698

A–Z listing of 150 medicinal plants, arranged by common standard name, with Latin name also provided. Information about each plant includes a detailed description, its habitat, distribution, current and traditional uses, history, folklore, toxicity, etc. Includes color photographs, botanical drawings, range maps. Includes essays on the medicinal plants of Africa, Australia and New Zealand, Central and South America, China, Europe, India, North America, the Middle East, and Oceania. Glossary, Latin name index, and subject index. Intended for general readers. Complements information found, for example, in *The complete German Commission E monographs*, *Herbal medicine: Expanded Commission E monographs* (Integrative Medicine Communications), and *PDR for herbal medicines*.

1247 Dietary supplements. 4th ed. Pamela
Mason. London; Chicago: Pharmaceutical

Press, 2012. 573 p.
ISBN 9780853698838
613.28   RM258.5

Title and imprint varies: 1st ed., 1995, had title *Handbook of dietary supplements: Vitamins and other supplements*; 2nd ed., 2001; 3rd ed., 2007.

This comprehensive resource covers the most commonly used vitamins, minerals, and dietary supplements in the United States, the United Kingdom, and Europe. Includes information on interactions with drugs. For pharmacists and other health professionals. Includes bibliographical references and index. Also available as an e-book.

1248 Drug facts and comparisons. Facts
and Comparisons. St. Louis: Wolters
Kluwer Health, 1982–
615.1 0277-9714   RM300.F33

Volumes from 1953–81 had title *Facts and comparisons*. *Drug Facts and Comparisons* adapted from Facts and Comparisons loose-leaf drug information service. Description based on "*Drug facts and comparisons 2013*," 67th ed., 2012.

Comprehensive drug information, intended as a reference source for health professionals. This edition incorporates 26 new drugs (cf. *Pref*). Organized by therapeutic use (14 chapters, e.g., nutrients and nutritional agents; hematologic agents, respiratory agents, central nervous system agents, gastrointestinal agents, and others), with each entry (monograph) giving detailed information and facilitating comparisons of different drugs with similar uses. A typical entry includes indications, administration and dosage, actions, contraindications, warnings and precautions, drug interactions, adverse reactions, overdosage treatment, and essential patient information. A "Keeping up" section provides information on new developments concerning orphan drugs and investigational drugs. Several appendixes include, for example: FDA new drug classification; Controlled substances; FDA pregnancy categories; Treatment guidelines; Normal laboratory values, and others. Index (generic names, brand names, group names, also synonyms, pharmacological actions, and therapeutic uses); manufacturer/distributors listing. Index lists generic names, brand names, and group names, many synonyms, pharmacological actions, and therapeutic uses for the agents included in this edition.

Available in electronic format as part of a Web-based version entitled Facts and Comparisons 4.0

Online, which also makes available several additional drug information resources.

1249 Drug information handbook. North American ed. Charles F. Lacy, Laura Armstron, Morton Goldman, Leonard Lance, Lexi-Comp, Inc., American Pharmaceutical Association. Hudson, Ohio; Washington: Lexi-Comp, Inc.; American Pharmaceutical Association, 1994–

615 1533-4511   RM301.12.D783

Publ. in cooperation with the Amer. Pharmacists Assoc. (APhA).

First ed., 1993/94. Available in North Amer. and internat. editions. Description based on 19th ed., 2010. Subtitle: A comprehensive resource for all clinicians and healthcare professionals. The 22nd ed.(2013) is the most recent edition available.

(Lexi-Comp's clinical reference library).

Concise, comprehensive, and user-friendly drug reference. Alphabetical listing of drug monographs, with new drugs and updates to monographs since the last edition. Includes detailed information in consistent format, such as dosage, drug interactions, adverse reactions (by occurrence, overdose, and toxicology), etc., with warnings highlighted. Appendix. Pharmacologic category index. For clinicians and healthcare professionals.

Several other comprehensive print pharmacology handbooks, also published by Lexi-Comp and frequently updated, include *Anesthesiology and critical care drug handbook* (1999– ; 10th ed., 2011); *Drug information handbook for nursing* (1998-; 14th ed., 2012); *Drug information handbook for advanced practice nursing* (1990– , 11th ed., 2010); *Drug information handbook for dentistry* (1996- ; 18th ed., 2012); *Drug information handbook for oncology* (2000- ; 11th ed., 2013); *Drug information handbook for psychiatry: A comprehensive reference of psychotropic, nonpsychotropic, and herbal agents* (1999- ; 7th ed., 2009); *Drug information handbook for the allied health professional* (1995- ; 12th ed., 2005); *Drug information handbook with international trade names index* (21st ed., 2012); *Geriatric dosage handbook* (1993- ; 18th ed., 2012); *Infectious diseases handbook: Including antimicrobial therapy & diagnostic test/procedures* (1994- ; 6th ed., 2006); *Natural therapeutics pocket guide* (2000- , 2nd ed., 2003); *Pediatric dosage handbook* (1992- ; 18th ed., 2011); and *Pharmacogenomics handbook* (2003- ; 2nd ed., 2006). Also available online as pt. of Lexi-Comp Online™ (http://webstore.lexi.com/Store/ONLINE).

1250 Drug interaction facts. David S. Tatro, Facts and Comparisons. St. Louis: Facts and Comparisons, 1988–

615.7045 0899-4951   RM302.D76

Description based on 2013 ed., edited by David S. Tatro.

Presents drug–drug and drug–food interactions. Drug interaction monographs are arranged alphabetically according to the principal drug affected. Interactions are assigned a significance rating between 1 and 5 (1=major, potentially severe effects; 5=minor effects), presented in three categories, i.e., onset, severity, and documentation. Each monograph has the following sections: Interacting drugs (including generic and trade names), clinical significance, effects, mechanisms and management, and discussion, with primary literature references. Indexed by generic, class, and trade names. Clinically significant interactions are identified in the index. Intended for health care professionals and pharmacists. Also available electronically through Facts and Comparisons 4.0 Online.

Drug interaction facts: Herbal supplements and food by Tatro is a companion volume; since 2005 also available in electronic format via Facts and Comparisons 4.0 Online.

A similar resource by the same publisher, published in loose-leaf and bound formats for many years, is Hansten and Horn's *Drug interactions: Analysis and management.* Several other Facts and Comparisons bound products include *A to Z drug facts, American drug index, ImmunoFacts, Ophthalmic drug facts, The review of natural products* edited by DerMarderosian et al., and others.

1251 Drug interactions: Analysis and management. Philip D. Hansten, John R. Horn. St. Louis: Wolters Kluwer Health, 2007–

RM302.D793

Description based on the 2010 edition. Also referred to as DIAM. "Adapted from Hansten and Horn's drug interactions analysis and management loose-leaf information service through the January 2010 update." Eight ed. (2013) is available.

Provides an analysis of the clinical importance of drug interactions and consideration of potential harm (with assigned "significance" numbers: 1 = avoid combination, 2 = usually avoid combination, 3 = minimize risk, 4 = no action needed, and 5 = no interaction). Includes prescription and nonprescription drugs as well as herbal medicines, with management options for each interaction. Not included are drugs of abuse and drugs used in anesthesiology. Bibliographical references and index, with generic drug names, class names, and trade names. Written for the use of health care providers who "prescribe, dispense, or administer medications."—*Pref.*

1252 Drugs in pregnancy and lactation: A reference guide to fetal and neonatal risk. Gerald G. Briggs. Baltimore: Williams and Wilkins, 1983–
618.32071
0897-6112   RG627.6.D79D798
Description based on 9th ed., 2011.

This updated edition summarizes data on specific drugs. Arranged in alphabetical order, each drug monograph provides the U.S. generic name, pharmacologic class, risk factor, fetal risk summary, breast feeding summary, and references, where available. Lists drugs which are contraindicated during breastfeeding, during pregnancy, and also drugs which cause human developmental toxicity. Three changes in format in this edition (cf. *Preface*): The FDA's risk categories, previously included (since 1979 when they first appeared), have been removed. Furthermore, information on drugs that are no longer available has been removed, i.e., drugs are still listed with the notation "withdrawn from the market see 8th edition." Another change is the addition to the index of prescription combination drugs; they are listed by trade name with the names of the individual drugs mentioned in the text. An appendix arranges the drugs by pharmacologic category, allowing comparison of drugs within the same pharmacologic class to determine different risk factors. Written for clinicians caring for pregnant women. Also available as an e-book.

Other resources are *Drugs for pregnant and lactating women* by Weiner, and *Drugs during pregnancy and lactation* by Schaefer. An online resource, Lact-Med (part of TOXNET) (http://toxnet.nlm.nih.gov/),

is a web-based peer-reviewed database with information on drugs and lactation.

1253 The 5-minute herb and dietary supplement consult. Adriane Fugh-Berman. Philadelphia: Lippincott Williams & Wilkins, 2003. xv, 475 p. ISBN 0683302736
615.321   RM666.H33.F835
Ready-reference resource, arranged alphabetically by botanical or dietary supplement, with Latin and biological names. Entries include concise description, appropriate dosage, pharmacokinetics, drug interactions, risks, etc.

For academic medical and public libraries.

1254 Guide to popular natural products. 3rd ed. Facts and Comparisons. St. Louis: Facts and Comparisons, 2003. xi, 367 p., col. ill.
615.321   RM666.H33.G85
First edition, 1999; 2nd ed., 2001.

Abridged from *The review of natural products*. Includes "more than 125 of the most commonly used herbs and natural products . . . each fully referenced and peer-reviewed"—*Publ. notes*. Alphabetical listing of products, with common names, patient information, references, and brief sections on botany, history, pharmacology, and toxicology. Color photographs, charts, and sources of natural product information. Index.

1255 Handbook of contemporary neuropharmacology. David Robert Sibley, Israel Hanin, Michael Kuhar, Phil Skolnick. Hoboken, N.J.: John Wiley & Sons, 2007. 3 v. ISBN 9780471660
615.78   RM315.H3434
Contents: (1) "Basic neuropharmacology"; (2) "Mood disorders"; (3) "Anxiety and stress disorders"; (4) "Schizophrenia and psychosis"; (5) "Substance abuse and addictive disorders"; (6) "Pain"; (7) "Sleep and arousal"; (8) "Development and developmental disorders"; (9) "Neurodegenerative and seizure disorders"; (10) "Neuroimmunology"; (11) "Eating and metabolic disorders."

Reference for nervous system neuropharmacology, with recent advances in neuropharmacology, drug development and therapy, and treatment of various diseases and conditions. Reference for graduate students, physicians and other health professionals, and researchers. A useful resource for academic and special libraries libraries. Also available online via Wiley InterScience (http://www.inter science.wiley.com/reference/hcn). Includes index.

1256 Handbook of drug-nutrient interactions. 2nd ed. Joseph I. Boullata, Vincent T. Armenti, Gil Hardy. New York: Humana Press, 2010. xxvii, 818 p., ill. ISBN 9781603273633

RM302.4.H355

First ed., 2004.

(Nutrition and health.)

Contents: Pt. I, "Approaching drug-nutrient interactions"; pt. II, "Influence of nutrition status on drug disposition and effect"; pt. III, "Influence of food, nutrients, or supplementation on drug disposition and effect."

Compilation of detailed information on both the scientific basis and the clinical relevance of drug-nutrient interactions, with recommendations for healthcare professionals to possibly better manage their patients who may be affected by these types of interactions. Also available as an e-book.

1257 Handbook of medicinal herbs. 2nd ed. James A. Duke, Mary Jo Bogenschutz-Godwin, Judi duCellier, Peggy-Ann K. Duke. Boca Raton, Fla.: CRC Press, 2002. 870 p., ill. (some col.) ISBN 0849312841

615.321   QK99.A1.D83

Publ. in 1985 under the title *CRC handbook of medicinal herbs.*

Provides well-documented information for 800 plant species having medicinal or folk medicinal uses. All entries include the species' scientific name and authority, the scientific name of the plant family, and one or two colloquial or common names. Most entries have four sections giving uses, folk medicinal applications, chemistry, and toxicity. Most plants are illustrated. Extensive tables, bibliography, and index. Also available as an e-book.

1258 Handbook of non-prescription drugs. American Pharmaceutical Association. Washington: American Pharmaceutical Association, 1967–. ill.

615.105 0889-7816   RS250.N66

Title varies: *Handbook of nonprescription drugs: An*

interactive approach to self-care. Description based on 17th ed., 2012.

Contents: sec. I, "The practitioner's role in self-care"; sec. II, "Pain and fever disorders"; sec. III, "Reproductive and genital disorders"; sec. IV, "Respiratory disorders"; sec. V, "Gastrointestinal disorders"; sec. VI, "Nutrition and nutritional supplementation"; sec. VII, "Ophthalmic, otic, and oral disorders"; sec. VIII, "Dermatologic disorders"; sec. IX, "Other medical disorders"; sec. X "Home medical equipment"; sec. XI, "Complementary therapies"; appendix I, "Pregnancy and lactation risk categories for selected nonprescription medications and nutritional supplements"; appendix II, "Safety issues with the use of selected natural products in pregnancy."

A compilation of facts on home remedies in 52 chapters with broad headings, such as asthma, diabetes mellitus, headache, musculoskeletal injuries and disorders, sexually transmitted infections, multicultural aspects of self-care, etc. Each chapter discusses the etiology of the condition; the anatomy, physiology, and pathophysiology of the affected systems; the signs and symptoms; the treatment and adjunctive measures; an evaluation of ingredients in over-the-counter products; and important patient and product considerations. Bibliographic references at the end of each chapter. Subject index. Useful for pharmacists, other health professionals, and consumers. Online content for the 17th edition is available through the subscription-based PhamacyLibrary portal (http://www.pharmacylibrary.com).

1259 Handbook of pharmaceutical excipients. 7th ed. Raymond C. Rowe, Paul J. Sheskey, Walter G. Cook, Marian E. Fenton. London; Philadelphia; Washington: Pharmaceutical Press ; American Pharmacists Association, 2012. xxviii, 1033 p., ill. ISBN 9781582121697

615.19   RS201.E87

First edition, 1986; 6th ed., 2009.

Comprehensive guide to the physical and chemical properties, uses, and safety of pharmaceutical excipients. Alphabetical arrangement. Cross-references and index, with listings of excipients by chemical, nonproprietary, or trade name. Includes comments by contributors. Several appendixes, including a "suppliers directory," a "list of monographs by functional category," and several others.

Also available online as part of MedicinesComplete (online version has title *Pharmaceutical excipients*).

1260 Handbook on injectable drugs.
> Lawrence A. Trissel, American Society of Hospital Pharmacists, American Society of Health-System Pharmacists. Bethesda, Md.: American Society of Hospital Pharmacists, 1977–
> 615.13 1544-1059   RM143.H36

Available in print and online versions. Description based on print version of the 17th ed., 2012.

Intended for use as a professional reference and guide to the literature on the clinical pharmaceutics of parenteral medications. Provides information on "accurate and appropriate" uses of drug therapy and important safety considerations.—*(Publ. note)* Incl. 332 drug monographs, listed alphabetically by nonproprietary name; cross-reference monographs incl. *AHFS drug information*®, administration, stability, brand names, and four compatibility tables for each drug.

Available online as part of MedicinesComplete. Also available in an interactive format for either computer or various mobile devices, ASHP's *Interactive handbook on injectable drugs: IV decision support*. For further information see http://store.ashp.org/default.aspx?TabId=190.

1261 Herbal drugs and phytopharmaceuticals: A handbook for practice on a scientific basis. 3rd ed.
> Max Wichtl, Josef A. Brinckmann, Michael P. Lindenmaier, F.-C. Czygan. Stuttgart [Germany]; Boca Raton, Fla.: Medpharm; CRC Press, 2004. xliii, 704 p., ill. (some col.) ISBN 3887631005
> RM666.H33.T43813

First edition, 1994; 2nd ed., 2001. Third edition edited and translated from the 2nd German ed. by Norman Grainger Bisset; German edition edited by Max Wichtl.

Translation of the revised and expanded 4th ed. of Max Wichtl's *Teedrogen und Phytopharmaka*.

Describes various aspects of herbal drugs used in tea preparation and phytopharmaceuticals. Includes 212 herbal drugs. Monographs have uniform structure. Each monograph contains Latin and English names, the pharmacopoeia to which a drug officially belongs, illustration, description, pharmacological names, plant source, synonyms, origin, constitutents, storage, and references. Includes British, Canadian, and U.S. regulation for herbal products. Several indexes. For pharmacists, physicians, food scientists, and students.

1262 Herbal medicine: Expanded Commission E monographs. Mark Blumenthal, Alicia Goldberg, Joseph Brinckmann. Newton, Mass.: Integrative Medicine Communications, 2000. 519 p. ISBN 0967077214
> RM666.H33

Based on *The complete German Commission E monographs*, this edition contains expanded monographs, color photographs, and more information about chemistry, pharmacology, dosage, administration, etc. Includes a comparison chart of leading herbal brands.

1263 Herbal medicines: A guide for healthcare professionals. 3rd ed.
> Joanne Barnes, Linda Anderson, J. Phillipson, Carol A. Newall. London; Chicago: Pharmaceutical Press, 2007. 710 p. ISBN 0853696233
> 615.321   RM666.H33

First edition, 1996; 2nd ed., 2002.

This revised and rewritten edition includes 152 herbal monographs. Describes phytochemical, pharmacological, and clinical aspects of each herb. Each monograph provides species, family, synonym(s), part(s) used, pharmacopeial and other monograph references, etc. Includes chemical structure drawings, color photographs, and a directory of product names and suppliers. Quality, safety, and legal requirements are addressed. Includes an overview of U.K. and European legislation concerning herbal products. Appendixes group herbs by their specific actions. Bibliographical references and index. Also available as a book and CD-ROM package and online as part of MedicinesComplete. A new edition (4th ed., 2013, print and onine access) is available.

1264 An illustrated Chinese materia medica.
> Jing-Nuan Wu. New York: Oxford University Press, 2005. 706 p., col. ill.

ISBN 0195140176

615.320951   RS180.C5.W785

Contents: introduction (including a history and theory of traditional Chinese medicine and modern research on Chinese medicinal herbs); illustrated materia medica (p. 31–669); appendix; selected bibliography; glossary; Latin (pharmaceutical) name index; English name index.

Alphabetical listing of medicinal materials (herbs, plants, and animal parts). Each entry includes a color illustration and follows the same outline format, providing a description under the following subheadings: Latin (pharmaceutical) name; English name; part used; flavor, property, and channel tropism; functions; clinical use and major combinations; dosage and administration; and precautions. Also available as an e-book.

1265 Illustrated manual of nursing practice. 3rd ed. Lippincott Williams & Wilkins. Philadelphia: Lippincott Williams & Wilkins, 2002. xiii, 1490 p., ill. ISBN 1582550824

610.73   RT41.I44

First edition, 1991; 2nd ed., 1994.

Updated and rev. edition.

Overview of all areas of nursing practice, clinical assessments, and intervention. Presents information according to the nursing process and body systems. Includes ethical and legal issues as well as complementary or alternative therapies. Appendixes on infection control, normal laboratory test values, common antibiotics, dangerous drug interactions, and therapeutic drug-monitoring guidelines. Index.

1266 Litt's drug eruptions & reactions manual: D.E.R.M. Jerome Z. Litt. New York: Informa Healthcare, 2010-. col. ill.

RL801

Title varies: Print editions from 1990s to 2003 had title *Drug eruption reference manual*; 2004-2009 (10th-15th ed.), *Litt's drug eruption reference manual including drug interactions*. Accompanied by CD-ROM. Updated annually. Description based on 18th ed., 2012; 19th ed., 2013 (*Litt's D.E.R.M.: Drug eruptions and reacting manual*) is available.

Contents: Introduction; Drug profiles A-Z; Descriptions of important reactions; Drugs that cause reactions; Index of synonyms and trade names.

This internationally recognized clinical reference guide provides information on adverse drug reactions (ADRs), side effects, and drug interactions to assist with diagnosis of skin eruptions caused by medications, including prescription and over the counter medications, biologics, and supplements. In alphabetical order by medication name, lists ADRs (skin, hair, nails, eyes, central nervous system and other body or organ systems) and describes common reaction patterns to certain drugs, drug-drug interactions, etc. Cross-references by drug and trade names. References. Written for dermatologists and other health professionals. Also available as an e-book.

Available to subscribers as an online database (Litt's D.E.R.M database, formerly: Litt's drug eruption global database http://www.drugeruptiondata.com/), regularly updated with new drugs, references, drug interactions, and reaction patterns and is searchable by drug names, drug reactions, drug categories, drug interactions, and drug combinations. A mobile version is also available (http://www.drugeruptiondata.com/info/index/type/mobile).

1267 Medicinal plants of the world: An illustrated scientific guide to important medicinal plants and their uses. Ben-Erik Van Wyk, Michael Wink. Portland, Ore.: Timber Press, 2004. 480 p., ill. (some col.) ISBN 0881926027

615.321   RS164.V295

Contents: "Medicine systems of the world"; "Plant parts used"; "Dosage forms"; "Use of medicinal plant products"; "Active ingredients"; "Quality control and safety"; "Efficacy of medicinal plant products"; "Regulation of herbal remedies and phytomedicines"; "The plants in alphabetical order"; "Health disorders and medicinal plants"; "Overview of secondary metabolites and their effects"; "Quick guide to commercialized medicinal plants."

Guide to 320 plants with color photos, alphabetically arranged by scientific name, with mention of common names in several different languages. Contains a "quick guide" chart with 900 plants, providing species, family, and common names, place of origin, plant parts used, related medicinal systems (African, Ayurvedic, Chinese, or European), and main indications. Chapter that cross-references indications to their main botanical therapies. Medicinal use by governmental bodies in pharmacopoeias is mentioned. Glossary, list for further reading, and general index. Written for general readers. A comparable title is *Herbal drugs and phytopharmaceuticals: A handbook for practice on a scientific basis*.

1268 MedicinesComplete. http://www
.medicinescomplete.com. Royal
Pharmaceutical Society of Great
Britain. London: Pharmaceutical Press.
2000– 610

Provides online access to the following drug information sources published by Pharmaceutical Press: *AHFS drug information*; *BNF for children*; *British national formulary*; *Clarke's analysis of drugs and poisons* by Moffat et al.; *Dietary supplements*; *Herbal medicines*; *Handbook on injectable drugs*; *Martindale: The complete drug reference*; *Pharmaceutical excipients* (print ed. has title *Handbook of pharmaceutical excipients*) by Rowe et al., *Remington: The science and practice of pharmacy*, *Stockley's drug interactions*, *Stockley's interaction alerts*, and more.

1269 Merck Index Online. http://www.rsc
.org/publishing/merckindex/index.asp.
Maryadele J. O'Neill, Patricia E.
Heckelman, Peter H. Dobbelaar, Kristin
J. Roman, Catherine M. Kenny, Linda
S. Karaffa, Royal Society of Chemistry
(Great Britain). Cambridge, U.K.: Royal
Society of Chemistry.
ISBN 9781849736701

RS51

Concise descriptions of more than 11,500 organic and inorganic chemicals, drugs, and biological substances, chosen for inclusion on the basis of their importance. Entries give formulas, alternate names, physical properties, CAS Registry Numbers, uses, toxicity, and journal and patent references. Includes links to ChemSpider records. Reference tables provide handy PDFs of common abbreviations, amino acids, common heterocyclic ring systems, nonproprietary name stems, radioactive isotopes, minerals, conversion factors, and more.

Basic search options include chemical and trademark names, CAS Registry Number and manufacturer, and properties such as molecular formula or weight. Also supports chemical structure and substructure searching and an Organic Named Reactions search. Downloadable image and mol

files. Users may create an RSC-ID to save queries, records, and lists.

First ed., 1989; 14th ed., 2006. Subtitle varies.

The 15th edition is available as an online database exclusively through the Royal Society of Chemistry; older editions are available as e-books. Also available in print.

1270 Mosby's dental drug reference.
Tommy W. Gage, Frieda Atherton Pickett.
St. Louis: Mosby, 1994–
615.10246176   RK701.M58

Description based on 9th ed., 2010; 10th ed., 2012, is available both in print and also as en e-book.

Contents: Therapeutic management of common oral lesions; Medically compromised patients; Individual drug monographs; Appendixes: (A) Abbreviations; (B) Aesthetics; (C) Combination drugs by trade names; (D) Controlled substances chart; (E) Disorders and conditions; (F) Drugs associated with dry mouth; (G) Drugs that affect taste; (H) Complementary and alternative medications and dietary supplements; (I) Pregnancy and pediatrics; (J) Preventing medication errors and improving medication safety; (K) Oral contraceptives; Generic and trade name index.

Alphabetical arrangement of drugs that dental patients may be taking, listed by generic name and indexed by brand name, with drug monograph information presented in a consistent format. Provides information on side effects, precautions, contraindications, and drug interactions. Also includes alternative therapies. Therapeutic and pharmacologic index. Accompanied by CD-ROM that contains color images of conditions resulting from drugs patients are taking, and also customizable patient handouts. The 9th ed. includes 33 new drugs approved by the FDA since the last edition. Intended for dental professionals, but also useful for health consumers. Ready-reference appendixes provide additional drug-related information. Also available as an e-book.

**1271 Mosby's drug reference for health
professions. 4th ed.** Maryanne
Hochadel. St. Louis, Mo.: Elsevier, 2014.
viii, 1736 p. ISBN 9780323077378
615/.1   RM301.12.H63

First edition, 2006 had title: *Mosby's drug consult for health professions*; 3rd ed., 2012.

"Designed as a concise, easy to use resource

for drug information for the busy healthcare professional . . . essential drug information in a user-friendly format."—*Introd*. Alphabetic listing of entries by generic name. Drug entries, with detailed explanation in the introduction, include generic & brand name; category & schedule; classification; mechanisms of action; pharmacokinetics; availability, indications & dosages; contraindications; interactions; diagnostic test effects; IV incompatibilities; side effects; serious reactions; precautions & considerations; storage; administrations. Appendixes (A)"FDA pregnancy categories and (B) "Normal laboratory values." Index and list of common abbreviations. Also available as an e-book.

1272 Natural medicines comprehensive database. http://www.naturaldatabase.com/. Jeff M. Jellin, Therapeutic Research Faculty. Stockton, Calif.: Therapeutic Research Faculty. 1995–

RM258.5

Available in a professional and a consumer version. Publication varies.

Compilation of natural medicines distributed in the U.S. Contains up-to-date clinical and research information for natural (i.e., herbal and and nonherbal) medicines and dietary supplements distributed in the U.S. Products can be found by most commonly used name, brand name (with editor's comments as appropriate or necessary), ingredient names, scientific names (botanical names), or popular names, with search features to find the safe use (with safety ratings based on evidence: likely safe; possibly safe; possibly unsafe; likely unsafe; unsafe), adverse effects (between natural and pharmaceutical products), interactions ("natural product/drug interaction checker"); also a "natural product effectiveness checker" for each natural medicine. Suitable for pharmacists, physicians, and students in the healthcare field, all types of medical libraries, and also for consumers. Also available in print version since 1999 (13th ed., 2013). Everything in the book is also contained in the web version, which has important added features, such as daily updates, additional search capabilities, patient education handouts, and hyperlinked references, to name a few.

Since 2010, many English and Spanish monographs dietary supplements and herbal remedies from the consumer version of this database have been added to MedlinePlus. This new content replaces the Natural standard monographs previously included in MedlinePlus.

1273 Nutraceuticals: A guide for healthcare professionals. 2nd ed. Brian Lockwood, Lisa Rapport. London; Chicago: Pharmaceutical Press, 2007. 426 p. ISBN 0853696594

615.854   QP144.F85

First edition, 2002.

Contents: (1) "Introduction"; (2) "Monographs"; (3) "Source, manufacture and analysis of major nutraceuticals"; (4) "Metabolism, bioavailability and pharmacokinetics of nutraceuticals"; (5) "Joint health"; (6) "Cardiovascular health"; (7) "Eye health"; (8) "Mental health"; (9) "Sleep enhancement"; (10) "Cancer prevention"; (11) "Bone health"; (12) "Respiratory health"; (13) "Women's health"; (14) "Weight management"; (16) "Skin health"; (16) "Oral health"; (17) "Sporting performance/enhancement"; (18) "Animal health"; (19) "Meta-analyses/systemic reviews"; (20) "Synergism, beneficial interactions and combination products"; (21) "Emerging nutraceuticals"; (22) "Adverse effects"; (23) "Quality"; (24) "Conclusions."

Examines the medical and scientific evidence for the use of nutraceuticals for prevention or treating various diseases. Presents new research, new products, and new therapeutic applications. Index. Also avaialble as an e-book.

1274 Ophthalmic drug facts: ODF. J.B. Lippincott. St. Louis: Facts and Comparisons Division, J.B. Lippincott; Wolters Kluwer Health, Facts & Comparisons, 1989–. v., ill.

617.7061 1043-1780   RE994.O64

Description based on 24th ed., 2012 "Ophthalmic drug facts 2013."

Up-to-date drug monographs for eye care professionals and students. Contains chapters organized according to therapeutic use; groups comparable drugs to provide comparative information. Additional chapters treat dosage forms, routes of administration, systemic drugs, and investigational drugs with information presented in a standardized format. Includes both prescription and over-the-counter products. Also includes charts, tables, illustrations, and extensive cross-references. Appendix lists orphan drugs and manufacturer & distributors index. Index lists generic, brand (in italics), therapeutic group names and many synonyms. Chapters include, for example, agents for retinal disease, anti-infective agents; anti-inflammatory agents; artificial tear solutions & ocular lubricants, contact lens care, dosages forms and routes of administration, ocular hypotensive agents, ophthalmic dyes, systemic medications used for ocular conditions, and many others. Also available as an online product.

1275 Phytochemical dictionary: A handbook of bioactive compounds from plants. 2nd ed. J. B. Harborne, Herbert Baxter, Gerard P. Moss. London; Philadelphia: Taylor and Francis, 1999. x, 976 p., ill.
ISBN 0748406204
572.2   QK898.B54P48
Covering more than 3,000 organic compounds occurring in plants, this dictionary is potentially useful to food scientists, nutritionists, plant biochemists, and biologists. Emphasizes economically important or biologically active substances, such as flavorings, scents, and antimicrobial compounds. Entries are arranged in five major bioenergetic categories of chemical compounds: carbohydrates and lipids, nitrogen-containing compounds, alkaloids, phenolics, and terpenoids. Compounds are grouped according to chemical class and subclass; chemical structures appear in nearly all entries, along with common name and synonyms, molecular weight and formula, Chemical Abstracts Service registry number, and brief description of use by humans or biological activity. References to the literature appear with the introduction to each section. Subject and species indexes are provided.

1276 PDR drug guide for mental health professionals. Thomson Medical Economics. Montvale, N.J.: Thomson Medical Economics, 2002–
615 1546-3443   RM315.P387
Description based on 3rd ed., 2007.

Written in nontechnical language, profiles psychotropic drugs commonly used in psychiatry, with recommended dosage, approved uses, physical and psychological side effects, food and drug interactions, etc. Also includes psychotropic herbs and supplements. Includes street drug profiles and a glossary of street drug names and color photos of psychotropic tablets and capsules. Indexed by generic and trade name and clinical disorder/symptom or drug class. Reference for health professionals taking care of psychiatric patients.

Related titles include *Physicians' desk reference: PDR, ADA/PDR guide to dental therapeutics* (American Dental Association), *PDR guide to drug interactions, side effects, and indications, PDR for herbal medicines, PDR for nonprescription drugs, PDR for nutritional supplements, PDR nurse's drug handbook, Physicians' desk reference for ophthalmic medicines, PDR guide to biological and chemical warfare response, PDR guide to terrorism response,* and other titles.

PDR and its major companion volumes are also found in the PDR electronic library.

1277 PDR for herbal medicines. Thomson Healthcare. Montvale, N.J.: Thomson, 1998–. col. ill.
615 1099-9566   RS164.P375; RS75.P554
Description based on 4th ed., 2007.
Contents: alphabetical index; therapeutic category index; indications index; homeopathic indications index; Asian indications index; dide effects index; drug/herb interactions guide; safety guide; common herbal terminology; herb identification guide; herbal monographs; nutritional supplement monographs.

Comprehensive resource on herbal medicines, with scientific data and findings concerning safety and interactions. Each monograph contains information on effects, contraindications, precautions, adverse reactions, and dosage.

Related titles include *Physicians' desk reference: PDR, ADA/PDR guide to dental therapeutics* (American Dental Association), *PDR drug guide for mental health professionals, PDR guide to drug interactions, side effects, and indications, PDR for nonprescription drugs, PDR for nutritional supplements, PDR nurse's drug handbook, Physicians' desk reference for ophthalmic medicines, PDR guide to biological and chemical warfare response, PDR guide to terrorism response,* and other titles.

PDR and its major companion volumes are also found in the PDR Electronic Library.

1278 PDR for nonprescription drugs.
Montvale, N.J.: PDR Network, 2012-
615.704 2169-2106   RM671.A1.P48;

RS250.P5

Title varies. Editions in 1980–98 had title *Physicians' desk reference for nonprescription drugs*; 1999–2005: *Physicians' desk reference for nonprescription drugs and dietary supplements*; 2006-2011: *PDR for nonprescription drugs, dietary supplements, and herbs.*

Description based on 34th ed., 2013.

Makes available essential information on nonprescription drugs. Contains therapeutic class overviews, drug comparison charts, and product information on over-the-counter medications. Arranged alphabetically by body system or condition, then by indication. Contains sections on supplements, vitamins, and herbal remedies.

Related titles include *Physicians' desk reference: PDR, ADA/PDR guide to dental therapeutics* (American Dental Association), *PDR drug guide for mental health professionals, PDR guide to drug interactions, side effects, and indications, PDR for herbal medicines, PDR for nutritional supplements, PDR nurse's drug handbook, Physicians' desk reference for ophthalmic medicines, PDR guide to biological and chemical warfare response, PDR guide to terrorism response*, and others.

PDR and its major companion volumes are also found in the PDR electronic library.

1279 PDR for nutritional supplements.

Medical Economics Company, Thomson Reuters. Montvale, N.J.: Medical Economics, Thomson Healthcare, 2001–. ill.

613 1534-3642   RM258.5.P37

Description based on 2nd ed. 2008.

Covers nonherbal nutritional supplements and provides FDA-approved descriptions and information on vitamins, minerals, sports nutrition products, probiotics, hormones, enzymes, cartilage products, and others, with detailed descriptions of the supplements, side effects, and potential interactions with prescription and nonprescription drugs. Contains summary information on published studies. Includes "Companion drug index," which lists common diseases, the prescription drugs to treat these diseases, their side effects, and the over-the-counter products to provide relief.

Related titles include *Physicians' desk reference: PDR, ADA/PDR guide to dental therapeutics* (American Dental Association), *PDR drug guide*

for mental health professionals, *PDR guide to drug interactions, side effects, and indications, PDR for herbal medicines, PDR for nonprescription drugs, PDR nurse's drug handbook, Physicians' desk reference for ophthalmic medicines, PDR guide to biological and chemical warfare response, PDR guide to terrorism response*, and others. PDR and its major companion volumes are also found online in the PDR electronic library.

1280 PDR electronic library. http://www .micromedex.com/products/pdrlibrary/. Ann Arbor, Mich.: Truven Health Analytics. 1998–

Publisher varies.

Provides access to FDA-approved package insert information contained in the *Physicians' desk reference: PDR*, the *PDR for nonprescription drugs,* and the *PDR for ophthalmic medicines*, as well as *PDR for herbal medicines* and the online version of *Stedman's medical dictionary.* Allows search and retrieval of data by brand and generic names of drugs, by manufacturers, and by prescribing categories, drug interactions, side effects, dosages, uses, contraindications, etc. Includes photos, charts, tables, and chemical structures. Intended users include pharmacists, drug information specialists, health care professionals, and consumers.

Also available on CD-ROM that contains the text of the print *Physicians' desk reference: PDR.*

1281 PDR guide to drug interactions, side effects, and indications. Montvale, N.J.: Thomson PDR, 2006–

615 1933-706X   RS75.P37

Formerly had title *PDR companion guide.*

This guide is based on eight clinical indexes: drug interactions index, side effects index, indications index, imprint identification guide, food interactions cross-reference, contraindications index, international drug name index, and generic availability guide. Serves as a complement to the (*Physicians desk reference: PDR*), *PDR for nonprescription drugs,* and *Physicians' desk reference for ophthalmic medicines.*

Related titles include *ADA/PDR guide to dental therapeutics* (American Dental Association), *PDR drug guide for mental health professionals, PDR for herbal medicines, PDR for nutritional supplements,*

PDR nurse's drug handbook, *PDR guide to biological and chemical warfare response*, *PDR guide to terrorism response*, and others.

PDR and its major companion volumes are available online in the PDR electronic library.

1282 PDR nurse's drug handbook. Delmar
    Cengage Learning. Clifton Park, N.Y.:
    Delmar Cengage Learning, 2000–. ill.
    615 1535-4601   RM125

Title varies: *PDR nurse's handbook*; *Physician's desk reference nurse's drug handbook*; *Nurse's drug handbook*. Description based on 2007 ed. of *PDR nurse's drug handbook*; 2013 ed. is available.

Description of the major prescription drugs, with phonetic pronunciation of drug name, drug classification, drug interactions, FDA warnings, etc. Includes various aids to prevent medication errors (e.g., listing of drug names that sound alike, administration and storage of drugs, etc.). Includes a visual identification guide. For nursing students, nurses, and other health care professionals.

Related titles include *Physicians' desk reference: PDR*, *ADA/PDR guide to dental therapeutics* (American Dental Association), *PDR drug guide for mental health professionals*, *PDR guide to drug interactions, side effects, and indications*, *PDR for herbal medicines*, *PDR for nonprescription drugs*, *PDR for nutritional supplements*, *Physicians' desk reference for ophthalmic medicines*, also *PDR guide to biological and chemical warfare response*, and *PDR guide to terrorism response*, and other titles.

PDR and its major companion volumes are available online in the PDR electronic library.

1283 Physicians' desk reference for
    ophthalmic medicines. Medical
    Economics Company. Montvale, N.J.:
    Thomson Healthcare, 2000–2012
    1535-461X   RE994.P57

Also called *PDR for ophthalmic medicines*. Annual.

Description based on 35th ed., 2007, by Douglas J Rhee et al. Publisher varies; now publ. by Thomson PDR. Ceased with 40th ed., 2012.

Contents: sec. 1, "Indices"; sec. 2, "Pharmaceuticals in ophthalmology"; sec. 3, "Suture materials"; sec. 4, "Ophthalmic lenses"; sec. 5, "Vision standards and low-vision aids"; sec. 6, "Product identification guide"; sec. 7, "Product information on pharmaceuticals and equipment."

Provides information and references on ophthalmic drugs and agents and instrumentation, equipment, supplies, lenses, vision standards, etc. used in ophthalmology and optometry, with detailed description prepared by the manufacturers. Indexed by manufacturer, product name, product category, and active ingredients. Color product identification section. Intended for eye care professionals. May also be useful to health consumers.

Related titles include *Physicians' desk reference: PDR*, *ADA/PDR guide to dental therapeutics* (American Dental Association), *PDR drug guide for mental health professionals*, *PDR guide to drug interactions, side effects, and indications*, *PDR for herbal medicines*, *PDR for nonprescription drugs*, *PDR for nutritional supplements*, *PDR nurse's drug handbook*, *PDR guide to biological and chemical warfare response*, *PDR guide to terrorism response*, and other titles.

PDR and its major companion volumes are available online in the PDR electronic library.

1284 Physicians' desk reference: PDR.
    Medical Economics Company. Oradell,
    N.J.: Thomson Healthcare, 1974–. ill.
    615.1 0093–4461   RS75.P5

Title varies: editions in 1947–73 entitled *Physicians' desk reference to pharmaceutical specialties and biologicals*. Description based on 67th ed., 2013. Imprint varies; now publ. by Thomson PDR, in cooperation with participating manufacturers. Available in print, on CD-ROM, and via the Internet (http://www.PDR.net). PDR and its major companion volumes are also found in the PDR electronic library on CD-ROM and as a web-based resource. Also available as part of Micromedex healthcare series.

"Contains Food and Drug Administration (FDA)-approved labeling for drugs as well as prescription information provided by manufacturers for grandfathered drugs and other drugs marketed without FDA approval under current FDA policies. Some dietary supplements and other products are also included"—*Foreword*.

Principal sections: (1) manufacturers' index, an alphabetical index by manufacturer's name; (2) brand and generic name index; (3) product category index; (4) product identification guide, showing tablets and capsules in color and actual size; (5) product information, the main section of the book, listing approx. 4,000 pharmaceuticals by manufacturer, giving full descriptions of composition, action, use, dosage, side effects, etc.; and (6) diagnostic products information section, arranged alphabetically by manufacturer. Product descriptions have been provided and approved by the manufacturers. Includes a national directory of drug information centers, alphabetically arranged by state and city, FDA use-in-pregnancy ratings list, state AIDS drug assistance programs, patient assistance programs, and also several other special drug-related lists and instructions.

Other PDR titles include *ADA/PDR guide to dental therapeutics, PDR drug guide for mental health professionals, PDR guide to drug interactions, side effects, and indications, PDR for herbal medicines, PDR for nonprescription drugs, PDR for nutritional supplements, PDR nurse's drug handbook, Physicians' desk reference for ophthalmic medicines, PDR guide to biological and chemical warfare response, PDR guide to terrorism response: A resource for physicians, nurses, emergency medical services, law enforcement, firefighters*, and other titles.

Other clinical information PDR products include the *PDR monthly prescribing guide* (drug reference designed specifically for use at the point of care), mobilePDR (software that allows retrieval of concise drug summaries), PDR.net (online source for FDA-approved and other manufacturer-supplied labeling information), and *PDR Pharmacopoeia pocket dosing guide*.

1285 Poisoning and toxicology handbook. 4th ed. Jerrold B. Leikin, Frank P. Paloucek. Boca Raton, Fla.: CRC Press/ Taylor & Francis Group, 2008. xlv, 1331 p., ill. ISBN 9781420044
615.9   RA1215.P65
First ed., 1998; 3rd ed., 2002.

Contents: sec. 1, "Medicinal agents"; sec. 2, "Nonmedicinal agents"; sec. 3, "Biological agents"; sec. 4, "Herbal agents"; sec. 5, "Antidotes and drugs used in toxicology"; sec. 6, "Diagnostic tests/procedures"; appendix; index.

Provides detailed information on approx. 900 drugs and poisons, including environmental toxins, and related special topics and resources. Includes listings of U.S. poison control centers and organizations that offer toxicology and teratology information services.

1286 Psychodynamic diagnostic manual (PDM). American Psychoanalytic Association, International Psychoanalytical Association, American Psychological Association, American Academy of Psychoanalysis and Dynamic Psychiatry, National Membership Committee on Psychoanalysis in Clinical Social Work. Silver Spring, Md.: Alliance of Psychoanalytic Organizations, 2006
0976775824

Intended as a complement to the DSM (*Diagnostic and statistical manual of mental disorders: DSM-IV-TR*) and ICD (*ICD-10 classification of mental and behavioural disorders*) classifications, it is described as "a diagnostic framework that attempts to characterize an individual's range of functionality—the depth as well as the surface of emotional, cognitive, and social patterns . . . based on current neuroscience, treatment outcome research, and other empirical investigations"—*Introd.*

1287 Rational phytotherapy: A reference guide for physicians and pharmacists. 5th ed. Volker Schulz, Rudolf Hänsel, Mark Blumenthal. Berlin; New York: Springer, 2004. 417 p.
ISBN 3540408320
615.321   RM666.H33.S3813
First ed., 1983, had title *Therapie mit Phytopharmaka*; 4th ed., 2001, *Rational phytotherapy: A physician's guide to herbal medicine*.

Contents: (1) "Medicinal plants, phytomedicine, and phytotherapy"; (2) "Central nervous system"; (3) "Cardiovascular system"; (4) "Respiratory system"; (5) "Digestive system"; (6) "Urinary tract"; (7) "Gynecologic indications for herbal remedies"; (8) "Skin, trauma, rheumatism, and pain"; (9) "Agents that increase resistance to disease."

Revised and expanded edition.

Practice-oriented introduction to phytotherapy. Includes selected herbal remedies considered by the authors to have pharmacological and clinical effectiveness, with information on dosage and form of application. "The authors are highly experienced in the field of postgraduate medical education and, with this work, present an indispensable reference book for the medical practice."—*Publisher's website* Also available as an e-book.

1288 Red book: Pharmacy's fundamental reference. Thomson Healthcare. Montvale, N.J.: Thomson Healthcare, 2004–. ill.

338 1556-3391   HD9666.1.D75

Volumes in 1941/42–1943/44 had title *Drug topics price book* (continues the "Red book price list section" of the *Druggists' circular*, issues semiannually 1897–1940); 1944–92 had title *Drug topics red book*; 1993–94, *Red book*; 1995–2003, *Drug topics red book*.

Description based on 114th ed. 2010

Contents: 1. Emergency information; 2. Clinical reference guide; 3. Herbal medicine guide; 4. Practice management and professional development; 5. Pharmacy and healthcare organizations; 6. Drug reimbursement information;

7. Manufacturer/wholesaler information; 8. Product identification guide; 9. Rx product listings; 10. OTC non-drug product listings. Advertiser index.

Product, pricing, and clinical & pharmaceutical reference information for prescription and over-the-counter (OTC) drugs, many with full-color photographs. Provides nationally recognized average wholesale prices and direct and federal upper-limit prices for prescription drugs. Also includes prices for reimbursable medical supplies and, for example, a vitamin comparison table of popular multivitamin products, a guide to herbal/alternative medicines, a list of FDA-approved new drugs, generics, and OTC products, and also a list of "Web sites worth watching." Includes poison control centers and manufacturers, pharmaceutical wholesalers, and third-party administrator directories. Intended for pharmacists and other health care professionals. For electronic delivery options, see http://www.redbook.com/redbook/index.html.

1289 The review of natural products. Ara DerMarderosian, John A. Beutler, Facts and Comparisons. St. Louis: Facts and Comparisons, 1996–

615 1541-1435   QK99.A1.R47

Volumes from 1898 to 1995 had title *Lawrence review of natural products*.

Alphabetically arranged monographs with Latin scientific names, common names, synonyms, historical names, botanical and other related information, and historical uses of products in folk medicine. Monograph entries also provide chemical and pharmacological information, interactions with drugs and other natural products, toxicology, patient information, use during pregnancy and lactation, and literature references. "Clinical overview" box at the beginning of each monograph. Primary index; therapeutic index. Intended for pharmacists and health care professionals.

Guide to popular natural products is an abridged edition of this title. Available as an e-book in Facts and Comparisons 4.0 Online.

1290 Stockley's drug interactions: A source book of interactions, their mechanisms, clinical importance and management. 9th ed. Karen Baxter. London; Chicago: Pharmaceutical Press, 2010. vii, 1792 p., ill. ISBN 9780853699149

615.7045   RM302.5

First ed. (1981) through 5th ed. (1999) had title *Drug interactions: A source book of interactions, their mechanism, clinical importance and management*; 8th ed., 2007. Description based on 9th ed.; 10th ed., 2013 has been published.

Comprehensive source of international drug interaction information, based on published clinical papers and reports, with British and American drug names. Covers drug-drug, drug-food, and drug-herb interactions. This edition contains approx. 3,700 drug interaction monographs, with more than 40,000 "drug interactions pairs" (*publ. notes*), 22,000 references and revision of previous text. Each monograph contains a summary, with details of the particular interaction, its clinical importance, and how to manage it. Interaction monographs are presented alphabetically in 38 chapters, grouped by therapeutic use or pharmacological activity. Includes some herbal supplements. More complete coverage of herbals can be found in *Stockley's herbal medicines interactions: A guide to the interactions of herbal medicines, dietary supplements and nutraceuticals with conventional medicines* and *PDR guide to drug interactions, side effects, and indications*.

Available online as part of MedicinesComplete and searchable by drug name (up to 12 drugs at once), synonyms and codes, international proprietary names, and drug groups.

Stockley's drug interactions pocket companion is an annual update of the less frequently published

Stockley's drug interactions. It contains the same, however abbreviated, information. This pocket edition does not include bibliographic data, pictures, tables, and graphics, but is up-to-date.

1291 Tyler's honest herbal: A sensible guide to the use of herbs and related remedies. 4th ed. Steven Foster, Varro E. Tyler. New York: Haworth Herbal Press, 1999. xxi, 442 p. ISBN 0789007053

615.321   RM666.H33T94

Title varies: 1st ed. (1981) had title *The honest herbal*; 2nd ed. (1987), *The new honest herbal*; 3rd ed., 1993. Provides references and peer-reviewed scientific data on the uses of herbs and herbal remedies. Includes approx. 100 herbs. Arranged in alphabetical order by common name, each entry describes the plant with the appropriate nomenclature, botanical information, the chemistry and pharmacology of its active ingredients, its traditional uses, positive and negative features when used for therapeutic purposes, folklore, and other facts. An evaluation by the author based on available evidence follows for each herb. Mentions possible safety concerns. Includes a chapter on laws and regulations. References to the literature. For general readers and as a starting point for scientists; index. Also available as an e-book.

Tyler's *Herbs of choice* (re-issued in 1999 as *Tyler's herbs of choice: The therapeutic use of phytomedicinals* and now in its third edition) provides related information.

1292 What your patients need to know about psychiatric medications. 2nd ed. Robert H. Chew, Robert E. Hales, Stuart C. Yudofsky. Washington: American Psychiatric Pub., 2009. xix, 421 p. ISBN 9781585623563

615.788   RM315.H328

Contents: "Medications in pregnancy"; "Antianxiety medication"; "Medications for treatment of insomnia"; "Antidepressants: Selective serotonin reuptake inhibitors and mixed-action antidepressants"; "Tricyclic antidepressants"; "Monoamine oxidase inhibitors"; "Mood stabilizers"; "First-generation antipsychotics"; "Second-generation antipsychotics"; "Treatment of attention-deficit/hyperactivity disorder in adults"; "Stimulants and nonstimulants for ADHD"; "Cognitive enhancers for treatment of Alzheimer's disease and other forms of dementia"; "Methods for treatment of alcohol dependence"; Index.

Provides relevant and easy-to-understand information about commonly asked questions regarding psychotropic medications. Information about each medication presented in a standard format: brand name; generic name; available strengths; available in generic; medication class; general information; dosing information; common side effects; adverse reactions and precautions; use in pregnancy and breastfeeding; possible drug interactions; overdose; special considerations. Accompanied by CD-ROM that contains PDF files of the pages as they appear in the book. Also available as an e-book via PsychiatryOnline.

Another well-regarded resource in this area is *Handbook of psychiatric drug therapy* (by Labbate).

1293 Wiley handbook of current and emerging drug therapies. Wiley. Hoboken, N.J.: Wiley-Interscience, 2007–. 8 v., ill. ISBN 9780470040

615.58   RM301.12.W55

Contents: pt. 1, "Introduction"; pt. 2, "Oncology"; pt. 3, "Immune system"; pt. 4, "Metabolic diseases"; pt. 5, "Infectious diseases"; pt. 6, "Emerging technologies and business opportunities"; pt. 7, "Global markets and national policy"; pt. 8, "New opportunities in drug discovery and pipeline development."

"Comprehensive reference to established and future drug treatments for more than 60 important diseases and indications in every major therapeutic area"—*publ. notes.* Current information and resource for biomedical and pharmaceutical research and drug discovery, including emerging technologies, markets, and information on the status of trials. Also available in a regularly updated version from Wiley (http://www.interscience.wiley.com/mrw/cedt).

Dispensatories and pharmacopoeias

1294 AHFS drug information. American Society of Hospital Pharmacists. Bethesda, Md.: American Society of

Hospital Pharmacists, 1989–. ill.
ISBN 10638792
615.1373   RS131.2.A47
AHFS Drug Information® (AHFS DI®)
Published since 1959. Description based on
2013 ed.
Earlier title: *American hospital formulary
service drug information.*

Provides comprehensive, evaluative drug information for physicians, nurses, pharmacists, and
other health care professionals. Arrangement by
pharmacologic-therapeutic classification. Within
each class, arranged alphabetically by generic name.
Gives comprehensive monograph for each drug,
including pertinent information such as administration, dosage, chemical stability, pharmacology,
uses, and cautions, including drug interactions and
interference with laboratory tests. Includes a section
on unclassified therapeutic agents. Indexed for proprietary (trade) names, pharmacologic-therapeutic
classes of drugs, synonyms, pharmacy equivalent
names (PENs), and acronyms of drugs. Use of symbol § indicates information omitted from the print
version which can be found at http://www.ahfsdru-
ginformation.com. Print edition kept current by
ongoing electronic updating.

Since 2000 also available in a variety of electronic formats, e.g., as part of MedicinesComplete.

Herbal companion to AHFS DI, with 52 herbal
monographs and 32 monographs on nutritional
supplements, complements this resource.

1295 American drug index. Norman F.
    Billups, Shirley M. Billups. Philadelphia:
    Lippincott, 1956–
    615 0065-8111   RS355.A48
    Description based on 56th ed., 2012; 57th
    ed., 2013 is available.

A listing of pharmaceuticals by generic, brand,
and chemical name, with brief information about
manufacturer, form, size, dosage, and use. This
edition has 16 major sections. The main section,
"Drug monographs," is arranged alphabetically,
with many cross-references. Generic names are in
lowercase, and all brand-name products upper/
lowercase as appropriate. Other sections include,
for example, common abbreviations used in chemotherapy regimens, common systems of weight
and measure, official container requirements for
U.S.P. drugs, and "drug names that look alike

and sound alike," and discontinued drugs. Also
includes a "manufacturer and distributor listing."

1296 British national formulary. British
    Medical Association, Royal Pharmaceutical
    Society of Great Britain. London: British
    Medical Association; Royal Pharmaceutical
    Society of Great Britain, 1957–. ill. (some
    col.) 0260-535X

Joint publication of the British Medical Association and the Royal Pharmaceutical Society of Great
Britain.

Prescribing, dispensing, and administering of
medications generally prescribed in the United
Kingdom, with mention of dosage, side effects,
contraindications, etc. Drugs are listed by generic
name (i.e., BAN), followed by brand name(s) available in the United Kingdom, with information on
strength, dosage, and price. Index of manufacturers and general index. Available online as part of
MedicinesComplete.

Also available, with some restrictions, online
from the publisher (http://www.bnf.org), via CD-
ROM, and as an intranet version.

1297 European pharmacopoeia. European
    Pharmacopoeia Commission., Council
    of Europe. Sainte Ruffine [France]:
    Maisonneuve, 1969–
    615.114   RS141.28.E95

Description based on 7th ed., 2010 (2 v.), complemented by two supplements published in 2010
and three supplements published 2011 and 2012.
Also available online.

Legally binding standards for medicines in the
countries that are members of the European Pharmacopoeia Convention. Contains the different types
of active substances used to prepare pharmaceutical
products: Various biological & chemical substances,
antibiotics, vaccines, radiopharmaceuticals, herbal
drugs, and homeopathic preparations, and others. Over 1,800 general and specific monographs,
general methods, and reagents, described and
illustrated by figures or chromatograms as appropriate. Further details at http://www.edqm.eu/en/
european-pharmacopoeia-publications-1401.html.

**1298 The International pharmacopoeia:
    Pharmacopoea internationalis.
    4th ed.** World Health Organization.

Geneva, Switzerland: World Health Organization, 2006. 2 v.

Title varies: 1st ed., 1951–59, *Pharmacopoeia internationalis*; 2nd ed., 1967, *Specifications for the quality control of pharmaceutical preparation*; 3rd ed., 1988–94, 5 v.

Contents: v. 1, general notices and monographs for pharmaceutical substances A–O; v. 2, monographs for pharmaceutical substances P–Z; dosage forms; radiopharmaceutical preparations.

Rev. ed., with consolidation of five volumes into two volumes, with new and revised monographs. Recommends specification for quality control of pharmaceutical preparation that can serve as references in any country. Includes mainly recommendations on widely used medicines important to WHO health programs to "achieve a wide global uniformity of quality specifications for selected pharmaceutical products, excipients, and dosage forms"—*Publ. website*. Also available electronically on CD-ROM. Amended by supplements. Further information and related links at http://www.who .int/medicines/publications/pharmacopoeia/over view/en/in dex.html, including a link to the current version of *WHO model list of essential medicines*.

1299 Martindale: The complete drug reference. William Martindale, Kathleen Parfitt. London: Pharmaceutical Press, 1999–

0263-5364   RS141.3.M4

First ed. (1883) through 31st ed. (1996) had title *The extra pharmacopoeia: Martindale*.

First through 15th eds. (1883–1912) comp. by W. H. Martindale and W. W. Westcott. Description based on 37th ed., 2011 (ed. Sean C. Sweetman) 2 v. (v. A and v. B). Now produced every two years.

"The aim of Martindale is to provide healthcare professionals with unbiased evaluated information on drugs and medicines used throughout the world."—*Pref.* This continuously expanded and revised resource is international in scope, covering prescription and nonprescription drugs. Vol. A, "Drug monographs," contains data on 5,930 drug monographs (from analgesics to vaccines), with 240 new monographs added to this edition and 171 removed. Vol. B, "Preparations, manufacturers, index" provides brief details of 161,700 proprietary preparations, a directory of 15,300

manufacturers and distributors, and a general index which covers drugs and diseases.

Available online as part of Micromedex Healthcare Series and MedicinesComplete. Both of these resources contain several additional drug resources.

1300 National drug code directory. http:// www.accessdata.fda.gov/scripts/cder/ndc/ default.cfm. Center for Drug Evaluation and Research (U.S.). Rockville, Md.: Center for Drug Evaluation and Research. 2001–

RS353

Continues print ed., published 1969–95. Web access available since 2001.

The National Drug Code (NDC) system provides product identification for human drugs, i.e., prescription drugs and selected over-the-counter products, including foreign drug products with commercial distribution in the United States. Searchable by proprietary name, NDC number (unique 10-digit, 3-segment number), active ingredient, or firm name. Background information is provided at http://www.fda.gov/Drugs/Information OnDrugs/ucm142438.htm.

1301 Pharmacopoeia of the People's Republic of China. English ed.
Zhonghua Renmin Gongheguo wei sheng bu yao dian wei yuan hui. Beijing, China: Chemical Industry Press, 2000. 2 v.
ISBN 7502529810

RS141.64.C5413

Rev. ed. Also called *Chinese Pharmacopoeia 2000*, abbreviated as *Ch. P 2000*.

Contents: "Membership of the 7th Pharmacopoeia Commission of the People's Republic of China"; "Editorial Board of the Pharmacopoeia of the People's Republic of China (Engl. edition)"; "Preface"; "History of the Pharmacopoeia of the People's Republic of China; Additions"; "Omissions, general notices; Monographs, pt. 1: Chinese materia medica, oils, fats, etc."; pt. 2, "Traditional Chinese patent medicine and simple preparations"; appendixes; index.

Official compendium on drugs, covering traditional Chinese medicines and most of the Western medicines. Contains 2,691 new and revised monographs (962 in v. 1 and 1,699 in v. 2) and a number of new and revised appendixes. Entries provide a description of the drug or substance, identification, information on reference standards and testing methods for purity, dosage, precaution, storage, and strength for each drug.

A new edition, *Pharmacopoeia of the People's Republic of China 2010* (pub. 2011), is available.

1302 The United States pharmacopeia.
20th rev. ed. United States Pharmacopeial Convention. Rockville, Md.: United States Pharmacopeial Convention, 1979–. ill.
615.1173 0195-7996   RS141.2.P5

Supersedes *The pharmacopoeia of the United States of America* and *The national formulary*. Merger of *Pharmacopoeia of the United States* and *American Pharmaceutical Association national formulary*. The combination of the two compendia in one volume (beginning with the 30th ed. [2007] in 3 v.) is entitled *The United States pharmacopeia–national formulary (USP-NF)*.

United States Pharmacopeial Convention (USPC); United States Pharmacopeia (USP); National Formulary (NF).

Kept up to date between revisions by supplements. Available in print, CD, and Internet versions. Also available in a Spanish-language edition (print only): *Farmacopea de los Estados Unidos de América. Formulario nacional*).

Description based on the three-volume *USP36-NF31* 2013 print ed. Contents: v. 1, table of contents; front matter; USP general notices; general chapters TOC; general chapters; reagents; reference tables; dietary supplements; NF general notices; NF monographs; complete index; v. 2, table of contents; general chapters TOC; USP general notices; USP monographs A–L; complete index; v. 3, table of contents; general chapters TOC; USP general notices; USP monographs M–Z; complete index.

An official compendium of drug information of the USPC, which is responsible for setting standards, test procedures, and specifications for drugs, biologics, dietary supplements, medical devices, and other health care products. The NF includes standards for excipients (inactive ingredients), botanicals, and other ingredients used in drug preparations. The USP(U.S. Pharmacopeia) website provides further information.

A related product is *USP dictionary of USAN and international drug names*.

1303 USP (U.S. Pharmacopeia). http://www.usp.org/. United States Pharmacopeial Convention. Rockville, Md.: United States Pharmacopeial Convention. 1997–
361.763; 615.1; 615.10218   RM300

Contents include: About USP; USP-NF; Food chemicals codex; Pending and non-U.S. standards; Reference standards; USP verified; Education; Healthcare quality and information; Worldwide activities; Meetings; Products.

The United States Pharmacopeial Convention (USP) sets standards for medications sold in the United States. This website provides an overview of USP and its history (time line 1820–2002; http://www.usp.org/aboutUSP/history.html), the USP-NF online (http://www.usp.org/USPNF/; see also related record for the United States pharmacopeia), and other publications; reference standards, patient safety programs; development of health care information; and other activities. Description for the USP-NF online (http://www.usp.org/store/products-services/usp-nf) provides information about available formats, special features of the online edition, differences between the editions, its legal status, other related topics. Information is presented for several different categories of users, including consumers, pharmacists, veterinary medicine professionals, manufacturers, and others.

Histories

1304 Chronicles of pharmacy. A. C. Wootton. London: Macmillan, 1910. 2 v., ill.
615.109   RS61.W7

Repr.: Boston: Milford House, [1971] (2 v. in 1); Tuckahoe, N.Y.: USV Pharmaceutical Corp, 1972.

In narrative form; describes the discovery and use of various drugs, medicines, and nostrums from ancient times through the 19th century. Includes some biographical material of famous apothecaries. Indexed.

Available online at https://archive.org/details/chroniclesofphar01woot.

1305 The development of American pharmacology: John J. Abel and the shaping of a discipline. John Parascandola. Baltimore: Johns Hopkins

University Press, 1992. xvii, 212 p., ill. ISBN 9780801844164

615/.1/092   RM62.A24P37

Contents: 1. From materia medica to pharmacology; 2. The education of a medical scientist; 3. Abel and the beginnings of pharmacology in American medical schools; 4. The growth of academic pharmacology in the United States; 5. Pharmacologists in government and industry; (6) The professionalization of a discipline.

Describes the early development and professionalization of pharmacology, also the growth of academic pharmacology as a discipline, patterned after programs at European universities. Includes biographical information on John Abel who can be considered the "father of pharmacology" in the U.S. Bibliographical notes, index. Another title by the same author, *Studies in the history of modern pharmacology and drug therapy*, provides through a collection of articles a more recent history of pharmacology and its subfields. These books are considered useful resources for researchers in the history of pharmacology and history of medicine.

1306 Discoveries in pharmacological sciences. Popat N. Patil. Singapore, Republic of Singapore; Hackensack, N.J.: World Scientific, 2012. xiv, 778 p., ill. (some col.), maps. ISBN 9789814355070

615.1   RM41

Contents: Pt. 1, "Drug discoveries"; pt. 2, "20th century drug discoveries, research, pharmacology education, laws and pharmaceutical companies."

Provides a history of the use of drugs & toxic chemicals and pharmacological discoveries from ancient times to the present, i.e., "a critical analysis of the major discoveries in pharmacology, including time, places and scientists involved."—*Pref.* Includes many interesting historical details related to ethnopharmacological and pharmacological discoveries and to traditional practices in various cultures, as well as drug discovery and pharmacotherapeutics in modern medicine and the growth of the drug industry. Also includes brief profiles of scientists. For pharmacologists, chemists, physicians, researchers, teachers, and graduate students. Also available as an e-book.

1307 Drug discovery: A history. Walter Sneader. Hoboken, N.J.: Wiley, 2005. viii,

468 p., ill. ISBN 0471899798

615.1909   RS61.S637

Contents: pt. 1, "Legacy of the past"; pt. 2, "Drugs from naturally occurring prototypes: (I) Phytochemicals; (II) Biochemicals; (III) Drugs from microorganisms"; pt. 3, "Synthetic drugs."

Presents an overview and review of the discovery of therapeutic compounds, from prehistoric times to the present. Chapters on plant products, hormones, antibiotics, and fungi and medicinal compounds developed from them as well as on the origins and discoveries of synthetic compounds. Includes chemical structures, bibliographical references, and index. Also available as an e-book.

1308 A guide to pharmacy museums and historical collections in the United States and Canada. George B. Griffenhagen, Ernst Walter Stieb, Beth D. Fisher, American Institute of the History of Pharmacy. Madison, Wis.: American Institute of the History of Pharmacy, 1999. xii, 143 p., ill. ISBN 0931292344

615.107473   RS123.U6G75

Title varies: 1956, *Pharmacy museums,* by George Griffenhagen; 1972, *Pharmacy museums and historical collections on public view, U.S.A.,* by Sami K. Hamarneh; 1981, *Pharmacy museums and historical collections on public view in the United States and Canada,* by Sami K. Hamarneh and Ernst Stieb; 1988, *Pharmacy museums and historical collections in the United States and Canada* (Publication American Institute of the History of Pharmacy, n.s.; no. 11). (Publication American Institute of the History of Pharmacy; n.s.; no. 18). Museums are described and listed in alphabetical order by state or province and city. Includes sites of historical pharmacy markers. Name index. Also available online from the American Institute of the History of Pharmacy (University of Wisconsin School of Pharmacy) at http://www.pharmacy .wisc.edu/american-institute-history-pharmacy/ histo rical-sources-pharmacy-faq.

1309 An historical account of pharmacology to the 20th century. Chauncey Depew Leake. Springfield, Ill.: Thomas, [1975]. xi, 210 p. ISBN 0398032777

615.109   RM41.L4
American Lecture Series no. 970.
Contents: ch. 1, "An historical account of pharmacology"; ch. 2, "Protopharmacology: Prehistoric empirical drug lore"; ch. 3, "Protopharmacology: Codified empirical drug use"; ch. 4, "Graeco-Roman medicine"; ch. 5, "The Muslim drug innovations"; ch. 6, "Drugs in medieval Europe"; ch. 7, "Drug development in the Renaissance"; ch. 8, "Drugs in the 17th and 18th centuries"; ch. 8, "The first part of the 19th century"; ch. 10, "Pharmacology in the second half of the 19th century"; ch. 11, "Progress and promise: Transition of pharmacology from the 19th century into the 20th."

Overview of the history of pharmacology. Name index; subject index. For historians of medicine and science and also general readers.

1310 The history of pharmacy: A selected annotated bibliography. Gregory J. Higby, Elaine Condouris Stroud, David L. Cowen. New York: Garland, 1995. xi, 321 p., ill. ISBN 0824097688
615.109   Z6675.P5.H53; RS61
Contents: pt. 1, "Bibliographies and general studies": (1a) "Bibliographies, encyclopedias, dictionaries"; (1b) "General historical literature and historiography"; (1c) "National studies"; (1d) "Company histories"; (1e) "Biographies"; pt. 2, "Special subjects": (2a) "Practice of pharmacy"; (2b) "Basic pharmaceutical disciplines"; (2c) "Materia medica (drugs) and drug therapy: General, pre-1600, post-1600"; (2d) "Laws and regulations"; (2e) "Professional pharmaceutical literature: Classics, historical studies"; (2f) "Professional and social aspects"; (2g) "Economic and business aspects"; (2h) "Education"; (2i) "Manufacturing (not including company histories)"; (2j) "Equipment and museology"; (2k) "Patent medicines and quackery"; pt. 3, "Pharmacy in the arts": (3a) "Architecture and interior design"; (3b) "Painting, sculpture, graphic arts, and photography"; (3c) "Creative literature"; (3d) "Music."

"Broad overview of the literature that emphasizes the most important and essential works" (*Introd.*), i.e., a selective guide to the secondary literature. Designed for graduate students and teachers. Author index.

Also available online from the American Institute of the History of Pharmacy (University of Wisconsin School of Pharmacy) website at

http://pharmacy.wisc.edu/american-institute -history-pharmacy/historica l-sources-pharmacy-faq.

1311 History of vaccines. http://www.history ofvaccines.org/. College of Physicians of Philadelphia. Philadelphia: College of Physicians of Philadelphia. 2010-
Historical rare books, medical journals, manuscripts, and archival materials used in the creation of this project are from The College of Physicians of Philadelphia Historical Medical Library, whose website is at http://www.collegeofphysicians.org/.

"Chronicle of the compelling history of vaccination, from pre-Jennerian variolation practices, to the defeat of polio in the Western Hemisphere, to cutting-edge approaches to novel vaccines and vaccine delivery. Aims to increase public knowledge and understanding of the ways in which vaccines, toxoids, and passive immunization work, how they have been developed, and the role they have played in the improvement of human health. Discusses some of the controversies about vaccination and some of the challenges, difficulties, and tragic events that have occurred in the use of vaccines."—*Website (About)*. "Timelines" (http://www.historyofvaccines .org/content/timelines/all) from 900 CE to the present includes , a multimedia "gallery" (http://www .historyofvaccines.org/gallery) with vaccine-related images and videos, a "history of the immunization schedule" (http://www.historyofvaccines.org/content/ history-immunization-schedule), and other interesting content. Useful resource for students, educators, and other general readers.

Further authoritative information on vaccines can be found, for example, in *History of vaccine development* by Plotkin and in *Vaccines* by Plotkin.

1312 Kremers and Urdang's History of pharmacy. 4th ed. Edward Kremers, George Urdang, Glenn Sonnedecker. Philadelphia: Lippincott, 1976. xv, 571 p., ill. ISBN 0397520743
615.409   RS61.K73
First edition, 1940, had title *History of pharmacy: A guide and a survey*; 3rd ed., 1963.

Contents: pt. 1, "Pharmacy's early antecedents": (1) "Ancient prelude"; (2) "The Arabs and the European Middle Ages"; pt. 2, "The rise of professional pharmacy in representative countries of Europe": (3) "Changing medicaments and the modern pharmacists"; (4) "The development in Italy"; (5) "The development in France"; (6) "The development in Germany"; (7) "The development in Britain"; (8) "Some international trends"; pt. 3, "Pharmacy in the United States": (9) "The North American colonies"; (10) "The Revolutionary War"; (11) "Young republic and pioneer expansion"; (12) "The growth of associations"; (13) "The rise of legislative standards"; (14) "The development of education"; (15) "The establishment of a literature"; (16) "Economic and structural development"; pt. 4: (17) "The American pharmacist in public service"; (18) "Contributions by pharmacists to science and industry."

A survey of the history of pharmaceutical science and a "sociohistorical view of pharmacy evolving as a profession in the Western world showing . . . the international character of pharmacy and its development"—*Pref.* Several appendixes (e.g., "Representative drugs of the American Indians," "Founding of state pharmaceutical associations," "Pharmaceutical literature: Some bibliographic historical notes," and others). Glossary, notes, references, and index.

1313 150 years of caring: A pictorial history of the American Pharmaceutical Association. George B. Griffenhagen. Washington: American Pharmaceutical Association, 2002. viii, 305 p., ill. ISBN 1582120404
615.106073   RS67.U6G754
"This book is primarily about the men and women who provided the leadership of the national professional society of pharmacists in the U.S.A. . . . and professionals who are responsible for the appropriate use of medication to achieve optimal therapeutic outcomes."—*Pref.* More than 300 illustrations. Chapters on the practitioners of pharmacy, pharmaceutical scientists, pharmaceutical educators, law enforcement officials, drug manufacturers, pharmaceutical distributors, women, minorities, students, and the military. Changes in terminology "to define a qualified practitioner of pharmacy" are described in ch. 41. Ch. 1 includes a list of articles published in the *Journal of the American Pharmaceutical Association* commemorating the APhA Sesquicentennial. Appendixes: (A) "APhA annual meetings 1852–2002"; (B) "APhA past president trivia"; (C) "Biographies

of APhA presidents 1852–2002"; (D) "The leadership of APhA 1852–2002"; (E) "Sources of information" (includes APhA code of ethics); (F) "Index of persons" (with indication of portrait and/or biographical sketch).

1314 Pharmacy in history. George Edward Trease. London: Baillière, Tindall and Cox, [1964]. vii, 265 p., ill., ports.
615.109   RS61.T7
Contents: pt. 1: "Our inheritance from ancient civilizations": ch. 1, "From folk medicine to Galen"; ch. 2, "From Galen to the Middle Ages"; ch. 3, "Early technology"; ch. 4, "Early alchemy"; pt. 2: "The chronological development of English pharmacy": ch. 5, "Introduction"; ch. 6, "The Roman occupation and the Dark Ages"; ch. 7, "From the Norman Conquest to King John"; ch. 8, "The thirteenth century, 1216–1307"; ch. 9, "The fourteenth century, 1307–1399"; ch 10, "The fifteenth century, 1400–1485"; ch. 11, "The early Tudors, 1485–1558"; ch. 12, "The reign of Elizabeth I, 1558–1603"; ch. 13, "The early Stuarts and the Commonwealth, 1603–1660"; ch. 14, "From Charles II to Queen Anne, 1660–1714"; ch. 15, "George I and George II, 1714–1760"; ch. 16," George III, 1760–1820"; ch. 17, "1820–1870"; ch. 18, "From 1870 to 1901"; ch. 19, "Pharmaceutical preparations of the 19th century"; ch. 20, "The twentieth century." Index.

Introductory historical survey of British pharmaceutical history. Contains quotations from the literature of the different periods of the development of pharmacy, and selected illustrations.

1315 U.S. Food and Drug Administration. http://www.fda.gov. Food and Drug Administration. Washington: Food and Drug Administration
The Food and Drug Administration (FDA) regulates foods, drugs, medical devices, biologics (vaccines, blood products, etc.), and radiation-emitting products (e.g., cell phones, lasers, microwaves, etc.). Searchable website with A–Z index (http://www.fda.gov/SiteIndex/default).

Major links include Drugs (http://www.fda.gov/Drugs/default.htm) which evaluates drugs before they can be sold and provides resources such as Drugs@FDA, Electronic orange book, and National drug code directory. Another FDA center is Food (http://www.fda.gov/Food/default.htm), with resources on foods and food safety, such as the GRAS (Generally Recognized as Safe) list of substances (http://www.fda.gov/Food/Ingredients PackagingLabeling/GRAS/SCOGS/default.htm), the "bad bug book" (http://www.fda.gov/food/food borneillnesscontaminants/causesofillnessba dbug-book/default.htm) and publications on food-borne illness, FDA food code, allergens, dietary supplements, etc. Additional FDA centers provide information on biologics, cosmetics, medical devices, radiological health, toxicological research, and veterinary medicine.

Other examples of resources provided at the FDA site include access to the "blue book" (i.e., *Requirements of laws and regulations enforced by the U.S. Food and Drug Administration*), oncology tools, patient safety portal, special health issues, and information on bioterrorism, trans fats, vaccines, xenotransplantation, and many other subjects and topics relating to human and animal drugs and biologics, foods, and medical devices. Information is tailored to the needs of different user groups, with separate pages for consumers, patients, health professionals, state/local officials, industry, press, women, and children. Frequently requested FDA documents can be accessed via an "electronic reading room" (http://www.fda.gov/foi/electrr.htm). Milestones in U.S. Food and Drug Law History 1820–2005 is available at http://www.fda.gov/AboutFDA/WhatWeDo/History/Milestones/default.htm.

Internet resources

1316 Drug information portal. http://druginfo.nlm.nih.gov/. National Library of Medicine (U.S.). Bethesda, Md.: National Library of Medicine. 2008–
"Gateway to selected drug information from the National Library of Medicine and other key government agencies . . . [with] access to over 12,000 selected drugs"—*About This Portal*. Can be searched by a drug's trade or generic name. Provides a summary of the information about the drug, and links to further related information, such as MedlinePlus, AIDSinfo (648), MEDLINE/PubMed®, LactMed, HSDB, Dietary supplements labels database, TOXLINE, DailyMed, ClinicalTrials.gov, PubChem, ChemIDplus, Drugs@FDA, and

others. For the public, health care professionals, and researchers. Information regarding the mobile version of this resource is part of NLM's Gallery of mobile apps and sites.

1317 Drugs, supplements, and herbal information (MedlinePlus). http://www.nlm.nih.gov/medlineplus/druginformation.html. National Library of Medicine (U.S.). Bethesda, Md: National Library of Medicine, National Institutes of Health, U.S. Dept. of Health and Human Services. 2003?–
Pt. of MedlinePlus®.
Generic or brand name drugs, arranged A–Z, with prescription and over-the-counter medication information from MedMaster™ (American Society of Health-System Pharmacists [ASHP]). For additional drug information, see the MedlinePlus Drug Therapy topic pages (http://www.nlm.nih.gov/medlineplus/drugtherapy.html). Also provides access to information on herbs and supplements from Natural Standard©. Additional herb and supplement information can be found via MedlinePlus Complementary and Alternative Therapies topics (http://www.nlm.nih.gov/medlineplus/complementaryandalternativetherapie s.html).

1318 Drugs@FDA. http://www.accessdata.fda.gov/scripts/cder/drugsatfda. U.S. Food and Drug Administration, Center for Drug and Evaluation Research. Washington: U.S. Food and Drug Administration, Center for Drug and Evaluation Research. 2004?
RM300
Includes FDA-approved brand-name and generic drug products. Searchable by drug name, active ingredient, new drug application number (NDA), abbreviated new drug application (ANDA), and biologics license application (BLA). Provides a drug's FDA history and helps with finding labels for approved drug products. Also provides monthly drug approval reports. Further information and answers to questions relating to this website can be found at http://www.fda.gov/Drugs/Information OnDrugs/ucm075234.htm.

Also from FDA, "Drug safety and availability" http://www.fda.gov/Drugs/DrugSafety/default.htm includes information for both consumers and health professionals on new drug warnings and other safety information. "Index to drug-specific information" (found under "Postmarket drug safety information for patients and providers") can be searched for drugs that have been the subject of some type of drug safety concern, with indication if a particular drug has an active FDA safety alert (cf. Website).

1319 FAQ drug information. http://www.nlm .nih.gov/services/drug.html. National Library of Medicine (U.S.). Bethesda, Md.: National Library of Medicine. 2000–

Produced by the National Library of Medicine (NLM).

Provides links to online information about drugs, supplements, and herbal information, and additional suggestions where to find this type of information. Includes links to national and international organizations.

1320 History of vaccines. http://www.history ofvaccines.org/. College of Physicians of Philadelphia. Philadelphia: College of Physicians of Philadelphia. 2010-

Historical rare books, medical journals, manuscripts, and archival materials used in the creation of this project are from The College of Physicians of Philadelphia Historical Medical Library, whose website is at http://www.collegeofphysicians.org/.

"Chronicle of the compelling history of vaccination, from pre-Jennerian variolation practices, to the defeat of polio in the Western Hemisphere, to cutting-edge approaches to novel vaccines and vaccine delivery. Aims to increase public knowledge and understanding of the ways in which vaccines, toxoids, and passive immunization work, how they have been developed, and the role they have played in the improvement of human health. Discusses some of the controversies about vaccination and some of the challenges, difficulties, and tragic events that have occurred in the use of vaccines."—*Website (About)*. "Timelines" (http://www.historyofvaccines. org/content/timelines/all) from 900 CE to the present includes , a multimedia "gallery" (http://www.history ofvaccines.org/gallery) with vaccine-related images and videos, a "history of the immunization schedule" (http://www.historyofvaccines.org/content/history -immunization-schedule), and other interesting

content. Useful resource for students, educators, and other general readers.

Further authoritative information on vaccines can be found, for example, in *History of vaccine development* by Plotkin and in *Vaccines* by Plotkin.

1321 MedWatch. http://purl.access.gpo.gov/ GPO/LPS81698. United States; Food and Drug Administration. Rockville, Md.: U.S. Food and Drug Administration
344.73041   HE20.4058

Produced by Food and Drug Administration (FDA).

"FDA gateway for clinically important safety information and reporting serious problems with human medical products."—*Home page*. Considered a valuable resource for consumers, pharmacists, physicians, and other health professionals regarding recalls and other news of drugs; medical devices; radiation-emitting products; vaccines, blood and biologics; animal and veterinary; cosmentics; and tobacco products. Online video discusses information available on site. Searchable or browsable for recalls by date, brand, or type of recalled products, with information available in a variety of formats (e.g., e-mail alerts, RSS feeds, adding a widget to Web pages, etc.).

1322 Traditional medicine (WHO). http:// www.who.int/topics/traditional_medicine/ en/. World Health Organization. Geneva, Switzerland: World Health Organization. 200?–

Defines traditional medicine according to MeSH (MeSH: Medical Subject Headings, 858) as "systems of medicine based on cultural beliefs and practices handed down from generation to generation. The concept includes mystical and magical rituals, herbal therapy, and other treatments which may not be explained by modern medicine"—*main page*. The site "provides links to descriptions of activities, reports, news and events, as well as contacts and cooperating partners in the various WHO programmes and offices working on this topics"—*main page*. World Health Organization (WHO) publications answer questions related to standardization and regulation.

1323 U.S. Food and Drug Administration. http://www.fda.gov. Food and Drug Administration. Washington: Food and Drug Administration

The Food and Drug Administration (FDA) regulates foods, drugs, medical devices, biologics (vaccines, blood products, etc.), and radiation-emitting products (e.g., cell phones, lasers, microwaves, etc.). Searchable website with A–Z index (http://www.fda.gov/SiteIndex/default).

Major links include Drugs (http://www.fda.gov/Drugs/default.htm) which evaluates drugs before they can be sold and provides resources such as Drugs@FDA, Electronic orange book, and National drug code directory. Another FDA center is Food (http://www.fda.gov/Food/default.htm), with resources on foods and food safety, such as the GRAS (Generally Recognized as Safe) list of substances (http://www.fda.gov/Food/Ingredients PackagingLabeling/GRAS/SCOGS/default.htm), the "bad bug book" (http://www.fda.gov/food/food borneillnesscontaminants/causesofillnessbadbug book/default.htm) and publications on food-borne illness, FDA food code, allergens, dietary supplements, etc. Additional FDA centers provide information on biologics, cosmetics, medical devices, radiological health, toxicological research, and veterinary medicine.

Other examples of resources provided at the FDA site include access to the "blue book" (i.e., *Requirements of laws and regulations enforced by the U.S. Food and Drug Administration*), oncology tools, patient safety portal, special health issues, and information on bioterrorism, trans fats, vaccines, xenotransplantation, and many other subjects and topics relating to human and animal drugs and biologics, foods, and medical devices. Information is tailored to the needs of different user groups, with separate pages for consumers, patients, health professionals, state/local officials, industry, press, women, and children. Frequently requested FDA documents can be accessed via an "electronic reading room" (http://www.fda.gov/foi/electrr.htm). Milestones in U.S. Food and Drug Law History 1820–2005 is available at http://www.fda.gov/AboutFDA/WhatWeDo/History/Mile stones/default.htm.

1324 WHO drug information. http://www.who.int/druginformation. World Health Organization. Geneva, Switzerland: World Health Organization
1010-9609   RS189.W47

Quarterly journal, available since 1987 in print and also online since 1996.

Provides an overview of topics relating to drug development and regulation that are of current relevance, with the latest international news, prescribing and access of medicines worldwide. Also introduces newly released guidance documents. Includes lists of proposed and recommended International Nonproprietary Names for Pharmaceutical Substances (INN). For health professionals and policy makers. Further information and links to INNs, the current 16th ed. (Mar. 2009 and Mar. 2010 update) of the *WHO model list of essential medicines*, and other related WHO publications can be found at http://www.who.int/medicines/publications/en/.

1325 WISER (Wireless Information System for Emergency Responders). http://wiser.nlm.nih.gov. National Library of Medicine (U.S.). Bethesda, Md.: U.S. National Library of Medicine. 2005–

"A system designed to assist first responders in hazardous materials incidents . . . including substance identification support, physical characteristics, human health information, and advice on containment and suppression guidance."—*Home page*. "Information is presented to the emergency responder, Hazmat Specialist, and EMS Specialist in the order that is most relevant to their respective roles."—*About page*. Content from HSDB (Hazardous substance data bank) and from CHEMM (Chemical hazards emergency medical management) http://chemm.nlm.nih.gov. Further information on other data sources and about applications available (for phone, tablet, and desktop) on the About page. This resource is also listed on NLM's Gallery of mobile apps and sites.

11 *Psychiatry*

1326 Health and psychosocial instruments (HaPI). http://www.ovid.com/site/catalog/DataBase/866.jsp?top=2&mid=3&bottom=7&subsection=10. Ovid Technologies, Inc. Ovid Technologies, Inc., Behavioral Measurement Database Services Behavioral Measurement Database Services, Ovid Technologies, Inc., Behavioral Measurement Database Services. New York: Ovid Technologies

Comprehensive bibliographic coverage of a wide variety of evaluation and measurement tools for health and psychosocial studies for practitioners, educators, researchers, and students.

1327 PEP archive. http://www.p-e-p.org/. Psychoanalytic Electronic Publishing. London: Psychoanalytic Electronic Publishing

The PEP Archive is a full-text, indexed, and hyperlinked collection of more than 20 premier journals on psychoanalysis since 1920, the full text of the *Standard edition of the complete psychological works of Sigmund Freud*, the complete correspondence of Sigmund Freud with other leading physicians and psychoanalysts of his time, and more than 20 other classic books by noted psychoanalytic authors. Also available in CD-ROM format.

1328 PsychiatryOnline. http://www.psychiatryonline.com. American Psychiatric Publishing, American Psychiatric Association. Arlington, Va.: American Psychiatric Publishing. 2005–
RC435

Also called American Psychiatry Online Library (APOL).

Online system providing access to several psychiatry journals and reference texts in psychiatry and psychopharmacology, CME & self-assessment tools, citation linking, and "see also" links. Examples include *American journal of psychiatry* and several other psychiatry journals; the *DSM-IV-TR* and DSM-5, both part of the DSM® Library (http://dsm.psychiatryonline.org/dsmLibrary.aspx); the *American Psychiatric Association practice guidelines for the treatment of psychiatric disorders, American Psychiatric Publishing textbook of psychiatry, American Psychiatric Publishing textbook of psychopharmacology, What your patients need to know about psychiatric medications*, and other titles. Also includes an alphabetic list of topics of interest to psychiatrists, other health professionals, and also general readers.

Guides

1329 American Psychiatric Association practice guidelines for the treatment of psychiatric disorders. American

Psychiatric Association. Arlington, Va.: American Psychiatric Association, 2006. xii, 1600 p. ISBN 0890423830

616.89   RC480.A528

The American Psychiatric Association (APA) has published recommendations about the practice of psychiatry since 1851. Since 1991, the APA has been involved in the practice guideline development process to ensure the development of reliable and valid guidelines consistent with the recommendations of the American Medical Association and the Institute of Medicine (24). Practice guidelines provide recommendations to help make treatment decisions supported by the best available evidence from current research and expert consensus. In addition to providing recommendations that may improve patient care, the guidelines may also be used for education by medical students and residents and psychiatrists seeking recertification, other mental health professionals, and the general public.

Since 2006, APA practice guidelines for the treatment of adult patients and details of the guideline development process are available as part of PsychiatryOnline. The American Academy of Child and Adolescent Psychiatry (http://www.aacap.org/) provides guidelines for the treatment of psychiatric disorders of children and adolescents.

1330 Clinician's thesaurus: The guide to conducting interviews and writing psychological reports. 7th ed. Edward L. Zuckerman. New York: Guilford Press, 2010. xviii, 395 p. ISBN 9781606238745

616.890014   RC480.7.Z83

Provides guidance and standard mental health terms and descriptors that can be used in the interview process for patient assessment and evaluation and for preparing reports. Pt. I, "Conducting a mental health evaluation"; pt. II, "Standard terms and statements for wording psychological reports"; pt. III, "Useful resources." References codes from the *Diagnostic and statistical manual of mental disorders* and the International classification of diseases, ninth revision: Clinical modification (ICM-9-CM) online edition. Intended for students and mental health professionals. Also available as an e-book.

Bibliography

1331 Core readings in psychiatry: An annotated guide to the literature. 2nd ed. Michael H. Sacks, William H. Sledge, Catherine Warren. Washington: American Psychiatric Press, 1995. xxv, 944 p. ISBN 0880485590

616.89   RC454.C655

First edition, 1984 (ed. Michael H. Sachs, William H. Sledge, and Phyllis Rubinton).

Contents: pt. 1, "Basic sciences: Biological, psychological, and social" (ch. 1–10); pt. 2, "Psychopathology" (ch. 11–30); pt. 3, "Assessment" (ch. 31–35); pt. 4, "Treatment" (ch. 36–51); pt. 5, "Normality and development" (ch. 52–66).

"Designed to be an introduction and guide to the entire psychiatric literature"—*Introd.* Broad survey, presenting 66 topical chapters by mental health specialists, with selected annotated literature citations. New areas of study since the previous edition include AIDS, neurospychiatry, models of psychoanalytic thoughts, child development, and medical economics. Resource for clinicians, educators, and students.

1332 Guide to mental health motion pictures. http://www.nlm.nih.gov/hmd/collections/films/mentalhealthguide/index.html. National Library of Medicine (U.S). Bethesda, Md.: National Library of Medicine U.S. Dept. of Health, Education, and Welfare, National Institutes of Health. 2012

Administered by the National Library of Medicine's Historical Audiovisuals Collection (HAV). Compiled and Edited by: Sarah Eilers; Technical Assistance: Nancy Dosch, Anatoliy Milikhiker, Anthony Vu.

This online guide contains references to approximately 200 films and videorecordings produced from the 1930s to 1970 dealing "with mental or psychiatric disorders as defined or recognized at the time the films were produced, as well as their corresponding causes and treatments. . . . The mental disorders found in these productions include anxiety, depression, psychosis, schizophrenia, substance abuse, and bipolar, dissociative, and personality disorders. Some films also consider as mental disorders topics that are not so classified today, such as alcoholism, homosexuality, and marital or maternal dissatisfaction. Therapies and treatments include psychiatric interviews, counseling and talk therapy, electro-convulsive therapy, frontal lobe surgery (lobotomy), pharmaceuticals, art therapy, residential treatment programs, and community-based treatment programs."—*Introd. and Scope*. Includes title, date of publication, running time, conditions/therapies, names, abstract, and link to the full catalog record in LocatorPlus (52) for each item. Subject index.

Further information on additional content and a selected list of notable titles can be found at http://www.nlm.nih.gov/hmd/collections/films/mentalhealthguide/scope.h tml. It is part of the NLM films and video collections http://www.nlm.nih.gov/hmd/collections/films/index.html#A0

which includes more than 5,300 films and video recordings from 1900 to the present.

Other online guides to NLM's historical audiovisual collections include, for example, *Guide to tropical disease motion pictures and audiovisuals* http://www.nlm.nih.gov/hmd/collections/films/tropicalguide/index.html and *National Library of Medicine's Motion pictures and videocassettes about the Public Health Service and its agencies* http://www.nlm.nih.gov/hmd/pdf/motionpicture.pdf. A print title is *Mental health motion pictures*.

Classification

1333 The ICD-10 classification of mental and behavioural disorders: Clinical descriptions and diagnostic guidelines. World Health Organization. Geneva, [Switzerland]: World Health Organization, 1992. xii, 362 p.
ISBN 9241544228
616.890012   RC455.2.C4I34
Adopted by the World Health Organization, Jan. 1993. A related title is *The ICD-10 classification of mental and behavioural disorders: Diagnostic criteria for research*, published by WHO in 2003.

Developed from ch. 5 of the *International statistical classification of diseases and related health problems*. An internationally agreed-upon psychiatric classification system, with descriptions

of clinical features for each disorder, diagnostic guidelines, and codes for mental and behavioral disorders.Includes index. Full text available online at http://www.who.int/classifications/icd/en/bluebook.pdf. A companion volume is *Lexicon of psychiatric and mental terms*.

Another major title in the area of classification of mental disorders is *{record}Diagnostic and statistical manual of mental disorders*.

Development of ICD-11 is underway with expected completion in 2015. See details at http://www.who.int/classifications/icd/en/.

1334 Intellectual disability: Definition, classification, and systems of supports. 11th ed. American Association on Intellectual and Developmental Disabilities. Washington: American Association on Intellectual and Developmental Disabilities, 2010. xvi, 259 p., ill. ISBN 9781935304043
616.8588   RC570.C515
First ed. (1921)–10th ed. (2002) had title: *Mental retardation: Definition, classification, and systems of support*.

AAIDD (American Association on Intellectual and Developmental Disabilities)

Written by the AAIDD Ad Hoc Committee on Terminology and Classification, consisting of 18 experts in disability, medicine, policy, special education, law, and other fields.

Contents: Pt. I, "Understanding intellectual disability and its assessment"; pt. II, "Diagnosis and classification of intellectual disability"; pt. III, "Systems of support"; pt. IV, "Implications."

In the 11th ed., the AAIDD presents its first official definition of the term "intellectual disability" (formerly mental retardation) and diagnostic system of intellectual disability based on three criteria: significant limitations in both intellectual functioning and adaptive behavior expressed in conceptual, social, and practical adaptive skills and age of onset before the age of 18.

Contains current and authoritative information on defining, classifying, and diagnosing intellectual disability and systems of support for people living with intellectual disability. Disability is being considered within the context of an individual's personal and environmental factors, and what support might be appropriate to improve a person's functioning and quality of life. Discusses various dimensions of support areas in a person's life, i.e. resources or strategies that promote the development, education, interests, and well-being of a person. Includes tables, figures, a glossary, references, and index, also historical definitions of mental retardation as formulated by the American Association on Mental Retardation (AAMR) and the American Psychiatric Association (APA). Intended for professionals in developmental disability, clinical psychologists, physicians, psychiatrists, students, and others. *User's guide intellectual disability: Definition, classification, and systems of supports* provides practical advice on how to use this resource.

1335 Psychodynamic diagnostic manual (PDM). American Psychoanalytic Association, International Psychoanalytical Association, American Psychological Association, American Academy of Psychoanalysis and Dynamic Psychiatry, National Membership Committee on Psychoanalysis in Clinical Social Work. Silver Spring, Md.: Alliance of Psychoanalytic Organizations, 2006 0976775824

Intended as a complement to the DSM (*Diagnostic and statistical manual of mental disorders: DSM-IV-TR*) and ICD (*ICD-10 classification of mental and behavioural disorders*) classifications, it is described as "a diagnostic framework that attempts to characterize an individual's range of functionality—the depth as well as the surface of emotional, cognitive, and social patterns . . . based on current neuroscience, treatment outcome research, and other empirical investigations"—*Introd*.

Indexes; Abstract journals; Databases

1336 NLM gateway. http://gateway.nlm.nih .gov/. National Library of Medicine (U.S.). Bethesda, Md.: National Library of Medicine. 2000–

RA11

As announced in 2011, "the NLM® gateway has transitioned to a new pilot project from the Lister Hill National Center for Biomedical Communications (LHNCBC)."—*Website* The new site focuses now on two databases: Meeting abstracts and Health services research projects. All of the other resources previously accessed through the NLM gateway are available through their individual sites. For a list of these databases previously available via the NLM gateway see http://gateway.nlm.nih.gov/ about.jsp.

The NLM gateway previously allowed simultaneous searching of information resources at the National Library of Medicine (NLM)/National Center for Biotechnology Information (NCBI) with an overview of the search results presented in several categories (bibliographic resources, consumer health resources, and other information), with a listing of the individual databases and the number of results within these categories. Previously included were, for example, MEDLINE/PubMed and the NLM Catalog as well as other resources, including information on current clinical trials and consumer health information (MedlinePlus) and many others.

1337 PsycINFO. http://www.apa.org/ psycinfo/. American Psychological Association. Washington: American Psychological Association. [n.d.] 150.5 0033-2887 BF1.P65

The most comprehensive index to the literature of psychology, indexing more than 1,200 English-language journals and reports and providing descriptive, nonevaluative abstracts. Formerly published in print as *Psychological abstracts* (ceased with 2006). Coverage has varied widely over the history of this title, extending back to 1872 in part. Abstracts are arranged by subject categories following the *Thesaurus of psychological index terms*. Coverage of books and dissertations, dropped in 1980, was resumed in 1992. Coverage of foreign-language materials was dropped in 1988. The database replaces associated indexes such as *Cumulative author index to Psychological abstracts* (1959/63–1981/83) and *Author index to Psychological index, 1894–1935, and Psychological abstracts, 1927–1958*.

1338 PubMed. http://www.ncbi.nlm.nih.gov/ pubmed. U.S. National Center for Biotechnology Information, National

Library of Medicine, National Institutes of Health. Bethesda, Md.: U.S. National Center for Biotechnology Information. 1996–

PubMed®, developed and maintained by the National Center for Biotechnology Information (NCBI) at the National Library of Medicine® (NLM). Provides a search interface for more than 20 million bibliographic citations and abstracts in the fields of medicine, nursing, dentistry, veterinary medicine, health care systems, and preclinical sciences. It provides access to articles indexed for MEDLINE® and for selected life sciences journals. PubMed subsets found under the "Limits" tab are: MEDLINE and PubMed central®, several journal groups (i.e., core clinical journals, dental journals, and nursing journals), and topical subsets (AIDS, bioethics, cancer, complementary medicine, dietary supplements, history of medicine, space life sciences, systematic reviews, toxicology, and veterinary science). "Link-out" provides access to full-text articles.

For detailed information see the PubMed fact sheet at http://www.nlm.nih.gov/pubs/factsheets/pubmed.html and also MEDLINE®/PubMed® resources guide (http://www.nlm.nih.gov/bsd/pm resources.html) which provides detailed information about MEDLINE data and searching PubMed.

Information regarding the mobile version of this resource is part of NLM's Gallery of mobile apps and sites.

Dictionaries

1339 American psychiatric glossary.
8th ed. Narriman C. Shahrokh, Robert E. Hales. Washington: American Psychiatric, 2003. ix, 255 p. ISBN 1585620939
616.89003   RC437.S76
First five editions, 1957–80, had title *A psychiatric glossary: The meaning of words most frequently used in psychiatry*. Seventh edition, 1994.

Includes "Outline of schools of psychiatry." Concise compendium of psychiatric terminology, with brief definitions. Incorporates the nomenclature of the *Diagnostic and statistical manual of mental disorders: DSM-IV-TR* of the American Psychiatric Association. More than 500 new terms in this edition. Includes abbreviations, tables of psychiatric medications and commonly abused drugs,

legal terms, psychological tests, research terms, and list of mental health resources, with pertinent websites. Considered a standard reference, intended for professionals and also laypersons.

1340 APA concise dictionary of psychology.
American Psychological Association. Washington: American Psychological Association, 2009. xi, 583 p. ISBN 9781433803918
150.3   BF31
A careful abridgement of the 2006 APA dictionary of psychology, at a lower price. Defines some 10,000 terms instead of 25,000. An even shorter condensation of the original is APA college dictionary of psychology.

1341 APA dictionary of clinical psychology.
1st ed. Gary R. VandenBos, American Psychological Association. Washington: American Psychological Association, 2013. xi, 636 p.
616.89/1403   RC467.A63
Based on *APA dictionary of psychology*, contains approx. 11,000 selected entries, with appropriate revisions where necessary. Contains, for example, entries on the diagnosis, prevention, and treatment of emotional and behavioral disorders; biological and cognitive foundations of mental health; etc. Cross references, a guide to use, and appendixes, with biographical entries of important figures in the history of clinical psychology, and various treatment approaches.

1342 APA dictionary of psychology. Gary R. VandenBos, American Psychological Association. Washington: American Psychological Association, 2006. ISBN 9781591473800
150.3   BF31.V295
Over 25,000 terms and definitions encompassing such areas of research and application as personality, development, interpersonal relations, memory, motivation, perception, cognition, language, and communication, among others. Provides coverage of psychological concepts, processes, and therapies across all the major subdisciplines of psychology— including clinical, experimental, social, developmental, personality, school and educational, industrial and organizational, and health. Amply cross-referenced, directing the user to synonyms

and antonyms, acronyms and abbreviations, related terms and concepts. Four appendixes, each gathering entries thematically into one synoptic listing, covering biographies; institutions, associations, and organizations; psychological therapies and interventions; and psychological tests and assessment instruments.

1343 The Blackwell dictionary of neuropsychology. J. Graham Beaumont, Pamela M. Kenealy, Marcus Rogers. Cambridge, Mass.: Blackwell Publishers, 1996. xix, 788 p., ill. ISBN 0631178961
612.803   QP360.B577

Extended entries by international contributors provide a broad perspective on the study of neuropsychology. Entries cover key topics. Alphabetical organization and cross-referencing provide immediate access to the complex vocabulary of this field. Enhanced by illustrations and tables.

1344 The Cambridge dictionary of psychology. David Ricky Matsumoto. Cambridge, U.K.; New York: Cambridge University Press, 2009. xviii, 587 p. ISBN 9780521854702
150.3   BF31

Seeks to offer an international, cross-cultural, and interdisciplinary approach. Covers concepts sometimes omitted from dictionaries of psychology. Supported by a body of contributors with international origins. Available as an e-book.

1345 Campbell's psychiatric dictionary. 9th ed. Robert Jean Campbell. Oxford; New York: Oxford University Press, 2009. xx, 1051 p. ISBN 9780195341591
616.89003   RC437.H5

First ed., 1940; 8th ed., 2003. Early editions had title *Psychiatric dictionary*.

A standard dictionary in the field of psychiatry and allied professions, this expanded edition contains the extensive terminology of psychiatry, neuroscience, cognitive and clinical psychology, and related fields, with many new words and encyclopedic treatment of many terms. Also contains brief biographical entries. Useful for specialists as well as for non-specialists.

1346 Comprehensive dictionary of psychoanalysis. Salman Akhtar. London: Karmac, 2009. xiii, 404 p.

ISBN 9781855754713
150.19503   BF173.A5767

Encyclopedic dictionary of psychoanalysis, intended for faculty, researchers, and students. Provides definitions of psychoanalytic terms and concepts and explains the origin of each term. Cites references in connection with each entry. Includes many applied psychoanalysis terms as well as terms that have become obsolete. Contains an annotated list of psychoanalytic glossaries and an extensive list of references. Also available as an e-book.

Complements the *International dictionary of psychoanalysis*.

1347 Comprehensive glossary of psychiatry and psychology. Harold I. Kaplan, Benjamin J. Sadock, Robert Cancro. Baltimore: Williams & Wilkins, 1991. xi, 215 p., col. ill. ISBN 068304527X
616.89003   RC437.K36

Concise definitions of terms from the behavioral sciences, psychiatry, psychology, and social work, neurochemistry, neuroimmunology, and neurophysiology. A new edition, *Sadock's comprehensive glossary of psychiatry and psychology*, is scheduled to be published.

1348 Dictionary of cognitive science: Neuroscience, psychology, artificial intelligence, linguistics, and philosophy. Olivier Houdé, Daniel Kayser, Vivian Waltz, Christian Cav. New York: Psychology Press, 2004. xxxv, 428 p. ISBN 1579582516
153.03   BF311.V56713

Translation of *Vocabulaire de sciences cognitives* (1998), a collaborative effort of 60 (mostly French) scholars. Presents 130 terms drawn from five major disciplines of cognitive science: neuroscience, psychology, artificial intelligence, linguistics, and philosophy. Instead of merely defining those terms, the editors divide them into sections corresponding to the five areas and explain them within the context of the applicable disciplines. Concluding each entry is a bibliography of selected sources, updated from the original French version. Not as broad and in-depth as its nearest competitor, *The MIT encyclopedia of the cognitive sciences*, still a good resource for definitions of basic concepts in cognitive science, making it suitable for students. Available as an e-book.

1349 Dictionary of ethical and legal terms and issues: The essential guide for mental health professionals. Len Sperry. New York: Routledge, 2007. xi, 277 p. ISBN 0415953219

174.2   RC455.2.E8.S655

Contents: pt. 1, Dictionary of ethical and legal terms; pt. 2, Ethical issues and considerations; pt. 3, Legal issues and considerations; appendix: Key legal cases and legislation impacting mental health practice; index.

Concise guide to the key ethical and legal issues and considerations; codes and statutes; and key legal opinions, legislation, and regulations relevant to everyday mental health practice in the United States. Pt. 2 and 3 present particular topics in some detail, with definitions of key terms. Intended for graduate and undergraduate students and as a ready-reference source for mental health practitioners. Also available as an e-book.

Legal and ethical dictionary for mental health professionals by Ahia is another resource in this area, containing definitions provided in a legal context. Also includes mental health acronyms and codes of ethics of several professional associations (e.g., American Counseling Association, American Psychological Association, and others).

1350 Dictionary of existential psychotherapy and counselling. Emmy Van Deurzen, Raymond Kenward. London; Thousand Oaks, Calif.: SAGE, 2005. 228 p. ISBN 0761970940

616.891403   RC489.E93.V357

Includes existential terminology and concepts; biographies of major philosophers (this dictionary is "considered generally philosophical" [*Introd.*] by the authors), psychotherapists, and theorists ("non-existential writers considered to have contributed to existential thinking" —*Introd.*); and related subjects not exclusively existential (e.g., humanistic psychology). Alphabetically arranged, with cross-references and many quotations. Includes bibliographical references (p. 222–228). For both general readers and professionals. Also available as an e-book.

1351 A dictionary of hallucinations. Jan Dirk Blom. New York: Springer, 2010. xiv, 553 p., ill. (some col.), ports. ISBN 9781441912220

RC553.H3B56

Provides a history of the concepts related to hallucinations, illusions, and sensory distortions, with an "alphabetical listing of key terms and concepts as derived from the historical and contemporary literature."—*Pref.* Comprehensive, up-to-date listing of words, terms, concepts, and people associated with its subject. Alphabetically arranged, each entry gives a definition and its etymological origin, information on who introduced the term and its year of introduction, current usage, material on etiology and pathophysiology, cross-references to similar concepts, when appropriate, source references to relevant literature. Illustrated. Also available as an e-book.

1352 The dictionary of psychology. Raymond J. Corsini. Philadelphia: Brunner/Mazel, 1999. xv, 1156 p., ill. ISBN 158391028X

150.3   BF31.C72

More than 13,000 entries as well as nine appendixes on such topics as terms used by the DSM-IV manual of mental disorders, prescription terms, measuring instruments, and brief biographies of noted psychologists through history.

1353 A dictionary of psychology. 3rd ed. Andrew M. Colman. Oxford; New York: Oxford University Press, 2009. xi, 882 p., ill. ISBN 9780199534067

150.3   BF31

Revised in part since the 2nd edition of 2006. Also known as the *Oxford dictionary of psychology*. Clear, concise descriptions offer extensive coverage of key areas, including cognition, sensation and perception, emotion and motivation, learning and skills, language, mental disorders, and research methods. Entries extend to related disciplines, including psychoanalysis, psychiatry, the neurosciences, and statistics, and are extensively cross-referenced for ease of use, covering word origins and derivations as well as definitions. Also includes appendixes covering over 800 commonly used abbreviations and symbols as well as a list of phobias and phobic stimuli, with definitions.

Illustrations and brief bibliography. Available as an e-book.

1354 Dictionary of psychopathology.
Henry Kellerman. New York: Columbia University Press, 2009. xvii, 278 p.
ISBN 9780231146500
616.89003   RC437

Some 2,000 short entries in alphabetical order. Deals with aspects of personality, diagnosis and treatment, specific symptoms and syndromes, and the vocabulary of the field. Cross-disciplinary in scope, and intended to be relevant for students, academic researchers and clinical practitioners in the disciplines of psychology, psychiatry and social work. Brief bibliography of similar works.

1355 A historical dictionary of psychiatry.
Edward Shorter. New York: Oxford University Press, 2005. ix, 338 p.
ISBN 0195176685
616.89003   RC438.S53

Contains key terms and concepts for psychiatry and the neurosciences, trends in psychiatry, pharmacological developments, and social themes. Includes important individuals, places, institutions, and dates in the development of psychiatry, with emphasis on the mid-19th century to the present. Bibliographical references and index. For clinicians, scientists, and general readers. Available as an e-book.

1356 International dictionary of psychoanalysis = Dictionnaire international de la psychanalyse. A. de Mijolla. Detroit: Macmillan Reference USA, 2005. 3 v. ISBN 0028659244
616.891703   RC501.4.D4313

Translation of French *Dictionnaire international de la psychanalyse*, ed. Alain de Mijolla, 2002.

Contents: v. 1, A–F; v. 2, G–Pr; v. 3, Ps–Z.

Considers the history and modern practice of psychoanalysis and its subfields, including the relationship between psychoanalysis and other disciplines. International resource, with 1,569 entries. The American edition contains more than 200 new articles, which include discussion of concepts, the history of psychoanalysis in different countries, and biographies of major deceased psychoanalysts and their major works. Multilingual glossary (from English into French, German, Italian, Portuguese,

and Spanish). Includes 19th- and 20th-century chronology. Also available online via Gale virtual reference library.

1357 The language of mental health: A glossary of psychiatric terms.
Narriman C. Shahrokh. Washington: American Psychiatric Publishing, 2011. viii, 338 p. ISBN 9781585623457
616.89003   RC437.L28

Up-to-date terminology, including commonly-used abbreviations, psychiatric measures, medications, and legal terms that are commonly used in the mental health field. Written for mental health professionals, but also useful for health consumers, i.e., patients and their families. Also available as an e-book.

1358 Lexicon of psychiatric and mental health terms. 2nd ed. World Health Organization. Geneva, Switzerland: World Health Organization, 1994. 108 p. ISBN 924154466X
616.890014   RC436.5.L49
First edition, 1989.

"The second edition . . . is designed as a companion volume to the *ICD-10 classification of mental and behavioural disorders*. Contains some 700 terms that appear in the text of the ICD-10 and that, in the judgment of experts, require definitions. Some of these, common to both ICD-9 and ICD-10, have been reproduced, with minor modifications" (*Introd.*, p. 2) from the 1st ed. Included are names of psychiatric diseases and conditions, names of signs and symptoms, and related psychopathological terms, terminology used in psychiatric classification, and also some mental health terms.

A pdf version is available at http://whqlibdoc. who.int/publications/924154466X.pdf.

1359 Lexicon of psychiatry, neurology, and the neurosciences. 2nd ed. Frank J. Ayd. Philadelphia: Lippincott Williams & Wilkins, 2000. vii, 1104 p.
616.803   RC334.A96
First edition, 1995.

This enlarged edition provides brief descriptions of psychiatric and neurological diseases and disorders and related terminology, with journal and book references cited within entries. Also includes concise information about psychiatric drugs, with comments on adverse reactions and interactions with other drugs. Subject index.

Directories

1360 Information gateway for psychiatry residents and fellows. http://www .psychiatry.org/residents. American Psychiatric Association. Arlington, Va.: American Psychiatric Association. 2006–

Part of the American Psychiatric Institute for Research and Education (APIRE) http://www .psychiatry.org/researchers/apire, a division of the American Psychiatric Association (APA).

Gateway for psychiatry residents and fellows, providing online information on the various subspecialties in psychiatry (e.g., child and adolescent, geriatric, addiction, forensic, psychosomatic psychiatry, and others) and their training requirements. Website also provides various "in training resources" links. Information on the individual programs are provided via FREIDA online (291), AMA's fellowship and residency electronic interactive database.

Directory of psychiatry residency training programs, a print resource, has been discontinued.

1361 Substance Abuse and Mental Health Services Administration (SAMHSA). http://www.samhsa.gov. Substance Abuse and Mental Health Services Administration. Rockville, Md.: Substance Abuse and Mental Health Services Administration
362.21; 362.29   RA790.6

Substance Abuse and Mental Health Services Administration (SAMHSA), part of U.S. Dept. of Health and Human Services (HHS).

SAMHSA has as its mission "building resilience and facilitating recovery for people with or at risk for mental or substance use disorders . . . gearing all of its resources . . . toward that outcome."—*About Us* Searchable website. Provides resources for prevention, treatment, and rehabilitation services for patients with various forms of mental illness and addictions. Includes three centers: SAMHSA's Center for Mental Health Services (CMHS), Center for Substance Abuse Prevention (CSAP), and Center for Substance Abuse Treatment (CSAT). Examples

of SAMHSA resources include "Find substance abuse and mental health treatment" (http://www .samhsa.gov/treatment/) with clickable maps to locate different programs throughout the United States, and links to various related publications (http://store.samhsa.gov/home). Provides the latest data (http://www.samhsa.gov/data/) on alcohol, tobacco, and illegal drugs as well as other statistical data and resources.

Handbooks

1362 APA ethics office. http://www.apa.org/ ethics/homepage.html. American Psychological Association. Washington: American Psychological Association. 2002

Areas covered include but are not limited to the clinical, counseling, and school practice of psychology; research; teaching; supervision of trainees; public service; policy development; social intervention; development of assessment instruments; conducting assessments; educational counseling; organizational consulting; forensic activities; program design and evaluation; and administration. Provides links to full-text ethics information: "Ethical Principles of Psychologists and Code of Conduct"; "Ethics Committee on Services by Telephone, Teleconferencing, and Internet"; "Guidelines for Ethical Conduct in the Care and Use of Animals"; and more. Available online from APA in HTML, PDF, and MS Word formats.

1363 Assessment scales in old age psychiatry. 2nd ed. Alistair Burns, Brian Lawlor, Sarah Craig. London; New York: Martin Dunitz, 2004. 383 p.
ISBN 1841841684
618.97689   RC473.P78

First edition, 1999.

Contents: (1) "Depression"; (2) "Dementia" ("Cognitive assessment"; "Neuropsychiatric assessments"; "Activities of daily living"; "Global assessments/ quality of life"); (3) "Global mental health assessments"; (4) "Physical examination"; (5) "Delirium"; (6) "Caregiver assessments"; (7) "Memory functioning"; (8) "Other scales."

Collection of psychiatric rating scales that support the valid measurement and diagnosis of signs and symptoms of mental disorders in older people. Includes approximately 200 scales, i.e., all scales from the previous edition and also additional scales, with commentaries. Includes a section covering neuropsychological tests. Also available as an e-book.

1364 Cambridge handbook of psychology, health, and medicine. 2nd ed.
Susan Ayers. Cambridge [England]; New York: Cambridge University Press, 2007. ISBN 9780521605
616.0019   R726.5.C354
Description based on 1st ed., 1997.
Interdisciplinary encyclopedic handbook, intended primarily as a reference text for psychologists and health professionals. Addresses areas of psychology relevant to medicine and behavioral factors in relation to medical conditions. Chapters are arranged alphabetically, with many cross-references. Includes bibliographical references and index. Also available as an e-book.

1365 Clinical handbook of psychiatry and the law. 4th ed. Paul S. Appelbaum, Thomas G. Gutheil. Philadelphia: Wolters Kluwer Health/Lippincott, Williams and Wilkins, 2007. xiii, 322 p. ISBN 0781778913
344.73041   KF2910.P75G87
First ed., 1982; 3rd ed., 2000.
Contents: ch. 1, "Confidentiality and privilege"; ch. 2, "Legal issues in emergency psychiatry"; ch. 3, "Legal issues in inpatient psychiatry"; ch. 4, "Malpractice and other forms of liability"; ch. 5, "Competence and substitute decision making"; ch. 6, "Forensic evaluations"; ch. 7, "Clinicians and lawyers"; ch. 8, "The clinician in court"; index.
Provides up-to-date information for clinicians on "how law affects practice, and how psychiatry can contribute to the law" (*Pref.*) and discussion of its interrelated clinical and legal aspects. Each chapter has the following seven sections: Case examples, legal issues, clinical issues, pitfalls, case example epilogues, action guide, and suggested readings. Available online to subscribers via Books@Ovid.

1366 Clinical manual of psychiatry and law. 1st ed. Robert I. Simon, Daniel W. Shuman. Washington: American

Psychiatric Publ., 2007. p.
614/.15   RA1151.S56
Contents: (1) Psychiatry and the law; (2) The doctor-patient relationship; (3) Confidentiality and testimonial privilege; (4) Informed consent and the right to refuse treatment; (5) Psychiatric treatment: tort liability; (6) Seclusion and restraint; (7) Involuntary hospitalization; (8) The suicidal patient; (9) Psychiatric responsibility and the violent patient; (10) Maintaining treatment boundaries: clinical and legal issues. Appendix A: Suggested readings; Appendix B: Glossary of legal terms; Index.
Covers a variety of topics concerning the requirements and legal regulations of psychiatric practice, including treatment issues that may lead to liability and malpractice law suits.
Clinical handbook of psychiatry and law covers topics such as confidentiality and privilege, legal issues in emergency psychiatry and inpatient psychiatry, forensic evaluations, the clinician in court, and others.

1367 Clinician's thesaurus: The guide to conducting interviews and writing psychological reports. 7th ed.
Edward L. Zuckerman. New York: Guilford Press, 2010. xviii, 395 p. ISBN 9781606238745
616.890014   RC480.7.Z83
Provides guidance and standard mental health terms and descriptors that can be used in the interview process for patient assessment and evaluation and for preparing reports. Pt. I, "Conducting a mental health evaluation"; pt. II, "Standard terms and statements for wording psychological reports"; pt. III, "Useful resources." References codes from the *Diagnostic and statistical manual of mental disorders* and the International classification of diseases, ninth revision: Clinical modification (ICM-9-CM) online edition. Intended for students and mental health professionals. Also available as an e-book.

1368 Concise rules of APA style. American Psychological Association. Washington: American Psychological Association, 2005. ix, 212 p., ill. ISBN 1591472520
808.06615   BF76.7.C66
Compiled from the 5th ed. of the *Publication manual of the American Psychological Association*,

this handy work covers topics such as concise and bias-free writing, punctuation, spelling, and capitalization, italicizing and abbreviating, the use of numbers, metrication and statistics, tables and figures, footnotes and appendixes, and quotations. Provides very helpful reference examples, including those from electronic and audiovisual media, a cross-reference to the publication manual, and a checklist for manuscript submission.

1369 Companion to psychiatric studies.
8th ed. Eve C. Johnstone. Edinburgh, [Scotland, U.K.]; New York: Churchill Livingstone, 2010. x, 834 p., ill.
ISBN 9780702031373
616.89   RC454.C635
First ed., 1973; 7th ed., 2004.
Written originally as a learning tool for U.K. trainees in psychiatry, this resource can also be considered a useful reference resource in the U.S. and elsewhere. It provides an introduction to psychiatry, including early concepts. Includes various tables (e.g., "Ancient times until 18th century" and "The modern era—18th century until the present day"), with the state of knowledge at the time, notable events, advances, and individuals. Includes a summary of the development of academic psychiatry, psychoanalytic theories, the international classifications of mental disorders, and also addresses future classifications. Each chapter on the various psychiatric disorders provides an historical introduction, definitions, clinical presentation and symptoms, acute and chronic phases of psychiatric disorders, epidemiology, risk factors, etiology, prognosis, treatment, and also related disorders. Also available as an e-book.

1370 The complete writing guide to NIH behavioral science grants. Lawrence M. Scheier, William L. Dewey. New York: Oxford University Press, 2007. 506 p.
ISBN 9780195320275
362.1079   RA11.D6C65
Contents: ch. 1, Peer review at the National Institutes of Health; ch. 2, Drug abuse research collaboration in the 21st century; ch. 3, A brief guide to the essentials of grant writing; ch. 4, Sample size, detectable difference, and power; ch. 5, Exploratory/developmental and small grant award mechanisms; ch. 6, Funding your future: what you need to know to develop a pre- or postdoctoral; training

application; ch. 7, Unique funding opportunities for underrepresented minorities and international researchers; ch. 8, R01 grants: the investigator-initiated cornerstone of biomedical research; ch. 9, P50 research center grants; ch. 10, P20 and P30 center grants: developmental mechanisms; ch. 11, The K award: an important part of the NIH funding alphabet soup; ch. 12, T32 grants at the NIH: tips for success; ch. 13, SBIR funding: a unique opportunity for the entrepreneurial researchers; ch. 14, Federal grants and contracts outside of NIH; ch. 15, The financing and cost accounting of science: budgets and budget administration; ch. 16, Documenting human subjects protections and procedures; ch. 17, Navigating the maze: electronic submission; ch. 18, Revisions and resubmissions; ch. 19, Concluding remarks: the bottom line. Appendix 1: The NIH Web sites; Appendix 2: NIH institutes, centers, and their websites.

Presents important considerations in developing research proposals and funding mechanisms for both junior and established researchers. Provides practical information on how to construct and write successful grants, electronic grant submission, revising research proposals, etc. Useful to researchers, clinicians, and educators in a wide variety of subject areas who are interested in submitting grants to the NIH.

1371 Comprehensive handbook of personality and psychopathology.
Michel Hersen, Jay C. Thomas. Hoboken, N.J.: John Wiley and Sons, 2006. 3 v., ill.
ISBN 0471479454
618.9289   RC456.C66
Presents an overview of the foundations of major theories of personality, covering such broad topics as personality and everyday functioning, adult psychopathology, and child psychopathology. Each section compiled by experts in their fields. Available as an e-book.

1372 Comprehensive handbook of psychopathology. 3rd ed. Patricia B. Sutker, Henry E. Adams. New York: Kluwer Academic/Plenum, 2001. xviii, 970 p., ill. ISBN 030646490X
616.89   RC454.C636
First edition, 1984; 2nd ed., 1993.
"Resource textbook that covers both general

and specific topics in psychopathology . . . useful to researchers, practitioners, and graduate and other advanced students in the mental health professions"—*Pref*. In six main parts: (1) "Issues in psychopathology"; (2) "Neurotic and psychotic disorders"; (3) "Personality disorders"; (4) "Disorders associated with social and situational problems"; (5) "Disorders associated with physical trauma and medical illness"; (6) "Disorders arising in specific life stages." Chapters by specialists focus on overviews of clinical description, research, and theories, with extensive references. Indexed. Also available as an e-book and via Credo reference.

1373 Comprehensive handbook of psychotherapy. Florence Whiteman Kaslow, Jeffrey J. Magnavita, Terence. Patterson, Robert F. Massey, Sharon Davis Massey, Jay Lebow. New York: Wiley, 2002. 4 v., ill. ISBN 0471018481
616.8914   RC480.C593

Contents: v. 1, *Psychodynamic/object relations* (ed. Florence W. Kaslow); v. 2, *Cognitive-behavioral approaches*; v. 3, *Interpersonal/humanistic/existential*; v. 4, *Integrative/eclectic*.

Intends to present the state of the art of psychotherapy, including history, theory, major schools, practice trends and research, reflecting the globalization of the field. Written from a biopsychosocial perspective. Author and subject index in each volume. For graduate students, faculty, clinicians, and researchers. Some volumes available as e-books.

1374 Diagnostic and statistical manual of mental disorders = DSM-5.
5th ed. American Psychiatric Association, American Psychiatric Association. Arlington, Va.: American Psychiatric Association, 2013. xliv, 947 p. ISBN 9780890425541
616.89/075   RC455.2.C4

First ed., 1952; 4th ed. (1994) has title *Diagnostic and statistical manual of mental disorders: DSM-IV*; 4th ed., 2000 (text revision) *Diagnostic and statistical manual of mental disorders: DSM-IV-TR*.

Details of the DSM-5 development process can be found at http://www.DSM5.org/.

Contents: Section 1, DSM-5 basics: Introduction; Use of the manual; Cautionary statement for forensic use of DSM-5; section II, Diagnostic criteria and codes; section III, Emerging measures and models; Appendix contains "Highlights of changes from DSM-IV to DSM-5, "Glossary of technical terms," "Alphabetic listing of DSM-5 diagnoses and codes (ICD-9-CM and ICD-10-CM)," "Numerical listing of DSM-5 diagnoses and codes (ICD-9-CM)," "Numerical listing of DSM-5 diagnoses and codes (ICD-10-CM)," "DSM-5 advisors, and other information."

Considered an essential resource for mental health professionals and a reference for clinical practice to facilitate more reliable diagnoses of psychiatric disorders and viewed by clinicians and researchers as the accepted classification system for psychiatric disorders. "This edition of DSM was designed first and foremost to be a useful guide to clinical practice . . . applicable in a wide diversity of contexts . . . intended to facilitate an objective assessment of symptom presentations in a variety of clinical settings — inpatient, outpatient, partial hospital, consultation-liaison, clinical, private practice, and primary care—as well in general community epidemiological studies of mental disorders."—*Pref*. Contains all diagnostic critera plus systematic description of disorders, using a numerical code system. Includes an explanation of the code system and instructions for its use, description of disorders, glossary, classification, history, alphabetic and numeric listing of diagnoses, and indexes of symptoms, diagnoses, and codes. Corrects factual errors, updates codes, and reflects new information since the previous edition. Instructions for use are followed by the diagnostic criteria for each of the DSM-5 disorders, along with descriptive text.

"Harmonized with the World Health Organization's International Classification of Diseases (ICD), the official coding system used in the United States, so that the DSM criteria define disorders identified by ICD diagnostic names and code numbers. In DSM-5, both ICD-9-CM and ICD-10-CM codes (the latter scheduled for adoption in October 2014) are attached to the relevant disorders in the classification . . . disorders included in DSM-5 were reordered into a revised organizational structure meant to stimulate new clinical perspectives. Corresponds with the organizational arrangement of disorders planned for ICD-11 scheduled for release in 2015.—Preface. Available online via Psychiatry-Online/DSM® Library.

Desk reference to the diagnostic criteria from DSM-5 is an abbreviated version with only the DSM-5 classifications, diagnostic criteria sets and codes, and usage instructions. It is intended to be a supplement for clinicians and should be used in conjunction with the full DSM-5. *Making the DSM-5: Concepts and controversies* and *Intelligent clinician's guide to the DSM-5* are helpful resources to explore and understand the changes from DSM-IV to DSM-5 and their implications to clinical practice.

1375 Drug information handbook. North American ed. Charles F. Lacy, Laura Armstron, Morton Goldman, Leonard Lance, Lexi-Comp, Inc., American Pharmaceutical Association. Hudson, Ohio; Washington: Lexi-Comp, Inc.; American Pharmaceutical Association, 1994–

615 1533-4511   RM301.12.D783

Publ. in cooperation with the Amer. Pharmacists Assoc. (APhA).

First ed., 1993/94. Available in North Amer. and internat. editions. Description based on 19th ed., 2010. Subtitle: A comprehensive resource for all clinicians and healthcare professionals. The 22nd ed.(2013) is the most recent edition available. (Lexi-Comp's clinical reference library).

Concise, comprehensive, and user-friendly drug reference. Alphabetical listing of drug monographs, with new drugs and updates to monographs since the last edition. Includes detailed information in consistent format, such as dosage, drug interactions, adverse reactions (by occurrence, overdose, and toxicology), etc., with warnings highlighted. Appendix. Pharmacologic category index. For clinicians and healthcare professionals.

Several other comprehensive print pharmacology handbooks, also published by Lexi-Comp and frequently updated, include *Anesthesiology and critical care drug handbook* (1999– ; 10th ed., 2011); *Drug information handbook for nursing* (1998-; 14th ed., 2012); *Drug information handbook for advanced practice nursing* (1990– , 11th ed., 2010); *Drug information handbook for dentistry* (1996- ; 18th ed., 2012); *Drug information handbook for oncology* (2000- ; 11th ed., 2013); *Drug information handbook for psychiatry: A comprehensive reference of psychotropic, nonpsychotropic, and herbal agents* (1999- ; 7th ed., 2009);

Drug information handbook for the allied health professional (1995- ; 12th ed., 2005); *Drug information handbook with international trade names index* (21st ed., 2012); *Geriatric dosage handbook* (1993- ; 18th ed., 2012); *Infectious diseases handbook: Including antimicrobial therapy & diagnostic test/procedures* (1994- ; 6th ed., 2006); *Natural therapeutics pocket guide* (2000- , 2nd ed., 2003); *Pediatric dosage handbook* (1992- ; 18th ed., 2011); and *Pharmacogenomics handbook* (2003- ; 2nd ed., 2006). Also available online as pt. of Lexi-Comp Online™ (http://webstore.lexi.com/Store/ONLINE).

1376 Ethics resources and standards. http://www.psychiatry.org/practice/ethics/resources-standards. American Psychiatric Association. Arlington, Va.: American Psychiatric Association

Produced by the American Psychiatric Association (APA).

Provides online access to APA's ethics-related publications, originally published in print version in 2001: *Opinions of the Ethics Committee on the principles of medical ethics: With annotations especially applicable to psychiatry*, which includes the APA's procedures for handling complaints of unethical conduct, and *Ethics primer of the American Psychiatric Association*.

1377 Gabbard's treatments of psychiatric disorders. 4th ed. Glen O. Gabbard. Washington: American Psychiatric, 2007. xxvi, 960 p., ill. ISBN 9781585622

616.891   RC480.T69

First edition, 1989, had title *Treatments of psychiatric disorders: A task force report of the American Psychiatric Association*, 4 v.; 2nd ed., 1995 (2 v.), and 3rd ed., 2001 (2 v.), had title *Treatments of psychiatric disorders*.

Contents: pt. 1, "Disorders usually first diagnosed in infancy, childhood, or adolescence" (ed. E. B. Weller and J.F. McDermott); pt. 2, "Delirium, dementia, and amnestic and other cognitive disorders" (ed. S.C. Yudofsky and R.E. Hales); pt. 3, "Substance-related disorders" (ed. H. D. Kleber and M. Galanter); pt. 4, "Schizophrenia and other psychotic disorders" (ed. R. L. Munich and C.A. Tamminga); pt. 5, "Mood disorders" (ed. A. J. Rush); pt. 6, "Anxiety disorders, dissociative disorders, and adjustment disorders" (ed. F. R. Schneier, L.A. Mellman, and D. Spiegel); pt. 7, "Somatoform and factitious disorders" (ed. K.A. Phillips); pt. 8, "Sexual and gender identity disorders" (ed. S. B. Levine and R. T. Segraves); pt. 9, "Eating disorders" (ed. A. S. Kaplan and K. A Halmi); pt. 10, "Personality disorders" (ed. J.G. Gunderson); pt. 11, "Sleep disorders" (ed. K. Doghramji and Anna Ivanenko); pt. 12, "Disorders of impulse control" (ed. Susan L. McElroy).

Current approaches, treatments, and therapies for common psychiatric disorders and mental illnesses. Provides comprehensive descriptions of the disorders and covers multiple approaches, including pharmacologic, psychodynamic, behavioral, cognitive, family, individual, and group treatments, recognizing evolving knowledge and preferred treatments as well as acceptable alternatives. Includes data from new and controlled studies. Includes bibliographical references and index. Useful for graduate research and health professionals. Available in electronic format as part of PsychiatryOnline.

1378 Handbook of child psychology.

6th ed. William Damon, Richard M. Lerner. Hoboken, N.J.: John Wiley and Sons, 2006. 4 v., ill. ISBN 0471272876
155.4   BF721.H242

This four-volume set reflects the current understanding of child psychology, focusing on the concerns of a new century. Now in its sixth edition, it is the definitive child psychologist's guide to current research findings. It serves as a sourcebook, encyclopedia, and research review.

1379 Handbook of clinical child

psychology. 3rd ed. C. Eugene Walker, Michael C. Roberts. New York: Wiley, 2001. xx, 1177 p., ill.
ISBN 0471244066
618.9289   RJ503.3.H36

First edition, 1983; 2nd ed., 1992.

Contents: sec. 1, "Child development"; sec. 2, "Diagnostic assessment of children"; sec. 3, "Problems of early life"; sec. 4, "Problems of childhood"; sec. 5, "Problems of adolescence"; sec. 6, "Intervention strategies"; sec. 7, "Special topics."

This edition reflects the growth of the field of child psychology in recent years, providing background information in child development and

"consideration of more specific disorders of childhood . . . in the context of human development"—*Pref*. Includes bibliographical references and indexes. Intended as a reference work for graduate students, researchers, and clinicians. Also available as an e-book.

1380 Handbook of clinical health

psychology. Susan P. Llewelyn, Paul Kennedy. Chichester, West Sussex, U.K.; Hoboken, N.J.: J. Wiley, 2003. xvii, 605 p., ill. ISBN 0471485446
616.0019   R726.7.H3542

Comprehensive overview of the practice of clinical health psychology. Provides authoritative summaries of research evidence in health care and demonstrates how findings are put into practice. Useful detailed and integrated reference work for clinical and health psychologists in academic, practice, and training settings. Available as an e-book.

1381 Handbook of clinical health

psychology. Thomas J. Boll, Suzanne Bennett Johnson, Nathan W. Perry, Ronald H. Rozensky. Washington: American Psychological Association, c2002–2004. v. 1–3. ISBN 1557989095
616.89   R726.7.H354

Vol. 1, *Medical disorders and behavioral applications* (ed. Suzanne Bennett Johnson, Nathan W. Perry, Jr., and Ronald H. Rozensky); v. 2, *Disorders of behavior and health* (ed. James M. Raczynski, Laura C. Leviton); v. 3, *Models and perspectives in health psychology* (ed. Robert G. Frank, Andrew Baum, and Jan L. Wallander).

Explores the role of behavior and psychology in the development, progression, intervention, and treatment of a wide range of medical conditions related to disorders of behavior and health. Emphasizes health-related behavior changes. For researchers and practitioners in clinical psychology. Includes bibliographical references and index.

A more recent publication in this subject area is *Comprehensive handbook of clinical health psychology*.

1382 Handbook of clinical psychology.

Michel Hersen, Alan M. Gross. Hoboken,

N.J.: J. Wiley & Sons, 2008. 2 vol., ill. ISBN 9780470008874

616.89   RC467.2.H357

Vol. 1, Adults (33 chapters); v. 2, Children and adolescent (32 chapters)

Same structure for both v. 1 and 2: Contents: pt. I, General issues; pt. II, Theoretical models; pt. III, Research contributions; pt. IV, Diagnosis and evaluation; pt. V, Treatment; pt. VI, Special issues.

Contains historical perspective on treatment, ethical & legal issues, professional roles and practice, cross-cultural psychology, psychoneu-roimmunology, cognitive-behavioral treatment, psychopharmacology, pediatric psychology, problems in infancy, child maltreatment, to name a few of the areas addressed. Intended for graduate students and professionals in the field of clinical psychology and mental health. Available as an e-book.

A more recent addition to this subject area is *Oxford handbook of clinical psychology*, available in print and as an e-book.

Handbook of clinical psychology competencies, available in print and as an e-book, addresses "general competencies" (v.1), "intervention and treatment for adults" (v. 2), and "intervention and treatment for children and adolescents" (v.3).

1383 Handbook of contemporary neuropharmacology. David Robert Sibley, Israel Hanin, Michael Kuhar, Phil Skolnick. Hoboken, N.J.: John Wiley & Sons, 2007. 3 v. ISBN 9780471660

615.78   RM315.H3434

Contents: (1) "Basic neuropharmacology"; (2) "Mood disorders"; (3) "Anxiety and stress disorders"; (4) "Schizophrenia and psychosis"; (5) "Substance abuse and addictive disorders"; (6) "Pain"; (7) "Sleep and arousal"; (8) "Development and developmental disorders"; (9) "Neurodegenerative and seizure disorders"; (10) "Neuroimmunology"; (11) "Eating and metabolic disorders."

Reference for nervous system neuropharmacology, with recent advances in neuropharmacology, drug development and therapy, and treatment of various diseases and conditions. Reference for graduate students, physicians and other health professionals, and researchers. A useful resource for academic and special libraries libraries. Also available online via Wiley InterScience (http://www.interscience. wiley.com/reference/hcn). Includes index.

1384 Handbook of eating disorders. 2nd ed. Janet Treasure, Ulrike Schmidt, Eric van Furth. Chichester, U.K.; Hoboken, N.J.: Wiley, 2003. xvi, 479 p., ill. ISBN 0471497681

616.8526   RC552.E18.H36

First edition, 1993, had title *Handbook of eating disorders: Theory, treatment, and research.*

Overview of the developing field of eating disorders, including obesity, with many advances in knowledge and understanding since the previous edition. For researchers and clinicians. Also available in a condensed version entitled *The essential handbook of eating disorders*. Also available as an e-book.

1385 Handbook of neurologic rating scales. 2nd ed. Robert M. Herndon. New York: Demos Medical Publ., 2006. xiv, 441 p. ISBN 1888799927

616.8/0475   RC348.H296

First ed., 1997.

Contents: ch. 1, Introduction to clinical neurologic scales (Robert M. Herndon and Gary Cutter); ch. 2, Generic and general use scales (Robert M. Herndon); ch. 3, Pediatric developmental scales (Roger A. Brumback); ch. 4, Pediatric neurologic and rehabilitation rating scales (Raphael Corcoran Sneed, Edward L. Manning, and Cathy F. Hansen); ch. 5, Amyotrophic lateral sclerosis clinimetric scales: Guidelines for administration and scoring (Benjamin Rix Brooks); ch. 6, Scales for the assessment of movement disorders (Stephen T. Gancher); ch. 7, Multiple sclerosis and demyelinating diseases (Robert M. Herndon and Jeffrey I. Greenstein); ch. 8, Assessment of the elderly with dementia (Richard Camicioli and Katherine Wild); ch. 9, Clinical stroke scales (Wayne M. Clark and J. Maurice Hourihane); ch. 10, Peripheral neuropathy and pain scales (Robert M. Herndon); ch. 11, Diagnostic headache criteria and instruments (Elcio J. Piovesan and Stephen D. Silberstein); ch. 12, Scales for assessment of ataxia (Robert M. Herndon); ch. 13, Assessment of traumatic brain injury (Risa Nakase-Richardson, Frances Spinosa, Charles F. Swearingen, and Domenic Esposito); ch. 14, Health-related quality-of-life scales for epilepsy (James J. Cereghino); ch. 15, Rehabilitation outcome measures (Samuel T. Gontkovsky and Risa Nakase-Richardson); ch. 16, Human immunodeficiency virus–associated cognitive impairment (Giovanni Schifitto and Michelle D. Gaugh); ch. 17, Summary and conclusions (Robert M. Herndon).

Reference source on methods of measurement and rating scales used in neurology to assess neurologic disease. Useful in the design of clinical trials and for interpreting the literature of clinical trials in neurology.

1386 Handbook of psychiatric education.
Jerald Kay, Edward K. Silberman, Linda Pessar. Washington: American Psychiatric, 2005. xiv, 379 p., ill.
ISBN 1585621897
616.890071173   RC459.5.U6.H36
Contents: (1) "Preclinical undergraduate curricula"; (2) "Psychiatric clerkships"; (3) "Undergraduate electives"; (4) "Evaluation of students"; (5) "Administration of the residency program"; (6) "What and how to teach in the residency program"; (7) "New teaching technologies and approaches for medical students and residents"; (8) "Teaching psychiatric residents to become effective educators"; (9) "The accreditation process: Challenges and benefits"; (10) "Evaluation of residents"; (11) "Special problems and challenges in the residency program"; (12) "Special events in the residency program"; (13) "Recruitment of residents"; (14) "Major issues in psychiatric education."

Reference guide for academic psychiatric educators with focus on undergraduate and graduate medical education issues and recent changes in medical education. Describes the role of technology in psychiatric education. Includes, for example, sections on electronic reference sources, new teaching technologies, online continuing education sources, and finding medical information on the Internet. Includes bibliographical references and index. Also includes a brief version of *Handbook of psychiatric education and faculty development*, publ. 1999, which includes information on careers in academic psychiatry, psychiatric residency, psychiatric administration, etc.

1387 Handbook of psychiatric measures.
2nd ed. A. John Rush, Michael B. First, Deborah Blacker, American Psychiatric Association. Washington: American Psychiatric Association, 2008. 828 p., 1 CD-ROM. ISBN 9781585622

616.89075   RC473.P78.A46
First ed., 2000.
Contents: sec. 1, "Introduction to the handbook"; sec. 2, "General measures (non-disorder specific)"; sec. 3, "Measures related to DSM-IV diagnostic categories"; appendix A, "DSM-IV-TR classification"; appendix B, "List of measures included on the CD-ROM"; appendix C, "Index of measures"; appendix D, "Index of abbreviations for measures." General index.

Rev. ed. Compendium on rating scales, tests, and measures that may be useful in caring for patients with mental illness and in understanding and using clinical measures. Overview text for each chapter and a text section for each measure. Test sections for each measure include goals, description, practical issues, psychometric properties, clinical utility, and references to suggested readings. Accompanying CD-ROM includes complete copies of measures that are in the public domain, or for which copyright was granted, and also the text of the *Handbook of psychiatric measures* in searchable form.

1388 Handbook of psychology. 2nd ed.
Irving B. Weiner. Hoboken, N.J.: Wiley, 2013. 12 v. 29 cm.
ISBN 9780470619049
150   BF121
Takes advantage of ten years of research since the first edition of 2003. Separate volumes on the history of psychology, research methods, behavioral neuroscience, experimental psychology, personality and social psychology, developmental psychology, educational psychology, clinical psychology, health psychology, assessment psychology, forensic psychology, and industrial and organizational psychology. Signed chapters with extensive lists of significant works. Author and subject indexes for each volume. Available as an e-book.

1389 Handbook of the psychology of aging.
6th ed. James E. Birren, K. Warner Schaie, Ronald P. Abeles, Margaret Gatz, Timothy A. Salthouse. Amsterdam, Netherlands; Boston: Elsevier Academic Press, 2006. xxi, 564 p., ill. ISBN 0121012646
155.67   BF724.55.A35H36
Twenty signed essays delve into the psychology of aging from a variety of perspectives. Beginning with questions raised by theoretical issues in aging,

articles discuss cognitive neuroscience, lifespan theory, how reading and language relate to aging, as well as what can be learned from problem solving, motivation, and even attitudes toward aging. Volume concludes with consideration of wisdom, memory, and religion in later life. Readable essays that present some weighty material in comprehensible form. A useful volume for both general and research collections.

1390 Handbook of research methods in clinical psychology. Michael C. Roberts, Stephen S. Ilardi. Malden, Mass.: Blackwell, 2003. xi, 455 p., ill. ISBN 0631226737
616.890072   RC467.8.H36

Title varies: also called *Blackwell handbook of research methods in clinical psychology*

Contents: pt. 1, "Clinical psychology research"; pt. 2, "Research designs"; pt. 3, "Topics of research."

Treatment of research methodologies used in clinical psychology (e.g., experimental design, statistical analysis, validity, ethics in research, cultural diversity, and the scientific process of publishing) and applications of research to the fields of child and adult psychopathology. Scholarly resource for researchers and students. For academic libraries. Includes bibliographical references and index. Full text available online via Credo Reference and netLibrary.

Another resource, publ. in 1999, also entitled *Handbook of research methods in clinical psychology*, by Kendall, covers similar ground.

1391 The Harvard guide to psychiatry. 3rd ed. Armand M. Nicholi. Cambridge, Mass.: Belknap Press, 1999. xiv, 856 p., ill. ISBN 067437570X
616.89   RC454.N47

First edition, 1978, had title *The Harvard guide to modern psychiatry*; 2nd ed., 1988, had title *The new Harvard guide to psychiatry*.

Contents: pt. 1, "Examination and evaluation"; pt. 2, "Brain and behavior"; pt. 3, "Psychopathology"; pt. 4, "Principles of treatment and management"; pt. 5, "Special populations"; pt. 6, "Psychiatry and society."

This edition considers advances since 1988, which includes the release of DSM-IV (Diagnostic and statistical manual of mental disorders: DSM-IV-TR), neurobiology of mental disorders,

neuroimaging, psychopharmacology, increased use of psychoactive drugs, advances in molecular biology, etc. The "Psychiatry and society" section has chapters on race and cultures in psychiatry, ethical issues, psychiatry and managed care, and psychiatry and the law. Bibliographical references and index. For mental health professionals, general readers, and academic and public libraries.

1392 Mental health in America: A reference handbook. Donna R. Kemp. Santa Barbara, Calif.: ABC-CLIO, 2007. xiv, 315 p. ISBN 1851097899
362.2   RA790.6.K45

Part of Contemporary World Issues series.

Contents: (1) "Background and history"; (2) "The twenty-first century: Problems, controversies, and solutions"; (3) "Worldwide perspective"; (4) "Chronology"; (5) "Biographies"; (6) "Facts and statistics"; (7) "Documents, reports, and nongovernmental organizations"; (8) "Legislation and court costs"; (9) "Organization"; (10) "Selected print and nonprint resources."

Explores mental health policy and attitudes toward mental illness from the 19th century to the present; changing definitions and explanations of mental illness; and the various treatments of mental illness. Includes chronology of approaches to mental illness, statistics, legislative information, a glossary, and annotated bibliography of current literature, including websites. Index. Useful for health professionals, researchers, and students. Also available as an e-book.

1393 The mental measurements yearbook. Oscar Krisen Buros, Buros Institute of Mental Measurements. Highland Park, N.J.: The Mental Measurements Yearbook, 1941–
016.1512;   Z5814.P8B932
016.159928 0076-6461

A monumental collection of standardized measurements, now in its 18th ed. Each edition follows much the same pattern and is intended to supplement rather than supersede earlier volumes. References are numbered consecutively and each has cross-references to reviews, excerpts, and bibliographic references in earlier volumes. Information for each test includes title, intended population, author and publishers, scoring, availability of forms, parts, levels, and computer-assisted scoring, cost, time to administer, and a statement concerning validity and reliability. Tests cover English-language materials. Often referred to by the name of its founder, Buros.

Also available online via EBSCO.

1394 PDR drug guide for mental health professionals. Thomson Medical Economics. Montvale, N.J.: Thomson Medical Economics, 2002–
615 1546-3443   RM315.P387
Description based on 3rd ed., 2007.

Written in nontechnical language, profiles psychotropic drugs commonly used in psychiatry, with recommended dosage, approved uses, physical and psychological side effects, food and drug interactions, etc. Also includes psychotropic herbs and supplements. Includes street drug profiles and a glossary of street drug names and color photos of psychotropic tablets and capsules. Indexed by generic and trade name and clinical disorder/symptom or drug class. Reference for health professionals taking care of psychiatric patients.

Related titles include *Physicians' desk reference: PDR, ADA/PDR guide to dental therapeutics* (American Dental Association), *PDR guide to drug interactions, side effects, and indications, PDR for herbal medicines, PDR for nonprescription drugs, PDR for nutritional supplements, PDR nurse's drug handbook, Physicians' desk reference for ophthalmic medicines, PDR guide to biological and chemical warfare response, PDR guide to terrorism response,* and other titles.

PDR and its major companion volumes are also found in the PDR electronic library.

1395 Procedure coding handbook for psychiatrists. 4th ed. Chester W. Schmidt, Rebecca K. Yowell, Ellen Jaffe. Washington: American Psychiatric Pub., 2011. xiii, 192 p. ISBN 9781585623747
616.890012   RC465.6.S36
First ed., 1993; 3rd ed., 2004. CPT (Current Procedural Terminology, 856).

Contents: ch. 1, "Basics of CPT"; ch. 2, "Introduction to documentation of psychiatric services"; ch. 3, "Codes and documentation for psychiatric services"; ch. 4, "Codes and documentation for other mental health services"; ch. 5, "Codes and documentation for evaluation and management services"; ch. 6, "Medicare"; ch. 7, "Commercial insurance issues"; ch. 8, "Putting it all together for accurate coding"; ch. 9, "FAQs and problem scenarios." Appendixes: A, "The CPT coding system: How it came to be, how it changed"; B, "The Health Insurance Portability and Accountability Act (HIPPA)"; C, "Modifier"; D, "Place of service codes for Medicare"; E, "1997 CMS documentation guidelines for evaluation and management services (abridged and modified for psychiatric services)"; F, "Vignettes for evaluation and management codes"; G, "Most frequently missed items in evaluation and management (E/M) documentation"; H, "Documentation templates"; I, "ECT patient information, consent form, and record template"; J, "Examples of Relative Value Units (RVUs) (2010)"; K, "National distribution of evaluation and management code selection by psychiatrists"; L, "American Psychiatric Association CPT coding service and additional resources"; M, "Medicare carriers and administrative contractors"; N, "Centers for Medicare and Medicaid services regional offices."

Explains the structure and function of CPT, how to use the psychiatric therapeutic procedure codes, and how CPT affects the practice of psychiatry. Also available as an e-book.

1396 Publication manual of the American Psychological Association. 6th ed. American Psychological Association. Washington: American Psychological Association, 2010. xviii, 272 p., ill. ISBN 9781433805592
808/.06615   BF76.7

Now in its 6th edition, the APA manual remains an indispensable tool for research and writing in psychology and related disciplines. Revisions and updates reflect the current landscape of scholarship, especially the impact of the Internet and online technology: advice on how to cite digital source materials and audiovisual media, word-processing software, online submission to journals, and retention and sharing of digitized data. Also of interest: discussion of plagiarism issues, advice on copyright permission, and suggestions for cover letters when seeking publication.

1397 The psychologist's companion: A guide to writing scientific papers for

students and researchers. 5th ed.
Robert J. Sternberg, Karin Sternberg.
New York: Cambridge University Press,
2010. x, 366 p, ill.
ISBN 9780521195713
808/.06615   BF76.8

A guide to scientific writing for students and researchers covers such topics as steps in writing library research papers, guidelines for data presentation, references for psychology papers, submitting work to journals and publishers, commonly misused words, Internet resources, and American Psychological Association guidelines for psychology papers. Updated since the 4th edition of 2003. Reflects revised guidelines in the 6th edition of the Publication manual of the American Psychological Association, the continuing impact of Internet tools on literature searching, and practical issues such as ethics and how to submit a manuscript. Intended for both students and early career faculty members and practitioners. Appendix provides a sample psychology paper. Bibliography. Index. Available as an e-book.

1398 Psychologists' desk reference. 3rd ed.
Gerald P. Koocher, John C. Norcross,
Beverly Greene. New York: Oxford
University Press, 2013.
ISBN 9780199845491
616.89   RC467.2

First edition, 1998; 2nd ed., 2005.

Contents: pt. I, Assessment and diagnosis; pt. II, Psychological testing; pt. III, Individual adult treatment; pt. IV, Couples, family, and group treatment; pt. V, Child and adolescent treatment; pt. VI, Biology and pharmacotherapy; pt. VII, Self-help resources; pt. VIII, Ethical and legal issues; pt. IX, Forensic matters; pt. X, Financial and insurance matters; pt. XI, Practice management; pt. XII, Prevention, consultation, and supervision.

Provides essential information (e.g., assessment guidelines, diagnostic codes, test information, etc.) and provides greater emphasis on evidence-based and research-supported practices and diversity issues. Detailed table of contents for 145 chapters, cross-references, and index. Also available as an e-book. For mental health professionals.

1399 Rating scales in mental health.
3rd ed. Martha Sajatovic, Luis F.
Ramirez. Baltimore: Johns Hopkins

University Press, 2012. ix, 502 p., ill.
ISBN 9781421406664
616.89/075   RC473.P78 S245

First ed., 2001; 2nd ed., 2003.

Contents: Diagnostic scales in psychiatry; Anxiety rating scales; Depression rating scales; Bipolar disorder rating scales; Psychosis rating scales; Global psychopathology and functioning rating scales; Social/family functioning rating scales; General health rating scales; Insight assessment rating scales; Involuntary movement rating scales; Health care satisfaction and attitude rating scales; Quality of life rating scales; Substance abuse rating scales; Suicide risk rating scales; Impulsivity/aggression rating scales; Eating disorders rating scales; Premenstrual dysphoric disorder rating scales; Sleep disorders rating scales; Sexual disorders rating scales; Geriatric rating scales; Rating scales for children.

Organized into 21 categories, this reference contains frequently used tests/rating scales in psychiatry. Indexes by test name and abbreviation. Each rating scale is reviewed and includes a description of the scale, the time needed to administer the scale, copyright holder, etc. Includes bibliographic references to the scale. Introductory material contains a history of ratings in psychiatry, an overview of the psychiatric interview in relation to the use of rating scales, a section on statistical evaluation of the outcome data, and other useful material. Considered an essential resource for students, researchers, and mental health professionals/practitioners.

1400 The SAGE handbook of
developmental disorders. Patricia A.
Howlin, Tony Charman, Mohammad
Ghaziuddin. Los Angeles ; London:
SAGE, 2011. xxi, 564 p., ill.
ISBN 9781412944861

RJ506.D47; S24

Contents: pt. 1, Overview; pt. 2, Disorders with a known genetic cause; pt. 3, Disorders with complex yet unknown causes; pt. 4, Environmentally induced disorders; Author index; Subject index.

Covers medical and genetic aspects of developmental disorders, reflecting a global viewpoint. Clearly describes each disorder, including its history, causation, social-emotional, motor and neurobehavioral function, implications for clinical practice, interventions , etc. A valuable resource for graduate students, researchers, faculty, and professionals. Also available as an e-book and via Credo reference.

1401 The Sage handbook of health psychology. Stephen Sutton, Andrew Baum, Marie Johnston. Thousand Oaks, Calif: SAGE Publ., 2004. xiii, 432 p., ill. ISBN 0761968490

616.0019   R726.7.S24

Contents: ch. 1, Context and perspectives in health psychology; ch. 2, Epidemiology of health and illness: a socio-psycho-physiological perspective; ch. 3, Biological mechanisms of health and disease; ch. 4, Determinants of health-related behaviours: theoretical and methodological issues; ch. 5, Health-related cognitions; ch. 6, Individual differences, health and illness: the role of emotional traits and generalized expectancies; ch. 7, Stress, health and illness; ch. 8, Living with chronic illness: a contextualized, self-regulation approach; ch. 9, Lifespan, gender and cross-cultural perspectives in health psychology; ch. 10, Communicating about health threats and treatments; ch. 11, Applications in health psychology: how effective are interventions?; ch. 12, Research methods in health psychology; ch. 13, Assessment and measurement in health psychology; ch. 14, Professional issues in health psychology.

Comprehensive interdisciplinary handbook reflecting international health psychology research and issues. For advanced students, researchers, and practitioners. Includes bibliographical references and index. Also available as an e-book.

1402 What your patients need to know about psychiatric medications. 2nd ed. Robert H. Chew, Robert E. Hales, Stuart C. Yudofsky. Washington: American Psychiatric Pub., 2009. xix, 421 p. ISBN 9781585623563

615.788   RM315.H328

Contents: "Medications in pregnancy"; "Antianxiety medication"; "Medications for treatment of insomnia"; "Antidepressants: Selective serotonin reuptake inhibitors and mixed-action antidepressants"; "Tricyclic antidepressants"; "Monoamine oxidase inhibitors"; "Mood stabilizers"; "First-generation antipsychotics"; "Second-generation antipsychotics"; "Treatment of attention-deficit/hyperactivity disorder in adults"; "Stimulants and nonstimulants for ADHD"; "Cognitive enhancers

for treatment of Alzheimer's disease and other forms of dementia"; "Methods for treatment of alcohol dependence"; Index.

Provides relevant and easy-to-understand information about commonly asked questions regarding psychotropic medications. Information about each medication presented in a standard format: brand name; generic name; available strengths; available in generic; medication class; general information; dosing information; common side effects; adverse reactions and precautions; use in pregnancy and breastfeeding; possible drug interactions; overdose; special considerations. Accompanied by CD-ROM that contains PDF files of the pages as they appear in the book. Also available as an e-book via PsychiatryOnline.

Another well-regarded resource in this area is *Handbook of psychiatric drug therapy* (by Labbate).

Histories

1403 After Freud left: A century of psychoanalysis in America. John C. Burnham. Chicago: The University of Chicago Press, 2012. 274 p., ill. ISBN 9780226081373

616.89/17   RC503.A38

Contents: Introduction; pt. 1, "1909 to the 1940s: Freud and the psychoanalytic movement across the Atlantic"; pt. 2, "After World War II: The future of Freud's legacy in American culture."

"Leading historians of psychoanalysis and of American culture reflect on what happened to Freud's legacy in the United States . . . Essays suggest a variety of new parameters in the histories of psychoanalysis and of American society and culture, at first in 1909 and in the decades after Freud left . . ."—*Introd.* Written on the occasion of Freud's centennial visit to the U. S., with a comprehensive introduction and examination of Freud's ideas in the United States. Includes a chronological guide to events.

1404 A century of psychiatry. Hugh L. Freeman, Servier Research Group. London: Mosby-Wolfe Medical Communications, 1999. 2 v., ill., ports. ISBN 0723431744

616.89009   RC438.C457x

Collection of historical essays and biographies of mostly American and European psychiatry and psychiatrists, with one chapter on "non-Western psychiatry." Organized by decade, with ten chapters and subsections covering various topics and themes on the "innovations . . . [and] . . . dark periods in the history of psychiatry" (*Foreword*). For example, chapters on convulsive therapy, emergence of psychoanalysis, history of the *Diagnostic and statistical manual of mental disorders*, psychoneuroendocrinology, psychopharmacology ("Psychopharmacology 2000"), and others. Includes a list of significant events in psychiatry. Illustrated with photographs. List of further readings. Written for general readers.

1405 Diseases of the mind. http://www.nlm
.nih.gov/hmd/diseases/index.html. Lucy
D. Ozarin, National Library of Medicine
(U.S.). Bethesda, Md.: U.S. National
Library of Medicine, National Institutes
of Health, Health & Human Services.
2006-
    362.210973   RC443
Michael North, editor; written by Lucy Ozarin; web design by Young Rhee and Roxanne Beatty.

Part of the National Library of Medicine's History of medicine.

Contents: "Introduction"—"Early psychiatric hospitals & asylums"—"Benjamin Rush, M.D.: 'The Father of American psychiatry'"—"The 1840s: Early professional institutions & lay activism"— "19th-century psychiatrists of note"—"19th-century psychiatric debates."

"Traces the beginnings of some of the earliest asylums for the mentally ill in colonial America and their evolution into large state hospitals also discusses the humane treatment of patients, the dilemma of the chronically ill and forcible commitment."—*Introd.* Includes many images, including portraits of prominent early psychiatrists and images of 19th-century hospitals.

1406 Fragments of neurological history.
    John Pearce. London: Imperial College
    Press, 2003. xvii, 633 p., ill., ports.
    616.809   RC338.P436
A collection of articles in the history of neurology and medicine. Includes, for example, biographical reviews (e.g., Galen and Vesalius), chapter entitled "Illness of the famous, and some medical truants," and chapters on anatomical and neurophysiological phenomena, dementias, headaches, cranial

nerve and various other neurological disorders, and the origins of insulin and aspirin. For neurologists, neuroscientists, physicians, and general readers. Includes bibliographical references and index. Also available as an e-book.

1407 The genesis of neuroscience.
    A. Walker, Edward Laws, George
    Udvarhelyi, American Association of
    Neurological Surgeons. Park Ridge, Ill.:
    American Association of Neurological
    Surgeons, 1998. ISBN 1879284626
    616.8009   QP353
Contents: ch. 1, Origins of neuroscience; ch. 2, From Galen through the 18th century: an overview; ch. 3, The evolution of encephalization; ch. 4, The spinal cord; ch. 5, The peripheral nerves; ch. 6, Clinical and pathological examination of patients with neurological disorders; ch. 7, Manifestation of cerebral disorders: headache, epilepsy, sleep disorders, and cerebrovascular disease; ch. 8, Congenital anomalies of the nervous system; ch. 9, Infections and inflammatory involvement of the central nervous system; ch. 10, The evolution of neurosurgery; ch. 11, Neuroscience comes of age. Appendixes (A)The arts in the evolution of neuroscience; (B) Medical fees throughout the ages; (C) Historical glossary of neurological syndromes; (D) Bibliography of writings by A. Earl Walker; Index.

Describes the origins of neurology and neurosurgery from prehistoric times until the 19th century. Includes portraits of many neurologists and neurosurgeons. Other titles in this area include *Fragments of neurological history* and *History of neurology*.

1408 The history and influence of the
    American Psychiatric Association.
    Walter E. Barton, American Psychiatric
    Association. Washington: American
    Psychiatric Press, 1987. xvi, 400 p., [16]
    p. of plates, ill., ports. ISBN 0880482311
    616.89006073   RC443.B35
Follows "the development of psychiatry in America through the founding and growth of the American Psychiatric Association"—*Pref.*

1409 History of neurology. Fielding H.
    Garrison, Lawrence C. McHenry.

Springfield, Ill.: Thomas, [1969]. xv, 552 p., ill., facsims., ports.

616.809   RC338.G36

Contents: ch. 1, Ancient origins; ch. 2, The Middle Ages and the Renaissance; ch. 3, The seventeenth century; ch. 4, The eighteenth century; ch. 5, The nineteenth century: Neuroanatomy; ch. 6, The nineteenth century: Neurophysiology; ch. 7, The nineteenth century: Neurochemistry; ch. 8, The nineteenth century: Neuropathology; ch. 9, Clinical neurology; ch. 10, The neurological examination; ch. 11, Neurological diseases.

A re-publication of Garrison's *History of neurology*, previously published in 1925 as a historical chapter in Charles L. Dana's *Textbook of nervous diseases*.

Presents a broad survey of neurology from antiquity to the beginning of the 20th century. Other more recent titles in the history of neurology are, for example, *A short history of neurology: The British contribution*, *The genesis of neuroscience*, *Fragments of neurological history*, and Stanley Finger's *History of neurology*, to name a few.

1410 The history of psychiatry: An evaluation of psychiatric thought and practice from prehistoric times to the present. Franz Alexander, Sheldon T. Selesnick. New York: Harper & Row, [1966]. xvi, 471 p., illus., ports.

616.89009   RC438.A39

In four parts: "The age of psychiatry," "From the ancients through the modern era," "The Freudian age," "Recent developments." A comprehensive history of psychiatry, with chapter notes and extensive bibliography. Index.

1411 A history of psychiatry: From the era of the asylum to the age of Prozac. Edward Shorter. New York: John Wiley & Sons, 1997. xii, 436 p., ill.

ISBN 047115749X

616.89009   RC438.S54

Contents: ch. 1, "The birth of psychiatry"; ch. 2, "The asylum era"; ch. 3, "The first biological psychiatry"; ch. 4, "Nerves"; ch. 5, "The psychoanalytic hiatus"; ch. 6, "Alternatives"; ch. 7, "The second biological psychiatry"; ch. 8, "From Freud to Prozac."

Presents the history of psychiatry and psychiatric thinking from the late 18th century to the present, with its major scientific and cultural developments and its major personalities. Also available

as an e-book. Complementary to this book are *American therapy: The rise of psychotherapy in the United States* by Engel and *Masters of the mind: Exploring the story of mental illness from ancient times to the new millennium* by Millon et al.

The title *150 years of British psychiatry* covers important developments in Great Britain, and *One hundred years of psychiatry* presents a general review of 19th-century psychiatry in Germany.

1412 History of psychiatry and medical psychology: With an epilogue on psychiatry and the mind-body relation. Edwin Wallace, John Gach. New York: Springer, 2008. xlix, 862 p.

ISBN 9780387347073

616.89009   RC438

This resource traces the history of psychiatry, taking its social, political, and philosophical contexts into consideration. Covers classical antiquity, Middle Ages, Renaissance, and Enlightenment, the growth of psychiatry as a medical specialty, and also important concepts and topics in psychiatry, including psychoanalysis, psychopharmacology, clinical psychology, and psychosomatic medicine. Scholarly work for educators, graduate students, and also general readers. Provides extensive bibliographical references to other histories of psychiatry. Index. Also available as an e-book.

1413 One hundred years of American psychiatry. American Psychiatric Association. New York: Columbia University Press, 1944. xxiv, 649 p., illus., ports., facsims., tables (part fold.)

RC435.A6

Contents: "Presenting the volume," by Gregory Zilboorg; "Introduction," by J. K. Hall; "The beginnings: From colonial days to the foundation of the American Psychiatric Association," by R. H. Shryock; "Psychiatry in Europe at the middle of the nineteenth century," by H. E. Sigerist; "The founding and the founders of the association," by Winfred Overholser; "The history of American mental hospitals," by S. W. Hamilton; "A century of psychiatric research in America," by J. C. Whitehorn; "American psychiatric literature during the past one hundred years," by H. A. Bunder; "The history of psychiatric therapies," by William Malamud; "The history of mental hygiene," by Albert

Deutsch; "Military psychiatry: The Civil War, 1861–1865," by Albert Deutsch; "Military psychiatry: World War I, 1917–1918," by E. A. Strecker; "Military psychiatry: World War II, 1941–1943," by Albert Deutsch; "A century of psychology in its relationship to American psychiatry," by T. V. Moore; "American psychiatry as a specialty," by H. A. Bunker; "Legal aspects of psychiatry," by Gregory Zilboorg; "The influence of psychiatry on anthropology in America during the past one hundred years," by Clyde Kluckhohn.

"Intended to be a historical synthesis of a century of American psychiatric evolution, of the birth and development of a medical specialty . . . intended to represent a survey of psychiatry as a growing cultural force"—*Introd.* Commemorates the 100th birthday of the American Psychiatric Association. Includes a selection of early psychiatric books (p. 226–69) and periodicals (p. 269–71). Illustrations.

Another title, *Three hundred years of psychiatry, 1535-1860*, presents original sources to support the study of the history of psychiatry.

1414 Resources on the history of psychiatry. http://www.nlm.nih.gov/hmd/pdf/historypsychiatry.pdf. Emily Martin, Lorna A. Rhodes, National Library of Medicine (U.S.). Bethesda, Md.: National Library of Medicine. [2004]

Contents: (1) "Overview"; (2) "Prehistory of psychiatry"; (3) "History of asylums"; (4) "History of psychotropic drugs"; (5) "Race in psychiatry"; (6) "Women, children, and the history of psychiatry"; (7) "Psychiatry, war, and violence"; (8) "Forensic psychiatry"; (9) "Radical cures: Psychosurgery and ECT"; (10) "Miscellaneous notable resources."

Bibliography of selected historical materials from the HMD and NLM collection, including publications ("scientific monographs, federal or state reports, personal accounts, conference proceedings, legal briefs, armed service publications, mass market publications, teaching materials, monographs on psychiatric ethics, treatment, or social effects, manuscripts, audiovisual materials, ephemera, and so on"—*Overview*) from the 19th century to the 1970s. For scholars interested in the history of psychiatry.

1415 World history of psychiatry. John G. Howells. New York: Brunner/Mazel,

[1974, c1975]. xxv, 770 p., ill.
ISBN 0876300824
616.89009   RC438.H67

Follows the development of psychiatry, exploring different eras, stages (primitive, rational, religious, somatic, harmonization) and regions, in the context of "cultural, economic, geographical, political and ecological factors"—*Introd.*

Treatises

1416 Kaplan & Sadock's comprehensive textbook of psychiatry. 9th ed. Benjamin J. Sadock, Virginia A. Sadock, Pedro Ruiz, Harold I. Kaplan. Philadelphia: Wolters Kluwer Health/Lippincott Williams & Wilkins, 2009. 2 v. (lix, 4520, I-138 p.), ill. (some col.), map. ISBN 9780781768993
616.89   RC454.C637

First ed., 1967; 6th ed., 1995, had title *Comprehensive textbook of psychiatry*; 7th ed., 2000; 8th ed., 2004.

Encyclopedic textbook of clinical psychiatry, with close integration between the basic and clinical sciences and with both established and new approaches to psychotherapy. Rewritten and revised, with 50 new chapters in this edition, on topics including genetics and neural sciences, clinical psychiatry, and psychopharmacology. Charts, tables, diagrams, and illustrations, including color plates of major psychiatric drugs.

Also available in an electronic version, searchable by keyword, topic, chapter or image, with cross-references and links to PubMed.

Statistics

1417 Mental health, United States. National Institute of Mental Health (U.S.). Rockville, Md.: U.S. Dept. of Health and Human Services, Public Health Service, Alcohol, Drug Abuse, and Mental Health Administration, National Institute of Mental Health, Div. of Biometry and Epidemiology, 1983–. v.
362.2/0973 0892-0664   RA790.6.M463

Substance Abuse and Mental Health Services Administration (SAMSHA).

Description based on *Mental health, United States, 2010* (Substance Abuse and Mental Health Services Administration), publ. 2012.

Contents: Section (1), Introduction; (2) Mental health of the population; (3) Providers and settings for mental health services; (4) Payers and payment mechanisms; (5) States: People, providers, and payers; (6) Data gaps; (7) Tables; Appendix (A), Data source descriptions; (B), Glossary; (C) Medication lists.

Contains statistical reports and data on trends in mental health services, derived to a large extent from national surveys conducted by SAMSHA (Substance Abuse and Mental Health Services Administration) Center for Mental Health Services in collaboration with various major national, state, and professional associations. Three new sections in this edition: Section 1 contains an editorial on likely future directions and an overview of the mental health field over the past 100 years; Section 2 reports on the current status of mental health statistics, and Section 3 on the current status of mental health services. Section 4, as in previous editions, provides current mental health statistics. Electronic full-text of several recent volumes available from the SAMSHA National Mental Health Information Center website at http://purl.access.gpo.gov/GPO/LPS24728.

Internet resources

1418 American Psychiatric Association. http://www.psych.org. American Psychiatric Association. Arlington, Va.: American Psychiatric Association. 1996–? The American Psychiatric Association (APA), founded in 1844, is an international specialty society, currently representing 33,000 physician leaders in mental health"—*main page*.

Provides professional resources, in training resources for medical students (http://www.psychiatry.org/medical-students) and residents & fellows (http://www.psychiatry.org/residents and http://www.psychiatry.org/residents/in-training -resources), as well as mental health information for consumers (http://www.psychiatry.org/mental-health).

Information on mental disorders, including intellectual and behavioral disorders, substance abuse disorders, an overview of research at the APA, DSM-IV (*Diagnostic and statistical manual of mental disorders: DSM-IV-TR*), practice guidelines (*American Psychiatric Association practice guidelines for the treatment of psychiatric disorders*), links to international psychiatric websites, links to psychiatric education organizations, psychiatric organizations by country, clinical issues, subspecialties within psychiatry, APA statements on ethics (Ethics), and links to additional "outside" resources.

1419 Diseases of the mind. http://www.nlm.nih.gov/hmd/diseases/index.html. Lucy D. Ozarin, National Library of Medicine (U.S.). Bethesda, Md.: U.S. National Library of Medicine, National Institutes of Health, Health & Human Services. 2006-

362.210973 RC443

Michael North, editor; written by Lucy Ozarin; web design by Young Rhee and Roxanne Beatty.

Part of the National Library of Medicine's History of medicine.

Contents: "Introduction"—"Early psychiatric hospitals & asylums"—"Benjamin Rush, M.D.: 'The Father of American psychiatry'"—"The 1840s: Early professional institutions & lay activism"— "19th-century psychiatrists of note"—"19th-century psychiatric debates."

"Traces the beginnings of some of the earliest asylums for the mentally ill in colonial America and their evolution into large state hospitals also discusses the humane treatment of patients, the dilemma of the chronically ill and forcible commitment."—*Introd.* Includes many images, including portraits of prominent early psychiatrists and images of 19th-century hospitals.

1420 Drug abuse (MedlinePlus). http://www.nlm.nih.gov/medlineplus/drugabuse.html. National Library of Medicine (U.S.). Bethesda, Md.: National Library of Medicine. 2000?–

A health topic in MedlinePlus.

Contents: Overviews; Latest news; Diagnosis/symptoms; Treatment; Prevention/screening; Specific conditions; Related sssues; Pictures and photographs; Games; Clinical trials; Research; Journal articles; Dictionaries/glossaries; Directories; Organizations; Newsletters/print publications; Law and policy; Statistics; Children; Teenagers; Men; Women; Seniors; Other languages.

Collection of links on substance abuse from a variety of government agencies, professional associations, and organizations, such as the National Institute on Drug Abuse, the Office of National Drug Control, Substance Abuse and Mental Health Services Administration (SAMHSA), National Library of Medicine, American Medical Association, American Academy of Family Physicians, and others. Also links to related MedlinePlus topics, e.g., alcoholism, prescription drug abuse, and substance abuse, to name a few.

1421 Institute of Medicine (IOM). http://
www.iom.edu/. Institute of Medicine.
Washington: National Academy of
Sciences. 1998–

The Institute of Medicine (IOM, 24), one of the U.S. National Academies, has the mission to "serve as adviser to the nation to improve health" and "provides independent, objective, evidence-based advice to policymakers, health professionals, the private sector, and the public"—*main page*. Offers a list of all publications by the IOM since 1970 (http://www.iom.edu/Reports.aspx), which cover a broad range of topics, including aging, child health, a variety of diseases, global health, health care quality, minority health, nutrition, public health, public policy, preventive medicine, women's health, and many other areas. The National Academies Press (http://www.nap.edu) provides online access to the publications of the four National Academies, i.e., National Academy of Sciences (456), National Academy of Engineering, IOM, and National Research Council.

1422 National Institute of Mental Health.
http://www.nimh.nih.gov/. National
Institute of Mental Health (U.S.).
Bethesda, Md.: National Institutes of
Health. 1995?–
616.89   RA790.A1

Part of National Institutes of Health (NIH).

Provides funding for research on mind,

brain, behavior, and behavioral disorders; for research on the causes, occurrence, and treatment of mental illness; and for mental health services, including major projects such as the Human Brain Project and neuroinformatics research in support of this project. Contains topics useful for the public concerning adult and pediatric psychopathology. Provides extensive information on a variety of mental health topics (http://www.nimh.nih.gov/health/index.shtml), links to NIMH publications and other resources, and to mental health information available via MedlinePlus (http://www.nlm.nih.gov/medlineplus/mentalhealth.html). Site index.

**1423 Substance Abuse and Mental
Health Services Administration
(SAMHSA)**. http://www.samhsa.gov.
Substance Abuse and Mental Health
Services Administration. Rockville, Md.:
Substance Abuse and Mental Health
Services Administration
362.21; 362.29   RA790.6

Substance Abuse and Mental Health Services Administration (SAMHSA), part of U.S. Dept. of Health and Human Services (HHS).

SAMHSA has as its mission "building resilience and facilitating recovery for people with or at risk for mental or substance use disorders . . . gearing all of its resources . . . toward that outcome."—*About Us* Searchable website. Provides resources for prevention, treatment, and rehabilitation services for patients with various forms of mental illness and addictions. Includes three centers: SAMHSA's Center for Mental Health Services (CMHS), Center for Substance Abuse Prevention (CSAP), and Center for Substance Abuse Treatment (CSAT). Examples of SAMHSA resources include "Find substance abuse and mental health treatment" (http://www.samhsa.gov/treatment/) with clickable maps to locate different programs throughout the United States, and links to various related publications (http://store.samhsa.gov/home). Provides the latest data (http://www.samhsa.gov/data/) on alcohol, tobacco, and illegal drugs as well as other statistical data and resources.

12 Public Health

1424 Agency for Toxic Substances and Disease Registry (ATSDR). http://www.atsdr.cdc.gov/. Agency for Toxic Substances and Disease Registry, U.S. Department of Health and Human Services. Atlanta: Agency for Toxic Substances and Disease Registry. 1999–

Agency for Toxic Substances and Disease Registry (ATSDR), part of U.S. Dept. of Health and Human Services (HHS).

Provides health information and takes public health actions to prevent harmful exposures and diseases related to toxic substances (e.g., recent examples: childhood lead poisoning prevention, drinking water concerns, anticipating the health concerns of climate change, etc.). Includes A–Z index by main topic (http://www.atsdr.cdc.gov/az/a.html), information about toxic substances, various data resources (e.g., access to the Hazardous Substance Release/Health Effects [HazDat] database, National Exposure Registry, and others), emergency response information, hazardous waste sites, a toxic substances portal (http://www.atsdr.cdc.gov/substances/index.asp), and many other information sources.

1425 American Public Health Association (APHA). http://www.apha.org/. American Public Health Association. Washington: American Public Health Association. 1998–

RA421

Searchable website of the American Public Health Association (APHA), an organization representing public health professionals, with the mission to protect Americans and their communities from health threats. Provides links to 29 sections (http://www.apha.org/membergroups/sections/aphasections/) representing major public health disciplines or public health programs and selected links to a wide variety of public health topics and resources (e.g., A–Z Health Topics at http://www.apha.org/advocacy/ and Public Health Links at http://www.apha.org/about/Public+Health+Links/). APHA participates in Partners in Information Access for the Public Health Workforce, a collaborative project to provide public health professionals with access to information resources to help them improve the health of the American public.

1426 CDC WONDER. http://purl.access.gpo.gov/GPO/LPS18322. Centers for Disease Control and Prevention (U.S.). [Atlanta]: Centers for Disease Control and Prevention. 1998–

RA643

CDC WONDER (Wide-ranging online data for epidemiologic research), developed by the Centers for Disease Control and Prevention (CDC), provides a search interface and access to a variety of reports, bibliographies on health-related topics, recommendations, and guidelines, and public-use data sets about mortality, cancer, HIV/AIDS, and others topics. Additional information and answers to a variety of questions can be found at http://wonder.cdc.gov/wonder/help/faq.html. For public health professionals and the general public.

1427 Health services research and public health information programs. http://www.nlm.nih.gov/hsrph.html. National Library of Medicine (U.S.). Bethesda, Md.: National Library of Medicine, U.S. National Institutes of Health, Dept. of Health and Human Services

Lists resources from multiple National Library of Medicine (NLM) programs, including collaborative projects (e.g., HSR information central), links to several databases, e.g., HSRProj (Health Services Research Projects in Progress), HSRR (Health Services and Sciences Research Resources), Health Services/Technology Assessment Text (HSTAT), American Indian and Asian American Health, and others. Provides preformulated PubMed search filters and search strategies. Its outreach and training resources, with links to their full text, include "Finding and using health statistics," "Health economics: information resources," Health technology assessment 101 (HTA 101), "Public health information and data tutorial," publications, and informatics. Also provides access various online publications, informatics resources, and links to additional information and related products.

1428 Indian Health Service (IHS). http://www.ihs.gov/. U.S. Department of Health and Human Services. Rockville, Md.: U.S. Department of Health and Human Services

Part of U.S. Department of Health and Human Services (HHS).

Searchable website. Provides detailed information to many IHS resources and links to American Indian sites, nationwide programs, information about IHS headquarters and area offices, press releases, reports, fact sheets, health care delivery to members of federally recognized tribes, and other information.

Also useful is the Native Health Database at https://hscssl.unm.edu/nhd/.

1429 Injury data and resources. http://www.cdc.gov/nchs/injury.htm. National

Center for Health Statistics. Atlanta: National Center for Health Statistics

"The purpose of this Web site is to provide an overview of injury morbidity and mortality data and statistics available from the National Center for Health Statistics (NCHS) and other sources and to provide details on injury surveillance methodology and tools to assist in data analysis"—*main page*. Provides links to a variety of resources, including the International Collaborative Effort (ICE) on Injury Statistics (http://www.cdc.gov/nchs/injury/advice.htm), relevant coding schemes, and additional resources (e.g., WISQARS: Web-based Injury Statistics Query and Reporting System, CDC WONDER, Faststats, and others).

1430 National Center for Health Statistics (NCHS). http://www.cdc.gov/nchs/. National Center for Health Statistics (U.S.), Centers for Disease Control and Prevention (U.S.). Hyattsville, Md.: Centers for Disease Control and Prevention. 1990s–

RA409

NCHS is the primary agency for compiling and making available American health and vital statistics and data sets. Searchable website, with topically arranged site index. Its home page provides links to various resources in several categories, including What's new; Health e-stats; Information showcase; Top ten links; surveys and data collection systems (data collected through personal interviews and systems based on records, with data from vital and medical records); and microdata access (including links to NCHS public-use data files and documentation and state data). Surveys and data collection systems include the National health and nutrition examination survey (NHANES), National health care survey (NCHS), National health interview survey (NHIS), National immunization survey (NIS), Longitudinal studies of aging (LSOAs), National vital statistics system (NSS), and Injury statistics query and reporting system. Examples of linked resources include *Faststats a to z* and Health, United States. Details on NCHS publications and information products are provided at http://www.cdc.gov/nchs/products.htm.

NCHS serves as the World Health Organization's (WHO's) Collaborating Center for the Family of International Classifications for North America

(North American Collaborating Center [NACC] established in 1976) and is responsible for coordinating all official disease classification activities in the United States, in close cooperation with the Canadian Institute for Health Information (CIHI), Statistics Canada, and the Pan American Health Organization. A portal to the disease classifications in North America (e.g., International classification of diseases, Ninth Revision, Clinical modification: ICD-9-CM and International classification of functioning, disability, and health (ICF)) is provided at http://www.cdc.gov/nchs/icd.htm.

1431 WISQARS. http://www.cdc.gov/injury/ wisqars/index.html. National Center for Injury Prevention and Control. Atlanta: National Center for Injury Prevention and Control. 2000–

HB1323.A2

WISQARS (Web-Based Injury Statistics Query and Reporting System), National Center for Injury Prevention and Control of the U.S. Centers for Disease Control and Prevention; CDC Injury Center.

Described as "an interactive database system that provides customized reports of injury-related data."—*Main page* Injury statistics presented in two categories, i.e., fatal U.S. injury statistics and national estimates of nonfatal injuries treated in U.S. hospital emergency departments, each with links to tables, charts, tutorials, help, and FAQs. CDC's Injury Center (http://www.cdc.gov/injury/) provides links to a variety of injury related topics, fact sheets, and overviews on injury response, violence prevention, and prevention of unintentional injuries.

The National Center for Health Statistics (NCHS) also makes a variety of injury data and resources available at http://www.cdc.gov/nchs/ injury.htm.

Guides

1432 Bioterrorism and public health: An Internet resource guide. John G. Bartlett, eMedguides.com. Princeton, N.J.; Montvale, N.J.: Thomson/ Physicians' Desk Reference, 2002. xi, 305 p. ISBN 1563634279
025.063633497   RC88.9.T47.B566

Contents: http://www.loc.gov/catdir/toc/fy036/2002 523094.html

Provides brief descriptions and ratings of websites from government, public health agencies, educational institutions, and research centers. Addresses bioterrorism concerns raised by Sep. 11. Covers bioterrorism public health advisories and guidelines, clinical resources on bioterrorism, health and safety guidelines, and hazardous materials. Also addresses psychosocial issues. Can be supplemented with other, more up-to-date online resources, such as Biodefense and Bioterrorism (MedlinePlus) and the website of the Institute for Biosecurity, Saint Louis University School of Public Health (http://www.bioterrorism.slu.edu/bt.htm), which links to ready-reference material and a variety of government, academic, and professional Internet resources. For medical and academic libraries, as well as public libraries.

1433 Bioterrorism: Guidelines for medical and public health management. Donald A. Henderson, Thomas V. Inglesby, Tara Jeanne O'Toole. Chicago: American Medical Association, 2002. xvii, 244 p., ill. (some col.) ISBN 157947280X
363.32   RC88.9.T47.H46

Provides guidelines for emergency and public health personnel and other health professionals following a bioterrorist attack: how to recognize and diagnose infections (e.g., anthrax, smallpox, plague, etc.) and how to manage survivors of such an attack. Includes a chapter entitled "Bioterrorism preparedness and response: Clinician and public health agencies as essential partners." Includes bibliographical references and index.

Can be supplemented with more up-to-date online resources, such as Biodefense and Bioterrorism (MedlinePlus) and the website of the Institute for Biosecurity, Saint Louis University School of Public Health (http://www.bioterrorism.slu.edu/ bt.htm), which links to ready-reference material and other government, academic, and professional Internet resources. For medical and academic users.

1434 The food safety hazard guidebook. 2nd ed. Richard Lawley, Laurie Curtis, Judy Davis, Royal Society of Chemistry (Great Britain). Cambridge, U.K.: RSC

Pub, 2012. xi, 533 p.
ISBN 9781849733816
664.001579   RA601.L39
First ed., 2008.

Contents: Sect. 1, Biological hazards; sect. 2, Chemical hazards; sect. 3, Allergens; sect. 4, HACCP (hazard analysis critical control point) and food safety management systems; sect. 5, Food safety legislation; sect. 6, Sources of further information; Abbreviations and acronyms; Subject index.

Concise, accessible reference which supplies the technical and scientific information that food safety professionals require. It is "intended as a guidebook rather than an encyclopedia, and has been conceived as a portal for the immense and ever expanding body of scientific knowledge that exists for food."—*Pref.* Covers a wide range of biological and chemical food safety hazards, including potential and emerging food safety hazards. Also available as an e-book.

Current authoritative updates and reports concerning issues of food safety can be found at "Food safety" (Centers for Disease Control and Prevention) http://www.cdc.gov/foodsafety/ and Food-Safety.gov http://www.foodsafety.gov/.

**1435 The new Blackwell companion
   to medical sociology.** William C.
   Cockerham. Malden, Mass.: Wiley-
   Blackwell, 2010. xvii, 596 p., ill.
   ISBN 9781405188685
   362.1/042   RA418

Global and comprehensive survey of the emerging field of medical sociology, or the study of the impact of cultural constructs on medical understanding and practice. Provides a definition of the field and its importance for health care research. This new edition offers 24 articles grouped around major themes such as Health and Social Inequalities, Health and Social Relationships, Health and Disease, and Health Care Delivery. The 2001 edition, *The Blackwell companion to medical sociology* by the same author, remains useful for the 17 summaries of regional or national health care practices around the world. Each chapter has bibliographical references. Indexes by author and subject. Available as an e-book.

**1436 A practical guide to global health
   service.** Edward O'Neil, American
   Medical Association. Chicago: American

Medical Association, 2006. xxxv, 402 p.
ISBN 1579476732
610.73/7   RA390.U5O54

OMNI Med ("loosely translated from the Latin meaning 'health care for all'" [*Pref.*]) is a nongovernmental organization founded by the author in 1998.

Contents: ch. 1, Overcoming obstacles: cultural and practical guidelines; ch. 2, Travel, health, and safety guidelines; ch. 3, The Omni Med database of international health service opportunities; ch. 4, Cross-referencing guide to the database; ch. 5, Other relevant organizations; Appendix A, Useful web sites; Appendix B, About Omni Med.

"A health providers guide to the practical aspects of serving internationally, including data on more than 300 organizations that send health providers overseas" (*Publ. notes*). Organization profiles include concise descriptions, contact information, and practical information about length of service terms, personnel sought, areas served, and availability of funding, training, room and board, and other essential information (e.g., trip planning, travel and safety guidelines, commonly encountered illnesses, information about the culture of a particular country, etc.). Written for persons interested in medical volunteering. Glossary; bibliography.

Caring for the world: A guidebook to global health opportunities, also available as an e-book, is a resource for finding out about health opportunities abroad, with a directory of relevant government and non-government organizations, educational opportunities, funding resources, and trip planning.

**1437 Secondary data sources for public
   health: A practical guide.** Sarah
   Boslaugh. Cambridge, [England]; New
   York: Cambridge University Press, 2007.
   x, 152 p. ISBN 052169023
   362.10727   RA409.B66

Part of Practical guides to biostatistics and epidemiology.

Contents: ch. 1, "An introduction to secondary analysis"; ch. 2, "Health services utilization data"; ch. 3, "Health behaviors and risk factors data"; ch. 4, "Data on multiple health topics"; ch. 5, "Fertility and mortality data"; ch. 6, "Medicare and Medicaid data"; ch. 7, "Other sources of data"; appendixes: I, "Acronyms"; II, "Summary of data sets and years available"; III, "Data import and transfer".

This guide lists the major sources of secondary data for health-related subjects that are important in epidemiology and public health research. They are often stored in different locations and not necessarily easily accessible. Examples include the National hospital discharge survey, the Healthcare cost utilization project, the Behavioral risk factor surveillance system, the National health and nutrition survey, Medicare public use files, Web portals to statistical data, etc. Description of each resource includes title, focus, core section, data collection, and information on accessing data and ancillary materials. Includes bibliography and index. Also available as an e-book.

Bibliography

1438 American health care in transition: A guide to the literature. Barbara A. Haley, Brian Deevey. Westport, Conn.: Greenwood Press, 1997. xii, 336 p. ISBN 0313273235

362.1/0973   RA395.A3H3426

(Bibliographies and indexes in medical studies ; no. 14). This annotated bibliography includes periodical articles and government publications, covering the literature 1979–1996. Index.

1439 Grey literature report. http://www.greylit.org/. New York Academy of Medicine Library. New York: New York Academy of Medicine. [1999]– 362.1 1931-7050

A publication of the New York Academy of Medicine Library http://www.nyam.org/library/

Grey literature is defined as "that which is produced on all levels of government, academics, business and industry in print and electronic formats, but which is not controlled by commercial publishers" (Cf. *Website*, New York Academy of Medicine "What is Grey Literature?" http://www.greylit.org/about. Considered an alerting service to new grey literature in health services research and various public health topics, assisting researchers and librarians with the identification of this literature for both reference and collection development purposes. The Academy's entire Grey Literature Collection can be searched by keyword(s), with further refinements

being offered. Also included on the website is an A–Z list of grey literature producing publishers (http://www.greylit.org/publishers/list), the New York Academy of Medicine Library's collection policy for grey literature (http://www.greylit.org/about/collection-development-policy), and other relevant links. The publications are cataloged in the New York Academy of Medicine Library online catalog.

1440 Health services research methodology core library recommendations, 2007. http://www.nlm.nih.gov/nichsr/corelib/hsrmethods.html. AcademyHealth, National Library of Medicine (U.S.). Bethesda, Md.: National Library of Medicine. 2007

Produced by AcademyHealth; National Library of Medicine (NLM); National Information Center on Health Services Research and Health Care (NICHSR). Although dated 2007, website is reviewed and updated regularly.

List of books, journals, bibliographic databases, websites, and other media; useful for collection development librarians and researchers interested in health services research methods. Lists both "core" materials and "desired" materials in areas such as general health policy, health economics, health services research, public health, and several others. The NICHSR website (http://www.nlm.nih.gov/nichsr/outreach.html) lists links to several other recommended lists, including Health economics core library recommendations (2011), Health outcomes core library recommendations (2011), Health policy core library recommendations 2011 (also called Core health policy library recommendations), and other information.

1441 Healthy work: An annotated bibliography. Namir Khan, Nina Nakajima, Willem H. Vanderburg, Ken Jalowica, Esther Vanderburg, David Vanderburg. Lanham, Md.: Scarecrow Press, 2005. xiv, 359 p. ISBN 0810852853

016.61362   Z6675.I5.K48; RC967

"The purpose of this annotated bibliography is to bring together diverse bodies of literature related to human work in a manner that supports preventive approaches to work design and organization.

An overview of relevant literature for occupational health and safety specialists, industrial hygienists . . . so that they and other professionals can understand why our workplaces have become primary sources of physical and mental illness"—*Pref.* Includes bibliographical references and indexes. Author index and keyword index.

1442 Medicine, health, and bioethics: Essential primary sources. K. Lee Lerner, Brenda Wilmoth Lerner. Detroit: Thomson/Gale, 2006. lvii, 513 p., ill. ISBN 1414406231
174.2   R724.M313
(Series: Social issues primary sources collection)

Contains complete primary sources or excerpts of documents and publications published 1823–2006, illustrating major biomedical issues. Each entry includes the complete text or an excerpt with complete original citation, subject area, historical context, significance. For students, health professionals, and also general readers. Available online via Gale virtual reference library.

1443 Resource guide for disaster medicine and public health. http://disasterlit.nlm .nih.gov. National Library of Medicine (U.S). Bethesda, Md.: National Library of Medicine

Developed by the New York Academy of Medicine through a contract award from the National Library of Medicine (NLM). Produced by National Library of Medicine (NLM}, Specialized Information Services (SIS) Disaster Information Management Research Center's (DIMRC) list of "disaster medicine and public health literature" list at http:// sis.nlm.nih.gov/dimrc/medscilit.html.

Described as a gateway to freely available Internet resources and a searchable database of full-text linked resources. It provides access to an extensive list of disaster medicine and public health literature (e.g., expert guidelines, factsheets, websites, research reports, articles, and other tools) from government agencies, professional associations, and non-profit organizations. A partial list of the sources scanned for this guide can be found at http://disasterlit.nlm.nih.gov/help/organizations. php. Print materials or materials available through paid subscriptions are not included in this guide.

Another resource is DIMRC's webpage of

"Disaster apps and mobile optimized web pages" http://disasterinfo.nlm.nih.gov/dimrc/disasterapps .html which includes content delivery on specific mobile platforms.

Indexes; Abstract journals; Databases

1444 The bioterrorism sourcebook. Michael R. Grey, Kenneth R. Spaeth. New York: McGraw-Hill Medical Publ. Div., 2006. xxxiii, 549 p., ill. ISBN 0071440860
303.625   RC88.9.T47; G746

Contents: section I, Clinical principles and practices (ch. 1–9); section II, Infectious agents (ch. 10–16); section III, Biotoxins and category B and C agents (ch. 17–20); section IV, Chemical weapons (ch. 21–26); section V, Nuclear and radiation syndromes (ch. 27–30).

Clinical and public health guidance preparing for and responding to immediate and long-term bioterrorism-related conditions. Provides concise and essential information on the various aspects and agents of a bioterrorist attack and the expected consequences, with synopses, illustrations, tables, charts, and practical tips. Selected bibliography; index. Also available as an e-book.

The CDC's "Emergency Preparedness and Response" site, "intended to increase the nation's ability to prepare for and respond to public health emergencies" (http://www.bt.cdc.gov/) provides extensive information resources for bioterrorism, chemical, and radiation emergencies, natural disasters, and other threats.

Additional resources in this area include, for example, *Bioterrorism and public health* (2002), *Bioterrorism preparedness* (2006), also available in print and online, and others.

1445 Food safety handbook. Ronald H. Schmidt, Gary Eugene Rodrick. Hoboken, N.J.: Wiley-Interscience, 2003. xiii, 850 p., ill. ISBN 0471210641
363.192   TP373.5.F67

"The intent of this book is to define and categorize the real and perceived safety issues surrounding food, to provide scientifically non-biased perspectives on these issues, and to provide assistance to the reader in understanding these issues. While the primary professional audience for the book includes food technologists and scientists in the industry and regulatory sector, the book should provide useful information for many other audiences."—*Pref.*

Thirty-eight chapters written by specialists are divided into eight sections: characteristics of food safety and risk; biological food hazards; chemical and physical food hazards; systems for food safety surveillance and risk prevention; food safety operations in food processing, handling, and distribution; food safety in retail foods; diet, health, and food safety; and worldwide food safety issues. Chapters have bibliographies. Index. Also available as an e-book.

Current authoritative updates and reports concerning issues of food safety can be found at "Food safety" (Centers for Disease Control and Prevention) http://www.cdc.gov/foodsafety/ and Food-Safety.gov http://www.foodsafety.gov/.

1446 Food Safety Research Information Office at the National Agricultural Library. http://fsrio.nal.usda.gov/index .php. National Agricultural Library (U.S.), Food Safety Research Information Office. Beltsville, Md.: National Agricultural Library, Food Safety Research Information Office. 2002–

TX537

Produced by National Agricultural Library (NAL); Food Service Research Information Office (FSRIO).

A major component of this searchable website is its "Research Projects Database" for locating information on food safety and related research. Categories currently in use in this database include food and food products, food composition and characteristics, food quality characteristics, food handling and processing, on-farm food safety, diseases and poisonings, sanitation and pathogen control, contaminants and contamination, government policy and regulations, methodology and quality standards, human health and epidemiology, education and training, facilities and sites, and pathogen biology.

Complements information found, for example, in *Food safety handbook*, *Food safety: A reference handbook* by Redman, *Foodborne disease handbook* by Hui, and two books with the same title, but different authors, i.e., *Foodborne diseases* by Cliver et al., and *Foodborne diseases* by Simjee.

1447 Global health. http://www.cabi.org/ publishing-products/online-information -resources/global-health/. C.A.B. International., Great Britain. Wallingford, Oxfordshire, U.K.: CABI. 1973–

RA441

Formerly known as *CAB health*.

Global health, 1973– (derived from *CAB abstracts* and *Public health and tropical medicine* databases; *Global health archive*, 1910–83 (derived from six former print abstracting sources). Includes records from the Bureau of Hygiene and Tropical Diseases to 1983.

Online databases available through CAB Direct, OvidSP, EBSCO, Dialog, and others. Indexes journals, books, book chapters, conference proceedings, and other resources, mostly English-language publications, but also in other languages. Useful databases for searching the international health and public health literature, in addition to searching MEDLINE and EMBASE. For researchers, health professionals, policy makers, and students.

1448 Handbook of environmental health. 4th ed. Herman Koren, Michael S. Bisesi. Boca Raton, Fla.: Lewis Publ., 2003. 2 v., ill. ISBN 1566705363

363.7 RA565.K67

First ed., 1980; 3rd ed., 1996.

Contents: v. 1, Biological, chemical, and physical agents of environmental related disease; v. 2, Pollutant interactions in air, water, and soil.

Includes various environmental health topics, issues, and hazards such as emerging infectious diseases and microorganisms, air quality and its effect on ecosystems, toxicology, and effects of the environment on humans. Describes interactions between humans and the environment and how they affect health and welfare of individuals of individuals. Comprehensive bibliography (v. 1, p. 647–702) and indexes. Also available as an e-book.

1449 Handbook of epidemiology. Wolfgang Ahrens. New York: Springer, 2005 ISBN 3540005668

Contents: sec. 1, "Concepts and methodological approaches in epidemiology"; sec. 2, "Statistical methods in epidemiology"; sec. 3, "Applications of epidemiology"; sec. 4, "Research areas in epidemiology."

Comprehensive overview of the field of epidemiology, reviewing "key issues, methodological approaches, and statistical concepts"—*Pref.* Includes areas such as molecular epidemiology, health systems research, ethical aspects, and good epidemiological practice, to name a few. Each chapter presents basic concepts, standard procedures, methods, and recent advances in the field. Intended as a reference source for health professionals involved in health-related research. Detailed table of contents and list of contributors. No index. Also available as an e-book. A second edition was published in 2011.

Oxford handbook of epidemiology for clinicians by Ward is another resource in this area.

1450 The handbook of health behavior change. 3rd ed. Sally A. Shumaker, Judith K. Ockene, Kristin A. Riekert. New York: Springer Pub. Co, 2009. xxxi, 827 p., ill. ISBN 9780826115454

613   RA776.9.H36

First ed., 1988; 2nd ed., 1998.

Contents: Sect. I, Health behavior change and maintenance: theory and techniques; sect. II, Interventions for lifestyle change; sect. III, Measurement; sect. IV, Obstacles and predictors of lifestyle change and adherence; section V, Lifestyle change and adherence issues within specific populations; Sect. VI, Lifestyle change and adherence issues among patients with chronic diseases; Sect. VII, Lifestyle change and adherence : the broader context.

It is recognized that many acute and chronic diseases can be prevented or lessened by increased attention to adopting and maintaining healthy behaviors. Health behavior change is considered the key to preventable diseases. This excellent handbook addresses health behavior change both in theory and practice, with current studies, interventions, and strategies, e.g., alteration of lifestyle, such as no longer smoking, changing eating habits, increasing physical activity, adherence to a medication regimen, practicing safe sex, etc. A valuable resource for both graduate and undergraduate

students and health professionals. Includes tables and figures. Index. Also available as an e-book. A new edition is expected to be published in 2014.

1451 Health information for international travel. http://purl.access.gpo.gov/GPO/LPS3580. Phyllis E. Kozarsky, Paul M. Arguin, Ava W. Navin, U.S. Centers for Disease Control and Prevention. Atlanta: U.S. Dept. of Health and Human Services, Centers for Disease Control and Prevention. 1974–

Part of the Centers for Disease Control (CDC) Travelers' health website (http://wwwnc.cdc.gov/travel/default.aspx). Also called "Yellow book" or "CDC yellow book." Description based on the 2014 ed., also issued in print with title *CDC health information for international travel: The yellow book.* Previous print editions issued since 1989 as a serial, *International travel health guide.*

Contents: Ch. 1, "Introduction"; ch. 2, "The Pre-travel consultation"; ch. 3, "Infectious diseases related to travel"; ch. 4, "Select destinations"; ch. 5, "Post-travel evaluation"; ch. 6, "Conveyance and transportation issues"; ch. 7, "International travel with infants and children"; ch. 8, "Advising travelers with specific needs"; ch. 9, "Health considerations for newly arrived immigrants and refugees". Appendix (A), "Promotion of quality in the practice of travel medicine"; (B), "Essential electronic resources for the travel medicine practitioner"; (C), Travel vaccine summary table; (D), "The HealthMap system." Also contains separate lists of tables, maps, boxes, and figures.

Provides comprehensive information on vaccination requirements and recommendations for international travelers concerning health risks.

The World Health Organization's website, International travel and health, also offers extensive travel information.

1452 HealthSTAR (Ovid). http://www.ovid.com/site/products/ovidguide/hstrdb.htm. National Library of Medicine (U.S.). Sandy, Utah: Ovid Technologies. 2000–

Ovid HealthSTAR (HSTR); HealthSTAR (Health Services Technology, Administration, and Research).

"Comprised of data from the National Library of Medicine's (NLM) MEDLINE and former HealthSTAR databases . . . contains citations to the published literature on health services, technology, administration, and research. It focuses on both the clinical and non-clinical aspects of health care delivery. . . . Offered by Ovid as a continuation of NLM's now-defunct HealthSTAR database. Retains all existing backfile citations and is updated with new journal citations culled from MEDLINE. Contains citations and abstracts (when available) to journal articles, monographs, technical reports, meeting abstracts and papers, book chapters, government documents, and newspaper articles from 1975 to the present." —*Publ. notes*. A list of NLM's retired databases, including the original HealthSTAR database, can be found at http://www.nlm.nih.gov/services/pastdatabases.html.

Relevant content on health services research, health technology, health administration, health policy, health economics, etc., can also be found in MEDLINE®/PubMed®, NLM® Gateway, and also CINAHL® (101).

1453 International health regulations
   (2005). http://www.who.int/ihr/
   publications/9789241596664/en/index.
   html. World Health Organization.
   Geneva, Switzerland: World Health
   Organization. 2007
   IHR

Rev. ed., with the new regulations in force on June 15, 2007. Also publ. as a print edition. Supersedes *International health regulations (1969)*, publ. in several different print editions. Title varies: previously called *International sanitary regulations*.

Part of WHO's Global Alert and Response http://www.who.int/csr/en/

Considered a code of practices and procedures for the prevention of the spread of disease, "in consideration of the increases in international travel and trade, and emergence and re-emergence of new international disease threats" (*Publ. notes*), with the goal of preventing and protecting against the international spread of disease. Related WHO websites are "International health regulations"(http://www.who.int/topics/international_health_regulations/en/) and "Alert, response, and capacity building under the international health regulation news" (http://www.who.int/ihr/en/).

1454 International travel and health. http://www.who.int/ith/en/. World Health

Organization. Geneva, Switzerland: World Health Organization. 2005–
                         RA638.I58
Description based on the 2011 online edition. Also available as a print edition. Selected chapters of 2012 are free online.

Contents: ch. 1, "Health risks and precautions: General considerations"; ch. 2, "Mode of travel: Health considerations"; ch. 3, "Environmental health risks"; ch. 4, "Injuries and violence"; ch. 5, "Infectious diseases of potential risk for travellers"; ch. 6, "Vaccine-preventable diseases and vaccines"; ch. 7, "Malaria"; ch. 8, "Exposure to blood and body fluids"; ch. 9, "Special groups of travelers"; ch. 10, "Psychological health"; ITH 2011 country list: 1. "Yellow fever vaccination requirements and recommendations"; 2. "Malaria situation"; ITH Annexes: 1. "Countries with risk of yellow fever transmission and countries requiring yellow fever vaccination"; 2. "International health regulations."

Provides information on the main health risks for travelers at specific destinations with different modes of travel. Website also provides related links on, for example, disease outbreaks (e.g., avian influenza, drug-resistant tuberculosis, etc.), International health regulations (2005) and others. Intended for medical professionals; also useful to consumers.

Health information for international travel is another resource for travel information.

1455 The law and the public's health.
   7th ed. Kenneth R. Wing, Benjamin
   Gilbert. Chicago: Health Administration
   Press, 2007. xiii, 391 p.
   344.7304   KF3775.W5
Contents: ch. 1, "The law and the legal system"; ch. 2, "The power of the state governments in matters affecting health care"; ch. 3, "Government power and the right to privacy"; ch. 4, "The constitutional discretion of the state and federal governments to limit or condition social welfare benefits"; ch. 5, "Government regulation of health care providers and payers"; ch. 6, "The scope of discretion of administrative agencies in matters affecting health and health care"; ch. 7, "The fraud and abuse laws"; ch. 8, "The antitrust laws: Government enforcement of competition"; ch. 9, "Malpractice: Liability for negligence in the delivery and financing of health care"; ch. 10, "Health care

business law: Legal considerations in the structuring of health care entities and their transactions."

Intended as an introductory text for schools of public health and law-related courses, this book can also serve as a reference book in the health care field. Provides an introduction to the law, the legal system, and principles applicable to the delivery and financing of health care but is not considered a treatise on health law. Includes bibliographical references and index. Also available as an e-book.

1456 Medical response to terrorism: Preparedness and clinical practice. Daniel C. Keyes, Jonathan L. Burstein, Richard B. Schwartz, Raymond E. Swienton. Philadelphia: Lippincott Williams & Wilkins, 2005. xiii, 449 p., ill. ISBN 0781749867

2005 362.18   RC88.9.T47.M43

Contents: pt. 1, "Agents of terrorism and medical management"; pt. 2, "All-hazards preparedness for terrorism."

Describes various biological agents (anthrax, plague, smallpox, etc.) and threats, including chemical, biochemical, and nuclear terrorism. Provides guidance with the preparedness for emergency situations and with the diagnosis and management of exposure. Includes practice drills and disaster simulations. Bibliographic references and index. Also available asa an e-book.

1457 Mental health in America: A reference handbook. Donna R. Kemp. Santa Barbara, Calif.: ABC-CLIO, 2007. xiv, 315 p. ISBN 1851097899

362.2   RA790.6.K45

Part of Contemporary World Issues series.

Contents: (1) "Background and history"; (2) "The twenty-first century: Problems, controversies, and solutions"; (3) "Worldwide perspective"; (4) "Chronology"; (5) "Biographies"; (6) "Facts and statistics"; (7) "Documents, reports, and nongovernmental organizations"; (8) "Legislation and court costs"; (9) "Organization"; (10) "Selected print and non-print resources."

Explores mental health policy and attitudes toward mental illness from the 19th century to the present; changing definitions and explanations of mental illness; and the various treatments of mental illness. Includes chronology of approaches to mental illness, statistics, legislative information, a glossary, and annotated bibliography of current literature, including websites. Index. Useful for health professionals, researchers, and students. Also available as an e-book.

1458 NLM gateway. http://gateway.nlm. nih.gov/. National Library of Medicine (U.S.). Bethesda, Md.: National Library of Medicine. 2000–

RA11

As announced in 2011, "the NLM® gateway has transitioned to a new pilot project from the Lister Hill National Center for Biomedical Communications (LHNCBC)."—*Website* The new site focuses now on two databases: Meeting abstracts and Health services research projects. All of the other resources previously accessed through the NLM gateway are available through their individual sites. For a list of these databases previously available via the NLM gateway see http://gateway.nlm.nih.gov/about.jsp.

The NLM gateway previously allowed simultaneous searching of information resources at the National Library of Medicine (NLM)/National Center for Biotechnology Information (NCBI) with an overview of the search results presented in several categories (bibliographic resources, consumer health resources, and other information), with a listing of the individual databases and the number of results within these categories. Previously included were, for example, MEDLINE/PubMed and the NLM Catalog as well as other resources, including information on current clinical trials and consumer health information (MedlinePlus) and many others.

1459 POPLINE. http://www.popline.org/. Johns Hopkins University Bloomberg School of Public Health, Information and Knowledge for Optimal Health Project. Baltimore: Johns Hopkins University Bloomberg School of Public Health

HQ766

A free resource, maintained by the Knowledge for Health Project http://www.k4health.org/ at the Johns Hopkins Bloomberg School of Public Health/ Center for Communication Programs and funded by the United States Agency for International Development (USAID) http://www.usaid.gov/.

Database on reproductive health with international coverage. Provides bibliographic citations with abstracts to English-language published and unpublished biomedical and social science literature, with links to full-text documents, RSS feeds for topical searches, and other special features. POPLINE subjects (http://www.popline .org/poplinesubjects) in 12 main categories: Adolescent reproductive health; family planning methods; family planning programs; gender; health communication; HIV/AIDS; maternal and child health; population dynamics; population law and policy; population, health, and environment; reproductive health; sexually transmitted infections.

1460 Praeger handbook of Black American health: Policies and issues behind disparities in health. 2nd ed. Ivor Lensworth Livingston. Westport, Conn.: Praeger, 2004. 2 v. (xlvii, 911 p.), ill., maps. ISBN 0313324778
362.1/089/96073   RA448.5.N4H364
First ed., 1994.

Contents: v. 1 (pt.I), Cardiovascular and related chronic conditions (ch. 1–6); v. 1 (pt. II), General chronic conditions ch. 7–13; v. 1 (pt. III), Lifestyle, social, and mental outcomes (ch. 14–26); v. 2 (pt. IV), Sociopolitical, environmental, and structural challenges (ch. 27–38); v. 2 (pt. V), Ethics, research, technology, and social policy issues (ch. 39–47).

This rev. and exp. ed. addresses crucial issues in disparities in health status and access to health care for African Americans, with identification of preventive strategies, interventions, and possible solutions (e.g., ch. 47, "Eliminating racial and ethnic disparities in health: A framework for action"). Index. For professionals and students in public health, medicine, health psychology, health policy, medical sociology, nursing, and possibly other areas of research, education, and study. Also available as an e-book.

Handbook of African American health, available both in print and as an e-book, provides authoritative current information on the physical and psychological health of African Americans.

Craig Haynes' *Ethnic minority: A selected annotated bibliography*, publ. in 1997, remains a good bibliography to start research in health disparities, complemented by "A selected, annotated list of

materials that support the development of policies designed to reduce racial and ethnic health disparities," available online via http://www.ncbi.nlm.nih .gov/pmc/articles/PMC385308/.

Healthy People, National Institutes of Health (NIH), and the Centers for Disease Control and Prevention (CDC) have as a goal to support research that advances the elimination of health disparities among ethnic groups and among the various vulnerable and at-risk populations. Other resources exploring and documenting minority health and health disparities with the goal of promoting racial parity include, for example, "National Library of Medicine Strategic Plan for Addressing Health Disparities 2004–2008" (http://www.nlm .nih.gov/pubs/plan/nlm_health_disp_2004_2008. html), "Native-American health" via MedlinePlus, NLM's "Native American health," (http://www .nlm.nih.gov/medlineplus/nativeamericanhealth .html), "Hispanic American information outreach" (http://sis.nlm.nih.gov/outreach/hispanicameri- can.html), "Minority health information outreach" (http://sis.nlm.nih.gov/outreach/minorityhealth .html), and other websites.

1461 Proctor and Hughes' chemical hazards of the workplace. 5th ed. Nick H. Proctor, James P. Hughes, Gloria J. Hathaway. Hoboken, N.J.: Wiley-Interscience, 2004. xi, 785 p.
615.902   RA1229.P76
First edition, 1978; 4th ed., 1996.

Contents: (1) "Introduction: Toxicological concepts"; (2) "The chemical hazards"; (3) "CAS number index"; (4) "Index of compounds and synonyms." Detailed contents at http://www.loc.gov/ catdir/toc/ecip0410/2003024018.html

Covers the effects on human health of chemicals likely to be encountered in various places of work. Each monograph includes chemical formula, CAS number, Threshold Limit Value, synonyms for the chemical, physical properties, uses, routes of exposure, toxicological information, carcinogenicity, mutagenicity, fetotoxicity, clinical effects of overexposure and treatment, and significant odor characteristics. For health professionals and students. Available online from Wiley http://online library.wiley.com/book/10.1002/0471662666.

Other titles in this area include, for example, *Sittig's handbook of of toxic and hazardous chemicals and carcinogens* and *Sax's dangerous properties of industrial materials.*

1462 Public health in the 21st century.
Madelon Lubin Finkel. Santa Barbara, Calif.: Praeger, 2011. 3 v., ill.
ISBN 9780313375460
362.1   RA424.8.P83
Vol. 1, Global issues in public health; v. 2, Disease management; v. 3, Current issues in public health policy.

Contains essays on a wide variety of global public health issues written by a large number of international scholars. Covers historical developments and current issues in public health, diseases and their treatment and prevention, health disparities, health policy issues, ethics and human rights issues, patient safety, public health practice and education. Also discusses emerging issues and threats to public health. Valuable resource for public health professionals. Also available as an e-book and online via Credo reference.

1463 The public health law manual.
3rd ed. Frank P. Grad, American Public Health Association. Washington: American Public Health Association, 2005 0875530427
First edition, 1965, had title *Public health manual: A handbook on the legal aspects of public health administration and enforcement*; 2nd ed., 1990, had title *Public health law manual: A handbook on the legal aspects of public health administration and enforcement.*

"The purpose of this manual: Achieving the most effective use of legal powers; recognition of legal problems and their management; effective use of available legal assistance; improving communication between the public health and legal professions; continuing dialogue"—*Foreword.* Intended for use by health care professionals and public health administrators in planning, developing, and implementing public health programs. Deals with basic legal procedures in public health enforcement—restrictions of persons; permits, licenses, and registration; searches and inspections; embargo, seizure, etc.—and with legal administrative techniques of public health administration. This edition emphasizes issues in environmental health law, legal aspects of personal health services, right to privacy, "right to die" issues,

and discussion of various related issues. Provides an overview of public health policies and public health law and a summary of international responses to SARS, bioterrorism, global warming, etc.

1464 PubMed. http://www.ncbi.nlm.nih.gov/pubmed. U.S. National Center for Biotechnology Information, National Library of Medicine, National Institutes of Health. Bethesda, Md.: U.S. National Center for Biotechnology Information. 1996–
PubMed®, developed and maintained by the National Center for Biotechnology Information (NCBI) at the National Library of Medicine® (NLM). Provides a search interface for more than 20 million bibliographic citations and abstracts in the fields of medicine, nursing, dentistry, veterinary medicine, health care systems, and preclinical sciences. It provides access to articles indexed for MEDLINE® and for selected life sciences journals. PubMed subsets found under the "Limits" tab are: MEDLINE and PubMed central®, several journal groups (i.e., core clinical journals, dental journals, and nursing journals), and topical subsets (AIDS, bioethics, cancer, complementary medicine, dietary supplements, history of medicine, space life sciences, systematic reviews, toxicology, and veterinary science). "Linkout" provides access to full-text articles.

For detailed information see the PubMed fact sheet at http://www.nlm.nih.gov/pubs/factsheets/pubmed.html and also MEDLINE®/PubMed® resources guide (http://www.nlm.nih.gov/bsd/pm resources.html) which provides detailed information about MEDLINE data and searching PubMed.

Information regarding the mobile version of this resource is part of NLM's Gallery of mobile apps and sites.

1465 State cancer legislative database program (SCLD). http://www.scld-nci.net/mtcindex.cfm. National Cancer Institute. Bethesda, Md.: National Cancer Institute, National Institutes of Health
Databases providing summaries of state laws and resolutions on the major cancers and cancer-related topics. Considered a resource for a variety of audiences, including universities and research centers, professional organizations, and the public.

1466 Statistical handbook on infectious diseases. Sarah Watstein, John Jovanovic. Westport, Conn.: Greenwood Press, 2003. xxiii, 321 p., ill., maps. ISBN 1573563757

614/.07/27   RA643.W33

Contents: (A) Nationally notifiable diseases; (B) Human Immunoficiency Virus (HIV) and Acquired Immunodeficiency Syndrome (AIDS); (C) Malaria; (D) Sexually transmitted diseases; (E) Tuberculosis; (F) Foodborne diseases; (G) Waterborne diseases; (H) Infectious disease worldwide: present issues, emerging concerns; (I) Vaccine-preventable diseases; (J) Infectious disease elimination and eradication; (K) Bioterrorism and biological warfare; Appendix: World Health Organization (WHO) regions. Glossary.

"Comprehensive statistical overview of the status of infectious disease worldwide . . . often hard to find, or difficult to interpret . . . a carefully selected array of tables and charts of authoritative statistical information, placing valuable statistics into context with introductory text" (*Publ. notes*). Selection from a variety of print and web-based sources. Includes bibliographical references (p. [315]–318) and index. For general readers and students as a good starting point for research. Also available as an e-book.

1467 Wallace/Maxcy-Rosenau-Last public health and preventive medicine.
15th ed. Robert B. Wallace. New York: McGraw-Hill, 2007. xxxiii, 1367 p. ISBN 9780071441

614.44   RA425.M382

Title varies: 1st–7th eds. had title *Preventive medicine and hygiene*; 14th ed., 1998, had title *Maxcy-Rosenau-Last public health and preventive medicine*.

Contents: sec. 1, "Public health principles and methods"; sec. 2, "Communicable diseases"; sec. 3, "Environmental health"; sec. 4, "Behavioral factors affecting health"; sec. 5, "Noncommunicable and chronic disabling conditions"; sec. 6, "Health care—planning, organization, and evaluation"; sec. 7, "Injury and violence."

This revised and updated edition includes 82 chapters, providing essential information on the delivery of public health services, coverage of new diseases and policy issues, a new chapter on bioterrorism and emergency preparedness, and inclusion of more Web-based resources for further reading. Includes bibliographical references and index. Also available as an e-book.

1468 WHO child growth standards. http://www.who.int/childgrowth/en/index.html. World Health Organization. Geneva, Switzerland: World Health Organization. 2006

Since the late 1970s, the National Center for Health Statistics/WHO growth reference has been in use to chart children's growth. It was based on data from a limited sample of children from the United States and is now considered less adequate for international comparisons. In 1997, WHO, in collaboration with the United Nations University, undertook the Multicentre Growth Reference Study (MGRS), which is a community-based, multicountry project with more than 8,000 children from Brazil, Ghana, India, Norway, Oman, and the United States. The new standards are the result of this study, which had as its goal "to develop a new international standard for assessing the physical growth, nutritional status and motor development in all children from birth to age five"—*press release*. The first new growth charts released (Apr. 2007) include weight-for-age, length/height-for-age, and weight-for-length/height growth indicators as well as a Body Mass Index (BMI) standard for children up to age 5, and standards for sitting, standing, walking, and several other key motor developments.

The title of the print version is *WHO child growth standards: Length/height-for-age, weight-for-age, weight-for-length, weight-for-height and body mass index–for–age: Methods and development*.

1469 Women's health USA (WHUSA). http://purl.access.gpo.gov/GPO/LPS21379. U.S. Dept. of Health and Human Services, Maternal and Child Health Bureau. Rockville, Md.: U.S. Dept. of Health and Human Services, Maternal and Child Health Bureau. 2002–

"An illustrated collection of current and historical data"—*main page*.

Part of Health Resources and Services Administration (HRSA), within the U.S. Dept. of Health and Human Services (HHS)

Description based on WHUSA 2012 ed. Online access to previous editions is included.

Contents: Population characteristics; Health status; Health services utilization; HRSA programs women's health.

Collection of current and historical data on health challenges facing women, with information on life expectancy and addressing topics such as postpartum depression, smoking, alcohol, illicit drug use, etc. Brings together the latest available information from various government agencies (HHS, U.S. Dept. of Agriculture, U.S. Dept. of Labor, U.S. Dept. of Justice).

Other notable women's health and policy websites include, for example, Women's health (MedlinePlus) http://www.nlm.nih.gov/medlineplus/womenshealth.html , Women's health resources http://whr.nlm.nih.gov/, Womenshealth.gov http://www.womenshealth.gov/health-topics/; The Kaiser Family Foundation's Women's health policy http://kff.org/womens-health-policy/.

1470 World health and disease. 3rd ed.
Alastair Gray, P. R. Payne. Buckingham [England]; Philadelphia: Open University Press, 2001. 352 p., ill. (some col.) ISBN 033520838X

614.42   RA651.G65

First edition, 1985, had title *Health of nations*; [2nd] rev. ed., 1993. Vol. 3 of *Health and disease* series.

Contents: ch. 1, "Introduction"; ch. 2, "World patterns of mortality"; ch. 3, "Mortality and morbidity: causes and determinants"; ch. 4, "Livelihood and survival: A case study of Bangladesh"; ch. 5, "The world transformed: Population and the rise of industrial society"; ch. 6, "The decline of infectious diseases: The case of England"; ch. 7, "Health in a world of wealth and poverty"; ch. 8, "Population and development prospects"; ch. 9, "Contemporary patterns of disease in the United Kingdom"; ch. 10, "Explaining inequalities in health in the United Kingdom"; ch. 11, "Food, health and disease: A case study."

Presents a global view of human health. "Examines contemporary and historical patterns of health and disease in the U.K. and the rest of the world. The book draws on the disciplines of demography, epidemiology, history, the social sciences and biology"—*Pref.* Index and annotated guide to further reading and to selected Internet resources. Intended for students, health professionals, and others.

Encyclopedias

1471 Encyclopaedia of occupational health and safety. 4th ed. Jeanne Mager Stellman, International Labour Organization. Geneva, Switzerland: International Labour Organization, 1998. v. 2–4, ill. ISBN 9221092038

616.980303   RC963.A3.E53

Prepared under the auspices of the International Labour Organization.

1st ed., 1930, had title *Occupation and health*; 2nd ed., 1971; 3rd ed., 1983. Sometimes cited as *ILO encyclopedia of occupational health and safety*.

Contents: v. 1, *The body*; v. 2, *Hazards*; v. 3, *Chemicals, industries and occupations*; v. 4, *Guides, indexes (index by subject, index to chemicals, and guide to units and abbreviations), directory of experts*.

Consists of a collection of signed articles on the basic information available in the field by international specialists, with recent bibliographic references. In 105 chapters, entries cover various aspects of toxicology, occupational illnesses and injuries, diseases of migrant workers, and institutions active in the field of occupational health. Preventive safety measures are stressed, and technical and social solutions to problems are offered. Intends to provide "theoretical and ethical underpinnings to the ongoing work of achieving the goal of social justice in a global economy"—*Pref.*

Table of contents with search interface to access words and phrases in the text (http://www.ilocis.org/en/contilo.html).

1472 Encyclopedia of aging and public health. Sana Loue, Martha Sajatovic. New York: Springer, 2007. 843 p. ISBN 0387337539

Interdisciplinary resource for professionals in the fields of public health and geriatrics. Contains entries on health and diseases of adults as they age, and quality and accessibility of care for an aging population. Includes biological, psychosocial, historical, ethical, and legal aspects. Entries include references and resource lists. Also available as an e-book.

1473 Encyclopedia of biostatistics. 2nd ed.
P. Armitage, Theodore Colton.
Chichester, U.K.; West Sussex, U.K.: John
Wiley, 2005. 8 v. ISBN 047084907X
610.21   RA409.E53
First edition, 1998 (6 v.). Description based on rev.
and enl. ed., 2005 (8 v.).

Contents: v. 1, A–Chap; v. 2, Char–Dos; v. 3,
Dou–Gre; v. 4, Gro–Mar; v. 5, Mas–Nui; v. 6, Nul–
Ran; v. 7, Rao–Str; v. 8, Stu–Z, index.

Biostatistics can be defined as the application of
statistical methods to the life sciences, medicine, and
the health sciences. Clinical epidemiology, clinical
trials, disease modeling, epidemiology, statistical
computing, and vital and health statistics are some
examples of the areas covered. This edition contains
more than 1,300 articles, with approximately 300
revised and 182 new entries. New topics include, for
example, applications of biostatistics to bioinformatics, study of the human genome, and outbreaks of
infectious-disease epidemics. Bibliographies, many
cross-references, author index, and a selected list of
review articles. Also available as an e-book.

1474 Encyclopedia of bioterrorism defense.
Richard F. Pilch, Raymond A. Zilinskas.
Hoboken, N.J.: Wiley-LISS, 2005. xiii,
555 p., ill. ISBN 0471467170
363.32   HV6433.3.E53
Single v. containing 136 entries written by 99 expert
contributors on topics related to bioterrorism in
fields of social, natural, and physical sciences; engineering; policy; and government. Articles explore
interdependent issues surrounding science, legislation, international government relations, and social
response related to the existence and potential use
of biological warfare. Entries provide references,
further reading suggestions, and Web sites. Most
articles provide background in their main subjects,
and some specifically address historical topics,
such as the Palestinian Islamic Jihad and Weather
Underground groups. Thorough index with cross-
references. Recommended for public and academic
libraries. Available as an e-book.

1475 Encyclopedia of epidemiology. Sarah
Boslaugh. Los Angeles: Sage, 2008. 2 v., ill.
ISBN 9781412928
614.403   RA652.E533
Reader's guide topics: "Behavioral and social

science"; "Branches of epidemiology"; "Data"; "Diseases and conditions"; "Epidemiological concepts";
"Ethics"; "Genetics"; "Health care economics and
management"; "History and biography"; "Infra-
structure"; "Medical care and research"; "Specific
populations"; "Statistics and research methods";
"Women's health issues."

Approximately 650 articles of varying length
on basic epidemiologic concepts. Covers research
methods, statistical information relating to diseases, biographical information, etc. Each article
includes bibliography and "see also" references.
Useful as a supplementary resource for health professionals and general readers. Available electronically through Sage eReference and also via Gale
Virtual Reference Library.

1476 Encyclopedia of health and behavior.
Norman B. Anderson. Thousand Oaks,
Calif.: Sage, 2004. 2 v. ISBN 0761923608
610.3   R726.5.E53
Contents: v.1, A–G; v.2, H–W.

Health and behavior as an area of study can be
defined as an interdisciplinary field of health science, health care, and public health that focuses
on the interaction of behavioral, psychological,
emotional, social, cultural, and biological factors
with physical health outcomes. Approximately 200
entries such as stress and health, pain management,
social support, health, smoking, health promotion
and disease prevention, and HIV/AIDS. Includes
policy and organizational issues, including health
care costs. Cross-references. Appendix with online
resources and an annotated listing of organizations.
Author and subject indexes. For scholars, health
professionals, and also general readers. Also available as an e-book.

**1477 Encyclopedia of infectious diseases:
Modern methodologies.** Michel
Tibayrenc. Hoboken, N.J.: Wiley-Liss,
2007. 747 p., [24] p. of plates: ill. (some
color), maps (some color).
ISBN 0471657328
362.1969003   RA643.E53
Provides coverage of modern multidisciplinary
approaches and applications of newly developed
technologies to the study of infectious diseases and
their surveillance and control. Emphasis is on medical applications. Articles on AIDS, malaria, SARS

and influenza, evolution of pathogens and the relationship between human genetic diversity and the spread of infectious diseases, uses of various technologies, and various specialized topics (e.g., bioterrorism, antibiotics, using a geographic information system to spatially investigate infectious disease, representation of infectious diseases in art, and others). Includes list of web resources. For an academic audience. Also available as an e-book.

Encyclopedia of infectious diseases, by Turkington et al. (part of the Facts on File library of health and living series), is also a useful resource, intended for health professionals, general readers, and public libraries.

1478 Encyclopedia of obesity. Kathleen
  Keller. Los Angeles: Sage, 2008. 2 v., ill.,
  port. ISBN 9781412952385
    362.196398003   RC628.E53
"Reader's guide" topics: biological or genetic contributions to obesity; children and obesity; dietary interventions to treat obesity; disordered eating and obesity; environmental contributions to obesity; health implications of obesity; medical treatments for obesity; new research frontiers on obesity; obesity and ethnicity/race; obesity and the brain or obesity and behavior; obesity as a public health crisis; psychological influences and outcomes of obesity; societal influences and outcomes of obesity; women and obesity; worldwide prevalence of obesity.

This interdisciplinary resource explores a variety of topics on obesity, health conditions, and issues related to obesity. Written in nontechnical language and intended as a starting point for different audiences, from scholars to the general public. References at the end of each entry. Glossary and index in both volumes. Available online via Sage eReference.

**1479 Encyclopedia of primary prevention
  and health promotion.** Thomas
  Gullotta, Martin Bloom, Child and
  Family Agency of Southeastern
  Connecticut. New York: Kluwer
  Academic/Plenum, 2003. xi, 1179 p., ill.
  ISBN 0306472961
    613.03   RA427.8.E53
A sponsored publication of the Child and Family Agency of Southeastern Connecticut.

Pt. 1, "Foundation topics in primary prevention and health promotion," includes, for example,

sections on definitions and the history of health promotion, and ethical considerations. Pt. 2, "Primary prevention and human health promotion topics," covers a wide range of interdisciplinary topics, such as aggressive behavior, environmental health, creativity, suicide, and violence, to name a few. Included are strategies that work or are promising, as well as those that do not work. International resource, written in a standard format that allows cross-comparison.

1480 Encyclopedia of public health. Lester
  Breslow. New York: Macmillan Reference
  USA; Gale Group, 2002. 4 v., ill., map.
  ISBN 0028653548
    362.103   RA423.E53
Approx. 900 alphabetically arranged entries with brief bibliographies in the key areas of public health, with topics such as epidemiology, environmental health, drug abuse, bioterrorism, etc. Includes overviews, definitions, and biographical entries. Each entry begins with an outline of the article. Glossary entries explain key terms. Extensive use of cross-references. Appendix includes text of core documents and publications of historical importance in the field of public health. A broad outline is found at the back of v. 4. Index. For general readers, students, and health professionals. Also available as an e-book.

Other public health encyclopedias include *Encyclopedia of public health* by Kirch and *International encyclopedia of public health*.

1481 Encyclopedia of women's health.
  Sana Loue, Martha Sajatovic, Keith B.
  Armitage. New York: Kluwer Academic/
  Plenum, 2004. vii, 710 p.
  ISBN 0306480735
    613.04244   RA778.E5825
Covers the history of women's health as well as current topics and issues. Interdisciplinary resource, including topics from medicine, psychology, law, and other areas and perspectives. Also includes alternative and complementary health topics. Suggested readings. Written for both general readers and health professionals. Also available as an e-book and via Credo reference.

**1482 Essentials of medical geology:
  Impacts of the natural environment
  on public health.** O. Selinus, B. J.
  Alloway. Amsterdam, Netherlands;

Boston: Elsevier Academic Press, 2005.
xiv, 812 p., ill. (some col.)
ISBN 0126363412
614.42   RA566.E87
Contents: sec. 1, "Medical geology: Perspectives and prospects"; sec. 2, "Pathways and exposures"; sec. 3, "Environmental toxicology, pathology, and medical geology"; sec. 4, "Techniques and tools"; appendixes: (A) international reference values; (B) Web links; (C) glossary.

Medical geology, considered an emerging discipline, is defined by the International Working Group on Medical Geology as the science dealing with the relationship between natural geological factors and health in man and animals. Chapters address such topics as natural distribution and abundance of elements, uptake of elements from a chemical or biological point of view, geological impacts on nutrition, volcanic emissions and health, radon in air and water, arsenic in groundwater and the environment, fluoride in natural waters, water hardness and health effects, GIS in human health studies, and histochemical and microprobe analysis in medical geology. Reference tables, graphics, and maps. Index. Also available as an e-book.

1483 International encyclopedia of public health. Harald Kristian Heggenhougen, Stella R. Quah. Amsterdam, Netherlands; Boston: Elsevier/Academic Press, 2008. ill. (some color), maps (some color).
ISBN 9780122272
362.103   RA423
Six-volume set.
Provides comprehensive coverage of current important public health topics, including global aspects of public health issues, various health care systems, containment of infectious disease outbreaks, and many others. Approx. 500 peer-reviewed articles, with bibliographies, cross-references, and many illustrations. Alphabetically arranged entries. Subject classification (30 sections) in v. 1. Index. Also available as an e-book.

Dictionaries

1484 Dictionary of environmental health.
David Worthington. New York: Spon Press, 2002. ISBN 0415267242

616.9803   RA566.W68
(Clay's library of health and the environment)
"Provides a one-stop reference to over 3,000 common and not so common terms, concepts, abbreviations, acronyms, and a wealth of supporting data . . . suitable for . . . environmental and public health practitioners and students . . ."—*Publ. description.* Appendix I: Units and measurements; Appendix II: Abbreviations and acronyms. Cross-references, bibliographical references, and index. Available as an e-book.

1485 A dictionary of epidemiology. 5th ed.
Miquel S. Porta, International Epidemiological Association. Oxford; New York: Oxford University Press, 2008. xxiv, 289 p., ill., maps.
ISBN 9780195314496
614.403   RA651.D553
First ed., 1983; 4th ed., 2001.
Defines and explains basic and advanced epidemiologic terms and methods for clinical research and public health practice. This edition provides a broad range of covered topics, including biostatistics, bioethics, community and public health, demography, and microbiology. It includes new terminology from biostatistics and various subspecialties of epidemiology (e.g., pharmaco-epidemiology and genetic and molecular epidemiology). Definitions range from one word to short essays that incorporate tables, graphs, charts, mathematical formulas, and diagrams. The more common terms are defined, with cross-references from their synonyms. Also available as an e-book.

1486 Dictionary of pharmacoepidemiology.
Bernard Bégaud. Chichester [England]; New York: Wiley, 2000. x, 171 p.
ISBN 0471803618
615.103   RM302.5.B443
English translation of Bernard Bégaud's *Dictionnaire de pharmaco-épidémiologie*, 1998.

Online access available from WileyInterScience Online Books (http://onlinelibrary.wiley.com/book/10.1002/0470842547) and also via netLibrary.

As defined in this dictionary, pharmacoepidemiology is the "study of interactions between drugs and populations, or more specifically, the study of the therapeutic effect(s), risk and use of drugs, usually in large populations, using epidemiology and methods of reasoning," and the work is written for "regulatory authorities, pharmaceutical physicians, lawyers, pharmacists, researchers, evaluators and students"—*Foreword*. Complements epidemiology dictionaries.

1487 A dictionary of public health. John
Last. New York: Oxford University Press,
2006. ISBN 9780195160
362.1003   RA423.L37

Provides approximately 5,000 definitions of varying length (some include explanation and discussion as well as pointing to further information online) for many specialized terms found in the public health vocabulary. Also included are brief biographical entries for "historically significant people who have contributed to the advance of public health"—*Pref*. Bibliography and references. Electronic version via Oxford Reference Online.

**1488 Dictionary of public health
promotion and education: Terms and
concepts. 2nd ed.** Naomi N. Modeste,
Teri S. Tamayose, Helen Hopp Marshak.
San Francisco: Jossey-Bass, 2004. xii, 177
p. ISBN 0787969192
613.03   RA440.5.M634
First edition, 1996.

This expanded edition, intended for public health professionals and students, provides definitions for frequently used terms in public health education and promotion and related public health disciplines. Emphasizes "terms relevant to the four settings of health promotion and education—community, workplace, primary care, and school"—*Foreword*.

Includes a list of health and professional organizations, references, and recommended reading. Also available as an e-book.

**1489 Health services cyclopedic dictionary:
A compendium of health-care and
public health terminology. 3rd ed.**
Thomas C. Timmreck. Sudbury, Mass.:
Jones and Bartlett Publishers, 1997. xii,
860 p., col. ill. ISBN 0867205156
362.1/068   RA393.T56
First ed. (1982) and 2nd ed. (1987) had title: *Dictionary of health services management*.

(The Jones and Bartlett series in health sciences)
This rev. and exp. ed. contains terminology and definitions from the fields of health services and medical care, health administration, health care reform, public health, environmental health, epidemiology, managed care, and other related areas.

**1490 Illustrated dictionary and resource
directory of environmental and
occupational health. 2nd ed.**
Herman Koren. Boca Raton, Fla.: CRC
Press, 2005. 701 p., ill.
ISBN 1566705908
616.98003   RA566.K59
First edition, 1996, had title *Illustrated dictionary of environmental health and occupational safety*.

Interdisciplinary resource covering a variety of fields (for example, epidemiology, microbiology, toxicology, and computer science) relevant to environmental and occupational health and safety, with approximately 16,000 terms and cross-references for synonyms, abbreviations, and acronyms. The resource directory lists professional and government organizations. For professionals, students, and general readers. Also available as an e-book.

**1491 Lewis' dictionary of occupational
and environmental safety and health.**
Jeffrey W. Vincoli. Boca Raton, Fla.: Lewis,
2000. 1093 p., ill. ISBN 1566703999
363.1103   T55.L468

Comprehensive resource for the terminology of the interdisciplinary area of industrial safety and environmental health. Includes approximately 25,000 definitions.

Available online via CRCnetBASE.

1492 Medical statistics from A to Z. 2nd ed.
Brian Everitt. Cambridge, U.K.; New
York: Cambridge University Press, 2006.
vi, 248 p., ill. ISBN 0521867630
610.727   RA407.E943
First ed., 2003.

Contains approx. 1,500 terms with definitions and references for further reading. Written in non-technical language. For health professionals and students. Also available as an e-book.

Another more recent title by the same author is *Encyclopaedic companion to medical statistics*.

1493 Slee's health care terms. 5th ed.
Debora A. Slee, Vergil N. Slee,
H. Joachim Schmidt. Sudbury, Mass.:

Jones and Bartlett Publ., 2007. 700 p.
ISBN 9780763746155
362.103 RA423.S55
First ed., 1986; 4th ed., 2001. Also called *Health care terms*.

Provides concise definitions for terms from a wide range of disciplines in the healthcare field, including administration, organization, finance, statistics, law, and governmental regulation. Many cross-references. Pays particular attention to acronyms. Terms used in definitions are italicized to indicate the term is defined elsewhere in the dictionary; related terms may be grouped together under one term, such as the many entries under the term "hospital." Intended for all types of healthcare consumers.

Directories

1494 Health.gov. http://www.health.gov/.
Office of Disease Prevention and Health Promotion. Washington: U.S. Department of Health and Human Services

Coordinated by the Office of Disease Prevention and Health Promotion, Office of Public Health Service, U.S. Dept. of Health and Human Services (HHS).

"Portal to the Web sites of a number of multi-agency health initiatives and activities of the U.S. Department of Health and Human Services (HHS) and other Federal departments and agencies."—*Main page* Provides links to general health information (e.g., Healthfinder, National Health Information Center [http://www.health.gov/nhic/], MedlinePlus, and others), special initiatives (e.g., Healthy People, Dietary guidelines for Americans 2010, and others), health news, the major federal agencies (U.S. Dept. of Health and Human Services and its agencies, Office of Disease Prevention and Health Promotion [http://odphp.osophs.dhhs.gov/], Office of the Surgeon General [http://www.surgeongeneral.gov/]), and other key government agencies with "direct health responsibilities" (e.g., Dept. of Defense [DoD], Environmental Protection Agency [EPA], Dept. of Veterans Affairs [VA], Occupational Safety and Health Administration [OSHA], and others).

1495 A practical guide to global health service. Edward O'Neil, American

Medical Association. Chicago: American Medical Association, 2006. xxxv, 402 p.
ISBN 1579476732
610.73/7 RA390.U5O54
OMNI Med ("loosely translated from the Latin meaning 'health care for all'" [*Pref.*]) is a nongovernmental organization founded by the author in 1998.

Contents: ch. 1, Overcoming obstacles: cultural and practical guidelines; ch. 2, Travel, health, and safety guidelines; ch. 3, The Omni Med database of international health service opportunities; ch. 4, Cross-referencing guide to the database; ch. 5, Other relevant organizations; Appendix A, Useful web sites; Appendix B, About Omni Med.

"A health providers guide to the practical aspects of serving internationally, including data on more than 300 organizations that send health providers overseas" (*Publ. notes*). Organization profiles include concise descriptions, contact information, and practical information about length of service terms, personnel sought, areas served, and availability of funding, training, room and board, and other essential information (e.g., trip planning, travel and safety guidelines, commonly encountered illnesses, information about the culture of a particular country, etc.). Written for persons interested in medical volunteering. Glossary; bibliography.

Caring for the world: A guidebook to global health opportunities, also available as an e-book, is a resource for finding out about health opportunities abroad, with a directory of relevant government and non-government organizations, educational opportunities, funding resources, and trip planning.

Histories

1496 Health and British magazines in the nineteenth century. E. M. Palmegiano. Lanham, Md.: Scarecrow Press, 1998. ix, 282 p. ISBN 0810834863
016.6 Z6673.P288; RA776.5
Bibliography of 2,604 entries based on headlines and captions in major British Victorian serials (selected mainly from the *Wellesley index to Victorian periodicals 1824–1900*), providing a synopsis of health issues during this period that demonstrates "the evolution of popular thinking about the

practice of human health . . . and outlines major concepts and investigates the formation of essential categories still in use, such as ideas of wellness and unwellness, the meaning of care and care-givers, and the productive status of being healthy"—*Publ. notes*. Indexed by author and subject.

1497 Historical dictionary of the World Health Organization. 2nd ed.
Kelley Lee, Jennifer Fang. Lanham, Md.: Scarecrow Press, 2013.
ISBN 9780810878587
362.1   RA8
First ed., 1998.
(Historical dictionaries of international organizations series)

Provides information on the history of the World Health Organization (WHO) and its contributions to international health cooperation, with emphasis on the last 20 years. Includes a new introduction to WHO agencies & programs, an extensive bibliography on WHO documents and writings about WHO, and a chronology of selected major events in the history of international health organizations. Includes appendixes, for example, constitution of WHO, chronological list of member states, and WHO directors. Related information available on the World Health Organization (WHO) home page.

1498 A history of public health. Expanded ed.
George Rosen, Elizabeth Fee, Edward T. Morman. Baltimore: Johns Hopkins University Press, 1993. xci, 535 p. ISBN 9780801846458
614.4   RA424.R65.R68
First edition, 1958.

An eight-part history of public health from earliest times to the present. Includes bibliography; list of memorable figures with brief biographical sketches; list of public health periodicals, arranged by country; list of worldwide public health societies and schools. Bibliographical references (p. 473–506). Subject and author indexes.

Another title by the same author, *Preventive medicine in the United States, 1900-1975: Trends and interpretations*, remains a useful resource.

1499 Plagues and politics: The story of the United States Public Health Service.
Fitzhugh Mullan. New York: Basic Books,

1989. 223 p., ill. ISBN 0465057799
353.00841   RA445.M75
Contents: ch. 1, 1798–1889, "Sailors, sinecures and reform"; ch. 2, 1890–1911, "Science, immigrants, and the public health movement"; ch. 3, 1912–20, "Public health warriors"; ch. 4, 1921–35, "Public health within limits"; ch. 5, 1936–48, "Calamity, necessity, and opportunity"; ch. 6, 1949–60, "The coming of HEW"; ch. 7, 1961–68, "Public health at the new frontier"; ch. 8, 1969–80, "Care, cost, and prevention"; ch. 9, 1981–89, "New politics, new plagues."

An illustrated history of the Public Health Service from 1798 to 1989, dealing with infectious diseases (e.g., malaria, yellow fever, typhus, etc.) and also with diseases such as AIDS, cancer, and others. Includes list of Surgeons General of the United States Public Health Service (active between 1871 and 1989) and Assistant Secretaries for Health (Dept. of Health and Human Services/Health Education and Welfare). Bibliography; index. For general readers. Also available as an e-book.

1500 Public health image library (PHIL).
http://phil.cdc.gov/Phil/. Centers for Disease Control and Prevention. Atlanta: Centers for Disease Control and Prevention. [1998]–

Public health image library (PHIL), created by a working group at the Centers for Disease Control and Prevention (CDC); National Library of Medicine (NLM).

Collection of a variety of single images, image sets, multimedia files, etc., with current and historical content about people, places, scientific subjects, etc. FAQ section (http://phil.cdc.gov/Phil/faq.asp) provides detailed information. Useful for public health professionals, scientists, librarians, teachers, and students.

This website also provides links to other CDC and NLM image libraries (e.g., Images from the history of medicine and Visible Human). Complements other medical image collections such as Health education assets library (HEAL) and Images-MD (http://www.springerimages.com/imagesMD/).

1501 The value of health: A history of the Pan American Health Organization.
Marcos Cueto. Washington: Pan American Health Organization, 2007.

239 p. ISBN 9781580462631

362.1   RA10.C8413

(Scientific and technical publication; 600) Pan American Health Organization (PAHO)

Contents: ch. 1, The origins of international public health in the Americas; ch. 2, The birth of a new organization; ch. 3, The consolidation of an identity; ch. 4, For a continent free of disease; ch. 5, Health, development, and community participation; v. 6, Validity and renewal.

History of PAHO, contributions of individuals in PAHO, and also contemporary issues. Endnotes, bibliography, and index.

1502 WHO historical collection. http://www.who.int/library/collections/historical/en/print.html. World Health Organization. Geneva, Switzerland: World Health Organization. 2000s–

Produced by World Health Organization (WHO); part of WHO Library and Information Networks for Knowledge (LNK).

Covers conferences before the founding of the WHO, WHO official records, International Sanitary Conventions (since 1851), and official records, reports, and other published materials from the Office International d'Hygiène Publique (OIHP), the health organization of the League of Nations (UNRRA). Includes materials on plague, cholera, and yellow fever, and also more recent epidemics; international classifications and nomenclatures of diseases; and public health and medicine monographs on public health in different countries and languages. Related links are, for example, WHO-LIS: World Health Organization library database and WHO archives (http://www.who.int/archives/en/index.html). The distinctions between the WHO library, the WHO archives, and WHO records are described at http://www.who.int/archives/fonds_collections/partners/en/index.html.

1503 World epidemics: A cultural chronology of disease from prehistory to the era of SARS. Mary Ellen Snodgrass. Jefferson, N.C.: McFarland & Co., 2003. vii, 479 p. ISBN 9780786416622

614.49   RA649.S65

Presents information on world epidemics from pre-historical times to publication date (i.e., 2003). Arranged chronologically by "estimated time spans

and exact dates.of incidents of contagion across the globe."—*Pref.* Includes citations from personal and public documents, comparative charts of types of infections, and estimates of the number of people affected by each epidemic. In addition to the chronology and information on important healers and researchers, provides several appendixes: (A) "Epidemic diseases and sources"; (B) "Historic writings and disease"; (C) "Timeline of writings on disease"; (D) "Authors of major works on disease". Bibliography (general resources; resources by diseases) and index. For general readers, students, and researchers.

A related website is "Contagion: Historical views of diseases and epidemics" http://ocp.hul.harvard.edu/contagion/, a digital collection of Harvard University's Open Collections Program that makes available historical materials from Harvard's libraries, archives, and museums. It provides background information on epidemics worldwide. This Internet resource includes digitized copies of books, serials, pamphlets, and manuscripts, with plates, engravings, maps, charts, and other illustrations.

Statistics

1504 Atlas of health in Europe. 2nd ed. World Health Organization.; Regional Office for Europe. Copenhagen, Denmark: WHO Regional Office for Europe, 2008. vii, 126 p., col. ill., maps. ISBN 9789289014106

614.4/24   G1797.21.E55 W5

First ed., 2003.

Contents: 1. Demography; 2. Life and death; 3. Diseases; 4. Lifestyles and environment; 5. Health care.

The WHO Regional Office for Europe consists of 53 member states.

This resource updates the 2003 ed. It pulls together health and disease-related statistics, with "new data on relevant health issues in the WHO European Region . . . to better reflect the new challenges confronting public health. Rich and elaborate data from various sources have been gathered, systematized, grouped and reformatted to help readers to go through them and gain an overall picture of health in the Region, to the extent it can be expressed in figures."—*Foreword.* Data covered are from 1980 at the earliest to 2006 at the latest, depending on the data available in countries. For undergraduates through faculty/researchers, also general readers. A freely available PDF version available at http://www.euro.who.int/__data/assets/pdf_file/0011/97598/E91713.pdf

1505 County health rankings & roadmaps. http://www.countyhealthrankings.org/. Robert Wood Johnson Foundation, University of Wisconsin Population Health Institute. Madison, Wisc.: University of Wisconsin Population Health Institute. 2010–

RA407.3

Part of the County Health Rankings & Roadmaps program, a collaboration between the Robert Wood Johnson Foundation and the University of Wisconsin Population Health Institute. Further information at http://www.countyhealthrankings.org/about-project.

A map of the U.S. allows to click on individual states to show county-by-county health data and the rank of the health of "nearly every county in the nation."—*Website*. Provides data of the overall health of each county and helps with understanding the factors that affect health (e.g., income, limited access to health foods, air and water quality, smoking, obesity, etc.) Offers various display options for data. FAQs (http://www.countyhealthrankings.org/faq-page) answer general and methodology questions. For all audiences.

1506 European health for all database (HFA-DB). http://data.euro.who.int/hfadb/. World Health Organization Regional Office for Europe. Copenhagen, Denmark: World Health Organization Regional Office for Europe. 2000s–

Description based on Jan. 2013 version.

Provides basic health statistics and health trends for the member states of the WHO European Region, with approximately 600 health indicators, including basic demographic and socioeconomic indicators; some lifestyle- and environment-related indicators; mortality, morbidity, and disability; hospital discharges; and health care resources, utilization, and expenditures. Can be used as a tool for international comparison and for assessing the health situation and trends in any European country. Help available at https://euro.sharefile.com/d-sb7422ab51e54f20b.

1507 Faststats A to Z. http://www.cdc.gov/nchs/fastats/Default.htm. National Center for Health Statistics (NCHS). Hyattsville, Md: U.S. Dept. of Health and Human Services, Centers for Disease Control and Prevention, National Center for Health Statistics

Provides topic-appropriate public health statistics (e.g., birth data, morbidity and mortality statistics, and health care use) and relevant links to further information and publications. Includes state and territorial data, with clickable map for individual state data. Also includes data derived from the "Behavioral Risk Factor Surveillance System (BRFSS)," which compiles data for 16 negative behaviors.

1508 Health, United States. http://purl.access.gpo.gov/GPO/LPS2649. National Center for Health Statistics, National Center for Health Services Research. Rockville, Md.: National Center for Health Statistics. 1975–

An annual report on trends in health statistics.

The report consists of several main sections: complete report; "at a glance" table; highlights; a chartbook containing text and figures that illustrate major trends in the health of Americans; and a trend tables section that contains 150 detailed data tables. Includes extensive appendixes and an index. Hyperlinks to tables and graphs, which are available in formats such as Excel, PowerPoint, and PDF.

New for the 2012 edition is a special feature on emergency care.

Easy access to related online resources provided by the National Center for Health Statistics (NCHS).

1509 Health data tools and statistics from PHPartners. http://phpartners.org/health_stats.html. Partners in Information Access for the Public Health Workforce, National Library of Medicine (U.S.). Bethesda, Md.: U.S. National Library of Medicine, National Institutes of Health, Dept. of Health and Human Services

Contents: County and local health data; State health data; Individual state data; National health data; Global health data; Statistical reports; Demographic data; Geographic information systems (GIS); Training and education; Health information technology and standards; Tools for data collection and planning.

Provides lists of selected links with brief annotations to assist in locating public health data and statistics. Part of The Partners in Information Access for the Public Health Workforce (PHPartners) website (http://phpartners.org/index.html) which is described as "a collaboration of U.S. government agencies, public health organizations and health sciences libraries, with the mission of helping the public health workforce find and use information effectively to improve and protect the public's health."—*About page.* Its topics pages include, for example, bioterrorism, dental public health, HIV/ AIDS, nutrition, obesity, public health genomics, and other relevant information for public health professionals and researchers.

Additional highly useful sites in this area are, for example, Health services research and public health information, HSR information central, and National Information Center on Health Services Research and Health Care Technology.

1510 Health in the Americas. Pan American Sanitary Bureau. Washington: Pan American Health Organization, Pan American Sanitary Bureau, Regional Office of the World Health Organization, 1998–. v., ill.

610/.8s; 362.1/09181/2   RA10.P252

Published by Pan American Health Organization (PAHO); "Salud en las Américas."

Title varies: Previously had title *Summary of reports on the health conditions in the Americas* and *Health conditions in the Americas.* Description based on 2007 ed. (2 v.): v. 1, Regional analysis; v. 2, Country-by-country assessment.

Health data, facts, health trends, and related information for Central and South America, with emphasis on health disparities. Provides a vision for the future of health and health challenges in the Americas. Also available online through netLibrary; both print and online versions in English or Spanish.

A complement to this publication is *Health statistics from the Americas,* publ. in print format 1991–98, and now online (2003 ed. http://www .paho.org/english/dd/pub/SP591.htm and 2006 ed.

http://www.paho.org/English/DD/AIS/HSA2006 .htm).

1511 Healthy people. http://www.cdc.gov/ nchs/healthy_people.htm. National Center for Health Statistics (NCHS). Hyattsville, Md.: Centers for Disease Control (U.S.), National Center for Health Statistics

RA395.A3

Contents: Healthy people 2000; Healthy People 2010; Healthy People 2020; Progress Reviews; Publications.

"Healthy People provides science-based, national goals and objectives with 10-year targets designed to guide national health promotion and disease prevention efforts to improve the health of all people in the United States." —*Home Page.* Previous reports include *Healthy people 2000* (http:// purl.access.gpo.gov/GPO/LPS3745) and *Healthy people: The Surgeon General's report on health promotion and disease prevention: Background papers: Report to the Surgeon General on health promotion and disease prevention.* "Healthy People DATA 2010," an interactive database system accessible via CDC WONDER provides various reports and data. A search interface providing searches for published literature related to Healthy People 2010 was added to the "special queries" section of PubMed.

Also available in print format: *Tracking healthy people 2010.* Progress Reviews and publications are added to the website regularly.

1512 Healthy women. http://www.cdc.gov/ nchs/data/healthywomen/womens chartbook_aug2004.pdf. Centers for Disease Control and Prevention (U.S.); National Center for Health Statistics (U.S.). Hyattsville, Md.: National Center for Health Statistics, Centers for Disease Control and Prevention, U.S. Dept. of Health and Human Services. 2004

RA408.W65

Title varies: Suggested title for website: *Healthy women: State trends in health and mortality;* suggested citation for print version, publ. in 2004 as *Women's health and mortality chartbook* by K. M. Brett and Suzanne G. Hayes.

PDF of *Women's Health and Mortality*

Chartbook, developed by NCHS with support from the Office on Women's Health. It describes the health of people in each state in the U.S. by sex, race, and age by reporting current data on critical issues of relevance to women.

Other publications in this area include *Women's health data book: A profile of women's health in the United States,* ed. by D. Misra, a collaborative publication by the Jacobs Institute of Women's Health and the Henry J. Kaiser Family Foundation (Kaiser Family Foundation) since 1992, complemented by *State profiles on women's health: Women's health issues,* publ. since 1998.

1513 HHS Data Council. http://aspe.hhs.gov/datacncl/. United States.; Dept. of Health and Human Services.; Data Council. Washington: U.S. Department of Health and Human Services. 200?–

RA407.3

"The HHS Data Council coordinates all health and human services data collection and analysis activities of the Department of Health and Human Services, including an integrated data collection strategy, coordination of health data standards and health and human services and privacy policy activities."—*Website.*

Provides access to key health and human services data and statistics. Covers information sponsored by federal, state, and local governments. Complements other government resources such as USA.gov and FedStats. Links to health and human services surveys and data systems sponsored by federal agencies and leads to websites and other key resources that contain statistics and data. Additionally, HealthData.gov http://www.hhs.gov/open/datasets/index.html provides access to datasets, various tools, and applications using data about health and healthcare.

1514 National vital statistics system (NVSS). http://www.cdc.gov/nchs/nvss.htm. National Center for Health Statistics (U. S.). Hyattsville, Md.: National Center for Health Statistics. 2000s–

A unit of the National Center for Health Statistics, which is responsible for the official vital statistics of the United States: births, deaths (annual mortality data, monthly provisional mortality data,

cause-of-death data by age, race, sex, etc.), marriages, divorces, and fetal deaths. Has contact information for obtaining vital records from states and territories. Provides access to a vital-statistics information sources portal (http://www.cdc.gov/nchs/data_access/VitalStatsOnline.htm), with links to publications and information products (http://www.cdc.gov/nchs/products.htm), including *Advance data*, *Vital and health statistics reports* (also referred to as "series reports" and "rainbow series"), and many others that can be identified via a NCHS Web search or a helpful site index at http://www.cdc.gov/az/a.html.

1515 Statistical record of health and medicine. Gale Research Inc. Detroit: Gale Research Inc., c1995–c1998. 2 v. 362.10973021

1078-6961   RA407.3.S732

Description based on 2nd ed., 1998.

Compilation of U.S. national, state, and municipal health and medical statistics from a variety of sources. Provides statistics on health status of Americans, health insurance, health care costs and expenditures, medical professions, international rankings and comparisons, etc. Further detailed notes on scope and coverage in the introduction and the sources from which the information is drawn. Keyword index.

Can be supplemented by more recent resources, for example, *Chronology of public health in the United Sates* (by Wright), which covers events back to 1796, but mainly since 1900, as well as various government websites containing health and medical statistics.

1516 WHOSIS. http://www.who.int/whosis/. World Health Organization. Geneva, [Switzerland]: World Health Organization. [1994]–

Published by World Health Organization (WHO).

Provides description and online access to statistical and epidemiological information, data, and tools available from WHO and other sites: mortality and health status, disease statistics, health systems statistics, risk factors and health services, and inequities in health. Provides links to several databases: WHOSIS database, with the latest "core health indicators" from WHO sources (including *The world health report* and

World health statistics), which make it possible to construct tables for any combination of countries, indicators and years, Causes of death database, WHO global infobase online, Global health atlas, and Reproductive health indicators database.

As of 2011, WHOSIS has been incorporated into WHO's Global health observatory(GHO) which provides additional data & tools, and also more analysis and reports.

1517 Women's health USA (WHUSA).
  http://purl.access.gpo.gov/GPO/
  LPS21379. U.S. Dept. of Health and
  Human Services, Maternal and Child
  Health Bureau. Rockville, Md.: U.S. Dept.
  of Health and Human Services, Maternal
  and Child Health Bureau. 2002–
"An illustrated collection of current and historical data"—*main page*.

Part of Health Resources and Services Administration (HRSA), within the U.S. Dept. of Health and Human Services (HHS)

Description based on WHUSA 2012 ed. Online access to previous editions is included.

Contents: Population characteristics; Health status; Health services utilization; HRSA programs women's health.

Collection of current and historical data on health challenges facing women, with information on life expectancy and addressing topics such as postpartum depression, smoking, alcohol, illicit drug use, etc. Brings together the latest available information from various government agencies (HHS, U.S. Dept. of Agriculture, U.S. Dept. of Labor, U.S. Dept. of Justice).

Other notable women's health and policy websites include, for example, Women's health (MedlinePlus) http://www.nlm.nih.gov/medlineplus/womens health.html , Women's health resources http://whr .nlm.nih.gov/, Womenshealth.gov http://www.womens health.gov/health-topics/; The Kaiser Family Foundation's Women's health policy http://kff.org/ womens-health-policy/.

1518 The world health report. http://
  www.who.int/whr/. World Health
  Organization. Geneva, [Switzerland]:
  World Health Organization. 1995–
  614.405 1020-3311   RA8.A265

Pt. of WHOSIS: WHO statistical information system.

"Every year . . . takes a new and expert look at global health, focusing on a specific theme, while assessing the current global situation. Using the latest data gathered and validated by WHO, each report paints a picture of the changing world."— *Website* Website also provides links to the full-text reports 1995–2005, each with a focus on a special theme: 1995, "bridging the gaps"; 1996, "fighting disease, fostering development"; 1997, "conquering suffering, enriching humanity"; 1998, "life in the 21st century: a vision for all"; 1999, "making a difference"; 2000, "health systems: improving performance"; 2001, "mental health: new understanding, new hope"; 2002, "reducing risks, promoting healthy life"; 2003, "shaping the future"; 2004, "changing history"; 2005, "make every mother and child count"; 2006, "working together for health"; 2007, "a safer future: global public health security in the 21st century"; 2008, "primary health care: now more than ever"; 2010, "health systems financing: the path to universal coverage"; 2013, "Research for universal health coverage". No reports for 2009, 2011, or 2012. Also available in print.

1519 World health statistics. http://www
  .who.int/gho/publications/world_health
  _statistics/en/index.html. World Health
  Organization. Geneva, Switzerland:
  World Health Organization. 2005–
                        RA407.A1
1939/46–96 publ. as *World health statistics annual = Annuaire de statistiques sanitaires mondiales* (print version).

Part of WHOSIS: WHO statistical information system.

Provides online access to the 2005-2013 reports. Description based on 2013 online edition (http://www.who.int/whosis/whostat/EN_WHS 2011_Full.pdf).

Contents: pt. I, "Health-related millennium development goals"; pt. II, "Global health indicators"; tables: 1. "Life expectancy and mortality"; 2. "Cause-specific mortality and morbidity"; 3. "Selected infectious diseases"; 4. "Health service coverage"; 5. "Risk factors"; 6. "Health systems"; 7. "Health expenditure"; 8. "Health inequities"; 9. "Demographic and socioeconomic statistics."

"Annual compilation of health-related data for its 193 Member States . . . includes a summary of the progress made towards achieving the health-related Millennium Development Goals (MDGs) and associated targets . . . using publications and databases produced and maintained by the technical programmes and regional offices of WHO. Indicators have been included on the basis of their relevance to global public health; the availability and quality of the data; and the reliability and comparability of the resulting estimates. Taken together, these indicators provide a comprehensive summary of the current status of national health and health systems."—*Introd.* Derived from multiple sources, depending on each indicator and the availability and quality of data. Every effort has been made to ensure the best use of country-reported data – adjusted where necessary to deal with missing values, to correct for known biases, and to maximize the comparability of the statistics across countries and over time (cf. Introd.) A print version is also available.

Internet resources

1520 Agency for Healthcare Research and Quality (AHRQ). http://www.ahrq. gov. Agency for Healthcare Research and Quality (U.S.). Rockville, Md.: Agency for Healthcare Research and Quality. 1990s
Searchable website ("search AHRQ" and "A–Z Quick Menu") provides access to a variety of resources, with links to clinical and consumer health information, research findings, funding opportunities, data and surveys, quality assessment, specific populations (minorities, women, elderly, and others), and public health preparedness (bioterrorism and response). Links to a large number of full-text documents, including links to the tools, literature, and news in patient safety (e.g., *AHRQ patient safety network*) and tips on how to prevent medical errors.

1521 amfAR. http://www.amfar.org. American Foundation for AIDS Research. New York; Washington: American Foundation for AIDS Research. 1999–
"amfAR™, the Foundation for AIDS Research, is one of the world's leading nonprofit organizations

dedicated to the support of AIDS research, HIV prevention, treatment education, and the advocacy of sound AIDS-related public policy."—*Website*
Provides basic HIV/AIDS facts and statistics, HIV testing, information about various therapies (approved or under development), young people and HIV/AIDS, women and HIV/AIDS, global initiatives, and many other related topics and links.
"amfAR global links," formerly know as *HIV/ AIDS treatment directory*, and "HIV/AIDS treatment insider," available 2000-5, have ceased publication. *The AmFAR AIDS handbook: The complete guide to understanding HIV and AIDS*, a comprehensive guide to help readers understand HIV/ AIDS, treatment options, and how treatment decisions are made, has not been updated since 1999.

1522 Biodefense and bioterrorism (MedlinePlus). http://www.nlm.nih.gov/ medlineplus/biodefenseandbioterrorism. html. National Library of Medicine (U.S.), National Institutes of Health (U.S.). Washington: U.S. National Library of Medicine, National Institutes of Health, Dept. of Health and Human Services. 2000–
A Health Topic within MedlinePlus. Contents: Overviews; Treatment; Prevention/Screening; Alternative medicine; Coping; Specific conditions; Related issues; Pictures and photographs; Research; Journal articles; Dictionaries/Glossaries; Directories; Organizations; Law and policy; Children.
Collection of links from a variety of government agencies, professional associations, and organizations, with representative bioterrorism resources selections from the Centers for Disease Control and Prevention (CDC), National Institute of Allergy and Infectious Diseases, American Medical Association, American Academy of Family Physicians, American Psychiatric Association, Dept. of Homeland Security, and others. Related information also at Disaster preparation and recovery (MedlinePlus) and Emergency preparedness and response (CDC), for example.

1523 CDC: Emergency preparedness and response. http://www.bt.cdc. gov/. Centers for Disease Control and Prevention (U.S.). Atlanta: Centers for Disease Control and Prevention. 200?–

CDC's primary source of information and resources for preparing for and responding to public health emergencies. Provides extensive information on specific hazards, e.g., bioterrorism, bombing, chemical emergencies, Gulf oil spill 2010, natural disasters and severe weather, radiation, mass casualties, etc. Emergency preparedness and response A-Z index can be accessed at http://emergency.cdc.gov/az/m.asp.

Related sites include, for example, Biodefense and bioterrorism (MedlinePlus) and Disaster preparation and recovery (MedlinePlus).

1524 Centers for Disease Control and Prevention (U.S.). http://www.cdc.gov/. Centers for Disease Control and Prevention (U.S.). Atlanta: Centers for Disease Control and Prevention, U.S. Dept. of Health and Human Services. 1998–

The Centers for Disease Control and Prevention (CDC), part of the Dept. of Health and Human Services (HHS), is considered "the principal agency in the United States government for protecting the health and safety of all Americans and for providing essential human services" (*Website*). Involved in public health efforts to monitor health, to prevent and control infectious and chronic diseases, injury, workplace hazards, disability, and environmental health threats. Works with partners in the U.S. and worldwide, such as the World Health Organization.

"About CDC" (http://www.cdc.gov/about/organization/cio.htm) provides information about the centers, institutes, and offices associated with the CDC, linking each to its own website and associated information resources. Examples include the National Center for Health Statistics [NCHS], National Center for Environmental Health (NCEH), National Center for Injury Prevention and Control (NCIPC) "Injury Center" (http://www.cdc.gov/ncipc/), National Office of Public Health Genomics, Coordinating Office for Global Health (http://www.cdc.gov/cogh/index.htm), Coordinating Office for Emergency Preparedness and Response (http://www.bt.cdc.gov/), to name a few. An A–Z index (http://www.cdc.gov/az/a.html) provides information on many diseases and other health topics found on the CDC website, with new topics frequently added. CDC WONDER provides a search

interface to a variety of health-related topics and statistics. For health professionals and general users.

CDC: Emergency preparedness and response is CDC's primary source of information for responding to public health emergencies.

"MMWR: the first 30 years" http://stacks.cdc.gov/mmwr is a recent addition to the CDC website. It contains the first 30 years of *Morbidity and mortality weekly report* (*MMWR*) issues in digital format and is considered an important resource for public health professionals, historians, researchers, and others. For current editions of *MMWR*, see http://www.cdc.gov/MMWR.

1525 Disaster preparation and recovery (MedlinePlus). http://www.nlm.nih.gov/medlineplus/disasterpreparationandrecovery.html. National Library of Medicine (U.S.), National Institutes of Health (U.S.). Washington: National Library of Medicine. 2000–

Disaster preparation and recovery guides for the public from various organizations including the Dept. of Homeland Security, Federal Emergency Management Agency, American Red Cross, and Centers for Disease Control and Prevention. Listing of MedlinePlus "related topics" pages and links, e.g., Biodefense and Bioterrorism (MedlinePlus), coping with disasters, posttraumatic stress disorder, safety issues, and others.

1526 Drug abuse (MedlinePlus). http://www.nlm.nih.gov/medlineplus/drugabuse.html. National Library of Medicine (U.S.). Bethesda, Md.: National Library of Medicine. 2000?–

A health topic in MedlinePlus.

Contents: Overviews; Latest news; Diagnosis/symptoms; Treatment; Prevention/screening; Specific conditions; Related sssues; Pictures and photographs; Games; Clinical trials; Research; Journal articles; Dictionaries/glossaries; Directories; Organizations; Newsletters/print publications; Law and policy; Statistics; Children; Teenagers; Men; Women; Seniors; Other languages.

Collection of links on substance abuse from a variety of government agencies, professional associations, and organizations, such as the National

Institute on Drug Abuse, the Office of National Drug Control, Substance Abuse and Mental Health Services Administration (SAMHSA), National Library of Medicine, American Medical Association, American Academy of Family Physicians, and others. Also links to related MedlinePlus topics, e.g., alcoholism, prescription drug abuse, and substance abuse, to name a few.

1527 Enviro-health links. http://sis.nlm.nih.gov/pathway.html. National Library of Medicine (U.S.), National Institutes of Health, U.S. Dept of Health & Human Services. Bethesda, Md.: National Library of Medicine. 2010–

Part of NLM's Specialized Information Services (SIS) "Pathways for public health information" website, with selected links to Internet resources on environmental health and toxicology topics and issues. Includes both NLM and outside resources. Covers arsenic and human health; climate change and health; developing and using medicines for children; dietary supplements; education, careers, and outreach in toxicology and environmental health; environmental justice; epigenomics; hexavalent chromium and other chromium compounds; imported (Chinese) drywall; indoor air; keeping the artist safe; laboratory safety; lead and human health; mercury and human health; nanotechnology and human health; outdoor air; pesticide exposure; tobacco, smoking and health; toxicology; toxicogenomics; water pollution; and West Nile virus.

In addition to "Enviro-health links" also provides "Disaster health links" (e.g., chemical emergencies, disaster recovery, fires and wildfires, floods, earthquakes, and many others) and "Targeted populations" (e.g., American Indian health, Asian American health, K-12 science and health education, multi-cultural resources for health information, women's health, and others) links. Guidelines for the selection of resources outside of NLM are spelled out at http://sis.nlm.nih.gov/enviro/envirohealthlinkscriteria.html.

This website is also part of SIS "Environmental health & toxicology" (http://sis.nlm.nih.gov/enviro.html), a comprehensive site with reliable information on chemicals & drugs, diseases and the environment, occupational safety & health, poisoning, risk assessment, toxicology, and pesticides

"especially for emergency responders, health professionals, the public, researchers/scientists, students/educators, and toxicologists."*Website*. Links to guides & tutorials, advice on what specific resources to use, and additional related information. Joining the Listserv, subscribing to the RSS feed, or following the site on Twitter allows users to keep up-to-date. Another website in this area is ATSDR toxic substances portal (the US Dept. of Health and Human Services' Agency for Toxic Substances and Disease Registry) http://www.atsdr.cdc.gov/substances/index.asp, "providing trusted health information to prevent harmful exposures and diseases related to toxic substances."—*Website*.

1528 Foodborne outbreak online database (FOOD). http://wwwn.cdc.gov/foodborneoutbreaks/Default.aspx. Centers for Disease Control and Prevention (U.S.), National Center for Emerging and Zoonotic Infectious Diseases (U.S.). Atlanta: Centers for Disease Control and Prevention, U.S. Dept. of Health and Human Services. 2011-

Produced by Centers for Disease Control and Prevention (CDC). This database is described as a "web-based platform for searching CDC's "Foodborne disease outbreak surveillance system" database (http://www.cdc.gov/foodsafety/fdoss/surveillance/index.html) which "captures outbreak data from local and state health departments on agents, foods, and settings responsible for foodborne illness . . . provides access to national information and is intended to be used for limited descriptive summaries of outbreak data."—*home page*. Includes causes for foodborne illness outbreaks, such as contaminated foods and beverages, exposure to animals, contaminated water, etc.

Other databases in this area:

Foodborne outbreaks (CDC) http://www.cdc.gov/foodsafety/outbreaks/index.html

Outbreak alert! database (Center for Science in the Public Interest CSPI) http://www.cspinet.org/foodsafety/outbreak/pathogen.php, and

Foodborne illness outbreak database (http://www.outbreakdatabase.com), a continually updated database that describes outbreaks occurring since 1984. Guidelines and tips for using this database are provided.

1529 Global health atlas. http://apps.who
.int/globalatlas/. World Health
Organization. Geneva, Switzerland:
World Health Organization. 2003–

RA441

Title varies: WHO's *Communicable disease global
atlas*; *Global atlas of infectious disease*; *Global atlas
of infectious diseases: An interactive information
and mapping system.*

World Health Organization Internet resource
"bringing together for analysis and comparison standardized data and statistics for infectious diseases at
country, regional, and global levels. The analysis and
interpretation of data are further supported through
information on demography, socioeconomic conditions, and environmental factors."—*Website*.
Searchable database which allows users to create
reports, charts, and maps (e.g., geographic areas
can be selected to create maps of diseases). Links to
related sites, e.g., *Global atlas of the health workforce* and others.

1530 Globalhealth.gov. http://globalhealth
.gov/index.html. U.S. Dept. of Health and
Human Services. Washington: U.S. Dept.
of Health and Human Services. 1990s–
Produced by HHS Office of Global Health
Affairs (OGHA). Title varies: Global Health.gov;
GlobalHealth.

Provides access to information about major
global health topics, such as avian influenza, HIV/
AIDS, malaria, etc. and links to partner organizations (e.g., WHO, PAHO, and others) and information on international travel, health regulation,
refugee health, and related areas. CDC's Coordinating Office for Global Health (http://www.cdc
.gov/cogh/) provides additional information and
resources.

1531 Global health library. http://www.global
healthlibrary.net/php/index.php. World
Health Organization. Geneva, Switzerland:
World Health Organization. 2005–
Produced by Global Health Library (GHL); World
Health Organization (WHO); the Knowledge
Management and Sharing Department of WHO
(WHO/KMS).

A WHO collaborative project with many partners worldwide, such as U.N. bodies, national libraries of medicine, various public health

institutes, academic and special libraries, and
others. Points to reliable health information from
various providers and in various formats. Provides
access to the international scientific and technical literature and links to further information and
access to global and regional indexes and international agencies (e.g., PAHO, WHOLIS, various
directories, and other information via its Global
Health Library Virtual Platform. Designed for different users and user groups, including health professionals, patients, their families, and the general
public.

1532 HealthMap. http://www.healthmap.org/.
Clark Freifeld, John Brownstein,
Children's Hospital [Boston] Informatics
Program, Harvard-MIT Division of
Health Sciences and Technology. [New
Haven, Conn.]: Clark Freifeld and John
Brownstein. [2006–]
616.9 RA643; RA566
Title varies: HEALTHmap: Global disease alert
mapping system.

"Brings together disparate data sources,
including online news aggregators, eyewitness
reports, expert-curated discussions and validated
official reports, to achieve a unified and comprehensive view of the current global state of infectious diseases and their effect on human and
animal health."—*About page*. Official alerts from
WHO are available via *Disease outbreak news*,
which is part of WHO's "Epidemic and pandemic
alert and response (EPR)" website (http://www
.who.int/csr/don/en). EuroSurveillance (http://
www.eurosurveillance.org/), a program of the
European Centre for Disease Prevention and
Control (http://www.ecdc.europa.eu), is another
data source. Uses marker icons (square-shaped:
Country-level marker; round: state, province, and
local) and low or high "heat index". Provides links
for information on particular diseases to Wikipedia, the World Health Organization (WHO),
the Centers for Disease Control and Prevention (CDC), PubMed, and Google trends. Available in different views, i.e., as map, satellite, or
hybrid map.

A detailed overview of the HealthMap system
is available as part of Health information for international travel in "*Yellow book*: Appendix D: The
HealthMap system."

1533 Health Resources and Services Administration (HRSA). http://www.hrsa.gov/. Health Resources and Services Administration. Washington: Department of Health and Human Services. 1999–
Health Resources and Services Administration (HSRA), pt. of U.S. Dept. of Health and Human Services (HHS).

HRSA provides leadership and direction for various major national programs, such as organ donation and transplantation, HIV/AIDS, drug pricing, programs related to rural health, health information technology, telehealth, emergency preparedness, and bioterrorism. Also provides information and data on the health professions, a "geospatial data warehouse," health workforce analysis and other reports, and a variety of other topics and links to related sites both within the HRSA and other agencies and programs.

1534 Health services research methodology core library recommendations, 2007. http://www.nlm.nih.gov/nichsr/corelib/hsrmethods.html. AcademyHealth, National Library of Medicine (U.S.). Bethesda, Md.: National Library of Medicine. 2007
Produced by AcademyHealth; National Library of Medicine (NLM); National Information Center on Health Services Research and Health Care (NICHSR). Although dated 2007, website is reviewed and updated regularly.

List of books, journals, bibliographic databases, websites, and other media; useful for collection development librarians and researchers interested in health services research methods. Lists both "core" materials and "desired" materials in areas such as general health policy, health economics, health services research, public health, and several others. The NICHSR website (http://www.nlm.nih.gov/nichsr/outreach.html) lists links to several other recommended lists, including Health economics core library recommendations (2011), Health outcomes core library recommendations (2011), Health policy core library recommendations 2011 (also called Core health policy library recommendations), and other information.

1535 Healthy people. http://www.cdc.gov/nchs/healthy_people.htm. National

Center for Health Statistics (NCHS). Hyattsville, Md.: Centers for Disease Control (U.S.), National Center for Health Statistics
RA395.A3
Contents: Healthy people 2000; Healthy People 2010; Healthy People 2020; Progress Reviews; Publications.

"Healthy People provides science-based, national goals and objectives with 10-year targets designed to guide national health promotion and disease prevention efforts to improve the health of all people in the United States." —*Home Page*. Previous reports include *Healthy people 2000* (http://purl.access.gpo.gov/GPO/LPS3745) and *Healthy people: The Surgeon General's report on health promotion and disease prevention: Background papers: Report to the Surgeon General on health promotion and disease prevention*. "Healthy People DATA 2010," an interactive database system accessible via CDC WONDER provides various reports and data. A search interface providing searches for published literature related to Healthy People 2010 was added to the "special queries" section of PubMed.

Also available in print format: *Tracking healthy people 2010*. Progress Reviews and publications are added to the website regularly.

1536 HIV InSite knowledge base. http://hivinsite.ucsf.edu/InSite.jsp?page=KB. Laurence Peiperl, Paul Volberding, P. T. Cohen, Merle A. Sande, University of California, San Francisco, San Francisco General Hospital (Calif.). San Francisco: University of California. 1996(?)–
025.174; 616.9792; 362.1969792; 616.979201
Online adaptation of *The AIDS Knowledge Base* (AKB), which appeared in several print editions (1st ed., 1990; 2nd ed., 1994; 3rd ed., 1999).

Contents: Epidemiology of HIV; Natural Science of HIV; Diagnosis and Clinical Management of HIV; Clinical Manifestations of HIV; Infections Associated with HIV; Malignancies Associated with HIV; Transmission and Prevention of HIV; HIV Policy.

Continually updated online resource covering HIV/AIDS clinical topics and also access to selected related materials (e.g., guidelines, fact sheets, journal articles, etc.), including both links within the

HIV InSite and outside resources. For academic libraries.

1537 HSR information central. http://www .nlm.nih.gov/hsrinfo/. Bethesda, Md.: National Library of Medicine (U.S.), National Institutes of Health, Dept. of Health and Human Services. 1993–
HSRIC = Health Services Research Information Central

Contents: HSR general resources: Data, tools, and statistics; HSR social media resources; Education and training; Grants, funding, and fellowships; Guidelines, journals, other publications; Key organizations; Legislation; Meetings and conferences; State resources. HSR topics: Aging Population Issues; Comparative effectiveness research (CER); Child health services research; Evidence-based practice and health; Technology assessment; Health care reform, health economics, and health policy; Health disparities; Health informatics; Public health systems and services research; Quality; Rural health. Alphabetic index (all websites in alphabetic order).

Developed by the National Library of Medicine to serve the information needs of the health services research community, in partnership with other government agencies and institutes (e.g., Agency for Healthcare Research and Quality (AHRQ), National Cancer Institute, the Cecil C. Sheps Center for Health Services Research, and the Health Services Research and Development Service [HSR&D] at the Veterans Administration, and others). Provides selected links which are intended to represent a sample of available information.

1538 International health (MedlinePlus). http://www.nlm.nih.gov/medlineplus/ internationalhealth.html. National Library of Medicine (U.S.). Bethesda, Md.: National Library of Medicine. 2000?–
A Health Topic within MedlinePlus. Provides extensive global health information, with access to various online reference resources, links to major organizations (e.g., Centers for Disease Control, World Health Organization), foundations (e.g., Henry J. Kaiser Family Foundation), research, journal articles, law and policy information (e.g., International Health Regulations [2005]), WHO and UNICEF statistics, etc. Links to related MedlinePlus topics, such as Traveler's Health and Health system (MedlinePlus).

1539 Kaiser Family Foundation. http:// www.kff.org/. Henry J. Kaiser Family Foundation. Menlo Park, Calif.: Henry J. Kaiser Family Foundation. 2000– 362.1; 361.7
The Henry J. Kaiser Family Foundation is an independent philanthropy focusing on major health care issues. Website contains statistics on Medicare, Medicaid, the uninsured in each state of the United States, minority health, etc. Links to resources on health policy covering such topics as women's health policy, HIV/AIDS, and media programs. A wide variety of resources are accessible via the following tabs found on the website: (1) Kaiser Health News(http://www.kaiserhealthnews.org/): search for recent daily reports and webcasts; (2) State-HealthFacts (http://kff.org/statedata/): source for state health data; (3) Global Health Facts (http:// kff.org/globaldata/); (4) Perspectives; and more.

1540 Malaria atlas project (MAP). http:// www.map.ox.ac.uk/. Malaria Public Health and Epidemiology Group, Centre for Geographic Medicine, Kenya, Spatial Ecology & Epidemiology Group, University of Oxford, UK. Nairobi, Kenya; Oxford, U.K.: Centre for Geographic Medicine, Kenya; University of Oxford. 2006–
Funded by the Wellcome Trust, United Kingdom.

Provides an overview of the MAP project and enables viewers to browse worldwide malaria and malaria-control data and also allows the submission of new data. Offers health links (e.g., malaria, general health, and food security and health), global and regional links, and links to malaria-related organizations. Also provides research-related links, including libraries, a listing of online resources, databases for literature searching, tutorials, and information about various software tools. Further details about this project and its future plans can be found on the MAP website.

1541 National Center for Environmental Health. http://www.cdc.gov/nceh/. National Center for Environmental

Health (U.S.), Centers for Disease Control and Prevention (U.S.). Atlanta: Centers for Disease Control and Prevention

The National Center for Environmental Health (NCEH) has the mission to maintain, improve, and promote a healthy environment. Its searchable data resources page (http://www.cdc.gov/nceh/data.htm) and its A–Z index (http://www.cdc.gov/nceh/az/a.html) provide links to a variety of public environmental data sources, health topics, query engines, and other key resources. Highlights the major data systems with a national scope where public health and environmental data can be downloaded from the Internet. For health professionals and students.

1542 National Information Center on Health Services Research and Health Care Technology (NICHSR). http://www.nlm.nih.gov/nichsr/. National Library of Medicine (U.S.). Bethesda, Md.: National Library of Medicine, National Institutes of Health, U.S. Department of Health and Human Services. 2002–

Health services research (HSR); NICHSR; National Library of Medicine® (NLM®).

NICHSR coordinates NLM's HSR information programs, with links to databases and retrieval services, HSR information central, presentations, publications, and other information. An alphabetic list (http://www.nlm.nih.gov/hsrinfo/alphahsre.html) of related websites provides a large number of HSR-related links: Federal agencies; associations; data sets and data sources; epidemiology and health statistics; evidence-based medicine and health technology assessment; funding; health policy and health economics; informatics; public health; rural health; state resources; disparities, and others.

A related page is NLM's Health Services Research & Public Health Information Programs, a website that lists resources from multiple NLM programs.

1543 National Institute of Environmental Health Sciences. http://www.niehs.nih.gov. National Institute of Environmental Health Sciences. Research Triangle Park, N.C.: National Institute of Environmental

Health Sciences. 1994?–

RA565

Website of National Institute of Environmental Health Sciences (NIEHS).

Contents: Health and Education; Research; Funding Opportunities; Careers and Training; News and Events; About NIEHS.

Presents information and resources for several user groups, including health professionals, research scientists, teachers, children, and the general public. Includes a list of environmental health topics (i.e., A–Z list of conditions and diseases linked to environmental exposures), access to specialized databases and software, resources of the NIEHS library and information services (http://www.niehs.nih.gov/research/resources/library/index.cfm), NIEHS bioethics resources (http://www.niehs.nih.gov/research/resources/bioethics/index.cfm), and other information resources.

1544 National Institute of Mental Health. http://www.nimh.nih.gov/. National Institute of Mental Health (U.S.). Bethesda, Md.: National Institutes of Health. 1995?–
616.89   RA790.A1

Part of National Institutes of Health (NIH).

Provides funding for research on mind, brain, behavior, and behavioral disorders; for research on the causes, occurrence, and treatment of mental illness; and for mental health services, including major projects such as the Human Brain Project and neuroinformatics research in support of this project. Contains topics useful for the public concerning adult and pediatric psychopathology. Provides extensive information on a variety of mental health topics (http://www.nimh.nih.gov/health/index.shtml), links to NIMH publications and other resources, and to mental health information available via MedlinePlus (http://www.nlm.nih.gov/medlineplus/mentalhealth.html). Site index.

1545 National Institute on Drug Abuse (NIDA). http://www.nida.nih.gov. National Institute on Drug Abuse (U.S.). Rockville, Md.: National Institute on Drug Abuse. 1995–

NIDA is part of the National Institutes of Health (NIH).

Addresses questions and supports research on health aspects of drug abuse and addiction as well as drug addiction treatment. Educational resources and materials on drugs of abuse are presented for several different user groups: students and young adults, parents and teachers, medical and health professionals, and researchers. Includes links to publications and "DrugFacts" (http://www.drug abuse.gov/publications/term/160/DrugFacts) with information on effects of drug abuse, health effects of specific drugs, prevention and treatment, research reports, survey data, and other information.

1546 Occupational Safety and Health Administration (OSHA). http://www .osha.gov/. Occupational Safety and Health Administration. Washington: U.S. Dept of Labor, Occupational Safety and Health Administration. 199?–
344.73   KF3570.Z9

Access to OSHA programs and services. Includes information on OSHA standards on safety, preventing injuries, and protecting the health of American workers. Provides access to the OSHA occupational chemical database (http://www.osha .gov/chemicaldata/), originally developed by OSHA in cooperation with EPA. Safety and health topics include biological agents (avian flu, food-borne disease, ricin, etc.), OSHA standards for carcinogens, construction (key standards and compliance activities), emergency preparedness (e.g., national safety and health standards for emergency responders), ergonomics (with focus on musculoskeletal disorders), hazard communication (e.g., workplace chemical safety programs), maritime industry, and many other subjects (see A-Z index http://www .osha.gov/html/a-z-index.html).

1547 Pan American Health Organization (PAHO). http://www.paho.org/. Pan American Health Organization, World Health Organization. Washington: Pan American Health Organization. 1990s–
RA438.A45

Published by World Health Organization (WHO); United Nations.

PAHO is WHO's regional office for the Americas, an international public health agency with the mission to improve health and living standards of the countries of the Americas.

Searchable website, with detailed information about PAHO's governance and mission, links to basic health indicators, core health data, country health profiles, trends and situation analysis, information products, and other related information. Includes, for example, Regional core health data initiative (http://www.paho.org/english/dd/ais/coredata .htm), including access to PAHO's Basic country health profiles for the Americas (http://www .paho.org/English/DD/AIS/cp_index.htm), which provides mortality statistics for the Americas and health profiles for all countries in North and South America.

Provides access to PAHO electronic books (English and Spanish) at http://www.paho.org/ Project.asp?SEL=PR&LNG=ENG&ID=360.

A related title is *Health in the Americas*.

1548 Partners in information access for the public health workforce. http:// phpartners.org/. U.S. National Library of Medicine. Bethesda, Md.: U.S. National Library of Medicine, National Institutes of Health, Dept. of Health and Human Services. 2003–

"Collaboration of U.S. government agencies, public health organizations, and health sciences libraries which provides timely, convenient access to selected public health resources on the Internet . . . [with the mission of] helping the public health workforce find and use information effectively to improve and protect the public's health."—*Website*

Provides links to the individual partner websites, such as Agency for Healthcare Research and Quality (AHRQ), American Public Health Association (APHA), Association of Schools of Public Health (ASPH), Association of State and Territorial Health Officials (ASTHO), Centers for Disease Control and Prevention (CDC), MLANET: Medical Library Association, National Library of Medicine, and several other organizations. Provides extensive information on several public health topics (currently to bioterrorism, environmental health, and HIV/AIDS). For additional information and links see the Partners in Information Access for the Public Health Workforce fact sheet at http://www.nlm .nih.gov/nno/partners.html.

1549 Public health genomics. http://www .cdc.gov/genomics/default.htm. Centers

for Disease Control and Prevention
(U.S.). Office of Genomics and Disease
Prevention. Atlanta: Centers for Disease
Control and Prevention. 2006–
610.711; 599.935072;
362.1; 576.5072   RB155
The Office of Public Health Genomics (OPHG) is a
center within the Centers for Disease Control and
Prevention (CDC).

Public health genomics "focuses on the effective
and responsible translation of genomic research
into population health benefits."—*About page*.
OPHG promotes the integration of genomics into
public health research, policy, and practice. Its
activities are related to genomics and health, family history, population research, and related areas.
Provides a variety of educational links about genetic
research. The Human Genome Epidemiology Network (HuGENet; http://www.cdc.gov/genomics/
hugenet), for example, helps "translate genetic
research findings into opportunities for preventive
medicine and public health" through guidelines,
workshops, case studies, and more.

1550 Public health image library (PHIL).
http://phil.cdc.gov/Phil/. Centers
for Disease Control and Prevention.
Atlanta: Centers for Disease Control and
Prevention. [1998]–
Public health image library (PHIL), created by a
working group at the Centers for Disease Control
and Prevention (CDC); National Library of Medicine (NLM).

Collection of a variety of single images, image
sets, multimedia files, etc., with current and historical content about people, places, scientific subjects, etc. FAQ section (http://phil.cdc.gov/Phil/
faq.asp) provides detailed information. Useful for
public health professionals, scientists, librarians,
teachers, and students.

This website also provides links to other CDC
and NLM image libraries (e.g., Images from the
history of medicine and Visible Human). Complements other medical image collections such as
Health education assets library (HEAL) and Images-
MD (http://www.springerimages.com/imagesMD/).

1551 Public health law program. http://
www2a.cdc.gov/phlp/lawmat.asp.
Centers for Disease Control and

Prevention (U.S.), Dept. of Health and
Human Services. Atlanta, Ga.: Centers for
Disease Control and Prevention, Dept. of
Health and Human Services. 200?–
Pt. of the (CDC) website with information on
a variety of areas and subjects related to public
health law and legal issues, including a list of state
public health departments.

Includes emergency preparedness-related statutes, regulations, orders, reports, and legal tools;
publications such as bench books, winnable battles, and public health concerns; and directories
to counsel at state, selected local, and bodering
countries.

**1552 Smoking and health resource
library (CDC)**. http://nccd.cdc.gov/
shrl/QuickSearch.aspx. Centers for
Disease Control and Prevention (U.S.).
Atlanta: Centers for Disease Control and
Prevention. 1990s–
Pt. of CDC's "Smoking & tobacco use" site http://
www.cdc.gov/tobacco/.

Continually updated database. Indexes and
abstracts tobacco-related "articles from medical and
professional journals; books and book chapters;
dissertations; reports; conference proceedings and
papers; government documents from federal, state,
local, and foreign entities; fact sheets and policy
documents from U.S. and international non-profit
organizations, and other documents. New citations
include recently published tobacco-related articles
from peer-reviewed journals of behavioral, scientific, and medical literature."—*Publ. description*.

Examples of other resources are "Tobacco,
smoking and health" http://sis.nlm.nih.gov/enviro/
tobacco.html (pt. of Enviro-Health Links, Smoking
(MedlinePlus)   (http://www.nlm.nih.gov/medline
plus/smoking.html), and other smoking-related
entries in MedlinePlus.

1553 Special populations. http://sis.nlm
.nih.gov/outreach/specialpopulations
anddisasters.html. National Library of
Medicine (U.S.). Bethesda, Md.: National
Library of Medicine. 2008–
Part of the National Library of Medicine's Enviro-
health links.

Contents: Disabled; Seniors; Hearing impaired;
Visually impaired; Women and gender; Pregnancy;

Children; Diabetes; Native Americans; Foreign language materials; Información en Español; Guidance for organizations and governments; Guidance for employers; Law and policy; Lessons learned from prior disasters; Searches from the National Library of Medicine.

Additional selected NLM resources for disaster preparedness and response can be found on the Environmental health and toxicology home page, http://sis.nlm.nih.gov/enviro.html.

1554 U.S. Dept. of Health and Human Services (HHS.gov). http://www.hhs. gov/. U.S. Dept. of Health and Human Services (HHS). Washington: U.S. Dept. of Health and Human Services. 1997–

HV85

"United States government's principal agency for protecting the health of all Americans and providing essential human services, especially for those who are least able to help themselves."—*About page*

HHS works closely with state and local governments. The Department's approx. 300 programs are administered by 11 operating divisions, including eight agencies in the U.S. Public Health Service and three human services agencies. A guide to information resources, i.e. "HHS information resources directory," is available at http://www.hhs.gov/about/referlst.html. This site also provides, for example, information on key initiatives (e.g., HealthCare.gov, FoodSafety.gov, InsureKidsNow.gov, for example), news and a news archive, information on prevention of diseases and a healthy lifestyle and on diseases and conditions, health information privacy, human research protections, health information technology standards, laws and regulations, and policies and guidelines. The current HHS website is searchable at http://www.hhs.gov/. Archival access to older materials (e.g., speeches, materials of historical or research interest, etc.) is available at http://archive.hhs.gov/. Historical Highlights and Past Secretaries, from 1798-2009, can be found at http://www.hhs.gov/about/hhshist.html.

1555 WISER (Wireless Information System for Emergency Responders). http://wiser.nlm.nih.gov. National Library of Medicine (U.S.). Bethesda, Md.: U.S. National Library of Medicine. 2005–

"A system designed to assist first responders in hazardous materials incidents . . . including substance identification support, physical characteristics, human health information, and advice on containment and suppression guidance."—*Home page*. "Information is presented to the emergency responder, Hazmat Specialist, and EMS Specialist in the order that is most relevant to their respective roles."—*About page*. Content from HSDB (Hazardous substance data bank) and from CHEMM (Chemical hazards emergency medical management) http://chemm.nlm.nih.gov. Further information on other data sources and about applications available (for phone, tablet, and desktop) on the About page. This resource is also listed on NLM's Gallery of mobile apps and sites.

id="1"

13 Toxicology

1556 Dictionary of toxicology. 2nd ed.
Ernest Hodgson, Richard B. Mailman,
Janice E. Chambers, Robert E. Dow.
London; New York: Macmillan Reference;
Grove's Dictionaries, 2000. xii, 504 p., ill.
ISBN 033354700
615.9003   RA1193
Rev. ed. of *Macmillan dictionary of toxicology*,
1988. Title varies.

Designed as an introduction to the field of toxicology for students and for scientists in other disciplines. Most entries relate directly to toxicology, but others provide information that might be needed by toxicologists. For example, contains certain anatomical, biochemical, pathological, and physiological terms. This revised edition includes 800 new and 1,200 revised entries, with structure and CAS number for important toxic chemicals. Provides references to *Hazardous chemical desk reference* by Lewis (entries cross-listed as HCDR) and *Toxicological profiles* (Agency for Toxic Substances and Disease Registry, cross-listed as ATSDR). Online access to this edition available via Credo Reference (http://corp.credoreference.com/) as *Macmillan dictionary of toxicology*.

Guides

1557 Information resources in toxicology.
4th ed. Philip Wexler, Steven G. Gilbert,
Pertti J. Hakkinen, Asish Mohapatra.
Amsterdam, Netherlands; Boston:
Elsevier/AP, 2009. xlii, 1510 p., ill.
ISBN 9780123735935
First ed., 1982; 2nd ed., 1988; 3rd ed., 2000.
Enlarged and updated edition. A selective guide to the major print and nonprint media resources and online sources of information. Contains annotated bibliographies of books by subject and listing of journals, organizations, audiovisuals, and Internet and other digital resources, with a larger number of digital resources that in some cases replace print formats in this edition. Includes Ch. 1–21 devoted to U.S. resources, ch. 22–25 to international resources. Appendix I, "Toxicology data and information management," Appendix II, "Glossary of terms used in toxicology, 2nd ed.," and Appendix III, "Toxicological quotations: Famous, infamous, obscure." Index. Also available as an e-book.

Indexes; Abstract journals; Databases

1558 CCOHS. http://www.ccohs.ca/. Canadian
Centre for Occupational Health and
Safety. Hamilton, Ont.: Canadian Centre
for Occupational Health and Safety.
1999–

T55

Similar to TOXNET, the CCOHS site makes available a variety of occupational health and safety information. Data collections allow retrieval of aggregated information using simple chemical name searches. Access to the complete search features of CCOHS is by subscription, but much of the data is free of charge.

1559 CCRIS (Chemical carcinogenesis research information system).
http://toxnet.nlm.nih.gov/cgi-bin/sis/htmlgen?CCRIS. National Library of Medicine (U.S.), National Cancer Institute (U.S.). Bethesda, Md.: National Library of Medicine. 1990s

Part of TOXNET. Developed and maintained by the National Cancer Institute (NCI).

Currently contains approximately 9,000 chemical records with carcinogenicity, mutagenicity, tumor promotion, and tumor inhibition test results. Includes data from studies cited in primary journals, NCI reports, and other special sources. Test results have been reviewed by experts. For additional details, see TOXNET fact sheet at http://www.nlm.nih.gov/pubs/factsheets/toxnetfs.html.

1560 ChemIDplus. http://sis.nlm.nih.gov/chemical.html. National Library of Medicine (U.S.). Bethesda, Md.: National Library of Medicine

Part of TOXNET.

Database providing chemical synonyms, structures, regulatory list information, and access to structure and nomenclature authority databases used for the identification of chemical substances cited in the various NLM databases. Provides structure searching and direct links to many biomedical resources at NLM and on the Internet for chemicals of interest. More than 390,000 chemicals, including synsonyms and structures; searchable by name, synonym, CAS registry number, molecular formula, classification code, and structure (see TOXNET fact sheet at http://www.nlm.nih.gov/pubs/factsheets/toxnetfs.html).

1561 DART/ETIC (Developmental and Reproductive Toxicology/ Environmental Teratology Information Center database.
http://toxnet.nlm.nih.gov/cgi-bin/sis/htmlgen?DARTETIC. Institute of Environmental Health Sciences, National Center for Toxicological Research. Bethesda, Md.: National Library of Medicine

DART/ETIC is part of TOXNET (http://toxnet.nlm.nih.gov/).

Bibliographic database covering literature published since 1965 on reproductive and developmental toxicology. For additional details, see TOXNET fact sheet at http://www.nlm.nih.gov/pubs/factsheets/toxnetfs.html.

1562 The dictionary of substances and their effects. http://www.knovel.com/knovel2/Toc.jsp?BookID=527. S. Gangolli, Royal Society of Chemistry (Great Britain), Knovel. London: Royal Society of Chemistry. [2005]
615.9003   RA1193.D53
First edition, 1992; 2nd ed., 1999 (7 v.).

This edition is the updated electronic version of the seven-volume print edition. Continually updated, with interactive features, contains 5,310 substances. All substances are listed in the searchable interactive table Physical Constants of Chemical Substances, which lists basic properties, toxicity, synonyms, molecular structure, and links to full-text articles. Compounds can be searched and located by their names, synonyms, molecular formulas, occupational exposure limits, and other properties. Available through Knovel.

1563 Dietary supplement label database.
http://www.dsld.nlm.nih.gov/dsld/. NIH Office of Dietary Supplements, National Library of Medicine (U.S.). Bethesda, Md.: National Library of Medicine. 2013–

Joint project of the National Institutes of Health (NIH) Office of Dietary Supplements (ODS) and National Library of Medicine (NLM) Division of Specialized Information Services (SIS). Also referred to as DSLD.

DSLD, a document repository database, captures information on dietary supplement labels. Contains the full label contents from 17,000 dietary supplement products marketed in the U.S. and will eventually include 55,000 products available in the U.S. Obtained from the manufacturers' labels. Includes image of the product label, both

"DSLD on market" (i.e., label information from dietary supplement products that are currently on the U.S. market) and "DSLD off-market "(i.e., label information from dietary supplement products that have been discontinued or are no longer on the U.S. market). Allows for searching, browsing, sorting, and filtering; and data can be saved and analyzed. Answers many questions researchers and users of dietary supplements might have concerning ingredients shown on labels of specific brands, chemical ingredients, animal products, proven medical benefits, toxicity of specific ingredients, etc. Includes reference links leading to further explanation (e.g., unit conversion, daily value, dietary reference intakes, etc.), definitions (A-Z), also a frequently asked questions section and links to reference sources.

An earlier database, "Dietary supplements labels database: Brands, ingredients, and references," has been retired.

1564 Drug information portal. http://druginfo.nlm.nih.gov/. National Library of Medicine (U.S.). Bethesda, Md.: National Library of Medicine. 2008–
"Gateway to selected drug information from the National Library of Medicine and other key government agencies . . . [with] access to over 12,000 selected drugs"—*About This Portal*. Can be searched by a drug's trade or generic name. Provides a summary of the information about the drug, and links to further related information, such as MedlinePlus, AIDSinfo (648), MEDLINE/PubMed®, LactMed, HSDB, Dietary supplements labels database, TOX-LINE, DailyMed, ClinicalTrials.gov, PubChem, ChemIDplus, Drugs@FDA, and others. For the public, health care professionals, and researchers. Information regarding the mobile version of this resource is part of NLM's Gallery of mobile apps and sites.

1565 GENE-TOX (genetic toxicology).
http://toxnet.nlm.nih.gov/cgi-bin/sis/htmlgen?GENETOX. National Library of Medicine (U.S.), Environmental Protection Agency (U.S.). Bethesda, Md.: National Library of Medicine. 1990s–
Part of TOXNET. Created by the U.S. Environmental Protection Agency (EPA).

A database of genetic toxicology (mutagenicity) test results, containing information on approximately 3,000 chemicals. For additional details, see TOXNET fact sheet at http://www.nlm.nih.gov/pubs/factsheets/toxnetfs.html.

1566 Haz-Map. http://hazmap.nlm.nih.gov/.
National Library of Medicine (U.S.).
Bethesda, Md.: National Library of Medicine. 2000–
Haz-Map is part of TOXNET.
An occupational toxicology database designed for health and safety professionals and consumers seeking information about the health effects of exposure to chemicals and biological agents at work. For additional details, see TOXNET fact sheet at http://www.nlm.nih.gov/pubs/factsheets/toxnetfs.html.

1567 Health & environmental research online (HERO). http://hero.epa.gov/.
United States. Environmental Protection Agency. Washington: Environmental Protection Agency. 2009-

RA566.3
This continually updated database includes "more than 600,000 scientific references and data from the peer-reviewed literature used by EPA to develop its regulations . . . [including] IRIS, a database that supports critical agency policymaking for chemical regulation [and] health risks to humans and the ecosystem from pollutants and chemicals in the environment."—*Home page*. Mostly indexes peer-reviewed journal articles, but also other articles, books, book chapters, reports, patents, websites, computer programs, pamphlets, and other resources. Help with searching is provided. For lower-level undergraduates through professionals; general audience. Documents in the HERO database that have been cited in EPA risk assessments can be viewed via its "LitBrowser."

1568 Household products database.
http://householdproducts.nlm.nih.gov/. Specialized Information Services, National Library of Medicine (U.S.). Bethesda, Md.: Specialized Information Services, U.S. National Library of Medicine, National Institutes of Health, Dept. of Health & Human Services

TS175
Part of TOXNET®.

Provides information on potential health effects and composition of chemicals contained in common household products. Includes reference to health effects information contained in Material Safety Data Sheets (MSDS). Products can also be searched by type, manufacturer, product ingredient/chemical name and by health effects. Additional details concerning this resource can be found via TOXNET fact sheet at http://www.nlm.nih.gov/pubs/factsheets/toxnetfs.html.

1569 HSDB (Hazardous substances data bank). http://toxnet.nlm.nih.gov/cgi-bin/sis/htmlgen?HSDB. National Library of Medicine (U.S.). Bethesda, Md.: National Library of Medicine. 1990s
Part of TOXNET.

Factual database providing toxicology information relating to approximately 5,000 potentially hazardous chemicals, including information on human exposure, industrial hygiene, emergency handling procedures, environmental fate, regulatory requirements, and related areas. Data are fully referenced and peer reviewed by expert scientists. Further details are provided via the TOXNET fact sheet at http://www.nlm.nih.gov/pubs/factsheets/toxnetfs.html.

1570 IRIS (Integrated risk information system). http://toxnet.nlm.nih.gov/cgi-bin/sis/htmlgen?IRIS. National Library of Medicine (U.S.), Environmental Protection Agency. Bethesda, Md.: National Library of Medicine
A database from the U.S. Environmental Protection Agency (EPA). Part of TOXNET.

Toxicology data in support of human health risk assessments for more than 500 chemicals. Focuses on hazard identification and dose-response assessment. Also includes carcinogen classifications, unit risks, slope factors, oral reference doses, and inhalation reference concentrations. Produced by the U.S. Environmental Protection Agency (EPA). For further details, see TOXNET fact sheet at http://www.nlm.nih.gov/pubs/factsheets/toxnetfs.html.

1571 ITER (International toxicity estimates for risk). http://toxnet.nlm.nih.gov/cgi-bin/sis/htmlgen?iter. National Library of Medicine (U.S.). Bethesda, Md.: National Library of Medicine. 2004 (?)
Part of TOXNET. Compiled by Toxicology Excellence for Risk Assessment (TERA).

Contains chemical data in support of human health risk assessments for more than 600 chemical records. Data, produced by the U.S. Environmental Protection Agency (EPA), several international health organizations, and independent peer-reviewed parties, are presented in side-by-side comparisons. Further details are provided in TOXNET fact sheet at http://www.nlm.nih.gov/pubs/factsheets/toxnetfs.html.

1572 LactMed (Drugs and lactation database). http://toxnet.nlm.nih.gov/cgi-bin/sis/htmlgen?LACT. National Library of Medicine (U.S.). Bethesda, Md.: National Library of Medicine. 2006–
Part of TOXNET.

Database of drugs and other chemicals to which breastfeeding mothers may be exposed. Data on maternal and infant levels of drugs; possible effects on breastfed infants and on lactation; and alternate drugs to consider. For further details, consult TOXNET fact sheet at http://www.nlm.nih.gov/pubs/factsheets/toxnetfs.html.

Since Jul. 2011, records for complementary and alternative medicine (CAM) products (e.g., herbal dietary supplements derived from botanicals, nutraceuticals [i.e., natural and synthetic nonherbals]) relevant to breastfeeding are being added to the database, with a field for the particular products' scientific and species names. LactMed is expected to contain 100 CAM products which are frequently used by nursing mothers. A complete list of CAM records can be found using the search term "complementary therapies" in the main LactMed search box. Information regarding the mobile version of this resource is part of NLM's Gallery of mobile apps and sites.

1573 Micromedex products. http://www.micromedex.com/products/index.html. Truven Health Analytics. Ann Arbor, Mich.: Truven Health Analytics. [199?–]
Produced by Truven Health Analytics, formerly known as Thomson Reuters (Healthcare) Inc.

Intended for clinicians; academic program available. Includes a variety of resources for finding information on drugs, toxicology, emergency, acute care, and disease data as well as alternative medicine information. Drug resources include DRUG-DEX, DRUG-REAX, IDENTIDEX, IV Index, *Index nominum*, *Martindale: The complete drug reference*, POISINDEX, *Red book*, and REPRORISK. Emergency and disease data can be found, for example, in DISEASEDEX and alternative therapies in Alt-MedDex and other Thomson products. Searchable across either all databases, by specific database(s), and by groups of databases. Drugs can be searched by trade or generic drug name. Specific drug database search and drug topic search provide, for example, a drug evaluation overview, dosing information, pharmacokinetics, contraindications, precautions, adverse reactions, single and multiple drug interactions, IV compatibility, teratogenicity, therapeutic uses, and comparative efficacy.

A matrix of all Micromedex products and versions in this series, with listing of the individual titles, various format options, and indication of whether a particular title is also available in print can be found at http://www.micromedex.com/support/faqs/plat_matrix.html. Help with citing the various Micromedex versions is provided at http://www.micromedex.com/about_us/legal/cite/.

1574 NLM gateway. http://gateway.nlm.nih.gov/. National Library of Medicine (U.S.). Bethesda, Md.: National Library of Medicine. 2000–

RA11

As announced in 2011, "the NLM® gateway has transitioned to a new pilot project from the Lister Hill National Center for Biomedical Communications (LHNCBC)."—*Website* The new site focuses now on two databases: Meeting abstracts and Health services research projects. All of the other resources previously accessed through the NLM gateway are available through their individual sites. For a list of these databases previously available via the NLM gateway see http://gateway.nlm.nih.gov/about.jsp.

The NLM gateway previously allowed simultaneous searching of information resources at the National Library of Medicine (NLM)/National Center for Biotechnology Information (NCBI) with an overview of the search results presented in several categories (bibliographic resources, consumer health resources, and other information), with a listing of the individual databases and the number of results within these categories. Previously included were, for example, MEDLINE/PubMed and the NLM Catalog as well as other resources, including information on current clinical trials and consumer health information (MedlinePlus) and many others.

1575 PubMed. http://www.ncbi.nlm.nih.gov/pubmed. U.S. National Center for Biotechnology Information, National Library of Medicine, National Institutes of Health. Bethesda, Md.: U.S. National Center for Biotechnology Information. 1996–

PubMed®, developed and maintained by the National Center for Biotechnology Information (NCBI) at the National Library of Medicine® (NLM). Provides a search interface for more than 20 million bibliographic citations and abstracts in the fields of medicine, nursing, dentistry, veterinary medicine, health care systems, and preclinical sciences. It provides access to articles indexed for MEDLINE® and for selected life sciences journals. PubMed subsets found under the "Limits" tab are: MEDLINE and PubMed central®, several journal groups (i.e., core clinical journals, dental journals, and nursing journals), and topical subsets (AIDS, bioethics, cancer, complementary medicine, dietary supplements, history of medicine, space life sciences, systematic reviews, toxicology, and veterinary science). "Linkout" provides access to full-text articles.

For detailed information see the PubMed fact sheet at http://www.nlm.nih.gov/pubs/factsheets/pubmed.html and also MEDLINE®/PubMed® resources guide (http://www.nlm.nih.gov/bsd/pmresources.html) which provides detailed information about MEDLINE data and searching PubMed.

Information regarding the mobile version of this resource is part of NLM's Gallery of mobile apps and sites.

1576 PubMed health. http://www.ncbi.nlm.nih.gov/pubmedhealth/. National Center for Biotechnology Information (U.S.); National Library of Meidcine (U.S.). Bethesda, Md.: National Center for Biotechnology Information U.S.);

National Library of Medicine (U.S.). 2011-

Based on systematic reviews of clinical trials which help to determine which treatments and preventive measures work. Searchable database which allows access to clinical effectiveness research and reviews (CER). Easy-to-read summaries as well as full-text reviews & reports can help consumers and clinicians understand and use clinical research results. Information is drawn, for example, from NCBI bookshelf (http://www.ncbi.nlm.nih.gov/sites/entrez?db=books), PubMed, and published systematic reviews from the Agency for Health Care Research and Quality, National Cancer Institute, The Cochrane Collaboration (see related entry Cochrane Library, and many others. A comprehensive listing of collaborators and other information about this resource at http://www.ncbi.nlm.nih.gov/pubmedhealth/about/.

1577 Specialized Information Services
(SIS). http://sis.nlm.nih.gov. National Library of Medicine (U.S.). Bethesda, Md.: National Library of Medicine

Specialized Information Services (SIS) is a division of the National Library of Medicine (NLM) and is responsible for information resources and services in toxicology (e.g., TOXNET) and Enviro-health links. Includes topics such as children's environmental health, indoor and outdoor air pollution, and biological warfare, to name a few; chemical information (ChemIDplus search system with access to nomenclature and structure authority files used for identification of chemical substances cited in the NLM databases); HIV/AIDS resources (for example, AIDSinfo (648); drug and dietary supplement information (e.g., Dietary supplement label database; directories (e.g., DIRLINE); and hotlines (e.g., Health hotlines (http://healthhotlines.nlm.nih.gov/). Each topic has its own website created for a specific audience (the public, researchers/scientists, health professionals, students/educators, and emergency responders), reference tools, listservs, and additional related links. Also provides websites for and about specific populations and specialized topics in minority health (for example, American Indian health, arctic health, and Asian American health). Further detailed information concerning SIS is provided via a fact sheet by Division of Specialized Information Services at http://www.nlm.nih.gov/pubs/factsheets/sis.html.

1578 State cancer legislative database
program (SCLD). http://www.scld-nci.net/mtcindex.cfm. National Cancer Institute. Bethesda, Md.: National Cancer Institute, National Institutes of Health

Databases providing summaries of state laws and resolutions on the major cancers and cancer-related topics. Considered a resource for a variety of audiences, including universities and research centers, professional organizations, and the public.

1579 TOXLINE. http://toxnet.nlm.nih.gov/cgi-bin/sis/htmlgen?TOXLINE. National Library of Medicine (U.S.). Bethesda, Md.: National Library of Medicine. 1990s–

Part of TOXNET.

"A bibliographic database providing comprehensive coverage of the biochemical, pharmacological, physiological, and toxicological effects of drugs and other chemical from 1965 to the present. . . . Contains over 3 million citations, almost all with abstracts and/or index terms and CAS Registry Numbers. *Toxline* references are drawn from sources grouped into two major parts, TOXLINE Core and TOXLINE Special, both of which offer a variety of search and display capabilities"—*TOXNET fact sheet* (http://www.nlm.nih.gov/pubs/factsheets/toxnetfs.html).

1580 TOXMAP. http://toxmap.nlm.nih.gov/toxmap/main/index.jsp. National Library of Medicine (U.S.). Bethesda, Md.: National Library of Medicine. 1995–

RA1190

As part of TOXNET, TOXMAP addresses toxicology and environmental health information needs. Uses maps of the United States to show the amount and location of toxic chemicals released into the environment. Data shown in TOXMAP come from the U.S. Environmental Protection Agency's Toxics release inventory (TRI) and Superfund programs (http://www.epa.gov/tri or http://www.epa.gov/superfund/), HSDB (Hazardous substances databank), TOXLINE, Agency for Toxic Substances and Disease Registry (ATSDR), USGS national atlas (http://www.nationalatlas.gov), and U.S. Census (http://www.census.gov). Users can create their own geographic region or select from a list of predefined regions. Provides various search options and links to other environmental health and toxicology resources. For further details, see TOXNET fact sheet (http://www.nlm.nih.gov/pubs/factsheets/toxnetfs.html).

1581 TOXNET (Toxicology data network).
   http://toxnet.nlm.nih.gov/. National
   Library of Medicine (U.S.). Bethesda, Md.:
   National Library of Medicine. 1998–
TOXNET: Toxicology data network, part of the Specialized Information Services (SIS) division of the National Library of Medicine (NLM) at http://sis.nlm.nih.gov/, responsible for information resources and services in toxicology, environmental health, chemistry, and other specialized topics.

Managed by the Toxicology and environmental health information program (TEHIP) of the NLM, TOXNET is a group of searchable databases that can be used separately or in combination (TOXNET multi-File; http://toxnet.nlm.nih.gov/cgi-bin/sis/htmlgen?Multi) to locate toxicology data, literature references, and information concerning environmental health and toxic release of chemicals. It can also identify chemicals that cause specific effects and provides links to PubMed.

TOXNET includes the following databases: ChemIDplus, HSDB (Hazardous Substances Data Bank), TOXLINE, CCRIS (Chemical Carcinogenesis Research Information System), DART/ETIC (Developmental and Reproductive Toxicology/Environmental Teratology Information Center database), GENE-TOX (Genetic Toxicology), IRIS (Integrated Risk Information System), ITER (International Toxicity Estimates for Risk), LactMed (Drugs and Lactation), Toxics Release Inventory (TRI), Haz-Map, Household Products Database, and TOXMAP. The TOXNET interface, originally designed and developed prior to the Internet, is being redesigned and will be released in 2014.

Information regarding the mobile version of this resource is part of NLM's Gallery of mobile apps and sites.

Encyclopedias

1582 Comprehensive toxicology. 2nd ed.
   Charlene McQueen. Oxford, U.K.:
   Elsevier, 2010. 14 v., ill. (some col.)
   ISBN 9780080468686
   615.9   RA1211

Contents: v. 1, General principles; v. 2, Cellular and molecular toxicology; v. 3, Toxicology testing and evaluation; v. 4, Biotransformation; v. 5, Immune system toxicology; v. 6, Cardiovascular toxicology; v. 7, Renal toxicology; v. 8, Respiratory toxicology; v. 9, Hepatic toxicology; v. 10, Gastrointestinal toxicology; v. 11, Reproductive and endocrine toxicology; v. 12, Developmental toxicology; v. 13, Nervous system and behavioural toxicology; v. 14, Carcinogenesis.

This edition provides updated content for all volumes. Comprehensive review of toxicology, presenting biological effects of toxicants across the different areas of toxicology, with emphasis on the action of chemicals on human systems. Each chapter contains a listing of peer-reviewed articles, reviews, and related websites. Also available as e-book, with enhanced features for cross-referencing and linkage.

1583 Encyclopedia of clinical toxicology:
   A comprehensive guide and reference
   to the toxicology of prescription
   and OTC drugs, chemicals, herbals,
   plants, fungi, marine life, reptiles
   and insect venoms, food ingredients,
   clothing, and environmental toxins.
   Irving S. Rossoff. Boca Raton, Fla.:
   Parthenon, 2002. xiv, 1507 p.
   ISBN 1842141015
   615.9003   RA1193.R67
Approximately 6,000 alphabetically arranged entries on toxic substances that adversely affect or destroy health or cause death. Mainly human data, with data on animals where insufficient data on human toxicity are available. Entries mention synonyms and use, toxic effects, and treatment, where appropriate. An appendix, "Alternative nomenclature," functions as an index.

1584 Encyclopedia of toxicology. 2nd ed.
   Philip Wexler, Bruce D. Anderson, Ann
   de Peyster. Boston: Elsevier Academic,
   2005 0127453512
   First edition, 1998.
Contents: v. 1, A–Dib; v. 2, Dib–L; v. 3, M–Ser; v. 4, Sev–Z, index.

Comprehensive survey of toxicology, with approximately 1,150 entries. Provides an introduction to the different areas of toxicology and includes experimental, applied, and regulatory toxicology entries. Contains entries on the Chernobyl and Three-Mile Island incidents, a history of the U.S. environmental movement, and also new areas such as computational toxicology, nonlethal weapons, and others. A–Z arrangement, cross-references, and references to primary and secondary literature. Index. Online edition available via Elsevier Science Direct.

1585 Encyclopedic reference of immunotoxicology. Hans-Werner Vohr. Berlin; New York: Springer, c2005. xxi, 730 p., ill. (some col.) ISBN 3540441727
616.07/903 QR180.4.E55
"Immunotoxicology . . . focuses on the undesirable effects of chemicals on the immune system. The exposure of humans . . . to such agents may be intentional (drugs) or unintentional (environment) . . . The side effects may lead to over-activation of the immune system, or equally to immunosuppression. The end points of dysregulation are therefore also varies: allergies, cancer, autoimmunity, poor resistance to infection." (*Pref.*). Intended for scientists and advanced students. Also available as an e-book.

1586 Essentials of medical geology: Impacts of the natural environment on public health. O. Selinus, B. J. Alloway. Amsterdam, Netherlands; Boston: Elsevier Academic Press, 2005. xiv, 812 p., ill. (some col.) ISBN 0126363412
614.42 RA566.E87
Contents: sec. 1, "Medical geology: Perspectives and prospects"; sec. 2, "Pathways and exposures"; sec. 3, "Environmental toxicology, pathology, and medical geology"; sec. 4, "Techniques and tools"; appendixes: (A) international reference values; (B) Web links; (C) glossary.

Medical geology, considered an emerging discipline, is defined by the International Working Group on Medical Geology as the science dealing with the relationship between natural geological factors and health in man and animals. Chapters address such topics as natural distribution and abundance of elements, uptake of elements from a chemical or biological point of view, geological impacts on nutrition, volcanic emissions and health, radon in air and water, arsenic in groundwater and

the environment, fluoride in natural waters, water hardness and health effects, GIS in human health studies, and histochemical and microprobe analysis in medical geology. Reference tables, graphics, and maps. Index. Also available as an e-book.

1587 Patty's toxicology. 6th ed. Eula Bingham, Barbara Cohrssen, F. A. Patty. Hoboken, N.J.: John Wiley & Sons, 2012. 6 v., ill. ISBN 9780470410813
613.6/2 RA1229
Previous editions had title *Industrial hygiene and toxicology*. Now publ. separately as *Patty's industrial hygiene* and *Patty's toxicology*.

Contents: v. 1, Toxicological issues related to metals and metal compounds ; Neurotoxicology and radiation ; Compounds of inorganic nitrogen, carbon, oxygen and halogens; v. 2, Hydrocarbons ; Organic nitrogen compounds; v. 3, Organic halogenated hydrocarbons ; Aliphatic carboxylic acids ; Ethers ; Aldehydes ; Ketones; v. 4, Alcohols ; Esters ; Epoxy compounds ; Organic peroxides ; Glycols and glycol ethers ; Synthetic polymers ; Organic sulfur compounds ; Organic phosphates; v. 5, Toxicological issues ; Inorganic particulates ; Dusts ; Products of biological origin ; Pathogens; v. 6, Mixtures ; Interactions; Physical agents ; Cumulative subject index; Cumulative subject index, v.1-6 ; Cumulative chemical index, v. 1-6 ; Cumulative CAS index, v. 1-6.

Updated edition of a standard reference for occupational health and toxicology professionals, with comprehensive toxicological data for industrial compounds. Entries include CAS numbers, physical and chemical properties, threshold limit values (TLVs), permissible exposure limits (PELs), maximum workplace concentrates (MAK), and biological tolerance values for occupational exposures (BAT) for each compound. New subjects include, for example, comprehensive chemical policy, flavorings and the food industry, metalworking fluids nanotechnology, pharmaceuticals, and others. Also available as an e-book.

Dictionaries

1588 Dictionary of environmentally important chemicals. D. C. Ayres, Desmond Hellier. Chicago: Fitzroy

Dearborn, 1999, c1998. xi, 332 p., ill. ISBN 1579582060

TD196.C45.A97

Chemicals included appear on three of the following regulatory agency lists: American Conference of Governmental Industrial Hygienists, European Community Directives of Dangerous Substances, German Commission for Investigation of Health Hazards of Chemicals in the Work Area, International Agency for Research on Cancer, and the United States Environmental Protection Agency list of priority pollutants (1995). Selected additional chemicals included were chosen when considered a risk to the general public. Few synonyms are given, so use of a chemical synonyms dictionary such as *Gardner's chemical synonyms and trade names* or *Gardner's commercially important chemicals* is recommended. Entries vary, but many are a page or two in length. A strength of the dictionary lies in the referrals to additional literature for each chemical. Includes brief glossary of acronyms and abbreviations, brief glossary of medical terms used, and a list of further reading (in addition to those given for individual chemicals).

1589 Dictionary of plant toxins. J. B. Harborne, Herbert Baxter, Gerard P. Moss. Chichester [England]; New York: Wiley, 1996. xv, 523 p., ill. ISBN 0471951072
615.95203   RA1250.D53

Provides a comprehensive source with concise entries on phytotoxins, i.e., poisonous substances produced by plants. Each entry mentions common name(s) with synonyms, chemical class and subclass, chemical structure, Chemical Abstracts Service (CAS) registry number, molecular weight, and chemical formula.

References to the primary literature. Includes subject, plant species, molecular formulas, and common plant/common toxin name indexes.

1590 The dictionary of substances and their effects. http://www.knovel. com/knovel2/Toc.jsp?BookID=527. S. Gangolli, Royal Society of Chemistry (Great Britain), Knovel. London: Royal Society of Chemistry. [2005]
615.9003   RA1193.D53

First edition, 1992; 2nd ed., 1999 (7 v.). This edition is the updated electronic version of the seven-volume print edition. Continually updated,

with interactive features, contains 5,310 substances. All substances are listed in the searchable interactive table Physical Constants of Chemical Substances, which lists basic properties, toxicity, synonyms, molecular structure, and links to full-text articles. Compounds can be searched and located by their names, synonyms, molecular formulas, occupational exposure limits, and other properties. Available through Knovel.

1591 IUPAC glossary of terms used in toxicology. http://sis.nlm.nih.gov/enviro/ iupacglossary/frontmatter.html. John H. Duffus, Monica Nordberg, Douglas M. Templeton, National Library of Medicine (U.S.). Bethesda, Md.: National Library of Medicine. 2007

International Union of Pure and Applied Chemistry (IUPAC).

Originally publ. (print and online) in *Pure and applied chemistry* 79(7) 2007: 1153–1344.

First edition, 1993, had title *Glossary for chemists of terms used in toxicology*, publ. (print and online) in *Pure and applied chemistry* 65(9) 1993: 2003–2122.

This second edition contains newly coined and redefined terms, with explanatory notes, from many disciplines that contribute to toxicology. Includes many medical terms, a list of abbreviations and acronyms used in the toxicology literature and names of international bodies and legislation, classification of carcinogenicity, and other related terminology. Includes bibliographical references.

1592 Lewis' dictionary of toxicology. Robert A. Lewis. Boca Raton, Fla.: Lewis, 1998. 1127 p. ISBN 1566702232
615.9003   RA1193.L48

Alphabetical arrangement. Contains common terms and definitions used in toxicology, environmental sciences, and many related fields. Cross-references for synonyms and related entries. For researchers and students.

Directories

1593 Poisoning and toxicology handbook. 4th ed. Jerrold B. Leikin, Frank P. Paloucek. Boca Raton, Fla.: CRC Press/

Taylor & Francis Group, 2008. xlv, 1331 p., ill. ISBN 9781420044
615.9   RA1215.P65
First ed., 1998; 3rd ed., 2002.

Contents: sec. 1, "Medicinal agents"; sec. 2, "Non-medicinal agents"; sec. 3, "Biological agents"; sec. 4, "Herbal agents"; sec. 5, "Antidotes and drugs used in toxicology"; sec. 6, "Diagnostic tests/procedures"; appendix; index.

Provides detailed information on approx. 900 drugs and poisons, including environmental toxins, and related special topics and resources. Includes listings of U.S. poison control centers and organizations that offer toxicology and teratology information services.

Handbooks

1594 Clarke's analysis of drugs and poisons: In pharmaceuticals, body fluids and postmortem material.
4th ed. Anthony C. Moffat, M. David Osselton, B. Widdop, Jo Watts. London: Pharmaceutical Press, 2011. 2 v., ill. 97808536697

First edition, 1969–75, 2nd ed., 1986, 3rd ed., 2004.

Contents: v. 1, pt. 1: 44 chapters (methodology and analytical techniques); Subject index; v. 2, pt. 2: 2,100 monographs (physical properties, analytical methods, pharmacokinetic data, ultraviolet, infrared and mass spectra, therapeutic and toxicity data of drugs and poisons); pt. 3: Indexes of analytical data; Subject index.

This revised and expanded edition, with more than 350 additional monographs since the last edition, provides analytical procedures used in analytical toxicology and data for drugs and poisons as well as applications of these techniques in areas such as forensic toxicology, workplace drug testing, drug abuse in sports, pesticide poisoning, and others. Drug and poison monographs provide physical properties, analytical methods, pharmacokinetic data, and toxicity data. Ultraviolet, infrared and mass spectra are included within the monographs, as well as therapeutic and toxicity data of drugs and poisons. Indexes of analytical data include, for example, CAS numbers, molecular formulas, therapeutic classes, color tests, molecular weights,

melting points, thin-layer chromatographic data, gas chromatographic (GC) data, high-performance liquid chromatographic (HPLC) data, ultraviolet absorption maxima, infrared peaks, mass spectral data of drugs and pesticides, reagents, and pharmacological terms. Subject index covering both volumes at the end of v. 1 as well as v. 2. An essential resource, intended for use primarily by forensic toxicologists, pathologists, and other scientists and students in these areas of study. Available online as part of MedicinesComplete.

Clarke's analytical forensic toxicology (2nd ed., 2013) is based on the content of v.1 of *Clarke's analysis of drugs and poisons*. It is intended as a text for undergraduate and graduate student use, *Clarke's analysis of drugs and poisons* is a reference resource for professional toxicologists.

1595 Goldfrank's toxicologic emergencies.
9th ed. Lewis Nelson, Lewis R. Goldfrank. New York: McGraw-Hill Medical, 2011. xxviii, 1940 p., ill. (some col.) ISBN 9780071605939
615.908   RA1224.5.G65

First ed., 1978, had title *Toxicologic emergencies: A handbook in problem solving*; 8th ed., 2006.

Guide to medical toxicology from a clinical perspective, with coverage of toxicologic emergencies (e.g., various medications, food poisoning, heavy metals, household toxins, toxic envenomations, etc.) and bioterrorism. Detailed information on how toxins affect the body and each organ in the body, with treatment guidelines, including use of antidotes. Also provides an historical perspective. Color plates (plants, mushrooms, spiders, snakes, marine life, dermatologic reactions). Includes bibliographical references and index. A website is associated with this edition. Available as an e-book.

Several other major publications in this area, publ. since 2000, include, for example, *Critical care toxicology: Diagnosis and management of the poisoned patient*, *Dart's medical toxicology*, *Ford's clinical toxicology*, and *Haddad and Winchester's clinical management of poisoning and drug overdose*.

1596 Handbook of industrial toxicology and hazardous materials. Nicholas P. Cheremisinoff. New York: Marcel Dekker,

1999. vi, 914 p., ill. ISBN 0824719352
615.902   RA1229.C472

Provides concise health and safety information for commercial chemicals and the health risks associated with them. For toxicologists, chemists, chemical engineers, and laboratory technicians. Includes information on safe handling and transportation of chemicals, worker protection, and emergency responses to spills. Alphabetically arranged glossary. Also available as an e-book.

1597 Handbook of pesticide toxicology.
2nd ed. Robert Irving Krieger. San Diego, Calif.: Academic Press, 2001. 2 v. (xxxiv, 1908 p.), ill. ISBN 0124262600
615.951   RA1270.P4H36

A major work on pesticide toxicology, with separate volumes on principles and agents. The 88 chapters are equally distributed between the two volumes. Many chapters contain numerous drawings of chemical structures, as well as other illustrations, photographs, and tables. Each chapter has an extensive bibliography. Index. Also available as an e-book.

1598 Handbook of poisoning: prevention, diagnosis, and treatment. 13th ed.
Bev-Lorraine True, Robert H. Dreisbach. Pearl River, N.Y.: Parthenon, 2001. viii, 696 p., ill. ISBN 9781850700388
615.9   RA1215.T78

First edition, 1955; 12th ed., 1987. Description based on 13th ed., 2002. Title varies; also called *Dreisbach's handbook of poisoning: Prevention, diagnosis and treatment.*

Contents: (1) "General considerations"; (2) "Agricultural poisons"; (3) "Industrial hazards"; (4) "Household hazards: Cosmetics, food poisoning, miscellaneous chemicals"; (5) "Medicinal poisons"; (6) "Animal and plant hazards: Reptiles, arachnids and insects, marine animals, plants."

Updated and revised edition, designed as a ready-reference manual, is considered a standard toxicology reference. Contains concise information for the diagnosis and treatment of poisoning. Also provides general information about prevention of poisoning and guidelines for consultations with medical toxicologists and regional information centers. For physicians and other health professionals. Bibliographic references contain listings of information resources about poisons and selected references for specific poisons. Also includes substances banned in the U.S. Index. Even though not updated since 2001, this handbook is nevertheless useful for researching poisoning diagnosis & management during the last fifty years.

More recent publications in this area are, for example, *Poisoning & drug overdose* and *Goldfrank's toxicologic emergencies.*

1599 Handbook of poisonous and injurious plants. 2nd ed.
Lewis S. Nelson, Richard Shih, Michael J. Balick, Lewis R. Goldfrank, Andrew Weil, New York Botanical Garden. New York: New York Botanical Garden; Springer, 2007. xviii, 340 p., ill. (chiefly color). ISBN 0387312684

RA1250.N46

This revised ed. of the 1985 *AMA handbook of poisonous and injurious plants* is a guide for medical clinicians to interpret symptoms of poisoning in adults or children and to identify common harmful plants. "It gives different perspectives on poisonous and injurious plants while remaining grounded in the integrative science of modern ethnobotany."—*Introd.* Sections of the book include botanical nomenclature and glossary of botanical terms; poisons, poisoning syndromes, and their clinical management; plant-induced dermatitis; gastrointestinal decontamination; and entries on individual plants (covering 155 genera). Entries give the plant's common and scientific botanical names, physical description, geographic distribution, toxic part and toxins, clinical findings, management of symptoms, and references. Recommended for academic and large public libraries.

1600 Handbook of toxicologic pathology.
2nd ed. Wanda M. Haschek, Colin George Rousseaux, Matthew A. Wallig. San Diego, Calif.: Academic Press, 2002. 2 v., ill. ISBN 0123302153
615.9   RA1211.H3196

First edition, 1991.

Vol. 1, *General toxicologic pathology*, provides an overview of the basic practice and the special techniques employed; also covered are risk assessment, experimental design, and statistical analysis. Contains several chapters on specific classes of environmental toxicants, for example, endocrine disruptors and heavy metals. Vol. 2, *Organ specific toxicologic pathology*, presents information in a standardized format, covering the different organ systems and the effects of toxic injury on a particular system. Available online via ScienceDirect.

1601 Handbook of toxicology. 2nd ed.
Michael J. Derelanko, Mannfred A. Hollinger. Boca Raton, Fla.: CRC Press, 2002. 1414 p., ill. ISBN 0849303702
615.9   RA1215.C73
Updated and enlarged edition of *CRC handbook of toxicology*, 1995.

Designed to locate basic toxicological information quickly. Organized into 33 chapters, with data arranged by toxicology subspecialty. Each chapter begins with a detailed listing of information presented. Most of the information is provided in tables and figures. This edition has expanded coverage of inhalation toxicology, neurotoxicology, and histopathology and several new regulatory chapters (on pesticides, medical devices, consumer products, and worldwide notification of new chemicals). Also new is the addition of information on ecotoxicology, in vitro toxicology, and basic male and female endocrinology and an overview of the toxicology of metals. Provides information on the care and use of laboratory animals. Bibliographical references and websites for further information. For professionals and students. Includes useful information for nontoxicologists in the areas of health, safety, and the environment. Index.

Available online via netLibrary and CRCnetBase.

1602 Handbook of toxic plants of North America. George E. Burrows, Ronald J. Tyrl. Ames, Iowa: Blackwell, 2006. xi, 307 p., ill. (some color), maps.
ISBN 0813807115
636.08959   SF757.5.B87
This ready reference volume is arranged by body system (e.g., plants affecting the blood, cardiovascular system, digestion, eyes, liver, neuromuscular system, reproductive system, respiratory system, skin, urinary system), reorganizing the content of the 1st ed. of *Toxic plants of North America* by Burrows et al. to emphasize toxic effects or disease syndromes that plants can cause in animals and humans. Aimed at veterinarians, animal scientists, farmers, and agricultural extension agents, the authors intend this guide to aid in identifying

suspicious plants that may cause illness or death in animals. Entries describe plant morphology and provide geographic distribution maps, color photographs, and line drawings. Details of plant toxicants, their mechanisms of action, signs of consumption, pathology, treatment or control, and plant taxonomy and ecology are provided. Appropriate for academic and public libraries supporting animal science and veterinary research and practice.

1603 Handbook on the toxicology of metals. 3rd ed. Gunnar Nordberg. Burlington, Mass.: Academic Press, 2007. xlvii, 975 p., ill. ISBN 9780123694
615.9253   RA1231.M52.H36
First edition, 1979; 2nd ed., 1986.
Comprehensive review of the effects of metals and metallic elements and compounds on biological systems, with emphasis on their toxic effects on human health. Provides access to basic toxicological data and also a general introduction to the toxicology of metallic compounds. Contains chapters on carcinogenicity of metal compounds, reproductive and developmental toxicity of metals, diagnosis and treatment of metal poisoning, principles for prevention of the toxic effects of metals, etc. Includes bibliographical references and index. Considered a standard work for physicians, toxicologists, and biomedical engineers.

1604 Hazardous chemicals desk reference. 6th ed. Richard J. Lewis. Hoboken, N.J.: Wiley, 2008. xx, 1953 p.
ISBN 9780470180242
604.7   T55.3.H3L49
First ed., 1987; 5th ed., 2002.
A compilation of basic hazard data concerning approx. 5,800 chemicals, extracted from Sax's dangerous properties of industrial materials, 11th ed., 2004. Over 500 new entries, many revised entries (updated physical properties and updated DOT classifications) in this edition. Some entries found in previous editions have been removed. Typical entries, filed alphabetically by compound name, include CAS registry number, molecular formula, molecular weight, synonyms, a "hazard rating" on a scale of 1–3 (where 3 is high hazard) or "D" if the data are insufficient, Department of Transportation (DOT) hazard code and classification, physical properties, indication of availability or consensus

reports (such as from the World Health Organization, International Agency for Research on Cancer, etc.), and a "safety profile" (a summary of reported hazards). Synonyms in English and also in Dutch, French, German, Italian, Japanese, and Polish. CAS number cross-index; synonym cross-index; DOT guide number cross-index. Also available as an e-book.

1605 Litt's drug eruptions & reactions manual: D.E.R.M. Jerome Z. Litt. New York: Informa Healthcare, 2010-. col. ill.
RL801

Title varies: Print editions from 1990s to 2003 had title *Drug eruption reference manual*; 2004-2009 (10th-15th ed.), *Litt's drug eruption reference manual including drug interactions*. Accompanied by CD-ROM. Updated annually. Description based on 18th ed., 2012; 19th ed., 2013 (*Litt's D.E.R.M.: Drug eruptions and reacting manual*) is available.

Contents: Introduction; Drug profiles A-Z; Descriptions of important reactions; Drugs that cause reactions; Index of synonyms and trade names.

This internationally recognized clinical reference guide provides information on adverse drug reactions (ADRs), side effects, and drug interactions to assist with diagnosis of skin eruptions caused by medications, including prescription and over the counter medications, biologics, and supplements. In alphabetical order by medication name, lists ADRs (skin, hair, nails, eyes, central nervous system and other body or organ systems) and describes common reaction patterns to certain drugs, drug-drug interactions, etc. Cross-references by drug and trade names. References. Written for dermatologists and other health professionals. Also available as an e-book.

Available to subscribers as an online database (Litt's D.E.R.M database, formerly: Litt's drug eruption global database http://www.drugeruptiondata.com/), regularly updated with new drugs, references, drug interactions, and reaction patterns and is searchable by drug names, drug reactions, drug categories, drug interactions, and drug combinations. A mobile version is also available (http://www.drugeruptiondata.com/info/index/type/mobile).

1606 National Library of Medicine Training Center. http://nnlm.gov/ntc/. National Library of Medicine (U.S.).

Bethesda, Md.: National Library of Medicine. 2003–

Produced by National Library of Medicine (NLM).

Provides access to online training materials used in conjunction with classes and courses offered by the National Training Center and Clearinghouse (NTCC), e.g., for PubMed{/record and {record}TOXNET.

1607 Patty's industrial hygiene. 6th ed ed. Vernon E. Rose, Barbara. Cohrssen, F. A. Patty. Hoboken, N.J.: Wiley, c2011. 4 v., ill.
613.6/2   RC967.P37

Previous editions had title *Industrial hygiene and toxicology*, recently published separately as *Patty's industrial hygiene* and Patty's toxicology.

Contents: v. 1, "Hazard recognition"; v. 2, "Evaluation and control"; v. 3, "Physical and biological agents"; v. 4, "Program management and specialty areas of practice."

Standard reference for occupational health and toxicology professionals. Also available as an e-book.

1608 Poisoning and toxicology handbook. 4th ed. Jerrold B. Leikin, Frank P. Paloucek. Boca Raton, Fla.: CRC Press/ Taylor & Francis Group, 2008. xlv, 1331 p., ill. ISBN 9781420044
615.9   RA1215.P65

First ed., 1998; 3rd ed., 2002.

Contents: sec. 1, "Medicinal agents"; sec. 2, "Nonmedicinal agents"; sec. 3, "Biological agents"; sec. 4, "Herbal agents"; sec. 5, "Antidotes and drugs used in toxicology"; sec. 6, "Diagnostic tests/procedures"; appendix; index.

Provides detailed information on approx. 900 drugs and poisons, including environmental toxins, and related special topics and resources. Includes listings of U.S. poison control centers and organizations that offer toxicology and teratology information services.

1609 Poisoning & drug overdose. San Francisco Bay Area Regional Poison Control Center., California Poison Control System. Norwalk, Conn.: Appleton & Lange, c1990-. v, ill.
615 11 1048-8847   RA1224.5 .P655

Description based on 6th ed., 2012.

Contents: Section I, Comprehensive evaluation and treatment; section II, Specific poisons and drugs: Diagnosis and treatment; section III, Therapeutic drugs and antidotes; section IV, Environmental and occupational toxicology; Index; extensive cross-references

Manual on the diagnosis and treatment of poisoning and drug overdose. "Provides practical advice for the diagnosis and management of poisoning and drug overdose and concise information about common industrial chemicals."—*Pref.* Contains information on common drugs and poisons, use and side effects of antidotes, emergency management, physical and laboratory diagnosis, methods of decontamination, etc. Also describes the medical management of chemical spills and occupational chemical exposures.

1610 Proctor and Hughes' chemical hazards of the workplace. 5th ed.
Nick H. Proctor, James P. Hughes, Gloria J. Hathaway. Hoboken, N.J.: Wiley-Interscience, 2004. xi, 785 p.
615.902   RA1229.P76
First edition, 1978; 4th ed., 1996.

Contents: (1) "Introduction: Toxicological concepts"; (2) "The chemical hazards"; (3) "CAS number index"; (4) "Index of compounds and synonyms." Detailed contents at http://www.loc.gov/catdir/toc/ecip0410/2003024018.html

Covers the effects on human health of chemicals likely to be encountered in various places of work. Each monograph includes chemical formula, CAS number, Threshold Limit Value, synonyms for the chemical, physical properties, uses, routes of exposure, toxicological information, carcinogenicity, mutagenicity, fetotoxicity, clinical effects of overexposure and treatment, and significant odor characteristics. For health professionals and students. Available online from Wiley http://onlinelibrary.wiley.com/book/10.1002/0471662666.

Other titles in this area include, for example, *Sittig's handbook of of toxic and hazardous chemicals and carcinogens* and *Sax's dangerous properties of industrial materials.*

1611 Sax's dangerous properties of industrial materials. Twelfth edition
ed. Richard J. Lewis. Hoboken, N.J.: John Wiley & Sons, Inc., 2012. 5 volumes

(xxviii, 4602 pages).
ISBN 9780470623251
604.7   T55.3.H3S3
Vol. 1, Introduction ; Dot guide number cross-index ; CAS registry cross-index ; synonym cross-index ; References; v. 2, General chemicals : entries A - C ; v. 3, General chemicals : entries D - G, v. 4, General chemicals : entries H - O; v. 5, General chemicals : entries P - Z.

This revised edition is a standard compilation of hazardous properties, covering some 28,000 materials, with 2,400 new in this edition. Vol. 1 includes an introduction explaining the entries, formats, sources, and codes. It also lists full references corresponding to the alphanumeric codes used in the entries. Contains "immediately dangerous to life or health concentrations (IDLHs)" for approximately 1,000 substances. Vols. 2 and 3 contain the entries, alphabetical by substance name; typical entries include synonyms, molecular formula, molecular weight, CAS Registry Number, a "hazard rating" (HR) of 1–3 (or "D" if there is insufficient data), properties, toxicity data with references, references to consensus reports in the literature, a Department of Transportation hazard code, and standards and recommendations from various agencies (OSHA, NIOSH, DOT, etc.) as to toxic concentrations. Most entries are one or two paragraphs; a few, such as DDT, run one or two pages. Considered an important resource for professionals in such areas as emergency response, industrial hygiene, safety and similar professions. Also available as an e-book.

1612 Sittig's handbook of toxic and hazardous chemicals and carcinogens. 6th ed.
Richard P. Pohanish, Marshall Sittig. Amsterdam, [Neth.]; Boston; Waltham, Mass.: Elsevier; William Andrew, 2012. 2 v. (xxvii, 3040 p.)
ISBN 9781437778694
615.9/02   RA1215 .S58
First ed., 1981, had title *Handbook of toxic and hazardous chemicals*; 2nd ed., 1985; 3rd ed., 1991, had title: *Handbook of toxic and hazardous chemicals and carcinogens*; 4th ed., 2001; 5th ed., 2008.
Vol. 1, A–K; v. 2, L–Z; appendixes 1-6.
Contents: "How to use this book"; "Key to abbreviations, symbols, and acronyms"; "Pesticide records A to Z"; "Bibliography"; "General guide to chemical resistance gloves"; appendixes: (1) "Oxidizing

materials";(2) "Carcinogens"; (3) "Glossary; synonym and trade name index-cross index"; "CAS number-cross index"; (4) "European/international hazard codes, risk phrases, and safety phrases"; (5) "Synonyms and trade name cross index"; (6) "CAS number cross index."

This updated edition presents concise chemical and safety information for approx. 2,200 toxic and hazardous chemicals, giving for each substance a code number, such as CAS (Chemical Abstract Service) number; RTECS number; DOT designation; EC (Commission of the European Communities); synonyms; potential exposure; incompatibilities; permissible exposure limits and determination in water; routes of entry, harmful effects, symptoms, points of attack, medical surveillance, first aid, decontamination, personal protective methods, etc.; suggested disposal method; and references for, about, and to sources of more information. Contains a glossary of chemical, health, safety, medical, and environmental terms used in this handbook. Useful reference for a variety of professions, including emergency response personnel, toxicologists, occupational doctors and nurses, special, technical, and university librarians, and many others (see *Pref*). Also available as an e-book.

1613 Toxic plants of North America.

http://onlinelibrary.wiley.com/book/10.1002/9781118413425. George E. Burrows, Ronald J. Tyrl. Hoboken, N.J.: Wiley-Blackwell. 2012.
ISBN 9781118413395
581.6/59097   QK100.N6

"Because of their ubiquity, there is a need for comprehensive treatment of toxic plants likely to be encountered in North America north of the Tropic of Cancer, growing wild or cultivated."—*Introd.* The 1st ed. originated from research on native plants toxic to livestock, while the 2nd ed. adds intoxication in humans and wildlife as well as the roles of secondary plant compounds and fungal infections in plants. The authors draw on the literature of toxicology, veterinary medicine, agronomy, chemistry, biochemistry, and physiology, as well as their own observations. Information for each plant family includes disease problems associated with it, toxicants and mechanisms of action, clinical signs of exposure, pathological effects associated with their toxicity, and principal treatments. Every

chapter ends with a bibliography. Distinct plant families are presented in 76 chapters; a separate chapter describes 44 plant families of questionable risk; and the final segment includes an explanation of how to identify toxic plants. Appendices include plant taxa grouped by their toxic effects, and a table of plants toxic to common pets. The index is thorough, listing scientific and common plant names and chemical compounds. Color plates, black and white line drawings, distribution maps, and chemical compound structures are dispersed throughout. Useful to researchers, professionals, students, and the general publlic. Also available as a print book.

1st ed., 2001.

Internet resources

1614 Agency for Toxic Substances and Disease Registry (ATSDR). http://www.atsdr.cdc.gov/. Agency for Toxic Substances and Disease Registry, U.S. Department of Health and Human Services. Atlanta: Agency for Toxic Substances and Disease Registry. 1999–

Agency for Toxic Substances and Disease Registry (ATSDR), part of U.S. Dept. of Health and Human Services (HHS).

Provides health information and takes public health actions to prevent harmful exposures and diseases related to toxic substances (e.g., recent examples: childhood lead poisoning prevention, drinking water concerns, anticipating the health concerns of climate change, etc.). Includes A–Z index by main topic (http://www.atsdr.cdc.gov/az/a.html), information about toxic substances, various data resources (e.g., access to the Hazardous Substance Release/Health Effects [HazDat] database, National Exposure Registry, and others), emergency response information, hazardous waste sites, a toxic substances portal (http://www.atsdr.cdc.gov/substances/index.asp), and many other information sources.

1615 Enviro-health links. http://sis.nlm.nih.gov/pathway.html. National Library of Medicine (U.S.), National Institutes of Health, U.S. Dept of Health & Human Services. Bethesda, Md.: National Library of Medicine. 2010–

Part of NLM's Specialized Information Services (SIS) "Pathways for public health information" website, with selected links to Internet resources on environmental health and toxicology topics and issues. Includes both NLM and outside resources. Covers arsenic and human health; climate change and health; developing and using medicines for children; dietary supplements; education, careers, and outreach in toxicology and environmental health; environmental justice; epigenomics; hexavalent chromium and other chromium compounds; imported (Chinese) drywall; indoor air; keeping the artist safe; laboratory safety; lead and human health; mercury and human health; nanotechnology and human health; outdoor air; pesticide exposure; tobacco, smoking and health; toxicology; toxicogenomics; water pollution; and West Nile virus.

In addition to "Enviro-health links" also provides "Disaster health links" (e.g., chemical emergencies, disaster recovery, fires and wildfires, floods, earthquakes, and many others) and "Targeted populations" (e.g., American Indian health, Asian American health, K-12 science and health education, multi-cultural resources for health information, women's health, and others) links. Guidelines for the selection of resources outside of NLM are spelled out at http://sis.nlm.nih.gov/enviro/envirohealthlinkscriteria.html.

This website is also part of SIS "Environmental health & toxicology" (http://sis.nlm.nih.gov/enviro.html), a comprehensive site with reliable information on chemicals & drugs, diseases and the environment, occupational safety & health, poisoning, risk assessment, toxicology, and pesticides "especially for emergency responders, health professionals, the public, researchers/scientists, students/educators, and toxicologists."*Website*. Links to guides & tutorials, advice on what specific resources to use, and additional related information. Joining the Listserv, subscribing to the RSS feed, or following the site on Twitter allows users to keep up-to-date. Another website in this area is ATSDR toxic substances portal (the US Dept. of Health and Human Services' Agency for Toxic Substances and Disease Registry) http://www.atsdr.cdc.gov/substances/index.asp, "providing trusted health information to prevent harmful exposures and diseases related to toxic substances."—*Website*.

1616 Toxics release inventory (TRI). http://toxnet.nlm.nih.gov/cgi-bin/sis/htmlgen?TRI. National Library of Medicine (U.S.). Bethesda, Md.: National Library of Medicine
Part of TOXNET.

"A series of databases that describe the releases of toxic chemicals into the environment annually for the 1987–2004 reporting years. *TRI* is mandated by the Emergency Planning and Community Right-to-Know Act and is based on data submitted to the EPA from industrial facilities throughout the U.S. These data include the names and addresses of those facilities, and the amounts of certain toxic chemicals they release to the air, water, or land, or transfer to waste sites. Information is included on over 650 chemicals and chemical categories. Pollution prevention data are also reported by each facility for each chemical"—*TOXNET fact sheet* at http://www.nlm.nih.gov/pubs/factsheets/toxnetfs.html.

1617 TOXMAP. http://toxmap.nlm.nih.gov/toxmap/main/index.jsp. National Library of Medicine (U.S.). Bethesda, Md.: National Library of Medicine. 1995–
RA1190
As part of TOXNET, TOXMAP addresses toxicology and environmental health information needs. Uses maps of the United States to show the amount and location of toxic chemicals released into the environment. Data shown in TOXMAP come from the U.S. Environmental Protection Agency's Toxics release inventory (TRI) and Superfund programs (http://www.epa.gov/tri or http://www.epa.gov/superfund/), HSDB (Hazardous substances databank), TOXLINE, Agency for Toxic Substances and Disease Registry (ATSDR), USGS national atlas (http://www.nationalatlas.gov), and U.S. Census (http://www.census.gov). Users can create their own geographic region or select from a list of predefined regions. Provides various search options and links to other environmental health and toxicology resources. For further details, see TOXNET fact sheet (http://www.nlm.nih.gov/pubs/factsheets/toxnetfs.html).

1618 TOXNET (Toxicology data network). http://toxnet.nlm.nih.gov/. National Library of Medicine (U.S.). Bethesda, Md.: National Library of Medicine. 1998–

TOXNET: Toxicology data network, part of the Specialized Information Services (SIS) division of the National Library of Medicine (NLM) at http://sis .nlm.nih.gov/, responsible for information resources and services in toxicology, environmental health, chemistry, and other specialized topics.

Managed by the Toxicology and environmental health information program (TEHIP) of the NLM, TOXNET is a group of searchable databases that can be used separately or in combination (TOXNET multi-File; http://toxnet.nlm.nih.gov/ cgi-bin/sis/htmlgen?Multi) to locate toxicology data, literature references, and information concerning environmental health and toxic release of chemicals. It can also identify chemicals that cause specific effects and provides links to PubMed.

TOXNET includes the following databases: ChemIDplus, HSDB (Hazardous Substances Data Bank), TOXLINE, CCRIS (Chemical Carcinogenesis Research Information System), DART/ETIC (Developmental and Reproductive Toxicology/Environmental Teratology Information Center database), GENE-TOX (Genetic Toxicology), IRIS (Integrated Risk Information System), ITER (International Toxicity Estimates for Risk), LactMed (Drugs and Lactation), Toxics Release Inventory (TRI), Haz-Map, Household Products Database, and TOXMAP. The TOXNET interface, originally designed and developed prior to the Internet, is being redesigned and will be released in 2014.

Information regarding the mobile version of this resource is part of NLM's Gallery of mobile apps and sites.

1619 Tox town. http://purl.access.gpo.gov/ GPO/LPS70098. National Library of Medicine (U.S.). Bethesda, Md.: National Library of Medicine. [2002]–

Companion to the TOXNET collection of databases.

An interactive guide that uses graphics, sounds, and animation to identify the types and sources of commonly encountered toxic substances and how they relate to public health and the environment. Intended for students, educators, and the general public.

1620 WISER (Wireless Information System for Emergency Responders). http:// wiser.nlm.nih.gov. National Library of Medicine (U.S.). Bethesda, Md.: U.S. National Library of Medicine. 2005–

"A system designed to assist first responders in hazardous materials incidents . . . including substance identification support, physical characteristics, human health information, and advice on containment and suppression guidance."—*Home page*. "Information is presented to the emergency responder, Hazmat Specialist, and EMS Specialist in the order that is most relevant to their respective roles."—*About page*. Content from HSDB (Hazardous substance data bank) and from CHEMM (Chemical hazards emergency medical management) http://chemm.nlm.nih.gov. Further information on other data sources and about applications available (for phone, tablet, and desktop) on the About page. This resource is also listed on NLM's Gallery of mobile apps and sites.

INDEX

Note: Numbers in bold refer to entry numbers. Numbers in roman type refer to mentions in annotations of other works.